D0723430

Dear Reader

Dear Reader

The Conscripted Audience
in Nineteenth-Century
British Fiction

Garrett Stewart

The Johns Hopkins University Press

Baltimore and London

© 1996 The Johns Hopkins University Press
All rights reserved. Published 1996
Printed in the United States of America on acid-free paper
05 04 03 02 01 00 99 98 97 96   5 4 3 2 1

The Johns Hopkins University Press
2715 North Charles Street
Baltimore, Maryland 21218-4319
The Johns Hopkins Press Ltd., London

Frontispiece: Antoine Wiertz, *The Romance Reader* (1853).
Musées royaux des Beaux-Arts de Belgique, Brussels.
Copyright © A.C.L. Brusssels

Library of Congress Cataloging-in-Publication Data

Stewart, Garrett.
Dear reader : the conscripted audience in nineteenth-century
British fiction / Garrett Stewart.
p.   cm.
Includes bibliographical references and index.
ISBN 0-8018-5282-X (alk. paper).—ISBN 0-8018-5283-8 (pbk. : alk. paper)
1. English fiction—19th century—History and criticism.
2. Authors and readers—Great Britain—History—19th century.
3. Reader-response criticism. 4. Point of view (Literature)
5. Narration (Rhetoric) 6. Fiction—Technique. I. Title.
PR878.A79S74   1996
823'.809—dc20   95-52372

A catalog record for this book is available from the British Library.

For Ian, a born reader

And for Renata, another reader born

Contents

Acknowledgments

𝒯he first thing to acknowledge is that this study of conscripted readers roped in many of its own right from the start. Anonymous NEH panelists may have had little choice but to read over each of the numerous proposals that came their way back in 1990; for the final choice they did exercise, however, they have, along with the beleaguered endowment, the gratitude of one among many disinterested literary scholars. At this early stage, Peter Brooks, James Kincaid, and Elaine Showalter—dearest of readers—were recruited to support the project when there was all too little of it to read. By the time there was all too much of it, a resourceful referee was commissioned by the Johns Hopkins University Press to help in evaluation and revision; when the identity of my most patient and discriminating reader, as the novelists used to say, was revealed to me, I found myself irredeemably in Jay Clayton's debt. The debts to other readers and advisers I more aggressively incurred. I garner the tacit approbation of these kind consultants—do I not, latest reader of mine?—simply by thanking them here: Emily Allen, Florence Boos, Marshall Brown, Lorna Clymer, Nataša Ďurovičová, Dino Felluga, Ed Folsom, Miriam Gilbert, Elisabeth Gitter, Tim Gould, Susan Gray, Eloise Knapp Hay, Jocelyn Lutz Marsh, Robert Pendleton, Donna Rudolph, Hilary Schor, Carol Tyx, Susan Wolfson, and Everett Zimmerman. With regard to any defects of fact or phrase introduced by these colleagues drafted into my prepublication audience, slips for which they are of course solely responsible, may the reviewers—those readers over whom one can, alas, exert no coercion—spare them in the fury of their discernment.

This is called reading. So far you're doing fine.

—Bookstore ad, *Chicago Reader*

Part 1

PRO LEGOMENON

Chapter One

Readers in the Making

What is a book no one reads? Something that is not yet written.

—Maurice Blanchot, "Reading"

Honoré Daumier, *Don Quixote Reading a Novel*
(1866). The Bettmann Archive

ℛeady now, reader? Easy then. That should put you in the right historical frame of mind, put you in mind of the right historical frame. For it did seem easier then, certainly more relaxed. Like the addressed and otherwise rendered nineteenth-century reader who is my subject of study, you are invited to take it slow while we back our way into the last century. We do so by moving from an unexpected modernist send-up of Victorian direct address, an early twist of phrase in E. M. Forster's 1907 *The Longest Journey*, to the underlying aesthetic of classic realism on which even this one rhetorical irony is by no means intended to pull the plug. On the way back to the nineteenth century, certain realist assumptions help mark out our course.

Literary reading serves desire in the world of form. Realist literary reading services desire in the form of a world. Until an insistence on the first condition with the rise of high modernism, two centuries of novel reading coasted along on the second presumption. Though the readers of realist fiction inhabit—at desk or fireside—the only third dimension on which the rectangular literary page can ever lay claim, such readers do everything in their imaginative power to overlook this fact when looking in on a created world. In Forster's *The Longest Journey*, written on the eve of experimental British modernism, the axiomatic paradox of a world's read presence—this abiding realist myth of narrative immanence—is coaxed almost to breakdown by way of travestying a Victorian rhetorical convention. *The Longest Journey* has barely begun when the hero, about to tell his family history, is assured by a fellow student that "If you bore us, we have books" (2:23).[1] The narrative proceeds now on the oddest of grounds, both anachronistic in its open address to the audience and disingenuous in claiming mandatory attendance: "With this invitation Rickie began to relate his history. The *reader who has no book* will be *obliged* to listen to it" (2:23; emphasis added). What was that? No *other* book? No *mere* book? Literary fiction is in this always multiple sense "obliging," pretending to necessitate the narrative attention for which it connives and to which it panders. Here is the traditional *captive audience* as a local rhetorical ploy, a tactical adjunct as well as an ultimate goal of the captivating tale. And such is, in turn, a tale for whose realistic manifestation as scene, if not for whose telling, you the obligated reader are always in part responsible—its coauthority and its conscript at once.

Nonsense—you might nonetheless retort to Forster's narrator—for surely you have other choices than to listen up. His calling you a reader only proves as much: proves your place as an independent agent only provisionally subject, for only so long as you continue reading this one book, to its author's rhetorical positioning. Forster's wry gesture would therefore rob from you, even while nominating you for, the book-reading credentials that are demonstrably your own. But even when designating you as a listener, Forster's gambit makes no effort to retrieve from the avocational reading of popular print matter something like the gripped listener of an earlier tradition of oral storytelling. Instead, the only voice to be heard is one lodged within the merely (and admittedly) *legible* plot, the represented voice of a character in recitation of his past. Forster's point is not meant to be subtle, just tricky. Anything less than the slamming together of such paradoxical terms—the "reader" of a novel made to confront, in supposed default of a book, the actual audition of that same novel's described scene—anything less aggressive in its self-contradiction might have been able to finesse yet again, for the ten thousandth time, and with all the cheerful effrontery of Victorian novelistic rhetoric, the twin pulls on the subject reader of classic fiction. These are, on the one hand, the draw of a credible world and, on the other, the lure of assured readerly status with respect to that world.

At play in such rhetoric is the premium placed on both manifested mimetic presence and attentive readerly presence, on willing submission to a made world but also on direct solicitation from a narrative voice. Only the mutually compelling appeal—compelling in both senses, like obliging—of these two facets of reading could keep in suspension their fields of force. There can be no mistaking it: The interest served by the cohabitation of textual markers like "the reader" with the undeconstructed presencing of told space, the collusion between cited narrating and narrated site, is for classic fiction nothing short of narrative interest itself—the coalition of suspended disbelief and cued self-consciousness. Moreover, the agency of reading thus delimited is not any the less institutional for being casually underspecified and endlessly mutable. The permutations of such a designated reading agent over the course of evolving fictional practice were effortlessly assimilated to, because they seemed virtually to enumerate, the aggregate reading public in its diversified channels of reception. Variants of the "dear reader" accumulated as a kind of institutional census taking sufficient unto the day when the novel had already carried that day, holding generic sway for decade after decade over leisured print consumption. All that has changed.

Hence this book: a stocktaking, a long view, a history in the employ of an interrogation. What made the great realist novels tick? How exactly were they synchronized to the reader's imputed (as well as real) desires? How much of the answer is to be unraveled from such fiction's now dated modes of address? And while we are at it, how else can the reader be named or contained by a classic realist text? These are questions that gain in interest with the decline of the realist form as canonical benchmark, if only because they offer the chance of attaching the heavily rhetorical structures called classic novels back to their not only intended but also internally foreseen social contexts, their programmed destinies in reception. In every manner of critical investigation, classic narrative comes into sharper focus as historical object the farther it withdraws from any immediate popular impact. Both a vanishing pastime, indeed vanishing craft, and a fading cultural stance, fictional reading has thus been ever more insistently theorized—as if with a certain unsaid urgency, if not elegiac plangency—during its gradual eclipse by other media. It is theorized here with a long look back at its glory days: the nineteenth-century British novel from Austen to Hardy. Classic fiction well knew what it had going for it, what kept it going: the reading subject. It is no surprise that the novelistic institution steadily sought to underwrite such an interested party, to insure its participation, to write it in.

I mentioned reading's cultural stance. You noticed that. In so doing I announce one frankly polemical impulse of this book: to return the particularities of the reading moment—its complex rhetorical specificities—to the study of culture within which they once seemed indispensable. The act of literary reading is not just a cultural disposition, part of an economy of leisure or an ideology of edification. It is also a locally positioned enterprise of reception within a socially inflected network of intertextual signals, a reception marked, precoded, co-optive. Literature does not simply reflect the social constructions of its period; it numbers itself among them. I stress the obvious in order to count on it when the going gets rougher. Not only entering culture on the books of an epoch, literature enters culture—penetrates and engages it—by the highly regulated routes of reading. It is not the mimetic model, therefore, which best grasps the relation between a text and its time but rather the rhetorical one: the model that covers exactly the space *between*, its negotiated traversals, its bizarre interchanges. In that space is textual subjectivity spawned and disseminated.

Subject: reading. Subject reading. Insofar as reading can become a subject—that is, a topic, or *topos*—in the very text it activates, and not merely reading in general but the very reading-in-progress that makes, let us say, a given Victorian novel happen as text, such reading has been, in a rather preemptive manner, made subject. In this relation alone subsists the reading subject—as Henry James, looking back on the Victorian achievement of George Eliot, saw so clearly: "In every novel the work is divided between the writer and the reader; but the writer makes the reader very much as he makes his characters."[2] In the encounter with classic fiction, you, reader, are therefore part of the script, though the stage directions are not always forthcoming. In view of this marked textualization of response, one can at least begin an analysis of the nineteenth-century fictional audience at the level of textual activity itself. You don't have to have been there. As distinct from the historical advent of a readership emerging en masse, and from the historicisms that attempt to canvass and graph it in retrospect, I am referring here to the very different level of the reading *event*.

This is an event time-bound in good part, to be sure, but not determined strictly by the social history of its day—an event that our own reading can thus work to re-create rather than merely to "place." So let me make plain at the outset the historical rather than aesthetic privilege I am attributing to the "dear reader" as synecdoche for a nineteenth-century literary public initially made available to us through the inferences of fictional reading. On the one hand, my argument is the opposite of any claim for reading as an ageless aesthetic activity. On the other hand, any attempt at "reading like a Victorian" moves in just the wrong direction when it finds the exemplary text "derived" from what we know in hindsight about nineteenth-century British social organization and its entrenched discourses. As a symptom but, more important, as a tool of cultural construction, fictional reading is inductive. In every sense it leads you on. This is precisely what is ideological about the classic novel as *literature*. This is also why the study of such reading is a prerequisite to any full contextualization. Narrative fiction works up and out from the individual (language, plot, personal agents) to the cultural totality, rather than dropping the particular into the general as its instance and its proof. The result is that criticism gets closest to its object when retracing just this inductive route. And such a procedure lays fewer traps for the critic than is often thought. No ideology of the literary need be subscribed to—even though its temptations must no doubt be felt—in order to reread the conscriptive strategies of Victorian fiction as a highly specialized set of ideological inculcations.

Contemporary reader of classic fiction, this, then, is your story, a tale often told before, often at your own expense, always about your own interpretive expenditures. You remain, though, not only the wearied hero of reading theory but the true worker of the literary work. To be on your side is to be just this side of the mute page, slotted for response, zoned for construction. The eighteenth-century pioneers of prose fiction, by any number of flamboyant ploys, peopled the novel with avatars of fictional attention, not infrequently with individual personifications of its readers. The habit became generic. Populated in this way with the image of its own increasing popularity, the novel in Victorian hands consolidated these devices for engraining the reader. Reading novels that absorb you, you are in every sense taken in, even as you yourself begin to "internalize." This is a large part of your story, as retold here. Toward this end, my subtitle. The emphasis on conscripted reading is an emphasis on the "audience in nineteenth-century British fiction": *in* as well as *of*. This is the audience not only narrated to but also narrated. At either level, you yourself—what is left of you in reading—must take on your role by taking the vacant place of engagement, mediate but intimate. What Dickens in private correspondence called the "many-headed"[3]—his dead metaphor for one body of readers with, so to say, a thousand seeing eyes—represents the potential multifariousness of the public as mob. Yet it is an unruly body politic only manifested, as no one knew better than Dickens, under the singularized plurality of the invested second person. In Blanchot's terms, the novel gets written with and in you alone.

Voluntary Conscription

But how exactly does reading, an activity carried out upon an inscription, become a site of conscription? In the event of a reading, fictional structure commandeers a response that it may also structure in replica as a described event. The rhetoric of narration passes thereby to the narration of rhetorical efficacy itself. Whether through direct address or structural parallel, at such times you as reader are not simply inscribed by prose fiction. Instead, as member of an audience, your private reading—along with that of every other reader—is actually convoked and restaged, put in service to the text. Either as an identifying notation or as a narrative event, this reading in of your reading—or of you reading—is what I mean by the notion of a conscripted response. Implicated by apostrophe or by proxy, by address or by dramatized scenes of reading, you are deliberately drafted by the text, written *with*. In the closed circuit of conscripted response, your input is a predigested function of the text's output—digested in advance by rhetorical mention or by narrative episode. As independent reading agent outside the story, your relegation by text to a delegate of attention within it converts you to either a second or a third person, either an addressee or a character, even if, in the latter case, only "the reader." It is the structured relation of these manifestations to each other within a reconceived notion of rhetoric, of figured response, that needs to be worked out across their separate exemplifications in these pages.

Your first and most obvious reservation about taking on such pages is inevitable. The conceptual terrain here is by no means methodologically untraveled. You're telling me. I can only hope to adjust the grounds for discussion enough to justify staking out this new—and double—course of inquiry, aligning the trope of the "gentle reader" with the embedded scene of reading. But where in the critical discussion of British fiction, you ask, is such an approach meant to intervene? Between sociohistorical studies of the popular audience, on the one hand, and so-called reader-response criticism, on the other—between approaches to a readership at purchasing or processing ends of the fictional contract—lies my interest (closer to the latter to be sure) in eventuated or achieved (rather than merely eventual) reading. This involves neither the simple redefinition of the text as an affective structure of effected meaning, as in reader-response aesthetics, nor the text's displacement, as in certain forms of cultural history, from linguistic event to social artifact, industrial object, or advertising medium. Eventuated reading does not just fall somewhere between textual and contextual analysis. It defines their common border. It thereby delimits a still textual horizon that is approachable by the procedures of narrative and rhetorical analysis. This is a way of saying that nothing in the recent work on the quasi-industrial production and social consumption of nineteenth-century fiction justifies discarding the analytic gains of a previous phase of critical analysis—from structural semiotics through deconstruction—where the poles of generated and received meaning are located within a textual *productivity* and its linguistic dissemination as well as within a system of manufacture and distribution.[4]

To say so is not to evade context but to seek for a way of registering it, from the inside out, as firstly a textual concern. Certainly the nineteenth-century novel begins in a cultural contestation about the role of fiction which it is forced, as well as rhetorically predisposed, to address. When Coleridge speaks of the social consequences of widespread literary scribbling as "that luxuriant misgrowth of our activity: a Reading Public!" he labels a mass of consumers at odds with the individuated force of a given reading experience.[5] Before Coleridge, Fanny Burney had put it only somewhat more neutrally in her preface to the epistolary novel *Evelina* (1778), with its "letters . . . presented to the public—for such, by novel writers, novel readers will be called."[6] Coleridge's tacit distinction between the private drama of reading and the lumpen consumption of the reading public, between the individuated reader and the literary collective, is just the distinction, as well as the potential link, which Jon Klancher sees "so-called reception theory" having "never deduced"—and to which his own study of romantic journalism is devoted.[7] Against the animus of Coleridge's "luxuriant outgrowth," as it even appears in the light condescension of Dickens' "many-headed," it is one central effort of nineteenth-century fiction to reprivatize such an overgrown commonwealth of reading within an undeniable sales economy. The carefully wrought mystifications to which this effort tends cannot be apprehended simply under the sign of consumption. On this point, I must second a caveat of Pierre Macheray's: "We must avoid turning all the problems posed by the work into the single question of its diffusion. In a word, we must not replace a mythology of the creator by a mythology of the public."[8]

This seems, though, to have been the effort of certain recent historicisms. The point here should be easy to make, but it needs to be clear from the outset. The noun *reader* (when designating more than a library user or book purchaser) escapes the concept of plurality and hence the hold of quantification. This is why there are no statistics that can genuinely round up the Victorian (or any other) general reader. It is also why any social history of the so-called reading public is not a study of the reader, let alone *a* reader, until it is informed by precisely that phenomenological detour, routed by language, along whose grooves, when people read, readers emerge, generated in process. The reader is a drastic abstraction of the self, spirited away from self-identity by text, a subjective construction spun out from moment to moment by the subvocal rematerialization of the graphic signifiers on the read, not just opened, page.[9] Reading voices, if you will. Reading also opens space. It thereby creates an occupied zone between text and interpretation whose terrain is too often reconnoitered from an aerial and hazy distance. The details of rhetorical emplacement are the first to go in the resulting blur.

The Situation of Reading

Reader, this is your story, then, but only if you do not quite recognize yourself in the accounts usually given of your textual situation. Too often adduced as simply a cover term for the manufacture of intelligible narrative continuity, you are not given credit for the complexity of your submission. The homogenized and depleted reader whose "responses" are logged in such accounts stalks its occasioning texts as the personification of meaning per se.[10] This tends to tame the more volatile reader you find yourself asked to be, and told you are, in nineteenth-century fiction, as well as to flatten those various scenes of narrated reading, or its parables, from which your role is to be extrapolated. Even when readers are formulated by criticism as more active players in the textual fray, their very autonomy may seem claustrophobic. Channeled by generic context, burdened by repertoires of response, hemmed in by horizons of expectation, the reader *in theory* is no match for the textual encounters you and I remember. With its ideal readers, superreaders, inferred readers, competent readers, model readers, zero-degree readers, intended readers, informed readers, preferred readers, virtual readers, specialized communities of readers, and all the other wan protagonists of response aesthetics, the contours of the actual *reading* tend to get lost in this faceless crowd.[11] What certainly gets overlooked is that double instantiation of the reader by petition and parable, direct address and narrative replication, which circumscribes response as a textual annexation. Neither confined to making meaning nor to being made by it as sheerly deciphering receptacle, the reader I have in mind, the reader I am in my mind while moving through a text, is there to establish, without ever stabilizing, a contact that grows elaborately contractual. Readers do more than underwrite the act of textual communication; they are conscribed, in short, by narrative's own economy as silent partners. In certain designated passages, that is, whether of invoked or actually dramatized reading, we will be concerned less with how a reader decodes a text than with how a text might encode—might teasingly encipher—its own reading.

That any of these aforementioned readers should have their own history *as readers* is important to agree upon at the start. It is a history literary and linguistic, philosophical and philological, a history at every point entangled in, but never reducible to, the social history of those economic and cultural agents who otherwise occupy the reader's time, place, and person. Though one may well share Tony Bennett's impatience with the way "textual and reading semiotics have been developed along the path of a mutually numbing symbiosis,"[12] still his historical-materialist corrective, via "reading formations," seems to rule out too much of the text's rhetorical contribution in "accounting for such *real* variations in the social destinies of texts as *have actually taken place*" (225; Bennett's italics). His question, in effect: How have particular texts been used by culture? Ours: How have such texts used their readers, then and now? Beyond the historical *application* of textual meaning in given contexts, that is, we need a more fundamental account of the means by which classic narrative writing *applies to* its own cultural moment of reception in two coordinated senses: appeals to and bears upon the reading event. This, again, is my double subject. Compared both with the reconstructed social agent, then, as well as with the implied reader who simply secures meaning by anchoring its preestablished codes—in contrast to the reader, that is, either as pawn of cultural indoctrination or as placeholder for textual signification itself—the reader you or I become, and the one whose evasive byways we will be striving to track through various narrative engagements in the following chapters, is a more figurative function sometimes cued by address, always keyed to (and frequently replayed by) plot.

These linked features of the reading act are bound to be uncoupled when both rhetorical and narrative facets of the novelistic text are vaporized by a militantly extraliterary sense of its cultural role. With treatments of prose fiction as combined mercantile product and ideological institution increasingly cut adrift from sophisticated theories of literary structure, the Victorian novel as text grows harder and harder to read. There is an irony here, as well as a disciplinary capitulation. For it is exactly the fictional work's true contextual dimension, the goal of such materialist-political reading, which falls victim to the vitiated methodologies of the textual. Cultural milieu, after all, is that context into which a novel, once written, is not only launched by being published and marketed, not only absorbed by being bought and read, but upon which it makes its mark by the protocols not just of attitude or behavior, whether class- or gender-determined, but of *literary reaction itself*, which the novel constructs, perpetuates, or reinflects. So it is that the textuality of narrative as an integrated structure becomes a *literary* as well as just a formal consideration (literature being a cultural category rather than a structural fact) immediately and only upon the apprehension by an audience that conscripted reading seeks to realize from within the text. Let me therefore put forward a working hypothesis to which these chapters will in various ways be asked to respond. The encoded presence of a reading consciousness to a narrative text—figured by apostrophe, for instance, or reduplicated by interpretive episode—can be isolated as *the* exemplary literary moment of the novel as narrative. As such, this is a "moment" in the sense (from physics) of a leveraging pressure. It marks not so much the literary imprint as the literary *impress*, which is only to be recognized—in the event—for the way it recruits the very reading it requires.

Second Person Present: "Reader, I Married Him"

When it comes to reading, examples are everything. Impressed attention, as an instance of conscripted reading, is never more forthright than in those direct addresses to the reader that accompany the novel from its inception through the nineteenth century and at least a little way beyond—and whose earliest manifestations I will be anatomizing in the next chapter. The *locus classicus* of this device in Victorian fiction is, of course, *Jane Eyre*'s climactic "Reader, I married him." We can take this minimal but in its own way exhaustive utterance as the model for a constitutive syntax of narrative, a virtual declension of its singular paradigm: the collaborative motivation, in other words, of second, first, and third person in an interdependent transitive—and transactional—grammar. The audience is singled out in the vocative; autobiographical heroine declared in the nominative; plot fulfilled in the verb of completed action; and the object of desire locked into place at last in the accusative. Two grammatical cases thus answer to each other across the preterite tense of reported event, preceded by the free-floating, parasyntactical "Reader"—and with no names mentioned anywhere. All is equally a pronomination, with your willingness to stand forward as "Reader" (here and now) thus collusive in the mutual embodying of heroine and hero (there and then). What this master sentence makes clear is that second person, even in a first-person narrative, invokes the only existential grounding possible for a fictional text. There is neither an "I" nor a "him" at the site of printed inscription, only the signifiers to this effect. But there *is* a reader in attendance, rhetorically hailed or otherwise.

Here deconstruction would interpose its strictures. On Derrida's show-ing, the vocative is the extreme, referentially eviscerating instance of all lit-erary language. Unlike nominative, genitive, and accusative cases, for instance, the vocative is for Derrida "not a category, a *case* of speech, but rather the bursting forth, the very raising of speech."[13] This notion highlights the sheer rhetoricity of the vocative, as does Jane's parasyntactic use of her "Reader" as the breakthrough into story of novelistic utterance per se. Such casting (up) of the audience within the text is identical in this sense with the enacted scenario of reading embedded in this and many another novel. Such a scene, though taking its assigned place in something like an overarching grammar of narrative and thus metonymically linked to the succession of episodes, is also metaphoric (synecdochic) for the whole—and hence in tropological re-lationship to what contains it. This is a relationship figurative, hence rhetor-ical. The point is worth insisting on. Whether hailed or staged, invoked or otherwise evoked, either version of the reader within the text is a means for calling out what a novel can never in its own right call forth.

If we concede that both nominating and dramatizing the reader, both ad-dressing and emblemizing the role of reception itself, are equally figurative moves on the part of the text (equal tropings or turnings, outward to what can never be textually internalized), then we might reconceive the relation between these devices as that between a *dialogic* and an *analogic* conscription. The trope of the invoked "dear reader" fabricates an entirely one-sided con-versation; however dear or gently predisposed, the reader can never talk back. Similarly, the trope of the emblemized reader figures a situation external to and precipitated by the text which that text has no way of literally, only of metaphorically, containing. To reiterate with example: Brontë's readers are no closer to being truly localized by that vocative than they are by a scene in which their interpretive work appears replayed by analogy, as, for instance, when Rochester dresses up as a gypsy, following an interim of decipherment in the charade episode, and decodes the surface features of Jane Eyre's phys-iognomy for marks of character (chap. 19)—even as such readers know of this scene only because they are processing another legible surface by the name of *Jane Eyre*. Emblemized in disguise, as it were, or hailed by common noun, the reader enters the text in a manner of speaking only. The reader is narra-tivized, that is, by fictional discourse—but only as a speechless figure of speech, now apostrophized, now displaced into narrative encounter.

In closing in on the narrower (vocative) case first, we might note the sidelining of the issue in two important commentators, Walter Ong and Wayne Booth. Their traditional approaches to the rhetorical gestures of prose fiction offer a clarifying point of departure. You may well have wondered with me, reader, where this most banal version of the figure—this present personification of yourself—came from in literary history, as well as where it went, that I could only be using it in this sentence with such an unmistakable antiquarian strain. What would it mean to ask what precisely happened to the "dear reader" trope in its ascendancy and decline across the transformation into and out of Victorian fiction? This is our question. Not: What happened to this trope? Rather: What would it mean to inquire, both closely and broadly, into its first vigorous, then "nervous," then doomed fortunes. I take that middle, that transitional, characterization from Ong's "The Writer's Audience Is Always a Fiction."[14] Jane Austen is discussed in passing as a pivotal figure for such a fictionalizing of the reader, though "the problem of the reader's role in prose narrative was by no means entirely solved" (17) by the time of her novels—as we will see in the fourth chapter. "Nervousness regarding the role of the reader registers everywhere in the 'dear reader' regularly invoked in fiction well through the nineteenth century" (17). This "nervousness" for Ong derives from the still unsettled transition into print culture from the oral tradition, unsettled for popular narrative in particular. "The reader had to be reminded (and the narrator, too) that the recipient of the story was indeed a reader—not a listener, not one of the crowd, but an individual isolated with a text" (17). A whole "history of literature," Ong adds, "could be written in terms of the ways in which audiences have successfully been fictionalized from the time when writing broke away from oral performance, for, just as each genre grows out of what went before it, so each new role that readers are made to assume is related to previous roles" (12). This present chapter leads off one speculative installment in just such a multivolume history.

What then, we ask again, would it mean to follow the fortunes of direct address through the Victorian novel down to an early modernist like Forster? The investigated fate of this trope—an effect faintly anachronistic even in its earliest appearances and self-consciously dated in its later uses, formulaic when not parodic—may summon up questions more definitive than the answers for which it holds out hope. How narrowly is the "dear reader" phenomenon to be demarcated? Grammatically only? Does mention in third person of "the reader" also count—and for what exactly? As the device grows mostly obsolete, into what other kinds of evoked reading might the formula of address be thought to relax or mutate over time?

Our second influential commentator on narrative rhetoric, Wayne Booth, passes over the question of address almost as briefly as Ong after him, with even less a sense of its centrality to his rhetorical project. "But let the gentle-hearted reader be under no apprehension whatsoever," he quotes from Trollope, since "the author and the reader should move along together in full confidence with each other."[15] As instance of a dated and overexplicit signaling that Booth claims to find at many points in Dickens as well (though in fact such moments are rarer than one tends to remember), Booth's example from Trollope is followed shortly by a discussion of Fielding's addressed reader "arrived at the last stage of our long journey" in *Tom Jones* (216). In Fielding, the journey motif is a kind of topographic figure for what Booth names as a "subplot" (216) with "its own separate denouement" (216), a contrapuntal drama of interaction between narrator and reader which has very little to do with our independent interest in the hero.[16] When one starts inquiring along these lines, a whole direction of effect is opened up: an axis of fiction, between narration and reception, which is by no means exhausted by the instances of address from which it cannot, nonetheless, be separated.

Reading In, Figuring Out

Before pursuing the vocative (or directive) aspect of conscripted reading in some detail in the next chapter, it is useful at this stage to be considerably more rigorous—meaning at least a little more semiotic—about the way in which not only direct address to, but enacted scenarios of, a narrative's reading agency may be taken to operate in tandem within a rhetorical conception of narrative textuality, and thus about the way they together establish the discursive situation of the reader. In the latter case of enacted reading scenes, the displacement from immediate reading to depicted site of narrative consumption involves the simultaneous mirroring and (hence necessary) evacuation of the reader from the scenes that represent her present activity in past action. This, too, we will be seeing in detail, is a no less rhetorically encoded, because no less figural, work of the text. We will also come to find that the scene of reading, however figured, is a unique permutation, indeed a revealing congestion, of the narrative codes given currency by Roland Barthes's *S/Z*. In reading about characters reading, decoding, responding, interpreting, you encounter in this curious textual fold the superimposition of your own hermeneutic practice upon that of the characters. The pressure from this superimposition sets the narrative text into recess from itself not just as story but as text. We will thus be working our way toward a tentative redefinition of the *mise en abyme* as precisely this intersecting and impacted (in a quite specific sense "reflexive") lamination of two of Barthes's primary codes. I refer to the direct crossing, the warping overlap, of narrated event and the vectors of interpretation, or in *S/Z*'s terms of the proairetic code (action in sequence) and the hermeneutic code (enigma and resolution).[17] It is a textual moment in which the reader's normal interpretation of action is converted to the very action of interpretation—when reading a scene, in other words, is internally reduplicated by a scene of reading.

And Barthes is of more help yet. In our effort to comprehend under the same systemic law the reader written in as momentary fictive character and the internal character figured (out) as reader—in other words, to collate as reciprocal functions the interpolated and the extrapolated audience—we need to go beyond the "implied reader" implied by Wayne Booth (inferred from his "implied author" and spelled out by Wolfgang Iser).[18] The shifting manifestation of the conscripted reader—now addressee, now delegated dramatis persona—finds an unexpectedly comprehensive account in one of the most suggestive distinctions in all of *S/Z*: between "character" in the ordinary sense and "figure" as the symbolic nexus that finds only occasional and partial incarnation in the semic bundles known in fiction as "persons" or "characters." For Barthes, the figure has no textual existence in pure form, only in the various amalgams of characterization. *S/Z* is concerned with such pervasive symbolic figures, such organizing abstractions, as "castration," "wealth," "the marriage of opposites," "the replicated body," and so forth—as they are felt to surface in, by intersecting, the narrower determinations of given characters and their semic profiles.

What, then, about the type of "figure" that might work to compose from within the text the image of our own attention to it, our very desire for story? The figure of responsiveness or penetrability, in this sense, might inhabit or contaminate various "characters" in a narrative, falling under the rule of a proper name only when crisscrossed by a certain number of other such figures, along with the various semes of personality, in that connotative knot we think of as character. Though Barthes never broaches the notion of the reading figure in particular, it may be that such a symbolic pattern of heightened attentiveness, of interpretive capacity, of passive reception, of vicarious subjection—any number of "characterizations" will do—could exist as a textual, rather than characterological, free agent. In this sense (sustaining as it does the intimate links between the figurative and broadly rhetorical functions of a narrative) the figure of response, the figure of reading, would pass back and forth between its grammatically isolated position as direct address, on the one hand, and, on the other, its partial contribution to the recognizable makeup of characters in the narrative itself. At such moments, a narrative agent may best be understood to take on the *character of a reader*. It is at just these moments, one might add, that the historicizing of the reader can begin. For here is a figuration of the receptive impulse isolated as agency within a given period's inflection of the broader cultural code of literary consumption.

These moments of surfaced readerly figuration are not without further structural complications, however, especially in the literal scene of reading. To recognize the most fundamental of these complications is to shift ground from the textual network to the phenomenology of its internalization in the reading act. This is still a matter of narrative structure—but now as an engineering of response. Imagine, for example (only by reading about it as follows, of course), a prototypical moment in classic fiction. A Victorian novel open before you, you are moving along comfortably enough as the narrative is unfolded to you, thick with external detail and heavy with subjectivity, spread wide and deep at once. The text has become a phenomenal world. Suddenly one of the subjects that people this world is described poised over a book. You thus see in your mind's eye a character engaged upon an act of obliviousness and withdrawal which is effected through means other than an immediate engagement with the space and time to which you have been introduced. The very world into which you have read your way, a narrative realm of intersecting (and collaborative) objectivity and subjectivity, is a world in and from which such a character has found a momentary intermission. Your denied access to the precise contour or texture of that intermission— even if the inlaid text is "read into evidence," quoted whole or in part, within the enclosing narrative in order to engage your own subjective response— has to do with the nature of reading as an *invisible* activity within a visible (or in fiction, visualized) posture of attention.

At the level of textual processing, then, the narrated activity of reading provides not a strict *mise en abyme* of reception but a regression with a difference. The difference is foundational. Classic realist fiction requires for effect a double *realization*: our activated sense, first, of the rendered social and physical world of the narrative and then, second and simultaneously, of that world as focused upon and filtered through the credible interior representation of characters' mental lives. As dual coordinates of realism, objectivity and subjectivity meet at right angles: one the horizontal principle of plot and shifting scene, the other the vertical axis of interiority and depth. When the realist scene of reading brings before you characters lost to the world of the narrative, they are dropped away into another *mise en scène* than the one to which you have been granted mental access. Your sense of visualizing such characters in their milieu is thus at odds with their being elsewhere caught up, their now reinhabited psychic space having nothing to do with the immediately narrated world it has previously served to confirm and interiorize. Such is precisely the tension at the base of textual experience—between mere inscription and the represented space it calls up in consciousness—which you are not normally encouraged to recognize about your own cogitation as reader. Across your encompassing activation of the larger narrative beyond such a reading scene, any sense of this cognitive discrepancy—between words taken in by the eye and the thereby visualized scenes that absorb you in turn—is a luxury which, in the hold of fascination, if not the heat of credence, you can never afford to let the text afford you. Even in the coils of a certain tutoring self-reference, this is the drastic ontological reflex that realism usually holds in check.[19] So it is that reading remains largely illegible in the genre whose plots necessitate so much mention of its everyday prominence.

The results cannot be overstressed in their effect on the narrative metaplot of conscriptive storytelling. It is for this reason, indeed, that the Victorian novel so often reaches for what I am calling parables rather than scenes of private interpretive reading. Extrapolation rather than direct recognition becomes the requisite mode of response. Reading along, you enter upon an episode from which you are signaled to extrapolate some adjusted orientation toward the continuing event of reading. Such moments provide variously disguised configurations of reading's activating energies. In doing so, these narrative episodes gain enough distance on the thing itself, on the private act of novel reading as an intersubjective textual engagement, to cast it into structural relief. These, then, are parables that at least fractionally refigure the isolated event of reading as, for instance, a public (that is, familial) ritual of oral recitation from book or memory, or, elsewhere, an act of hermeneutic decoding not necessarily literary, or even textual, in nature—at any rate, to be embarked upon quite apart from the ensconced and solitary engagement with a novelistic text. Instead of a character alone with a volume of fiction, we have (by what we might call concentric association) the oral recitation of biographical story (Dickens); the global trope of life as an inwardly audited silent tale (Charlotte Brontë); the world stage as itself an epitomizing volume of human effort, foible, and defeat (Thackeray, Meredith, Schreiner, Hardy); the posthumous intensity of expressive impulse released from all textual encumbrance (Eliot); or, increasingly toward the end of the Victorian century, all manner of vicarious, voyeuristic, mesmeric, and vampiric phenomena in which psychic usurpation, somatic doubling, or perversely gendered otherness doubles for the aesthetic distance—and transacted gap—between reader and read. And so it goes—unsaid: reading encrypted but persistent, made immanent in its own pantomimes of itself.

These and other such parables are the subject of much that follows, affiliated as they are with the intermittent turn to readers themselves in direct address. It is this conjoint operation that explains why the attention to be trained on—as well as trained by—the vocative case of Victorian narrative, though no less than philological, is not a linguistic or stylistic matter only. "Dear reader" is the proverbial tip of an iceberg; its occasional appearance marks the structure of participation, mostly submerged and invisible but now and then replayed by parable, which floats an entire fictional institution. And has done so right from the genre's start. When in 1625 Cervantes begins his "Prologue to the Reader" at the opening of the second part of *Don Quixote* with "gentle or even plebeian reader" (415), he has covered the bases to remind us of the derivation of address from the deference exacted by aristocratic patronage. But even the common rather than gentle reader is always a patron of the art of fiction, a contributor, a sponsoring because coresponsive supplement. Despite *Don Quixote*'s extended satire of overcredulous readerly investment, the first volume of the novel (1615) can close by ironically suggesting that eventual readers should model their reactions on something not unlike the Don's own (admittedly excessive) fascination with romance. This happens when the narrator, speaking for the chronicle's "said author," asks from "those that shall read it" only "the same credit that people of sense give to the books of chivalry that pervade the world and are so popular" (402-3). By your tacit extrapolation from the reading of chivalric romances within the narrative, the Don's extreme reaction thus mediates between the novel's popular intertexts and the readerly populace restructured on the spot through the suspended disbelief solicited by the present account of his adventures. Interpolated by prefatory or summarizing mention and extrapolating from the thematics of reading within the text, you are made to know your equilibrated place only through the cooperative making of it.

To say that the participatory logic of both address and parable reflects upon the license of institutionalized reading is not to suggest that the reflexive text can ever fully characterize, let alone dictate, its own effect. Here is where you come in—and hence where "the reader" can never be fully written in. The fictional text can only strive—only contrive—to model and so mandate, without ever being able to monitor, your response. Thus it is that interpolation (the text inscribing you by third-person reference or vocative tag) and extrapolation (you choosing to read yourself in parable) attest to deeply complementary motives of Victorian narrative, motives tacitly in play even when the text has not worked to manifest them together. For the impulse of classic fiction is to address your attention even when no second-person grammar gets in the way of story, as well as to narrate your place in its discourse even when no one (else)—no character—is made to read.

In the strictest sense, this double impulse is, of course, an impossible challenge to the novel's specialized variety of textual utterance, since through it all the plot must go on. I have found only one text that succeeds in mounting the two effects all but simultaneously, address and reflexive enactment, and only by an instructively reductive trick of referentiality. Accordingly, I have given it pride of place as the epigraph to this study. "This is called reading," it begins. The utterance is more than just fundamentally self-referential. It operates not as a self-enclosed enunciation, only as a provocation to its own reading event. It is not the text here that could really be said to be referring to itself as "this." Instead, the shifter effects a more rudimentary displacement. It is not reading matter that is the referent but rather the act of reading: what you are doing, from one part of speech to another, in making your way across this wryly patronizing second-person advertisement. "So far you're doing fine." Despite its capping direct address, this utterance is also a caught scene ("this") of reading, however minimal, immediate, and undernarrated. This "catchy" ad copy may thus be taken to conflate the two halves of this study in a rhetorical interpolation of attention ("you're") inseparable from the previous sentence's zero-degree extrapolation from the demonstrated to the instantaneously eventuated scene of reading. In the minimalism of this scenario, your extrapolation from it evokes the very site of attention not as place but as the mental space of cognitive duration itself.

Here I touch on the way in which an analysis of the reading analogue, the scene of extrapolated response in fiction, tends to converge with the familiar category of self-referentiality only to revise it. Miniaturized in that ad copy but soon to be exemplified at varying length, the kind of reflexive (rather than strictly autotelic) episode with which we will find ourselves concerned labors to develop a telos pointing outside the text. The analogic scene of reading, in all its rhetorically crafted and narratively charged determinants, is there to remind you—in deed—that form has a transitive as well as a static sense, designating the formative as well as the shaped. This, then, is the ultimate structural—or constructivist—dimension of extrapolated auto-allegory in the reading of classic fiction. It is not merely a form of reading. It seeks to form reading. It is structuration's way of trespassing from text to reception, in another sense from text to context. And so from one perspective it is the only true reflexive moment in fiction, the only moment genuinely turned back on itself *as moment* rather than merely as stretch of writing. Anything but page-bound and hermetically self-commenting, such an analogue of narrative attention is disposed—is stationed and poised—precisely to induce a *reflex* in that conscripted reader whose attention it configures from within. In just this way is conscription itself narrated, narrated when it is not simply effected by address.

Hence the types of "reader-making" (James) which divide across the next two introductory chapters. Where direct references in second or third person render by designating the reader at a given moment, embedded analogues render by portraying (whether or not also apostrophizing) the reading act, either literally or in camouflage. Here again is the byplay of dialogic (faintly interlocutory) over against analogic (latently parabolic) forms of the reading event, of interpolation (writing in the reader) and extrapolation (reading out from textual situation to deciphering stance). To secure and extend our understanding of their complementary functions, we need, from the start, the clearest possible estimate of the vocative function in prose fiction. To this end the next chapter is given over.

Methodological Forecast

It should already be clear how the emphasis of this book emerges from an interest in the relentless micromanagement of reaction in nineteenth-century narrative. The study thus begins at the same time in a dissatisfaction with accounts that tend to obscure this textual work: with, for instance, the positivism of the new economic and demographic studies in aggregate reading communities, with those tendencies in cultural studies that would level the text to the horizon of its social determinants, and even with the normative semiotics as well as hermeneutics of reader response. These are among the leading current paradigms by which fiction readers, in the name of their emancipation, are often disenfranchised as inventive (if never free) agents. Rather than figures in and of the text, enlisted agencies, they are reduced by these paradigms, respectively, to (a) sheer consumers of the novel's merchandized distractions, (b) processors of extraliterary cultural discourse when sieved through fiction, or (c) the standardized producers—in response—of a text's raw intelligibility both as narrative utterance and as thematic pattern. Whether the mass audience is merely pitched a product or actively sold an ideological bill of goods as well, in either case the third category of "response" seems no adequate name for the subjection of readers to their rhetorical programming by text.

Nor does the "interpellated" reader of bourgeois narrative, a radically conformist sort encountered lately in British cultural critique and its American counterparts (via Althusser's sense of the subject "hailed" into ideology), go any very great distance toward specifying the textual effect.[20] This notion of co-optation tends to back even farther away from textual work toward the amorphous working upon the reader of the text's cultural assumptions, taken as already shared while being tactically instilled. My point is not that the idea of interpellation is not true for narrative texts but rather that, as the final word, it is not true *to* them, to the particulars of their cultural insinuation. An ideologically oriented analysis of the notion of "hailing" might well, handled differently, make powerful connection, on the textual face of things, with the actual citation—and intended rhetorical incitation—of the Victorian novel reader. This is a reader often, for one thing, interpolated (hence interpellated) through the personifying force of direct address. But rather than beginning with this overt pinioning of the reader, a reader conscripted by being quite explicitly accosted, instead the notion of "hailing" tends to be generalized beyond linguistic or rhetorical recognition in its usual literary applications.[21] Response aesthetics is thus summarily shunted onto cultural critique, the constructive but also text-constituted reader translated to the socially constructed subject of a literary institution seen as ideological apparatus. In this way the concept of the interpellated reader can too quickly become merely an updated version of the intended and implied, the competent and model reader not of texts so much as of that cultural baggage with which they are inevitably freighted. What needs stressing, instead, is that the cultural logic of interpellation is a logic only manifest in fiction according to literature's own logistics: a set of minutely calibrated verbal strategies devised *by* narrative rather than a blanket fact *about* narrative.[22] On the score of apostrophe alone, the evidence of this study collects against Catherine Belsey's proposition that classic realism "interpellates the reader as a transcendent and non-contradictory subject" (78). This is, rather, what culture at large does with its social subjects. To the extent that it does so in part through narrative fiction—a prose literature that distinguishes itself, that justifies and markets itself, by its difference from other discursive forms—such fiction may be found hailing its figuratively dispersed, even though ultimately recuperated, reader by a far more destabilizing array of localizing rhetorical devices and interpretive instigations.

So how should one proceed? Some premises about my own line(s) of investigation are in order. (1) From a semiotics of narrative codes, I extract a manifold sense of the classic novel's "dear reader" as *sign*, not just narrative signpost. (2) From narratology, by extension, I assume a sense that both the explicit signification of the reader's act (by third-person mention or direct address) and the metanarrative figuration of such reading are best understood in relation to the textual energies of plot. (3) At the same time, from the poststructuralist rhetoric of tropes I take counsel on the buried strata of figurative language in all textual structure, from which any particularized figuration of the reader must emerge. (4) From historicist work (new and old) on the exigencies of the literary marketplace, including periodical and serial publication, I take my further view of the tactical urgency both of address and of the strategies of its suppression in certain narrative settings. (5) From the more linguistic discriminations of discourse analysis (in early Foucault), I derive a sense of subjectivity in enunciation which renders the narrator/audience dyad a reciprocal contingency and a slipping differential. (6) From deconstruction as it overlaps with this study of discursive positioning, I borrow terms for a resistance to the interlocutory figments of the communicative model when imported into narrative. (7) Burrowing even deeper beneath the normative functions of directed utterance, an intensified textual audition (oriented by an intersection of what can be thought of, in shorthand, as Derridean, Lacanian, and Kristevan models) lays my readings open at times to the differential phonograms as well as the transgressive puns of the novelistic undertext, both in their return (nostalgically) to a prescribal fluidity of language and in their reversion (psychically) to the unconscious-structured-like-a-language. (8) From a further psychoanalytic account of the textual function, as called up in part by the transactional (and often virtually transferential) gestures of reader apostrophe and its correlative figurations, I am led nonetheless, despite the breakdown of the communications paradigm, to a sense of the emotive dynamics of narrativized reception staged by the text itself. (9) And first of all, as well as finally, I situate this mutual dynamic of encoded reception within a literary history where the study of noncanonical texts (the now little-read Victorian best-sellers I review here, for instance) would make no historical (let alone aesthetic) sense if such texts are considered in artificial isolation from their own contemporaneous interaction with the culture of the canon, both its literary standards and their social cachet.

In short, then, I wish to demonstrate that the textual effects of both reader reference and enacted reading are systemically bound together as (1) a signifying function and (2) a narrative armature that together (3) trope rather than reproduce the reading experience within (4) a given set of publishing imperatives, mass-market expectations, and consumer constraints; trope it, in other words, (5) as a bifocal discourse of subjectivity divided between narrator and narratee which (6) exposes even while exploiting (in a word, deconstructs) any normative fiction of communication, while (7) coasting at times on an undulatory depth of lexical mutation and phonotextual viscosity that may nevertheless sustain (8) a mimed psychodynamic of reciprocal self-construction between storytelling "voice" and figured reader—(9) all of which can only be apprehended in its restless (and often allusive) permutations along the several pathways of a continually oscillating literary history. Toward such an evolutionary account of novelistic conscription, the next chapter's history of reader apostrophe is only the first of these paths forward.

Chapter Two

On Terms with the Reader
The Interpolated Audience

> The reader himself is always thoroughly anonymous, he is anybody, singular
> yet transparent. He does not add his name to the book (as our fathers used to do)
> but rather erases every name through his nameless presence and the humble,
> passive, interchangeable and insignificant gaze from whose gentle probing
> the book emerges written, dependent on nothing and on nobody.
>
> —Blanchot, "Reading"

An Interesting Book
(artist unknown, n.d.). The Bettmann Archive

*A*s a reader of classic fiction, you never know where your next "you" is
coming from. Even poetry can get into—by getting you in on—the act: the
act as event. On the eve of the nineteenth century, part of the narrative intertext of Wordsworth's *Lyrical Ballads*—the vestigial link of these poems
through the balladic tradition not only to minstrelsy but also to early novelistic device—surfaces in a direct interpolation of the audience as "gentle reader."
It is a device ordinarily foreign, of course, to the tradition of lyric reflection.
The address sneaks up on us in "Simon Lee" by beginning undemonstratively
with a descriptive emphasis closer to the French *on* than to the "you" of strict
second person. For "meet him where you will," Wordsworth writes of his
protagonist, "you see / At once that he is poor" (ll. 11–12). By the beginning of

the ninth stanza, we are still being invited into the text via this generalized mode of address: "Few months of life has he in store, / As he to you will tell" (ll. 55–56). But in the second quatrain of this stanza, the free-form "you" suddenly calcifies, by parody, into a rhetorical twin of the apostrophized and mockingly coddled reader of eighteenth-century fiction, complete with epithet and vocative. "My gentle reader, I perceive / How patiently you've waited" (ll. 69–70), notes the speaker, quite obviously "afraid" (as evinced even by his novelistic mode of address) "that you expect / Some tale will be related" (ll. 71–72). Such passive (if here restive) consumption of narrative is acknowledged by Wordsworth only to be rebuked and cured, for the next stanza continues with an echoing deflection of the earlier idiom "in store" (l. 55 above, for "to come"): "O reader! had you in your mind / Such stores as silent thought can bring"—with the further overtone of "stories" in "stores"—"O gentle reader! you would find / A tale in everything" (ll. 73–76).

Narrative, like beauty, is in the mind's eye of the beholder. And reading is textually invoked by Wordsworth primarily as a name for a certain interpretive receptiveness to the world apart from texts, a receptiveness that can only be blunted by the inflamed narrativity and blatant "appeal" (in both senses again) of the popular novel. Already prominent enough for dismissive allusion by Wordsworth, the interpolated reader of the eighteenth-century novel becomes a hallmark of complacent narrative fascination (though also much else) in Victorian fictional practice. Indeed, after a century more of novelized readers crowding the pages of literary production and menacing its rhetorical credibility, Gerard Manley Hopkins will think to criticize a poem of Robert Bridges, "On a Dead Child," for being, in effect, too much in the emotional key of reader address (despite its prolonged apostrophe to the dead child): indulging, that is, "a familiar commonplace about 'Reader, have you never hung over the pillow of . . . '!"[1] What Hopkins satirizes was already there for Wordsworth as a lowbrow intertext.

Building on such eighteenth-century precedents, the novel of the nineteenth century gets on by coming to no uncertain terms with the agency of its activation. It is likely to do so either through the use of a specific *term* for that agency ("audience," "public," "friends") or through some other negotiated understanding, either by name or by intimation, now by vocative deference ("gentle reader"), now by structural inference (emblematic scene). This and the next chapter divide up the alternatives between them. In the present consideration of direct reader reference, our tracing a hallmark of Victorian fiction back to an innovation of Dantean epic practice—and across an irregular and variegated topography in between, in both verse and prose—should show this tendency in process.

The mentioned reader, whether addressed in second person or ascribed in third, marks the site of an implicated response, however minimal, by which the reading subject is gradually taken for granted in the narrative text, granted to it and so assumed by it, assumed and presumed upon. And so the mentioned reader becomes an optionally explicit placeholder for that subjectivity constructed by, because requisite for, the execution of narrative not only as mass product but as supposedly private pleasure. To follow along the different contributory streams that feed into the rhetoric of fictional address in the emergent moment of the novel as genre is thus to theorize the reading subject as a manifold and discrepant construct: partly invoked like a muse manqué, partly written to as in a letter, sometimes chastened as if from pulpit or roadside tombstone, now conversed with as if in attendance, now alluded to in absentia and in prospect ("the reader" rather than "dear reader"), occasionally hectored as if by a courtroom prosecutor, here elevated to surrogate patron, there merely patronized, often bowed to, sometimes browbeaten, and everywhere, in a word, conscripted.

Any prehistory of the Victorian "dear reader" thus moves toward a theory of such a reading agency when and if it looks back not just to the underpinnings of direct address in the Western literary tradition, in Dante's *Divine Comedy*, but to the interplay of the saluted or commanded reader with the apostrophized muse of this same tradition—as well as with diverse influences from the editorial, epitaphic, juridical, and epistolary modes. A detailed enough attempt at genealogy begins in this way to confound and unravel the logic of address. Such a heterocosm of intertexts generates a kind of allusive overkill, so that readers may find themselves diversified beyond coherence by the same language that attests to, if only by tacitly requesting, their very attention. Individual reading subjects cannot take up a kaleidoscope of addressed or attributed positions without cost, without deficit of credible presence under any one sign; they cannot be all things at once, except to the textual system that admits to merely constructing them from phrase to phrase. Before narrowing in, then, on the postmedieval lineage of that most common form of interpolated literary attention, the direct address to a textual audience, we should find use for a broader account of literary apostrophe, not limited to reader invocation, as a tactic for the annexation of receptive consciousness to textual subjectivity. With this account before us, we will then be able to trace the transformation of conscriptive device from Dante's Italian epic into English through Spenser and Bunyan and, once converted to fictional maneuver in Fielding, from Scott on into the whole range of Victorian practices pitched between Dickens' muted, sentimental use of the trope and the outright parody of address in Thackeray.

In the Case of the Vocative

Even for linguistics, to say nothing (yet) of narrative poetics, this function of address has its anomalies. When Jakobson rethought the traditional breakdown of an utterance according to message, sender, and receiver, the last, or "appellative," dimension (over against the sender's expressive dimension) was termed "conative." It was thus separated entirely by Jakobson from the operations of the message itself: namely, the referential, poetic, phatic, and metalingual functions, concerned respectively with context, message (as message), contact, and code.[2] But when traces of the appellative reappear within the poetic or fictive message, the categorical ground begins to slip. How, for instance, does one understand the apparent conative residuum of direct "appeal" (as well as the phatic reassertion of readerly "contact") in the rhetoric of the literary apostrophe? One is tempted to insist that the poetic code can manifest direct address only on the code's own terms, relying exclusively on a verbal engagement with a wholly textual "narratee"[3]—with, that is again, Ong's entirely fictional audience in its strictly figurative investiture.

The second person—it cannot be overstressed—is a grammatical category in literature, not a receptive destination. The slack between discursive address and extranarrative appeal, then, between the reader *in* the fiction and the reader *awaiting* it, keeps in play two divergent models of language activity: narrative text and communicative speech act. To say so is to expand upon a passing disclaimer in Jakobson's own essay, when he remarks on the inevitable indeterminacy that attaches to the "'you' or 'thou' of the alleged audience of dramatic monologues, supplications, and epistles" (313). Add to his list of literary modes the mainstream novel (rhetorically descended or compounded, we will see, from all three) and you have my point. In the oscillation between ultimate textual recipient and a stand-in "dear reader," the actual reader is eased into the utopic space of address, whether spelled out or implied. To put the matter in terms of speech act theory: The illocutionary mode of "directive," along with the other vocative and imperative forms of reader address, serves to mime a perlocutionary (or extratextual) force that it can only inscribe, never effect.[4]

But that is only one half of a conscriptive procedure that can be traced back to a linguistic foundation. The orientation of a text toward its receiver, even from within the texture of its message, may be manifest through narrative extrapolations from, rather than mere appeals to, an attention thereby enacted rather than enjoined. I dwell on this correlation of effects to emphasize again the strictly textual or "poetic" (ultimately figurative) basis for both aspects of this study. On our way into a pair of chapters devoted to each in turn, we might sum up the dual issue in a terminology adapted once more from Jakobson. Just as the poetic function is tinged with the conative through direct address, so is it inflected with the metalingual function (where self-reflexive questions about the code emerge) in certain scenes of reading. For it is there that we encounter narrative reception defining, by performing, its own terms in progress. In short, reading's self-parable is the complement of apostrophe in a figurative analysis of narrative coding.

Jonathan Culler's influential essay on the repressed attention to apostrophe in the criticism of lyric poetry happens to follow his critique of reader-response theory in *The Pursuit of Signs*.[5] It does so, however, without making any direct connection to the phenomenon of reader address as a variant of lyric apostrophe (the vocative personification of the absent and abstract) and none to the novel as contiguous genre. Culler generalizes about "two forces in poetry, the narrative and the apostrophic," without considering their convergence in novelistic asides to the reader.[6] Apostrophe, Culler shows, "tropes not on the meaning of a word but on the circuit or situation of communication itself" (135). This is a circuit that would seem to include (though Culler has no occasion to say so), if only by triangulation, the reader as well as the odic abstraction. The latter would in this sense be subsumed to and hence naturalized by the I-thou economy of the former. By this I mean simply to suggest that the only way for an invoked presence, whether metaphysical abstraction or genius loci, to stand addressed by an apostrophic interjection (Shelley's "O wild West Wind," for example) is not for the odic addressee to hear such a summons while the rest of us merely hear, by reading, *about* it but rather for the figure (both senses) of address to stand momentarily in the very place of the reader as the (otherwise continuous) recipient of lyric utterance. Culler's omission of any reference to specified "reader" address notwithstanding (even in a romantic verse text like "Simon Lee"), the point he builds upon the metaphoric force of romantic apostrophe could scarcely be a larger one: "If, as we tend to assume, post-enlightenment poetry seeks to overcome the alienation of subject from object, then apostrophe takes the crucial step of constituting the object as another subject with whom the poetic subject might hope to strike up a harmonious relationship" (143). In the alienated world of withdrawn subjectivity (perfectly recapitulated, I would add, in the autonomous muteness of textual utterance and exchange), the trope of invocation marks the gap it can only pretend to close.

In light of Culler's emphasis on romanticism in his attempted restitution of apostrophe as a critical category, we might further hypothesize a transitional genealogy for that chief apostrophic form of prose narrative, the interruption of telling by hailing. It would run like this. Between the formulas of address ("Hail to thee, blithe spirit!") in the romantic lyric and the co-opted apostrophic form of nineteenth-century fiction (from Brontë's "Reader, I married him" to Kipling's "O Best Beloved!") would lie, even before the Victorian dramatic monologue (and exempting the mockery of predigested consumption in "Simon Lee"), the so-called conversation poem of Wordsworth or Coleridge. In texts like "The Eolian Harp" or "Tintern Abbey," however, the troping of dialogue by way of apostrophe (to bride and sister, respectively) is not exhausted at the level of such a rhetorical conceit. Nor is it in those apostrophic epitaphs by which Wordsworth was so frequently intrigued. Interlocution emerges as itself a metatrope of that natural interanimation that is often the poem's topic, as if all physical presence, all natural energy, were in a dialogue for which a given human exchange might at any moment serve as metaphor. Such texts inscribe in this way the saturated community of feeling—with other selves because with nature first and foremost—which lays claim to the figure of conversation as both instance and symbol, both metonymy and metaphor.

The presence of a silent dialogic partner in these poems confirms, in other words, the visionary agenda of their meditations on nature. The issue is not dissimilar in Victorian narrative, where the presence of an interlocutor is often, in and of itself, the utopian upshot of the narrative's social vision. Whether by interpolation or extrapolation, whether engaged by second person (or its deflected forms of third-person reader reference) or analogized by narrative episode, reading becomes itself a metaphor, vehicle to a tenor beyond itself—and beyond itself in the full valorization of such reach. Reading is read as community. By address or anecdote, apostrophe or parable, the Victorian novel conscripts the attention it solicits as a wholesale figure for the communicable legibility that alone can channel consciousness within the semiotic immersion of social existence. It is not enough that the private life be registered, made to signify; it must be conveyed in order to be known, yes, but it must also be known *to be conveyable*. Bombarded by signs, their singularity often effaced by corporate writing (journalism, bureaucratic directives, advertising, and so forth, all the discourses currently under analysis in Victorian scholarship), isolated Victorian subjects want their story told, however indirectly, as a story *told*. They want the image of a narrator—and thus of an auditor or reader. In this sense, the vicariousness of the novel does not stop at the level of narrative (which is also why, ultimately, it can be renarrated as an analogue or parable of itself, as we will see in the next chapter). The underlying—at times overbearing—psychic surrogacy of the Victorian novel has as much to do, in other words, with narration as with narrated story.

I give emphasis to a point that seems to me as hard to deny as to find discussion of. In our reading of classic fiction, we identify with narration itself as process; in our attention, with the telling per se; in our supposed listening, with at least one voice that does not go unheeded.[7] We heroize narrators—and reward them in turn with attention—as a projection of our own latent wish to be heard. Though we certainly identify with the tribulations of a William Dobbin, a Maggie Tulliver, an Arthur Clennam, a Clara Middleton, as readers we also identify with the pressure to narrate, the intention to tell, and almost as much with the omniscience of *Middlemarch* as with the first-person narration of *David Copperfield*. Our isolation as readers, doubled by the variously preserved and invaded privacy of fictional characters, a state taken in turn either as an inalienable autonomy or an alienated atomism—this radical privacy is thus relieved twice over by novelistic reception: first, by the appeal to our very capacity for vicarious participation in the lives of characters, even benign eavesdropping; and second (a fact less often recognized), by our tacitly acknowledged capacity, by receiving such narrative as a motivated enunciation, to alleviate the narrative agent's own emotional isolation, anthropomorphically rather than textually construed. Before and after all, at a bare minimum there is one thing you prove by reading: In the midst of inevitable social fragmentation, at least somewhere someone is paying the emotional price of attention.

Calling this premise of Victorian storytelling not just an anthropomorphic bias but a psychological bent is to begin engaging a deeper cultural fact that the coming chapters on Dickens and the Brontës will make inescapable. The nineteenth-century novel articulates a massive and unsaid paradigm shift that transpires in the rhetorical substratum of Victorian narrative textuality: a shift from philosophy (metaphysics, epistemology, ethics, aesthetics) to psychology (affect, its defenses and deflections, its willed transactions). Hence the mystified circular logic of narrative voice. "Reader, I married him" consummates two lines of desire at once, suspends two solitudes: that of narrator as well as that of heroine, a doubleness all the clearer in *Jane Eyre* because the two personae are interchangeable. One structural consequence of all this merits repeating. It is precisely because the reader's emotional identification with realist narrative is bifocal—now with a character making her way in the world, now with narrative consciousness itself, now representational, we might say, now phenomenological—that the space for parable is opened. It is only because you respond at two levels that in certain strategic circumstances the former can refigure the latter. It is only in this way that in reading about another's reading you can think to encounter your own.

Short of this, you may simply be reminded in passing that you are read-ing—by having your textual attention invoked by address. I began with Culler's stress on the psychodynamic of nineteenth-century poetic apostrophe because such a vocative format comes revealingly close to the novelistic model of di-rect reader engagement, even as much of the apostrophic effect attaches as well to such third-person references to an audience as "the perceptive reader will no doubt see . . ." This should be clear after we turn now, back past Culler's resuscitated interest in romantic apostrophe, to Dante's first vernac-ular proliferation of a more pointed, and narrowly rhetorical, apostrophe to the reader.

On the way, we touch again on that first point made by Culler about the lyric vocative, a rhetorical device that we need now to distinguish from reader address and its close correlate in reader reference. The distinction is so per-fectly obvious that it might well be missed without insisting on it. And in another sense, it doesn't hold at all. Let me do what I can to clarify. Lyric apos-trophe tends to fantasize its own present occasion. The troping of an audi-ence, by contrast, must always anticipate its occasion from the distance of the previously written (or subsequently printed) page. Lyric apostrophe, for Culler, is one of those moments that "say 'now'" (149). Within this fiction of instantaneous reception—in Shelley's "thou breath of autumn's being," for instance—the wind is imagined to be breathing on the lyric speaker even as he solicits its spirit, a naturalized muse forever in attendance. The reader's conscripted inspiration of (not just by) a text, however, is always a thing in prospect. In such an imperative as "thou, reader of these pages, please note that . . . ," no one but the author is present to the formulation of the thought; readers make do only with its later recognition. At the same time, though, just as such moments anticipate their own outcome, their own endpoint in reception, they also become a kind of self-fulfilling prophecy. A vocative of this sort is no sooner seen than achieved. It is for this reason that "the reader will see here," though apparently more accurate than "the reader sees here," is interchangeable with it in novelistic practice, each realizing on the spot its own eventuation.

All the varieties and derivatives of reader apostrophe thus differ from odic address by the time lag of their vocative, even as that lag is erased in reception. It is in such reception that the past time of writing or printing, of enunciation or dissemination, is displaced onto the time of textual activation. So that finally "dear reader" and "the reader" both "say 'now'" after all, but only, unlike "thou breath of autumn's being," by first manifestly absenting the Voice of the Author altogether. Another way to think of this, on the way back to Dante, is that when the role of the Muse is partly devolved upon the reader at the dawn of modern literature, the conjuring and resonant persona of the bard is usurped irreversibly by the silence of the printed page in circulation.

It is of course the epic dimension of address which has vanished so completely from the contemporary resurgence of the second person in postmodernist experimental fiction. Though not able to eradicate entirely such a grammatical option within literary rhetoric, modernism did what it could to administer the death blow to any epic pretensions on the part of the readerly "you." Programmatically outlawed in modernism, address went underground, extruded only in irony or parody, and then only rarely. Forbidden equally by the autotelic gestures of formal self-enclosure and by the often skeptical despair of such fiction's psychosocial content, the open invitation to response is wiped clean from the burnished surface of a modernist text that stresses inscape over outreach, as well as from a vision of community too besieged for the gesture of familiarity and affiliation sketched by address. Yet the habit of second-person summons, atrophied in the *fin de siècle* text and taboo in its high modernist successors, never actually dies. As if banked for decades rather than extinguished, the impulse toward interpolated attention flares up again in the postmodern involutions of the *nouveau roman*. Under communicative restraint for so long, the novel as genre is now bent out of shape by this indulgence of the second person. Rhetorical orientation, so entirely repressed in its own right, returns from within plot as a skewing of characterization itself. For in numerous contemporary texts "you" engorges both "I" and "she" or "he" as hero.[8] Where the modernist artifact often seems closed, self-contained, introvert, the postmodernist text grows so wholly porous to the circulation networks of its dissemination that the audience can appear in the text as the simulacrum of itself, an impertinent double of that immanent reader so long effaced by modernism.

Each reader is so inextricably wedded to every other reader in the atomized interchangeability effected by certain postmodernist narratives that one of the most extravagant of such novels ends in a precipitous marriage of its two principal readers, who bed down with each other and the book in hand:

"Now you are man and wife, Reader and Reader. A great double bed receives your parallel readings."[9] This is a novel whose plot is merely the turning of its own pages, a novel that opens with "you are about to begin reading Italo Calvino's new novel, *If on a winter's night a traveler*. Relax. Concentrate" (3)— in order to end eleven chapters later with the new husband saying to his Reader bride, "And you say, 'Just a moment, I've almost finished *If on a winter's night a traveler* by Italo Calvino'" (260). The devices of interpolation and extrapolation merge completely when the only site of narration is meant to set (up) the erotic scene of its very consumption. Concentrating on the former device in this chapter, I allude here to the grammatical recovery of second-person address in such writers as Butor, Pynchon, and Calvino, among others, mainly to show how the epic stretch toward tribal consolidation through narrative is inverted by a postmodernist textual circuitry that processes—and so pulverizes—all traces of social space into textual space. To appreciate this most recent turn—outside in—of narrativized rhetoricity in the discourse of fiction requires a clearer picture of address in the epic tradition itself and its early novelistic offshoots. We seek, in particular, a poetics (and linguistics) of address within a theory of reader representation.

Pensa, lettore: The Reflecting Reader

In the tradition of the oral epic, the bard's audience was all ears. Bardic "textuality" was thus saturated with tacit and global address. Epic *reading*, by contrast, encounters those more local devices necessary in scribal culture to retain—and impart—a sense of audience. Hence the advent of reader address in the vernacular Italian of the *Divine Comedy*, as debated by Auerbach and Spitzer.[10] Both agree that there is no precedent for such address in the classic epic and that its Latin appearances in Ovid and Martial were more on the order of appeals to a patron (Auerbach, "Dante's Addresses," 268). Auerbach includes the direct address of the "funeral inscription" or "epitaph" (269) as one kind of prototype—in a way separately developed in later work by John Freccero—but only so that Auerbach can distinguish it from the new loftiness of invocation in the twenty such addresses that punctuate the *Commedia*.[11] He points out that classic rhetorical theory, concerned with spoken oratory and its assumed presence of an audience, its a priori "public" (270), has no term for such moments of invoked attention, which have to be distinguished from the strict sense of an "apostrophe" (270), whether to a muse, a goddess, or an opponent. All rhetoric was in one sense apostrophic. What surfaces from these discriminations is a sense—not explored by Auerbach himself—that in the vernacular literature of a new print culture, reader address amounts to a trope of tropes. The previous, presumptive ground of all rhetoric, a present audience under exhortation, becomes that metatextual horizon of a modern literary culture that Dante, in definitive command of it, chooses to make explicit. He does so by stressing the linguistic artifact as directed expression. Reader address, as a particular exacerbation of the communicative paradigm, thus tends to come forward as an atavistic and fabricated index of literature's oral genesis: again, the rhetorical trace of rhetoricity per se, the troping of all tropology as the solicitation of attention by direct utterance.

Locating Dante's own specific reasons for inscribing his reader in this way will take us to the crux of Spitzer's demurral from Auerbach. Within the larger perspective of literary history, however, their claims serve mostly to reinforce each other. In Auerbach's view, the appeals to the reader's involvement and activity are pedagogic, even prophetic, with the poetic speaker, himself guided by Virgil, guiding the reader in turn into the untraveled reaches of the other world. Dante's exhortation to think, to imagine, to read with participation—*Pensa, lettore* ("Reflect, reader") (*Literary Language*, 302 n. 118)—is the most forthright of these addresses in the vocative mode of *O tu che leggi* ("O you, who read") (300 n. 117), for it asks no more than it occasions. If and when Auerbach seems to be emphasizing the visionary and pedagogic rather than merely descriptive powers of Dante's narrator, however, Spitzer balks at this characterization, especially in light of Auerbach's previous work. Spitzer insists instead that the reader's imagination is elicited and coached more as a function of *mimesis* itself than in direct service to the narrator's prophetic dispensation. The reader is singled out and guided forward more to render accessible the visions of the beyond than to transmit spiritual illumination about them (158).

When Auerbach later returns to his original argument about Dante in light of Spitzer's objections, he clarifies his emphasis on Dante's "ability to address the reader" as a mode less of spiritual "prophecy" than of literary "authority" (297). It is in this sense that "Dante created a public not for himself alone but for his successors as well" (312). But to what extent does this public take subsequent redefinition from the same rhetorical device that helps found it? For us, the question comes down to this: Given Auerbach's scrutiny of a vernacular epic at the dawn of widespread print culture, a literary genre laying formal claim to a public through the maneuvers of invocation, what can be borrowed from such a cultural moment for an understanding of the next great stage in the consolidation of modern literary practice: namely, the birth—in Georg Lukács's terms—of the novelistic epic out of the epic proper?

To what extent, for instance, does Henry Fielding's "comic epic-poem in prose" (the novelistic genre so designated in the preface to *Joseph Andrews*) secure an audience for the new vernacular form of narrative fiction through a return to the functions of address—and, more important, to all that they imply about the readerly compact—experimented with by Dante but excluded, for instance, from the Miltonic epic? Any full answer would await a look at two missing links in the evolution of the English novel as central cultural form. I refer to the nexus of allegorical texts by Spenser and Bunyan which serve to transfer the epic ambition in English through verse narrative into prose fiction.

This line of development is overlain, of course, with any number of other histories, including not only the epitaphic tradition (as Auerbach suggests) but the gradually secularized legacy of the literary Muse itself. So that to chart the course of that imperative/vocative dyad (*Pensa, lettore*)—as it passes in derivation, by the most graduated of stages, from Dante to the early novelists—is also to record the progressive subordination of the apostrophized Muse (or, in later terms, the aristocratic patron) to other structures of directed utterance.[12] From Muse to disinterested general reader is a gradual transformation littered with a number of specified and partisan invocations along the way. On Auerbach's showing, "nowhere does Dante speak like an author who looks upon his readers as customers" (301). This will come, but it awaits the rise of the novel within and from the combined capitalism and bourgeois individualism of mass print culture.

Readers Errant: Spenser's Knights to Bunyan's Buyers

Following Spenser's dedicatory sonnets to *The Faerie Queene*, the proem of the first canto inaugurates the prevailing format of apostrophe to the eponymous addressee, Elizabeth herself, as an overarching political, spiritual, and even stylistic muse. At a couple of later points, however, the invocatory pattern of direct address is what we might call narrativized. In this way does the definitive figure of the epic, the character of the knight errant, become in the other sense a figure for the reader, the reader apostrophized and admonished in the imperative mode: "Young knight, what euer that does armes professe, ... Beware of fraud" (I.iv.1.1–3). This is the same chivalric narratee who is pluralized in a later address: "Redoubted knights, and honorable Dames, / To whom I leuell all my labours end" (III.ix.1.1–2). None of this Spenserian latitude within the category of the apostrophized muse occurs in the studious classicism of Milton, who begins *Paradise Lost* by calling down inspiration on his head in order to proceed with its assurance from that point on: "Of Man's first Disobedience . . . Sing, Heavenly Muse." Unlike in Dante, the effort to "justify the ways of God to men" is handled without direct address, the reader induced to reflect without being told to do so. On the matter of apostrophe, it is instead Bunyan's allegorical version of the Christian quest as cultural epic in *The Pilgrim's Progress* which offers a more illuminating move toward the procedures of the novel.[13] After much sparring with his critics in second-person grammar, the opening "Author's Apology for his Book" finally deploys the vocative formula of summons or solicitation for something more like the dismissive rather than inviting "Come now": "Come, let my carper to his life now look, / And find there darker lines than in my book."[14] Further along, however, the second person widens to embrace, by circumlocution, the general reader at large: "This book it chalketh out before thine eyes / The man that seeks the everlasting prize" (5). As it "chalketh out" rather than "talketh out" its argument, we are that much further from the bardic origins of the epic.

From sighted words, then, the reader is now led on in this inaugural "Apology" to the refigured traverse of the text that processes them as a series of narrated events. "This book will make a traveller of thee" (5), Bunyan continues, rather in the mode of Spenser's questing reader. There follow more than a dozen rhetorical questions stationed to interrogate the reader's desire and hold out promise of its fulfillment. They are punctuated en route with another imperative in which the emphasis on writing goes so far as to suggest the text as the unmediated transcription of the narrator's own inner life: "Then read my fancies" (7). But it is the last two in the surrounding string of rhetorical interrogations which bring us closest to what one may think of as Bunyan's fathering of novelistic address: "Wouldst thou lose thyself, and catch no harm / And find thyself again without a charm?" (7). Rehearsing the Christian model of losing thyself to find thyself, Bunyan's question replays it with a more aesthetic sense of a going out of oneself in projective identification and return. Biblical dramaturgy is thus partially devolved upon textual phenomenology. But this identification, as in the case of the reader with the hailed knights in *The Faerie Queene*, is really a mode of self-exploration, here explicitly called self-reading: "Would read thyself, and read thou knowest not what / And yet know whether thou are blest or not, / By reading the same lines?" (7). Self-knowledge comes by indirection and allegory, the reader a questing decipherer who confronts herself in both the cryptology of narrative and the narratology of the inner life.

The(e) Reader: Attention Edited In

Bunyan's trope of the reader as encoded hero of a narrative apparently otherwise engaged is an idea willed to the novel of the next century and its descendants. And not least because it is an idea conveyed by the recurrent mechanisms of direct address. On the way into the narrative's central dream vision: "O then come hither / And lay my book, thy head, and heart together" (7). On the way out: "Now, reader, I have told my dream to thee / See if thou canst *interpret* it to me" ("Conclusion," 167; emphasis added). Narrative hermeneutics, seldom so openly invoked, takes at the same time an unexpected turn. To phrase it only somewhat anachronistically, Bunyan's text *novelizes* its readership into the new postepic muse, the audience as ultimate motivation, but here in a further reversal by which the audience helps the text read itself.

More than this, in the verse introduction to the second part of *The Pilgrim's Progress*, in 1684, the quasi-novelistic, psychologically identified, and entirely textual reader of the narrative is confessed as an operative of mercantile consumption as well as of aesthetic reception. The knight errant has become a purchasing citizen, the quester a book buyer. Of the sequel hereby being launched, Bunyan is content to rhyme: "may its buyer have no cause to say / His money is but lost or thrown away" (173). The third person, distancing and disinfecting the invoked financial transaction, has replaced the second-person "thou" of interpretation. The grammar is itself revealing. Despite Bunyan's thematic resistance to the capitalist ethic, here is the ethos of production and consumption muting the mechanisms of address. Nothing more pointedly marks Bunyan's transitional place in the giving way of an epic dispensation to the reign of the novel than this last deflected address. For the evolving genre of prose fiction, with its new muse the reader, the sphere of patronage becomes the marketplace proper.

Across the progress of the *Pilgrim* from 1668 to 1684, then, we see that terms for the protonovelistic evocation of an audience have been consolidated. With public success already gauged, the text can by the later date readily admit that its genuine destination is always "*the* reader," some buyer somewhere, never exactly you there. Yet though such terms may have been developed in the sequence of Bunyan's publishing venture, they are only the more vigilantly suppressed over the next two centuries of popular fiction in the frequent recourse to an intimate, ingratiating, and mock-interlocutory address. In the derivation of its structures from classic allegorical and epic models, that is, novelistic discourse has to be recoded on two fronts at once, not only narrational but also rhetorical. The latter requires, in turn, two stages of disengagement. First, novelization, as a never more than indirectly rhetorical mode, comes to involve a studied divorce of the openly didactic from the largely phatic structures of the apostrophic form. Second, issuing as it does in printed text, novelization entails the emptying out of pretended oratorical immediacy from the structures of address, a permission to fade freely, for instance, from second to third person, "dear reader" to "the reader"—and back again.

This last leeway in the parameters of reader invocation—with the incipient genre of prose fiction working to mold by denominating its audience—derives from another tradition as well. This is the fictionalized editorial device of appended commentary so often crossbred with the high-literary rhetoric of epic and allegory, with their invoked muses and dedicatory addressees. This admixture serves to generate the communal as well as the more obvious epistemological ground of prose fiction. Editors often intervene only to gloss the gap between story and reception. Feigned or not, scholarly modesty in the editorial vein requires a sustained distance from any presumption of immediate attention through second person. Thus Swift in *A Tale of a Tub* hails "the reader," "the judicious reader," "the gentle, courteous, and candid reader," "my reader," and only in the last paragraph before conclusion earns the right to speak not only of but *to* "thee, courteous reader."[15] In all this, your reality is averred in its only real aspect from the textual point of view: not as yourself but as one among many, and not at the time of writing, but only potentially. As "the reader" (when occasion arises) you are awaited rather than engaged as other by the text. You are on hold as well as on call.

Epithets, Epistles, Epitaphs, and Perorations: Fielding's "Comic Epic" of the Prose Reader

In Fielding's *Joseph Andrews*, this editorial procedure of indirectly ascribed rather than apostrophized attention is on view in the chapter of the main narrative where allusions to the reader (almost two score in all, nearly twice as many as in Dante's *Commedia*) first begin to coagulate. "We hope, therefore, a judicious reader will give himself some pains to observe" (1,7:27)—the indefinite article even more forthright here than the definite—is followed two paragraphs later by the personalization of that judiciousness in the proprietorial pronoun of "our reader." The editorial epithet has been replaced by the editorial possessive. Such reference to the reader tilts toward addressed rather than merely ascribed response by the last injunctive sentence of the chapter, though the skeptical reader, if not the otherwise disposed recipient of the utterance, remains in third rather than second person still: "If there be anyone who doubts all this, let him read the next chapter" (1,7:29). This is Dante's imperative formula without the direct vocative to lend it immediacy. In Fielding, as we just saw, the gradations are roughly as follows on the deflected way toward full frontal address: first *a* or *the* reader; next *my* or *our* reader; then, in effect, "let *any* remaining reader . . . ," itself merely an inclusive variant of the indefinite *a*.[16] In such a hierarchy, *a* reader, becoming *the* reader, assumes the role of *our* reader, the narratorial conscript, by being assimilated at the dispensing end to the patronizing grammar of that muted imperative "[You] let him read . . ."

Within Fielding's gathering narrative momentum, the incremental structure of address quite explicitly installs not merely an allusion to but an instance of two remaining provenances of the vocative without which its literary genealogy, on the way to and through Victorian fiction, would remain incomplete. Beyond the hedging third person of standard editorial inscriptions of "the reader," there is, first, the inscribed salutation of the letter form, descended in a literary vein from the epistles dedicatory of the poetic tradition into the epistolary novel itself (as Fielding has of course travestied in *Shamela*). Second, there is the more literal inscription of the tombstone epitaph. We touch base with both these precedents early on in Fielding's novel. In the "Dear Sister" of chapter 6, entitled "How Joseph Andrews Writ a Letter to His Sister Pamela," we find the text incorporating—self-consciously encasing—the mode of the Richardsonian epistolary novel it has already begun to satirize. It does so even as its salutational impulse will quietly co-opt at the discursive rather than diegetic level a similar intimacy of address to the reader. This is a mode of address whose formulaic ingratiations Fielding's narrative voice now rides upon, now ridicules.

And even before this, a tombstone inscription. The epitaphic matrix of both the narrative and its rhetoric emerges offhandedly in the second chapter of *Joseph Andrews*. It appears as one more passing turn of the comic screw in the attempt to secure a documented origin for the novel's hero. Indeed, the epitaphic prototype surfaces there in momentary conjunction with the inscription of a readership for the novel's own pages. Anticipating across the first two chapters that eddying of "the" to "our" reader replayed later, as we have seen, in more concentrated form in the seventh chapter, the text leads us through its first two inscriptions of the reading agency toward the direct address of the epitaphic form.[17] "*The* reader, I believe, already conjectures" (1,1:14; emphasis added), says the narrator in the first chapter. In the second, it is to the "opinion of *our* curious reader" (1,2:15; emphasis added) that he leaves the question of whether Joseph "had any ancestors before" his present parents. "However, we cannot omit inserting an epitaph which an ingenious friend of ours hath communicated." This epitaph's figurative arrest of human progress (the classic *Siste, viator*) both hails and minimally characterizes its own reader at once: "Stay, traveller, for underneath this pew / Lies fast asleep that merry man Andrew" (1,2:15).

The literal passerby of the epitaphic model, the halted "traveller," is of course an anticipatory sketch for reading as a journey by coach in Fielding's novel as a whole, with its familiar picaresque declension of that epic pattern we saw in Spenser's knight errant as reader or Bunyan's pilgrim "traveller." As the narrator explains in a trope to be dilated into a full-blown conceit in *Tom Jones*, it is for "the advantage of our reader" that respite is provided, so that "those little spaces between our chapters may be looked upon as an inn or resting-place" (2,1:73). Here is the manifest rhetorical figuration of the reading sequence which colludes at intervals throughout the novel with the less obviously figurative status of address. Whereas in the ordinary epitaphic strategy, a traveler becomes a reader only when riveted to the spot, in Fielding reading is traveling to begin with.

Then, too, any such allusion in fictional address to the epitaphic vocative—couched as the latter often is in an admonitory voice from beyond the grave—exaggerates to unmistakable clarity the tacit temporal lag of all reader apostrophe. No one is ever there directing a text toward us by the time we arrive on the scene of reading. On the downside of the Victorian realist epoch—as we will see after our spot check of address in the best-sellers of chapter 6—modernist narrative only closes itself off more resolutely from the moment of response than does Fielding or his nineteenth-century followers. Evading any obvious derivation from the artificial solicitations of incised memorials, modernist textuality thus becomes marmoreal in a different sense—not just polished by style but sheathed against penetration by the leisured reader. In this way it remains, after all, every bit as removed as is epitaphic writing from the time of consumption, every bit (and without pretense to the contrary) as dead to the moment of attention.

To be unabashed about this, as we know, is to have come a long way from the epic nostalgia—and vestigial communal voice—which helped authorize eighteenth-century fiction. Beyond the epithets that characterize in miniature, the epistlelike salutations that hail in passing, and the quasi-epitaphic injunctions that halt in progress, Fielding's battery of reader address and reader reference includes any number of asides that admonish or advise. These are circumscribed social or ethical perorations that resonate, in *Joseph Andrews* especially, against the more obvious sermonizing of his hero, Parson Adams. Moreover, a recent attempt by Alexander Welsh to link the origins of novelistic plotting to the rules of probabilistic evidence in contemporaneous legal theory happens to imply another oratorical prototype beyond the pulpit sermon for Fielding's habitual invocations of the reader. A passage like the one Welsh quotes for other purposes from *Tom Jones*—beginning "If the Reader will please to refresh his Memory, by turning to the Scene at *Upton* in the Ninth Book"—may suggest the prosecutorial nudge to a judge or jury (read: audience) as yet another model for those passages of résumé and reemphasis so characteristic of Fielding's reader guidance.[18] In this sense apostrophe would double back on its own origins by reversing its founding deviation, according to Quintilian, as a turning aside from the "your honor" mode of court oratory to a more strictly rhetorical interjection.[19]

Fielding himself, the reader will be pleased to remember, was appointed justice of the peace for Westminster the year before *Tom Jones* was published (1749), thereby assuming a career as a professional auditor of deferential address. A little more than two centuries later, the English novel's separate legacies of courtroom rhetorical plaint and erotic picaresque accomplish a strange convergence with the publication of Vladimir Nabokov's *Lolita* (1955). There, the "good-natured reader" from the preface to *Joseph Andrews*, presumptive model for the reception of an entire fictional genre, is sorely tested by Nabokov's ethically distressing cross between a spoof of the monitory seduction novel (his own version of *Shamela*) and a tragicomic novel of the open road. Wrought up by the first-person confessional mode of the narrator, Humbert Humbert, the insistent juridical gesture—from which all literary apostrophe derives by departing—is carried in reversion to alternately bathetic and defensive heights in such self-exculpating addresses as "Ladies and gentlemen of the jury," "Jurors!" and "Frigid gentlewomen of the jury."[20] These outbursts, and others like them, are interspersed with more formulaic acknowledgments of "the reader who knows the ropes" (23) and "my learned readers" (57). When not reaching for exoneration or universality ("Human beings, attend!" [124]), the narrator enjoins a more immediately textual effect—namely, a projective erotic identification imputed of necessity to the participant reader: "Imagine me; I shall not exist if you do not imagine me . . . trembling in the forest of my own iniquity" (129). Not unlike the prurient titillations induced in the addressed reader by the voyeuristic omniscience of Fielding's narrator, the kinship in erotic fantasy entailed by Humbert's story is ultimately distilled, in his punning German version of Baudelaire's famous apostrophe to the hypocrite reader as "frère," when the brooding semblance of Humbert as narrator—co-

conspirator in his erotic reveries of brutalized girlhood—is saluted as "Reader! *Bruder!*" (262).[21] Nabokov's spin on the modernist autonomy of the aesthetic object, and of the removed, aestheticizing impulse behind it, is thus to explode the presumptions of realist neutrality by comically rehearsing the whole history of vested interest and rhetorical address in the constitution of a genre. He does so, however, without giving up on an inherent elegiac dimension associated as well with the epitaphic origins of audience apostrophe, for Humbert ultimately turns away from readers hailed not only as jurors but as "My judges" (185) or "Your Honor" (185) to address Lolita herself from across a mutual fatality that renders epitaphic not only this but all of his other mentions of the reader: "Thus, neither of us is alive when the reader opens this book" (309).

A Cross Section of Intertexts

From the treacherous slopes of its decline, Nabokov excavates the rhetorical layerings that once went to consolidate the very genre of the realist novel. At the other end of prose fiction's literary history, our concern so far has been, instead, with the first sedimentation of these devices as formal determinants in the new order of literary narrative. To sum up the intertextual inventory we have been sketching out from the Dantean, then Spenserian epic down through Fielding's "comic epic-poem in prose"—a genealogy by only the most circuitous of routes—I venture the chart below. It begins with the epic formula of the narrative persona as guide, leading readers on by drawing them out—in short, educing rather than merely inviting attention. It includes, next, the most often noted influence on the "dear reader" trope of eighteenth- or nineteenth-century narrative rhetoric: the quasi-editorial ascription of response (more common than its direct address in second person). This is indeed the nearest correlate of novelistic direct address in two senses. It is near not only in literary-historical chronology but in textual positioning, since as part of a pseudodocumentary preface or afterword it may accompany the main narrative's fictive address within the same volume. Following these imprints of educative and editorial logic, the epic directive and the editorial pointer respectively, we move in review to even more oblique and divergent— but no less foundational—influences on the novel's effort to situate its audience. As we have seen, the vocative case of prose fiction emerges as a lingering composite not only of superannuated epic and editorially authenticated narrative but also of epistolary, epitaphic, and other apostrophic modes, sermonic and juridical among them (the last given below under the editorial paradigm with which its grammar—short of Nabokov's exaggerated apostrophes—most nearly coincides). The novel thus takes rhetorical form, in part, as a kind of open letter from beyond the grave of presence to the demoted but still invoked new muse of consumerist literacy, a letter that "patronizes" its readers in both senses, saluting and guiding that audience through a mode of address dimly reminiscent of the epistle dedicatory of earlier epic formats. The enjoined arrest of the epitaphic model combines with the imperative reflection of epic address to evoke as well the pulpit rhetoric (or sermonic imperative) of congregational meditation-upon-demand. Following along in this breakdown of tacit influences is the sixth, last, and least intertextual slot on the chart: namely, the generalized phatic motive of sheer reader contact, with or without epithetical attribution, the "purest" and least allusive form of (nonetheless "editorialized") intervention. These half dozen lines of influence upon the novel's dialogic gestures toward the answerable but unanswering reader fall out as follows, with each category overlapping in grammar and rhetorical force with several of the others at once:

Types of Address or Reference	Grammatical Mood	Rhetorical Mode	Literary Model
Directive (epic induction)	Imperative + Vocative	Exhortation	*Pensa, lettore* ("Reflect, reader")
Epistolary	Vocative	Salutation	Dear——— (Dear Reader)
Editorial (juridical)	Declarative	Prediction (veiled instruction)	The reader will . . .
Epitaphic (sermonic)	Imperative + Vocative	Command	*Siste, viator* ("Halt, traveler") (pause, reader)
Invocatory	Interjective + Vocative	Formal apostrophe	O Muse! (O Reader!)
Em/phatic	Vocative	Punctuation: contact/impact	Reader, I tell you . . .

And so the eventual communicative infrastructure of nineteenth-century narrative, its poetics of reader reference or address, has to do with the novel's broad and various engenderment in the preceding century out of allegorical and odic as well as epic modalities. It should therefore be further clarifying to note such converging modalities in a single narrative author as transitional as possible on all fronts: a writer not yet settled into the routine of narrative expectations in the novel as mainstream genre, one poised between eighteenth-

and nineteenth-century storytelling practice as well as between verse narrative and the novel, and poised moreover between the self-consciously polarized habits of a popular oral culture and a popular print culture, between bardic recitation and authored publication. Such a transitional figure is of course Walter Scott. In the laboratories of his verse narratives, he worked out the station—and stationing—of the audience which his historical novels would shortly help orchestrate for the evolving genre of prose fiction.

"Hear Then, Attentive to My Lay": Scott in Transition

In *Marmion* (1808), the familiar invocatory structure of an epic proem or epistle dedicatory is directed more openly at the English audience at large through the mediating dedicatees of Scott's own circle of friends. The "Introduction to Canto First," for instance, takes the form of an epistle to William Stewart Rose, Esq. This is a fact we may well forget as we are caught up in this extended prefatory matter, until an explicit vocative punctuates the close of the proem at the moment when "thou, my friend" is called upon to justify the present poetic endeavor, "For few have read romance so well" (ll. 249–50). The sudden drawing taut of communicative lines around the second-person addressee conveys something of the effect of the delayed apostrophe in a conversation poem by Coleridge or Wordsworth, though without the rendered dramatic setting. This emphasis on the communal figuration of the narrative urge is also one measure of Scott's place as a writer navigating between the revival of chivalric romance and the gradual solidification of nineteenth-century narrative technique.

This solicitation to his friend Rose now behind him, Scott can move forward into the text itself by general invocation: "Hear then, attentive to my lay, / A knightly tale of Albion's elder day" (ll. 326–27). With that ambiguous transferred epithet, "knightly," serving as a possible specification, at least in oral recitation, for the likely time of the tale's domestic performance in the households of the poem's audition, the imperative "Hear then" seems to reach past Rose to the audience at large of the published volume. This is an implication crystallized later in the closing explicit apostrophe—for the first time in Scott's narrative verse—to a more or less public audience: "*L'Envoy.* TO THE READER" Making good on the earlier pun, this benediction closes unmistakably upon the multiple site—and time—of evening reading: "To all, to each, a fair good night, / And pleasing dreams, and slumbers light!"—a nocturnal metonymy for the dreamlike aura of legend conveyed, here and elsewhere, by the rhythmic cadences of bardic verse. Scott's novels after *Waver-*

ley will, as we are to see in chapter 6, take up the responsibility of the author's bardic lineage under cover of an increasingly byzantine editorial superstructure. Even before his turn to fiction, however, Scott's verse apostrophes have already helped place the new readership just where the Victorian novel will want it: alert and on call, always potentially *at attention.*

"Pause You Who Read This": The Dickensian Imperative

When a novelist like Dickens turns away momentarily from addressing (though usually without mentioning) the kind of generalized middle-class cultural addressee inscribed by Scott, it is usually for a turn of satire, a turn into rhetorical travesty itself. Little Jo dies grievously in *Bleak House*, in a scene whose tearful audience we are meant to have no trouble recognizing (through our blurred vision) as ourselves, even as its closing rhetoric veers off into a harangue against the negligent aristocratic and clerical classes: "Dead, your Majesty. Dead, my lords and gentlemen. Dead, Right Reverends and Wrong Reverends of every order" (47:705), an apostrophe linked by one critic to the whole tradition of literary address to a royal patron.[22] Moreover, as a funeral sermon without public audience, the moment is epitaphic, and as so often in the tradition of epitaphic address, importunate. With omniscient narrative interrupted by monitory apostrophe, the epitaph's halted traveler becomes the interrupted consumer of plot.

It is another dimension of Dickensian address upon which Joyce draws for his stylistic parody in *Ulysses*. What "The Oxen of the Sun" captures in the scene at the lying-in hospital, beyond the melancholy cadences of Dickens' sentimental flourishes, is exactly the fluidity of address still available to Dickens despite his typical avoidance of the "dear reader" trope. Apostrophes penetrate and crisscross the passage, weaving together reader and character in a mutual subservience to a voice of authority which is actually pitched beyond the unspoken conventions of omniscience to an explicitly supernatural vantage. "Those who have passed on, who have gone before, are happy too as they gaze down and smile upon the touching scene," we read, followed by the enveloping ambiguity of command: "Reverently look at her as she reclines there."[23] The reader seems suddenly at one with the dead in the access impelled—and simultaneously permitted—by this imperative grammar of depiction.

Well before Joyce's satire, Victorian rhetoric is certainly not above transgressing mortal borders. It usually does so, however, more in the epitaphic than the visionary mode. In particular, the epitaphic turn may often serve in nineteenth-century fiction as the immediate imprint of the elegiac. If the seeds of the late-eighteenth-century graveyard school can be found lurking in Fielding's comic epitaph at the start of *Joseph Andrews*, so can those more pervasive elegiac tonalities of ensuing realist fiction, with their frequent returns to origins at the site of commemorated death. Dickens again comes to mind. The epitaphic mastertrope of Victorian narrative finds one of its fullest stagings in such a pervasively elegiac text as *Great Expectations*. Like *Joseph Andrews*, this is a novel that embeds its origin in a linked moment of epitaphic comedy and halted narrative traverse. The link comes about as follows. In remembering his wife-beating father, Joe Gargery explains that "it were my intentions to have put upon his tombstone that Whatsume'er the failings on his part, *Remember reader* he were that good in his hart" (7:77). Joe thereby borrows, if without punctuation, that seasoned alliance of imperative plus vocative crucial for Auerbach's view of Dante's inscribed reading as well as for the *Siste, viator* of the epitaphic format. Further, Joe, in his naiveté, strips the epitaphic cliché of its disingenuous figuration ("traveler") by calling the interested party a "reader" pure and simple. At which point we are made to recall, by being called back to, our own *present* reading.

A parallel combination of imperative plus vocative surfaces a few chapters later in a more than nostalgic, a virtually elegiac, transformation. All but indistinguishable from Joe's epitaphic blurring of the spirit of memorial with that of *memento mori*, the format returns this time, however, in the direct address of the narrative voice from the vantage of saddened retrospect. It is a highly uncharacteristic move for Dickens, justified only by the dramatized first-person narrative of Pip as speaking persona at the close of an ominous chapter in his history. Further, in its breathless interruption of the plot, it echoes the unpunctuated grammar of Joe's epitaphic composition: "Pause you who read this, and think for a moment of the long chain of iron or gold, of thorns or flowers, that would never have bound you but for the formation of the first link on one memorable day" (9:101). To cast this against the backdrop of epic precedent, Dickens—quite by literary-historical accident, no doubt—has hit upon a revealing alloy of Dante's *O tu che leggi* ("O you, who read") and *Pensa, lettore* ("Reflect, reader"). Though the burden of Dickens' digression is easy enough to take at face value, it manipulates in a unique way the pronominal "shifters" (Benveniste's term) of both tense and person.[24]

Where exactly, according to Dickens' narrator, are we to pause? After reading just what? The previous sentence? "Imagine," we have just been commanded, "one selected day struck out of [any life], and think how different its course would have been" (9:101). It is from that all but dead metaphor of "struck out" that the figuration of the next vocative structure derives, with its imagery of chains, links, and inextricable bindings derived by association from Pip's home near the forge and transferred by contamination to the seductive appeal of Satis House. At this point the verb "read" may itself be read to shift—under pressure of the demonstrative "this" as a localized rather than book-inclusive pointer—into the past tense of more immediate textual succession, as if to say, "You who (have just) read this ought now to lift your gaze from the page and turn it inward upon retrospect and conjecture." If so, this would honor the temporal lag that renders the present tense of reader invocation always something of a fiction. Such a circumscribed uncertainty of tense aside, it is a grammatical default within English usage itself—the absence of the second-person singular verb—which permits the typical sealing of a Victorian narrative contract. Pause each of you who reads this: the legitimate syntax of personal engagement. Pause you who read this, all of you: the aggregate ("the many-headed") quietly conscripted into the syntax of intimate address.

This commanded hiatus in *Great Expectations* is the exception that proves the rule, not only of Dickens' textual practice but of Victorian fiction generally. At one level, Dickens' narrative enjoins in this way an irruptive disjuncture. At another, it serves merely to characterize the inevitable, but virtually seamless, interstices of any text in production. By momentarily dispelling the grip of narrative involvement, this eccentric address spells out such a narrative's normative and founding hold on the reader: the hold of introjective identification itself. But in order to up the stakes, Dickens has actually turned the tables. We always read on because we take on the fictional psychology offered up to us. It is the anomalous gambit of Pip's transference in that passage, however, that passage from text to reader, the singular and signal genius of its displaced introversion, that, after having it for so long the other way around, the *character* actually identifies with his *reader* in the examined privacies of desire.

Further, Dickens' narrator has inscribed the audience apostrophe, and thus conscripted the reader, not so much within some historical lineage or allusive field as within an intertextual network. Imperative plus vocative, by seeming to command(eer) attention to a remembrance of things past—and always passing—outside the text, also rehearse the modalities of such attention within the convergent codes of literary address. On this understanding, such a moment of address does not evolve from (historically) so much as derive from (intertextually) that trope of reader-as-traveler (or knight errant) appearing not only in textual self-allegorizing from Spenser through Bunyan to Fielding and on to Trollope but in the eighteenth-century epitaph and its poetic manifestations.

The derivation may be even more attenuated elsewhere, while still conveying the same impulse toward textual contact. At the close of *Bleak House*, the heroine narrator is about to "part for ever" from "the unknown friend to whom I write" (67:932), yet the only sign of the "dear reader" format in this quasi-epistolary paradigm is a detached signifier sprung from the suppressed formula of apostrophe: "Not without much *dear* remembrance on my side" (67:932; emphasis added). Dear what? Esther has nothing to recall of you, the reader, except, paradoxically, your *future* perusal of her labors. The imputed "dearness" of any such relation can only be turned back upon the private recollections she has labored to transcribe: "much dear remembrance," that is, in the second sense of nostalgic introspection. As everywhere else in the fiction of the period, and never more openly, the "you to whom I write," the reader, is only a code name, only a figure, for sentiment itself in circulation.

In regard to our conscription by address or mention in Victorian fiction, then, the question is exactly: Where do we stand? If the intertextual checkpoints of reader reference and reader apostrophe trace a derivation reactivated in any *present* reading as part of that multichannel rhetorical system that articulates the Victorian novel from no fixed source of enunciation, neither is the point of reception likely to be stabilized in such a circuit. This is the case even across those novels which, though they may eschew the trope of the apostrophized reader per se, cannot be assumed in advance to do so. The option is always open. And when it comes to the vocative case, you never know on which frequency you may find yourself dialed in. Classic narration is neither as monologic nor as monolithic as it would appear in those critics who link it directly to all things hegemonic. And by the same token, to accept from book to book the Victorian text's rolling amalgam of your own rendered attention is to accept the nonsimultaneity of the subject positions so constructed, their nonidentity with themselves. With motives antithetical to Dickens', Thackeray's *Vanity Fair* simply compresses this discrepant array between a single set of covers.

"Brother Reader": Thackeray's *Hypocrite Lecteur*

Hypocrite, actor, shape changer: etymology itself sketches the range of roles for the *Fair*-goer in Thackeray's anticipation of Baudelaire's readerly compact and sibling rivalry, where the reader as *mon frère* is also part (satirically inflected here) of that familial surrogacy known as the Victorian literary audience. *Vanity Fair* is a narrative whose conduct motivates and exhausts by turns the whole arsenal of Victorian rhetoric, as marked in particular by the shifting terms of its apostrophized readership: a summoned sideshow audience perfectly anonymous even while personally compromised. In attending the *Fair*, we stand convened—as well as accused. We are charged (in both senses) with all the reading habits of an age at once. We thus become, each of us at once, that ubiquitous nobody of self-interested consumption.

The evidence leaps to mind—and can be typified in brief. Thackeray's first chapter keeps "Jones, who reads this book at his Club," at the safe distance of third person.[25] It is Dickens' "you who read this" pictured by satiric stand-in, jotting down his contempt in words prescribed for him by the text he rejects: "Yes; I can see Jones at this minute . . . taking out his pencil and scoring under the words 'foolish, twaddling,' &c., and adding to them his own remark of '*quite true*'" (1:15). The accompanying plate (fig.1) is like a fun-house mirror in which you resist recognizing the image of your own readerly impatience:

Figure 1. "Jones, who reads this book," from *Vanity Fair*

Later, too, quotation marks cordon off the parodistic voice of the huckster (anticipating Dickens' Reverend Chadband) in a narratorial aside: "I warn my 'kyind friends,' that I am going to tell a story of harrowing villainy and . . ." (8:81). But by the next paragraph this same narrator has returned his all but second-person addressees (accompanied by the possessive pronoun "my") to the more common, less proprietary "editorial" slot of a neutralized third person. There, we are assured that in the chapters to come the narrator will have plenty of opportunity to mock various characters by laughing at them "confidentially in the reader's sleeve" (8:81). Some of these travestied characters turn out to be various readers themselves, labeled either solo or *en bloc*. These subsets of Thackeray's mass public are singled out by such specialized ascription as "the most sentimental reader" (12:114) as well as by such equally particularized address as "oh fair young reader" (14:131) or "Be cautious then, young ladies" (18:172).

Yet any such gesture at a targeted minority among Thackeray's readership vanishes at other points into a sweeping embrace. We find this, for instance, in such a blanket rhetorical question as "Is it so or is it not so? I appeal to the middle classes"—or in the even more encompassing polemical gauntlet of "I defy any member of the British public to say . . ." (21:196). It is as if all the commonwealth were, as vain Fair-goers, part of his "public" in the narrower literary sense. Equally universal, though lapsed back to third-person declarative grammar, is the ascribed rather than addressed audience (spectatorial, theatrical) in the passing metaphoric observation that "it is only a comedy which the reader pays his money to witness" (19:180). Yet by the time the corrosive universality of Vanity is established in such a way as unmistakably to implicate this general reader, the fortunes of address are again reversed. Suddenly, all of the narrator's subsidiary, third-person narratees seem subsumed to the filiated attention of the following vocative thrust. It is a second-person salutation appearing, again within a rhetorical question, late along in the novel: "Which, I wonder, brother reader, is the better lot . . . ?" (61:586). Yet this interlocutory directness at once slips away again into the distanced and deferential third person of the clichéd "my respected reader" (64:622). Thus incriminated by tongue-in-cheek obeisance, our flattered attention is bandied about a little longer and then dropped by apostrophe into the last infantilizing theatrical metaphor: "Come, children, let us shut up the box and the puppets, for our play is played out" (67:666). We've never known where exactly we stood in the *Fair*, nor whether we had a leg to do it on. Now we know in going—in silencing characters by shutting up the box (the rectangular, three-dimensional form) which contains them—how the ludic kaleidoscope of address has itself been part of the shadow play before Vanity's mirror all along.

Readerly Dysposition

Vanity Fair, then, is a compendium and anatomy of the novelistic rhetoric it inherits. That its congested, ultimately conflicted, signaling of attention should accompany and compound nearly every other strategy of self-referential dislocation known to, and as, "modernist" textuality is no surprise.[26] Even so, *Vanity Fair* only concentrates to the point of cacophony what other Victorian narratives may indicate in their own less extreme way about reading's relation to the textual network that enrolls it for response. Any textual system oriented toward so many available and variable sites of reception has somehow to discharge this overload. The reader, split and multiplied, is the one available conductor of this discharge. And so you recognize yourself, finally, everywhere and nowhere in the discourse of a Victorian novel. As Dickens dimly intimates and Thackeray massively exaggerates, you become the second or third "person" of its narrative monologue by dint of the loss of all coherent *personality* of response. Since the mirror in which you are supposed to find yourself identified turns out to refract rather than reflect the image of reception, you end up splintered across all those instances of your unequatable designations.

Despite Thackeray's apparent design to impale as well as more generally implicate the reader, the layered associations of literary address appear operable in his novels, as in many others, only by way of a certain *disorientation*. The more often the reader is put in his (never quite the same) place, the more like a dysposition it seems. Being part initiates, part tutees, part confidants, part correspondents, part muses, part editorial pawns, and so forth, readers of English narrative from Fielding through Thackeray, Eliot, and beyond, tossed about in this way, can only fall back on the mysterious indetermination of the literary encounter: an encounter whose parameters are often replicated in miniature by the same text that elsewhere salutes its very audience. When this takes place, the reader's own place is taken, taken from you in order to be rehearsed or mirrored within plot. At which point you extrapolate your response on the basis of this internal modeling. All such moments of configured reading at one and the same time mock the rhetorical anachronism and confirm the potential subjective anarchy (or at least indetermination) of the "dear reader" trope: a posit(ion)ing of presence *to* the text that is only more of those words by which that text's own presence is manifest. And so it is once again that the two major aspects of this study—reading in apostrophe and reading in parable—can be advanced as complementary halves of the same study.

What is broadly rhetorical about such considerations—when both apostrophe and parabolic scene are recognized as equally figurative—is just what recommends such a rhetorical perspective as a check on any number of reductionist, however informative, market-oriented approaches to the industry rather than the work of Victorian fiction. So far from closing the text off from its context, a rhetoric of figured reading, a rhetoric rooted at one level in a linguistics of the vocative, offers the only *textual* (hence the only *readable*) registration of that context (the social world of reception) as it impinges most closely upon—by being invoked by—the novelistic utterance. It is at this point that I would like to extend J. Hillis Miller's insight into the operation of character in traditional fiction to include the characterized reader, as that inclusion may even end up revising (as in Brontë's *Villette*) our very notion of constructed subjectivity in the classic novel. In "The Function of Rhetorical Study at the Present Time," Miller, without mentioning direct address, sees the novel as taking the idea of personality or character to task—and all but to pieces—in a continuous cultural experiment, a heuristic exercise both contextual and reciprocal. "My hypothesis, then: the novel as the perpetual tying and untying of the knot of selfhood works, in the psychic economy of the individual and of the community, to affirm the fiction of character by putting it fictionally in question and thus short-circuits a doubt that, left free to act in the real social world, might destroy both self and community."[27] Another way to think of this: To whatever degree a text may let you see the labor of character construction in fiction (as, I would add, of "reader-making"), the artifice behind the attempted naturalization still measures its success against a presumed organic model: real people, individual readers. "Belief in the subject, in character, is thereby precariously maintained over the abyss of its dismantling" (213).

To substitute the idea of address or one-way dialogue—of utterance to a localized, if unnamed, subject—for the freestanding novelistic character in Miller's formula is therefore one further way to apprehend the decentering logic of audience apostrophe this chapter has been attempting to sketch. The variant and conflicting protocols of address—generating the reciprocal confounding of self and other in the dissemination of story—mount the virtual unraveling of interlocution in just the way that narrative's overt fabrication of coherent agency may deconstruct character. This is, of course, related to Culler's point about apostrophe in romantic verse: that it tropes rather than participates in a circuit of communication. But the analytic breakdown of reader presence does not halt at this logic of apostrophe. If personhood is called into question (and yet fortified under scrutiny) by characterization, in other words, then so, too, is the communicative model of novelistic dissemination artificially isolated (even as ratified) at two levels by classic narrative. It happens not only through vocative appeals to a constructed reading subject but by plotted scenes of narrative reception as the internal staging of a discourse circuit (scenes set off from within as concentric to narrative structure and eccentric to rhetorical address). Together, vocative and metanarrative modes operate yet again as twin features of rhetorical conscription, drafting the reader into (and as) text—even while keeping clear of all *mere* text the supposed autonomy of the social subject as occasional reader.

By either means, classic narrative rounds on itself to delimit its own conditions. These are the conditions that determine it in advance as well as those it puts on its own reception. The more historically specific an account one can render of the nineteenth-century texture of such devices, the closer one comes to monitoring in them the genesis—rather than merely the prehistory—of a certain dimension of the modernist moment. With the fading of the classic fictional paradigm went, once and for all, those built-in safety mechanisms that kept the ontological travail of hero or narratee from eroding the anchoring status of the self as reading agent. In modernist textual practice, even to smuggle back in the banished mode of apostrophe would be to beckon within a flaunted vacuum. Then, too, modernist parables of reading will come to encode mostly the subject's cognitive fluency within a world system constituted exclusively, rather than at privileged moments, by the exchange of signs. To a further, and furthering, look at this second aspect of conscription in its evolving modes—the analogic rather than quasi-dialogic means of "reader-making"—we conclude these preparatory chapters by turning here.

Chapter Three

Reflex Action
The Extrapolated Audience

> The moment when that which is glorified in the work *is* the work . . .
> this moment which cancels the author is also the moment when,
> as the book opens to itself, the reading finds its origin in this opening.
> Reading is born, therefore, at this moment when the work's
> distance from itself changes its sign.
>
> —Blanchot, "Communication"

Jean-Honoré Fragonard, *La lecture*
(1780s). Musée du Louvre, Paris

How can a novel situate within itself—and you certainly need not agree as yet that it can—the essential sitelessness of the reading act? When a book is transformed through reading into a text, it no longer is (or has) a volume but becomes instead a temporal event. All that is spatial about it, except for the imagined world it signifies, has been left behind along with the bodily posture of the reading agent. Is that posture, that apparent disposition toward a book, rather than reading's active dispossession of the subject, perhaps all that can be genuinely represented?

To investigate such external signs of textual internalization in the burgeoning realism of the eighteenth and nineteenth centuries, one might naturally turn at some point to their scenic depiction in visual art. A picture may be worth a thousand words, but it may also render the way in which the felt impact of such words remains unavailable to visual inscription. Put it for the moment, without leaving it, this way: Reading is a kind of picturing it is impossible, in any inward detail, to picture. In this sense, it is no surprise that numbered among the nondemonstrative, antitheatrical scenes surveyed by

Figure 2. Gerard Manley Hopkins, *Man in a Punt,* c. 1865.
Courtesy J. Handley-Derry

Michael Fried in *Absorption and Theatricality* (on French painting from the 1750s to the early 1780s) are a good many canvases centered upon the preoccupied consciousness—only dimly indicated in bodily form—of a reader.[1] The Fragonard at the head of this chapter doubles the absorptive effect of reading across the averted faces (the withdrawn "personalities") of the reader (no doubt aloud) and the listener/onlooker, both deflected in their "sitting" from the requisite frontality of portraiture. An obverse but entirely comparable effect is achieved in the sketch called *Man in a Punt* by Gerard Manley Hopkins (fig. 2). The frontality of the man's gaze, just where the heavily foreshortened composition would lead the viewer's eye toward it, is occluded by the book. Look at it this way: In reading's willed effacement of the subject, the self is lulled to anonymity.

The motif of private reading—or, more exactly, the tendency of pictorial representation to register and inflect the intensified privacy of all reading—persists into a later epoch and a later medium as well, namely photography. In 1971, the great Hungarian photographer André Kertesz published a volume organized around unposed photographs of solitary readers, photographs running from the early years of this century through the 1960s, under the title *On Reading*.[2] Separately the images are arresting and often witty; collectively, they unfurl a sustained thematization, mounted on the contingency of the caught visual image, of that most unphotographable of activities: the interiority of reading, where not only the reader's line of sight but also the mind's own focus evades and defies the camera's.

In one pair of Kertesz's pictures, costumed theatrical performers, oblivious to the camera, are caught reading in stolen moments backstage, escaped from one performance to a different one equally unseen by the camera—on an internal rather than adjacent stage. In another photo there is a seated child turned aside from her seated doll to the different ludic dimension, the different fantasy personifications and human replicas, of a text—lost in a passive absorption that is merely travestied by the blank stare of the limp doll.[3] Like most of the pictures, this image entertains with tacit precision the difference between the photochemical and the phenomenological senses of being *taken with* a book.

Still other photographs in *On Reading* contrast the invisible life of the reader with the textlike manifestation of the visible (the social) world. In response to modernity as a landscape of signs, there is a man halted in his tracks by a book in hand while photographed in long shot in front of a wall scrawled with graffiti: the scene of everyday life's involuntary reading. Most serendipitous of all, there is a man seated on the ground at the top of a wide brick embankment on the Seine (fig 3.). With its architectural structure spread out below him as if magnifying the open pages of his (to us, only faintly visible) volume, the mottled lineation of the bricks defines a slanted rectangular surface split in two by a vertical gutter—as if, quite unmistakably, by the spine of a book. Here is an image that reverses and complements the majority of the portfolio by suggesting not just the visibility of the reading act (or at least of its multifold external postures, each a story in itself) but also the very legibility of the visible—as the world's open book.

Figure 3. André Kertesz, from *On Reading*. Copyright © 1971 by André Kertesz. Used by permission of Viking Penguin, a division of Penguin Books USA Inc.

Absorbing Reading: Embedding the Scene of Affect

The implications of this last figuration, as a mastertrope for Victorian fiction to emerge briefly here in connection with *Vanity Fair*, will for the most part be tabled until chapter 10. For now, we need to reflect further not on the visualized or novelized text of experience but on the novelized experience of texts. Besides unmistakable episodes of novel reading, three related formats for extrapolating from a given narrative scene to the situation of its own reading appear most frequently in the traditional novel from Fielding through the next century: (1) the narrated reading of something other than a novel, as, for instance, a letter or journal or court affidavit, the tenor of whose reception is aligned in some way (closely or divergently) with literary response; (2) the oral (and so at least to that extent communal rather than private) delivery and reception of a narrative; (3) the interpretive conversation or debate (again interpersonal) following in the wake of a text either read or audited. By such reflex effects as well as by the interpolation of the reader through either direct address or third-person reference, the novel as text has moved to conscript and absorb what awaits it as contingent eventuality.

This takes us back to Michael Fried's conceptual dichotomy (as well as to his historical transition into the late-eighteenth-century rise of pictorial realism), as it can be found to turn in part on what painting and fiction may equally claim as the "figure" of reading. We now see that the absorbed reader in paintings by Chardin or Greuze stands in something of the same relation to the theatrical gestures of spectatorial solicitation in an earlier style of scenic treatment (where, in the most blatant cases, sight lines from painted figures tug the viewer into a space of overt display) as does the dramatized scene of reading in fiction to instances of histrionic direct address, which precede, without entirely disappearing into, the nineteenth-century ascendancy of literary realism. On the one hand, the captured look of a subject absorbed in a book is cognate with our own absorbed looking, our own reading of the canvas. On the other, in theatricalized depiction, the tableau's compositional (and hence ultimately "rhetorical") turn of gestural posturing (rather than scenic self-containment) is closely akin to audience apostrophe in literary textuality. In short, theatricality is to address as absorption is to narrative regress.

Of course, not every absorptive canvas pointedly reinscribes within its scene the spectatorial gaze that confronts it, just as not every pictorial theatricalization involves a painted figure staring out in undeflected address to its viewer. So, too, in prose fiction, metanarrative parables of reception, on the one hand, and audience apostrophes, on the other—the subjects of this and the previous chapter respectively, and of all that follows in various combinations—are complementary structural prototypes that need not appear in pure form to delimit a range of effect. These options push to extremes a choice of aesthetic emphases held in common to some extent by painting and fiction of the later eighteenth and nineteenth centuries. The history of the novel in this period differs in these respects from Fried's history of earlier realist painting largely in the sense that obliviousness to reception and its vocative markers in Victorian texts is not so complete as in an absorptive scene that has forgone all sense of self-conscious spectation and turned in upon its own depicted space. But just as absorption and theatricality, preoccupation and deliberate presentation, remain functional opposites in the configuration of pictorial space, so in the traditional novel do the embedded episode and the extruded reference indicate deep-going alternatives of figuration within an overriding logic of absenteeism and deferred contact.[4] In neither case, whether through salutation or parable, whether their roles are summoned in second person or summed up by disguise in third, are such subject readers, it bears repeating, anywhere to be found in the text, only figured. Nor is there any reason to suppose that the one method of conscription necessarily entails its counterpart in a given text. At least in principle they are independent functions, both of each other and of any real reader on hand. Yet the effort to bring into comparison instances of direct address with the rehearsed scene of reading—to register the exhortation in view of the homology, the directive apostrophe in light of the reflexive episode—should elucidate the underlying link between the gradually outmoded habits of the vocative and the persistence of reflexive evocation across three centuries of fictional practice, as represented briefly in this chapter by Fielding, Thackeray, and Proust.

This exemplification therefore depends on what has been accomplished so far. We have seen that the reader, the reader in critical rather than literary practice, is too often cast as the bloodless and passive scapegoat of the machinery of meaning rather than the adroit double agent of narrativity and reception. We have said, therefore, that a more flexible semiotics of reading would have to deduce a new wrinkle in the weft of codes, one able to enfold the rhetoric of marked response within the narrative system itself. We have seen that, in an expanded sense of such rhetorical marking, both addressed attention and its recessed scenarios are equally figurative, since they image or denominate that activating agent who cannot literally be there. We have said in addition that the inset dramaturgy of reading, quite apart from the apparatus of apostrophe, may involve a further phenomenological thrust that plumbs the very fundament of realism (in its register of consciousness itself).

Nor is direct address as simple a procedure as it might seem. Looking back over the long history of such address as a typifying artifice within the culture of print rather than oratory, we have seen the highly unstable dialogism of apostrophe (as if to a patron or muse or autumn wind) at work upon, even when not directed upon, the reader. We have therefore seen to it that our resulting inventory of reader address and reference does not petrify into a set of orderly derivations from a single source, that it records instead the way in which even the explicit addressee is dispersed across a palimpsest of associations, a laminate of allusion to other vocative sites. Since such a rhetorical inclusion (by interpolation) of an always external reader is in fact a frequent, though not necessary, systemic counterpart to the reading in—or better, reading out—of the reader in parable, a closer look at just this latter form of response (by extrapolation) is now in order, with examples ranging from Fielding's picaresque comedy through Thackeray's satire to Proust's involuted revery.

To begin with, a clarification. In broaching the notion of extrapolation as a structural function of narrative, I am speaking, and have been, about something other than—though not always separable from—the thematizations frequently built upon either plotted reading or its kindred forms of narrative consumption.[5] It might fairly be said that the Victorian novel is the genre whose historical context requires such a plot feature within the prescriptions of its realist aesthetic. Characters go about reading just as they work and marry, by the imitated laws of probability. Hence emplotted textual encounter. And given the social and economic project of Victorian fiction in an age of widening literacy—namely, the impetus to assimilate its own institution to the engineered leisure of a broad-based print culture—such probable reading, once turning up in plot, is made thematic in both its desire and its effects. Let me perhaps overdo a literary-historical distinction in order to underline it. Eighteenth-century novels teach us how to read them, and in the process they are not above pedagogic disclaimers, apostrophic words to the wise, and rhetorical pop quizzes along the way. Over the course of the next century, acclimation breeds a further ambition. Taking fictional competence for granted, nineteenth-century novels teach us less how to read them than what reading them might teach us. Yet if an extrapolative scene both figures and at the same time prompts a certain agenda for its own textual reception—figures it in the form of audited storytelling (Fielding) or theatergoing (Thackeray) or spatial perspective and its imaginative investments (Proust)—criticism does not go far enough simply to observe that the audience thereby triggers in reading a certain thematizing of fictional affect. At such moments, as well as in the literal scene of reading, you enter upon an enactment rather than a thematics: a narrative staging, a rehearsed event. It is an event whose reflexive nature (about which more at the end of this chapter) remains every bit as simultaneous with the reading act it internally reconstitutes as is the vocative that elsewhere names and directs the agent of that act.

There is an established position on certain closely related issues that can help to schematize—and hence steady our view of—the elusive problematic of mimed response. In Paul Ricoeur's tripartite understanding of narrative operations, the three orders of mimesis are oriented respectively toward the "figured" world being represented, the "configured" nature of the representation itself, and the "refigured" perception taking place at that border which, in oral narratives, for instance, "marks the intersection of the world of the text and the world of the hearer."[6] For Ricoeur the latent circularity of these distinctions generates the "hermeneutic spiral" (1:72), or in other words the "synergetic relation" (3:178) on which the "pact of reading" (3:162) is constituted—recalling the model of "pact and contract" in Pierre Macherey.[7] Then, too, the synergy developed by the reciprocal facets of the mimetic process anticipates the yet more fluid sense of the book/world relation in Gilles Deleuze and Felix Guattari. Ricoeur's sense of mutual encroachment among mimetic levels is not unlike the more radically indeterminate "rhizomatic" bond in Deleuze and Guattari between a no longer discrete text and the world outside it, which, perforce, includes that book's own reading: a psychic space thus "territorialized" by text, even as the text is forever invaded and colonized by response.[8]

Reading isn't easy to figure. That's why assorted metaphors abound in its accounts. *Event* is not one of them, however. Reading happens. Ricoeur's particular emphasis on the reading moment as a hermeneutic expenditure allows him to hold that the Aristotelian concept of *praxis* covers both real and unreal events, in other words not only ethics but poetics (1:46), and therefore to pursue more fully "the order of action implied by narrative activity" (1:46). This pursuit can logically be extended to include what we are after here: the reflex action of such praxis, the moment of its recognition as such. At issue is what takes place when Ricoeur's orders of mimesis, rather than just being dovetailed at their borders, are made to fold over themselves more completely. One facet of mimesis may end up imitating another. This special case of narrative praxis recalls, in fact, the overlapping subsets of the code of action (proairetic) and the code of interpretation (hermeneutic) in my first chapter's adaptation of Barthes, where interpretation is itself enacted, as well as the complication of Jakobson's categories in the second, with the return of the receiver from within the message, the conative within the poetic function. At such moments of categorical interpenetration, what Ricoeur would call the refigurative impact of storytelling, its orientation toward reception, may get rehearsed in advance through the configuring process of that very narrative by which any reaction must be induced. This happens most obviously when you read of your own reading, by name or exemplum, and are further read into the text by reading on. Mimesis is extrapolated to its own effect. Between configuration (mimesis as text) and refiguration (mimesis *sub specie* reception), then, lies the force field of conscription: the configurative drawing in of response not in the offing but in execution, the emplotment rather than mere prospect of the reading function.

The plan of this chapter is to move forward by progressive stages of parabolic decoding, taking up our three fictional test cases across the three centuries of major novelistic production. Each develops a less obvious, though no less potent, isomorph of novel reading than the one before it. We begin with the scene of reading in Fielding's *Joseph Andrews*, as figured primarily in the highly codified locus of oral storytelling (the Cervantesque embedded tale) and inflected there by the momentary interpolations of the audience through direct reference or address. (Note, on terminological grounds, that my use of *extrapolation* to suggest the shock waves of recognition set off—and sent out—by a given novelistic episode leads me frequently to the kind of miniaturized narrative occasion traditionally classed as the "interpolated tale," whereas my use of the term *interpolation* for the insertion into narrative of reader mention or address has no *necessary* connection with such episodes. For this chapter, I select examples of the deliberate coordination of these two devices only to clarify a certain collaborative link that is by no means routinely activated in classic fiction.) From Fielding's tandem manifestation of reader address and encoded reading episode, we move next to the omnivorous scene of reading in *Vanity Fair*, where both extrapolation and interpolation (each inducing the audience's recognition of its own vanity) end up seeming perversely coextensive. Reaching forward from this mid-Victorian landmark to the rarefaction of Proustian narrative rhetoric, we will find the discursive work of reader invocation and reader evocation further conflated. Here, too, we will take stock of the confrontation between reading's figured inwardness and a tropological deconstruction (in Paul de Man's sense) of the contradictions on which such representation seeks to rest.

Compared with Thackeray and Proust in their englobing snares of conscripted response, Fielding simply carries to a full pitch of structural explicitness the tried and tested formula of embedded narrative. What *Joseph Andrews* does in borrowing from the Cervantesque tradition of the inset tale, and then reframing it so that it renarrates the novel's own relays of response, cannot therefore be understood apart from the operations elsewhere in Fielding's text of direct address, to the reader as well as to other impinging abstractions like vanity. Neither can Thackeray's parable—of Vanity Fair as life's simultaneously performed and attended spectacle—be divorced from the personified address to *Vanity Fair*'s readership. Nor can even Proust's expatiations on reading, along with the subsidiary tropes that compose them, be severed in conception from a rare instance of apostrophized reading. These are representative cases from the history of fiction with the aid of which—before turning at length to Austen, Shelley, and the Victorians—we can sketch out the parameters of reading's embedded performance. As these examples suggest, this performance is often delimited by a closed system of apostrophe and parable, interpolation and extrapolation, through which fictional reading, too important to leave to readers, is doubly inscribed by the fiction itself. At the very least, these initial test cases, as instances of a twofold conscription, should introduce the range of indirection available to reader parable, whether in lieu of or in league with the direct modalities of address.

"*Lege*, Dick, *Lege*": Fielding's Reading Lesson

The last of the subsidiary tales in Fielding's *Joseph Andrews*—each of its predecessors concerned in various ways with the structure and motivation of narrative, its pace and reception—is cast in the explicit form of an oral reading rather than merely an oral narrative (as in the case of the lady's tale of Leonora or Mr. Wilson's autobiographical narrative). More than this, it is a *lesson* in such reading, with palpable inferences for the domestic dissemination of the novel as a whole. The tale in question is the story of Leonard and Paul, a story of disastrously misinterpreted intentions which gets aborted in midstream, its conclusion displaced by the rapid-fire events—with all their own disentangled misreadings—which lead to the novel's denouement. The embedded tale's narrative urgency thus cedes to that of a novel (and a genre) whose narrative format (and common reading condition, out loud from a printed text to a familial group of eager listeners) is one that this inset tale begins by replicating. For the story has been read aloud, haltingly at first, by the son of Parson Adams, mentor and surrogate father of the hero. Further, it has been set in motion by the father's Latin command to the son—the voice of culture speaking in the language of tradition—to "Read" ("*Lege*, Dick, *lege*").[9] Such is the virtual injunction that has gone out repeatedly to us from the pages of Fielding's text in the form of addressed attention ("Reader, you") or its ascribed counterpart ("the reader will"), the vocative or its third-person kin.

Whether by command or blandishment, by tease, false lead, or genuine clue, by arrest or deflection in the vested interest of plot, by whatever means, the reader is kept on explicit alert by Fielding's venture into the new fictional form. And this attention is at intervals refigured by parable in the analogous listening audiences of the dramatically reframed tales. These are tales whose recurrent claim on us is merely spelled out most explicitly by the pedagogic imperative "*Lege*, Dick, *lege*." Indeed, it is no accident that the sole common member of these inset audiences is the ethical touchstone of the novel as a whole, Parson Adams, on hand as eager recipient for the first two tales and impresario of the third by way of instruction for his son.

Even before the compressed and downward-spiraling Bildungsroman of Mr. Wilson—pedagogic countertext to the main narrative of Joseph's coming of age—there is "The History of Leonora, or the Unfortunate Jilt." This is a tale of frustrated desire told orally by the lady to her fellow passengers in the carriage during their journey between inns. As such, its mobile venue sketches a reflexive renarration of the discursive place of just such a tale in the novel as a whole, a novel figuratively interrupted at the breathing spaces and watering holes of chapter gaps, interrupted like a coach journey by the respite of inns en route (see 2,1: "Of Divisions in Authors"). Indulging the trope of reading-as-traveling familiar from both the prehistory and subsequent proliferation of the novel as genre, this microcosmic transit of narrative also entails another, this time psychodynamic, momentum. In this sense, the narrated *response* to this embedded narrative, not just the trajectory of its enunciation, further replicates in miniature the ambit of desire within which any such narrative, including the novel that contains it, may be received and pursued. If Parson Adams is later found "licking his lips" (3,4:188) in the delectation of Mr. Wilson's exemplary moral fable of decline and reformation, so too, on the verge of the earlier tale, is the least hint of the lady's story "abundantly sufficient to awaken the curiosity of Mr. Adams, as indeed it did that of the whole company, who jointly solicited the lady to acquaint them with Leonora's history" (3,3:84).

To call a scene of avidly received narration a parable of our response to the longer popular narrative that incorporates it is to suggest how close the analogue can come to the prototype. The difference here that makes for the parabolic curve of roundabout correlation is only that the one tale is oral, the other (the novel) written, at least before it is read aloud by someone at hearthside—or someone's son. "The lady proceeded in her story thus" (2,4:85), we hear after an early interruption. Following a chapter-length digression at an inn, however, we seem to have penetrated more deeply yet into the scene of narration, for third person has become first without any discursive shift signaled by quotation marks: "But to return to *my* story: As soon as Ballarmine was recovered . . ." (2,6:105; emphasis added). We may momentarily take the implied "I" behind "my," where before there was only "the lady," as Fielding's own persona breaking through. At least, that is, until this first-person pronomial shifter realigns itself along the I / thou axis in order to address collectively *her* rather than *his* own audience—namely, the ladies in the conveyance (Adams now afoot), rather than the general public *carried along* both by the novel as a whole and, of course, by this scene of narrative transport within it: "I shall not attempt, ladies, to describe Leonora's condition when she received this letter" (2,6:108). At the same time, this address could just possibly be construed as one of the gender-specific asides of Fielding himself elsewhere—a rhetorical gesture of narrative identification meant to suggest, in regard to the story's heroine and its auditors, that it takes one to know one. All we are certain of as we read is that the very mechanisms of directed response are being reapplied here to that circumscribed scene of oral narration and captive interest which is the model for the naturalized office of cultural transmission in the novel as print genre.

This is the artifice of interlocution sustained elsewhere in part by the rhetoric of direct address—and here reinscribed as a voluble intimacy: the dialogic ruse under all but inadvertent analysis within the analogic scene. To be sure, the fluid boundaries that define the typographic codes of narrative discourse in Fielding (governing quotation marks, for example) await their fuller regimentation in nineteenth-century generic practice. In flux as yet, they abet in *Joseph Andrews* the highly permeable demarcation of narrated internal listeners from the narrative's own encircling audience. Early as they appear in the history of the novel, these typographic instabilities highlight, in a rough-hewn way, an underlying doubleness in emplotted fictional encounter. The line between a readership being presented with a story and being found represented as audience within and by that story is often vanishingly thin. Over the long haul of subsequent generic refinements on through the Victorian ascendancy of the realist novel, this foundational and slippery doubleness, I'll be attempting to demonstrate, never goes away.

Certainly the interpenetration of story and its signaled receipt is sustained into the second of Fielding's major inset tales, Mr. Wilson's autobiographical narrative of profligate poet turned hack writer. "You are not more affected with this part of my story than myself" (3,3:174), says Wilson at one point in direct (and time-honored) oratorical address to his sometimes interlocutor, now passive auditor, Parson Adams. But once Adams again breaks in with an interrogative remark—his participatory interest a stand-in for ours—the wearing away of borders between the quoted and the merely denoted (as ordinarily cued by inverted commas) is also registered by a foreshortening of verb tense: "Sir, *says* the gentleman [Wilson], the profit which booksellers allowed authors for the best works was so very small, that . . ." (3,2:181; emphasis added). At such moments of muted enunciative rupture and diffusion, all is copresent and all discursive, the storytelling act eschewing the artificial differentia of tense structure and quotation marks together. The novel-length picaresque, with its running critique of the world's vanity, grows structurally as well as dramatically coterminous with the included sideshow of a corroborative shorter tale. Both are brought, not just seen, to bear *on us* as audience, here and now in our present act of reading along in one of Fielding's own "best works." *Lege, lege* is everywhere the operative apostrophe, even as that reading is figured as audition in a strategic demediation by which the scene of narration (Wilson telling) is made commutable with the narration of its very scene (Wilson's telling retold). Here is the revealing place of Fielding's Cervantesque borrowings in the formative history of British fiction. Inset or embedded tales are one thing, framed by narrative structures within which they are recessed into place. Fielding's carefully adjusted narrative inlays are another. These are stories counterset to fit flush with the discursive protocol of the inclusive narrative mosaic.

Furthermore, even when suspended at last, Mr. Wilson's tale is not all told. Its scene of eager reception rehearses that of the novel itself not least because the fact of his having fathered a young male child, Joseph by name, will eventually complete the main plot by straightening out its genetic crossed wires. No room is left for other than empathy and breathless anticipation when this crucial aspect of Wilson's earlier narrative leaks into the main novel to cement its happy coupling and so permit its closure. What readers might extrapolate from their reading of an inlaid storytelling like Mr. Wilson's tale is also that attention into which the novel's inclusive storytelling energy works to conscribe them: in short, a recognition of their place as functions of narrative impulse. When the reader's desire—figured as such (as we are to see in the next chapter by contrast with Austen) through a network of address that summons (by merely imputing) an overwrought delight verging on prurience—comes to crisis and consummation at the same moment as the hero's and heroine's, the sheer insatiable fascination of narrative, already rehearsed in the subsidiary tales and their own greedy reception, finds itself borne out at the level of the textual dynamic at large.

"Your Books or Your Business": Thackeray's Reading Scene

As one measure of the further stress to which this intersection between parable and apostrophe, between the represented and the directed audience, will later submit, we move forward to Fielding's satiric heir in the nineteenth-century, William Makepeace Thackeray. "O Vanity!" Fielding had written in *Joseph Andrews*, "I know thou wilt think that, whilst I abuse thee, I court thee, and that thy love hath inspired me to write this sarcastic panegyric on thee" (1,15:57). This charge—by which Vanity would insinuate herself exactly as secret muse rather than satiric butt—is ingeniously foisted off onto a fantasized conversation between equidistant personifications, Vanity herself on the one side, the reader on the other. Fielding, in short, would not object, as he closes the apostrophe by professing, "if thou [Vanity] shouldst prevail on the reader to censure this digression as arrant nonsense" (1,15:57). The reader, of course, has no way out of this logical double bind. Either you accede to the rhetorical force of this diatribe, or else, by siding with Vanity, you enact the relevance of the attack in your prideful blindness. Where you might expect direct address as a means of snaring you within the *vanitas* of the novel, instead the apostrophic formula is shunted onto a personification of vainglory from which you must work to distinguish your own third-person denomination as reading agent. Nothing in Fielding anticipates more directly the rhetorical machinations—and their conscriptive logic—attending the grammar of address in Thackeray's later satire.

There, the *vanitas* tradition is quite bluntly enlisted through the skewering moves of direct address. When the novel comes closest to addressing its own generalized satiric muse outright, the apostrophe takes shape as if it takes the novel itself as eponymous object: "O, Vanity Fair—Vanity Fair! This might have been, but for you, a cheery lass [Lady Crawley]" (9:83). This double-edged apostrophe to the Fair occurs just a short while after we have been actively reminded of the novel's title: "But my kind reader will please to remember, that this history has 'Vanity Fair' for a title, and that Vanity Fair is a very vain, wicked, foolish place" (8:80). For Thackeray's englobing apostrophe to Fair and *Fair* alike, the text has laid an even earlier groundwork. In the preface, the man "with a reflective turn of mind" becomes the second-person protagonist of the next paragraph: "When you come home, you sit down, in a sober, contemplative, not uncharitable frame of mind, and apply yourself to your books or your business." The phrasing hovers in an uncertainty pitched between "your account books or your other chores" and a conception more like "your reading or your work." Returning from the Fair to the enclave of one's books—as syntactically (at least) distinct from one's business—leaves open the possibility of the novel's own present scene of consumption: the domestic site for a very different sort of "application," by which one may make space within worldly affairs for a novel satirizing such worldliness. The real dailiness of transit between public and private is thus recruited to figure that illusory shuttling— illusory because not topographical, only terminological—between home and Fair, home and world. And if the domestic haven is subsumed to the Fair, so too is the *Fair*, as circumscribed by the home, incorporated within the Fair: not only its satiric mirror but a synecdoche for it. Reading is no escape from the cycle of commercial circulation. If we look in at the *Fair*, only to find that looking, that spectatorship, repeatedly thematized as voyeurism, class curiosity, gossipy snooping, and so forth, all within the system of worldly information as exchange value, then our reading—our role as readers—becomes inseparable from that of all the other citizen Fair-goers, busy bookkeepers of fiction as well as finance, vicarious addicts of life's theater, vain worldlings, titillated and escapist consumers. Every day is market day.

Writing of that self-conscious vein of prose fiction from Sterne to Thackeray (and we might well include Fielding here) in which "a special complexity and multi-layeredness entered the novel," Mikhail Bakhtin exemplifies his point by noting how "'intervalic' chronotopes appeared, such as, for instance, the chronotope of the theater"—a space-time folded into narrative by way of a certain reformulation of its larger pattern—in the manner (one of his own examples) of the puppet theater in *Vanity Fair*.[10] The Victorian novel provides dozens of further illustrations of such chronotopic doubling in which an embedded scene of reading—or its variant in a more disparate arena of representation and reception like Thackeray's puppet show—emerges from and reorients the reading of the text that incorporates it. This abyssal function becomes all the more disorienting as we move forward into another century to the sinuous self-referential evocations, for instance, of Proustian textuality, which do their work of situating the reader without, for the most part, the structural aid of vocative address.

Having examined the localized sites of extrapolated response in the so-called interpolated tales of an eighteenth-century novelist like Fielding, and postponing a closer look at their Victorian derivations in Dickens, Eliot, and others, we have turned to *Vanity Fair* for its global extrapolation (as reading event) from novel to the world it figuratively denominates. From this Victorian compendium as "book of the world" (see chapter 10), we move now to sketch the far reaches of the traditional novelistic agenda in the Proustian "world of the book." We therefore defer consideration of the interplay in high Victorian fiction between two intertwined legacies of the eighteenth-century novel—interpolated reference or address and extrapolated hermeneutic response—for a forward glance at the even more elusive (yet no less illustrative) fusion of these two devices in Proust's modernism. In an unremitting version of narrative's conscriptive logic in Proust, the reader's subjectivity seems to coauthor the text by a rhetorical *subjection*. It takes nothing less than some reading to bring this out.

"Reader, of the Enclosure": Proust's Holding Action

In distinguishing the present emphasis from the slippery associations attaching to the term "allegories of reading" in Paul de Man's work, we can go straight for that Proustian scene of reading from which de Man takes his inaugural and favored example, a passage dwelled on in his lead essay, "Semiology and Rhetoric," and returned to in his chapter titled "Figures (Proust)."[11] This is the episode of Marcel's closeted summer reading at Combray. Yet "readability" more than reading is actually the condition de Man is interested to find allegorized, here and elsewhere, by literature. Explaining away the more intuitive sense of one's read encounter with a narrated scene of textual engagement, de Man maintains that "we cannot *a priori* be certain to gain access to whatever Proust may have had to say about reading by way of such a reading of a scene of reading."[12] Certainly not, but we can gain access to what the text says (rather than "what Proust may have had to say") in the scene itself. De Man's own account actually goes a considerable distance in this direction. Informed by it, we can move on, as with Fielding and Thackeray, to trace out the connection in Proust between such an analogue or parable (rather than "allegory") of reading and its quasi-dialogic counterpart in direct address. The move forward and aside from the classic British tradition to a French modernist writer at the close of these introductory chapters is frankly strategic. It is meant primarily to engage on its own favored (Proustian) ground that influential approach of Paul de Man's which might otherwise seem to debar just the kind of investigation into the scene of reading for which this chapter prepares the way.

We begin, as de Man does, with Marcel taking up, and at once caught up by, a written narrative in *Swann's Way*. He has fled to it from the mandatory daylight and warm air enjoined by his grandmother. Yet in escaping from the assault of a summer noon into the reading closet of a darkened bedroom, Marcel assimilates to the intensity of the moment all the freshening outer life he has happily foresworn. A single sentence at once sets and detonates the scene. In a fraught periodic syntax, the "dark coolness" of Marcel's isolated chamber, protected from the blaze of summer, "matched my repose which (thanks to the adventures narrated in my book, which stirred my tranquility) supported, like the quiet of a hand held motionless in the middle of a running brook, the shock and the animation of a flood of activity." The passage must come to negotiate, according to de Man, a figurative "transfer" (65), entirely within the exchange systems of metaphor, a relay by which "the cool repose of the hand should be made compatible with the heat of action" (65)—namely the "torrent d'activité" he first translates as "flood." What passes as obvious, perhaps, in de Man's account (though he does not say so) is the displacement onto figuration of the masturbatory paradox of feverish passivity. But the hand deployed in turbulent repose has, and does, other work in the passage as well. De Man comments: "The persuasive power of the passage depends on the play on the verb 'supporter' which must be strong enough to be read not just as 'tolerate' but as 'support,' suggesting that repose is indeed the foundation, the ground that makes activity possible" (64).

But what ultimately turns the passage into an emblem of our own supported repose in reading, the paradoxically animated passivity of our own attention, seems to me another aspect of the "play on the verb" unnoted by de Man. Just as the dead metaphor of "stirred" (as in *stirring the passions*) anticipates "like a . . . hand," so does the image of the immobile hand as the only fixed point of reference in the subjectivized inrush of narrative activity call to mind not only that condition of repose which tolerates, or even founds, the textual phenomenon but that which actually *holds the book in place*. In the metonymic slide of contiguous association, that is, the vehicle of "hand" in relation to the tenor of reading's "repose"—in this metanarrative about reading narrative—finds itself demetaphorized by the associative force of contiguity itself. Ultimately, the hand is exactly that sole stationary support that anchors both any encounter with Proust's narrative and thus any homology it broaches with that remembered act of the narrator's hand-held reading.

I need here to reiterate a point not unlike the understanding this involuted passage turns inside out in order to clarify. In the broad range of the traditional novel's conscriptive effects, both the interpolation of the reader through reference or directive and the extrapolation of the reader's orientation from a narrative episode (by however direct or indirect an analogue) are tropes. They "turn away" to what can never actually appear *in* the text: its destination in mentality. In the case of the *Swann's Way* passage, this figural turn seems twice removed and hence circular. Here the analogy to reading may appear to recapitulate itself from within a preliminary figuration of just such textual engagement. Reading is like holding against a torrent with a hand that holds its own as if, come to think of it, it were gripping a book. Reading is like X, which is like reading. In this way, the literalized condition of reading may be found returning from within the very figuring of its effect. For the hand of the hero we substitute our own: extrapolation thus reduced to a kind of material tautology.

Interpolation is another matter in Proust, though not unrelated. Indeed, the hailing of the reader in a central passage from *Jean Santeuil* (1896–1900; published 1952) anticipates both the allegories of readability and the analogues of the reading act well over a decade later in *Swann's Way*. It does so, in part, by generating an ambivalence familiar to us from one of the earliest second-person addresses of *Joseph Andrews*: "You have heard, reader, poets talk" (1,8:32). There, the generalized tendency toward reading, rather than any present attention to a text in hand, seems to authorize the address—as if all "gentle readers" were in fact being celebrated for the literary predisposition that brings them to a text in the first place: "You, reader that you are . . ." We can at least agree that the effect would hardly be out of place in Proust. Further, the capacity of such address to refigure the scene of imaginative retreat, the self lost in a book, as the text's ultimate abyssal ground—this capacity can be seen in the unexpected vocative grammar of that passage from *Jean Santeuil*, an episode adduced by Georges Poulet to illustrate the transformation in Proust from "objective verity to that of art."[13]

In "a movement very rare for him, the novelist addresses the reader" with the following: "And you too, older than Jean, reader, of the enclosure of a garden situated on a height, have you not had sometimes the feeling that it was not only other fields, other trees that extended before you, but a certain country under its special sky?"[14] The trees in the foreground, nearest the enclosure upon which the reader is asked to remember leaning, "were like the real trees of the first plan of a panorama; they served as a *transition* between what you knew, the garden where you had come to visit, and that unreal, mysterious thing, a land that lay before you under the appearances of plains, developing richly in valleys, letting the light play upon itself" (Poulet, 22). As the vertical plane (of "real trees") becomes horizontal through the effect of illusion(ism), what begins in simile ("*plan* d'un panorama") spreads by linguistic slant echo to the "apparences de *plaines*" (emphasis added). The funneled perspective is in touch for a while yet with the physicality of landscape, though phasing over—and fading out into—something other: "Here are still real things . . . but farther away there is something else" (Poulet, 22). The transitional zone between real and unreal, actual space and the space of art (rather than reading per se)—such for Poulet is the recession from enclosure to the framed scenography beyond, from material immediacy to the distanced vista of the yet unrealized. The whole scene unfolds, according to Poulet's demonstrations, as what might be termed, in a dead metaphor made topographic, the very picture of aesthetic distance.

But the question of the aberrant apostrophe remains open. Why should Proust break ranks with his own modernist removal of text from the fiction of address—in such a lyrical rather than ironic passage—to call out the reader at just this point? Beyond noting the anomaly, Poulet does not explore the motive—or, more to the point, the effect. There is, however, much to go on in the larger shape of the long paragraph, especially its ultimate destination in a review of the activity of childhood reading. This, in its own right, structures a return to and recapitulation of the preceding chapter, entitled "Reading" ("Lectures"), in which the hero's rapt preoccupation with his favorite novel leaves him in "complete unmindfulness of his body," having "lost, at times, all awareness of the outside world."[15] We can now begin to recognize what puts a virtually self-fulfilling spin on the question attending Proust's exceptional direct address, "Reader, have you not felt?" It is a rhetorical question, finally, about the very working of fictional rhetoric, breaking as it does with the strictly mimetic contract (through the obtruded reminder of textuality and reception) only to ratify it anew. Suggested by this passage is that the act of engagement with a textual space begins in the condition of the reading agent's being poised at, or even leaning upon, the material base, brace, or "transition" between a real world and that framed and enclosed glimpse of distance, spatially bounded, upon which the opened pages of a book *seem* further to open back, open out. In Proust's extended but attenuated conceit, the later plans and planes of the "panorama" to which the transfigured landscape is likened hold out only a beckoning fabrication of three-dimensionality, into which one's imagination is drawn by the borderline of real trees. In at least one implied aesthetic tenor to this spatial vehicle, therefore, it is not just the arboreal enclosure "you had been leaning on" but the heft and density, the bulk and pulp, of a bound volume that offers one palpable foredrop to the receding world of fancy: physical prop for the amorphous scenography of textual visualization. The reader is explicitly, almost awkwardly, invoked, we may say, because it is our present reading that grounds the metaphor in an assured experience that memory need not be relied on to reproduce.

I turn now to a level of response—a level of reading practice—to whose ramifications this chapter will need to return. For under the weight of surrounding evidence in Proust's opulently layered paragraph, it gradually comes clear how the unexpected torsion of reader address is abetted by the materially resistant inversions and interruptions of its own grammar. This is a grammar that we need to hear, finally, in French: "Et vous-même, plus âgé que Jean, lecteur, de la clôture d'un jardin située sur un hauteur n'êutes-vous pas parfois le sentiment que . . . "[16] The standard English translation understandably, but unacceptably, straightens out the syntax, flattening the effect: "And you, reader, older though you are than Jean, have you not sometimes . . . felt that . . ." (125). As restored to its doubly strained inversion by Poulet's translator, "you, older than Jean," precedes the delayed appositive "reader," which is followed, before the main clause, by the prepositional phrase "of the enclosure of a garden situated on a height." What Proust's forced inversion has done is to shadow the grammar with another idiomatic predication, another normative verb phrase: *to read of* rather than *to have the feeling about*. When each member of the audience is thereby put on alert as "reader [,] of the enclosure of a garden," it is a characterization impossible to deny in respect to the present sentence. Turning upon the syntax as well as the fact of address, such is Proust's self-fulfilling grammar of rhetoric, his rhetoric of grammar. Vocative tautology becomes abyssal duplication when the tentative opening for a dialogic response (the rhetorical question) springs reading's analogic figuration instead. The text's reflexive tropology generates, in short, a perspectival topology of illusory textual space.

To rephrase the guiding binary opposition in the passage from *Jean Santeuil* as that between substantial and apparitional, real and illusionistic, is to connect it with the immediate context of the *Swann's Way* passage in Proust's sustained disquisition on the phenomenon—we would since say (and thanks to Poulet) the phenomenology—of reading. It is as if that yearning in *Jean Santeuil* past an immanent structure of support toward some imminent vista—a garden wall toward a receding and unreal perspective, an enclosure toward the mysteries it frames and to which it yields—is recast in Proust's masterwork to become, more explicitly, the imaginative immersion of the reader in narrative space, in all its "torrential" activation. From here on, this is a reader no longer addressed directly but represented instead by proxy in the narrator's autobiographical retrospect. Proust has thus driven one tradition of novelistic narrative to a certain lower and revealing limit: the tendency for classic texts to take upon themselves the encoding of their own parameters of reception. Its immediate impact impossible to "allegorize" perhaps, reading in Proust is captured instead in its mediacy. What happens in both our examples is thus up to the text *at hand*.

Response Foreshortened

As touched on in the first chapter, narrative reading is made possible by an extroversion of the fictional inner life: a mimesis of emotion as well as milieu whose only point of occlusion is the scene of reading itself when set off within plot. The representational charter by which narrators convey (relay, transfer) consciousness from narrated characters to the reading act—as if such textual consciousness somehow preexists our constitutive vivification of it (and can therefore be thought revived): this charter is abrogated in reading about reading. Characters may seem fully read by us, that is, except when they are reading. Hence the two Proustian examples at which we've been at work. As we are drawn to inhabit Marcel's reading consciousness, by none other than the penetrant empathy of reading itself, what we find at the heart of the analogies summoned to evoke his captivation, and ours superimposed upon it, is a figurative turn that turns the whole conceit into, I want to say, a parable of itself. The event of a reading becomes a replay *as mere figure* of reading's material condition in a held volume. So, too, as we inhabit Jean's consciousness while he is meditating on the nature of aesthetic manifestations (in its contextual relation to reading in particular); there we also discover a parable of the very reading—as spatiotemporal disposition of body as well as mind—which not only effectuates the text but is caught off guard when apostrophized by it.

To enlarge upon terms already introduced from Paul Ricoeur, reading absorbs the inner life otherwise available to configurative mimesis (the representation in this case of the immaterial life of imagination); in so doing, it transfers this absorption onto third-order mimesis, where we substitute our own "refigured" engagement for that of the character. Narrative at such moments may thus be felt to *theatricalize absorption* in the form of attention per se. I move here, of course, to borrow (and cross-wire with Ricoeur) the main terms of Michael Fried's argument. At which point, in the move between media, one must ask precisely how print, as distinct from brushed pigment, sets about replicating the fascination that activates its various scenes, by what subterfuge of phenomenological displacement it folds your own absorption into the fabric of characterization.

Just as the intertextual static generated by literary direct address tells you not so much that there is nobody really there talking to you as that there is no *one* at home to be hailed (I recur to an argument developed in the last chapter), so the analogic rather than (or in league with) the dialogic construct narrates your own lack of priority (as reader) to the world of which you read. As you are conscripted in either fashion to help constitute the inner life of a character—to undergo what overcomes Marcel in reading, and to do so mostly by the cognitive flux of deciphering it—you nevertheless find in yourself nothing to lend but what is already offered, nothing to invest but what is already vested in you by the text. Even as everything in the nature of textual realization depends on what you bring to the text, you are made to find it all there *before* you. In order to read aright, therefore, you are required or sometimes openly requested to become most yourself for Marcel's or Jane Eyre's sake. Yet it is their experience that consumes, if only by duplicating with a difference, your own. As fictional characters they are made up, but so for the moment are you of them. This doubleness, this circular logic, is always the case. The enterprise of reading rests on it. The scene of *their* reading only makes it the more precariously, vertiginously, apparent.

The introversion of reading in either Poulet's or de Man's account of Proust is a figuratively buttressed aesthetic autonomy—a veering from nature to culture—which invites historicizing in ways that fall well outside their sectors of concern. From a rather unexpected quarter, a dialectical-materialist vantage on the history of reading, in untranslated German scholarship by Erich Schön, can offer a diachronic long view of such aestheticism in its emergent phase. With methodological roots partly in German reception theory, Schön's study serves to complement not only the most searching work on the figurative sleights of the high modernist canon but also, and more directly, various Anglo-American understandings of the earlier rise of the novel as a middle-class form. In this larger context, it would seem that both passages from Proust instance once again the principle of ontogeny recapitulating phylogeny. In each, the hero's aesthetic maturation replays the world-historical stages in an allied liberation and routinization of the modern reading subject. This is a subject imaginatively freed up (unimpeded even by sounded language) to transgress textual borders into alternative and invented worlds—but only as this freedom is licensed and exercised within a psychoeconomy of the social subject. Schön's is thus a study of "reader-making" at a scale unanticipated by Henry James.

Its title renderable in English as *Loss of Sensuality, or The Transformations of the Reader*, with its subtitle *A Turn of Mentality around 1800*, Schön's book takes shape around a self-correcting set of cultural checks and balances. On the one hand, his meticulous research can demonstrate the final fading in the eighteenth century, even as vestigial social habit, of solitary reading out loud—with all the losses the new silent mastery incurred in regard to the palpable pleasures, the phonic materiality, of reading. On the other hand, across the evolving culture of that same eighteenth century, there developed an adjusted sensuous investment in the felt fictional world rather than the real resonating body of reading: in the psychic space made accessible, that is, by the representational rather than the material aspect of the text. Mixing what he designates as "civilization theory, historical anthropology, and sociological theories of symbolic interaction and the taking-over of roles," Schön wants to know what functions of reading disappear with the consolidation of its private and silent status, as well as what compensatory dimensions of the reading experience arose in the eighteenth century to adjust the deficit.[17] If the body had been the sensuous envelope of oral reading, it was also to just this degree a kind of cage. Giving up its physiological register—the musculature of enunciation—facilitates instead, if only by default, a turn toward what Schön calls "a controlled traffic in the specific reality of a literarily mediated world" (326).

Schön's question quickly takes him to the history of textual consumption as visually represented in German painting and graphic art, with its prevalent image of reading out of doors. The reading subject gets merged with nature in a way that borrows its prestige both from the medieval trope of nature as God's book and also from the general aestheticizing of natural landscape in the eighteenth century. Dismissing such practices of outdoors reading as anything approaching a statistical commonplace, Schön instead takes its picturing as part of a diffused propaganda for the new private textuality as a naturally rooted practice. At the same time, he notes in the subsequent decline of this pictorial trope a gradual codification of reading as the "crossing over" into a "literary reality" (327) all its own, with no spatial orientation (or excuse) necessary. If Proust's Jean Santeuil were painted leaning over a garden gate as a makeshift lectern for reading, his eyes averted from prospect to page, the scene would echo the motifs Schön has found in the visual representation of the eighteenth and early nineteenth centuries. Marcel's outright preference for his book's warmth over the sun's would then be only the final stage in this cultural transformation.

Emphasizing the first stirrings of such a privileged aesthetic in the latter half of the eighteenth century, Schön's argument is at its most steadily materialist in seeking to account for the "historical development" of what he calls "em-

pathetic competence" as one "process of modernization" (327). Such function-
alist "competence" is best understood when aligned with the reified division of
labor in an ascendant bourgeois culture. Reading not only continued mostly
indoors but, by the routines of the business day, was scheduled increasingly for
the lamplit evening hours, where its allotted time partook of the same work
ethic from which it seemed to seek respite: determined by the laws of efficiency
and self-improvement. The better one was at shifting gears, at plunging into
the created space of reading, the more productive was one's accession to information and to culture. Hence the subordination of reading to "free" time
and of free time in turn to "use" time (328) within the pragmatism of the *Bild-
ungsbegriff* (329)—the whole concept of mental developmentalism. To put it in
a way by no means unfamiliar to fiction readers of the next century, "empathetic
competence" was not only necessary for identification with the hero of the
Bildungsroman but turned the *roman* itself into part of the reader's own *Bild-
ung*. Here literature in fact took the lead among other reading, since it was
uniquely disposed to promote the rapid shifts of concentration necessary to
the mental equipment of the new bourgeois citizenry. The integration of literary with real world experience, at faster and faster speeds of alternation, was
therefore a learned skill of the modern subject, an aspect of cultural evolution
governed by the survival of the imaginatively fittest. In other words—my terms
now rather than Schön's—the novel tutored the bourgeois citizen at the dawn
of the modern era in the adaptive substitution of fictional phenomenology for
textual phonology.

But the dialectic need not be arrested at this first stage of antinostalgic synthesis in the ascendancy of the aesthetic. Not only does my historical argument
continue well past Schön's eighteenth-century turn of mentality, but what it
finds there is that the enunciatory murmur suppressed at the birth of fiction
often reasserts itself as a textual undertone in the novel's second full century.
This is where considerations of literary history may be profitably attached to
Schön's very different template for cultural advancement. A fictional tradition
conceived as having an explicitly postromantic phase (and well before Proust),
while building on what I would want to call the "phenomenological" (or "empathetic") competencies traced by Schön, may also mitigate the originary ban
of modern literary consumption—the silenced page—by tapping again the
phonemic textuality of just such a page. In this way do the densened phono-
logical effects of romantic verse, passed on in moderated form to the British
novel, mark the return of a repressed aural register in the subvocal materializations of Victorian style from Dickens and Charlotte Brontë through Robert
Louis Stevenson, a somatic complication of the gradually attuned affective fac-

ulty. Such effects by no means occlude the hard-won transparency of realist mimesis but rather, even in their phonic convolutions, get folded back into narrative momentum as a purposive aesthetic surplus. By latently engaging the bodily sensorium, they also compound rather than block the feeling of self-surrender to the broadly literary (not just the fictive) otherworld: the made space for which time is made—and by which competent reading subjects are co-opted through their own empathetic mastery.

With literary history culturally contextualized in this way, apostrophe and parable provide only two of the most obvious outward signs of such textual internalization. Mixing the eighteenth-century protocols of gothic intensity and epistolary intimacy, Jane Austen will satirize as well as extend this double logic of a reader at once external and internal to a text, with the reading agency consolidated as both a touchstone and a structuring device of gradually dispensed narrative. Mary Shelley will psychoanalyze this doubleness by concentric reframing, inverting in the process the gothic parody experimented with by Austen into a new metanarrative dynamic. The Victorian best-sellers will for the most part skirt round the unstable cloning of interiority induced by extrapolation, instead moderating the dislocations of conscribed response by the more sociable tethers of direct address. Dickens, however, reserving the mode of reader apostrophe primarily for satiric set pieces, will revel in the participatory inwardness of reading as social psychology, exploiting primarily by analogic models the interdependencies of character and audience. As Victorian fiction proliferates, the textual careers of interpolation and extrapolation continue to part and cross by turns, to exclude or entail, repel or embroil each other. Emily Brontë will work once more, as did Mary Shelley, to recruit the metanarrative leverage of multiple reframings as parabolic reading sites, Charlotte Brontë to marshal the frame-breaking options of supposedly extratextual apostrophe. In structural conjunction with an apostrophized audience, George Eliot will be found returning again, in *Daniel Deronda* especially, to the time-trusted parable of reading. It is located by her within a plot of explicit hermeneutic obsessions, one whose muted demonic aspect leads on not so much to the revived reading of gothics as to a veritable gothic of reading in the *fin de siècle*, with its recurrent implications for the perverse erotic sorcery of the textual encounter.

In view of such developments and devolutions, one takes up again this chapter's opening comparisons between the realist ascendancy in painting and fiction to inquire into the potential common denominators of realism's eclipse. What modernist painting does in Michael Fried's view to further the elision of specular self-consciousness within a self-absorptive objecthood of form is one thing. What literary high modernism does, having driven out address by the englobing stress on a textual density elevated at once over both traditional representation and normative communication, may be a similar thing. When the objecthood of the text is no longer its latency as an object of reading but rather the material surface of its signification, what has been rescinded is exactly the hermeneutic distance between the reflexive scene of reception and the hermeticism of scriptive "self-reference." Victorian narratives down through the coterminous textual allegories and reading parables drawn out in my last chapter, if they do not fully see this coming, nonetheless foreshadow it by not being able to see beyond the clearly marked crisis in reception which precipitates it: namely, the dubiety such narratives perform (as well as entertain) concerning the tenor of fictional consumption as passive, greedy, and depleting. Empathetic competence has become vicarious indulgence.

In the novel between Fielding and Proust, the prevalence of conscripted reading, whether by reference or reflex, does not in itself, however, erase de Man's doubts about the interpretive leverage accorded to such moments. Quite the contrary. It is therefore time—before embarking on the course of novel reading just charted out—to put forward more plainly, and in relation to each other, a guiding axiom and a resulting modus operandi. The axiom has to do with the reflex of reading precipitated by the traditional novel, the operational mode with the level at which that reflex gets registered. On both counts, my discussion is sufficiently informed by de Man to depart from exactly the impasse of his strictures. It is the premise of this book, in short, that the reflexive scene (at least once redefined) is just what it seems to be, if nothing more—textually privileged; and that this privilege is often most obviously legible in the quite specific demands it makes on reading.

For de Man, the fact that the unreadability—the undecidability—of writing may be found staged by a text in the self-contested densities of its own figuration invites (or constitutes in and of itself) a deconstruction that stops short of anything like the allegory of reading per se. For the latter is a contradictory project that overrules the very possibility it seeks to refigure. To winnow the complications through which de Man sifts at length, we may simply say that reading cannot be the signifier of its own immediate signified. You can't isolate the normative case of what you are (no longer quite) doing (i.e., straightforwardly reading) in reading *about* it. Unlike pictorial allegory, where a female representation may, for instance, bear the legend KARITAS (his example is Giotto) with clear intent, for Proust to print LECTIO on the frames of his stories would be to achieve no fixed designation of the act it requires as well as names (77). According to de Man, no autocommentary of this sort can "ground the stability of the text" (72). This may well be the case, but as distinct from the programmatic modernism of a Proust or a Joyce, no Victorian writing would have needed or sought (let alone known what to rest on) such grounding. In Victorian narrative, the base of the fictional enterprise is a social contract which, having a participation outside the text, could never be thought wholly contained or even exhaustively troped by the text. Such a base was simply *figured in* on occasion: either by an address manifestly directed beyond the borders of the text or by a scene whose narrative contours stand at something like a parabolic distance (how could it be closer?) from the scene of its reception.

If we have been on the right track with those passages from Proust, what makes them almost blithely ironic are their tautological somersaults. In the one, the hero reads feverishly as if only his hand were in ultimate control over the rush of impressions. So what else is new? In the other, the reader of a garden scene is asked if he has ever had an aesthetic experience based in such a scene. Inner and outer implode upon each other across a simile in the one, across the ambiguous grammar of an apostrophe in the other. But tautology is almost too comfortable a way to designate this. For a cognitive and emotive experience that might here be redefined wholly by reference to itself does not in fact quite coincide with itself. And the angle of deflection springs a reflex. Whatever exactly this feels like when it is happening, it is time to distinguish it from self-referentiality in the usual understanding of that term. I do so on behalf of subsequent chapters that will need to draw on this distinction. Episodes of writing (or their analogues): these are definably self-referential. The text at such places refers (by association) to its own articulation. But reading is an activity and a duration rather than, like writing, a material fact and its manifestation. I therefore reserve the term *reflexive* for those moments (rather than places) where the act of reading within the text—or its momentary approximation—registers as a reflex of and upon the text's own consumption. In so doing, these moments may also (not of necessity but often by design) bring back from historical attrition (in Schön's terms) the very body of phonatory self-consciousness as part of this reflex.

Unlike the self-referential inscription, the reflexive moment is an event rather than a site. Pace de Man, or with whatever inevitable aporias counted in, reflexivity marks an act of reading caught in the act. The concentric relation of a story's internal writing or even storytelling to its printed form in a bound novel, the relation on which metatextual self-reference is based, does not hold for scenes of reading. This is one way of putting the problem they raise for de Man. They seem to install a more complete substitution than synecdoche would suggest. In the process, though, they are often as densely *written* as any stretch of self-referential textuality. The resulting premise—become a practice—is as follows: conscripted reading is often a function of the scripted difficulties thrown in the path of a reading. In hereby forecasting the level of attention to be repeatedly invited in the pages to come, I mean simply to suggest that the textual demands (figural, syntactic, lexical, typographic, phonemic) upon the reader's processing of narrative may themselves be taken as part of the reflexive charge incident to reading-about-reading, thus qualifying de Man's sense that the process and its depiction are always irreconcilable. You can't know till you've been there, been there when, because never exactly where, they *seem* to coincide.

A Reading Seen

Lest this process be thought to elude larger aesthetic and psychic ramifications in the intensive nature of its linguistic concern, let me illustrate it from the "close reading" of another medium entirely. I will do so by way of one last return to Michael Fried's category of the absorptive scene. The interdisciplinarity (if that's what one calls it) fostered by this return is by no means gratuitous at this point in our introductory discriminations. For the extended look we'll be taking at a mid-nineteenth-century canvas concerned with the excesses of reading (and placed here as frontispiece) induces in its own right a reflex of viewing, one that redoubles and undoes its very thematic of righteously chastened vicariousness. The canvas happens also to intersect with an apostrophic discourse of addressed fascination so pervasive in the century that it can show up not only in popular and elite literary rhetoric but in magazine art reviewing and gallery catalogue copy.

The gallery in question is the Musée Wiertz in Brussels, dedicated to the work of Antoine Wiertz (1806–65); the magazine, the *Art-Journal* of 1869, which contemplates the 1853 canvas by Wiertz entitled *The Romance Reader*—and whose comments are reprinted in an early catalogue.[18] What that painting offers up is not so much described as narrativized by the anonymous reviewer for the *Art-Journal*. The "young girl reclining on her bed . . . has read throughout the night, . . . until now that the cool light of morning and reality dawns, she cannot release herself from the spell" (366). She sounds a little like the heroine of Thomas Hardy's *A Pair of Blue Eyes* (1873), who, in the opening chapter to the serialized version of the novel, is so frenzied to know the fate of the hero in the romance by which she is engrossed that she scans the table of contents and is prematurely convulsed by its tragic climax.[19] It may be no accident in this regard that Thomas Hardy, whom we know to have been more than once in Brussels, actually alludes to Wiertz's museum in *Tess of the D'Urbervilles*, if

not to the "Romance Reader" herself.[20] In any case, according to the British reviewer, at her bedside is "one who, under the guise of a very handsome young
man, is nevertheless Satan, as two satanic horns reveal," the devil plying his
trade by supplying the young girl with a continuous stack of romances. (Such
a source of spirit-wasting books may suggest the original bottomless pit.) What
is most eye catching about the journalistic commentary, however, and especially when excerpted in the museum catalogue, is its first sentence: "You behold a young girl reclining upon her bed, reading romances." With a second-
person grammar verging on the imperative, you are plunged into the scene by
an address calculated to replicate the instantaneous grip of the picture. This is
the prose version of a pictorial scene that may have (but that makes no) appeal.
Your viewer's gaze is not interpolated by reciprocation, by any direct look back
from the canvas (the pictorial equivalent of "dear reader" in something like
"you, viewer, are seeing here"). With your gaze nowhere explicitly invited, in
other words, by this detheatricalized scene (where even the horned tempter is
absorbed in his devil's work), looking is thus dramatized only by the relays of
extrapolation in this most reflexive of pictorial texts.

To begin with, the improbable mirror next to the girl's bed—upon which
a coronet is hung, as though it were the abandoned laurel crown of high-literary art—is positioned to arrange the dramatic shock of a *vanitas* (in which
Wiertz elsewhere specialized), one that never materializes here. Instead, the
mirrored plane of self-voyeurism is primed in this case for erotic fantasy or masturbatory narcissism. Although no skeleton is made proleptically visible in the
mirror as scourge of the flesh, however, we do see reframed the heightened
vulnerability of that flesh in its yet more exposed lassitude. Whatever self-in-
volved fantasies have previously been indulged with the aid or prop of the mirror, at this moment the young woman has no interest in its image of the heated
imaginings that fever her brow. All you see is that it amplifies and exaggerates
the indiscretion of your own point of view. In the intermission or aftermath of
its probable erotic function, it hangs there for you as the emblem of mimesis
itself in its sexual privilege. For, unmistakably, it is angled just so—just so as to
make available the scandal of all but full genital display. What the erotic romances are to the subject, so, then, is her nudity to you: the access that only
reflection, or call it representation, can maximize.

This is not all. As you see the female subject even more openly revealed to
you in the obtrusive looking glass, your vantage (your "reading" of the image)
is eroticized twice over. For you are seeing in her, by enhanced mediation, what
she is only reading about: the insatiability of sensual abandon. By an act of pictorial irony and poetic justice, she pays the price for being able, as it were, to

peer in upon the intimacies of others by being viewed in her own throes of vicarious titillation. Entered upon here is a surrogacy of desire, an exchangeable erotic positioning, that renders the subject viewer (as always), like the subject reader within the scene—and especially in the mirror by which her privacy is more fully betrayed to us—effectively *faceless* in the grips of another's story. As with the two readers in our example from Fragonard or the sketch by Hopkins (fig. 2), such is the self-effacing posture of deputized desire.

Beyond and including the girl's angled mirror, the inscription of a recurrent pictorial geometry draws out—by sketching forth—this irony of the textual voyeur herself espied. Wiertz's composition is a network of reversed lines and cocked limbs traced back to the physical as well as mental strain of its willed origin—the awkwardly maintained proximity of eye and book—at a point that recalls the Proustian hand supporting a torrent of inward action in reading. And just as the girl's face is framed by the bracketing angles of her two bent arms, intended both for reading (the hand holding the book) and its relief (the hand holding the handkerchief), so does another double angle arrest attention. This is of course the angle of spread legs and their mirror reversal, an inverted image hinged at the left knee. This meeting of knee and mirror is one of many acute angles whose pattern is reinstituted one more time to the far right of the canvas—just before the interruption of its own frame—by the inverted triangle formed by the side view of the mirror's frame as it meets the wall. Inscribed thereby, in a different plane, is yet another V shape echoing at once the just deflected pubic disclosure of the open legs, the fuller view in the mirror, and, to a lesser extent on the far left of the canvas, the slight perspectival cleft out of which the devil's work emerges, as if from the abyss.

A last and definitive touch: What only a very good reproduction of the painting can begin to reveal is that cast into shadow at the back of the mirror lies the cause of its forced angle away from the wall.[21] What in fact wedges open this unlikely gap is nothing less than a pile of discarded books—presumably more of the same romances—deliberately hidden from view behind it, perhaps on hold for another reading. The allegorical satire cuts both ways: In their opening upon new erotic worlds, books both assist in mirroring, by giving narrative form to, the girl's yearning and thus also facilitate (here in a mechanical reduction) the closed circuit of narcissism induced by their reading. However one diagnoses the dilemma, books are *behind it all*.

Put in the most encompassing terms, then, the painting's graphic principle is that of the triangle: the shape of arms held over shoulders; of bed slanted away from its horizontal footpost; of frame against wall; of thighs opened— and of their revealing obverse in the mirror (where the twain do converge and nearly lay bare). Averted from us in the insistent angularity of the composition, receding toward the subjective origin of the whole display, is in this sense the ultimate matching spread to the cleft thighs: namely, the forced triangle of the open book, its unseen pages spread to hungry view (hers alone, since we have her instead). Our eyes are drawn there in part, too, because the book occupies a kind of preemptive vanishing point for the narrowing lines of molding on the right wall of the bed closet. Moreover, besides the architectural triangle that thereby pinpoints the nameless because interchangeable book and the second triangle its open pages form in their own right, that clutched volume anchors another recognized triangulation that exceeds the absorptive scene. Completing, that is, the painting's schema of nervous zigzags in the third dimension of spectatorship is the governing triangulation of feverish pictured reader, steamy text, and the onlooker as reader manqué. This last is a spectatorial transgressor—you, by name—whose voyeuristic pleasure is less checked than unnervingly enhanced, as is the reading girl's in its own way, by the *mirror* of romantic prostration offered up in and by this canvas.

Finally, too, given the curious (there is no better word for it) conditions of exhibition surrounding the painting, one notes a further incriminating triangulation in the axis of spectation, strictly optical rather than pictorial—yet all the more psychological for this very reason, as well as rhetorical in its immediate fallout. In connection with the verbal orbit of this image, the second-person address precipitated in criticism by the canvas ("you behold a young girl")—though it shows up elsewhere in the description of Wiertz's paintings ("a grim Calabrian brigand, looking at you, and presenting his loaded carabine" [366])—is most emphatic in connection with "The Romance Reader" and two associated paintings (one of a man buried alive; one of an insane woman cooking her own murdered children). These are canvases that for years shared the same eccentric display, visible to the spectator only through "a little glazed round peep-hole" (366) in one of three white screens.[22] In both journal and catalogue account, therefore, the second person is the scopophiliac interloper snared by grammar because transfixed by private visual access. Standing before "The Romance Reader," you the hunched viewer, strenuously peering in upon the triangulated scene and scenario of displaced desire, would be made in every sense uncomfortably aware of the three-dimensional triangular funnel of your own scopic field—in other words the cone of vision itself—by which the tableau of debauch by proxy becomes available to you in turn under such conditions "as almost to appear a reality" (366). In your straining to see it as you once would have done through the peephole, as if through a chink in the young girl's own screened-off bedchamber, this effort of focus would itself only compound those ironies of spectation which may in part have moved even Wiertz's appreciative critic to note that, though the "idea desired to be expressed by this picture, is one of moral truth; the treatment, however, in itself is somewhat satanic" (366).

Appearing in the decade that saw the ultimate novelistic critique of romance reading and its erotic abasements in *Madame Bovary* (1857), Wiertz's 1853 scene of rank absorption and gothic (demonic) possession marks a revealing midpoint—and thematic watershed—for the chronology of this study. Its reflex of titillated attention falls somewhere roughly between Jane Austen's defense of any romance reading in moderation, even of the gothics, and a century's-end feel for the immoderation of all subjected textual encounter, undeterred nonetheless: that gothic of deputized and disembodied desire to which our intervening sequence of readings will now lead.

Part 2

IN THE EVENT OF A READING

Chapter Four

"Whomsoever It May Concern"
Austen's Open Letters to the Reader

Painting of the Romney school. *A Lady of the Eighteenth Century Reading* (n.d.). The Bettmann Archive

*O*ften enough in Austen the exact motives behind a character's satirized behavior "must be left to be guessed" (*Persuasion*, 14:143). In the monosyllabic and anapestic double stroke of that blithely awkward compound passive lie some of the poetry and much of the poetics of Austen's comic prose. The unsaid reciprocal agency of narrator and narratee—glimpsed in such phrasing as "must be left" (by the discourse) "to be guessed" (by you, the reader)—generates at the limits of omniscience the hermeneutic force field of the *lector absconditus*, presiding muse of postepic narrative. If Brontë's "Reader, I married him" encapsulates the transitive grammar of narrowly addressed storytelling, "must be left to be guessed" is its pertinent opposition in the earlier-nineteenth-century linguistics of narrativity. In the evolution of her seamless fictional form, Austen suppressed at least one debt to her own predecessors in the eighteenth-century novel by scuttling her epistolary drafts of *Pride and Prejudice* and *Sense and Sensibility*. We may begin by suspecting that the increasing rarity of reader salutation in her omniscient rhetoric testifies to the weight of that suppression.

The matter of this chapter is transitional. The matter with it, at first glance, may seem its reliance on negative evidence. My purpose is, first, to follow the transformation from the eighteenth-century to the nineteenth-century novel across the vanishing trace of reader apostrophe—not just its rapid disappearance but its *marked* exile—in the methodical "classicism" of Austen's comedy; and, second, to register the wake of that banished apostrophic habit (soon enough revived, if spottily, in later novelists) in those practices of manipulated and thematized reception which nevertheless keep continuity with previous fiction. The two purposes are scarcely at odds, since the continuity in question is mounted on the very exclusion of reader address. Many of the issues brought forward by the direct interpolation (placing) of a reader, that is, are now ruled on in Austen by a more diffused extrapolation (analogic displacement) of response, whereby whole novels, in their shaped emotional engagement, are opened to the reader as tacit addressee. This is why negative evidence regarding apostrophe need not come up empty handed.

What this chapter thus ultimately prepares for is an adjusted understanding of the resuscitation of address at certain diverse sites in Victorian fiction, popular and canonical alike. These loci of apostrophe and indirect reference will come to be understood not primarily as the return of the repressed, nor even (though in the best-sellers it is often little more) as rhetorical decor by way of anachronistic allusion. They answer a different structural need. Instead of the more regularly didactic apostrophes of the genre's formative stages, and after both the decline of direct address in the late eighteenth century and its further ironic isolation in Austen, the moment of invoked reading intrudes again into the Victorian novel as a more textually vexed function of prose fiction's never quite stabilized public relations. It is available as such for the further specification and questioning of intersubjectivity itself as a rhetorical operation. Even Victorian texts don't always come easily to their own reading.

In contrast to the locally implicated reader, linguistically manifested and site-specific, Wolfgang Iser's "implied reader" is to be recognized, in the transition between centuries, according to a more broadly epochal set of character traits. Without spelling out Austen's place in his sense of this evolution, nor paying any specific attention to direct address, Iser sees a more autonomous and wary reader of Victorian fiction emerging in rejection of the docile audience of the eighteenth century: a new reader more guarded than "guided,"[1] one who "had to discover the fact that society had imposed a part on him, the object being for him eventually to take up a critical attitude toward this imposition" (xiii). If one can accept in even a rough and provisional way that an eighteenth-century emphasis on "human nature" and the rules of "moral conduct" (xii) is transformed in the nineteenth to a stress on "subjectivity" (xiv), then the affective form of such literary subjectivity must be partly registered in the one-way interlocutory pressure of the vocative case. And if so, then such explicit invocation of reading may be accompanied in just this regard, and as structural complement, by its staged evocation: parable answering to apostrophe. Examined closely, however, these conjoint formal operations do not lend themselves so readily, or without internal complications, to that sweeping brand of periodization offered by Iser. This is what Austen, on the cusp between the two periods, serves to demonstrate whenever her work is noticed to offer not only a wry conspectus on human nature but a virtual *structuring* of subjectivity in the protocols of reading.

The speed and thoroughness with which Austen inherited, modulated, and ultimately threw over the tradition of vocative address is thus one clear measure of her shaping place in the nineteenth-century novel—even as subsequent Victorian practice was soon to lower once more the generic resistance to such intrusions. The more an audience is left alone by Austen's discourse, spared the prod of apostrophe, the more the reader's patient attention is conscripted by plot as the plot's own thematic premium: a capacious openness to unfolding event. It is by this route of affect that Austen enters the history of prose fiction at a moment primed for the transformation she works upon it. Her first completed novel, *Northanger Abbey* (1803; published 1818), pits the architecture of gothic plotting against the sentimental closure of the provincial romance, the influence of Ann Radcliffe against that of Maria Edgeworth, with all the rhetorical adjustments this requires. After examining the collaboration of minimal apostrophe and reflexive parable in *Northanger Abbey*, we will then be ready to recognize in a late masterpiece like *Persuasion* (1819) how the structural distribution, rather than mere tactical deployment, of readerly dynamics—precisely because not extruded as direct address—has become the very engineering of receptivity in the form of fiction.

What the gothics had already achieved by sidelining the Gentle Reader would serve Austen's very different realist purposes as well—and not only in *Northanger Abbey*. In the "Translator's Preface" to Horace Walpole's *The Castle of Otranto: A Gothic Story* (1765), for instance, we find a fictionalized prologue appended to the fiction of a found volume. This preface contains the novel's only mention of a reading audience. Specifically intended is the native "English reader," who is bound to be "pleased," the translator assures us, with the moral rigor and "rigid purity" that "exempt this work from the censure to which romances are but too liable" (5). Such is the unremitting virtue for which the coming narrative thrills are the unspoken reward. And in the grips of them, we want no reminder that we are actually—and merely—reading.[2] Immediacy is all. Narrative omniscience needs to be as cool and disinterested as possible to carry conviction, and departures from this norm in gothic fiction are few and readily noted.[3] Once participation has been corralled and milked dry, the gothics start down the slope of their denouement toward a moral achieved as a sanctifying afterthought. On the last page of *The Orphan of the Rhine* (1798), the harrowed principals are subordinated to an ethical principle, for they are said to have "presented, in the whole of their lives to the reflecting mind of the moralist, a striking instance of the imbecility of vice, and of the triumphant power of virtue" (360).[4] This is the brand of rote uplift which Austen is to satirize in *Northanger Abbey*, even as she relies on and subtly rewrites the kind of narrative trajectory to which it offers an arbitrary summation. In this way, she gradually reconceives the gothic's typical curve of plot—tension stretched to release, then tailing off into a brief reflective coda—as a function of the closural checks and balances of her own fictional aesthetic. Emptying the gothic of its narrative *material*, one might say, or translating it from the melodrama of villainy and peril to the psychodrama of social morality and domestic emotion, Jane Austen preserves its narrative *architectonics* for the new mode of domestic realism.

"The Bosom of My Readers": Austen's Singular Collective

By the third paragraph of *Northanger Abbey*, Catherine Morland had "read all such works as heroines must read to supply their memories with those quotations which are so serviceable and so soothing in the vicissitudes of their eventful lives" (1:39). The genial mockery is unmistakable, recruiting the reader's own intertextual savvy throughout this establishing segment. You need to know how novels usually go to get on with this one. When a new character comes on the scene: "It is expedient to give some description of Mrs. Allen, that the reader may be able to judge . . . how she will, probably, contribute to reduce poor Catherine to all the desperate wretchedness of which a last volume is capable" (2:42). This generically accustomed "reader," familiar with the conventions of novelistic outcome, is speedily eased into a position of direct address for the first (and all but the last) time in this novel. As the heroine and her new friend, Isabella, "shut themselves up to read novels together" (5:57), Austen launches one of her most famous digressions, an aside aimed at the reader by the indirection of a suppressed but understood vocative: "Yes, novels—for I will not adopt that ungenerous and impolitic custom so common with novel writers, of degrading by their contemptuous censure the very performances, to the number of which they are themselves adding" (5:57–58). The inferred grammar: "Yes, novel readers, novels." Or in other words: "Yes, reader, reading just like this." As the functional opposite of interjected negation (one of the ancillary markers of the "zero-degree narratee" in fiction, according to Gerald Prince), the muted apostrophe entailed by "yes" emerges into text as the dialogic trace of a tacit interlocution between author and reader.[5]

This modest frame-breaking device is a far cry both from the fabricated transparency of general gothic rhetoric and, at the opposite end of the spectrum, from the hortatory intensification of certain gothic infratexts: namely, the vocative rhetoric of the typical found manuscript, as parodied here in the voice of Catherine's suitor, Henry Tilney: "Oh! thou—whomsoever thou mayst be, into whose hands these memoires of the wretched Matilda may fall" (20:166). More is here than yet meets the eye, however. Despite the caricature of a gothic plot device, this overwrought wording will come to bear a telling resemblance, after all, to the closing sentence of Austen's novel. There, the gothic gesture is softened by that neutralized formula of address borrowed from the etiquette of the epistolary mode. With the hero and heroine overcoming the roadblocks to their marriage at last, their commitment all the stronger for it, Austen closes: "I leave it to be settled by *whomsoever it may concern*, whether the tendency of this work be altogether to recommend parental tyranny, or reward filial disobedience" (31:248; emphasis added). Despite the dismissive ironies in the course of plot, the rhetorical blatancies of the gothic seem still very much on the text's mind at this late point—and in more ways than one. For that last disclaimer parodically invokes the heavy-handed moralizing at the close not just of the gothics in general but of the very novel about which the heroine has earlier said, "I should like to spend my whole life in reading" (6:60). What Austen's last clause seems quite directly to lampoon, by alluding to while refusing to duplicate, is the penultimate paragraph of Ann Radcliffe's *The Mysteries of Udolpho* (1794). Radcliffe's rhetoric takes the reader as the unstated indirect object (as with Austen's "whomsoever it may concern") of narrative demonstrations now retroactively evaluated: "O! useful may it be to have shown . . . that innocence, though oppressed by injustice, shall, supported by patience, finally triumph over misfortune!" (577). Radcliffe then adds a telling specification of her ideal reader, for her novel will be judged a success only if it "beguiled the mourner of one hour of sorrow, or by its moral, taught him to sustain it" (577). Distraction and tutelage, *dulce et utile*: these are the twin benefits of a fictional genre assimilated momentarily to something like a generalized elegiac program, serving thereby the therapeutic function of working through the anxieties of mortality itself.

It is no little part of Austen's achievement, in her satiric distance from the gestures of narrative justification which encumber the didactic close of *Udolpho*, to have found in the very genre of the novel a more muted and encompassing model of human endurance in the face of death's closure: the lesson of duration itself, whose melancholies and reversals of fortune come bearing down on no stated and unambiguous "moral." This sense of the novel *read for life* (to adapt Catherine's exaggeration)—the novel as a paradigm for time and transformation itself—is first sketched out ironically in *Northanger Abbey* and then worked out with almost perverse assurance in *Persuasion*, where taking one's time is a prototype, indistinguishably, for right reading and for full living.

An additional knot in the intertextual logic of *Northanger Abbey* claims attention on our way—past the loaded close of that novel—to the metaplot of *Persuasion*. At the turning point of *Northanger Abbey*, Henry Tilney's attempted demystification of gothic skullduggery takes its bearings in a curious way from the literary system of which he is a part. As a prima facie defense against Catherine's suspicions about his father's treacheries, Henry offers the very fact of "literary intercourse" (24:199) in all its manifold array. Until this point, the "well-read Catherine" (23:186) is so exclusively versed in the gothics that the least hint of the father's previous history is translated at once into this macabre literary mode, so that (transforming the idiom "speaks volumes" into a less dead textual figure) rumors about him "conveyed pages of intelligence to Catherine" (23:189). Yet the world she imagines through her reading is a world that her very reading, together with the whole culture of mass literacy and textual dissemination, has long ago outmoded. This is Henry's point—and the deepest cultural irony of the novel's satire. Austen here reminds her own reader that the popularity of gothic fiction, as a phenomenon of public consumption, is enmeshed in a system of discursive and textual exchange—call it modern life—which renders anachronistic the medieval privacies and secretive machinations central to gothic plotting.

In this sense, Henry waxes sociological—even implicitly literary-historical—

in dismissing Catherine's fears of grotesque misdeeds: "Could they be perpetrated without being known, in a country like this, where social and literary intercourse is on such a footing: where every man is surrounded by a neighbourhood of voluntary spies, and where roads and newspapers lay everything open?" (24:199). That last is a term that will become, from *Sense and Sensibility* to *Persuasion*, a crucial Austenian touchstone. The adjective "open" takes part at this turn in a kind of sylleptic double sense in which the verb phrase "lay open" applies now to transit, now to disclosure and transmission, yet each as a function of the other in "social . . . intercourse." Further, Henry's mention of "literary" openness is not likely to refer in context primarily or exclusively to letter writing, for this sense of "literary" was obsolete by Austen's time.[6] Instead, what Henry means to evoke with "literary intercourse" may well be the lettered journalism of newspaper prose, the written correlative of gossip as "social" exchange. In any case, his phrasing cannot but reverberate also with the sense of humane or creative letters, thereby playing into that modern sense of "literature" just emerging in Austen's day (first *OED* citing, 1812). Even without this dawning acceptation of the term, the point holds: Gothic plotting cannot be actualized in the world in part because of how much the world knows about it from books, among other textual forms, currently in circulation. So begins the nineteenth-century fictional establishment. It ends—this study with it—in the massive aesthetic reversal whereby literature's "intercourse" with the subjected reader comes to seem a gothic phenomenon in its own right, piercing, hypnotic, entrapping, vampiric.

For now, Henry's debunking argument helps situate the novel that mounts it within the ascendancy of realism—and, in particular, within the rise of domestic comedy: generic antithesis of the gothic thriller. Yet once Catherine's suspicions of nefarious intrigue are replaced by anxieties every bit as real, by threats to amorous satisfaction every bit as lethal, the heroine's dilemma is referred away to our own generalized expectations as readers of fiction per se. This is a textual practice that comes to us mass-produced in printed form with the promise, after so and so many pages contracted for, of a certain kind of closural verisimilitude. Tutored by the build and payoff of gothic plotting, *Northanger Abbey* is not out to disappoint you in this regard. Nor is it about to let you take its pleasures without self-conscious recognition. Interpolation returns, in the form of reader reference rather than apostrophe, to point them up.

As you near the denouement of *Northanger Abbey*, yours is a stance toward narrative reception stipulated in one of the text's most densely self-referring asides: "The anxiety, which in this state of their attachment must be the portion of Henry and Catherine, and of all who loved either, as to its final event, can hardly extend, I fear, to the bosom of my readers, who will see in the tell-tale compression of the pages before them, that we are all hastening together to perfect felicity" (31:246). Idiom begins by anticipating the turn of fortune which the sentence as a whole works to postpone, since "the portion" of anxiety which currently falls to the lovers draws associatively upon the notion of a "marriage portion" or nuptial settlement. Next, you come upon that rare (for Austen) first-person "we" (the editorial plural) positioned to include a phrase whose constructed plurality is marked by the shift in number between noun and object of the preposition in the collective "bosom of my readers." Where Dickens will be found to evoke with some trepidation the singular plural of "the many-headed" (the multifarious) as a literate mob, Austen has mitigated the figure in advance—with the image of an audience whose hearts beat as one for resolution. This audience seeks, in other (loaded) words, the "perfect felicity" of fit closure—*per facere*: to see through, to complete—across the "pages" (metonymically, the story) hereby "compressed" (narratively condensed). In that very phrasing, however, lurks the textual as well as narrational evidence of pending closure, hinged around another twist of idiom. For the "compression" at issue is also, physically, the lessening number of pages pressed between the fingers of your right hand as the book nears completion. This is a diminishing thickness that becomes "tell-tale" in the slyly reversible sense of the tale left to tell. To summarize the effect of this prose density: Wordplay is always a playing upon the reader, so that, as we saw in the last chapter, the reflex of reading is never more layered than when it is flagged by the cognitive retardations of thickly self-referential discourse.

Opening toward Closure: Edgeworth, Fielding, Austen

One of the novels enlisted with high praise during the narrator's extended set piece in defense of novel-reading heroines in *Northanger Abbey*—namely, Maria Edgeworth's *Belinda* (third in a triad after Fanny Burney's *Cecilia* and *Camilla* [5:58])—is a narrative that closes even more self-consciously than Austen's, albeit not in the narrator's own voice.[7] In just this difference, and that of the reader's relation to it, resides Austen's innovation. In *Belinda* (1801), the salient self-referential exercises are delegated to a character of lightly cynical wit, Lady Delacour, who has pronounced early on that "nothing is more unlike a novel than real life."[8] Despite this, on the brink of resolution for the text's double marriage plot, she emerges as the impresario of disclosure as finality:

"'And now, good friends,' continued Lady Delacour"—as if offering herself, two pages from the novel's end, as vessel for Edgeworth's direct address to us— "'shall I finish the novel for you?'" (31:432). This striking version of metalepsis (in Gerard Genette's sense) transacts a shift in narrational stance which, in effect, suddenly incorporates you, the outer audience, within the scene.[9] Inside the plot of *Belinda*, there is general acquiescence among the assembled friends that Lady Delacour would sum up their desires in style, thus ably standing in for the providential narrator of popular fiction. It is, however, left to Belinda herself to speak in favor of that *duration*, crucial to Austen as well, which is the very stuff—and test—of any central character in a marriage plot. Belinda reminds Lady Delacour "that there is nothing in which novelists are so apt to err as in hurrying things toward the conclusion: in not allowing *time* enough for that change of feeling, which change of situation cannot instantly produce" (31:432; Belinda's own emphasis).

Austenian plotting is here anticipated and defended in advance, but with a signal difference. In *Northanger Abbey*, for instance, you are merely reading along, coasting toward closure, when the emotional turmoil that might beset you as participant in the imagined reality of events is overruled by your status as mere reader, with only so many "tell-tale" pages left. This is an important point for the history of the reading's reflex action. Whereas in *Belinda* characters become surrogate readers of their own destinies on the way to the consummation thereof, in Austen—and the tradition she advances—the analogic tables are turned. Rather than life suddenly getting refigured as a novel, novel reading builds to a climax as a distended and unidentified figure for life under the sign of a signifying duration: the perceptive taking of one's time on the way to "the end."

Before Maria Edgeworth, Henry Fielding offers an equally suggestive precedent for the interplay of narrative event and structural form in Austen's logic of plot: plot as a graduated disclosure for characters and readers alike. At about the midpoint of *Joseph Andrews*, leading up to a passionate reunion between Joseph and Fanny—and anticipating the final nuptial embrace that completes, with parodied readerly participation, the eroticized telos of the entire plot— you are elbowed by this apostrophe: "O reader! when this nightingale . . . saw his beloved Fanny in the situation we have described her, canst thou conceive the agitations of his mind?" (2,12:130). Invited to "behold" the couple, you are also assured that they embrace "without considering who were present" (2,12:130), yourself included. In all this titillation of the textual "point of view," allied as it is with the invocation of the reader as warrantee of emotional engagement, ground is being laid for the novel's discursive as well as narrative climax, where the trick of erotic disclosure—or better, the erotics of disclosure—is brought off one last and summarizing time.

On one recent account, the importance of this symptomatic climax as a precursor of the formal and ideological priorities of nineteenth-century fiction cannot be overemphasized. Michael McKeon's argument about the finale of *Joseph Andrews* has to do with the way social questions of worth are displaced entirely onto hermeneutic questions of birth, in particular birth under the sheerly epistemological conditions of uncovered genealogy.[10] What looks like a progressive antiaristocratic emphasis on the lowborn Fanny's fitness for the hero is deflected onto the sudden relief that she is not, as it has briefly seemed, his long-lost sister. The "truth" comes out only to foreclose the issue of class. Fielding's novel thus works to illustrate by recapitulating McKeon's sense of the genre's formative history in its play between value and evidence, ethics and epistemology.[11] But this development has a rhetorical, a figural, register that McKeon leaves unexplored. Taking Fielding's text up on its thematized epistemology—including the complicity of the addressed reader in the displacement of social by evidentiary issues, of value by revelation—helps trace by anticipation the meshing of plot momentum with ethical posture in the increasingly privatized value system of the realist aesthetic—and its conscripted reading—in Austen's work. To begin specifying in rhetorical terms the means by which the formal co-opts the moral in Fielding, with social mobility subordinated to the quest for origins within an avoided incest plot, is thus to note more closely the links between the delayed revelations within the narrative and the enunciative enterprise itself of withheld climax. With its various tactical maneuvers of postponed closure, such an economy of telling enlists, stalls, entices anew, derails, and then again retrieves and fulfills the reader's participatory activity.

Discourse in Fielding becomes, early on, an erotic choreography of expectation, an explicitly figured version of Barthes's narrative "striptease," as when Lady Booby's erotic perturbation over Joseph is called "a something she began to conceive, and which the next chapter will open a little further" (1,4:21).[12] Approaching a later crisis of erotic misrecognition, the discourse turns aside "to open to the reader the steps which led" to the confusion (1,12:69). What is subsequently to pervade Austen's novels as their unsaid modus operandi, the love affair with slow disclosure, is wrung by Fielding to a farcical voyeurism at the novel's amorous climax, when Joseph and Fanny are no longer kept from each other's arms by the fear of a sibling bond between them. Consummated at this point is the very eros of discovery for the characters themselves and, one last time, for the invoked reader as well: a carnal knowing. It is not simply a case of a social exigency (debates over personal worth and social mobility) passed off onto an epistemological—hence narratological—crux (who's who by birth). At a figurative level that complements McKeon's treatment, delayed resolution is itself devolved in the nuptial aftermath upon the dynamics of reception as spectation, with sexual unveiling imagined as revelation rather than divestiture: "Undressing to [Fanny] was properly discovering, not putting off, ornaments," taking "properly" now in the combined sense of "strictly speaking" as well as "with [marital] propriety." So it is that the tease of discursive retardation, often dovetailed en route with erotic deferral, finds relief in the (tastefully truncated) bed scene of achieved desire into which the reader is drawn by the last of the novel's privileged moments of vocative address: "How, reader, shall I give thee an adequate idea of this lovely creature!" (4,16:297). Efforts are quickly made, with the "idea" drifting over into a voyeuristic ideal: "[T]o comprehend her entirely, conceive youth, health, bloom, beauty, neatness, and innocence in her bridal bed . . . and you may place the charming Fanny's picture before your eyes"—even if her textual portrait only. The character in process has become the fixed image or "picture" of her own fulfillment. Such is the logic of closure, "properly . . . discovering" the achieved arc of desire (reader's as well as character's) in the moment of satiety.

I am reading this closing passage in terms deliberately crossed between Barthes's erotics and McKeon's dialectics to lay stress on exactly the seductions—or conscriptions—of the reading activity itself, variously addressed and configured, which get sidelined in McKeon's prevailing dichotomy of form versus content. I need, therefore, to tender a claim that this chapter can only be fully prepared for by the time it has worked through the figural network of deferred disclosure in *Persuasion*. The claim is this: In the commutation between plot and generic form, reading is a necessary *tertium quid*, ultimately the site of whatever dialectical synthesis a text seeks to stage for itself. *Joseph Andrews* is the last novel McKeon considers at length, and it leads him to his "Conclusion" about the rise of "the individual" and its impact on the history of the novel. "Hypostatized over against the individual, 'society' slowly separates from 'self' as 'history' does from 'literature,'" with the following result sketched out: "The autonomy of the self consists in its capacity to enter into largely negative relation with the society it vainly conceives itself to have created, to resist its encroachments and to be constructed by them." It is a point closely related to Iser's distinction (discussed in chapter 2) between the "reader" (rather than the "self") in the fiction of the two centuries: the docile social subject of the eighteenth turned to the warier hermeneutic agent of the nineteenth. To his own comments about the constitutive opposition between self and society in literary experience, McKeon adds: "The work of the novel after 1820 is increasingly to record this struggle" (419). Why 1820, and what happens on the immediate way there? Austen has, of course, no place in the coverage of his argument (from 1600 to 1740), but her novels of the self in society may be taken, in their formative and influential "realism," to facilitate a transition within that categorical instability of the novel which is McKeon's largest subject.

Clearly Austen's work would fall into that nineteenth-century tradition in which the previous dialectical reversals of romance idealism and naive empiricism, overturned but not resolved by extreme skepticism, are reversed again into the autonomous category of the "aesthetic," where questions of both truth and worth are together subsumed to those of *novelistic* value. This, at the generic level. At the textual level, another transition is at work upon the inherited material of the fictional tradition. This is a transition that thematizes the central logic of plot familiar from Fielding—namely, the reader-oriented escalation of disclosures—as what we might call in Austen an epistemological psychology of closed versus open characters in a world of "read" as much as lived encounter. In the process, the new aesthetic contract of fiction comes to depend on a no less endeared but a no longer so furiously adduced reader, one whose former epistemological anxieties about veracity and historicity, by now neither placated nor mocked, can be silently suspended in the delayed gratifications of sheer plot, even as these gratifications retain the eighteenth-century tendency to migrate between generic form and social content. To just such migration, and the reader's bordering place within it, this chapter must return in closing.

Reading per Suasion: Austen's "Book of Books"

To see *in action* the transvaluation of plot by the rhetoric of response, we turn from Fielding's discursive torque on the idea of slowly "opened" rather than delved character to those crisis points in Austen's social comedy when the veiled, the guarded, the withheld is thematically marked as an explicit betrayal of the social contract. The most damning, if understated, indictment of a character in *Persuasion* is in fact leveled in indirect discourse against the suavely villainous Mr. Elliot, who, long before his shady behavior has been made known, is diagnosed by the heroine as "rational, discreet, polished,—but he was not open" (17:173). This word has had a long career in Austen, since many of the major emotional turns in her first published novel, *Sense and Sensibility* (1811), can be taken to depend on more than half a dozen self-adjusting appearances of this term.[13] As such examples proliferate, it grows clear that what plot mandates in *Joseph Andrews* is in Austen the responsibility of character, the formal transformed to the psychological. By the time of *Persuasion*, only the briefest allusion to Mr. Elliot's personality as "not open" is enough, as we will see, to draw taut a similar, if merely implicit, network of associations. This network is the plot itself, which at the level of the domestic romance is structured to reveal the already recognized. This is the novel's aberration and its typifying genius. It follows from everything we saw worked out (while being worked out of the textual system) in the parodic excesses of *Northanger Abbey*. The "telltale" compression of pages—just so many for just so much artificial suspense—has been so thoroughly internalized as the psychodynamic of realist narrativity by the time of *Persuasion* that this last of Austen's novels—as a readily accepted rather than self-consciously signaled reading act—becomes a virtual generic parable.

Written last among her finished books and published posthumously, offering the capstone to Austen's formal experimentation in the marriage narrative, *Persuasion* boasts a plotter's plot, its symmetries and distensions quintessential to the work of the realist novel. Once madly in love with a sailor, the heroine was too readily convinced by her closest friend and surrogate mother, Lady Russell, that the match was imprudent. Transpiring long before the novel opens, this prehistory is all dispensed in retrospect. No sooner do we learn it than the hero returns as a wealthy sea captain, at which point the actual plot gets under way. Though the rejected lover's pride is still stung, his former love is gradually rekindled in the face of adversity, accident, looming complications, and numerous romantic blandishments on both sides. In the end, the past is recaptured, the future assured. Such a romance, by being both foreordained and at the same time narrowly rescued from accidental prevention, is merely the metaplot of all romance. Think of it this way. A couple is destined for union by all that precedes—all the planning that lies behind—the opening pages of a text. It is then the text's work to negotiate that union, to realize the prevenient scheme—and to do so in the form of a reunion, a return to originating intentionality, to a long-fallow and now realized desire. Love lost achieves recovery through rediscovery, as in Stanley Cavell's sense of "remarriage comedy."[14] The reader, in sum, knows for certain that the couple belongs together; reading is a way of getting them there. What is this, then, but the schematization of all romance plotting? What but an exposure of the works under cover of an ec-

centric detour? It is thus that the deviant plot of this one novel of foregone conclusions narrates the masterplot of the marriage novel itself, doing so in full
view of that readerly collusion that is necessary both to promote and to suspend momentum, to push toward the inevitable while sustaining the interest
of the undetermined. As Lady Russell says at one point, as if personifying the
very essence—and relaxed acceptance—of narrative development, "Time will
explain" (16:160). What I am at this point seeking to explain are the maneuvers,
now salient, now latent, by which the classic marriage novel, distilled here to
an incomparable assurance, is concerned to eventuate its own reading from
within a supposed internal unity. Though neither the thematic of reading nor
the codes of apostrophe are given prominence, still a formal homology is generated between the psychological regimen within the plot, namely patient duration, and the paced labor of its consumption. Extrapolation has become pervasive: the steadily reflexive reading act.

That *Persuasion* should involve not only an act of reading but the reenactment of reading's own values might seem too abstract a sense of things only
if we have forgotten the negative model set in place by the novel's first sentence. Brought forward there is an anatomy of the novel's claims on attention,
ironically reversed in the distorting mirror of a solipsist's self-preoccupation.
"Sir Walter Elliot, of Kellynch-hall, in Somersetshire," the novel opens; his consequence imparted by commas, emphatic, ponderous, he comes to us as from
the only prose that holds an interest for him, by taking an interest in him: the
honorific roll calls of the landed gentry. As soon as Austen's opening sentence
moves to the predication of this character—"was a man who, for his own
amusement, never took up any book but the Baronetage"—we realize that his
earlier denomination has the ring of just such who's-who prose, the cadences
of formulaic deference. The rest of the paragraph continues this inverted negative image of reading and its motives. Beyond "amusement," Sir Walter Elliot
also "found occupation for an idle hour, and consolation in a distressed one;
there his faculties were roused into admiration and respect" by the lineage of
peers and to "pity and contempt" as he considered the escalating number of
negligible claimants to nobility. In this litany of trivial response, what the reader
might well overlook is the way it offers a virtual compendium of the motives
for reading elsewhere and otherwise: amusement, occupation, consolation, in
other words distraction, engagement, solace; the lifting of spirit to the awe of
"admiration and respect" for heroic stature and, alternately, in an impulse here
debased, the "pity and fear"—withered for Sir Walter to "pity and contempt"—
of tragic catharsis. All the enticements of narrative are thus drafted in shadow

play, sketched in negation, except for the essence of Austen's chosen mode, entirely missing from Sir Walter's vision: the articulations of plot itself, of transformation over time.

The novel thus begins with a reduced—and reductive—model from which it must move, by moving on at all, to unleash itself. Sir Walter's *idée fixe* is fixity per se, the stasis and empty iteration of inherited rank, the list rather than the plot: more epitaphic than narrative. On "the page at which the favourite volume always opened," we find: "Walter Elliot, born March 1, 1760, married, July 15, 1784 . . ."—an inscription complete only at death. This patriarchal and aristocratic volume—not even a chronicle or story, merely the inert accumulation of defunct or functionless agencies subsumed to their baronial rubrics—is a more thoroughly calcified form of those historical writings that Anne, in the climactic chapter, refuses to accept in evidence of the feminine character: "Men have had every advantage of us in telling their own story . . . the pen has been in their hands" (23:237). In between the introduced baronetage on the opening page, that eviscerated, postbiblical "book of books" (1:38), and its unforeseen emendation twenty-four chapters later (when Sir Walter was at last "to prepare his pen . . . for the insertion of [Anne's] marriage in the volume of honour" [24:250]) is the expansive extent of the real story: as precisely a temporal extension, a duration, an endurance, a space in time leaving room, as the baronetage does not, for disequilibrium, digression, and expectancy, for the return of the past not replicated but transformed, for continuity not as frozen perpetuation but as forward momentum. In between, in a word, is plot.[15]

This is a plot whose shape as it emerges, whose central action, is to stave off the threat, not just of Anne and Wentworth never confessing their renewed affection, but of Anne succumbing in effect to her ideal place within the baronetage. The greatest threat to the daughter of Walter Elliot, at the level both of plot and of symbolic inference, is the interest Lady Russell has in her becoming the wife of her cousin and her father's namesake, William Walter Elliot, a lady of the Elliot line after all. This is a danger signaled by, as if always lying latent in, the ambiguous linguistic material of the heroine's own name. Establishing a subterranean linkage with the early relegation of Anne Elliot to her father's whims—"her word had no weight . . . she was only Anne," with its phonemic hint of phrasal truncation (Anne what? an appendage? an excrescence?)—is Mr. Elliot's later gingerly advance, a circumlocution that accidentally drives straight to the point: "'The name of Anne Elliot,' said he, 'has long had an interesting sound to me'" (20:197).[16] It is indeed the first name's monosyllable as "sound," its homophonic doubling for Christian name and indirect article, which is at issue. He continues: "and, if I dared, I would breathe my wishes that the name might never change." Looking to insinuate himself back into the favor of the titled gentry, and hence to perpetuate its genealogical stasis with his own ascension to it, this suitor could not but notice that *an Elliot* has just the right ring. And any such fantasy of changelessness is exactly the larger menace he represents.

Reading "An/ne Elliot" in the novelistic and ironized context of Austen's prose—reading it, that is, as a double-voiced register of structural short circuit in the marriage plot—is very different from reading it, disambiguated by mere listing, in the satirized "book of books." For the latter is that test of reception against the dead weight of which the novel has struggled to get going. Ultimately, as if to recompense our sensitized ear with what can only be called a benign, almost giddy pun, we come suddenly, three sentences from the end of the novel, upon the syntactically (and lexically) captured reciprocation of the lovers' achieved union. This culminating wordplay gains force by prying open a suggestion lurking in the hero's name from the beginning: "Anne was tenderness itself, and she had the full *worth* of it in Captain Wentworth's affection" (24:253; emphasis added). Fulfilling the psychic economies of desire, debt, and repayment in this novel, and compressed here within the separable etymologies of a name now "had" (along with its signified affection) by the heroine, the man that long ago got away—whose *worth went* irretrievably, it once would have seemed—is returned in the form, in the very terms, of reward.[17] Phrasal truncation, lexical homophony, syntactic doubleness: these disturbances measure at the microlevel the difference between the emotional deadlock of the potential match with Mr. Elliot and the recovered *meaning*, for Anne, of the departed Wentworth. It was a marriage with the former which would have fulfilled the daydreams of Anne's surrogate mother, Lady Russell: a domestic fantasy about how the title of the maternal parent should "be revived in the daughter"—who is in fact her "mother's self in countenance and disposition"—so she can take "the dear mother's place" in society (18:171–72). A matrilineage in name only (that is, by being still bound up with the patrilinear name), this detour around the deadlock of male succession does not really escape from the claustrophobic class-consciousness of inherited rank and its oppressive master narratives. And, of course, Lady Russell has been wrong before. Between the error that precedes plot and the one that would close it down prematurely, between Lady Russell's two gestures of persuasion, lies the heroine's story of self-determination.

Here Austen's debt to the plot mechanisms of the eighteenth-century novel runs deeper yet than the escalated revelations of comic pacing or the feverish

exigencies of the gothic. Austen is concerned with the very structuring of identity upon a grid of difference. The familial—and familiar—pattern that Anne
must avoid, if not the exact genetic content of the pattern, is the incest bind.[18]
Such a premature convergence of psychic energy is the perpetual enemy of
plot, at least plot as existential model: Miss Elliot marrying Mr. Elliot, patrilinear like unto like, the self stalled in a book of ingrown descent, a recurrence
that only another kind of return—the revival of fled love—could rectify. What
Fielding locates externally—symbolizes—as the figuration of psychic claus-
trophobia and blocked maturation in the specter of incest, Austen's characterization internalizes as an ominous failure of nerve. Such a supposedly sensible
alliance as Anne's with Mr. Elliot, rescuing the heroine from spinsterhood, is
avoided only—and here the imagery of narrowness and blockage is itself tacitly internalized and repaired—through intellectual disclosure and moral ventilation: through, in other words (Austen's meticulously chosen ones), the dead
metaphors of spatiality in the image of an *open* spirit.

Anne's complete antithesis is therefore the cloaked character who foils all
genuine emotional converse. This is, for her, fatal: "She prized the frank, the
open-hearted, the eager character beyond all others." Even Mr. Elliot's aversion to risk is phrased so as to be unflattering, for he is seen as "not at all open
to dangerous impressions" (21:203). Couched in the form of a laudatory double negation (not vulnerable to the unadvised), still the truth about Mr. Elliot—
that there is nothing coming in or out unguardedly—is hard to hide. Yet this is,
of course, just what makes him interesting, mysterious, what keeps you reading. More ominously than in *Sense and Sensibility*, the resistance to being "open"
which characterizes Mr. Elliot by temperament, and shrouds his past by design—this spur to plotted enigma and this deterrent to affection—is a symptom of scheming self-centeredness that might have duped a less perspicacious
heroine than Anne Elliot. It is her reward to be reunited, instead, with Wentworth, the man who returns into her life with an even more "glowing, manly,
open look" (7:86) than when she had driven him away.

But psychology and morality fall far short of exhausting the structural—
and ultimately cultural—implications for Austen's texts of narrative "unreserve."[19] My present interest in the recurrent word "open" and its variant forms—
for an author whose experiments in rendering the inner life through the extru-
sions of indirect discourse served to rewrite the history of realism in English
fiction—has primarily to do with the way the figure of "openness" straddles an
aesthetic and an ethical set of criteria. At the very foundations of prose fiction,
argues John Bender, socialization is a form of narrativization—and vice versa.
Indirect free style, so-called, where the inner reflections of a character are fully

assimilated to omniscient discourse, must pinion to liberate, invade the thought processes of human agents in order to "convert" them (in a double sense: sheer narrative transformation, Benthamite reformation of character) to fully legible subjects.[20] Mastered by "novelists from Jane Austen onward" (177), this intrusive ploy in the discursive arsenal of fiction is, for Bender, a form of mastery in the coercive sense as well. It is a gesture of control that emerges early in Austen, I would want to add, as the formal supplement of an ideology of innate or voluntary "openness." Following Bender's argument, one might further suggest that the ethical subscription to a stylistic device like *style indirect libre* is matched also, at the broader level of plotted temporality, by the valorized inscription of delay, retardation, and forestalled achievement as well as disclosure—in short by the formalizing of emotional tenacity and deferred gratification—as moral dimensions of the socialized self. It is thus, when form and value interpenetrate—when, in other words, social representation in fiction replays the modes of fictional mimesis itself—that the novel is installed as cultural institution.

Likewise, the thematic of openness in Austen, figuring an epistemological and hence discursive goal of narrative as well as a social good, may be offered as one touchstone of McKeon's argument when translated to the play between formal and thematic issues. What Austen's novels bring out is an ingrained generic reciprocation of consciousness and conscience, or in a word the coming to *know better*. This coincidence of realization and judgment occurs, of course, for the reader as well as the character—for the character as reader and the reader as ethical deliberator. It is at just this level that Austen's troping of openness as a textual as well as characterological function, especially in her last novel (and narratological summa), serves to place her fictional endeavor right where it belongs, on the threshold of the novel's second major (Victorian) phase. The transparency of character to discourse in fiction, as a symptom of the panoptic revamping of the social subject, finds its parallels in an epistemology inseparable from an ethics of the variously revealed and invisible inner life. The perspectives of both Bender and McKeon might thus be refocused in Austen around that act of scrupulous decipherment—called deliberative reading—which subserves and in its own way replays the gradual disclosure and temporal transformation of character.

The reader is thereby tacitly heroized through the demonstration of energies cognate with those harder won by the characters, the ability to stay with it, attend closely, adjust judgments, see them through—in short, to persevere without illusion, curious but not credulous, everywhere on alert. In *Persuasion* preeminently, as before it in *Northanger Abbey* parodically, your reading on, an expectancy checked by patience, becomes analogous to the characters' own readiness to unfurl in due time to each other. To describe this doubling over of form upon content in a way that I hope by now seems clear enough: the whole novel, in its gradualism of plot, is the parable from which you *extrapolate re-flexively* the very reading in which it coaches you in order to couch its own character psychology. By this means (to repeat) does reading in *Persuasion* become a figure for life: the reading you yourself do in its pages as well as the reading done within its plot by other subjects like you.

On the brink of the plot's final corrective disclosures, with Anne Elliot about to disabuse Lady Russell about the good intentions of Mr. Elliot, there is a thickened textual moment, compacted of dead metaphor and allusive simile, that sums up the relation of plot to the opening of character. Remembering her promise to spend the day with the Musgrove family, Anne must defer the moment of negative revelation: "Her faith was plighted, and Mr. Elliot's character, like the Sultaness Scheherazade's head, must live another day" (23:233). The fabled character who kept herself alive through the curiosity induced by her multiple storytelling becomes instead a figure for the postponement of an unmasking climax and the prolongation of a single plotline. Then, too, all this delay is structurally necessitated by the fact that Anne's "faith was plighted" in a different sense once before—and in effect still is. When all misapprehension is finally swept away and the couple can reunite at will, we are indeed told that "they returned again into the past" (23:243)—in both a mythical recuperation and a virtual elision of intervening plot.[21]

That the final revelation scene, of Wentworth's unchanged love for Anne, should arrive as a scene of reading—Anne devouring the letter of declaration he has just left her—helps to secure the bond between emotional maturation and reading insinuated on several different levels by the plot.[22] Anne reads her way to happiness as we have been reading on in her interest. Reading thus stands as a mode of desire—and, more, a mode of knowing—dependent on that "openness" that breeds affection. Nothing here is left to discursive chance. Dead metaphor has prepared and now detonates the point. Following her first meeting with Wentworth in the novel's unfolding plot, Anne's legibility to us through indirect discourse is sharply contrasted with her own frustrations as regards the intentions of her former betrothed: "Now, how were his sentiments to be read?" (7:85). As both logical and temporal adverb, "now" operates at once as the idiomatic marker for the onset of reasoned inference and as the gauge of an eight-year lapse in communicative facility between them. When, months later, Anne finally takes up the still warm seat from which the decisive note to her has been penned, "succeeding to the very spot where he had leaned and written" (23:240), she is able to *read him* in a way not previously anticipated: by a literal decipherment that is rounded back to figurality by his letter's own metaphor: "I had not waited even these ten days, could I have *read* your feelings as I think you have *penetrated* mine" (23:240; emphasis added). Only otherness is a two-dimensional *text*; self is an interiority and a *volume* permeable to insight. Yet in a novel, we read by penetrating each character in turn, right down to the final moment when their presumed third dimension, their depth, is again surrendered to the sheer confessed page of textual closure.

Yet even this Austen resists. Finally, that is, the novel's own reader, tacit addressee of the last chapter's opening interrogative—"Who can be in doubt of what followed?" (24:250)—becomes the manipulated narratee of its closing and elusive grammatical transformation: "She *gloried* in being a sailor's wife, but she *must pay* the tax of quick alarm for belonging to that profession which is, if possible, more distinguished in its domestic virtues than in its national importance" (24:253; emphasis added). The reunion scene of the canceled chapter had closed in metaphor with Anne having "to pay for the overplus of bliss by headache and fatigue" (264). This subjective economy is transformed in the last sentence of the published novel ("but she must pay the tax") to the status of a national levy. Even so, the phrasing is not what might have been predicted. Since Anne "gloried" in her connection to a public figure, she therefore "had to" pay the price: that would be the expected parallelism within the historical past tense of this narrative, with "pay the tax" following the "worth" of Wentworth as the culminating economic metaphor in the text.[23] Such a metaphor, in the past tense, would have carried the additional implication that, since this tax of anxiety is regularly collected, no actual tragic toll has ever (to the date of this writing) been exacted. Instead, the text's almost imperceptible but no less unsettling slide forward into the present tense ("must pay" rather than "had to pay")—for the insistence on a quickening uncertainty—brings the reader up short in a still nervously poised convergence of the time of story with the time of discourse.

Such a convergence enters upon the domain of reception in ways so suggestive that it will take a century of novel production to play them out. As the function of suspense common to both *Northanger Abbey* and *Persuasion* is exposed, overdrawn, and reinvested at a higher level, the earlier novel sketches forth an aesthetic of duration and disclosure that finds its culmination in what we might call the formalized tautology of desire in the plot of *Persuasion*: its falling-in-love-again pattern as a parable of generic expectation within a structure of withheld omniscience. So goes the Victorian realist novel in its turn, building on this high watermark of formalized content in Austen even as it returns to more complicated weaves of domestic with gothic melodramas. And so goes apostrophe, no longer an asset for some writers but rather a handicap, as Austen found, in the full play of the realist aesthetic. Only in the first-person "confessional" narratives of a novelist like Charlotte Brontë can reader apostrophe in any systematic way be counted on to advance—rather than digress, if not actually detract, from—the structuring of affect on which the novelistic aura depends.

I therefore find myself wanting to say that in the last closural sentence Austen lived to write, the nineteenth-century novel was placed on a new footing. Not just in its duration as a model for endurance, the Austenian novel has hereby devised for the reading act, by strictly technical means, a manner of leave-taking that leaves open. And it is no accident that the muted suspense of this closing sentence is prepared for by a particularly indicative trace of Austen's longstanding suppression of direct reader address. I refer again to the faint whiff of interlocution in the scarcely apostrophic third person of the pivotal rhetorical question "Who can be in doubt of what followed?" This is a far cry from the elaborate reading activity coagulated around the parallel moment of reader-anticipated "perfect felicity" at the close of *Northanger Abbey*. *Persuasion* removes its readers completely from the textual space of the very scenario whose affect it attempts to induce upon them. You are no longer in the text; it is in you. In this sense, with the subsequent grammar of the novel's last sentence, the ethic of openness as disclosure has been turned inside out to an aesthetic of minor indeterminacy within a formal logic of closure—a mode of paradoxical open-endedness.

The cornerstones of the novel in its formative era are thus transvalued into an interlocking set of epistemological and social terms upon which the Victorian novel will soon fasten. As captured in Austen's last sentence, the accepted unknowability of the future is heroized to a virtue when that future is seen contingent upon the sacrifices necessary to any attempted rapprochement between private desire and public role. Even the woman who does nothing but wait manages to partake of this conservative balance of self and society without which the realist novel could neither survive as plot structure nor imagine the stabilizing compromises that would in another sense survive the close of any one such plot. When Charlotte Brontë, speaking for and through her heroine at the close of *Villette*, refuses the domestic waiting game, she does a generic violence that only a complex invocation of the reader can begin to repair. When, by contrast, George Eliot's narrator in *Daniel Deronda* embraces future contingency—under the sign of historical destiny—as a triumph of moral expectancy, of virtue without assurance, that visionary text has brokered a new alliance between epistemology and social valuation.

These open-ended, reader-entangling closures—just for instance—are in some sense the indirect heirs of Austen's twofold revisionism. This is the generic corrective hinted by the parody of closural suspense in *Northanger Abbey*, as an epistemological joke based on the nature of printing itself (a "telltale" thickness of pages) and clinched by the subsequent displacement of that suspense in *Persuasion* out past the end of the text, furrowing the grammar of the last sentence in the process. Implicated readers in the decades to follow are located at those recurring pressure points where the epistemology of plot is subsumed to that broader knowingness of response, with its own ethics (now called aesthetics) computed in the bargain—in the textual economy, that is, of formalized content and thematized form. This is the interplay between conferred shape and its structured inferences. The reader alone marks, by knowing or not, the difference. The textualized reader, as we have noted before and have now seen by Austen's extended example, the subject reader textualized either by interpolation or by extrapolation, *makes* that difference.

Here again is where generic categories intersect with plot energies in ways that only the receptive audience, stationed between the intertextual field and the individual narrative, can fully register. Confronting again the historical moment of Austen's verisimilitude, emergent from an eighteenth-century dialectics of verity and value, we return to that shifting scale of affect that marks the interchange of form, its content, and its modes of responsive contentment. As concerns the specific plot resolution of *Persuasion*, a decidedly nineteenth-century categorical conflation finds ethics laying claim to epistemology as its favored instrument. With the hierarchies of rank no longer in question, as they were, for instance, in *Joseph Andrews*, but merely the ethics of overvaluing them, questions of worth now crowd out questions of birth even in the postponed decidability of the former. Under the sign of openness, epistemology *becomes* ethics. To be sure, the persistence of Wentworth's affection (his continued openness to romantic possibility) needs discovering as much as does the villainy of Elliot; in the moment of such disclosure, however, revelation melds with valuation—even at the metatextual level—rather than (as in *Joseph Andrews*) dissolving it. For what is thereby found out is the active presence (or absence) of a sensibility that approximates to an internal equivalent of the aesthetic pleasure solicited by the text itself as formal construct. It comes down to—or up to the generic level of—this: Mr. William Walter Elliot, Esq., in the thick of his tight-lipped scheming, would have little time for the subtle pleasures of a novel like the one in which he features; Captain Frederick Wentworth would. The hero thus stands in the line of reader identification both as narrative agent and as aesthetic sensibility. And the axis is rotational: As novelistic content comes up to your expectations as reader, you find yourself the persuaded and conscribed protagonist of the new form. But at the cost, you might ask, however persuasively levied, of what psychic outlay? How vulnerable is open? How suspect its receptivities? Such questions do not go unexamined in the rest of the century's fictional production.

To stand back sufficiently at this point is, therefore, to glance forward as well as behind in the progress of the novel. It is also to note how readily titles, strung together across a genre, may tell a tale broader than their own stories. By way of epistemological parody, as well as by a sweeping conversion of epistolary formats, we enter the nineteenth-century novel through the antechamber of *Northanger Abbey*, not only the namesake of a space extensively renovated but itself a corrective design, its plan a restructuring of gothic affect as well as a partly gothic structure in its own right. A site at once of abiding forms and their transformation, the *Abbey* is a space tenanted, and not altogether unmysteriously, by reading. But this is only the beginning. The rapidly sophisticated architectonic structure of Austen's new fictional form, solidified in the emerging edifice of classic realism, seems built up to obscure its underlying gothic foundations. Only in this way can a given novel aspire to anything like the new generic authority of a fully aesthetic *Persuasion*, where a fusion of truth and worth is achieved at the formal level through the reified aesthetic value of the true-to-life. When that reification comes forward as undisguised commodification, the antique *Abbey* has gone overtly commercial in the representative Victorian form of an *Old Curiosity Shop*: a licensed establishment—coextensive with its heroine's private residence—for none other than the serial vending of fiction. The Victorian publishing industry has hereby found its prototypical home. At the other end of the realist hegemony from Austen's novels, as nineteenth-century fiction edges toward the modernist impenetrability of the *Heart of Darkness*, the generic tables will have been so turned that a negative epistemology, an occlusion of ready truth, is now subsumed to aesthetic worth through the self-staged histrionics of identificatory relays among characters, narrators, and the dramatized zone of uncertain reception. By Conrad's point in the history of prose fiction, the genre's realist superstructure will not only have acknowledged but in many a late-century neogothic plot sought figuratively to *realize* the quasi-gothic materializations rather than plot materials by which it has all along engineered its effects. It will have done so, probing to the very bedrock of the novel's phenomenology, through the psychodynamic of fiction's own formal demands on reading.[24] As we move forward now from Austen, it will therefore grow ever more apparent how Catherine Morland, wishing to "spend [her] whole life" in the emotional expenditures of reading, remains a definitive patron saint of nineteenth-century fiction in the steady refurbishment of its continually remodeled premises.

Chapter Five

In the Absence of Audience
Of Reading and Dread in
Mary Shelley

Young Woman Reading Byron, the Forbidden (1869).
The Bettmann Archive

*W*hat do the least gothic novel ever written, *Persuasion*, and the most famous gothic novel ever written, *Frankenstein*, have in common? If nothing of substance, then the question turns us to form. Yet since there is no obvious structural resemblance, either, between Austen's omniscience and Shelley's dramatized frame tale, the question pays off only if it gets us to some deeper notion of narrative formation—or, more particularly, to the structure of reading fashioned by such formal determinants.

Well before the transitional pre-Victorian figure of Mary Shelley, with her wholehearted renewal of gothic materials, what Austen's comic realism has already managed to do is to draw off from the gothics flourishing in her day a formula that subtends their narrative peculiarities: a psychodynamic of novelistic reading per se which the lurid excess of the gothics was bound to maximize. Intensified in that melodramatic mode is the rhythm of contemplative (often moralizing) calm after narrative storm. In this way late-eighteenth-century gothic plotting tends to rehearse on its way toward closure the evolutionary outmoding of its very genre: the metamorphosis from sensation to sensibility. This takes place even as the latter mode retains—in Austen, for instance, and in *Persuasion* as much as in *Northanger Abbey*—something of the same pronounced emotional curvative which, though perfected in the gothics, came to seem inherent in the very temporality of narrative fiction.

Mary Shelley, of course, taps the gothic conventions in a more direct manner, while at the same time returning to the epistolary roots of Austenian realism for a full-blown but still curiously disembodied version of that "whomsoever it may concern" structure manifested by the respectively psychological and apocalyptic ironies of framing in *Frankenstein* and *The Last Man*. In the process, Shelley's stress is laid on credibility and dissemination as much as on rhetorical heightening and the necessities of resolution. The gothic atmospheres and mechanisms of the literary vernacular emerge *within* the plot of *Frankenstein*, for instance, as they have come to it: mediated and transmitted many times over, processed and dispensed, in a word *received*. Where Austen inherits and reworks the narrativity of late-eighteenth-century gothic plotting, its arcs of suspense, tribulation, subsidence, and evaluative retrospect, Shelley's revisionary emphasis falls more on its discourse in circulation: its overwrought paths of access between narrators and narratees. In Shelley as much as in Austen, therefore, you are not just implicated but schooled as coparticipant in that work of plotting which takes its bearings from the present modulation, rather than the mere promise, of response.

To linger even momentarily over the structural contrast between these two early nineteenth-century writers is to grasp in short order the breadth of effect opened up within the force field of conscription between, at one pole, the work of submerged interpolation in Austen (the marginalized "dear reader") and, at the other, the frame-ups of extrapolation in Shelley (the circumferential zones of reception). If Austen's gothic flirtations in *Northanger Abbey* enlist a melodramatic format which, in loose alliance with the shape of provincial romance, helped further codify for the history of fiction the reciprocal demands of anticipation and closure, Shelley's unabashed gothic plotting is a transgressive or deviant storytelling that pitches to crisis the narrative contract itself, psychologizing (under far more extreme narrative circumstances than in Austen) the very motives for the dispensing and receiving of stories. Furthermore, where Austen in *Northanger Abbey* checks the excesses of the gothic within the sphere of its acknowledged and harmless appeal, Shelley in *Frankenstein* chronicles the aftermath of the gothic's more dangerous exile from the mind's regimen. She does so through the withholding of supernatural narrative affect altogether from her hero, thereby constructing a mentality doomed by its very difference from the reader's own. As much as Austen's texts, therefore, Shelley's too are embroiled in the psychosocial protocols of literary acculturation. So that, once again, the analysis of narrative structures confronts most directly the workings of culture, and fiction's place in it, by staying alert to the structuration of the reading agency not only laid out by story but replayed by reading.

Yet such an agency, I stress again, is by no means the solid bourgeois citizen, the stabilized monolithic presence, of recent reductive accounts—but instead the very absenting of subjectivity both demanded and dramatized by the fictional text. Dependent as it is on your surrender to the deputized agents of narrative identification, textual transmission must evacuate consciousness before invading (and replacing) it. In this sense, Shelley's two major frame tales, *Frankenstein* (1818) and *The Last Man* (1826), undergo their own textuality, enact their own becoming-text, by invoking an attention whose personification they finally obliterate. They thereby subsume the scenario of reception under that aspect of reading which they can conscript but, beyond a certain point, never hope to specify. Everything about storytelling and transcription in them, everything about textual processing, everything about the transmissive function of language, everything, in short, about their own narrative impulse and textual premise comes forward toward that moment they attempt to circumscribe while leaving blank: the moment, plausible in one, impossible in the other, of their own reading. For one is a gothic thriller whose feverish stenographer lives on, and as if only, to tell of what he has heard and seen; the other a tour de force of dystopian futurism whose last author, sole survivor of a universal plague, has no conceivable readers left.

Mary Shelley's two most interesting novels serve therefore, in a revealing symmetry, to test the phenomenological bounds of fictional address as a function not only of textual circulation but of linguistic and cultural, even racial, continuance. What the nineteenth-century fiction industry takes for granted—namely, the normal routes of reception—Shelley instead takes to a denaturalizing limit. The very transmission of human consciousness in language is at stake in the rhetoric of her narratives. She wrote two novels, that is, in which the situation of the reader, even though in different ways emptied out of the text, is necessary to complete the thematic of storytelling within that text: a reader whose attention alone fulfills the communicative and confessional impulses of the characters themselves. Equally in *Frankenstein* and *The Last Man*, the story will out only if the reader's enacted absence is overridden—or underwritten—by textual activation, in short by reading.

In *Frankenstein*, the fated Creature, denied progeny, is able to leave behind no more than a story, which he tells to and through Victor Frankenstein, also the dying last of his family line, who in turn unfolds his version of the story to a ship's captain named Walton, who then transcribes it in a journal appended to letters that are, though read (at least by us), never definitively received by the sister back in England to whom they are addressed. Where narrative thus operates in *Frankenstein*, for Victor and his Creature alike, as an ultimately posthumous transmission to an always deferred present from a fatal past, operates in other words as a surrogate posterity, in *The Last Man* there is no one left alive to inherit the story of worldwide annihilation. It is a story that comes to us not by way of mystical vision but by way of a telepathically transcribed document from the future discovered by the Shelleys in the cave of the Cumaean Sybil. Narrative becomes the sole relic of the human race: an epic in the wake of culture itself. It is not read posthumously by those who outlive its events, for their number is none, but read proleptically by those (any of us) whom its very writing will (already) have outlasted. In *Frankenstein*, then, the reader receives the narrative of deviant creation as the event's only legacy. In *The Last Man*, the reader receives the text of racial extirpation as that eventuality's only solace, before rather than after the fact. In neither case, however, is the reader actually there to do so. Taken together as experiments in reading, these two texts jointly explore—by exaggerating from opposite directions—a phenomenological intuition one might phrase as follows: a sense that your most engaged reading takes place in your own absence, or in other words takes your place.

"With What Interest and Sympathy I Shall Read!"

No reader can miss the fact that Mary Shelley's *Frankenstein* is a novel preoccupied with storytelling and transcription, shaping itself by subsidiary narratives of all sorts—journals and confessional accounts framed and redoubled by the narrative event of epistolary broadcast. That the novel, in structure even more than in episode, is as much about reading as about writing, about narrative consumption as about narrative production, is perhaps less obvious. And this is because reading is most pointedly thematized by what we might call its encompassing absence. The issue only grows clear by the end. Even with Victor's entire narrative retold, and the Creature's within it, by Walton to his sister, the completed story never arrives at a *narrated* destination. Its frame functions, instead, more as an open bracket. Certainly you don't "see" the posted documents being read. There is no presentation of them by the butler, no parlor of breathless perusal, in short no *mise en scène* of receipt. All you can be sure of is that the letters, enclosing Walton's journal of Victor's story, have somehow made it your way.

But they do so—as at one level who could doubt?—only as they fade from documentary to fictional status: the first letter realistically placed and dated, except for the "editorial" avoidance of the year ("St. Petersburg, Dec. 11th, 17——), and then formally signed ("Your affectionate brother, R. Walton"); the second shifted toward the quasi-mystical ("Archangel"); the third merely dated, without site of origin, and mechanically initialed ("R.W."); the fourth, again without salutation or place of origin, dated in three stages (as if now by pure narrative chronology) and then yielding place to no closing signature. All that follows, twenty-four chapters later, is the eventual subsumption of epistolary narrator to novelistic character within the omniscient stage direction "Walton, in continuation." With more typographical cueing than in Austen, literary history is again telescoped by the local evocation of generic precursors. Like the Creature made rather than born, demonically cobbled together, the novelistic mode is pieced out before our eyes, born of epistolary directness, midwifed by a framing structure that remains vectored beyond plot's own closure. Walton disappears "in continuation," never to return in proper (or signatory) persona, but only to have his transcriptive role absorbed by the reading audience's own reactions. And just as there is no one there to sign off on the story, so there is no one seen to sign *for it*, as it were, in receipt. Mrs. Saville is nowhere to be found except in the address of the discourse, playing mere narratee in contrast to your role as reader. You therefore intercept the letters (the transcript of Frankenstein's extended monologue enclosed with the last of them) in her place, in place of the civilized reader "tutored and refined by books and retirement from the world" (letter 4:27).

Moreover, the chain of reception, and hence the psychology of reading, does not stop there. It doubles back on itself when even the scribe of Frankenstein's story wants part of the action at the receiving end: "This manuscript will doubtless afford you the greatest pleasure," Walton writes to his sister, "but to me, who know him [Victor] and hear it from his own lips—with what interest and sympathy shall I read it in some future day!" (4:29). In an ethos of internalized narrative energy, vicariousness goes deep.[1] As we began to see with Austen, reading becomes not just an extension of but a model for human experience, which Shelley's text seems to recognize as *vicarious at its source*. From the ranks of fictional characters, all of whom are narrated, emerge certain characters who not only live their lives so that they may become narratable, or in the absence of such life stories seek out the narratives of others to fill the void, but who await final engagement and understanding through the rerun of all such experience *as read*. With Dickens and the Brontës and Eliot still waiting in the wings of nineteenth-century narrative, here already is the emergent valence of the novel as Victorian cultural establishment. When, in the reading of *Frankenstein*, fiction structures desire in the form of its secondary processing *as story*, narrative has overstepped the bounds of art or commodity to become a prosthesis of social subjecthood.

Even to suspect as much is to question the newer methodological terrains of literary study, including the contested grounds of the proper disciplinary object itself: text versus context, as if the two were not structurally contiguous. Now is therefore a timely moment in these pages to italicize one corrective emphasis of this chapter—and of those to come. I want to insist that what a narrative artifact, as rhetorical construct, takes from the discourses of its culture—let us say in Shelley's case, for starters, the science-versus-poetry debate, evolutionary anxiety, gynophobia, class tensions, a dubious stance toward the romantic sublime, and so forth—is only half the picture, and very little of the story, if it is not correlated with what the narrative sends back into cultural circulation through the very form of its own discourse. This is to say that the critical reading of literature, precisely as an act of historical recovery, deserves the name only if it keeps its eye on rhetorical interplay as well as mimetic subtext, on fiction's "interface" with its reading subjects as well as on its image of their (other) social (because discursive) imbrications.

Reading, Revival, Reanimation

Read as literary construct, then, *Frankenstein* conflates two traditions of the British novel as Shelley has inherited them. First, it borrows those evidentiary mechanisms of the eighteenth-century text that were often attached as prefatory editorial footwork to prose fictions. Second, this device is crossbred in Shelley's novel with the epistolary mode of writing-to-the-moment. In this way the "editor," taking on the role of empassioned "correspondent," melds the corroborative with the affective dimension of textual force. The romantic transformation to which Shelley's inherited materials is submitted, however, results at the structural level from the arrest of the epistolary circuit, on the one hand, and, on the other, from the avoidance of its more overtly rhetorical derivative in the "dear reader" formula. Straddling these models, the vocative phrase "My dear Sister" (letter 3:21) appears in only one letter—as if serving a strictly rhetorical rather than epistolary function.

As such, this residuum of address is only part of a broad rhetorical campaign whereby the extrapolative force of the novel, the managed output of its fictional effect, is programmed in part through the novel's literary-historical input, as detailed in a variety of prefatory allusions having to do with the general literary topography of the period as well as with certain specific source texts. Anticipating how the "sentiments" of the novel may "affect the reader" (xiv), the preface assures the audience that the story is bent on "avoiding the enervating effects of the novels of the present day" (xiv). It cannot be missed that the binary opposition thus insinuated offers as the relevant counter to such fiction the surcharged and energizing novel, a text revived and reviving—the novel, in a word, *reanimated*. A fable emerges. Despite the moralizing condemnation of Victor's overambitious trespass upon forbidden ground, he seeks what Shelley achieves: the vivification of an inert form. And like Shelley, no matter how violent his deviant inventiveness, he can promise in the end, as he does to Walton, an "apt moral" (letter 4:28) in reward. The deliberate links throughout the text between Victor's laboratory exertions and the labor of fictional invention on Shelley's part serve to confirm this. They offer, by their supposed candor about the creative process, a check on the disingenuousness of this forcefully cautionary, because scarcely enervating, tale. For it is a tale about the allowable limits of what one is tempted to call regenerative pastiche, the very process that brought it about in the first place.

For all its avowed solicitude concerning the reader, though, there is no structural room in *Frankenstein* for the direct solicitation of the audience. One notes, by contrast, Mary Shelley's later short story, "Transformations" (1830), a supernatural narrative of doubling and physical malformation, pride and psychic transgression, very much in the mold of the 1818 novel. Without the distancing of the novel's frame, however, disallowing as it does all direct authorial address, the second paragraph of Shelley's story stalls upon its own reasons for being: "Why tell a tale of impious tempting of Providence, and soul-subduing humiliation? Why, answer me, ye who are wise in the secrets of human nature!"[2] Such an apostrophe, in the traditional combination of imperative and vocative, is the sort of interpolation ruled out by the dramaturgy (without commentary) of narration in *Frankenstein*. Instead, Shelley works a wholesale extrapolation of response displaced from the absent Mrs. Saville upon that individual reader who must proceed under the aegis of an *intended* but not necessarily achieved attention.

And the fable continues—as the story of a formative reading that blurs borders between plot and its preconditions in imaginative vulnerability. Just as textual reception awaits the narrative at or beyond its outer edge, so too, deep within the plot's chronological prehistory, can the will to reading be traced all the way back to the constitutive inclinations of narrative's desiring agents. "My education was neglected, yet I was passionately fond of reading." Thus Walton writes in the autobiographical mode (letter 1:16), yet giving anticipatory voice to the Creature's story as well. Eavesdropping later at the de Lacey cottage, the Creature will be initiated first into language, then into its cultural productions (Goethe, Plutarch, Milton), by his listening in on a quintessential family scene of hearthside reading aloud. In a more radical way than that in which the phrase is ordinarily taken, the Creature is *humanized by reading.* Yet this reading is placed in ironic juxtaposition to that undertaken by both his creators, Victor as well as Shelley. Victor's case is perhaps the clearest, by being the most extreme and complete. Whereas Mary Shelley, Walton, and the Creature each narrate as they have been programmed to do by their reading, indeed narrate an experience that would never have emerged in the same way but for their reading, it is Victor, spurred to creation by what he has (and hasn't) read, who is the only character to take charge explicitly of his own narration in an editorial role, as we are about to see, helping to guide its desired reading. In this, as in many other ways, he is of course very close to Mary Shelley as author and editor of her own published manuscript. The fecund monstrosities of her tale come to seem as terrible to her, so she would pretend, as Victor's brainchild does to him, a "hideous progeny" (xii) like his "hideous narration" (23:188) later.

Such a figurative crossing between discourse and story, between textual and anatomical invention, is subsequently reversed when metaphors of verbal creativity are incorporated into the language of transgressive creation—rather than narrative itself figured as monstrosity. Not only does Victor accuse himself (by the phrasal doubling of hendiadys) of being the "miserable origin and author" (10:96) of the Creature, but he refuses to make the same mistake twice, to "compose a female" (18:143), as if it were to be an act, again, of authorship rather than laboratory magic. This link between black magic and aesthetic conjuration is further tightened by the manner in which the compositional will to invention and the labors of the laboratory are conflated in Victor's own mind near the end of his story to Walton. "Frankenstein discovered that I made notes concerning his history; he asked to see them and then himself corrected and augmented them in many places" (24:199), his editorial rigor devoted "principally" to the task of "giving the life and spirit to the conversations he held with his enemy" (24:199). Not content to have breathed life into a pastiche, a random assemblage, of body parts, Victor now tries to animate the prose that records it. His will to power persists, that is, across two levels of "compositional" energy. Finally, too, the language of aberration and deformity surfaces in his description of this editorial purpose: "'Since you have preserved my narration,' said he, 'I would not that a mutilated one should go down to posterity'" (24:199)—that "posterity" by which the created and printed text alone, not its homologous Creature, is bid to replicate itself. Narrative mutilation, biological malformation—these are the paired defaults of "authorship" in Shelley's novel, from a negotiation between which all audience response must be processed.

Thus is confirmed a running parallel between the genesis plot and the story of its own literary generation. Just as Victor sutures together the Creature, so does Shelley, assembling her creation *Frankenstein*, also assemble the man for whom it is named: a composite, as he is, of two figures from the German ghost stories that Shelley read aloud with Percy Shelley, Byron, and Polidori.[3] Along with the effects of conversation about Erasmus Darwin and his reputed experiments in spontaneous animation (x), these stories coalesce in Shelley's unconscious, invade her dreams, and spawn the script of unholy creation that becomes, upon waking, her tale. Out of discrepant body parts, a humanoid shape; out of discrepant pieces, a newly articulated narrative, a narrative galvanized by the spark of creative inspiration: such is the offspring of writer and hero alike. Moreover, Shelley's dream (from the preface) of an artificial man, an artifice of life, stands to the novel as a whole—embryonically—as do Frankenstein's feverish conceptions to the confessional tale he ends up having to tell, reread, edit, and revitalize.

In this way the prefatory explanations of what James would call the "germ" of the text relate indirectly to the most deeply receded text-within-the-text of the story proper, a microcosm of its own gestation. This analogue of conception embedded in the resulting narrative is inscribed—under proscription—in the form of Victor's journal, containing his notes for the assembly and animation of the Creature. As the ur-text within this nest of tales, transcripts, and transmissions—a text stolen by the Creature shortly after the inception of his consciousness (15:124), never quoted from, and never seen again—it is the origin under erasure of all that follows. Providing for the Creature a primal reading lesson, the unfolded mystery of his origination, for us it is instead the un-readable journal within that read journal-like transcription that constitutes the largest part of the novel: the story of a constructed Creature within that creative construction—here, explicitly, a dreamlike dictation from the unconscious—which is fiction itself.

To pursue the comparison between Walton's journal and Victor's, tunneling back together, as they do, toward the mysterious inception of the story in Shelley's own reading, is to confirm the literary-historical overtones of her "progeny" trope. For the process of its gestation plays out in advance the nature of its fictionalized plot: the *making up*, in two senses, of a new hybrid form. I have suggested that at some level the reading that brings the Creature to compelled and compelling voice, the reading aloud at the de Lacey cottage, is what "humanizes" him. So, too, with the reading by Mary Shelley that went into his imaginative composition. Reframed thrice over by the novel's layered textual dissemination, the Creature erupts as a perversely fashioned organic entity in every sense *brought alive by reading*: Shelley's, Victor's, the cottagers', the Creature's own, Walton's, Mrs. Saville's prospectively, and finally, in the moment of extrapolation from all of them, your own.

"To Encounter Your Unbelief"

Everything points toward this emphasis on the nerved and sinewy grip of textual fascination upon an audience, including a sequence of derailed private narratives near the end of the novel that follow out—without being able to follow through on—Victor's final attempts, before he meets Walton, to confess in narrative form the mayhem he has indirectly perpetrated. His first effort seems designed to return his guilt over beastly creation to its progenitorial source, but his father "changed the subject of our conversation" (22:177). Next, as if to substitute for sexual initiation, he has assured Elizabeth that she will hear a tale of terrible explanation on her wedding morn (22:183). What is promised is the almost black-comic equivalent of a nineteenth-century male's coming clean about his unchaste past. Yet Elizabeth does not live long enough to hear what she might well suppose to be a sexual secret—meeting instead the Creature in the flesh. Where the urge to create was a sublimation of desire that deferred marriage in the first place, now the urge to "compose" the story in retrospect is all that is left of the maker's libido. To give yourself over in turn, as reader, to this central narrative logic with your own desire for the rest of the tale is thus to wed yourself to a fraught textual eros.

Once Elizabeth's murder has forestalled disclosure, Victor proceeds instead to give a "deposition" (23:189) to the local magistrate: a receiving agent stationed to externalize the self-policing that confession entails. And you don't hear a word of Victor's disclosure to this unnamed civil servant. You don't hear it because you know it full well. It is precisely, and in detail, the novelized story up to this point, all the events of plot without the extended discourse by which you have been led to interpret them. This circumscribed absence of an already familiar story, this ellipsis of recapitulation, is thus a hole in the narrative filled up, *pars pro toto*, by the narrative as a whole: another, more encompassing version (like the account of monstrous conception in Victor's unread journal) of a *mise en abyme* under erasure.

At first "incredulous," the magistrate is soon "attentive and interested" (23:189). At some points he would "shudder with horror; at others a lively surprise, unmingled with disbelief" characterizes his reactions. Just before the close of the novel, this figure of attention offers a retroactive sketch of your own reading, in all its Coleridgean "suspension of disbelief," as well as of the transferential investments that flow from that reading without passing over into credence. The hair-raising details of Victor's "deposition" are cordoned off from the magistrate's official role. To the surprise and frustration of Victor, a surprise—as we will see—bred of his own deprivations in the realm of fantasy, nothing he has said seems *actionable*. He calls for the "seizure and punishment" (23:190) of his monstrous creation, but his auditor has emerged from the story as merely, in effect, his reader, not his confessor, let alone his disciplinary agent. "He had heard my story with that half kind of belief that is given to a tale of spirits and supernatural events; but when he was called upon to act officially in consequence, the whole tide of his incredulity returned" (23:190). It is clear now that the magistrate did not "credit my narrative"—except, of course, as just that: a riveting narrative. Asked to go further into credulity, he "reverted to my tale as the effects of delirium" (23:190).

In its elided replay of the plot to this stage, this mere "tale" also sends us back to one of the novel's founding dramatic ironies. For it shows Victor punished in his failed confession to the magistrate by the very response on the latter's part—gothic fascination—whose possibility for Victor himself was abrogated in childhood, thus leading to his transgression and its narrative in the first place. Following on from (in order of disclosure across frame and tale) the interdict of Walton's father against his son's activating his book-fed fantasies of a seafaring life, and in turn Alphonse Frankenstein's contemptuous forbidding of Victor's reading in medieval science, there is the subsequent revelation of a textual proscription (or at least neutralization) earlier yet in the disentangled chronology of the plot. By way of explanation for his lack of squeamishness in rooting about among corpses in the graveyard, Victor recalls precisely what set him apart in childhood from the chain—that putatively humanizing nexus—of narrative reception passing now from the Creature through Victor to Walton and on to you. Or not so precisely, since the admission seems dragged out of a language that has no ready words for it. "In my education my father had taken the greatest precautions that my mind should be impressed with no supernatural horrors" (4:50). In what sense not "impressed"? Inured or altogether protected? Did the excitation of fantasy get tamed by reason or warded off by proscription?

Shelley's vulnerability to circumlocution, though not to nightmare, is seldom devolved upon Victor to more deviously revealing effect. Here is the core of her psychic diagnosis, yet it comes to us swathed symptomatically in the character's own self-protective obscuration. Even as Victor continues in what may seem a stiffly explicit diction, still the recalled interdict (or corrective discipline?) is filtered through the blurred screen of internalized denial: "I do not ever remember to have trembled at a tale of superstition or to have feared the apparition of a spirit" (4:50). Grammar abets his evasion through its own ambivalence. Does he remember never trembling? Or simply never let himself remember? If the former, is it a maintained childhood taboo or a gradual debility that has sustained his exemption from all gothic aggravation, his exclusion from the fostering romanticism of the negative sublime? Whether or not such a "tale" was any more available to Victor as a child than the visitations of specters, the basic privation is clear. With the father's own scare tactics amounting either to an outlawing of natural instinct or to a kind of aversion therapy through neutralized affect, here is how Victor's antiromantic childhood helps him in a starkly literal sense, and in a sweeping parody of Wordsworthian gestational maturation, to *father the man*: "Darkness had no effect upon my fancy, and a churchyard was to me merely the receptacle of bodies deprived of life" (4:50). An ounce of unadvised parental prevention ends up requiring an adult male's dead weight in cemetery refuse as raw material for an unhinged creative cure.

Indeed, Victor introduces this whole passage on the blocked imaginative passage of his childhood in a way that shows his "recourse to death" (4:50), his graveyard forays, as a displacement of a once denied access to the perturbations of the "supernatural tale" onto his present lust for forbidden thrills. The dead metaphors of this self-characterization demonstrate, in other words, how he has become, in the fever of dubious creation, his own electrified ghoul: a frenzied agent "animated by an almost supernatural enthusiasm" (4:50), without which his loathsome scavenging would have been "almost intolerable" (4:50). Denied a child's normal focus, and outlet, for imaginative unrest, never allowed the constructive anxieties of fairy tale or gothic narrative, Victor's arrested fictional development—ironically leaving him unprepared for the inefficacy of his later confession when taken as just such a tale of superstition—is an impoverishment from which the novel as a whole defends its readers. Portrayed in Victor's case is a kind of trauma by exclusion: the scarring *avoidance* of a narrative opportunity—or its potency—which (as with Shelley's novel, and others like it) might have indued a healthy sense of mystery, a responsible timidity before the unknown. Instead, the deficit of Victor's earliest reading comes to haunt him now, like the return of the repressed, in the form of the nameless magistrate's purely *readerly* interest in his tale.

The novel reader's more sophisticated response must be extrapolated by contrast. That Victor suffers for our interest as well as for his sins is the tried and tired logic of catharsis. The structure of Shelley's novel explores a fuller psychodrama. In between Walton's feeding off of the hero's suffering (Walton dependent, insatiable, passively snared by identification) and the foregrounded evacuation of the sister's response—in between the voracious and the unspoken—opens the zone of your potential critical distance as well as your complicity. At the other end of the century, the revival of the gothic genre takes up where these inferences in *Frankenstein* leave off. The socializing symbiosis of narrative and response that we will investigate in Dickens, the Brontës, Eliot, Meredith, and the other high Victorian novelists gives way in certain *fin de siècle* novels to an even less acquiescent sense of textual reception. In Bram Stoker's *Dracula*, for instance, the absentation that is reading, together with its annexation of otherness, becomes actively devouring. To engage with a text is figured there as a no longer passive dependency, derivative and harmlessly vicarious, but rather as a labor akin to vampirism itself, not animating the text so much as drawing off its life into the void of response.

In pursuing such implications, my last chapter will return more systematically to the mode of reading sketchily attempted here. For what we have seen with Shelley's text is how a novel that proceeds by "deconstructing" its own most famous creation, the Creature, as a mere structure of intertexts and inscriptions can turn out, at another level, to be reinscribing—and in the process conscripting—the rationalized (and here championed) irrationality of audience response. In certain bellwether texts at century's end, that is, as before them in

Frankenstein, textual self-referentiality develops simultaneously as reader reflex. After all (we have been reminding ourselves), this is exactly the path by which literary form engages culture: not by imitation so much as by a rhetoric of participation.

Homo Legens: In Posthumous Response

But before this late-century ferment in the tacit premises of response, as well as before the long march of the Victorian novel in its self-consciously *formalized* reception, there is Shelley's *The Last Man*. What do you, as reader, make of a narrative directed at an already absent audience, a universally decimated readership? Where could you possibly find room for yourself in such a textual hypothesis? If these questions seem somewhat overheated, if you think the futuristic conceit of *The Last Man* tends no more to perturb than in fact indirectly to confirm the ordinary conditions of literary reception, including the depletions of identity on which they depend, then in your resistance to the novel's immediate shock value as plot you have begun to divine its overriding parable. As it happens, though, even on the plot's own terms, *The Last Man* opens with a potential way out of its own flaunted deadlock. From the novel's visionary twist on the evidentiary or editorial fiction in its framing preface, you get an initial (albeit fantastic) explanation about how and why, and from where, you read. For this text of plague and its aftermath is actually transmitted, unbeknownst to its author not yet born, by way of prophetic rather than retrospective mediation.

The prefatory fable of *The Last Man* recounts how Shelley and her "companion" (Percy Shelley) chanced to discover the cavernous inner chamber of the Cumaean Sibyl, whose strewn "leaves" and "bark" (former pun intended) "were traced with written characters" (1,1:3), some of them in "modern dialects, English and Italian."[4] These inscriptions represent whole language systems that postdate the epoch of the Sibyl—and which are therefore prophetic at the level of medium (*langue*) as well as omen (*parole*). Shelley, as quasi-editorial persona, stands to these traces of the future as does Walton to Victor's memories of the past: their secretarial scribe and conduit. "Scattered and unconnected as they were, I have been obliged to add links, and model the work into a consistent form" (1,1:3–4). She thus turns the found fragments, as she had done before with the scattered gothic pretexts of *Frankenstein*, into a rearticulated whole: in this case an anatomy not of a betrayed humanoid but of humanity's own self-betrayal.

When Verney, the Last Man, arriving at the extirpated seat of Western culture in Rome, finds "writing materials on a table in an author's study," they are adjacent to leaves of a manuscript that "lay scattered about" (2,10:339). With this direct echo of those Sibylline leavings that inspire Shelley's transcription, Verney, too, takes up the pen: "I will leave a monument to the existence of Verney, the Last Man" (2,10:339). It is only here, four pages from the novel's end, that the Last Man tells us how he has decided to write for an absent posterity what we must suddenly presume to be the account we have all along been reading: a chronicle of the decline of the British monarchy, the republican advent and its failures, followed by the laying waste of the world by plague. "I also will write a book, I cried—[but] for whom to read? to whom dedicated?" (2,10:339). According to this very book, all present readers are long dead—and all your heirs. Reversing the trope of an author immortalized in words by surviving his body and sustaining his impression(s) across future generations, Shelley allows the only possibility of reception to be staked paradoxically, impossibly, on a resurrection of the past dead by the dead future. It is the audience itself, rather than the writer, who must be afforded a disembodied immortality.

Even more than in *Frankenstein*, the metanarrative balance of *The Last Man* is tilted toward a thematics of fictional inscription rather than fictional reception—and yet even more powerfully weighted, in the ultimate counterplay of extrapolation, toward an evocation of reading's uncanny dispensation. The entire narrative construct of *The Last Man*—climaxed in an act of writing not for posterity but for one's long-dead ancestors—is thus shot through with the spookiness of its own eventual reading, but only as the type of all such textual encounter. If there is something ghoulish about animating the "hideous progeny" of pilfered and recombined narrative matter in *Frankenstein*, both by writing and also by reading it, in *The Last Man* there is an even more palpably supernatural cast to the transactive event of writing read. But the supernatural is meant, as suggested, to trope rather than to trump the uncanny, to refigure the weirdness of reading rather than to explain it away.

This is never clearer than when Verney decides to begin his text (inseparable from the one we have been reading) with the "silly flourish" of a spectral apostrophe:

DEDICATION

TO THE ILLUSTRIOUS DEAD.

SHADOWS, ARISE, AND READ YOUR FALL!

BEHOLD THE HISTORY OF THE

LAST MAN

Here again, the at once disallowed and still operable reflexivity of this passage is registered in a lexical density mounted in its own way on contradictory determinations. Just as "arise" and "fall" set up a figurative antithesis that flouts the normal idiomatic deployment of these same words, so the notion of a "history" of the as yet unarrived future, read from the point of view of the past, raises a comparable specter of paradox. It does so only to overcome it with a new order of implausible but immanent discourse, addressed as summons to the always absent. Further, the alphabetic (if not phonemic) drift at "and read," in tempting though unactivated internal echo with "dead," teases out just that phobic realization, just the "dread," that otherwise goes unsaid in this quasi-epitaphic epigraph: the foregone conclusion of its foregone finality.

This passage thus points up a third way—beyond the epistolary and editorial mechanisms discussed in connection with *Frankenstein*—by which Mary Shelley's textual practice works its subtle transformations on her eighteenth-century forebears. The vocative and imperative grammar of reader address, banished (except for the salutation "My dear Sister") by dramatic structure in *Frankenstein*, emerges near the close of *The Last Man* bearing not only traces of editorial and epistolary formats (an unanswered missive of critical commentary from the future) but, more directly than in most novels, traces of the epitaphic prototype as well. The apocalyptic equivalent of a tombstone's *Siste, viator* ("Halt, traveler") is deployed by Shelley in a complete reversal of its generic norm. Instead of the past dead speaking to the living in the midst of life from the site of an incised text, the already dead are addressed from the brink of extinction by the last of their human line. It is thus that you as readers of Verney's last words, two and two-thirds centuries before, must—by (effacing) definition—be included in this address and hence mourned even as implored. The paired structural principles of this study here explosively collide. Interpolated by the vocative plus imperative format of "SHADOWS, ARISE," you have no choice but to extrapolate from this summoned multitude of the doomed future your own present emptiness in taking up this book, taking on its narrative, and so taking *in* the Last Man's words.[5]

I dwell on the oddity, the radical affront, of this structure because it has a normative as well as a bizarre dimension, offering comment on the conditions of textual reception even when not, as it were, in extremis. Generically, *The Last Man* can command an audience eager for futuristic narrative, reversing the mass catastrophe of such narrative (the end of civilization in this case) by mass appeal (the present consolidation of a readership). This is at least what happens at one (recuperative) level. An attentive collectivity becomes in this manner the utopia for which inadvertent genocide is the dystopian double. Yet this meta-trope is offered at the very time in the evolution of a mass readership when, as we saw in our first chapter, a widening anxiety in the high-literary discourse of the period has begun to recoil from the "epidemic" of literacy that seemed to be cheapening the art of reading. In this sense, the mass annihilation of Coleridge's loathed "reading public" at the hands of a fellow romantic author (albeit popular novelist) begins to resemble, among its other structural functions, a fable—or is it a devilish parody?—of withering elitism. We need to come back to this possibility in a moment.

In an essay by Paul de Man on the phenomenological criticism of Georges Poulet, the latter is seen to find in reading a kind of localized self-immolation. "I begin," Poulet is quoted as claiming, "by letting the thought that invades me . . . reoriginate within my own mind, as if it were reborn out of my own annihilation."[6] In de Man's gloss, this *"moment de passage* changes from a temporal into an intersubjective act or, to be more precise, into the total replacement of one subject by another" (95–96)—as Walton by Victor, for instance. This chapter's interest in Shelley's metanarrative "sequel" to *Frankenstein* amounts, then, to this: that *The Last Man*, too, in tandem with and in containment by its preface, has also shifted ground from temporality to intersubjectivity, from a realm where death is one name for the terminus of duration to a realm where death is a figure for identification. As Frankenstein enacts and *The Last Man* announces, you as reader are dead on arrival to any text that, as you take it in, takes you out of yourself. In Jane Austen, reading prolonged over time teaches a manner of duration and epistemology, a process of gradually opened subjectivity, known as life. In Mary Shelley, borrowing more directly from the gothic (without the conversion of its formulas, as in Austen, to the mere form of heightened climax yielding to relaxed coda), reading teaches that manner of psychic removal only sometimes called death.

And if this is the case, then the suspected cover story of world plague as in fact a fantasized revenge on the mass audience—that grotesque antitrope of receptivity—is not only covered for in turn but structurally justified by recourse to the inevitable privatizing of response in the transferential surrenders of the reading act. Such is the phenomenological solitude that empties out not an audience en masse but a single, if no longer individuated, reading subject. The lumpen collectivity of mass readership, that feared contradiction of the literary sublime itself, is hereby provisionally reconceived by Shelley—less perhaps to refute than merely to defuse the threat—as the hollowing out of consciousnesses, one by one, that is the very precondition of literary self-transcendence—or call it vicariousness.[7] So it is that the cultural artifact known as narrative text once again enacts rather than merely assumes its more than sociological place within a culture of reading. The emotive room opened by this particular text, the subjective space hollowed for present empathy, thus operates to defend against, or at least to defer, that radical evacuation of all sentient response predicted by its plot.

From this perspective, we may see more clearly how the edging out of address in *Frankenstein* permits the truncated dialogic (or interpolative) inference of its epistolary structure to coincide finally with the analogic (or extrapolative) force of reading at its farthest reach. Exactly the kind of audience apostrophe that *Frankenstein* disallows by its concentric structure of dramatized telling is reincorporated with fatalistic defiance for *The Last Man*. The public face of Victorian fiction may be taken as one long retreat from this latter extremity. In this way, these paired chapters on Austen and Shelley can be seen to lead—given the very exclusions (and devious returns) of invoked reading in both authors—toward the thick of address in the mainstream popular novel of the subsequent period. Remaining attentive to that address, however, is only one way of monitoring how the reader *figures* in Victorian fiction, as these same two chapters (on novels mostly avoiding direct reader reference) have gone to demonstrate. Both Austen and Shelley configure their reading audience less in the spotlight of address than in the reflected light of their overarching narrative structure as a psychotherapeutic mechanism. Just this is what constitutes their most important anticipation of the Victorian novel, where direct address to the readership, even though prominent, is no more determinate than other means of conscription.

More than pre-Victorian chronology has thus aligned our first two nineteenth-century fictional exemplars. In their generic divergence, Jane Austen and Mary Shelley attest to a shared tendency. Both the marital plot at the core of classic realism and the fantastic anomalies of the subcanonical gothic are found to program reception by complementary means, to convert the reader to an operative of the text. They do so by routes inherent to their differing attractions as stories while also constitutive of their readers as pliant imaginative subjects at leisure with a text. Austen inculcates the patient attention she demands as a mode of sensibility plotted out by characters within the narrative (Anne and Wentworth)—and then valorized by counterexample (Mr. Elliot). In *Frankenstein*, Shelley trains the heightened attention she needs by plotting out the psychic delegation, as well as sustained responsiveness, on which the narrative fascination of her texts depends—and then ratifies a centrist position by satirizing the extremes: on the one side, abject mental capitulation (Walton);

on the other, emotional withdrawal from gothic seductions altogether (Victor). This dialectic makes *Frankenstein* Shelley's version of *Northanger Abbey*. Victorian literary history will tend to confirm this early alignment of authors even as it pursues the separate tracks of their generic divergence. For what appears at first, and at most, complementary in these opposing narrative ventures will, by the end of the century, begin to seem like a masked commonality (hence chapter 13): namely, that nagging interrogation of psychosocial autonomy which is incident to narrative subjection of any kind, more obvious in fictions of the gothic revival than in psychological realism in good part because the former so often give parabolic shape to the psychic exactions of the latter.

Polarized motivations of gothic formula—travesty in *Northanger Abbey*, revival in *Frankenstein*—may have in common, we have seen, the pressure they exert upon self-conscious response. In the one case, Austen advances the suggestion that "literary intercourse" would itself preempt not only the unchecked medieval cruelties of gothic invention but the untempered reactions of her characters. It would do so, perhaps, by the double force of over*exposure*: by modern communicative networks that forestall the enclaves of festering autocratic power upon which the gothic depends (this much is explicit), as well as (in an inviting further inference) by the sheer generic overfamiliarity of the form's hyperbolic conventions. Once more, the psychodynamic of reading becomes the site of cultural negotiation. It is a case of fictional affect not simply reflecting historical transformation but in part catalyzing it. From the opposite direction, within an unstinted requisition of gothic formula, Mary Shelley puts forward a not dissimilar suggestion: namely, that "literary intercourse" (a reading subject's being conversant, say, with the gothic form in particular) might have done more for her hero than he was able to permit. It might have leeched off some of his perverse energies and checked his tendency to turn his own life into a gothic plot. As it can do for you, too, if need be. In each case, then, fiction both implants and actually performs its own recommendation.

But this is no more to isolate the full extent of audience manipulation in these texts than it would be to say that each equally, by positive and negative example, interpellates the middle-class reader into a supposedly antifeudal ideology of voluntary marital union and personal industry only nominally free from the aristocratic dead weight of inherited property rights and the social hierarchies of the landed classes. Values are *imbued* by the generic implications of the text, to be sure, but they are also *incurred* in the act of reading. This chapter can't afford to be held, in other words, to the narrow parallel between gothic parody and gothic reappropriation in *Northanger Abbey* and *Frankenstein* respectively. *Persuasion* and *The Last Man* are more fully steeped in their own promotion as humanizing textual events—as well as their own countercurrent of interrogation and encroaching critique. Taking shape in this way is a sliding scale whereby aggravated self-absentation begins to seem like merely an over-explicit form of the sympathetic self-abnegation on which all narrative empathy must turn. Seen from this angle, along such a disclosed common axis, Austenian sensitivity shades over into a perverse susceptibility at just those moments when the ideal deciphering subject (communal and textual both)—posited as open, apprehending, patient, tentative, sensitized, empathetic, hence vulnerable and soon engrossed—appears too close for comfort to the Walton-like subject avid and apprehensive to begin with, vicarious, dependent, intentionally preoccupied and readily surrendered, the subject caught up and lost in narrative, abdicating to it, inhabited and drained by it.

Before examining the encoded scenes of readerly subjection from Dickens through Eliot which test by extrapolation the psychic investments of realism well before the *fin de siècle* crisis of generic confidence, however, we need to canvass the best-sellers of the period, those texts most evidently in touch with the audiences they tend to designate by name. We do so in order to comprehend the range of their allegiance to that classic eighteenth-century habit of reader apostrophe that is variously marginalized (swept to the periphery) in Austen's comic realism and Shelley's revived gothic, as before them respectively—by the end of the preceding century—in Edgeworth's comic romance and Radcliffe's prototypical gothic (to name two of the direct influences on Austen). Such a minimizing of address may be found perfected in Austen and Shelley, though, precisely because the withdrawal from routine interpolation has taken place alongside the wholesale extrapolation of plot as a discipline—and a diagnostic—of reading. Well beyond any and all nodding recognitions of the reader, that is, falls (into structural place) a crucial dispensation of the text as the immanent modeling of response. In the Victorian novels that follow, "dear reader" is often no more than the shadow image of such an encompassing machination.

Chapter Six

In "Dearing" the Reader
Popular Fiction, 1814–1918

Walter Langley, *Memories* (1885). City Museums and
Art Gallery, Birmingham

𝒫opular fiction has its tacit and pervasive intimacies as well as its direct endearments. The former justify the latter, making "dear reader" seem the mere token of a comprehensive affect. Emotion recollected in the privileged tranquility of a space afforded: the romantic naturalizing of poetic effect. Recollection's filtered emotion as the next best thing to the vividness of reading: the promotional rhetoric of Victorian fiction. "Memories," like more far-fetched imaginings, get s(t)imulated by narrative art on page or canvas, where absent (because invented) feeling is made present, endeared to reception by the mix of familiarity and otherness. This is a sense of things captured in Langley's 1885 painting, which in part renders what it cannot help but engender in many a contemporary viewer: the emotive time lines of domestic nostalgia. In its literary manifestations, the affective dynamic is very little altered even when the narrative topic is historical adventure or exotic romance. While excluding all immediate experience but its own perusal, popular art (painting or its internal emblem here, reading) induces an artifice of recaptured or borrowed feeling in its most impressionable audiences, an emotive fusion of estrangement and interiorization which can eventually be indulged by the adult viewer (reader) as well as by the child's responsive imagination. Such is the affect of identification, cultivated in early years by popular representation and then supplied in perpetuity. Recalling Erich Schön's thesis in chapter 3, we may want to add that reading, no less than painting, is in just this way designed to let the world in—or at least the limitless tracts of literature's fantasized otherworld, replacing the surrendered pleasures of bodily phonation in oral reading with the imagined vistas of alternative spatial habitations. We might want further to say that reading becomes as a result a kind of threshold or casement in its own right—hence, no doubt, the frequency of readers stationed at open windows in Schön's own gallery of examples from German painting.

So, too, with Langley, a representative British painter of the Newlyn school, in whose *Memories* the exterior scene impinges upon three generations of familial domesticity through the medium of window and book alike. In an exception that only proves the rule of the outdoor settings favored by this late-century movement in landscape painting, Langley's perspective angles its compositional vectors forward toward the indoor scene of formative reading while also back toward the world of scope and contingency on which that interior opens. Poised expectantly at the border of the world beyond her window, the adult woman, fingering a net and looking up abstractedly from whatever might previously have caught her eye in the open book before her, seems almost in the presence of a younger female self reared on illustrated reading, with its own internally reframed visual prospects. Taking the canvas in this way as a diachronic palimpsest incorporating a *mise en abyme*, a text whose muted sentimental melodrama needs a version of the very reading it depicts, we see the "memories" of the title both in formation and in retrieval within the same scene, each associated with a faraway look in the eyes. And if the adult, perhaps the mother, is yearning for her fisherman husband, now at sea or beneath it, and touching him by metonym in the net, the eros of this snared memory cannot be separated from that early reading, figured in the foreground, which first trains and later sublimates such romantic desire. All the diffused affect and remembered affection upon which this picture depends, like the included popular literature from which its own effect is to be extrapolated, all the eroticism (marginalized) and textual nurture (front and center), can at other times, and in another medium, be distilled (purified, refined, or, of course, tinctured by satire) in the literalized endearments of a reader by the surrogate intimacies— and even, once again, the phonic g/ratifications—of Victorian textual rhetoric.

The very cadence of "dear reader" has an inevitable curvature and phonemic resonance: the perfect chiasm tailing off from the stem of the second word to repeat with a fading vowel the consonant bracket of the first: deer/reed/(d)er. Even the phantom clasp of an elided *r* between epithet and noun makes it seem a catchier, a smoother, a more inescapable collocation.[1] As a prototype of address, it is the salute to attention from which all others—and their number is legion—derive. To follow along the avenues and byways of such derivation requires something between a history and a spectrum analysis. It may also require some preliminary justification in the absence of competing accounts.

One comes to suspect that the questions to which the following remarks about nineteenth-century popular fiction seek to feel out an answer must, in the past, have appeared either too obvious to escape mere intuition or too out of the way to prompt research. For whatever reasons, what seems from one point of view an inviting line of inquiry has remained unpursued in scholarship on the nineteenth-century novel. I will respond to its invitation by putting it this way: Given the history of a period during which, not only in hindsight but in progress, the high-literary text was beginning to be categorically pitted against the lowbrow best-seller, what would looking into the frequency and habitual forms of direct reader address in the most often read novels of the Victorian century have to show about the invocative technique—equivalent or divergent, borrowed or eschewed—of their more demanding counterparts? What light is shed by the publishing ephemera of the period upon those novels by which, whether or not hailed through apostrophe, we are still held? Austen skirted or mocked the vocative. Shelley shackled it to epistolary or epitaphic exaggeration. Between parodic and hypertrophic extremes lies the ordinary unlabored usage of subsequent generations, casual, sometimes flaccid, always in relaxed continuity with eighteenth-century norms. To what effect? To effect what? How does the vocative give off its various signals, navigating reaction as it makes a narrative text over to—and over into—the event of its own reading?

Only examples, though not examples alone, can lead to a useful position on this issue. I have in mind interpolative passages of reader reference and address from Ainsworth, Bulwer-Lytton, Reade, Kingsley, Corelli, Haggard, Kipling, Stevenson, and others, on into the turn of the century, including the surfacing en route of such formulaic inscriptions of response in the more seriously regarded fiction of Hawthorne and Trollope.[2] These were the novelists who *spoke to* their audience with greatest frequency and gusto, their texts streaked and veined with cues to attention. I mean this, of course, figuratively, there being no one there for these writers to speak to, even via print; the novel-reading public, once inscribed, is itself entirely figurative. Having seen this *in theory*, we will now watch for its evidence in popular practice.

The habit of reader address or designation in fact depends for its striking fluidity on just this sheerly figurative status. In the classic form of apostrophe, invoked reading is a prosthesis of authorial discourse: a masked doubleness within enunciation (Culler) which projects in the form of commanded attention the very intentionality of an utterance. Addressed or merely mentioned reading—to review certain theoretical articulations in the introductory chapters—thus "refigures" (Ricoeur) the sphere of consumption. It does so through an already figurative return of the conative (and even the phatic) from within the poetic function (Jakobson) as the very *figure of speech*: the primal index of communicative motive from which all other textual rhetoric may be felt to derive. As one might imagine from the banishment of the vocative to peripheral status in Mary Shelley's novels, the popular insistence on an addressed literary populace in the subsequent best-sellers is no less an orientation of text toward consumption, no less a gambit in the contradictory presencing of merely pending attention. The "terms" on which nineteenth-century fictional narrative thereby sought to stand with the consuming public are to be marked by the way these texts singled out readers figured alternately as "gentle," "worthy," "courageous," "courteous," "benevolent," "cultivated," "kind," "good," otherwise merely "general," or all things to be wished at once, as, for instance, in "Dear, good, gentle, Christian friends." What we will want eventually to rest on such address, collectively, is a sense of the way in which the routine inscription of a receptive public may not only clarify by contrast but amplify by cultural context the discursive position of that mass audience's more ambitious kin: the conscripted readers of the high-literary novel in Eliot, Meredith, Hardy, and the like.

The focus of this survey will be divided, even in its forward momentum. In garnering evidence from dozens of best-selling fictions mostly unread today, we will also be gleaning certain recurrent figurations of the reading act which will claim separate treatment later: most important, the world as book (to which a given novel necessarily attaches itself as supplement) and the transcendence of spatiotemporal limits by texts addressed beyond life to an audience death cannot abolish. Chapter 10 will explore the former trope; the latter, already familiar from the structural ironies of Mary Shelley's *The Last Man*, will take its place within the ramified metaphors of reading as supernatural transgression in chapter 13. Indeed, the reading act interpolated through apostrophe, especially when explicitly linked to editorializing gestures continuous with eighteenth-century reader address, actually corroborates the former of those recurrent figures—the conceit of the world's book—at a fundamental level of text production. For if the world is already a book, then an excerpt or translation of it, even one called a novel, is on the face of it more of an editorial than an inventive process. We begin, then, with Walter Scott, who by compartmentalizing reader address in editorial prefaces serves nevertheless to measure its generic necessity and set its terms. He does so by maximizing the thematic as well as rhetorical work of just the sort of prefatory material which would for the most part lose its prominence, even while gradually regaining its frequency, in the subsequent narrative practice of Victorian mainstream fiction.

Front Matter as Front: Scott's Public Faces

One of the most definitively popular writers of the century cannot be disabled by his almost immediate canonization from casting light on the tradition of best-sellers for which his historical romances were the century's generic high watermark. In Scott's invention of the historical novel as we know it (the virtual oxymoron of its generic status absolved under the dispensation of the aesthetic), the nineteenth-century regime of fiction finds not only its quintessential mixed mode—the romance of the real—but its exemplary latitude in audience address. Fictionality is so readily accepted, verisimilitude rather than historicity so entirely the desideratum, that no fiction of editorial transmission need be cogently sustained except for the sake of a joke. It is a joke the reader is in on, and addressed by, from the start. Where the catchall category of the aesthetic may be taken to have subsumed the debates of the previous century about historicity versus fabulation—as Michael McKeon's work on eighteenth-century fiction (see chapter 4) serves to predict—it now spawns its own division between art per se, whether that of antiquarian craft or novelistic construction, and everyday storytelling: between the ambitious and the idle even within the commercialized circuits of the literary product. It is this tension that is often in play between the layered authenticating personae who stand in for the long-anonymous "author of *Waverley*." And in just this regard, even the absence of such personae in the debut novel is instructive. For *Waverley* (1814) thematizes within plot, and then reframes by authorial commentary, much the same debate about the habits and laxities of popular reading which will be structured into the secondary annotational machinery of Scott's later novels. What is subsequently edited into view has already been editorialized from the start.

On this score, the penultimate chapter of *Waverley* passes over into the last, the "Postscript, Which Should Have Been a Preface," across a revealing verbal echo. The cup "filled" in a wedding ceremony, having become the wish "fulfilled" of happiness ever after, is edged over from plot to discourse: "Our journey is now finished, *gentle reader*; and if your patience has accompanied me through these sheets, the contract is, on your part, strictly *fulfilled*" (72:491; emphasis added). Such is the slide between story and its supervening narration (by author this time, as by various editors later) over which the "gentle reader" is called forth to officiate. But that reader's gentility does not remain unscathed, since Scott explains that he has put what amount to his prefatory remarks last rather than first because "most novel readers, as my own conscience reminds me," tend to skip such introductory material, often beginning with "the last chapter" (72:491–92). If you don't recognize him in yourself, you nonetheless know the kind of reader Scott is writing about, for you have read of him in this very novel. Racing to last chapters for the thrill of a climax, skipping introductions—all this seems symptomatic of that "desultory course of reading" (3:49), weighted heavily to romance, which is analyzed early on as an aspect of young Waverley's permissive upbringing. It is an attitude implied as well by a later direct address to a certain assumed number of impatient readers: "I beg pardon, once and for all, of those readers who take up novels merely for amusement, for plaguing them so long with old-fashioned politics" (5:63).

Impatient or impercipient reading is more than a literary or even textual default. It is a way of going blind to the world. This is a notion seeded deep by Scott in one of *Waverley*'s earliest figures of speech, an instance of that mastertrope of nineteenth-century fiction to which chapter 10 will return us: the idea that even narrating is a kind of reading—a reading in the "book of humanity." Without an editorial persona yet deployed to boast of sifting through documents to purvey a coherent narrative, here the author himself is cast into the secondary role as transmitter of the already recorded. This occurs by recourse to that trope of the *legibility* of space and time derived from the theological figuration of the world as God's book. As secularized and historicized by Scott, it is this same figuring of inscription as decipherment which passes through countless permutations, popular and arcane, in the course of the Victorian novel: "It is from the great book of Nature, the same through a thousand editions, whether of black-letter, or wire wove and hot-pressed, that I have venturously essayed to read a chapter to the public" (1:36). Author as reader (aloud) of life's indelible story, reader as contractual partner, closure as narrative and discursive fulfillment for the latter as well as the former—thus are Scott's interlocked metafictional premises articulated in his first novel. Even in increasingly belabored disguise, the editorial reframings of his subsequent narratives only follow suit. Half a decade after *Waverley*, for instance, the fictional narratorship of *Ivanhoe* (1819) has disappeared behind the claims to antiquarian research by one Laurence Templeton, whose dedicatory epistle to "The Rev. Dr. Dryasdust, F.A.S," fears that the latter will mistakenly confuse his chronicle "with the idle novels and romances of the day" (521). All of this is of course more send-up than cover-up, wholly deflected in its epistemological or historiographic debate by the clear reign of aesthetic fabulation.

In *Old Mortality* (1816), the supposed author/compiler, Peter Pattieson, makes no bones about the novelistic expectations that will greet his published labors. Uncertain about how to wrap up his story, he actually canvasses the novel-reading public in the person of one Martha Bucksbody: "Knowing her taste for narratives of this description, I requested her to look over the loose sheets . . . and enlighten me by the experience which she must have acquired in reading through the whole stock of three circulating libraries" (Conclusion: 478). Much debate follows, in a dialogue that becomes a brief essay on the economies of closure: How much future to dispense (rather than dispense with) to how many of the major and minor characters? Allowing just enough of the traditional coda to be teased out of him by the voiced curiosity of this stand-in reader, Mrs. Bucksbody, Scott's stand-in persona immediately completes his task of gracious farewell to the reader: "In like manner, gentle Reader, . . . I take the liberty to withdraw myself from you for the present" (Conclusion: 482). There is appended, however, a "Peroration" by the subsequent editor, Jedediah Cleishbotham, promising his "most courteous Reader" more tales for undoubted approbation "by the unanimous voice of a discerning public" (Conclusion: 483). It is in this confidence that the deferential pedant can chirp out his obsequious syllabic gesture in closing: "I *rest, est*eemed Reader, thine as thou shalt construe me" (emphasis added). Thus does the narrative mediator, even twice removed from the plot, give his own persona and opinions, even his own existence, over to the constructive or interpretive energies of the novel's reading public.

"We Can Assure Our Readers": Ainsworth and Bulwer-Lytton

Across much of the Victorian period, beginning before Dickens and continuing well after, W. Harrison Ainsworth mined the Scottian vein of historical romance along such a broad stratum of popular sentiment that his language further eroded the boundaries between editorializing and conversational narrative voices. Dialing down Scott's techniques of documentary verification, a justificatory aside like the following in Ainsworth's hugely popular chronicle of the robber Dick Turpin, *Rookwood* (1834), is entirely typical: "Exaggerated as this description may appear, we can assure our readers that it is not overdrawn."[3] When Ainsworth chose to introduce the novel's reissue with a preface (1849), no tonal distance is placed between the textures of historical romance and this retrospective prologue. Free entirely of Scott's weighty and pseudonymous scholarly mechanics, the preface insists that the novel has been composed with "an eye rather to the reader's amusement than his edification," the same "benevolent reader" who has put in a brief appearance in the last paragraph of the novel proper (L'Envoi: 394).

In this way does the very predominance of third (rather than second) person in such reader inscription seem derived in Ainsworth, in a quite roundabout fashion, from the real or fictive editorial practice of the preceding century down through Scott. This tendency toward third-person mention rather than second-person address persists across Ainsworth's career in a typical Victorian fashion, as in the 1840 *Tower of London*, where "we have endeavoured to make the reader acquainted with the general outline of the fortress" (152).[4] Just as editors introducing a chronicle to their readers are more likely to speak of *the* reader (the reader of what follows) than of *my* reader (of these prefatory remarks), so do narrators adopt that impersonal mode of inferred (rather than directly invoked) readership even in the absence of front matter. Ainsworth's consolidation of editorial and narrative voices is therefore entirely in line with the composite tradition out of which he is working—and out of which he produces such a popular new amalgam. The distinction (once an obvious partition) between introductory matter and the saga whose momentum it initiates, between preface and romance chronicle, has become, though manifestly a textual fact, no longer so markedly a rhetorical one.

So let us see where, following the nineteenth-century novel through its mutations as pseudodocument, we have come so far. With "the reader" invading the precincts of the novel from the sphere of editorial apparatus in order to secure from within narrative an available vantage comparable to the remove of an introductory overview, much of the distance between editorial and narratorial tones in Scott has already been closed by the early Victorian period. Almost the whole difference, then, between the editorial and the narratorial "reader," each with its impersonal "the," is apparent in a single distinction: that between the integral evidentiary introductions of the former period and the secondary nature of the Victorian preface, "advertisement," or afterword. The latter may well follow only a good while after the first printing and may be revised from edition to edition—in view primarily of the novel's ongoing *reception*, not its epistemological basis or aesthetic status. Put it this way: If the interpolatory address of such supplementary material seems structurally essential, it is likely to have found its way into the main text from the beginning.

A further example from the very eve of the Victorian period: the relation of novel to ex post facto prefaces in the case of Bulwer-Lytton's 1828 *Pelham*, a benchmark success in the silver-fork school of aristocratic romance. This is the first-person "fashionable novel" that established its author's reputation as, along with Ainsworth, one of the two most formidable literary contemporaries of the early Dickens, defining between them the narrative and rhetorical setting of that popular literary scene onto which Dickens made his own spectacular entrance. The main body of *Pelham* closes with the first-person narrator showily unleashing one of the techniques of the professional author he is here, within plot, becoming. He writes now from a self-imposed and improving retirement "among my books," addressing his valedictory remarks to a "gentle reader" similarly situated, hoping that his autobiographical "confessions" will provide the kind of instruction in their turn which his own "mute teachers" offer him.[5] Exaggerating the communicative bias of popular narrative to the point of imagined interlocution, the narrator issues a most improbable invitation to "thee," his second-person reader, "to come and visit me in the country," where it shall be found that "my conversation" is by no means "much duller than my book" (22:444). A page later, the apostrophic address is directed beyond yet another untraversable barrier: "my friend, my brother, have I forgotten thee in death?" (22:445).

In *Pelham's* link between reader address and posthumous invocation, the device of apostrophe has been bared in its extreme and liminal case: narrative's always quasi-epitaphic address to a reader's passing interest manifested here in its reverse form as transcendental appeal from the living to the dead. By comparison with dead kin, other absences—yours, say, to the world of the text—seem far more readily negotiable. Four more paragraphs remain of *Pelham*, in the course of which a trope to be increasingly drawn upon in the subsequent history of the Victorian novel down through Meredith, and already familiar from Scott, is introduced by Bulwer. This is the conceit that any given human chronicle borrows its legitimacy—and its legibility—from the greater text of the world itself. It is in this sense that the present narrator declares himself as offering, perforce, no more than "one true, and not utterly hacknied, page in the various and mighty volume of mankind" (22:445). This is Scott's "great book of Nature," Meredith's Book of Egoism to come, indeed that "book of books" that Austen has travestied in Sir Walter Elliot's preoccupation with the volume of the baronetage. It is the book now offered by Bulwer, in excerpted form, to the "kind reader" (22:447) of the leave-taking last paragraph, the reader as deciphering social subject.

Lodging a diatribe in his subsequent 1840 preface against "the Reader" in the guise of publisher's referee, the professional critic as bane of popular fiction, Bulwer the public man comes out even more explicitly in favor of mass taste in his later 1849 "Advertisement." His intuitive populism has by now blossomed into a full-scale cultural agenda, where literary pursuits are singled out as contributing to an ameliorating social evolution. By this sanguine logic the "middle class"—that collective noun taking its characteristic plural verb in British English—"have become more instructed and refined, . . . fused with the highest in their intellectual tendencies, reading the same books, cultivating the same accomplishments" (456). Be it elevating or leveling, call it hegemony. Emphasis falls again, a little further along, on the sudden and happy proliferation of "cheap books" that are "addressed, not . . . to the passions, but to the understanding and the taste" (456). Even his choice of verb—"addressed . . . to"— speaks with the rhetorical bias of his epoch. With the spread of reading, in short, comes the democratization of culture without the decline of refinement. Such is Bulwer's boast. This effect even trickles down, through "that inexpressible diffusion of oral information," to the lower classes, that "great reality—the People" (456)—or, as he calls them just before, the "operatives" (456).

Literary history rewards this liberal optimism with a curious footnote toward the end of the Victorian period, in a brief scene of extrapolated rather than interpolated reading. What we find remarked upon in the first chapter of Conrad's *The Nigger of the "Narcissus"* (1897) is perhaps the lowest level of intellectual attainment to which Bulwer-Lytton's fiction itself, in printed form, may directly appeal: bare literacy itself. Conrad is describing Old Singleton fixated on a book: "He was intensely absorbed . . . reading 'Pelham'" (1:17). In his own bid for popularity within a modified adventure genre far removed from the silver-fork pretensions of Bulwer's novel, Conrad allows his narrator to be pulled up short: "The popularity of Bulwer Lytton in the forecastles of Southern-going ships is a wonderful and bizarre phenomenon. What ideas do his polished and so curiously insincere sentences awaken in the simple minds of the big children who people those dark and wondering places of the earth?" (1:17). The occasionally patronizing tone taken toward these nautical "operatives" is one familiar from Bulwer-Lytton himself in regard to the industrial lower classes. Of the fictional literacy of these seamen, Conrad asks: "What meaning can their rough, inexperienced souls find in the elegant verbiage of his pages?" (1:17). Whatever it is, it must involve the appeal of otherness, of the unfamiliar. At which point we are caught up—by extrapolating from the sailors' reading to our own—in the further inference that Conrad's seagoing adventures might justifiably make at least as much claim, by way of a comparable exoticism, on more civilized and sedentary readers like you and me.

Where Conrad waxes quizzical, however, Bulwer-Lytton is all mainstream confidence. The role of the popular novel in mid-Victorian culture seems to him clear and unquestioned. He is the cheap-book maker par excellence, able to speak alike to middle and upper echelons of society, while also able to promulgate his sentiments to the illiterate lower orders through those mysteries of cultural dissemination and oral "diffusion" celebrated in the 1849 "Advertisement." No clearer promotional statement exists in the mid-Victorian era from the pen of a popular novelist (and intermittent parliamentary figure) about the power of publication to reform and renew a public; about "cheap books" as cultural currency; about reading as an exercise in social engineering; about narrative, whether or not punctuated by the vocative, as nonetheless a manner and a strategy of "address."

From Cloister to Hearth: Reade's Readers and Others

Even as Bulwer, after *Pelham*'s coup in the silver-fork market, went on to yet greater sales in the best-selling genre of historical fiction, other popular stars were rising as well. Charles Reade had one of the century's most extraordinary commercial successes with *The Cloister and the Hearth* (1861). Narrating the lives of the parents of Erasmus in the fifteenth century, the novel adjusts its authorial stance along the two chief routes we have been following out: the editorializing leverage of authorial upon narrative voice, achieved either by local rhetoric or by prefatory device, and the grammar of designated attention itself, whether direct or indirect address, vocative, imperative, or more neutrally declarative. From the "general reader" of the first paragraph, we traverse almost seven hundred pages to the second-person emotive guidelines of the climactic passage, where the narrator asks for his characters "your sympathy, but not your pity."[6] This intended "appeal" of the novel has been built in from the start, a function of the narrator's own self-characterized role as "interpreter"— a translator, that is, of the "stern page" of some "musty chronicle" (1:19) into the vitality and pathos of felt story. Marketed here is nothing less than the epic function in a postoral epoch, transferred from tribe to nation, orality to literacy. Bearing with it all the didactic self-consciousness of an editorial gloss, and yet breaking directly into the initial chapter of narrative from its more expected prefatory remove, Reade's opening thereby orchestrates his audience's response in prospect—and in direct address: "For if I can but show *you* what lies below that dry chronicler's words, methinks *you* will correct the indifference of centuries, and give those two sore tried souls a place in *your* heart—for a day" (1:19; emphasis added). That only a brief textual hiatus intervenes between this and the scene setting of "It was past the middle of the fifteenth century . . ." measures how far the justificatory logic of Victorian fiction has come from the structure of Scott's segregated editorial framing.

And this is only one line of development. More rhetorical experiments in the mode of address take place in the formative through middle years of the Victorian period than we have yet accounted for. Here Ainsworth the popular novelist and Carlyle the philosophical narrative artist, standing in exemplary opposition, may stand for a larger division of textual labor. There is a crucial difference, for instance, between two superficially similar moments which can begin sketching the picture. When in 1834 Ainsworth has the narrative of *Rookwood* track the sea journey of a character, his "we are going at the rate of twenty knots an hour . . . and the reader must either keep pace with us, or drop astern" (4,6:321) is a narrativization of discourse worlds apart from the participatory urgency of Carlyle's challenge to the reader of the same year in *Sartor Resartus*: "Forward with us, courageous reader; be it towards failure, or towards success! The latter thou sharest with us; the former also is not all our own."[7] Reading subordinated to duty is a notion kept clear, for the most part, of the Victorian novel's leisure ethic. The rigor rather than the vacation of reading is therefore seldom stressed, at least until George Eliot. Ainsworth's trope of the voyaging audience casts back instead to the picaresque figurations of journeys in eighteenth-century fiction, whereas Carlyle's image of forward motion, against unspoken inertia and resistance, anticipates the hermeneutic self-consciousness of such later novelists as Eliot, Meredith, or Conrad.

In Carlyle's second chapter, "Editorial Difficulties," an instance of imperative (couched as permissive) grammar avoids the head-on confrontation of second-person address without loss of rhetorical importuning: "Let the British reader study and enjoy, in simplicity of heart, what is here presented him, and with whatever metaphysical acumen and talent for Meditation he is possessed of" (1,2:10). Not until *Middlemarch* or *Daniel Deronda* will such a call go out to the reader of prose fiction, and then only between the lines. It is there that the internal reciprocity of enjoyment and study, dramatic engagement and necessitated meditation, narrative drive and hermeneutic return will be activated by demonstration rather than manifesto: emplotted for extrapolation rather than exhorted by interpolation. In the first Victorian decade, however, the various traces of editorial incursion into the prefatory admonishments and discursive asides of novelistic prose can perhaps best be appreciated by a fairly stark contrast with the more uncompromising intervention from the interpretive taskmaster of Carlyle's fictionalized scholarly persona. A facile trick like Charles Kingsley's in his best-selling *Westward Ho!* (1855)—"Let us take boat, as Amyas did, at Whitehall-stairs, and slip down ahead of him under old London Bridge"[8]—is a far cry from Carlyle's activated, "courageous" interpreter. Such an overly literal version of reading-one's-way-into-a-scene will later, on the way toward modernism's contempt for address, find itself pitched to blatant artifice in a writer like George Gissing, who opens *Workers in the Dawn* (1880) with the following imperative grammar: "Walk with me, reader, into Whitecross Street,"[9] where sedentary reading and enjoined ambulation are archly at odds.

The "Indulgence" of Readers in Hawthorne

To remain for a while longer in the mid-Victorian period, however, we turn for consideration to the two greatest writers, one American, one British, to manipulate the explicitly named reader through the established popular protocols (rather than irregular importunities) of reference and address. Probably no British novelist of the period before Anthony Trollope more regularly alludes to the agency of reception than does Nathaniel Hawthorne, not only in his tales and sketches but in his major novels. From "the indulgent reader" of the opening page of "The Custom-House" preface to *The Scarlet Letter*, to "the reader" who "must understand" two pages later (1:8), through the presentation of a rose to this same reader plucked from the very scene being described (1:40)—a veritable flower of rhetoric—and on to such later mock-confessional gestures as "to hold nothing back from the reader" (20:153), the novel has already set the tone of Hawthorne's persistent conscription of response.[10] Such mentions of the reader's activity have, once again, broken down the distinction between the quasi-editorial asides appropriate to an authorial preface and the conduct of narrative prose to follow. In the next year's *The House of the Seven Gables* (1851), the lexically equivalent "reader" mentioned on the last page of the preface and the first of the novel ("The reader may perhaps choose to assign an actual locality . . . "; "which, if adequately translated to the reader, would serve to illustrate . . . ") are in every way identical twins. *The Blithedale Romance* (1852), another year later, continues in this manner, running the gamut from the innocuous "as the reader probably knows" (4:656)—a predictable formula lent an unexpected twist, however, when used of the hypothesized extranarrative experience of a fictional character—to the yet more textually provoking "let the reader abate whatever he deems fit" (9:693). This ostensible control on the reader's part over the implications of the narrative, this supposed consensual relation to the text, is only, of course, the disingenuous flip side of conscription.

Such salient interpolations of the reading audience, in *Blithedale* and *The House of the Seven Gables* before it, may well be designed as a check on the sort of unstinted absorption in the narrated scene which Hawthorne parodies in that earlier novel. This moment of captivation by text in *The House of the Seven Gables* involves the spectacle of train passengers devouring railway novels by letting their plots swallow them up in transit: "Some, with tickets in their hats, ... had plunged into the English scenery and adventures of pamphlet novels, and were keeping company with dukes and earls" (17:572).[11] Escapism as self-evacuation is what the same railway fiction fails to provide a year later for the more sophisticated Coverdale, narrator of *The Blithedale Romance*, who reads along in only partial distraction a novel "purchased of a railroad bibliopolist" which is mostly "soporific" in effect (17:761). You are to revel in the contrast to your own challenging and engrossing choice of fiction. At one tongue-in-cheek moment in *The House of the Seven Gables*, in fact, a self-accusatory charge of soporific storytelling ends up imputing (by protesting feebly against it) a virtually hypnotic languor it is your place to deny. I refer to the high-handed false modesty of a parenthetical allusion to the novel reader's response which interrupts the rendered aftermath of the story told by the mesmerist and would-be novelist Holgrave to Phoebe Pyncheon: "He now observed that a certain remarkable drowsiness (wholly unlike that with which the reader possibly feels himself affected) had been flung over the senses of his auditress" (14:534). Hypnotic disclosure is comically rewritten as a stupefying digression, only to highlight all the more forcefully the magnetic fascination of the inset narrative on which you have just eavesdropped. Interpolation thus converges with extrapolation: reader reference with a scene of oral narrative crucial both to Hawthorne's developing plot and to the responsive disposition on the reader's part—rapt attention—which that plot labors to evolve from within its own discourse.

"But Can You Forgive Her, Delicate Reader?": Trollope and the Interrogated Audience

In Anthony Trollope, the oscillation between designated or apostrophized textual attention and a localized reflex of reading operates differently from the comparable interplay in Hawthorne, even as it effects a similar convergence of interpolative interventions with circumscribed scenes of configurative reading. Among the most prolific of the century's best-selling authors, Trollope made an all but incessant claim on the reading public. With so much unbroken commerce between his output and the popular uptake, between pen and reception, it is no wonder that the discourse of his omniscient narration should become increasingly relaxed and direct, likely at any moment to implicate the alert and cooperative readership that it has steadily habituated to its procedures.[12]

Written after the solidification of Trollope's popularity with the Barchester series, the Palliser sequence begins with *Can You Forgive Her?* (1864–65), in which reader reference and address are even more prevalent than before. From the interrogative title forward, the novel displays all the modes of apostrophe and rhetorical inscription by which the audience in Trollope is recruited and then conducted through a text. Given the indefatigable production of this serial novelist, one imagines that those frequent declarations across publishing intervals—to the effect that "the reader will remember"—may be mnemonic prods almost as much for the writer as for his audience as he picks up his own thread. In *Can You Forgive Her?*, for instance, reference to the memory of "the attentive reader" (1,38:388) is followed in the second volume by "The reader will, perhaps, remember their last interview" (2,6:55). These ascriptions of narrative mastery can also be pitched into second person: "Gentle reader, do you remember Lady Monk's party . . . ?" (2,58:180). More obtrusive is the kind of presencing of the reader within the plot noted previously in Ainsworth and Kingsley—and making a belated ironic appearance in Gissing: "I will now ask the reader to go down with me to Nethercoats that we may be present with John Grey when he received [the letter]" (1,36:372).

Not only does *Can You Forgive Her?* defer by title to the reader's ethical sense, even while tacitly presuming upon the outcome of text-long deliberations in this regard, but it respects this textual duration when chastising itself for a premature posing of the question. Nearing the close of the first volume, the narrator balks at his own potential jumping of the gun, again in second-person address: "But can you forgive her, delicate reader? Or am I asking the question too early in the story?" (1,37:384). After two paragraphs in this vein of plot-arresting meditation, we have moved from a premature vocative to a compensatory imperative: "Come;—let us see if it be possible that she may be cleansed by the fire of her sorrow" (1,37:384). Yet for all the self-marked awareness of textual sequence and its ethical consequence, Trollope's stress on the reading act results finally in an even more quintessentially Victorian notion about the semiosis of experience. For on the way to the final sounding of the novel's keynote—"Oh! reader, can you forgive her?" (2,70:311)—we have already passed through a telling assertion in the same paragraph: "the causes were as I have said, and such was the true reading of her thoughts" (2,70:311). As the narrative reads the inner life of its character, we have yet another variation—muted and internalized—of that nineteenth-century mastertrope familiar from Bulwer-Lytton and Charles Reade, as before them from Scott. This is the book of human nature or the "stern page" of human chronicle, lying open for quotation or translation by each new novelist. It is also, of course, what Austen dramatized in the reciprocal reading of each other over time by Anne Elliot and Frederick Wentworth. Whenever we are reminded of our reading along in Trollope, our activity borrows conviction from this epistemological archetype.

Hawthorne, as suggested, is Trollope's nearest American peer in the combined notation and invocation of the reading act—familiar, confident, and emphatic. In the mainstream of the British realist tradition, however, Trollope serves more obviously as a kind of multivolume clearinghouse for the strategies of address and directive in the middle decades of the century. As the popular market for prose fiction continues to expand and its contributors to multiply, one would only expect the devices for securing and channeling a reader's attention, devices whose range is fairly well consolidated by midcentury, to pass through a distracting variety of nonetheless identifiable permutations. Such expectations are entirely borne out by the best-sellers that followed, along with Trollope, after the early triumphs of Dickens and Thackeray.

In an explicitly interrogatory mode anticipating Trollope's, there is Mrs. S. C. Hall's *Can Wrong Be Right?* (1861), serialized in the *St. James Magazine* three years before the appearance of *Can You Forgive Her?* The entire novel is cast up as a letter—and "lesson"—from grandmother to granddaughter about the young girl's tragic forebears and their heroic endurance. "If the records I have written have not taught it, my story has been told in vain:"—followed by her title in caps, turned now to exclamation: "WRONG CAN NEVER BE RIGHT!"[13] An entire illustrative narrative is reduced to the heuristic staving off of a paradox, a moral tale begun in the language of a merely rhetorical question and ended in the sheer semantics of tautology. "I would not have chronicled these memories," the grandmother adds, "but that I desired you should know the facts of what might hereafter be repeated to you or to your children as the Romance of Brecken Hall" (438). Fictional practice has thus sealed again—from within narrative itself this time, rather than from some prefatory vantage—yet one more Victorian contract with the regime of the aesthetic under the banner of the exemplary, of "Romance" under the dispensation of the real. Middle-class narrative stands forth once more as an armature of cultural indoctrination cast up moreover, and increasingly, as the closural refiguring of its own consumption.

Can Wrong Be Right?—Victorian moralistic potboiler par excellence—thus writes, and reads for us in the writing, the fable of its own efficacy even as fabulation. The Victorian novel has also come forward here, by sanctimonious exemplar, as an unabashed apparatus of domestic maintenance, securing an ethical line of descent under the guise of preserving a family history. (Its closest precedent, as we will see in chapter 8, is Collins' collection of stories two years before, under the title *The Queen of Hearts*.) In just this form of familial appendage, the novel as institution, surrendering nothing of its ethic to its confessed aesthetic, continues to flourish with those various audiences it continues to invoke or evoke, address or encode. In the case of the most widely read writers of the later Victorian period, such lodestones of popular sensibility as Marie Corelli, George du Maurier, H. Rider Haggard, Rudyard Kipling, and Robert Louis Stevenson, the bearings of their reader address continue to measure the orientation of the audiences they magnetize. And as the escalating and often indiscriminate market for fiction swells further, the mordant critique of this hypertrophic publication in writers like George Gissing and George Moore is found to enter into certain curious affiliations with the public stance of the best-sellers.

"Dear, Good, Gentle, Christian Friends!": Corelli's Marked Appeal

From the pinnacle of her popular renown, Marie Corelli offers an especially illuminating case. Her narratives are saturated by the invocation of her audience, on whom she fastens with often garrulous abandon, even as she anathematizes the sort of "reader" she makes no effort to reach: the paid professional lackey of the publication industry against whom Bulwer-Lytton had an earlier occasion to rail. It is the first-person male persona of her novel *The Sorrows of Satan* (1895) who lashes out for her against this new subclass of referees: those "'readers,' I learned, were most of them novelists themselves, who read other people's productions in their spare moments and passed judgment on them."[14] Long after she could count on an assured and lucrative way into print, her bitterness was unabated, though directed mostly now against the press that continued to dismiss her. There is, for instance, the epistlelike "To American Readers" prefixed to *Holy Orders: The Tragedy of a Quiet Life* (1908), where we are lectured about trusting the author's reputation to her work rather than to rumors about it.

"And now what else remains?" begins the coda of Corelli's best-selling first novel, *A Romance of Two Worlds* (1886). "A brief farewell to those who have perused this narrative, or a lingering parting word?"[15] It turns out to be the latter, for the valediction dilates across two fulsome paragraphs of moralistic admonition in the following vein: "Be sure, good people, be very sure that you are *right* in denying God for the sake of man" (17:308; Corelli's emphasis). Such "good people" apparently rallied round their author, for the "New Edition" of 1887 brings to unprecedented completion the dialogic gesture of Corelli's prefatory and valedictory engagements with the Victorian audience by printing selected commendatory responses of her readers as an "Appendix" of "genuine epistles"—after ten of which inserted documents her own voice strikes up again in peroration. In *Wormwood: A Drama of Paris* (1890), apostrophes like

"Dear, good, gentle, Christian friends!" (2,4:64) clot the text with the most leaden of ironies, often tending toward the clichéd imperative: "Sit in judgment on yourselves, my readers, before you venture to judge *me!*" (2,7:135; Corelli's emphasis). Later still in *Wormwood*, the public that has been made privy to the narrator's confessions is gallicized to *"mes amis"*—and then returned to the English immediacy (even within anonymity) of the singular "Mark me here, good reader, whosoever you are!" (3,1:3). By the mark of inscription (*"me* here"), the remarking known as attention is thus built into the very grammar of Victorian textual address—"whosoever" the strictly figurative "you" may be at the other end.

Reader Redress: Recrimination and Reprisal

As the competition for audience increased toward the end of the century, the "gentle reader" grew harder to locate and rely on. The jaded audience had to be won over—or even hectored into identification. An extreme form of the latter tactic appears in the Baudelairean harangue against the reader in George Moore's autobiographical *Confessions of a Young Man* (1888). "Hypocritical reader, you draw your purity garments round you. . . . Hypocritical reader, think not too hardly of me; hypocritical reader, think what you like of me, your hypocrisy will alter nothing."[16] The rest of the passage seems in fact designed to spell out the implications of Baudelaire's famous lines in his introductory poem, "Au lecteur," from *Fleurs du mal* (1857)—"Hypocrite lecteur,—mon semblable,—mon frère!"—by detailing just such a (re)semblance in a manner that anticipates both the phenomenology of reading and the satire of righteous response in Oscar Wilde's *Picture of Dorian Gray* two years after Moore's *Confessions*. For "in telling you of my vices," writes Moore to his audience in the heated escalation of his refrain, "I am only telling you of your own; hypocritical reader, in showing you my soul I am showing you your own; hypocritical reader, exquisitely hypocritical reader, you are my brother, I salute you" (12:190). Before the stringency of his naturalist phase, this moment in the French-schooled work of Moore is entirely symptomatic—and proleptic.

Erupted here into English literary tradition is one vocative measure of the decline of reader address in that wholesale modernist recoil from communalistic literary rhetoric which takes Baudelaire, and in fiction Flaubert, as early heroes. Given the philistinism and *hypocrisie* of the mass *lecteur*, it came to seem beneath literature's dignity to enter into even the pretense of dialogue with such a constituency. The insistence on literature's inherently closed form can thus also be construed as a retreat from mass contamination into art's impregnable fortress. In the last decade of its fading reign, the Victorian realist novel, long ago born into the aesthetic, dies away again into this self-protective aestheticism, into feminist naturalism or experimentalism, or into exotic romance, into Wilde, the New Woman novelists, or the male romances and neogothic fables of Stevenson, Haggard, du Maurier, Stoker, and others. With it goes that blanket confidence in the readership betokened by interpolation. Apostrophe is either muzzled or returned to the dramatized confines of fictionalized editorial paraphernalia.

"To the Hesitating Purchaser": Jockeying for Audience at the *Fin de Siècle*

At the height of Robert Louis Stevenson's popularity in the adventure genre, his text could solicit its reader with a certain aplomb, but only in a comic vein, never when such distractions would dispel the charge of exotic excitement. His prefatory verses to *Treasure Island* (1883), for instance, are addressed with confident good grace to "To the Hesitating Purchaser." Such a potential buyer stands assured—in a humble candor that operates also as a boast—that there is nothing to expect from this new novel which has not delighted readers of past classics in the adventure genre. Stevenson is of course participating in the revival of the "male romance" for boys which is not only part of the period's reaction against the high "feminine" solemnities of George Eliot but a function as well of the new emphasis on specialized genres and their mass-marketing.[17]

In the generic crossfire at the end of the century, and beyond such open appeals to the purchaser as in Stevenson, the revival of both gothic romance and exotic adventure involves various tactical uses of address in the actual conduct of the narrative, often to distance and so legitimate a putatively authentic document, elsewhere to strip away all sense of textual mediation in the worked urgency of response. The latter tendency is most apparent, for instance, in Rudyard Kipling, the former in Stevenson and H. Rider Haggard. When Kipling's narrator in *Kim* (1901) veers climactically into an imperative grammar of immediate attention—"Behold him . . . ascending Shamlegh slope, a just man made perfect"[18]—he is drawing on the tradition of second-person address manipulated for dramatic rather than conversational illusion. Via the flaunting of a textual paradox in *Kim*, the reader is commanded, and so permitted, to behold such actions in the (supposed) stead of the very record that enjoins their manifestation, for "there is none to enter them in a book" (15:268). This histrionic presencing of the scene, by recruiting the immediacy of second-person address, is linked not just to the general devices of children's fiction ("See him climb"). It also shares, in particular, a rhetorical texture with the spontaneous vocatives—"O Best Beloved"—of Kipling to his children in the *Just So Stories* in particular: a kind of filial distillation of Victorian popular fiction's general effort at an intimacy of tone, whether epistolary or dramatic in derivation.

If the immediacy of *Kim*, in its paradoxically unbooked drama, styles itself as more than literary, quite often the adventure genre advertises itself, in an equally disingenuous way, as something less than literary, requiring a different—more editorial—stance toward its readers. Narrated by Allan Quatermain, Haggard's *King Solomon's Mines* (1885) opens with just such an authorial disclaimer: "I wonder why I am going to write this book; it is not in my line. I am not a literary man."[19] Quatermain's introduction closes as follows: "But if you whose eyes may perchance one day fall upon my written thoughts have got so far as this, I ask you to persevere" (14). The effect of this apostrophic circumlocution is of course to privilege the contingent destination of the manuscript, rather than the certainty of print circulation. A similar effect is produced by the editorial framework of Haggard's *She* (1887), where the narrative is precipitated by the receipt of a letter delivered to an unnamed "editor" (clearly Haggard himself, author of a previous adventure novel that has called him to the letter writer's attention). This letter from L. Horace Holly contains an astonishing manuscript in his hand. "Of the history itself the reader must judge," we hear in the introduction, since the editor (Haggard) has "made up my mind to refrain from comments."[20] Passing the buck by passing on the book, deferring both the epistemological and hermeneutic burden by giving over the text to the reader's unglossed perusal, Haggard chooses a far less intrusive framing gambit than many preceding novels of the period. At the same time, the permeation of main narrative by an editorial rhetoric of address is encouraged by this laissez-faire stance, with Holly himself as narrator taking no more responsibility for interpretation than the editor: "The reader must form his own opinion on this as on many other matters" (28:209). Furthermore, the transmission of the manuscript—unlike Walton's to Mrs. Saville (or in *Wuthering Heights*, for instance, Lockwood's to who knows whom)—is potentially (and explicitly) a financial matter involved in the Victorian publishing industry: "P.S.—Of course, if any profit results from the sale of the writing, should you care to undertake its publication, you can do what you like with it" (Introduction: 5).

Beyond editorial validation as a low-level intrusion on the narrative, Haggard tends to wield the apostrophic function only when that function can itself be exoticized, rendered in fact *supernatural*. Take *Beatrice* (1894), where an odd warp in the contours of an invocatory imperative opens the text to its postmortem narratees. "Say—what are we?"[21] the narrator seems to be asking his readers. But the locus of reception suddenly shifts across an implausible imperative grammar: "Tell us, you who have outworn the common tragedy and passed the narrow way, what lies beyond its gate? You are dumb, or we cannot hear you speak" (Envoi: 319). With the textual condition projected onto the metaphysical, no one can ultimately answer back to a such a narrative—certainly not that audience (of ghostly readers? supernal auditors?) which the author would hope to convert to agents of narrative revelation.

Even in the deferral of arrived revelation, this is merely business as usual, albeit in a unique exaggeration. Moreover, this baroque closure suggests in reverse a more normative logic not just of fictional characterization but of fictional address as well. Pressing past the narrated lives of its invented agents, the nineteenth-century novel frequently, and not always implicitly, turns toward the reading audience—in an expanded epitaphic mode—to complete the psychological or spiritual interpretation of already concluded event. That this one narrator in *Beatrice* should get no answer from auditors no longer in the Victorian world is the exception that proves the rule of the genre's familiar complementation by response. Furthermore, a device that might have seemed innocent enough, "pure" rhetoric, in *Pelham*, where Bulwer's narrator addresses his dead brother in the coda, tends now, after seven intervening decades of Victorian fictional experiment, to reveal the eerie overtones of reader emplacement within such narrative ventures: the summoned presence within manufactured absence which constitutes recruited attention. This aberrant logic will loom larger in subsequent chapters, as its inherent spookiness—there is no better word for it— is further dwelled upon by the novels of Dickens, Charlotte Brontë, Meredith, Eliot, Wilde, Stevenson, and others. The mortal economies of narrative and transmission which trouble these works can instead be both tossed off and shaken off in the more transparent rhetoric of many best-sellers.

In short, once more: "I am not a literary man." This is one pole of late Victorian appeal, exploited by the adventure novelists who hawk their tales as less pretentious (as well as, despite appearances, more authentic) than elaborate literary productions. At the other pole—with art-for-art's-sake aestheticism in between, excluding address for its own programmatic reasons—we find, for instance, the New Woman writers, whose reformist animus is advanced as *more* rather than less portentous than familiar literature, high or low. At either pole, the timeworn practice of direct address seems too routine for the break being

made, in one direction or the other, from the dialogic networks of psychological realism and its communitarian implications. Reader apostrophe suits neither the tall tale that is credible only if free of all rhetorical posturing nor the
psychosocial exemplum too rigorous for the ruses of persuasion.

Odd Women Out

Nor does apostrophe consort well with formal experimentation. To begin
with, soliciting an audience by direct interpolation has a way of carrying the
weight of the given, the generic: Dear reader—of this and *other stories like it.*
This impulse does not readily attach itself to the defiantly new, as both late-
century decadence and subsequent high modernism are driven to insist by the
calculated exclusion of such rhetoric. Without implying that for a true literary
avant-garde there can be no readers in the traditional sense at all, no familiar
access to the sealed arena of verbal experiment, there is, however, another motive for the suspension of apostrophe well this side of such hermetic aestheticism. On the eve of this century, even best-selling New Woman novelists tend
to leave the vocative ploy behind along with the otherwise ingratiated readers
of traditional nineteenth-century fiction. Confident (or confidential) familiarity of address seems little in keeping with the muted reformist agenda of such
writers as Sarah Grand, Grant Allen, Emma Frances Brooke, Mona Caird, Olive
Schreiner, or the more renowned male authors in this line, Hardy and especially Gissing in *The Odd Women* (1893). Theirs is a social corrective managed
more by case study than by apostrophic harangue—and sometimes thrown
over altogether for a more expressive experimentation, in which formal deviance matches social defiance.[22] In neither case would a certain coziness of address catch the right tone. For all the occasional simulated heat of its rhetorical urgency, reader address is usually *complacent* in a kind of root sense: at ease
with. If addressed at all in the New Woman novel (as we will see shortly in Olive
Schreiner), the reader is likely, instead, to be put very much on the textual spot.
There is a further aspect to the issue as well, one recommending against the
cultural associations of interpolated response. New Woman fiction often involves not the companionable reading of a story but the resistant, if tacit,
rereading of inherited stories en masse, a rereading through the now corrective lenses of an adjusted feminist vision. This tendency is in fact localized by
an interknit series of reading scenes in Sarah Grand's *The Heavenly Twins* (1893),
scenes from which we are to extrapolate our own revisionist reading of the
male canon from the heroine's incremental efforts to come to terms over the
years with *The Vicar of Wakefield.*[23]

For a number of reasons, then, the recourse to apostrophe wanes in the New Woman novel—or narrows to a more pointed effect. Then, too, literary history can help enlarge the context in which to view the feminist valences of this tapering off. Looking back over the curious shadow cast by such late Victorian rhetorical stringency in the general suspension of address, back across the long march of nineteenth-century sentimental realism, one comes to suspect a tacit—and not necessarily straightforward—gender thematics of apostrophizing rhetoric at least from midcentury. It has been argued elsewhere about such earlier writers as Gaskell and Eliot that there was something unique to the (supposedly long-suppressed) female narrative voice in its liberated gravitation toward the open forum of popular narrative, something that allowed direct appeal to audiences in these writers (through apostrophe or otherwise) to assert what was before a predominantly masculine stance of public authority through oratory.[24] It seems just as likely, however, that well after the earlier Victorian female novelists had made their mark (drawing no less than Trollope or Thackeray, for instance, and far more than Dickens, on the device of reader invocation), the New Woman writers, on reflection, might have sensed something more conventionally *feminizing* (as in Gaskell; or in Corelli, even petulant) in the paraepistolary intimacies of standard Victorian address—either this, or, at other points, the too-much-protesting voice of masculinist command and pronouncement which some found too strident in George Eliot and few in any case strove to assume.[25] Part of the "newness" of these New Woman writers would thus be to forestall either stereotypical tendency. Indeed, contrasting her own work with that of Eliot's, Schreiner writes as if she might have had the very habit of audience apostrophe in mind: "Her great desire was to teach, mine to express myself, for myself and to myself alone."[26] The occasional detours from this desire into direct address in Schreiner's most important novel, as we are soon to see, are tied to a thematic rather than just a rhetoric of reading as inculcation.

Another factor in any deployment of the interpolated reader: Besides its frequent recourse to generic expectation, as well as to potential gender tonalities, the solicitation of an audience (through either apostrophe or third-person allusion) inevitably drags in the issue of textual mediation, and with it the possible avowal of sheer fictionality in the representation of events. One's sense of a loose coalition, therefore, between the sociological exposés of the New Woman fiction and those of naturalism would militate against anything resembling the apostrophized fiction reader. Here extremes meet, since the impulse toward reportorial credence lent to male adventure tales by frameworks of editorial rhetoric also works to forbid or minimize direct address within the plot's diaristic logging of extraordinary events. Like *She* or *Dr. Jekyll and Mr. Hyde*, the stories of the New Woman also tend to be told straight, documented with a more or less cool omniscience or shorn of overt rhetoric by dramatic occasion, as, for instance, in the exploration of feminine subjectivity in dream states or in openly pedagogic dialogue.

The most powerful and enduring of the New Woman novels by a female author, Schreiner's *The Story of an African Farm*, may serve to sum up much of what we have seen in this chapter both about the byways of direct address and about the independent trope of reading the world: in other words, about the rhetorical logistics of interpolation as well as about the overdetermined cultural logic of extrapolation. For the most part in Schreiner's novel, the pressing energies of direct address are funneled through the rhetorical immediacy of dialogue, especially in the heroine's central feminist pronouncement. "Do you think," she asks rhetorically, "if Napoleon had been born a woman that he would have been contented to give small tea-parties and talk small scandal?" (2,4:192). The rapt auditor in this case, and your stand-in, is the meditative farmhand Waldo, who shortly gives voice to a broader audience reaction: "When you speak I believe all you say; other people would listen to you also" (2,4:195). Indeed, to just the extent that the novel's main chance for reformist discourse is channeled through the heroine in this one famous chapter, we are not entirely surprised to find an occasional incursion of second-person address punctuating the surrounding narrative or descriptive surface apart from dialogue— though address of this sort is not likely to come trailing epithets of endearment. The first such moment is exemplary, since it involves the enjoined reading of a human condition figured in a dead metaphor associated as much with writing as with sheer notice: "for, *mark you*, the old dream little how their words and lives are texts and studies to the generation that shall succeed them" (1,4:58; emphasis added). Address from narrator to reader violates no norm of dramatic presence if even the represented experiences within plot are taken to be textualized and decipherable, from the point of lived inscription on into the future; taken, that is, to be fragments, once again, from "the big world's book" (2,4:198).

Although the late-century fortunes of direct address can be seen most clearly in the generic polarity between male adventure yarns and New Woman narratives—the former often packaged by editorial voucher as found documents, the latter entering directly into circulation with neither assured nor courted audience—there is nonetheless a curious amalgam of the two in a novella by a past master of the adventure mode. As we prepare to watch the last bastions of addressed narrative give way before the juggernaut of modernist textual *signification*, we may usefully linger, by way of summation, over a parable of Victorian reading energies and their perverse gendering developed from within one of H. Rider Haggard's own exotic sea adventures. First, though, a comment is in order on the altered perspective briefly demanded by this discussion. While shifting focus, with Haggard's text, from the reader address that characterizes so many of the previous best-sellers to a scene (or extended scenario) of reading—an episode of textual encounter from which our own is to be extrapolated—it is the whole point of this study that we have not thereby departed very far from the apostrophic motive. The two gestures of inclusion, interpolation and extrapolation, are complementary.

We move from one to the other, now, in part to speculate about the disappearance of the former into the latter in a certain strain of late Victorian writing concerned with the entrance of the woman into the marketplace of ideas. Haggard's *Mr. Meeson's Will* (1888) has cast his heroine as a novelist—almost as a false lead—in order to explore, through a set of bizarre circumstances, not her own writing (or reading) habits so much as the way in which the female figure in fiction is often reduced to the inscribed body of simulated (because still only textual) spectation, material exhibit for the deciphering masculine voyeur. Allegorizing this in a lightly satiric key, Haggard may be thought to prepare the way for those alternative representations of feminine desire itself, in confrontation with patriarchal culture, which characterize the New Woman novels of the next decade. If so, then the evolving forms of fictional rhetoric may help chart the transition. Such issues raise themselves at just this turn in my argument about apostrophized response in the nineteenth-century bestseller, that is, because the metanarrative scenes in question sketch forth the enthralled textual attention that direct address might otherwise have been intruded to solicit or confirm.

"It May Strike the Reader as Very Strange": Haggard's Erotics of Inscription

Augusta Smithers, heroine of *Mr. Meeson's Will*, is a frustrated best-selling author of a first novel, financially cheated by her contractual obligations to the huge Birmingham firm of Meeson's. After she happens to become engaged to the proprietor's son, even more improbable developments lead her to be pitched overboard with the father in the subsequent shipwreck of a passenger liner. Washed to a forlorn shore with him and a few other survivors, Augusta arrives at the moral crux of the novel: whether to sacrifice herself, out of love for the son, to allow the dying and now repentant father to write a last will that would reverse his recent disinheriting of the young man. The trouble is that, in order to facilitate such a will, Augusta the writer must at once become written. For in the absence of all normal writing materials, the amended will can only be inscribed on her neck and shoulders by a sailor, one Bill Jones, primed to undertake the tattooing assignment. If she had wanted, for instance, "a fancy pictur [*sic*] of your young man, I might manage it on your arm," but for a "doc-cyment" of the sort in question "one wants space."[27] Instead of indulging herself with an erotic fetish, then, she must in her own person become a legal one, the carrier rather than the object of paternal lenience.

As plot will have it, Augusta stalwartly submits to the painful inscription (fig. 4).

Figure 4. Illustration from *Mr. Meeson's Will*

She then delivers the mark of patriarchal intention into a court of law, where the very admissibility of her text, of herself as text—sight unseen—is ponder-ously debated, only to have its words read into evidence at last (fig. 5) in an eroticized spectacle of disclosure which saves the day and helps unite her with her lover.

Figure 5. Illustration from *Mr. Meeson's Will*

This union is witnessed by his embrace of the heroine's body, marked as it is by the material index, the wounded flesh, of familial sanction and continuity. If woman in the standard Victorian marriage plot may at any point operate merely as signifier of patriarchal intentionality, sign and prize of the hero's coming into his majority, then the instance of fiancée as corporeal text of the father-in-law's will is a farcical reduction of that signifying function. At this point Haggard's marriage plot needs a turn for the better. In the closing chapter we see Augusta's husband writing "cancelled" across the document that had impoverished her, the contract for her best-seller, *Jemima's Vow*—naming, as the title does, the domestic equivalent of legalistic obligations. With these contractual vows abrogated, the woman is released from their entailments, but only once she has become a "doccyment" in her own right: virtual legal tender in the adjudications of the power structure. In a nightmare inversion of female expressivity, the heroine, writing to be read, achieves the deserved reward of her popular success only after being read in her own person.

And not just by the staring court. For, in her own readable figure, Augusta

Smithers becomes the novel's title figure. Synecdochically, she stands before us as *Mr. Meeson's Will* incarnate: eponymous heroine of the illustrated novel that the Victorian reader here sees—and I choose the verb advisedly—to completion. She is thus a fairly precise illustration, as the illustrations of her go to show, of that chiastic (and, in our terms, extrapolative) logic referred to at several points, with different examples, by Peter Brooks in *Body Work*: a "semiotization of the body" matched by the "somatization of story."[28] Through it all, the juridical rhetoric in this climactic courtroom scene of actionable decipherment cagily doubles for the interpretive signals of a more familiar novelistic rhetoric. The judge, that is, speaking with the dubiousness of a critical reader, nonetheless succumbs to credulity with the ultimate cliché of documentary verification in those exotic late Victorian thrillers of which Haggard is to become the best-selling master: "The whole tale is undoubtedly of a wild and romantic order, and once again illustrates the saying that 'truth is stranger than fiction'" (21:262). Thus concludes the story's tacit insight into the seductions of "romantic" reading, its waver between titillation and authentication, the very tease of credence in the whole tradition of exotic popular narrative. Moreover, that Augusta the best-selling novelist has, in effect, given over her body for money (albeit money promised to another rather than to herself)—and done so through the intermediation of text—is no small part of this story's uneasy comment on the risk of debasement lurking in its popular venue.

Toward its inclusive conscription of the reading imagination, Haggard's parable of gendered inscription is unusually exhaustive: at once biological, erotic, generic, and textual. The woman's body is always in one sense the conduit for patriarchal succession. So much, first, for woman as wife: potential gestational vessel awaiting the biological imprint of the male will. Second, erotically, the woman's body is reinscribed into that male line of succession as object of desire and exchange. Third, generically, the fetishized female form is the very figure for the spectacle either of family melodrama or of exotic romance, what Barthes sees as the striptease of narrative disclosure itself. Finally, at the fourth—the textual (or metatextual)—level, there is a further, passing, and transitional detail that spells out the fullest suggestion of the story, a detail all the more deeply entrenched for its being strategically forgotten at the story's climax.

In the decisive courtroom scene, that is, nothing is mentioned about an intermediate bit of prudent jurisprudence by which the legality of the woman as document can be ratified. This earlier scene transpires in the chapter called "How Augusta Is Filed," involving the brainstorm by which the court registrar hits on "something better than a certified copy of the will," namely "a photographic copy" (17:213). Confident that "the dark lines of cuttle ink upon Augusta's neck would . . . come out perfectly," the photographer "took two or three shots at her back and then departed, saying that he would bring a life-size reproduction to be filed in the Registry in a couple of days" (17:215–16). The printer's ink of the much reduced novelistic illustrations is of course all we actually see, except as we visualize the life-size Augusta in court, the novelist as text, embodying her own deposition. In short, between the authoress-as-readable at the start of the novel and the female-body-as-legible in the climactic trial by evidentiary ordeal, what has intervened is the photographic equivalent of literary textuality: the character-as-document, a textual figuration to be archived and read upon demand. The magnifying glass in the judge's hands is a further tease. Reaching for one of our own, in order to make out the writing that was so clear in the earlier plate, we find what we might have suspected: that the fuller text is mere undecipherable hatching (fig. 6). All that is legibly incised there is the woman's body itself. It is what we are all there, and all we are there, to read.

In this extravagant way, the writing woman as popular novelist finds herself denuded and reduced to the mere figure of public reading. Such reading is localized as an encounter with the present text itself at only two late moments

Figure 6. Detail of illustration from *Mr. Meeson's Will*

in the novella, moments of ironic conscription. After the untoward events leading up to the courtroom scene, the subsequent and inevitable marriage of the couple is couched in the rhetoric of mock astonishment: "And now, *it may strike the reader* as very strange, but, as a matter of fact," within ten days of the trial, "there was a small-and-early gathering at St. George's, Hanover Square" (22:269; emphasis added). At the metanarrative level, then, the faked surprise of this interpolative gesture points the way after all: toward the extrapolative force of the narrative as a parable of its own consumption. Capping the story's demotion of autonomous authorship (woman novelist) to the mere allure of novelistic effect is the last scene of the narrative, where we encounter for the first time the heroine with pen in hand. She is working away, but not on a new novel of her own. She is busy instead with a plan to divest some of her husband's inherited wealth in order to found "an institution for broken-down authors" (23:285). Augusta has thus become a missionary Odd Woman straight out of Gissing, but with her feminine defiance directed now at the general malaise of Grub Street, her own narrative voice silenced for the time being in selfless authorial philanthropy. With his protagonist finished off by such heroized diminution, Haggard performs one last turn of reader-response irony designed to break through the frame of fiction into the precincts of current event. This is the story's second instance of conscripted response through a third-person interpolation. Haggard has removed his heroine, on whose shoulders much has already rested, from her marital bed to the "writing-table to work out that scheme on paper which, *as the public is aware*, is about to prove such a boon to the world of scribblers" (23:286; emphasis added). Narrative is thus dissolved completely, if only momentarily, into a late Victorian public discourse of authorial hardship and economic inequity—with the corrective to such cultural ills already putatively in place.

Plot hereby outstrips itself to eventuate in the ameliorative social scene of its own reparation. The effect is compensatory, but it does not erase what—and how—we have read. For *Mr. Meeson's Will*, critique of the Victorian publishing industry as corporate octopus, is also an unblinking (if cockeyed) acknowledgment of the eroticized thirsts that industry seeks by turns to inflame and to slake. If there is any doubt that the woman's body is typically summoned in nineteenth-century popular fiction to receive the inscription of male desire, you have only to wait for the next chapter on a prototypical Victorian heroine half a century before Augusta: Dickens' Little Nell.

Finally, there may also appear in Haggard's treatment the tipped hand, or jabbed elbow, of a specifically literary-historical agenda dearer yet to Haggard's heart, or should we say closer to the bone: the bone he picks with the feminizing reign of that literary eminence known disparagingly as Queen George (Eliot, that is). The generic oddity of Haggard's whole plot, setting high seas adventure against courtroom deliberation, exotic melodrama against debunked familial litigation, sets off these ill-sorted components in a way that begins to look like a wholesale setup—or, speaking coolly, a metalepsis: a shift from story to authorial operation. After having lashed us to the mast of attention with his shipwreck saga, that is, the ranking purveyor in his day of male bravura and masculinist bravado seems almost to bait the reader: So you still want to *read a woman*, do you? Well, stay tuned.

Toward the Superannuation of the Vocative

Despite the late Victorian tendency toward rhetorical—and specifically apostrophic—restraint which characterizes the New Woman narrative, among other emergent genres, nevertheless old habits fade slowly. A deliberate rhetorical throwback, from the pen of none other than George Moore, can clarify the sea change undergone by the whole tradition of interpolated response. Long after having blasted the "hypocritical reader" in *Confessions of a Young Man*, Moore is willing to forgive the sin and retain the rhetorical trope. His blithely anachronistic recourse to a genially interpolated readership should help close out the lineage of address whose wider implications, for popular fiction and beyond, we will then attempt to set in perspective. Two years after his controversial 1916 novelization of the gospels, *The Brook Kerith*, Moore saw to the private printing, in an edition of twelve hundred and fifty copies, of *A Story-Teller's Holiday*. It opens with a colorful dream sequence from which the narrator wakens in a virtually pre-Victorian, almost Dantesque form of vocative punctuation: "The dreaming traveller is none other, O reader, than thy friend George Moore, come to entertain thee once more."[29] The festive trope jostles oddly with the book's preface, couched as the lamented "Leave-Taking" of a "great many readers" (2)—those, presumably, who will perforce have no access to this private edition.

In that preface Moore "can hear a reader saying to himself" that "our author has done well to retire into a literary arcanum" (2), for, as another member of this reading chorus adds, "he wished to write for men and women of letters, and this class is not recognized by the libraries as readers of books" ("A Leave-Taking": 1). As in Thackeray, such interpolation is only a parody of the phenomenological status quo. Writers always put words into our mouths; it is all we have there as we read them. And even such direct address is no more Victorian in character than the accompanying sense that even the specialized and dwindling, if still fit, audience borrows its communal form from the cultural exchange mechanisms of bourgeois domesticity: "I have faith in the good sense of all my readers, for they are not a heterogeneous crowd, but a family, and every one of the family knows how steadfast the persecution of my writings has been" (1). Spoken like a patriarch. In Moore's confrontation with the dawn of a modernism for which his naturalistic swerve from high Victorian realism helped clear the way, his once "hypocritical readers" are not only his *frères* but his dependents. As children of the vanishing age, they constitute that small sector of the Victorian collective on which he must continue to count for response.

E. M. Forster's illustrative Edwardian career had begun as Moore's was winding down, with Forster entering the fictional scene as a more ironic tactician of address. Even within its author's already transitional status as an early-twentieth-century novelist, *Howards End* (1910) is uniquely transitional: a palinode for lingering Victorian values on the way to the more technically austere modernism of his long-delayed next novel, *A Passage to India* (1924). In the gradually thinning instances of reader mention and address across the course of *Howards End*, the narrative may be read to bleed apostrophe from the Forsterian rhetorical system. It does so in service to a psychology of reticence working in ironic conjunction with omniscient disclosure.

Margaret Schlegel, heroine of the spirit, knows the things that go unsaid, whereas Forster the narrative artist must find ways to communicate them to the reader. This tension becomes productive, thematic. In the novel's first chapter of reflective commentary after the epistolary opening, you the practical reader of more traditional narrative are caught off guard by seeming to be put on it: "To Margaret—I hope that it will not set the reader against her—the station of King's Cross had always suggested Infinity" (2:12). After an unfolding brief disquisition on the metaphysics of railway termini, there follows a more direct second person: "If you think this ridiculous, remember that it is not Margaret who is telling you about it" (12:13). Holding to these filmy apprehensions only at a certain level of spiritual intuition, Margaret would never desecrate such perceptions by bringing them to words. Though this is meant to let Forster's heroine off the hook, you, his reader, are still designated as the sort who would be unduly contemptuous if she did try to formulate these nebulous emotions. In this way, the novel's first and last mention of "the reader" (isolated in the traditional singular) has given way across this very paragraph to the collective and more aggressive pegging of a rigidly empirical "you" that we might best understand as derived from Thackeray's omnivorous satire via Gissing's scouring realism. This is the "you" that recurs at intervals for the first half of *Howards End*, until such a defensive communal audience, class-bound in its impercipience, has been educed away from its prejudices for the more free-ranging speculative effects of the novel's second half.[30]

Faced with the pivotal incident of Leonard Bast's experimental dawn walk, for instance, and with the enthusiasm over it expressed by both Schlegel sisters, you are cast, more blatantly than ever before, into the complacent role of colonialist privilege: "You may laugh at him who have slept nights out on the veldt, with your rifle beside you and all the atmosphere of adventure pat" (14:124). This is the ironic nadir of your occluded participation in Forster's restorative romance of the real. Interpolation has done its work by tagging, aggravating, and thus exorcising a whole spectrum of erroneous reaction. It has done so through a network of goading address in the first half of the novel which has contributed to the dismissal (both senses) of the late Victorian popular audience: an audience jaded alternately by realism and exotic adventure—and hence unequipped for Forsterian symbolic fable. What we have briefly reviewed, then, is the manner in which both mentioned "reader" and apostrophized "you" finally collude, from within this mandarin text, in the expurgation of the demotic by the hieratic.

Gentling the Reader Out

It should be possible at this resting spot in our evidence (and at this literary-historical point of no return) to gather from such a litany of solicited reader attention—a rhetorical subcode running from Ainsworth to Haggard, Bulwer-Lytton to Corelli, Scott to Moore—certain patterns of development which these examples have been collected to detect, especially in light of the options for apostrophe and address willed to the Victorian novel from the previous century of fictional rhetoric. To review briefly this prehistory: The widely varying degrees of "dearness" attached to the addressed reader in the eighteenth century are sometimes intimate (the personal letter as intertext), sometimes studiously disinterested (the editorial preface as prototype), sometimes importunate and admonitory (epitaph and pulpit rhetoric both). And all such address may ultimately be tracked even further back, through the tradition of epic or allegorical address, to literature's founding invocations to the Muse, fountainhead of all representational motive. Much later, in the restlessly other-directed experiments of nineteenth-century fiction, we encounter the simultaneously domesticated and externalized version of such inward inspiration in the hypostatized populace of response. The demotic muse of destination is, in Dickens' phrase, "many-headed" indeed. Paradoxically enough—or at least striving for the dignity of paradox in the face of a mere sleight of hand—the novel in its second century tends to subpoena the reader's attention as founding authority, summoning inspiration from its own eventuality as read text. In this way does the dethroned muse of nineteenth-century prose fiction become the continuous musing response of a new audience often addressed one on one by the text.

Jane Austen and Mary Shelley have served us as transitional figures in complementary ways, making their own separate stands against that inscribed reduction of the reader to mere narrative signpost which they might otherwise have borrowed straight from the eighteenth-century novelists who went before. Austen's comedy at times broadened (in every sense) to debunk even this outer edge of her narratives, this orientation toward their audience. Shelley formally overruled all quasi-phatic contact by displacing it onto framing structures, gothic and apocalyptic by turns. But Austen and even the Shelley of *The Last Man* were already behind us when this chapter moved out from the more immediately transitional figure of Scott into the full panoply of address in the Victorian best-seller.

What we might well have anticipated in scanning a representative swath of evidence—that the device of reader apostrophe and its approximations would be widespread but unassuming, smoothly subordinate for the most part to the momentum of plot—turns out to be the case. Narrative is propelled even as interrupted in this way (in "minor" as well as canonical fiction of the period), interrupted in the manner of scattered punctuation. There is nothing approaching a full dismantling of mimesis in the name of semiosis and its transmissive mechanisms. Notably, too, what emerges from a comparison of the vocative or declarative case of audience recognition in what we might call blockbuster (as against cornerstone) texts of the Victorian era is that there is no literary priority, either in terms of originality or chronology, in the deployment of such reader reference and address. This is to some extent, of course, another way of remarking that the Victorian period enjoyed less of a distinction, at least for a long while, between mandarin and popular levels of textual endeavor. Rifts of course did appear—and widen. But even as the century progresses, novels, elite and otherwise, seem to borrow from each other in equal measure as regards the considerable variations—or motivated suppressions—of such address.

What is finally hardest to retrieve for the historical imagination, then, especially from the contemporary vantage of a modernist fiction in widespread eclipse by visual and auditory media alike, is what the vocative filiations between narrative practices at every level of literary aspiration make indisputable about the Victorian period: a shared sense of a *public*, whether apostrophized or not, at the receiving end of textual discourse. This seems very far indeed from the concerted sealing off of narrative representation as modernist textuality. Moreover, what the discourse circuits of these Victorian texts bespeak as well as further articulate is a shared sense of their public in the *representative* sense (predominantly "the reader" rather than "readers"), each conscripted reading agent a stand-in for the mass. Victorian literary narratives high and low are directed, in short, to a collective of individuated response.

One further exemplary moment from the middle years of nineteenth-century rhetorical practice should assist in distilling the tendencies from which it only pretends to distance itself. When "the Author of this Romance last appeared before the Public," writes Hawthorne in the preface to his final novel, *The Marble Faun* (1860), he had the habit, he confesses, of addressing the unspecified (but very particularly imagined) reader to whom any author "implicitly makes his appeal."[31] In looking back on this inclination as if it had been by now wholly subdued, he reaches even farther back to recall the origin of such devices in the prefatory habits of a bygone epoch: "The antique fashion of Prefaces recognized this genial personage as the 'Kind Reader,' the 'Gentle Reader,' the 'Beloved,' the 'Indulgent,' or, at coldest, the 'Honoured Reader'" (853). Hawthorne speaks next in the idiom of republican federation, suggesting in such personifications of the mass audience a *demos* convened by a more than mimetic act of "representation." Though he "never personally encountered, nor corresponded through the Post, with this Representative Essence," nonetheless such a "Gentle, Kind, Benevolent, Indulgent, and most Beloved and Honoured Reader" was, if not in so many words, once his—his, he adds metaphorically, "in spite of the infinite chances against a letter's reaching its destination, without a definite address" (853). Yet "address" there was in the other sense, however indefinite, as well as "appeal" in more ways than one. It is all of this which Hawthorne now makes a gesture of renouncing, no longer presuming upon "the existence of that friend of friends, that unseen brother of the soul" (854) who was once personified as an ideal reader—the externalized alter ego incident to so much literary apostrophe. Surrendering both epistolary and invocatory prototypes, as well as the fraternal intersubjectivity and transferential projection on which they lean, Hawthorne will be more matter of fact this time out, more formal. "I stand upon ceremony," he explains, his remarks "here offered to the Public" without any intimate characterization of such an audience. For all this disinterested stance, however, an old pattern soon renews itself. The very first sentence of the novel proper recovers the mentioned readership familiar from Hawthorne's fiction of the early fifties, introducing four characters "in whose fortunes we should be glad to interest the reader" (857).

This turn is as minimal as it is difficult to dismiss. All interest promised by fiction is in the self-interest of the author, even when that authorial desire remains sequestered behind the editorial plural; all reader mention or apostrophe in nineteenth-century narrative splits this conditioning fact into a rhetoric of solicitation over against an imputed response in kind. Specific rhetorical evidence for this goes in all directions at once. Grammatically, it crosses person, gender, and even at times number in a virtually indiscriminate mix. Socially, it crosses boundaries of gender and class, youth and age, in its allusion to a shifting conglomerate of response. Textually, it touches here and there upon self-references to the narrative's own structure. Metaphysically, it may even (in Bulwer-Lytton or Haggard) cross from life to death in the ambition of its reach. Lacing loosely together the "yous" and "gentle readers" and imperative predicates ("Let the British reader") in a welter of disparate contexts, only a single common thread can be detected. Not one of the passages I have found (or quoted) could have turned up in Conrad, Lawrence, or (except by parody) Joyce or the Woolf of *Orlando*, in American writers of this same early-twentieth-century period, or in any other typical high-modernist narrative that comes to mind. At the same time, few of these passages would seem, in isolation, decidedly out of place in Fielding or Sterne. They represent a continuum long in store for a break. Yet within that continuum, few demarcations hold firm. Each "the" or "our" or "gentle" or "dear" reader is, in an important sense, the same as every other, however laden with epithets or specified by context. Each mentioned or addressed reader is simply that obtruded *fact* of reading in which Victorian fiction can afford to bask—if only because it can confidently assert (and so reactivate) such reading from page to page.

But having said this, I must return to an earlier point as well, one upon which the second chapter has already begun to lay emphasis: namely, that the individual reader so addressed, from paragraph to paragraph or book to book, is by no means stabilized (in the way criticism, mostly silently, assumes) by such local address. The fundamental indeterminacy of second-person grammar itself holds the key. You are there for the asking, singular or plural. But such conscription inducts each and every one of you into a discursive system within which no one of you is ever more than made room for, never really set in place. When decoded rather than mystified, in short, Victorian apostrophe performs its own protomodernist critique in and upon itself, decentering the social (become literary) subject it purports to inscribe or address. The discrepancies of address thus abet this decentering every bit as much as does the avoidance of all apostrophe in the structured evacuations of response one finds in a novel of vicarious displacement like *Frankenstein*.

In regard to the slackening of such address at the end of the century, there are a pair of overriding causes in the mainstream material we have examined. The explanations seem contradictory only at first blush: the return of romance on one side (including aestheticism's romance of art as well as the gothic revival), and on the other the displacement of the realist aesthetic by the putative reality of naturalism, as in the halfway house of certain New Woman novels. These new departures move in opposite directions from the deserted center of literary realism, with its heavy dependence on the formal structure of marriage comedy—the one, for instance, into the throes of macabre fantasy, the other into an active grappling with turbulent social concerns. Yet what Haggard does by way of framing his exotic adventures, or Stoker and Stevenson their horror stories, in the evidentiary footwork of first-person documents (reminiscent of Mary Shelley) is no more obvious a rejection of the commanding authorial apostrophe of certain mastertexts and best-sellers alike than is the withdrawal, in many of the New Woman plots, from the complacent domestic ingratiation of address to an open-eyed sociopolitical diagnosis. It is the latter that often drives out the exemplary *confidence* (both taken for granted and bestowed) of novelistic rhetoric, not only the assurance of the narrative but its reassuring asides to the reader. These manifestations of fictional control are replaced either by the documentary directness of narrativized reportage or by what one might call the new interior naturalism of female subjectivity.

What, then, have we seen in sum? Beyond the common denominators of recurrent formulas, there are at least three suggestive tendencies in the matter of audience acknowledgment which our surveyed examples of reader inscription have brought out, in sketchy detail but sharp enough outline:

First, there is a frequent and ever increasing tendency in the Victorian bestseller—from Bulwer-Lytton through Corelli to Haggard—to arrive (or at least end up, in subsequent editions) enveloped in prefatory or other (often retroactive) framing materials, whether fictionalized or not. Such (re)packaging is sometimes testamentary in emphasis (how to vouch for the story), sometimes hermeneutic (how to take it), with a given novel often passing through further reprints accreting more of the same. In any case—and this point is fundamental to a contextual sense of Victorian fictional reception—belated prefaces and "advertisements" only serve to sustain the feeling of immediacy regularly associated with serial publication in the first place. For just this reason, such prefatory material is more or less unique to the premodernist phase of novel production. Later fictional modes tend to be more clearly divorced from the temporal moment of their reception, from that sphere of affect which is inevitably different, but not necessarily updated rhetorically, from edition to edition. The modernist novel is also more clearly cut loose, as text, from its status as narrated story. Its textual condition is one upon whose origin, intent, and subsequent fortunes there is often nothing pertinent to observe from a position outside it. For the Victorian novel, instead, to indulge in such communicative buffer zones between story and response, to mediate textuality by the prefatory discourse of its publication, is an ongoing measure of its relation to the evolving community (even generational lineage) of its readership.

Second, this multiplication of reader positions in the Victorian mainstream novel is further compounded by the more and more common allusion, often disgruntled or satiric, not only to the divergent demands of audiences prudish versus tolerant, refined versus vulgar, sophisticated versus unlettered, but to the full gamut of institutional response. This includes everything from the publishing house and its referee network through the public forum of journalistic opinion—all intermixed with the individuated affect of private domestic reading. Resulting from such internal inscription of a whole range (and prehistory) of responsive postures, whether documentary or fabricated, is therefore the fact that the readership by turns accosted and cajoled, rued and wooed, mutates as object of address across the shifting and often discrepant categories of eager leisured reader, avocational skeptic, censorious professional critic, publisher's "reader," and so forth.

Third, then, the range and potential discrepancy of address in question turns on an antithesis between art and commerce, literary communication and industrial commodification, which declares itself—on the way toward modernism—not only as a polemical thrust but as a rhetorical ambivalence in the very structures of narrative address. Following out the dichotomous path marked off by these internal oppositions between creativity and productivity—or elsewhere between ivory tower and marketplace, private library and railway bookstall—we are brought up short by the rhetorical spectacle of a popular technique moved to inscribe its own supersession.

This needs a minute more. We have already seen how far from formal stability in the positioning of a subject, if not always from authorial complacency, is the effect of discrepant address across both single Victorian novels and the genre as a whole. But even understood in the aggregate as a genre's candid attempt to call out the reader upon whom it depends, novelistic apostrophe and its related forms remain one common measure of a critical truism about the decline of the whole popular Victorian literary ethos. What criticism has come to see as the collapse of the nineteenth-century "Easy Book" into the modernist Text (I borrow here a formulation from Hugh Kenner) resulted from a crisis that had long been afoot, in ways unmentioned by Kenner, as a rhetorical tension within the former.[32] It is apparent there, just for instance, in a rhetorical allegiance now torn, now just pulled, between the merely literate audience and George Moore's "men and women of letters." Looking back, we recognize that Moore has simply rephrased a dissonance in the century's literary output as a whole. Conflicting the novel's signals to response, this is a growing tension that results not only in a vocative or declarative endearing of the reader in quite divergent ways from author to author but in the progressive outmoding of this very device.

It is thus that the diametrical opposition between high and low takes one of its most immediate tolls on the very figure that often sketches it forth. It is one thing to recognize that the tonal spectrum of reader address within the Victorian novel increasingly registers a suspicion of commercialized and unreflective reading—in anticipation of one modernist problematic. It is another thing to recognize that the entire apparatus of apostrophe—as well as the broad popular readership that could once have been lazily embraced by unspecified address—is thus thrown into question. Though helping at one stage, through the nuances and ironies of its formulations, to block out the terms of an escalating difference between Book and Text (the modified extremes, for instance, of railway novels and George Eliot's "works"), reader address is gradually but irrevocably demoted to that negative demotic pole against which modernism's closed form closes ranks. Third-person references as well as direct apostrophes are stigmatized, that is, as the overly companionable and artificially intimate gesture of a more properly impervious textual object. From its service as virtual megaphone for the popular novel's mystique of untroubled communal discourse—as well as (still within the reach of this mystique) for certain more dubious, probing, or satiric voices from its cultural heights—direct address is eventually held hostage to the evolutionary outmoding of both popular romance and domestic realism. As abused and timeworn protagonist of this story of Victorian story, then, the "dear reader" is seen to have led a decidedly checkered career—now heroized interpretive initiate, now mere factotum of rhetorical effect—on down through its final excommunication from the modernist novel as text. In the course of a single century of literary experimentation, "dear reader" has gone before our eyes from transformed and subjectivized literary patron to persona non grata, the first obvious casualty of the no longer casual read. The postepic muse has become a founding modernist scapegoat.

To appreciate more fully what was inevitably to be surrendered with the advent of this hard-won modernism, and what was thus for so long clung to as prose fiction's intrinsic hold over (and fix on) its audience—to sense, in other words, the full extrapolative agenda to which the interpolated "dear reader" was often in tow—is the work of the more extensive readings to come. For now, one further point, by catching up matters at issue in the last chapter, should help open our way forward. Though the Victorian novel's discrepant variety of address tends, on the one hand, to scatter any stable emplacement of readerly attention, still, on the other hand, even the absence of explicit address in the period is never final or fixed. A corollary observation would suggest that even the most aggressive modes of apostrophe in Victorian best-sellers may well inhabit the same rhetorical atmosphere as the structuring absences of attention exploited by Mary Shelley's gothic and apocalyptic formats. With the binarism of address versus its absence involving no absolute negation, the phenomenon might best be described as a toggle effect: "dear reader" either on or off at a given turn, but the wiring always securely in place. This is why the unmentioned reader can carry a submerged charge in its own right even in premodernist texts that actively eschew the apostrophic mode (the novels of naturalism or aetheticism, say). Let us call it the *unmentioning* of the reader—and see it as a strategic rhetorical retreat that leaves in its wake no cognitive deficit.

The protocols of assumed response are so ingrained in the Victorian literary enterprise by the time of its explosive last years that the audience exerts a certain passive pressure on the fictional text, a certain mass(ive) immanence. This is the case however much that audience is contested, attenuated, or incriminated—and even when its status is not spelled out in so many (familiar) words as "reader," "populace," "public," or "friends." It is indeed a main tenet of this study that conscribed response, if it is worth definition to begin with, cannot be narrowly confined to the moment of direct inscription. The tacit reader's hovering availability of access, constituting the virtual ether of the fictional medium, is what remains even as the routines of address grow dated or otherwise tactically unwarranted. It remains, that is, in the form of the latent psychic absentation necessary to activate a text. Whether covered over by excess denomination or not, this latency of reader investment generates by vicarious subjection a preternatural immediacy of response to be pursued across the next half dozen chapters before being investigated, in the last, as a kind of gothic phenomenon in its own right.

Chapter Seven

Telling Time
Reading Round the Dickensian *Clock*

Reading the Bible to Grandpa (n.d.), drawn from the
painting by E. W. Perry. The Bettmann Archive

𝒯o move from a sample best-seller list of the nineteenth-century fiction industry to the most popular major writer of the period requires more adjust-
ment in rhetorical orientation than one might suppose. For in Dickens, with
respect to address, less is more; and with respect to extrapolative moments,
much is often even more than it seems. Such is the saturation of his work by
the presumption—and attempted programming—of response. It should thus
be instructive to enter the Dickens canon at its first great crisis of confidence
in regard to public reception. The intent of this chapter is to think through the
sagging sales and eventual collapse of Dickens' journal, *Master Humphrey's Clock*
(1840–41), in light of the running metanarrative of readerly fascination which
constitutes its frame—a publishing failure despite its being launched with the

serialization of his hugely popular *The Old Curiosity Shop*. We need to consider this failure in relation to the elaborately implicated reading of Dickens' narrative production—and its continuous repackaging—across both that piecemeal novel and its weekly frame. For at issue in his serial venture are the conditions of publication as the conditions of textual self-publicity in Victorian fiction. This chapter thus reads a novel not in its social context but in the nearest *readable* thing to it: the rhetorically freighted apparatus of its mercantile circulation. It reads, in other words, *The Old Curiosity Shop* as it was read by its first Victorian audience, stretched out as showpiece installments in a weekly commercial as well as artistic experiment, an experiment staged as a communal but at the same time pseudodomestic scene of narrative consumption: an exclusive private reading club.

This chapter will therefore be examining the way Dickens encircles as well as embeds a novel with the coordinates of response. For the serialized *Master Humphrey's Clock* apportions its storytelling so that the public fact of fiction, of narratives both massively produced and massively consumed, is not only framed but *contained* by an artifice of parafamilial intimacy and virtually clandestine interchange. As the next chapter will then further investigate, this containment goes to the core of Dickens' conservatism. It draws boundaries having to do not only with the politics but also with the social psychology of industrialized urban existence—and with the place of reading within it. This region of reading—at once courted, counted on, and figuratively reconstructed in Dickens—is the place of continuous imaginative displacement through a projective, and ultimately self-protective, identification with otherness.

Across the entire rhetorical conglomerate of *Master Humphrey's Clock* as a serial mechanism, the Dickensian conscription of response shows its characteristic textual economy. With direct address withdrawing to the margin, the narrative's ongoing parable of reading seems raised to unusual clarity by the periodical coefficient. In the laboratory of this failed venture, we can thus watch Dickens forging the rhetorical agenda of his exemplary Victorian career. Dickens' rhetoric strives for an omniscience so unchecked and a melodrama so uninterrupted that his narrative resists breaking step for the specification of attention. Once upon a time—and you are there. Ideal Dickensian audiences don't wish to be reminded that they *read* of Paul Dombey as they are riveted to his decline. Entrancement is more complete without a rhetorical entrance permit. By contrast, Thackeray's wry designation of his audience by discrepant and irreconcilable terms—"Jones at his club," "fair young readers"—is a tactic calculated to divide and conquer. Dickens wants no contest at all, no tension in our voluntary openness to his narrative. Readers are not typically interpolated in Dickens because their special sympathy with the text is meant to be too immediately intuitive for invitation or caveat, directive or blandishment. You are not to feel yourself either lumped with or singled out from the attentive multitude. Either way, the privilege of anonymous intimacy would be lost.

In the etymological sense of "inter-polate," then, Dickens avoids polluting or adulterating the flow of event in order not to cloud the power of its transparency. At the same time, to the degree that interpolation is strategically forgone through the general suspension of reader address, to just this extent Dickens' readers, no longer referred to, are regularly led to infer their role from within an enacted scene of decipherment or interpretation. Such in Dickens is the closed system of conscripted participation. In *Master Humphrey's Clock*, the lengths to which Dickens goes in adjusting the poles of this homeostatic field— the textual economy of interpolation and extrapolation, apostrophe and parable—bring out another way of understanding the transformation of narrative rhetoric since the decline of oral and the ascendancy of print culture. As never so clearly before, the Dickensian novel, in widening its Victorian readership, gives up on the myth of an addressed *audience* precisely to consolidate a reading *public*. But his is a public whose singular response to a given story, every reader for yourself alone, comes to define for Dickens the very condition of Victorian social organization as an individuated collective.

There can be little doubt that Dickens' first novel (and first runaway publishing success), *The Posthumous Papers of the Pickwick Club*, was, as "Papers" suggests, a prolonged reading course for this Victorian populace. Though not directly interpolated by the so-called interpolated tales that punctuate Mr. Pickwick's adventures, this public encounters, along with these tales, the repeated scene of the hero's distracted or soporific reading thereof. Implicitly called upon to react both to these stories and to Pickwick's lack of response, readers are thus positioned to extrapolate from Pickwick's imperviousness to their own more capacious imaginative grasp.[1] This is the best reason for remembering that *The Posthumous Papers of the Pickwick Club* is named for itself as book, as dossier, an archive containing subsidiary manuscripts by other hands along with the edited transcripts of the Pickwick Club. Figuratively, both *Master Humphrey's Clock* and *The Old Curiosity Shop* are also named for themselves as books, as narrative localizations, as reading spaces.

Accommodated Reading

From April 1840 to November 1841, a weekly journal purporting to record the now exclusively narrative transactions of a more sedentary men's club than

Pickwick's, a reading group hosted by Master Humphrey and known as "the Clock," provides the framing occasion for the serialized appearance of both *The Old Curiosity Shop* and *Barnaby Rudge*. The *Clock* thus puts itself forward as a venue for the accommodation, in two senses, of Dickensian readers: a facilitation of their continuing interest and also its furnished setting in Master Humphrey's rooms. At the eventual collapse of the periodical after the public's lukewarm response to all but the novels themselves, Dickens narrates the death of Master Humphrey and the sealing off in perpetuity of his quarters—long-standing scene of narrative's oral exchange—according to the stipulations of his last will and testament (see figs. 7 and 8). Secured in this way is a commodious and still-furnished memorial to the eccentric but nonetheless socialized forum that lent rendered ear to the narrated reading aloud of those two Dickens novels (among other assorted tales and anecdotes).

This concluding move of Dickens' frame narrative thus inverts, normalizes, and hence mitigates the notion lurking in Shelley's *The Last Man*: that every text, having a kind of immortality, may to such an extent be foreseen to outlive its audience and, by so doing, to inscribe the annihilation of that audience. In Dickens, by contrast, narrative is a tomb we are enlivened by visiting. On the score of encoded reading, it should be stressed that the alignment of these two otherwise incommensurate literary productions, a futuristic novel and a weekly magazine, provides no merely arbitrary contrast. As a measure of the institutional entrenchment of fiction in the nineteenth century, their contrast marks the distance between the dystopian candor of Mary Shelley's romanticism and the guarded *sociability* of one of the founding efforts of the Victorian literary epoch: the ritualizing of a mass audience, periodic and routine.

Underlying this latter effort in the first of Dickens' three self-directed journals (to follow are the far more successful *Household Words*, 1850–59, and *All the Year Round*, 1859–95) is a motive that reverses an emphasis in Austen as well as in Shelley. What develops, that is, in *Master Humphrey's Clock* is an inverse ratio, rather than direct parallel, between openness and narrativity. Master Humphrey himself seems to have no qualms about the symbiotic relationship between his own social retreat and the disclosed secrecies of the London panorama he takes as his narrative object. By contrast with Austen, omniscience begins to be celebrated in Dickensian fiction not so much for its place on a continuum with social "unreserve" as for its compensatory aesthetic service within the isolated urban individualism of Victorian communal organization. To this end, Dickens contrives by the very title of *Master Humphrey's Clock* a canny rescue of the ethos of romance from within the mechanic periodicity that mere clockwork might seem to suggest. For this title is not only the quaint name of an antique machine, a trusty timepiece from whose hidden cabinet at hearthside the weekly installations of the journal are supposedly drawn forth—and around which they are read in sociable camaraderie by an intimate group of aged and crotchety romantic bachelors. It is also the name bestowed metonymically on this very club of readers at their surrogate familial fireside. The chief aesthetic appliance of Victorian domesticity, the novel as reading event, is hereby espoused—by this coterie of familyless readers—as their only form of the very domesticity that reading is otherwise meant to replenish rather than replace.

The real strain on Dickens' rhetoric of the reading event, as one might expect, comes when the publishing effort thus framed ends in failure. This was the first setback in the spectacular ascendancy of Dickens' career, for the journal as a whole never achieved anything like the popularity of the *Sketches by Boz*, *Pickwick*, or his contribution to *Bentley's Miscellany* in the form of *Oliver Twist*. This time out Dickens was losing touch with the very audience he had for the first time chosen to figure in the Clock's circle of addicted readers. Dickens may be said to have foundered on his own attempt at novelistic self-commentary. Popularity, he seems to have sensed in finally giving up the journal, must be renewed from text to text rather than simply reviewed. Dickens is ultimately to explain, in a kind of "in memoriam" for the journal, how he had originally assumed that the reading populace would be more interested in the implicit study of its own reactions, as staged through Master Humphrey's reading circle, than it turned out to be. It was as if Dickens were learning a lesson on behalf of the nineteenth-century novel at large: that narrative must sustain before it can reframe the reading process; that fables of its preoccupation with the perverse and strange are best kept subordinate to an action that is otherwise occupied; that metanarrative can succeed only under cover of plot.

It is, therefore, not in the frame story alone but in the interplay between tale and serial apparatus, *Shop* and *Clock*, that we find the links forged between narrative and its metatext which are to become the stock-in-trade of later Victorian fiction. These include a freely shifting mode of reader address (under unusual restraint in Dickens, except when it bursts out almost parodically in the *Shop*) and a recurrent network, rather than constrictive bracket, of enacted textual encounter and response, transmission and interpretation. In *The Old Curiosity Shop*, as it is set off by and ultimately set loose from *Master Humphrey's Clock*, the Dickensian literary product (hence the Victorian novel in prototype) learns indirectly to claim rather than openly to reproduce a concerted hermeneutic attention, to render in parable rather than portray in so many words the passivity and stasis—and the imputed fullness—of the reading act. The novel as it came to be known over much of a century thus learns to summon and deploy the attentive, reflective, and interpretive impulses without attempting to invade (by representing) the unreadable inwardness of reading itself.

Reading Reception: The Double Cover Story

In laying stress on the eccentric psychology of reading rather than of writing when bringing out *The Old Curiosity Shop* within the *Clock's* serial format, Dickens had everything to gain because he had, of course, everything to hide. In May of 1837, his beloved sister-in-law, Mary Hogarth, seventeen years old, was taken from life in his very arms. That this was a nearly crippling loss worked out by being worked up in fiction is a truism of a full century's worth of biographical commentary on Dickens. Nothing could, on its own terms, be truer. Mary died, and what in her absence she came to represent, since already in the form of a memory (a psychic representation), needed little transformation to pass into literary effect. In *The Old Curiosity Shop* five years later, Nell Trent as *character* is already the *idea* of virginal death, the novel its rumination as idea under the guise of plot, with the heroine fleeing a death that she is all the while narrowing in on. But that rumination itself is made part of the fiction, even when not part of the plot: part of the frame if not the fable. It is for this reason that criticism ignores the deepest conversionary subterfuge of biography-turned-fiction whenever it treats *The Old Curiosity Shop* as one of fourteen separate volumes in the Dickens canon. In that light it is cut away from origin and reception, cast free of grieving; it becomes merely a story, not still an act, of mourning. Since it was not first a separate novel, its strategic place in the newly launched *Master Humphrey's Clock* is what narrativizes, as it were, its full spectrum of emotional involvement, from occulted autobiography through public response. Heavily underwritten by biographical *affect* at its source, it is only the "reframing" of the story which permits the generalizing of its *effect* as narrative art, "popular" rather than private.

Needing his fictional creativity (as never before) for an exercise in personal expression, and so needing all the more urgently to secure his readership in its own independent sphere of attention, Dickens thought he had found a workable pretext in the prolonged dramatization of just such an audience. With his new serial experiment, on a weekly rather than a monthly basis, he gambled upon what he mistook as the perfect means for addressing his public without having to recede behind the evidentiary smokescreens of edited papers (*Pickwick*) or disappear so completely into the narrative voices of *Oliver Twist* or *Nicholas Nickleby*. When Dickens masks himself as Master Humphrey, execu-

tive narrator of a sequence of subsidiary stories, and does so to mask his readers in turn as the ex officio members of a reading circle, he has rendered the
poles of intent and reception thoroughly fictionalized. He then proceeds to insert into this framework as momentously personal and unashamedly therapeutic a story as he was ever to tell. My emphasis falls on exactly the bipolar
nature of this narrative preconditioning in *Master Humphrey's Clock*. It is not
enough that Dickens vanish behind his most fully, almost tediously characterized persona, the Master himself. His readership, too, must undergo an equivalent personification in order for a symmetrical relation to be established in the
cathartic displacements incumbent on the text. It is thus that veiled autobiographical confession is transposed to the phenomenology of investment, an
unprocessed excess of the personal read off as a textual energetics of intersubjectivity. In tracing out the valences of this transposition, this disposition of
affect, what I am after is an account of how the suppression of input (autobiography) is abetted by the steady management of output (melodramatic effect), how sponsoring motive is transferred (and transvalued) to the heightening of response.

And this is not the only wholesale conversionary tactic—of private grieving
into the textual rituals of indoctrinated reception—deployed by Dickens in this
experiment with narrative reframing. The private goes public in another way
as well, involving the placement of Nell's pain in the context of industrial devastation and proletarian backlash. Individual tragedy—and private mourning—
are brazenly cast against the broader, potentially eclipsing backdrop of statistical suffering and death, with its consequences in social and political crisis.
Nothing less would do in order to avoid the danger that his story might seem
too embarrassingly private or merely too thinly personal. The autobiographical and the political, the barely transmuted domestic trauma and the socioeconomic counterplot about an underclass on the brink of insurrection, meet
on the ground of their mutual cover story: Master Humphrey's collective. They
meet, that is, on the ground—if only the false bottom after all—of reader reaction. It is not enough that private grief and public grievance should be jock-
eyed to complement each other. They are asked to figure each other within a
defusing fable of response itself. It is by such deflections and conversions that
Dickensian narrative, even at its most confessional, works to *impress* the reader.

"The Book of Her Heart": Reading as Primal Scene

It might be said that Little Nell herself, if only intermittently, reads herself
to death. In so doing, she can be seen to struggle toward the recovery of a lost

site of reading—rendered once and unreturned to—from which time has severed her. The pattern of her itinerant solace in texts recalls the literary motif
of reading as journeying which runs in English from Chaucer's pilgrim narratives through Spenser and Bunyan down through Fielding and on into the casual tropes of the early-nineteenth-century best-sellers. In *The Old Curiosity
Shop*, the pattern may be summarized as follows: Nell reads, reads of a journey (*Pilgrim's Progress*), journeys while she reads, indeed while we read on; is
herself both read and misread along the way; and when she is through moving on, works herself free through more reading, until all that is left is our reading of her—and this only (and twice over, as we will see) in funerary retrospect.
In the "little tale" (6:98) Quilp has forced his wife to extract from Nell, the girl's
memories of better days go as far back as, and no farther than, a quintessential scene of Victorian reading aloud at the family hearth: "I used to read to him
[her grandfather] by the fireside, and he sat listening, and when I stopped and
we began to talk, he told me about my mother, and how she once looked and
spoke just like me when she was a child" (6:97). Deep within the prehistory of
plot itself, story begets story. And this recollected mutuality of discourse, a
written text inspiring an oral intimacy, is, of course, the Dickensian family
scene par excellence.

Metaphors of reading do not stay put in this novel. Long after Nell can no
longer read in peace to her grandfather, she herself comes to be figuratively
misread by him when he appears self-defensively "content to read the book of
her heart from the page first presented to him, little dreaming of the story that
lay hidden in its other leaves" (9:120). Nearing her last days, Nell in her solitude
is left—in yet another inversion within the pattern of enacted reading—with
"none but the stars, to look into the upturned face and read its history" (52:484).
An idiomatic sense of "reading one's fate in the stars" is turned upside down
by that conceit, even as you read on from a position of virtually extraterrestrial
omniscience—rectifying the deficit of human indifference in the heroine's life.
All the while, ordinary down-to-earth reading is all Nell herself has for solace,
though without the idyllic reciprocity of conversation in the remembered
scene by the fireside. The kindness she used to provide for her grandfather is
now offered by others to her, as when "the schoolmaster would bring in books,
and read to her aloud; and seldom an evening passed, but the bachelor came
in, and took his turn of reading" (55:508).

This is still going on a hundred and fifty pages further into her decline, as
her final circle of acolytes "read and talked to her" (72:655). But it is ultimately
that primal scene of reading with her grandfather to which the discourse,
though not the plot, shortly returns her. For it is no accident that Nell's ex-

pression in final repose, transcending by seeming to erase time, recovers a prelapsarian peace first associated with the scene of communal (familial) reading: "Yes," the narrator has it, in a zero-degree direct address to the reader marked out by this rhetorical asseveration, "Yes, the old fireside had smiled upon that same sweet face" (71:654).[2] The reader has heard no mention of this hearthside space since the early confession to Mrs. Quilp, yet it is to just this realm of lost grace that death has won a way back.

"Curious Speculation," Psychic Investment

Whatever energies may be routed and in turn released by the marked recurrence of the scene of reading across the length of plot, in whatever alignment with that reading of yours which activates this plot, such energies have come a long way from the impedances of the opening pages. There, the very motive for reading on is so laden with dubiety, so throttled and compromised by the threat of voyeuristic indulgence, at best so rhetorically worried, that Nell's straightforward perusal of improving literature comes subsequently upon the plot as an easing respite from its own vexed gambit of narrative "speculation," of suspect psychological investment. The novel's first chapter is organized, that is, around both senses of "curiosity": a mode of response as well as an object of interest. "'It would be a curious speculation,' said I [Master Humphrey], after some restless turns across and across the room, 'to imagine her [the young girl Nell] in her future life, holding her solitary way among a crowd of wild grotesque companions'" (1:56). Curiosities are what one would otherwise assume the "Curiosity Shop" had to offer rather than to rouse. Yet even in this participatory sense of the word, to whom is Master Humphrey directing this fairly blatant narrational lure? In eventual effect, he has a way of talking to himself which is also through himself to the reader.

Indeed, Master Humphrey pulls himself up short upon the second iteration of his own "dealings" in the curious, his own quasi-economic "speculation." He breaks off exactly where his favored adjective is caught slipping over toward something more like "odd" than like "quizzical": "It would be curious to find—" (1:56). Except for Dickens' narratorial activity, of course, there is nothing to find, only something to construct in words. "I checked myself here, for the theme was carrying me along at a great pace, and I already saw before me a region on which I was little disposed to enter." The reader can only assume that Humphrey means simply to be rebuking his own instincts for the macabre or morbid in using a code word, "theme," imported from the literary manifestation of such instincts. The rhetorical force of this passage is a cliff-hanger, but its structural logic is a fracture in discourse, induced by recoil from confessed fiction making and its emotional risks. This recoil is all the more tactical when we realize that the story will finally be claimed as an autobiographical set of memories—those of Humphrey himself, not to mention (deliberately not to mention) those of Dickens—with all the wounding exposure their retelling can be assumed to entail. There are, then, already two *I*'s in play and at work here, two "voices," two "egos." There is Master Humphrey the old man, a single-minded embodiment of the urge toward narrative, an eccentric meditative figure smitten with the odd jumble of impressions he has seen and beginning to imagine a future, a destiny, a story; and there is Master Humphrey the official narrative agency, who needs (according to the scheduled clockwork of such storytelling) to retard all inordinate speculative foreshortenings to make time for plot. The latter's obligation to clear room for any tale delivered from his clock case is phrased, in fact, as an exercise in pure duration: the mission "to beguile time from the heart of time itself" (Penguin appendix, 678).

In anthropomorphizing this narrative mandate as the work of one of Humphrey's two "egos," above, I had in mind a set of terms introduced by Michel Foucault in "What Is an Author?" and never, so far as I know, taken up for fictional analysis (Foucault's own examples being philosophical or theoretical discourses). Yet these are terms by which Foucault's widespread influence on the study of the novelistic institution might be formally specified through a linguistics of discursive emplacement as well as a generalized politics of omniscience and surveillance.[3] Once more we find that the contextual study of narrative within the interlocking discourses of its historical moment (penal, bureaucratic, mercantile, and so forth) tends to simplify narrative's active orientation toward its contemporaneous readership if it does not submit narrative discourse itself to the pressures of analysis.

In Foucault's account of the "author-function" within the grammatical agency of a text, everything turns on the ordinary "signs of localization" in a semiotics of enunciation—that is, "[p]ersonal pronouns, adverbs of time and place, and the conjugation of verbs," which he designates with the linguistic term from Benveniste as "shifters."[4] These signs are traded off and abraded between the loci of divergent subject positions, as, for instance, between the work's biographical signatory and its executive agency, between, let us say, authorial and narratorial "egos." This exchange or tension would occur, for instance, between Dickens as valorizing "first ego" and the "second ego" (Foucault's terms) of a first-person narrator like Pip or David Copperfield—or here, for a few chapters, the characterized narrator Master Humphrey. When these two egos work away at each other against the grain, as they always do in the very process of coming into distinction, the strictly relational and relativistic "'author-function' arises out of their scission—the division or distance of the two" (144). In their definitive and collateral slippage, they become de-cisive. So that (departing from Foucault) it is in the crevices of their frictional byplay that manifestations of the *reader function*, as well, may be detected.

Though held to a strictly linguistic application, Foucault's choice of the term *ego* for these discursive emplacements may well recall Freud's emphasis on "His Majesty the Ego" in his early essay "Creative Writers and Day-Dreaming."[5] Designated thereby is the radiating center of any creative fiction, around which are arrayed various distorted mirror images of the conceiving self when embodied as central hero. In an application of Foucault's template to narrative fiction, the magisterial or executive ego, in (purely textual) tension with the persona delegated to do the telling—especially when that deputized and second "ego" is himself a character (as with Master Humphrey)—this "first ego," precisely to avoid the egoism of autobiography, must share its "function" with the "second ego" of conducted narrative, as in turn with its further portioning out into various characters. Otherwise (Freud now) the disclosed authorial daydream—or nightmare (mourning, say)—would appall rather than appeal, supposedly repulsing attention by its masturbatory self-absorption. Hence the relation of the *Shop* to the *Clock*. Dickens' framing design displaces the autobiographical suspicions (of undue libidinal fixation) so completely from author to prosecuting narrator of the serial that the contradictions generated between the motive to disclose (and luxuriate) and the tendency toward reticence can be played out in the oscillations of discursivity itself, all extranarrative psychology momentarily suspended.

To see this in (self-curtailed) action, we may pick up the text again where we left off. Following upon the grammatically marked "scission" of "I checked myself," the narrative enters upon a further cleft in personae bridged by pronominal shifters. For the fairly neutral idiom of "I checked myself" is strained into virtually schizoid discrepancy in the next sentence: *"I agreed with myself that this was idle musing, and resolved to go to bed, and court forgetfulness"* (1:56; emphasis added). Into this discrepancy, this default—between Humphrey as narrative momentum (enunciating subject) and Humphrey as character— the reader is inevitably slipped, the audience's own propellant curiosity at once solicited and rebuked. This is to say that the truncated drama of self-checked discursive energy is staged in such a way that it structures *in you* the very response (overanxious fascination) it is stationed to postpone. The ethical register of plot in Austen, as the patient shaping of duration, is shifted here to the psychological register, where for Dickens it can be shifted in turn from the impulsions of autobiography to those of fictional narrativity. Before returning to such narrative plotting, it should be said that what Foucault's differential linguistics of enunciation has to offer our largest interest in the localization of the reader function will only emerge fully once we have remade Victorian fiction's own way toward that cynosure of its hermeneutic mission in Eliot's *Daniel Deronda*. For now, with the doors of the *Shop* thrown open to us and the *Clock* pacing our access, we submit to the grip of the curiosity function, from which narration cannot afford to release reception too soon. In the deflection of private catharsis into plot dynamic, the discursive effort is everywhere to unload authorial responsibility upon sympathetic participation: in complicity with, to *conscript*.

"The Friendly Reader" Redirected

Instead of racing to conclusions, the self-checked narrator must, as we have been seeing, take his time, let the tale take its own time, not try to beat the Clock. Within the short space of two chapters, however, the supposed independent momentum of the story has so gained a lock on your imagination that the characterized narrator can recede into an unspecified omniscience, his departure passed off as a bowing (out) to the autonomy of the world that his words have so cogently manifested: "And now that I have carried this history so far in my own character and introduced these personages to the reader, I shall for the convenience of the narrative detach myself from its further course" (3:72). A very slow fuse has hereby been lit. Thirty chapters after Master Humphrey has made his precipitous exit from the novel, leaving "those who have prominent and necessary parts in it to speak and act for themselves" (3:72), the smooth surface of narration is exploded by an equally self-conscious intervention. This narrational self-signaling—via reader reference—occurs at the start of a chapter routing us back from Nell's traumatic pastoral to those other characters left undeveloped in the city. Before your unprepared eyes, narrative rhetoric swells to the bursting point: "As the course of this tale requires that we should become acquainted, somewhere hereabouts, with a few particulars connected with the domestic economy of Mrs. Sampson Brass, and as a more convenient place than the present is not likely to occur for the purpose"—now is as good a time as any—"the historian"—the who? where did he come from?—"takes *the friendly reader* by the hand, and springing with him into the air, and cleaving the same at a greater rate than ever Don Cleophas Leandro Perez Zambullo and his familiar travelled through that pleasant region in company, alights with him upon the pavement of Bevis Marks" (33:319; emphasis added).

In some mystified meeting of "the hand" holding the pen and that holding the book, you are to imagine yourself transported once again, as Master Humphrey had put it earlier, "for the convenience of the narrative." As anticipated in chapter 1, this very moment of discursive flourish has found its way as exemplary (rather than exceptional) instance of Dickensian apostrophe into Wayne Booth's general account of the Victorian rhetoric of fiction.[6] My own sense, instead, is that the reader's friendship (seldom more sorely tested than by this contrivance) can be so laboriously invoked by Dickensian narrative in this exotic and digressive simile, and in another intrusion closely following, precisely because it can elsewhere be taken for given.

We see the same *un*characteristic device in operation four chapters further on in this London section. The interplay between plot and discourse is once more at issue, and Dickens again whips up (without really resuscitating) an earlier editorial formula for ascribed reader response (here in Shandeyesque exaggeration): "Kit—for it happens at this juncture, not only that we have breathing time to follow his fortunes, but that the necessities of these adventures so adapt themselves to our ease and inclination as to call upon us imperatively to pursue the track we most desire to take—Kit, while the matters treated of in the last fifteen chapters were yet in progress, was, *as the reader may suppose,* gradually familiarising himself more and more with Mr. and Mrs. Garland, Mr. Abel, the pony, and Barbara" (38:362; emphasis added). As against this overblown instance, the convivial sympathies or intuitions of the Dickensian reader are not regularly encumbered by mention. No opacity of discourse is let fog the lens of narration. But if reading, in all its "ease," "inclination," and "desire," ordinarily goes without saying, why not here?

I take the link between these two exceptional passages, four chapters apart in that central section of *The Old Curiosity Shop*, to be tactical as well as (and largely because) atypical. They are part of the novel's immediate design to roughen its discursive texture at this particular turn of plot, to call our attention to a narrative energy that can no longer go (forward) unexamined. Signaled discourse, having given way to the weight of story long enough to instill the latter's momentum as a chain of events taking their own autonomous time to unfold, returns at exactly the point in the novel where it must begin working to deflect the plot from its greatest threat: the specter of its triviality as sheer story. The narrative purview must be wrenched open to take cognizance of larger social issues—specifically the environmental spoilage and human desperation of industrial labor (and worse: industrial unemployment). The immediate effects of this social crisis are registered through deracination, poverty, suffering, itinerancy, starvation, and death. Though, point by point, these are

in effect Nell's problems too, they cannot be circumscribed by the eccentric vic-
timage of a single teenage girl, for they tell a larger tale of economic destitution. At the same time, they cannot be allowed to annihilate the poignancy of
her tale. Dickens could, of course, have skirted this political material altogether.
Instead he renders it twice over, first as a comic "revolution" in London, then
in its proper place as a social crisis in an outlying industrial town—once figurative, once literal, and each time associated with the self-conscious guidance
of narrative discourse.

And, still within the plot, this self-consciousness is itself double: authorial as
well as neutrally discursive. For it is just here, upon rejoining the satirized London scene, that there is about to appear for the first time in the story, *in propria
persona*, the character who will turn out to be its narrator (not to mention its
reader aloud, and finally its author), a character known to us so far, unless we
have forgotten by now, under the name of Master Humphrey. This character
(re)enters the plot in the detective role—and under the sustained incognito—of
the "single gentleman," obsessive seeker after Nell. The stated contingency of
such a (no more than) "convenient place" for his introduction, even as it protests
too much its own fortuity, is the only false lead in the chapter; everything else
is tightly overdetermined—if visibly so only in retrospect. The narrator—call
him Humphrey or Dickens—can no longer keep his distance. His autobiographical investment surfaces precisely when needed to keep the importance of
a single domestic tragedy like Nell's from being obliterated by social crisis.

The reemergence of discursive impulse in the form of a compulsive character is an immediate precipitant, as well, for further plot material yet unactivated. The single gentleman's "loud double knock" (34:331) educes from her
previous hiding place the heretofore unseen servant girl to be known as the
Marchioness. She is the one major character left to take the stage of narration,
and whose doubling of Nell—in age, innocence, stature, and selfless duty—
will provide an alternate happy ending to the chronicle of brutalized girlhood.
As detective, the single gentleman needs to be let into the story; as narrator in
disguise, he needs the character who will survive the object of his quest as the
very principle of survival. Indeed the Marchioness "never came to the surface
unless the single gentleman rang his bell, when she would answer it and immediately disappear again" (36:349). That's what narrative agents (rather than
characters) are for: to bring what is needed precisely *to the surface*.

Moreover, the matter of withheld identity in connection with the single
gentleman is itself the mask for a double stratum of "identification," emotional
but also structural. At one level, we do not have to guess, or find credible, the
single gentleman's belatedly disclosed *identity as* Master Humphrey (much

lamented in commentary on this novel as a retroactive concoction) in order to appreciate Humphrey's (the erstwhile narrator's) *identification with* the single gentleman as the renewed narrative impulse (plot-unraveling functionary) behind the whole remaining story. Here is someone else, besides you and the narrator, curious to a fault. And discursive structure corroborates the psychology of response. When the novel's personified narrative focus (Master Humphrey talking our way into the novel), having dropped out of plot for thirty-some chapters, seems to return in the form of an unmotivated discursive clotting (complete with a twice-mentioned "reader") timed to the intrusion of a figure of undermotivated (or at least undisclosed) curiosity, a figure obsessively in search of stories about the heroine, such a return is linked to the agency of narration, that is, by a formal as well as psychological inevitability.

Clues continue to accumulate. When the single gentleman insists on giving no name in letting an apartment above the Brasses' shop, Dick Swiveller responds with a typical snippet of poetry which renders alliterative the logic of his interlocutor's withheld name in the novel as a whole: "'If any mistake should arise from not having the name, don't say it was my fault, sir,' added Dick, still lingering. 'Oh blame not the bard—'" (33:346). Under the camouflage of his comic self-aggrandizement as poetaster, Dick—who is "invariably" chosen by the single gentleman "as his channel of communication" (36:347) from here on—is also recording the narrative's own exculpation: blame not Dickens for any mistakes, or mistakings of identity, incident to the unsaid.

Keeping "the Many-Headed" in Place

The first explicit purpose of the single gentleman upon his introduction is to summon into the neighborhood as many Punch exhibitors as possible, in hopes of acquiring information about Nell from the one troupe of players he knows to have encountered her. It is this device that allows narrative *tout court* to refigure itself as street theater, mass entertainment, finally a sop to the mob. Given that the entire novel is a kind of Punch show (with Quilp, for instance, playing both Punch and the finally vanquished devil of the puppet theater's standard scenario), it is part of the single gentleman's links to the discursive machinery of the text as a whole that his interrogation of the Punch players rapidly becomes annexed to the exhibition itself by way of a theatrical (or textual) metaphor, providing its "epilogue" (37:353) upstairs in the room where he grills the players. It is there that he is found later, pacing in meditation "over the wondering heads of Mr. Swiveller and Miss Sally Brass" (37:362). Such a swift twist on the idiom of mystification further dissolves the architecture of this space into a cognitive field of detection and retraced plot: a purview, indeed an *over*view, to which these baffled characters are structurally subordinate.

The passage describing in detail the way in which the single gentleman discomfits the neighborhood of Bevis Marks by his paid invitation to traveling Punch players was much cut at the manuscript stage, for reasons of space in this overlong weekly number.[7] Gone from the published version is a passage that describes the Punch showmen as "social benefactors" (701 n. 1)—an obvious irony that only veils the deeply Dickensian sympathy with popular entertainments. Gone, too, is the inflated speculation about whether "political economists" would have to "deduce a new theory of supply and demand" from the persistent appearance of yet new exhibitors (as long as the single gentleman stood ready to pay) or merely to "cite" these "facts" in "support of an old [theory]" (701 n. 2). It is tempting to think that, under pressure to cut, Dickens was only too happy to see dropped such unabashedly explicit tipping of his hand as paid popular entertainer. But only because such inferences were by now redundant. Never more than in his new weekly serial, Dickens is obviously dependent on those same laws of "supply and demand" which in other forms he was also busy thematizing in the installments of its first included novel.[8]

The edited, less cluttered text of this chapter allows the reader to register all the more immediately the political reverberations, loud and hollow, of a remaining irony in the published version. A heightened description that reads like a trial run, though entirely tongue in cheek at this point, for the scenes of the Gordon riots in *Barnaby Rudge* (that next set of serial installments in *Master Humphrey's Clock*), the passage concludes as follows: "It was sufficient, in short, to know that Bevis Marks was *revolutionised* by these popular *movements*, and that peace and quietness fled from its precincts" (37:354; emphasis added). With the pun on political "movements" in describing the sheer milling about of an anxious audience, the implied notion of an "upheaval" or "overturning" in the neighborhood is the closest Dickens comes to evoking that proletarian "revolution" threatened at the time by the Chartist uprisings.[9] What thus happens to this stuffy business district is no more than the farcical upending of its routine by mass entertainment: the comic analogue of a political revolt.[10]

As mentioned in my first chapter, there is another philological wrinkle earlier in Dickens' prose (before the etymological recovery and political gutting of phrases like "movements" and "revolutions" in *The Old Curiosity Shop* itself) which connects mass consciousness in general with Dickens' narrative audience in particular. It does so through the evolution under his pen of a classical epithet ("*the many-headed* multitude") into an adjectival substantive for *Pickwick*'s description of its hero being pelted by "little tokens of the playful disposition of the many-headed" (19:340).[11] Four years later, this comic pejorative for the rabble has become a sarcastic term for Dickens' own narrative public. In correspondence of 1840, Dickens responds to Forster's suggestion about cutting a potentially misleading passage in none other than *The Old Curiosity Shop*: "Of course I had no intention to delude the many-headed."[12] The textual occasion is trivial. Nonetheless, in that stray remark we get a sense of the hydra-headed collectivity to which Dickens thought himself directing his texts. So near to the mob, and yet—such is the Dickensian agenda—so far. Plot itself depends on this distance in *The Old Curiosity Shop*. In an age of industrial destitution and mass infant mortality, where revolution is a persistent threat, the story of a single dying child may well expect to clear space for its reaction only by acknowledging all that hedges it round. In any case, it cannot remain the reclusive Master Humphrey's story as we have initially come to know him. It must instead be given over to omniscience—if only in the (at first unadmitted) person of his pseudonymous double, that other (more widely traveled and less hermetically romantic) single gentleman. Only in this way can Dickens ratify that private tale on behalf of a sociology, rather than an ingrown psychology, of devastation, whose potential consequences in mass revolt are both testified to and staved off by literary response. Then, too, this *non*metaphoric specter of revolution is shortly to enter the novel in a context even more subtly disarmed, in part by the preparation already laid for a connection between mass entertainment—including by extension popular narrative, especially of a Punch-like variety—and the energies otherwise routed into collective violence.

The famous episode in question finds Nell in the industrial chaos of a town modeled on Birmingham, where Dickens, merely in describing the scene as local color for his plot, still manages, as we will see, to insinuate the transcendental value of narrative itself in an age of economic crisis trapped between degrading labor and (more dangerous yet, in Dickens' view) the explosive social unrest bred of industrial *un*employment. Against the grasping and uninterrupted self-employment of Quilp in the city, his rank and resourceful possessiveness, this is the absolute dispossession, the paralyzing poverty, of the system's human detritus.[13] It is a spectacle by which Nell—like Dickens—seems horrified as much for its effects as for its causes, as sickened by the violence and bloodshed of sporadic revolt as by the deprivations of blighted lives.

During the first of Nell's two nights in this wasteland, in return for a spell of warmth at a furnace tender's industrial hearth, she provides him, just by her presence with the grandfather, "new histories" for him to read in the surrogate library of his "furnace fire" (44:442)—where all representation is immediately and literally consumed. Nell is, as always, the very stuff of narrative. The novel's subtext of reading here takes one of its crucial turns toward the meta-text. As Nell is read by this industrial victim, so is she by the Victorian middle class: for solace and uplift by their own more comfortable fires. No scene marked out for extrapolated response could be easier to gauge. It comes accompanied, as we are to see, by a muted interpolation as well in the next chapter, one that turns the tables by asking incredulously what Nell could possibly need to have narrated *to* rather than about her. The buildup to this disruptive loop of rhetoric is itself unflinchingly rhetorical. For on her second night in the industrial precincts, Nell encounters the full nightmare from which the furnace tender has beaten a retreat into readerly daydream. There, despite the prolonged and rhetorically inflated dwelling on the misery of their conditions, "unemployed laborers" are seen with diminished sympathy as "maddened men, armed with sword and firebrand, spurning the tears and prayers of women who would restrain them," and thus destined "to work no ruin half so surely as their own" (45:424). Such is the nature of Dickens' reactionary social diagnosis. It ends with the benighted status quo lamented even while rendered irresistible. Nothing can mitigate the ugliness and grievous plight, certainly not armed uprising, nothing except as it might be relieved (such is always the implication in Dickens) by the gradually ameliorative efforts of an empathetic middle class whose enlightenment and engagement would in part be attributable to passages like these: narrative exposés stopping short of radical harangues, editorialized but nondemagogic renderings, essayistic detours within improving fictions. For those, alone, who need such reading.

"Who Shall Tell the Terrors": Narrative Transcending Itself

The most unexpected thing about this passage is that for all its immediacy—an indirect discourse filtered through Nell's assaulted consciousness—it closes down on the locus of its own inadequacy and/or redundancy precisely *as narrative discourse*. The whole central paragraph of diagnosed and indicted revolutionary rage funnels to a single interrogative-turned-exclamatory grammar that takes the Dickensian readership almost by name and entirely by surprise: "Who shall tell the terrors of the night to that young wandering child!" Facile rhetorical gesture though this may be, it is not an easy sentence. On consideration, it seems derived from an idiomatic matrix like "Who can tell just how terrible this all was for Nell?" But in its actual phrasing, idiomatic language pulls in different directions at once. Who shall/should tell/discern/describe the terrors of the/this night to/for that young wandering child?/! In one direction, the narrator would seem to cede the very privilege of his mimesis: Who among us would boast the powers, either of empathy or of representation, needed to relate how terrifying to Nell this night has been? A familiar enough move. Preterition: a figure by which summary mention is made of a thing in professing to omit it. Eight clausal variants of "night, when . . ." have plowed us through Dickens' long paragraph, an overview dramatically achieved by the time its very possibility has been dismissed. In another direction of that capping rhetoric's loose phrasing, however, if the reader is drawn to the gravitational field that gives the idiomatic "tell . . . to" an upper hand in this grammar, then a different emphasis is pressed: Who should presume to enlighten Nell on the subject of night's worst terrors, this or any night's? What does Nell need with narrative realism when she has seen reality?

This sense of the exclamatory interrogative, with its less expected rhetorical question, carries a suggestion whose plot equivalent is the earlier scene where Nell, alone among the audience, falls asleep at a Punch show, having already lived through its waking equivalent (16:185). Just as Nell needs to attend no violent escapist melodrama when all she seeks is the escape from one of her own, so does she need no narrative of a social tragedy for which, as Theodor Adorno once observed, she is herself positioned as the narrative scapegoat.[14] Yet it is possible to rephrase one grammatical thrust of Dickens' rhetoric in that climactic exclamation in a way that more fully accounts for its tacit self-valorization as far as the reading public is concerned. The gist is this: Now that you know from narrative what Nell has gone through, both traversed and endured, you know better than to think she needs to learn from it what you have learned. By such another (again rare) gesture at the "friendly reader," Dickens' novel hereby compounds its scene of extrapolation at the furnace (Nell as readable character) with a passing interpolation of the many-headed by direct address. You, readers, are thus intercepted by this rhetoric at the far limit of an indirect discourse which, while putting in question its own access to Nell's consciousness, also turns outward to you instead—you in her stead. And any doubts of your own, as reading audience, are set to rest on the spot, reminded as you are that you, not Nell, do indeed need such narrative—but only if, and partly so that, you are not required to gain all your tragic knowledge through suffering it directly. What has thus happened in this brief rhetorical address to a wholly unindividuated reader ("who shall tell!") is that two mutually exclusive collectivities are made to veer apart once and for all across a self-emptying apostrophe: the illiterate suffering masses and the novel-buying public—them in their despair, you in your empathy.

This focus on the functional narrativity, rather than just the narrative, of human misery is prolonged into the next episode. Nell herself—the once avid reader who has now seen it all, she to whom nothing need be told—becomes in the scene immediately following the Birmingham transit a narrative agent in her own right. When she encounters the schoolmaster again and "told him all" (46:435), it is a case of the child giving lessons in life to the master. As with Frankenstein's tale to the magistrate, Dickens' audience is made privy to none of her story in her own words, since it has already heard it, far better yet, in Dickens'. Nonetheless, the force of extrapolation is not absent even from this absent scene of narrative delivery. After her recitation, "[w]hat more was thought or said, matters not" (46:435). Yet again you are positioned to fill in the blank of response, with the "more" of the schoolmaster's reaction merely standing in for your own.

In assessing the social deflections of the novel's rhetoric, including the risks it runs with a degrading of politics to insulated melodrama, Dickens' revisions are once more revealing. His deletions can again be found to turn the manuscript into not just a more streamlined narrative but a veritable palimpsest of strategic suppressions. Writing to Forster that, in view of the number running over length, he had "something in my eye near the beginning which I can easily take out,"[15] and saying no more about it, Dickens dropped a long additional passage of depicted industrial anguish at the start of the chapter that leads Nell to the furnace fire. It is a passage that closes by personifying bourgeois hypocrisy in the figure of a "portly gentleman" who, in his self-satisfaction that evening, "standing in the best streets in town," looks around him with gratification at the tokens of culture and leisure, dismisses the charge of "Misery!" threatening from the margins, and plumes himself on living in a city whose ennobling attractions include none other than its "Museum of Natural Curiosities" (705 n. 1). Luxuriating in a complacent display of curiosities is a self-satisfaction too close for comfort to be included at the center of a supposedly withering social indictment. Into a *mise en abyme* of this sort Dickens' entire *Shop* of curiosities could topple headlong.

Entrusted Narrative: "That Few Could Read . . .
without Being Moved to Tears"

So much for the keeping of aesthetic distance. Narratives cannot afford this mistake, and their instances are multiplied as the novel draws to a close in order to broadcast their emotional hold on an audience. Storytellers continue to be handpicked for the part. Following on from the schoolmaster as conduit for Nell's tale, there is another close double of the single gentleman in that aged "bachelor" with whom Nell meets up in her rural retreat, known to her there as the "universal mediator" (52:486). It is, in fact, through the "medium" of the bachelor's letters to his aged brother in the city, Abel Garland, that Nell's story is able eventually to reach those most concerned with her fate in exile—and this just before we discover the parallel relationship between the single gentleman and his own long-lost brother, Nell's grandfather. Dwelling on his new acquaintance, the "mediator" in his letters "had told . . . such a tale of their wanderings, and mutual love, that few could read it without being moved to tears" (68:69). Dickens' narrative being just "such a tale," and the letters requiring therefore no quotation, the novel seems accompanied here by a simultaneous gloss on its own sentimental reception.

When Mr. Garland arrives to hear more from his brother in person, it is the single gentleman who instead takes up the story where the other bachelor's mediation has suspended its account: "I have a short narrative on my lips . . . and will try you with it." Like the novel we have been reading, which is hereby recircumscribed within a more encompassing family chronicle, the single gentleman's oral rather than written story goes forward without room for vocal intercession, without any "readerly" protestation or assent: "Pausing for no reply, he . . . proceeded" to tell of his lasting love for his elder brother, now Nell's grandfather. It is a love founded on the fact that—at the deepest stratum of the novel's regressive structure—the elder brother was forever "telling him old stories" to solace his sickly childhood (69:636). Yet again, as with Nell's own earliest memories of reading to her grandfather, the storytelling dispensation emerges as indistinguishable from the genealogical foundations of the narrative text—both for the plot and, as we are now in a position to work out, for its autobiographical subcode. Reading is once more slotted into place as a kind of familial primal scene.

The story of the generations continues. When the Trent (rather than Garland) brothers grew older, they "became rivals too soon," with both "their hearts settled upon one object"—an erotic object replacing "old stories" as emotional stimulus. The younger brother deferred to the elder's passion in gratitude for previous storytelling kindnesses, as if substituting remembered for present desire, and left the country. But the object of desire, true to form, continues to renew itself. In the daughter of the resulting marriage, "the mother lived again," that "Good Angel of the race" (69:637). This genetic and spiritual replication is sustained as well into the next generation, with Nell's mother leaving our heroine orphaned at a point when the mother is "the same in helplessness, in age, in form, in feature—as she had been herself when her young mother died" (69:637). The "Angel of the race" is precisely *that*: never a thriving *genius loci*, an angel of the house, but an image from the otherworld presiding over a bloodline of fatality. Such, two chapters later, is the higher condition Nell herself has achieved, tolled away by the threefold repetition of "She was dead" within the span of ten sentences (71:652–54)—as if once, interchangeably, for each generational stage of that persisting familial configuration. In this she remains also the scapegoat of contemporaneous social blight as well as of romantic nostalgia. At the hovel of an unemployed laborer back in the novel's industrial inferno, Nell was shown the corpse of the man's "third dead child, and last" (45:427). Compressed to one end-stopped generation, this pattern of death in triplicate, when further distilled to sheer rhetorical emphasis at Nell's deathbed, has thus twice over been taken up by iteration from story into discourse, becoming, in its destiny as mere syntactic recurrence, all the more clearly epitaphic rather than diachronic, elegiac rather than narrational—an iterative working through. Which brings us back full circle to the question of whose reworking, and of whose death?

By the time the single gentleman's last brief "narrative" has been unfolded, a familial matrix is established which turns out to be structurally isomorphic with Dickens' own relation to the sponsoring trauma of the narrative. The long-withheld (and autobiographically occulted) family structure behind the story—providing its very mainspring both as quest (via the single gentleman's searches) and as postmortem evocation (via Dickens' elegiac motives)—has in fact been thrown into unique relief by our longtime (though unacknowledged) narrator's one explicit "narrative." According to this narrative, the single gentleman has returned from exile to seek out the very "image" of the woman, two generations before, whose love was forbidden to him by his family ties. Dickens himself has also (indeed thereby) returned from a protective distance on a not dissimilar relationship. Here, then, is the deepest parallel between textual plot and authorial catharsis. For Dickens must confront again, in fiction, his devotion to a woman whose love was denied to him by her equivalent status as a *sister-in-law*—though in this case not wife of his brother but sister of his wife. With the generations collapsed (on the one side of the parallel) by the physical as well as spiritual equivalence between Nell, her mother, and her grandmother—as successive avatars of the "Angel of the race," dead three times over—we are left (on the other side) with an only apparent difference. Mary Hogarth was dead before Little Nell, if you will, was born; by the time of *The Old Curiosity Shop*, Mary is not there to be (even conceivably) embraced again, whereas within the story Nell has been alive for most of the single gentleman's quest. Even the single gentleman's finding of Nell, however, could not have brought back her grandmother—that sister-in-law three times removed by death—but only her image, her idea, the idea of her as already in the past. And even this finding of Nell *in time*, in the nick of or the realm of time, is by structural definition impossible. What is left of her for the "narrator," when his plotted quest is through, is only her "figure" in both senses, her peaceful shape as image. Neither could Dickens make Mary live again for himself, only for others en route. For you, a narrative; for him, a transposed mourning. In the mind of the single gentleman—Dickens' delegate inside that narrative—as for Master Humphrey, elegist from outside, Nell will always be dead before one gets there: already a figural (and figurative) signifier rather than living signified.

In this way belatedness becomes very much the burden of nostalgic literary structure as well as of nostalgic psychology. Even narrative discourse gets there too late: "They did not know that she was dead, at first" (72:655), with the cadence of that anticlimax reverberating across two levels of plotting. The "they" referred to in context is *not* actually the group headed by the single gentleman and misled by Nell's grandfather into thinking her still alive upon their arrival. In grammatical fact, within the retrospective story now disclosed about Nell's dying, the "they" refers instead to that small coterie of Nell's melancholic entourage attending upon her right through to the unperceived instant of her release. Twice over, that is, Nell has been *found dead*, first slipped from the world unnoted in the moment of her going, then come upon as if still in this life and suddenly discovered (long) gone. Hence, twice over, the need for story where the death has been, for a compensatory discourse in which, just as for the reader, Nell's death can only be reacted to, even on the scene, as verbally reenacted, as told. Her death, like Mary Hogarth's before her, becomes the occasion of sheer narrative, a scene of secondary reception rather than unmediated response. Death told becomes elegy.

There is, moreover, a specialized literary semiotics that bears on the conversion of Nell's elliptical death into the stuff of retroactive story—and thus bears, ultimately, on Dickens' autobiographical fable. Evinced by the kind of condensed "internal duplication" of organizing narrative structure offered by these tragic tale tellings is the "metatextual" *mise en abyme*: installed, according to Lucien Dallenbach, "to operate as 'instructions' to enable the reader to perform his/her task more easily: imitating, as if in a mirror, the actions of a reflection; reading the work in the way it wants to be read."[16] Yet Dallenbach adds a forthright question ("to put it more radically") that presses him forward to the consideration of one final category. He wonders whether it might be "just possible that by using the linguistic model to conduct our study we have blinded ourselves to [one final] kind of reflexion" (100). Upon further consideration, then: "This new *mise en abyme*, because of its ability to reveal something in the text that apparently transcends the text, and to reflect, within the narrative, what simultaneously originates, motivates, institutes and unifies it, and fixes in advance what makes it possible, seems to merit the name of *tran-*

scendental mise en abyme in our inventory" (101). Yet in the sliding subjectivity and self-consuming (Foucauldian) egoism, as it were, of Dickens' serial frame, this apparent outplaying of the text can be found encoded as a still textual, still discursive matter after all: a semiotics of conscripted response rather than that of encrypted origination.

A last example of this process occurs just before the closure of plot cedes to the autobiographical revelations of the serial apparatus. In the concluding account *of* (not yet recognizably *from*) the single gentleman, we are told of "his" efforts (not to be "my" until he stands confessed as Master Humphrey in the frame) to follow the tracks of Nell's journey on the basis of her "last narrative." This is, presumably—we have nothing else to go on—that story of her travel and travail up through the industrial turning point: the story we hear about, without hearing again, when she "told all" to the schoolmaster. On the gentleman's retroactive (and recursive) trek, the last-mentioned friend of the wandering girl's to be revisited is the furnace tender, into whose running narrative at fireside she herself, and her grandfather, were readily assimilated. To render emphatic the meeting of the single gentleman with this memorable benefactor of the heroine, omniscient narration dips into a parenthetical direct address. It borrows the shifter of present tense (as well as the "ego" position of the narratorial "I" in the objective case) without an actual second-person pronoun or vocative, singling out one destination among all the other familiar stops: "and trust me that the man who fed the furnace fire was not forgotten" (Chapter the Last: 670). What could be more innocent, more negligible? "And, make no mistake about it, the man . . .": This is the sense of the idiomatic imperative. What can the direct object, "me," possibly add—in "trust me"—to such a vernacular second-person address? Certainly no ordinary reader, thus momentarily addressed, is going to be prepared by this for the coming revelation of "me" as the single gentleman: the biographical "ego" represented by the narrative voice. Yet even at this stage the interpolating "trust me" can be taken to admit in passing the way in which the readerly assumption of a grammatical first person (validating our second-person status as implied narratees) is never entirely covered over by the structure of impersonal or omniscient narrative. The "I" behind the text will out, if only by implicature in the axis of address.[17]

"I May Confide to the Reader Now"

Even with the Mary Hogarth myth lurking in the background, then, biography alone neither explains nor exhausts the structural intricacies I have been attempting to trace out. It merely replays them, as it were, before the fact. That is why the abyssal displacement in operation here remains a textual, a *readable* construct, designed precisely as the reflex construction of its reader. This is a process that becomes all the clearer in view of a striking moment in the textual history of *Clock* rather than *Shop*. Nearing the completion of the serial frame, and working under the combined obligation of a pressing deadline and a space requirement, Dickens is discovered complaining about the exigencies of invention. As he worries how to work a transition from the draining conclusion of the *Shop* to the resumption of the *Clock*, faced with four more pages available to him in the weekly number, he writes to Forster that "I am at present in what Leigh Hunt would call a kind of impossible state—thinking what on earth Master Humphrey can think of through four mortal pages."[18] Exposed here, as if it were anything but the status quo of fictional invention, is that overload and potential short circuit in the relays of the author function which none other than the reader function will in the upshot be recruited to discharge. Troubled by his own "impossible" role as the author rather than reporting conduit of another's thoughts, Dickens is beset by the compositional equivalent of a reader's impulse to abdicate his imagination to the narrative agency itself: the phenomenological transfer by which the reader (according to Georges Poulet) is found "to be the subject of thoughts other than my own."[19] Yet what is there left to say of—or by—the narrator (Master Humphrey) when his function is consumed in the course, the discourse, of his own narrative?

Nothing but to admit as much. Dickens' solution is as structurally economical as it is opportunistic: to make the narrator disappear into what we have *already* read. If Dickens can sufficiently identify with Humphrey as frame narrator in the latter's efforts to facilitate closure, then he has hit upon exactly the thematics of identification he needs to finesse his own closure in Humphrey's voice. It is a case of what we might call self-fulfilling empathy. In this way does the biographical detour I have allowed myself in this chapter (ranging from Dickens' grieving over Mary to his fretting over his compositional burdens)—this recourse to external evidence—derive whatever pertinence it has from its entire redundancy to structure, its external reduplication of it. Discourse has already carried the closural point *in advance*, sustained the very burden of intersubjectivity. Instead of twisting himself into the mental disposition of his delegated storyteller, Dickens instead lets the tables be turned. The frame narrator, formerly Humphrey, is made to give himself over to what Dickens himself "would think" on such an occasion, thereby owning up (as the single gentleman) to his anything but disinterested involvement in the story all along.

"I may confide to the reader *now*, that in connexion with this little history I had something upon my mind—something to communicate which I had all along with difficulty repressed—something I had deemed it during the progress of the story, necessary to its interest to disguise, and which, *now* that it was over, I wished, and was yet reluctant to disclose" (679; adverbial emphasis added). The first "now" points to the teller's present discourse, the second to the internally narrated scene of postnarrative interrogation at his clockside. Just as between the two persons, early on, of "I checked myself" (between narrating and narrated agent), or later the equivocated persons of "[I say] trust me," so here, in the "scission" between the two "nows" of discourse and story, is the scene set for the answering here and now of reception. Thus does response develop its own grammatical parameters.

Continuing at this level of conscripted effect, Humphrey's revelation next builds across a simultaneously mounting and self-collapsing grammar: "The younger brother, the single gentleman, the nameless actor in the little drama, stands before you now" (680). In a micrological reprise of the whole plotted course of story to this point of disclosure, the ordinary framework of serial grammar—one character after another passing in review—is subsumed instead to apposition and a singular predicate, an equative predication: I am he in all of these guises. Under unsettling duress—a constraint to be "thinking what on earth Master Humphrey can think of"—Dickens has arranged at just this juncture to shunt such a coerced imaginative participation onto the very dynamics of reading. A single plot revelation thus uncovers the working of any plot in reception. It is all a matter of discursive identification, not disclosed identity.

Here is what we might call the foregone conclusion of this autobiographical surprise: that it would be all but impossible *not* to forge such identifications (as Master Humphrey here confesses to) in the act either of telling or of merely reading. For it is no small point to be made about Master Humphrey's final—and, for Dickens, creatively hard-won—investment in the story he narrates that Humphrey has also been assuming all along the audience's role by *reading that same story*: activating aloud its written text not only for his cronies but also for himself again. He is *your* double as much as the single gentleman's on one side or Dickens' on the other. Which is to say that you as reader are positioned, situated, conscripted at a point equidistant between biography and fictional narrativity, facilitating the transmutation of the one into the other through your own emotive investment in the latter's felt truth to life. You *are* what you read, a sometimes harrowing fact to which Humphrey's final disclosure is meant to testify. Bringing back Ricoeur's terms from the third chapter, we may say the weight of *Master Humphrey's Clock* upon *The Old Curiosity Shop* is to impress upon narrative structure more clearly than ever how "prefigured" autobiographical sentiment can be "configured" by fictionality to "refigure" the sentiments of an audience—an audience thereby partially contained within the dimensions of mimesis itself.

All this points to a self-inflicted limitation in certain forms of recent Victorianist criticism. So-called discourse analysis, for instance, in bypassing Foucault's own linguistic analytic (among other reading strategies), averts attention from one of the decisive environing contexts of classic realism. This is the valorized postromantic discourse of fellow feeling and empathetic surrender which has its own grammar of elided subjectivities and displaced objects, not to mention its own vocative delegations of ego and identification. And this discursive instrumentation, in turn, draws power from one of the deepest-going archetypes—or discourses, if you will—of aesthetic operation in a posttheological culture. Just as we found the narratorial conduct of Dickens' text, at the level of its enunciatory markers, made to mesh with its framing labors of orientation, so is its narrowly conceived autobiographical component arranged to articulate the novel's encompassing *mythic* function. At this juncture (of text and cultural context) certain methodological ramifications are again worth reflecting on. Anything called cultural studies cannot profitably overlook, for long, the ways in which a literary text may in its own right study, rather than merely instance, its culture. In its newer historicist forms, critique often widens the aperture of textual registration to a whole lateral field of discursive interaction—or at least passive interchange. Just as often, though, the achieved scope comes at a price, ignoring the abiding cultural context for the immediate historical one. Novels are thereby seen to realize their sign functions within a sociocultural space properly broad but artificially shallow. Against this tendency, it is crucial to recall that texts may be acts (as well as objects) of cultural anthropology.

In this respect, alongside the psychic displacements set in motion by Dickens' devices of serial closure and containment, an unexpected parallel with Jane Austen takes clarifying shape. In *Persuasion*, we remember, a merely symbolic incest, an incest *in name only*, is the emblematic threat to narrative momentum: Anne Elliot marrying herself back into the Elliot line. In *The Old Curiosity Shop*, the taboo against radical endogamy would also leave the stain of a strictly symbolic (but still illicit) eros, a familial transgression akin to incest. Such a taint would not only contaminate any desire on the part of a narrative agent to track Nell—any desire, that is, which is not at least a couple generations displaced from fraternal rivalry. It would also, and simultaneously, appear to defile any Victorian gentleman's residual desire for his wife's sister. In Austen, of course, sheer *openness* seems to deflect the cultural specter of such an incestuous deadlock; figured in this way is a receptiveness at the level both of plotted psychology and also of the reader's willingness for suspense, duration, and the patient differentiations upon which they depend. In Dickens, by contrast, a cathartic death is needed—and then a frame tale to depersonalize it, to render it public property. In both Austen and Dickens equally, though, the machinations of deferral enact their own inaugural logic: Oversameness, resisted differentiation, is a tendency overcome in advance in order for narrative to perform not only its structural function but its communal service.

In *The Old Curiosity Shop*, what everyone notices as the violative overtones of the grandfather's relation to Nell thus take on a different coloration in the shadow of the serial frame. The old man's *use* of the heroine is exactly the appropriation of the other which narrative structure seeks to repair by a corrective figuration. Stopping short of a quasi-incestuous introversion, the creative outlet of Master Humphrey's inbred bachelor cadre of nonprocreative subjectivities remains a kind of social compact in the mode of affective outreach. Not only a reduced collective in themselves, more to the point they widen their circle through texts, *taking in* otherness in order to replenish their confederation. In Dickens' metropolitan social diagnosis, that is, reading may in its own right begin to rectify the isolating impulse toward imaginative (rather than genetic) self-sameness whose equivalent in tribal society is the retreat from exogamous congress which religious interdict, rather than the secular ethic of reading, traditionally works to check. From Dickens forward, however, as later chapters will investigate, it grows harder to keep clean this cleansing function of literature as cultural ritual, to detach its vicariousness from either voyeurism or scapegoating.

Reading's "Ghostly Converse"

In the penultimate paragraph of *The Old Curiosity Shop*, we read that the Shop itself has been leveled to make way for a new "fine broad road . . . in its place" (Chapter the Last: 672). Though Kit cannot locate exactly in "reality" the site of his former devotion, he can summon it in narrative, and his children "would often gather round him of a night and beg him to tell again the story of good Miss Nell who died" (671). Retelling, textual replication, is already a privileged figure in this passage, since one of these very children is characterized as "an exact facsimile and copy" of his wife's brother (671). The discourse's own self-copying pleonasm ("facsimile and copy") only drives the point home. If we accept the fact that renewing life in the flesh is to some extent like textual multiplication, then a corollary trope would suggest how narrative renewal

(Kit's story of Nell told over, not to mention Dickens' of Mary) is like life in facsimile. As with Nell's narrative to the schoolmaster, of course, this is certainly not a story we need to have repeated at this late stage, even in condensed form. Instead, the scene of the tale's habitual retelling, rather than introducing a microcosm of the novel as executed narrative, provides a final rehearsal of its effect, its affect, as a familial ritual: the Victorian novel in its calculated *rereadability*.[20] "Such are the changes," adds the narrator with a fabled simile, "which a few years bring about, and so do things pass away, *like a tale that is told!*" (672; emphasis added). The time-trusted biblical analogy—a not too distant variant on the book of the world—actually reverses novelistic expectation in this case. Rather than aesthetic form being like life, life's closure is like art's. With narrative become the model for life, it is only fitting that the only Old Curiosity Shop left standing is the one on the shelf, just now over, at least over for now—its story passed away but always recoverable.

The Shop is gone, *The Shop* remains. But what about the carefully preserved Clock and the "society" or reading circle itself metonymically "christened 'Master Humphrey's Clock'" (678)? The titular Clock in this sense points away from the time-marking function of narrative (the periodical figured as clockwork mechanism of textual disgorgement) toward the communalizing figure of readership as a "society." Moreover, Master Humphrey has "caused my will to be so drawn out"—a willed desire prolonged, a document inscribed—so that the site of reading is itself in trust. By the will's provisions, "when we are all dead, the house shall be shut up, and the vacant chairs still left in their accustomed places," to facilitate an ongoing "ghostly converse" (678). This mausoleum of narrative is the true tomb of Nell, visited after the figural death of the author, as it were, by a perpetual community of "Clock" members enrolled—conscripted—simply by reading.[21]

Stripped of the ordinary contamination of property rights, euphemized out of the sphere of production, such is the sole legacy of a teller as teller: the disposition of the social space organized by his storytelling. The spectral postmortem trope of spatial maintenance for the "Clock" society, as for the *Clock*—a preserved domain of convivial transmission to be reinhabited simply by the activation of "converse" between tale and reception—takes on even more specifically novelistic resonance in the context of certain peculiar details that we have already learned about Master Humphrey's reading group. The "vacant chairs" mandated in perpetuity, for instance, will not be entirely new to the premises, since there have always been not one but two extra chairs "placed at our table when we meet" (678). This is done in case there is ever the wish to "increase our company" (678). It is a motive never far from the mind of a Victorian popular author.

In this way, the sustaining homology between Humphrey's privatized enclave and the simultaneously public but subjective space of Dickens' audience is impossible to avoid. Not only does this surrogate domestic microcosm of the Victorian reading public boast a minimal plurality of spaces (two) standing open for an increased "readership," waiting for you and yours as it were, but it also numbers among its present audience—inexplicably at first, and as the only member of the society initially mentioned at all—a "deaf gentleman" with whom his host spends many nights "communicating" romantic fancies. By sign language? By lip reading? Nothing is offered in explanation at the outset, but we are told later that the deaf gentleman "produced a little set of tablets and a pencil to facilitate our conversation."[22] Despite these material aids, "I scarcely know how we communicate as we do, but he has long since ceased to be deaf to me," writes Dickens the writer. That last phrase operates as a contextually reactivated dead metaphor for an interlocutor who never fails, let us say, to "lend an ear." Dickens has thus summarily refigured the eccentric companion as placeholder for the reader at large. For deafness is of course the state of reception in which a writer's "voice" first speaks to any and all readers, even though the text in hand may then be further broadcast to actual auditors by the oral emission of its written signs. Moreover, the "deaf gentleman" (like the single gentleman whose tale he is about to hear) is a man whose "humour" it is "to conceal" his name; according to the pseudonymous Master Humphrey, otherwise the single gentleman, "as he has never sought to discover my secret, I have never sought to penetrate his" (677). Call this odd symbiotic duo the figured interdependence of a pseudonymous Dickens, doubly withdrawn behind his assorted personae ("Boz," "Master Humphrey"), and any anonymous reader—to whom tales appear like clockwork from the mechanism of a serial, and in the presence of a "society," both christened "the Clock"—call it this, and the bizarre details have zeroed in on a familiar model of fictional "communication" and response.

Dickens constructs a "society" so exclusively devoted to such narrative communion that the analogy of storytelling to life at large in the closing words of the single gentleman's narration ("like a tale that is told") might in fact be taken to dramatize a closed obsessional world of reclusion and monomania. Yet you don't suspect this for a second. You get the real point: Only for as long as you are reading does "the Clock" comprise your only "society." And anyway, *The Old Curiosity Shop* ultimately goes forth into that other social, if less sociable, world on its own, without its periodical frame as buffer (except in the form of an editorial apparatus in certain scholarly editions). Still, of course, the closural conceit of the "tale told" remains in place, denaturalizing the tragedy of Little Nell, defusing its excess, sealing the redemptive promise of her perpetuity through rereading. When all is done by being merely said, and your "trust" *formally* secured by every sleight of grammatical sequence and every structural analogue, the no more than figuratively "revolutionised" neighborhoods reached by Dickens' weekly numbers are set right again. Such is the attempted sociology of reading mounted upon the passive romanticism both of *The Clock*'s communal appeal and of "the Clock" as its own already inscribed community. For Dickens any such theory of reading, if we want to call it that, is always at the same time a philosophy of the self in the world. This is a controlling fact of his prose which will emerge more clearly, for him as for us, once the entire serial experiment of *Master Humphrey's Clock* is behind him, its deficiencies realized, its motives reviewed. The apparatus attached to the collected issues of the journal offers a dossier of such second thoughts.

Figuring the "Empty Space" of Response

With Boz reasonably sure of his audience and of his voice before it, but uncertain about the best strategy for holding and enlarging that audience, ultimately for naturalizing it, he threw *himself*, as it were, into an experiment from which he later backed—loquaciously—away. His retrospective "prefatory" material to the serial brings out the social basis of popular fiction, as well as Dickens' populist craftsmanship, in ways that scholarship has generally overlooked—interested more in the two novels that emerged from the *Clock* than in the encasing mechanics of production which sought to formulate and orient the nature of novel reading for the contemporaneous audience. Well before his final obituary for the weekly serial, Dickens can be found rereading the elapsed matter of his own *Clock* text as a tacit parable of, rather than an ineffectual call for, sustained emotional participation. The cultural institution of the Victorian novel undergoes in the process one of its most sedulous apologias. It does so precisely by defining the psychic distances on which the culture itself, as well as its necessitated fictions, is thought to depend.

It is in the preface to the "First Cheap Edition" of *The Old Curiosity Shop* (1848) that Dickens finally looks back at how the serial "wisely" became "one of the lost books of the earth" (Penguin, 41–42). Considerably in advance of this palinode for the defunct journal, however, Dickens has anticipated his return to monthly numbers in an open letter "To the Readers of 'Master Humphrey's Clock,'" addressed with an atypical Dickensian salutation to "Dear

Friends" and suggesting "a better means of communication between us."[23] Such intercourse would only confirm the myth of the "Clock" itself: a parafamilial reading group funded by a rich stash of assorted manuscripts by various hands, read aloud and by turns among the disinterested members in a vicarious narrative communication shared and reciprocal. Other material in his several retrospective assessments (even in progress) of the short-lived journal will flesh out this mythic *topos* as a full-fledged mythology of urban cultural identity and its purported alleviations through narrative.

In prefacing the first collected issue of journal numbers, released while *Master Humphrey's Clock* was still in publication, Dickens is trying to account for his reintroduction of certain characters from *Pickwick*—as more than a ploy to increase sales with a surefire commodity from the proven past. "When he sought"—writes the author about his own motives—"to interest his readers in those who talked, and read, and listened, he revived Mr. Pickwick and his humble friends."[24] He did so "not with any intention of reopening an exhausted and abandoned mine, but to connect them in the thoughts of those whose favourites they had been, with the tranquil enjoyments of Master Humphrey" (689). These nostalgic revenants are not there for their own sake, in other words, but for yours, and not so that you should enjoy them, exactly, but so that you should imagine Humphrey's enjoyments of his clock-case tales by comparison with your previous delight in *Pickwick Papers*. The hubris of this touchstone is hardly outshone by the warm glow of its mock humility. The reader, we are told, can perhaps best understand the power of the present stories, in their hold on their dramatized auditors, by remembering how captivating Dickens' *own* stories (as if there is any difference) are and have always been. The real problem, however, is not with the return of the Pickwickians but with the vested members of the Clock circle themselves. "Having brought himself in the commencement of his undertaking to feel an interest in these quiet creatures, and to imagine them in their old chamber of meeting, eager listeners to all *he had to tell, the author* hoped—as authors will—to succeed in awakening some of his own emotions in the bosoms of his readers" (689; emphasis added). Here is the phenomenology of reading by any other name—authorial feeling animated by proxy in those who realize his prose in their own cognitive operations. Yet as part of the mechanism by which the private feeling for Mary should be "awakened" as a narrative feeling for Nell, the very logic of transmission is thrown off by the slippery third-person grammar—in which "all he had to tell" attaches more to the "author" than to "Master Humphrey" (a more distant antecedent). Yet again there is a blurring of boundaries between the two avatars of narrative origin. Yet again the reader function is manifested in the crevices or "scission" of discursive instability—and projected here onto a figured commune of "eager listeners."

The effect persists—across a continuing grammatical instability. "Imagining Master Humphrey in his chimney-corner, resuming night after night, the narrative,—say, of the *Old Curiosity Shop*—*picturing to himself* the various sensations of *his* hearers . . . and how all these gentle spirits would trace some faint reflection of their past lives in the varying current of the tale—he has insensibly fallen into the belief that they are present to his readers as they are to him" (689–90; emphasis added). Dickens thus explains his authorial interest in picturing "his"—Humphrey's, not his own—"hearers" and conceiving their reaction in the form of a two-staged identification: with the internal life of characters in their independent identification, in turn, with stories received if not produced in their own image, along the autobiographical "trace" of "some faint reflection." A sliding (and ultimately elided) scale of response is thus marked out. Humphrey's listeners see themselves in the place of Humphrey as narrator of his stories, as, by extension, Dickens assumes his own readers will see themselves in those same listeners. But by not actually describing the emotive transformations of response, the "author" seems at least dimly to realize that he has put at risk the whole procedure, "has forgotten that like one whose vision is disordered he may be conjuring up bright figures where there is nothing but empty space" (690). Unoccupied by a given reader's activated response, this "space" is, after all, the always "empty" zone of intersubjectivity itself.[25] This is precisely the burden of that metanarrative substitution that puts Master Humphrey back into the plot of *The Old Curiosity Shop* as the single gentleman. Enunciator becomes character. In the case of the Master of ceremonies at his own reading circle, the reader aloud becomes an eventually admitted participant—ultimately, indeed, the sine qua non not just of readerly activation but also of narrative agency (quest and detection) within the very tale that occupies his present time.

"The Reader Must Not Expect to Know Where I Live": Our Mutual Secrets

There are few readers made acquainted with the Clock confederates (explicitly not confidants), Dickens supposes, "who would have them forgo their present enjoyments, to exchange those confidences with each other, the absence of which is the foundation of their mutual trust" (690). That word again: "confidence." Elsewhere, it has been the term for the personal names that both Master Humphrey and the deaf gentleman, in their mutual anonymity, refuse to "confide," even as it is the term for the revelation of narratorial identity in the novel's coda, where Master Humphrey has a secret to "confide to the reader now" (Penguin, 679).

The very same privacy we are presumed to respect in the Clock members is thus the privacy we are led to expect of them in their narrated dealings with each other. This has a kind of logic—as already articulated in the *Clock*'s opening sentence, where we find Master Humphrey's direct mention of the reader in his or her exclusion from full companionship: "The reader must not expect to know where I live" (Penguin, 673). Like the uncertain topographical location of the razed Curiosity Shop, the location of the Clock—the very space of storytelling—is everywhere and nowhere, with any audience for it convened on the (variable and impalpable) spot. This would, as I say, boast a self-contained logic, but Dickens does not stop there. His preface has more to insinuate with that last unexpected subordination, "the absence of which is the foundation of their mutual trust." Trust is born not of knowledge but of its withholding, so that the characters attached to the clock and its *voluminous* case function as a group, keep their stories in trust for each other as it were, precisely because their own histories are withdrawn behind the arena of collective response. It is as if, not ever certain that you could know the truth of otherness, all you can found a society upon, or in microcosm a reading group, is the certainty of this impasse. But into and across the space of this negative trust, this trust in negativity—lest it remain a vacuum—must flow the more open nature of fictional narrative (among other modes of circulated textuality). This is a specialized mode of writing which is virtually unmatched in its publicizing—up to a certain limit—of the interior life.

More perhaps than Dickens knew, and more than has been noticed since, such variously halting drafts of his novel-reading compact as we find in prefatory and parenthetical material of this sort are also a compressed interpretation of the whole Victorian social contract—and of reading's place within it. Social subjects trust only when allowed to retain their deepest privacy: This is liberal polity in embryonic formulation. But to keep all from being clandestine and repellant, culture infuses the public sphere with narratives that tell individual secrets over the signature and under the guise of otherness. Narratives like those exchanged at Humphrey's clockside envision a community of response which compensates for the unknowable nature of source and destination, speaker and listener, teller and reader. What we can never know of or reveal to others, even the secret we may *be* (as well as keep) to ourselves, is what we often cannot help but know in responding to fictional narrative. It is this response, not anything more about them in particular, that Dickens had hoped the subsidiary participants in the Clock group would evoke even in their effacement as characters. They are there, as we have seen, simply so that the Dickensian narrator can imagine us imagining our way into the position of their imaginative investment.

As with Dickens' prefatory exits from the *Clock* serial, such things are perhaps never clearer than when made baldly explicit. Three novels later, in the paradoxical opening farewell to the separate publication of *Dombey and Son* in 1848, where the serializing narrator again yields place to the authorial signator of a bound volume, all is salute, be it coming or going: "I cannot forego my usual opportunity of saying farewell to my readers in this greeting-place, though I have only to acknowledge the unbounded warmth and earnestness of their sympathy in every stage of the journey we have just concluded" (41). Fielding's coach as figure for narratorial progress pales almost to dead metaphor, while "unbounded" comes forward as a virtual pun for the previously uncollected status of the monthly numbers. So far, though, all is fairly routine. It is the second and last paragraph of this brief prefatory valediction which shows the attempted transcendence of authorial ego into popular sociology. Alluding to the audience's potential sadness over Paul Dombey's death, Dickens adds, "I hope it may be a sorrow of that sort which *endears* the sharers in it, one to another" (emphasis added). After the dim figural subtext of the first paragraph, here is the seeded matrix of this whole rhetorical gambit: the unsaid "dear" reader whose relationship of "warmth and earnestness" is meant now to be displaced sideways into a community of fellow feeling, each reader endeared to every other as well as to the cathartic impresario of the narrative itself. "This is not unselfish in me," Dickens closes. "I may claim to have felt it, at least as much as anybody else; and I would fain be remembered kindly for my part in the experience." Since Dickens created "it," the sorrowful plot turn, even as he was feeling it, the analogic dodge hidden behind the sense of parallel communities hereby movingly enlarged (Dickens with his audience, each reader with all others) can scarcely escape suggesting the reader's cocreative role in the actualization of that death scene, first as an occasioned feeling and then as the ground of a social cohesion. As even more extensively dramatized with the story of Little Nell, the Victorian cult of death tips its hand as the (usually occulted) origin of an entire fictional aesthetic in reception.

The local rhetoric of *Dombey and Son* goes so far as to confirm, in ways unexpected at this stage in Dickens' fiction, the communitarian force of its rhetorical send-off. Amid the chill of young Paul's fateful christening, there is a fleeting detail, cordoned off in a single sentence, which explicitly pits the ambience of Dombey, stone-cold man of business, against the sentimental warmth which, according to the preface, will come to both author and reader alike in the saddening experience of Dickens' novel. In Dombey's library, textual intimacy or endearment is unthinkable: "The bookcase, glazed and locked, repudiated all familiarities" (5:109). Just the opposite is what books are for. To convey this seems one of the overdetermined motives, a chapter before, for an atypical moment of reader reference within the paragraph-to-paragraph conduct of Dickensian narrative. The purpose in this case is scarcely to "repudiate" but rather to appropriate the protocols of "familiarity" as a textual effect: "It is half-past five o'clock, and an autumn afternoon, when the reader and Solomon Gills become acquainted" (4:90). In a much reduced and less intrusive form of the ornate "become acquainted" trope from *The Old Curiosity Shop*, the temporal pinpointing lifts its logic from a description, just two sentences back, of Gills' "tremendous chronometer" (4:89). It is the very punctuality of a character's spatiotemporal world into which the Dickensian discourse dips expeditiously to endear us—to narrator as well as character in the mutualities of fictional intimacy.

And having interpolated us so amicably into a system of reading as community, Dickens follows it up with the tacit extrapolation warranted by a later passage like this, when Florence has availed herself of a book, perhaps from the same library in her father's house, and sits over it daydreaming of Edith, her destined stepmother, as a new friend and protector. The terms are the same, an impetus toward intimate community now dramatized as an urgent yearning, yet even here it is a motive not attached to internal characterization alone. The emphatic participial beat of the prose cadence announces a ceremonial moment that hardly seems exhausted by the homely scene itself within this one-sentence detail of plot: "Florence was, one day, sitting reading in her room, and thinking of the lady and her promised visit soon—for her book turned on a kindred subject—when, raising her eyes, she saw her standing in the doorway" (30:501). Not only does "kindred" borrow its charge from the familial relationship so eagerly anticipated by the isolated heroine, but a further inference is stirred: As Florence's deed of reading is cousin both to her better thoughts and to their immanent fulfillment, so is the reading of Dickens imagined to claim kin with your own finer feelings, as themselves a yearning, like Florence's, for a more expansive fellowship, one that a novel like *Dombey and Son* can only—but this is no small thing—half satisfy.

This is the typical work of extrapolation rather than interpolation in Dickens. Far more commonly than with such a gesture as "become acquainted," the relation of narrator to reader, even of author to reader, as emotional familiars extending together their imaginative acquaintanceship is left for prefaces to spell out. Yet everything in *The Old Curiosity Shop*, in its original release to a curious public, has acted this out. What is left when we cannot open to each other is the open book, in the name of whose openness we can convene our own veiled individuality in a shared emotion masked in any one of us but common to us all. The domestic novel becomes both a rallying point for the deficits and reticence of the public domain and an emotive focus for the inexpressible. Reading is where we go, not to be made whole or made one so much as to be made mutual with others in our separateness, where the secrets we share in only one sense—hold in common without telling—are displayed without incrimination, if only up to a certain point, as those of others: the fears and yearnings, say, of a girl named Nell and a young man named Swiveller. Pictured here is the labor of social bonding that the public institution of Victorian fiction is ritually proliferated to insure.

But the Clock must always run out. "For . . . when their tales are ended and but their personal histories remain, the chimney-corner will be growing cold, and the clock will be about to stop for ever" (690). This elegiac prolepsis is made good on by the final disposition of the frame tale. Constituted as storytellers, not characters—but only as they are all participants in a narrative activity designed to hide their own stories while telling others—the listeners to story within the *Clock*, when eventually thrown back on their own histories, will have lost the very energy that convenes and buoys them. It is thus that they can only die away—narratively, their vicarious will for life spent; textually, their purpose consumed in the course of inset stories framed by their attention. And where there is death pending, there may well be a legacy in mind, a will prepared, even a final resting place enshrined: at last, in Master Humphrey's preserved chambers, the very temple and tomb of ritual reading. This is the space of assembly, in perpetuity, which we have seen provided for by Humphrey's legal will, the realm reserved for "ghostly converse" (Penguin, 678). A visionary space, it has been twice envisaged, first by George Cattermole in a plate accompanying the first chapter and later in an endpiece by Hablot Browne.[26] The first (fig. 7) offers a ceremonial view of the emptied chamber, the still waiting place of story, an illustration in keeping with the cool preview of this sacrosanct memorial by the narrator; the second (fig. 8), when Clock and *Clock* are actually disbanded at the same moment, gives the disarray of sudden and unplanned evacuation, with various manuscripts, including one titled "Barnaby Rudge," still strewn about amid the jumble of furniture. Together the illustrations contrast the tonality of narrative closure in the offing, a thing of formal serenity, with the seldom chosen moment of human arrest.

Figure 7. Illustration from *Master Humphrey's Clock*

In both cases, your voyeuristic access to the emptied scene of reading invades

Figure 8. Illustration from *Master Humphrey's Clock*

a region whose suspended narrativity has arrived as the silence of the grave: the outer limit of all discursive community.

Short of this, the Victorian novel is there to convene the disparateness it cannot repeal. Reading is thereby advanced as a knowing discipline of the fancy designed largely to divert an acknowledged (rather than denied) otherness within the social subject (either divisiveness or self-mystery) toward a less disruptive otherness beyond it (fictional character and event). This is the inherent bond between fiction and culture's ritual basis. The question then remains: How does a given novel, when not investigating these matters in direct exposition, otherwise set about modeling a transaction with its audience designed to reconcile the often contradictory terms of the Victorian social compact, based as it is on a humanist individuality that seems by turns yearned for (as the ego ideal of the centered subject) and painfully inescapable (as a knot of isolated and socially unincorporable drives)?

One version of literary history amounts to an archive of such transactions—and the rhetorical understandings that make them more or less explicit. What a text's invitation to privacy and its thematization of interiority combine to warrant in Dickens' ordinary practice as a representative Victorian writer is, as it happens, a wholesale revision of both the nested engineering of disclosure in Mary Shelley and the ethic of openness in Austen. On the one hand, increasingly entrenched procedures of blanket omniscience (with the first-person deflections of the *Clock* a clarifying exception) tend, as contrasted with Shelley's practice, to vitiate the leverage made available by framing and denarrativize its graduated access to inwardness. On the other hand, a romantic metaphysics of the psyche, fetishizing the mind's secret springs of power, deflates the communicative value of "unreserve" so prominent in Austen, placing emphasis instead on the disclosures of discourse rather than those of dialogue. But here, too, something is always held back. In comparison with the audience for Austen or Shelley, Victorian readers are left with a more flexible and strangely invasive, but still limited, medium of storytelling. Beyond its laying open of character, the novel has evolved into a mediation that can reach its readers by rhetoric or rehearse their response by parable—but which, such readers need to think, can never actually penetrate to that deepest inwardness they have left safely behind for the book in hand.

What we have seen so far in Dickens thus lends itself to summary as follows: As Little Nell reads herself—and is read—to death in *The Old Curiosity Shop*, a new Victorian reader is born in the serial frame. This is a reader continuous with the inscribed or apostrophized audience of the formulaic bestsellers but one conscripted less blatantly, inducted instead through the psychodynamic relays of characterization and narration. In this one text and in the tradition it illuminates, the determinants of such reading go well beyond that privately eroticized and incognito mourning performed by Dickens. The novelistic issue concerns, instead, the more generally fetishized suffering of Nell's story—of nubile distress as the virgin page of ripe (written) but as yet unenjoyed (unread) text. Here is an erotics of reading which remains merely tacit as a Victorian narrative staple until (for the sake of example) the inscribed or textualized female bodies of Rider Haggard's exotic romances (*Mr. Meeson's Will*, *She*) half a century later.

In this light, the readings to come may be seen to detail the gradually exposed terms of the Victorian narrative contract so one-sidedly negotiated by the framed event of *The Old Curiosity Shop*. The psychopathology Dickens' text narrowly evades, the class unrest it derails or travesties, and the morbidity it labors to disinfect—these all come back to haunt the Victorian mainstream narrative. After various further suppressions and transvaluations in both high Victorian writers and the lesser best-sellers alike, these disturbances to both the civic authority of fiction and its ritual function return most notably, on the one hand, in the class warfare of literary readership itself in Gissing and, on the other, in the vicarious neurosis of textual encounter in the gothicized reading ethos of his *fin de siècle* peers. How little of this potential textual trouble is let surface in Dickens may suggest just how clearly he saw it coming.

Chapter Eight

On *Abymes*
The Regress of Reception in Collins and Late Dickens

Frontispiece to Wilkie Collins, *The Queen of
Hearts* (New York: Peter Fenelon Collier,
Publishers, 1900)

$\mathscr{I}$t is high time to place *Master Humphrey's Clock* in the larger context of nineteenth-century fictional reception. It was just this context, after all, which the
Clock had been geared to count on. This chapter will examine how certain Victorian structures of publication promote the reformulation of their own con-
stituent narratives as renditions of, rather than merely venues for, the reading
function: sites of enacted consumption rather than simply incitations to response. The *Clock*'s ultimate inference about receptive subjectivity in literary
transaction (an inference further explored in the serialization of *A Tale of Two
Cities* two decades later) helps draw out certain related implications in a para-
novelistic text by Wilkie Collins: the enframed story anthology called *The*

Queen of Hearts, whose individual narratives originally appeared, as it happens, in Dickens' second serial, *Household Words*. The setting of Collins' text—a domestic locus of narrative writing read aloud—bears closer relation, however, to the quasi-familial premises (both senses) of the earlier serial, *Master Humphrey's Clock*. For what Dickens' *Clock* enacts at intermittent length in its framing interludes, what *The Queen of Hearts* subsequently bears out, and what *A Tale of Two Cities*, within and beyond its encasement by the monthly journal *All the Year Round,* will later carry to such lengths (trying for heights) of visionary self-involution is a much-advertised fact of Victorian fictional prose: its household status as a fund of verbal diversion and improvement available all the year round. Such fiction emerges as an aspect of both leisure economy and social ideology whose hearthside perpetuation the nineteenth-century novel not only represents but abets—even at times (hence the present chapter) represents itself abetting.

The Queen of Hearts appeared in 1859 at the height of the Victorian fiction industry's confidence in a congregated and harmonized public. The widening gulf to come between railway bookstall and ivory tower, lending library and "arcanum" (George Moore's term), market practice and mandarinism is, of course, the schism that hastens the breakdown of the Victorian literary populace (its paying public as a civic collective) into mass audience versus modernist *clientele*. No better representative of the earlier arrangement can be found than the intended readership of Dickens' friend and associate Wilkie Collins; and no better text than this publishing venture of 1859 which is really more of a *marketing* venture, symptomatic as such of the period's whole mode of popular narrative circulation.[1] Through the clanking mechanics of its central conceit, *The Queen of Hearts* turns out to narrate the always more or less familial context of narrative attention upon which Collins', not to mention Dickens', other successes less explicitly rest. Like Dickens' frame tale, this is a text having no need to include you by salute; plot itself inculcates its own use for you and yours. And it does so, in 1859 again, the year before the publication of Collins' first and definitive sensation novel, *The Woman in White*, whose intensified Dickensian agitations of melodramatic response, and those of its whole subgenre, are thus justified in advance as socially *normalizing* aberrations.

"Our Anxious Literary Experiment": W(h)iling Away the Time

The frame narrative of *The Queen of Hearts* offers a veritable parody of a patriarchal household interrupted in its generational continuity—and impatiently awaiting renewal. The story concerns the elderly narrator and his two brothers, quirky misogynistic recluses cohabitating in the temporary absence of the narrator's son, a young man scheduled to return home soon after recuperating from a wound inflicted in the Crimean War. To the consternation of the three aged brothers, their retreat—their secluded phallocentric Eden at the "Glen Tower"—is to be invaded by a beautiful young woman, Jessie Yelverton, who, by the terms of her father's will, must spend six weeks each year rusticating under the narrator's care. The purpose of this prescribed interval is to effect a routine purge of "the evil influences of society over the characters of women in general."[2] Jessie thus enters the story as the unwanted "Queen of Hearts" in this bachelor enclave, yet it is only after the duration of her enforced stay has nearly elapsed that the plot—and the metaplot—begin thickening together.

It is at this turn that the narrator receives a pleading letter from his son, who harbors an as yet undeclared passion for this "spoiled darling of society" (12). He begs his father that she be kept at the Tower for the extra ten days necessary to insure his arrival, so that he might propose marriage and thereby indirectly serve the purposes of her dead father in rescuing Jessie once and for all from the defeminizing vortex of the social swirl. It is only in the quiet confines of the Tower, he suspects—away from the temptations of her life as a female free agent in a culture of increasing social license—that he can be sure of prevailing upon her affections. His father, the narrator, is moved; but what to do? What can keep a spirited urban girl voluntarily enthralled for ten days?

Despite the trepidations of the father *as character*, who should know better than a fictional narrator? The answer to the problem is nothing less than the collected stories before us, projected back into a context of dramatized manuscript preparation and then forward to the scene of their nightly recitation. He decides, in short, to while away her time with story. Various tales are written out by the narrator himself as well as commissioned from his brothers, some autobiographical, some secondhand but launched by first-person authentications, all conceived to rivet attention and renew desire. Narrative desire only, of course; for this Scheherazade in reverse must have her own itch for narrative kept alive long enough for it to be transferred to another kind of passion. Where the "box of novels" (31) originally provided to amuse her has failed to do so, still the stories succeed. We suspect why. Not only are they urgently delivered aloud, rather than left with her in her solitude. They also bear the testamentary traces of first-person experience that Collins mobilizes for his own later "sensation novels." More to the point, they involve just often enough some of the same irresistible narrative ingredients of these later novels: the lurid mix of coincidence and treachery, supernatural overtones, dark family secrets, crim-

inal detection, insanity and incarceration, hairbreadth escapes—the whole ar-
mory of excitations that both exaggerate and exhaust the sedentary reader's
urge for a more thrilling daily milieu. Then, too, the stories are textually su-
pervised, when not actually written or rewritten, by the narrator, who redis-
covers, so to speak, the Wilkie Collins in himself, explaining, "I had hardly been
more than an hour at my desk before I found the old literary facility of my
youthful days, when I was a writer for the magazines, returning to me as if by
magic" (52). Further, the narrator's schooled literary tact, as well as his literary
dexterity, will come to his aid by way of moderating the excesses of his yet
more sensationalist brother Morgan, who provocatively overstates his narrative mandate: "'I understand,' [Morgan] said, taking a savage dip at the ink, 'I'm
to make her flesh creep, and to frighten her out of her wits. I'll do it with a
vengeance!'" (52). As long as the "vengeance" is meant idiomatically, this is
roughly the spirit of their fictional cabal, but its startling effects must be kept,
as in the sensation novel itself, within allowable bounds, the narrator therefore
reserving "to myself privately an editorial right of supervision over Morgan's
contributions" (52).

There is, moreover, a sociology as well as a psychology of story involved in
the book's obverse version of the *Arabian Nights*. Nothing is said about it by
Collins' narrator, but all the telling goes to show it. The parable thus unfolded
is at the core of the Victorian fictional institution's domestic privilege. For
across the narrative subdivisions of the ten "Days" that follow, and the subdivided chapters of the separate tales that further mark them off on the plot's
internal calendar, what happens is not merely distraction but tacit inculcation.
What the duration of the heroine's apprenticeship in narrative response thus
does for her, besides forestall her departure, is to train her precisely in the patient domestic virtues, the sympathy and focus, the emotional involvement required for the consummation of the hero's need for a Victorian wife. Between
the skittishness of adolescence and the maturation of desire which permits
commitment come therefore the lessons of narrative, of narrative in and of itself, regardless of its particular subject matter. To fill up evening after evening,
the tales read aloud by this curious surrogate family (of multiple patriarchs and
a daughter-in-law-in-training) are, like popular Victorian fiction at large, stories
that engage, redirect, enlarge, and concentrate—often inflame and deplete—
feeling. And more.

These tales resemble Victorian commodity fiction, not just Victorian storytelling, in another way as well. In this they solidify their obvious parallels
with the stories dispensed from Master Humphrey's Clock, though designed
not to solace the domestic deficit of aged bachelors in a reading club but rather

to apprentice a young woman in connubial maturity. As with the stories stored in the clock case, whose telling is thus *taken out* from time itself, the brothers' deliberately time-consuming tales are also, without explanation, all written down rather than simply told, except for the two or three that happen to be found wholesale among their papers. Why should these grumpy siblings, none of them practiced or practicing authors, want to read from manuscripts hastily prepared rather than to deliver orally the stories they have in them to tell? Why should this be the case—unless to nail down the analogy between such an unlikely parlor game and the larger arena of consumed textuality, of literary print in circulation, where stories are better crafted than in oral exchange, more gripping in their tightness of construction? This is no doubt why the unmentioned particulars of Jessie's reaction to any of the stories are *given* only in one sense, taken for granted as entirely displaced by your own response as simultaneous public for their textual dissemination.

And this is not the whole of it. The net of response is not only cast wide but folded back into the marital prospects upon which the plot closes in and down. For such published matter is what the heroine and the son will one day read aloud to each other once she has abdicated her throne as Queen of Hearts and accepted the domestic pedestal instead, especially now that she seems to be mastering what one might call the essential domestic lesson of Victorian literary culture, its husbandry of the inner life: to substitute the private expansiveness of narrative excitation for the frenetic and wasting pleasures of too much society; or in other words to purify desire through aesthetic exertion. In the same year that George Eliot's *Adam Bede* diagnoses the spirit of an age "prone to"—as if prostrate before—the leveling continuity between "excursion trains, art-museums, periodical literature, and exciting novels" (52:557), the eventual master of the "sensation novel" has his work cut out for him. For Collins must labor in effect to separate the latter half of the catalogue—periodical stories made more exciting yet in quasi-novelistic format—from the former, to extricate literary fascination from the world of unalloyed sensation for which the heroine is feared to yearn.

However hoodwinked she may be about the motive for her extended sojourn, Jessie's own sense of its high occasion oddly confirms and extends the narrator's, since the storytelling will be both intimate and formal, embracing—but only to tame it—something of the self-gratifying erotic display of the high life it interrupts. For "the readings . . . take place in her own sitting-room," with Jessie "in magnificent evening costume," regretting that she hadn't "brought with her from London the dress in which she had been presented at court the year before" (61). As pictured by the frontispiece to *The Queen of Hearts*, by contrast with the illustrations of Master Humphrey's clockside, Collins' fictional site more openly incorporates the world's vanity that it means to cure, panders to the same indulgence it works to chasten by not openly chastising.

Another thing less to overlook than to bear in mind, as the Victorian audience would have done: These stories had all been published before by Collins, many in Dickens' *Household Words*. They are thus already institutionalized products of the literary mainstream before they are renarrativized into motivated distractions within this one improbable plot—already bought and sold before their present strategic recirculation in a new and nearly five-hundred-page narrative form. But instead of this anthology structure—with its unabashed ploy of marketing rebound tales—serving to vitiate the allegory of Victorian story in service to marital domesticity, the fact of reprinting actually corroborates the social—*because* commercial—fable. The previous salability of stories already in public circulation builds into the heart of this extemporaneous paternal experiment, that is, a tried and tested Victorian format of domestic consolidation through written and read entertainments. With all the book's disparate stories held in readiness under one roof, such are the *home truths* taught by fiction through the very fact of its printed circulation as household words. By parody and exemplum at once, Collins' narratively fixated heroine is thus a placeholder for the Victorian *captive audience* as a willingly indoctrinated subject.

In *The Queen of Hearts*, Collins has hit upon (or lifted from Dickens) a frame structure that allows him, in the act of recirculating already popular tales, to bracket and transvalue the entire popular aesthetic of an age, to say nothing of the sensationalist subgenre just around the corner. The craft of the novel subserves a veritable ethic of patience, of acceptance, of willing deflection from immediate gratification. Such is the moral—and morale—taught by the form of all stories, as well as the content of many, and reconstituted here as the very metatext of their reception: both the regimen and the social regime of reading. That Jessie's forestalled departure to the arms of the world has been a kind of sexual sublimation effected through story is a point clinched by a passing detail of the denouement. With all the stories gone through and the son now arrived, with offstage disclosures made on both sides and the marriage commitment sealed, Jessie "showed charmingly" (471) her appreciation for all the narrator has done by asking, quite "simply," we are told, "May I stop at the Glen Tower a little longer?" By the very word "stop" this Queen of Hearts reveals how entirely she has internalized the plot, the complot, of arrested worldliness in deference to the marital mating—and waiting—game. Though the narrator gets her sly point at once, he responds with a sly naiveté of his own:

"If you think you can get through your evenings, my love." Just a few lines from the end, the cultural logic of Collins' whole text comes clean in that single conditional: either sexual proximity or narrative magnetism, whatever gets you through the night.

Like Jessie, nineteenth-century fiction here comes of age. What Jane Austen's novels instill by their very structure as dilatory marital narrative, Collins' quintessential Victorian text of recurrently renewed narrative energy—renewed under the guise of postponed and ripening emotional reward—replicates at the even more explicitly institutional level. This is the story of Victorian story in its domestic, but only because mercantile, function. Finally, though, there is yet another way to take this, to receive it, one that inverts only to confirm the terms of response. If this portrayed exercise in the reading aloud of personally drafted manuscripts is, in all its important domestic aspects, the functional equivalent of having a volume of a periodical like *Household Words* on hand, stocked with just the number of stories necessary to keep one going till the next issue, then a further and reciprocal inference comes forward. The recognition that stories, once distributed as literary productions within the machinery of the fiction industry, can be so readily recast as privately drafted accounts by the three brothers only redounds to the deepest fiction of such fiction as intense personal communication—in marketplace as well as parlor. (This would come as no surprise to Master Humphrey, alleviating his own grief through the narrative agency of the single gentleman—as Dickens through both.) Marketing is taken to enhance rather than to compromise the intimacy of storytelling. Readers are always dear, however dear a published fiction may be. In view, then, of Collins' self-promoting legerdemain in the retelling (and reselling) of his tales, it seems an opportune moment to renew the largest methodological claim of this study: that ideology, Victorian or otherwise, is not just a factor but a narrative *function* of literary textuality in circulation, a structural and rhetorical instrumentation of its venues—and avenues—of exchange.

An adjacent publishing venture may further clarify the place of Collins' text in the print culture of its day. In the same year as *The Queen of Hearts*, and drawing also on stories primarily published for the first time in *Household Words*, Elizabeth Gaskell brought out a two-volume anthology called *Round the Sofa* (1859), naming by title the site of its narrative dispensary at the regularly attended couchside of an invalid Edinburgh widow.[3] The contrast with Collins' setup is so complete because the formats are so fully complementary. They each envision an anomalous case that differs from, only more clearly to delineate, the standard reception of published fiction as a pleasure to be cultivated within the routine pressures of domestic management. The general principle is clear:

Where leisure is at a premium, narrative's place is secure. But where leisure is a tautology—with the carefree life of a young socialite (Collins) or the housebound monotony of an invalid (Gaskell)—narrative justification comes more urgently to the fore. While Gaskell takes the familiar route of therapeutic distraction with stories sufficiently eventful to relieve a sofa-ridden confinement, Collins rearrays his melodramatic tales as homeopathic medicine: agitations for the too easily aroused. You would seem to be the ideal audience for a narrative outlet like *Household Words* (Dickens' subsidiary anthologists suggest between them) if you are either a shut-in or a gadabout. The tonic of storytelling appeases either extreme—even while these exceptions further normalize the norm. In between fidgety youth and infirm decline, that is, and factoring in the purchase (rather than oral exchange) value of stories when not disseminated gratis, the ordinary patterns of domestic consumption make room for reading as a commercialized mode of leisure distraction. By the continuously adjusted measures of supply and demand, the price is always right.

The candid mention of publication in a much later chain of stories reprinted by Thomas Hardy, under the title *A Group of Noble Dames* (1891), sets that volume off from the mid-Victorian anthologies so far examined, even as the frame of the collection seems a deliberate cross between the Pickwick Club and Master Humphrey's circle of eccentric gentlemen. Only after the first of Hardy's ten tales has unfolded do we get—afterthought that it is—the retrospective construction of its narrative scene: "It was at a meeting of one of the Wessex Field and Antiquarian Clubs that the foregoing story, partly told, partly read from a manuscript, was meant to do duty for the regulation papers."[4] Entirely welcome, it is a story shared with "the inclusive and intersocial character" of the club's membership when their planned field trip is interrupted by rain. Moreover, this opening tale, "The First Countess of Wessex," though not entirely read rather than told, is nonetheless given shape by the professionally drafted text of the local historian, a "manuscript . . . prepared, he said, with a view to publication" (57). As is the case with stories shared in turn by the old surgeon, the rural dean, the sentimental member, the church warden, and so forth, the very act of trying out such a manuscript on Hardy's own audience fulfills its print ambitions. It also consolidates a hard-won camaraderie that the closing frame acknowledges as improbable in the separate members' ordinary walks of life. For many of them, the "easy intercourse" of tale-telling would be replaced by the "barest nod of civility" on "the following market day" (270). Further, "the President, the aristocrat, and the farmer" know full well "that affairs political, sporting, domestic, or agricultural would exclude for a long time all rumination on the characters of dames gone to dust for scores of years" (271). If only in the moment of disbanding, it has become clear that suspended self-interest has been the very ticket of admission to this reading group. These antiquarians thus offer a plausible microcosm of the late Victorian reading community only by constituting an artificial confederation to begin with, bound together solely by the Dickensian "trust" in narrative as a surrogate intimacy.

"Our Two Fields of Action": The Mitigation of *Hard Times*

Well before Hardy's interlinked chain of tales, Collins' mid-Victorian *Queen of Hearts* had not only cashed in but further economized on Dickens' experiment in *Master Humphrey's Clock*, finding a genuine (if transparently obvious) plot for his parable of response. In motivating his heroine's immobilization as passive audience, Collins thus avoided what Dickens came to fear he was doing with Master Humphrey's circle of response, "conjuring up bright figures where there is nothing but empty space." Never again would Dickens leave his pages at the mercy of such a possibility. From there on, unswervingly, through sustained monthly rather than weekly numbers over much of the next quarter century—and, symptomatically perhaps, with less direct address to a self-conscious reading audience (another lesson learned by Collins as well as Gaskell) than in most of the other major mid-Victorian novelists, certainly less than in Thackeray, Brontë, or Eliot—Dickens is committed to edging that "empty space" out where he takes it to belong: just off the page. You are not very often to be reminded directly of your interest in reading, its dubious passivity, and not certainly as the very axiom of a narrative situation.

There are strategic moments in Dickens, however, when the metatextual "emptiness" of conjured response—the circumscribed latency of reception—works its way back into narrative view. Dickens returns to such prescribed but unwritten—such conscripted—reception twice explicitly, though in very different fashion. He does so each time by way of a novelistic finale of an envisioned future, framed in each case within an ongoing (and thus future-oriented) journal guided by his own editorship: first in a closural fillip (*Hard Times*, published in *Household Words*, 1854), then in a full-scale coda (*A Tale of Two Cities*, in *All the Year Round*, 1859). The first instance is for Dickens unprecedented in the directness of its pseudoepistolary address, a climactic rhetorical moment preceded by an apostrophic clutter it is meant to transcend.

At times the audience address in *Hard Times* has been targeted at lampooned interest groups, as in the vocative barrage of "Utilitarian economists,

skeletons of schoolmasters, Commissioners of Fact, genteel and used-up infi-
dels, gabblers of many little dog's eared creeds, the poor you will always have
with you" (2,6:125).[5] In this most satiric of Dickens' novels, the apostrophes are
at their most Thackerayan. The novel's last paragraph, however, wants it, and
has it, otherwise, turning on a single noun phrase, "Dear Reader," meant to
counter much psychic deprivation in the novel. When Dickens has the Small-
weeds in *Bleak House* boast of denying themselves the irrelevant distractions of
reading, their attitude recalls the Gradgrind asperity of *Hard Times* as much as
the antisupernatural constraints on reading imposed by Alphonse Frankenstein. With Frankenstein's injunction against gothic excitement extended here
to all fiction, the "house of Smallweed" has systematically "discountenanced
all story-books, fairy tales, fictions and fables" (21:342). "Don't you read, or get
read to?" asks Mr. George of the old grandfather, in an exhaustive summary of
the hearthside conditions of Victorian narrative dissemination. "No, no" in
reply. "We have never been readers in our family. It don't pay" (21:351). Also forbidden as a child to take comfort from literature, in the penultimate paragraph
of *Hard Times* Louisa Gradgrind projects her future life as a reader (to children
not her own) as that of a woman "grown learned in childish lore" (3,9:226), a
virtual scholar of the fancy. It is this lore "without which . . . the plainest national prosperity figures can show will be the Writing on the Wall" (3,9:226).
Only one kind of reading can forestall another, and it is the former variety that
now emerges victorious in a single phrase: Dickens' apostrophic epithet for his
own audience.

Louisa's self-predictions have just been guaranteed by narrative omniscience—"these things were to be"—when Dickens' prose, for the first and last
time in his major fiction, drops into the most formulaic mode of audience
address: "Dear reader! It rests with you and me, whether, in our two fields of
action, similar things shall be or not" (3,9:297). The whole rudimentary mechanics of address is spelled out in this parsed grammar of apostrophe: the exclamatory vocative followed by the first- and second-person pronouns that constitute the poles of address. All seems to be coming to "rest" in our perception,
our reception, until the idiom revises itself into paradox. What "rests with you
and me" is action, action "in our two fields"—whether just (the obvious meaning) in our separate lives as citizens or also ("two fields" each) in our dovetailed
functions as narrator and participant reader, the latter role thus heroized in its
own right, as well as apostrophized, in the last lines of its own present "action."
Typifying both the optimism and the self-promotion of Dickensian fiction,
Hard Times leaves us suspecting that, though you can certainly distinguish be-

tween social and aesthetic engagement, you cannot finally have one without the other. In any case, it is wholly characteristic of Dickens' rhetoric that one of its rare addresses to the reader should come at the liminal moment where the boundaries of sheer story are purposefully reached beyond.

Such a blending of meditative "rest" and the dividend of social action, of reading and all the rest it might entail, is even more clearly the case (because staged as such in connection with a separately envisioned narrative event) at the close of *A Tale of Two Cities*. Generated there is a novelistic climax that predicates as the crucial "field" of future action the very story that the novel has just seen to a finish: the trope of renewal through continued narrative interest. It is a trope so prevalent in Dickens that it may even invert itself by way of variation. *Dombey and Son* (1848) comes to mind, by contrast with the familial retelling of Nell's story by Kit. As often at the final resting places of his plots, Dickens effects a studied play between transpired events and their immanent narrative shape. When old Dombey and his grandson *"go about* together, the story of the bond between them *goes about*, and follows them" (69:975; emphasis added). This echoic phrasing rewrites present ambulation as the embodied equivalent of transmission, of a narrative sent abroad. At the same time, the compromising reasons behind Dombey's expiatory devotion—his long neglect of Florence, the child's mother—are delicately withheld by her, for "that story never goes about." Such a narratively implied power of story, especially under a necessitated suppression, depends as much on extrapolation from the reader's own rapidly elapsing textual experience as in novels like *The Old Curiosity Shop* and *A Tale of Two Cities* which come to terminus with the sanctifying scenes of their own perpetuity in reception.

It is all done with angled mirrors: the narrative discourse slanted to become an image of itself as retold oral story. The mirroring surface need never be turned directly outward, to catch the reader in the act, in order to conscript your recognition by internal analogue. In *Dombey and Son*, you are singled out from a potential audience denied that status by a diegetic ban on telling, even while it is the fact of your already having been told the story which takes the measure of heroized restraint on Florence's part within the plot. Such is the tantalizing disingenuousness of Dickens' fictional license that it can thrive by violating its own provisos, invade the privacy it sacralizes. Such is the force of Dickensian extrapolation that its effects can survive their own denial—either this or, as in *A Tale of Two Cities*, outlast their own setting. And when the hero of that novel, Sydney Carton, is brought to the point where, at his apotheosis, he becomes the mere present occasion for an eventual familial discourse akin to reading, this climax also has everything to do, we will find, with the relation of "secrets" to "death" posed in a digressive episode of meditation early in the novel.

A Tale of Two Citings: Toward a Prolepsis of Present Reception

The excursus in question from *A Tale of Two Cities* is especially disquieting because the passage will turn out to be not at all as digressive as it seems. "A wonderful fact to reflect upon, that every human creature is constituted to be that profound secret and mystery to every other" (3:44). Similar ruminations lead on to thoughts of death as "the inexorable consolidation and perpetuation of the secret that was always in that individuality [of friend, neighbor, lover], and which I shall carry in mine to my life's end" (3:44). The passage then closes upon a weighty query: "In any of the burial-places of this city through which I pass, is there a sleeper more inscrutable than its busy inhabitants are, in their innermost personality, to me, or than I am to them?" (3:44). This ominous rhetorical question, however, in its interpolated address to each of us in our secrecies, pales by comparison with the sleight of reader extrapolation in a preceding sentence: "No more can I turn the leaves of this dear book that I loved, and vainly hope in time to read it all" (3:44). Though the deictic force of the demonstrative shifter "this" seems to take as antecedent some exemplary book in the imaged urban scene of the speaker, its only *present* referent is the very text on whose page the pronoun appears and which, since I too am reading it, localizes the measure of my own remaining time as well. The day will come when this book will no longer be mine to read through again either. The novel thus obtrudes itself as its own memento mori. Such thoughts of mortality are just what the passage, in its reflexivity, asks the reader of this, or any, book to "reflect upon." I reflect further upon their presence in this passage largely because of its close coordination with the notion advanced in the preface to *Master Humphrey's Clock*: that the secrecies of individuality, of "innermost personality," are not only inalienable in their own right but constitute the underlying bond of social cohesion, communal "trust." Fiction's place in all this, as we have been taking its Dickensian measure, is to offer—in its opening of and to the otherwise private—a psychic prosthesis of the compart*mentalized* Victorian mind.

Dickensian fiction knows its place, this place, and keeps it. This is part of what *A Tale of Two Cities* has to tell about novelistic tale-telling. Trusting others to leave us ultimately to our sole selves, despite the disclosures of narrative, is a way of trusting also that there is something there to be left alone. Call it radical subjectivity. Or individuality. Dickens suggests that though narrative is the very structuring function that keeps such individuality in place, it does so not because it can fill or fulfill it but only because it is an institutionalized activity designated directly to suspend the extremity of such inwardness, to give us something else in its place. Individuality in this sense needs the novel not to speak but to honor its silences, by diversion. The novel as theorized (it is nothing less) by Dickens, both early and late, cannot pretend either to dismantle or to transcend the division between public and private; it inhabits the gap; it becomes their very *difference*.[6] The relation between Dickens and Collins in the parables generated by their narrative structure is again revealing. Where *The Queen of Hearts* suggests that prose narrative quarantines sensationalism within fiction in order to mature domestic sensibility as the very context for such fiction, Dickens, with a different emphasis, implies that novels cordon off an arena for the fictional histrionics of disclosure in order to secure elsewhere the untouched recesses of interiority.

Fictional representation meets its admitted limit for Dickens, that is, when the secreted nature of the inward life is supposed to brook no further representation. In *Bleak House*, for instance, Lady Dedlock lives in fear of her shame, once published abroad, becoming actually textualized, "chalked upon the walls" (41:632) for all to read. She is terrified of being surrendered to public narrative. But can there be any doubt that, in the public narrative of Dickens' novel, we are meant to assume her carrying the secret of her original feeling for her dead lover, in every nuance and wound, straight to her grave? The Victorian popular novel never violates its "trust," never presses you into thinking that the deepest core of the inner life is transmissible as a text or renewable in shared reading; rather, the novel is instituted to keep you at a tolerable distance from yourself and others, and for the most inevitable of reasons: that there is no getting closer. The novel is itself a wholesale, communally sanctioned evasion, a deflection from the mute intractable nature of an abiding inwardness —finally, Dickens would suggest (in his most pervasive anticipation of psychoanalysis) a *self*-secrecy—harbored and masked by so-called privacy. As etymology implies, privacy is a social, sometimes even a familial, (de)privation, a subtraction of self from the communal. It is there that the often further isolation of individuality can be appeased, its dead spots smoothed over by the quasi-public, semiprivate work of fiction, whether encountered in solitude or read aloud to another in the so-called privacy of the home. This is the tale of "innermost personality" and its solacing approximations—hence evasions— which *A Tale of Two Cities* ends up telling.

Amid the French Revolution's convulsive rewriting of history, Dickens' an-

tihero, Sydney Carton, is a routine law writer in fitful service to the conservative maintenance of the British system. When he ultimately chooses death in
the place of the man, Charles Darnay, whose wife he loves, Carton has become
the self-appointed victim of a public scene of reading: Dr. Manette's Bastille
letter accusing the entire Darnay line. This is a scene of reading portrayed in a
manner as far as can be imagined from a novelistic encounter (your own so far)
with the melodramatic reporting of the same historical iniquities, even if read
aloud. Dickens' single breathless sentence: "In a dead silence and stillness—the
prisoner under trial looking lovingly at his wife, his wife only looking from him
to look with solicitude at her father, Doctor Manette keeping his eyes fixed on
the reader, Madame Defarge never taking hers from the prisoner, Defarge
never taking his from his feasting wife, and all the other eyes there intent upon
the Doctor, who saw none of them—the paper was read, as follows" (3,9:348).
To call what follows a "narrative" (3,10:361) is only to highlight its difference, in
the event of reception as well as the style of presentation, from the alternative
chronicle of aristocratic cruelty in *A Tale*. When the tribunal's resulting verdict
is reached, a new story of compensatory bloodletting replaces the old. It is one
in which Carton, instead of Darnay, promises to keep up his disguised narrative part. Says the spy Barsad, just before another day's roster of expected ex-
ecutions: "You must . . . , Mr. Carton, if the *tale* of fifty-two is to be right" (3,13:
382; emphasis added). It is just such a figuration of the remaining story, as story,
which remains to be developed by Dickensian rhetoric—in what one can only
call, again, a proleptic retrospect. In the process, two implicit mystiques of
Dickensian narrative are destined to converge as never before: the oral and the
oracular, the dream of a rhetoric of such visionary directness that ordinary inscription would only enfeeble it.[7]

To being with, the innocent seamstress who goes to the scaffold just before
Carton (a woman whose trade affords a benign contrast to the remorseless
recording of Madame Defarge's sinister knitwork) laments near her death that,
being illiterate, she cannot send a last message to her orphaned cousin:
"Poverty parted us, and she knows nothing of my fate—for I cannot write—
and if I could, how should I tell her! It is better as it is" (3,15:403). Carton echoes,
"Yes, yes; better as it is"—and before another page has turned in Dickens' own
writing, the hero himself goes to a death beyond self-expression. By contrast,
yet another female victim of the guillotine is now mentioned in passing as if
to underscore the scriptive alternative that Dickens so explicitly eschews for his
hero: "One of the most remarkable sufferers by the same axe—a woman—had
asked at the foot of the same scaffold, not long before, to be allowed to write
down the thoughts that were inspiring her" (3,15:404). Instead, Carton's "sub-

lime and prophetic thoughts" are to remain inward, private, subliminal—except in the omniscient text that inscribes their anticipations. This now takes place in the anaphoric cadences of Carton's internalized "I see," an unpronounced form of enunciation fourteen times repeated at the head of so many clauses in the paradoxical future present. His predictive inner speech confirmed only by a history that outlasts him, it summons for the novel's audience much of what such a readership knows to have come to pass between Carton's once-upon-a-time and the Victorian present of the novel's retrospective stance.

The question remains just how this one novel fancies its readers to have learned such a history, which is another way of asking how it imagines—and enacts—its own history being passed on into legend. Carton in his dying vision foretells rather than inscribes, and then only to himself, the succession of his namesake, Lucie Darnay's child. He envisions how "my name is made illustrious . . . by the light of his. I see the blots I threw upon it, faded away" (3,15:404). Anticipated next is yet another namesake for Carton, born to Lucie's son and brought by his father to Paris only when every "trace of this day's disfigurement" has been rubbed clear, the very word "trace," like "blots" before it, a partly textual figure for the scars of history. Once and for all, it might seem, the patrilinear cruelties of a dead regime are scoured clean by the familial inheritance of a name without stain, entitled only by love. The undeniable sentimentality of this conception is nonetheless entirely premeditated by the novel's motifs of textuality. Just as Carton in his prophetic vision persists in the yet again replicated word of his name, so does word of his deed find transmission in the last moment of his epiphany. From the limit of his dying, he glimpses rather than inscribes a tale told of him rather than read: "—and I hear him tell the child my story, with a tender and faltering voice" (3,15:404). Rescuing narrative pure and simple from the various devastations of historical inscription, the Dickensian hero dies here—just here, and knowingly—so that story might live to tell of it.

But there is a symptomatic catch. The story of Carton's life and death—as it will be told again, by Lucie's grandson among others—cannot in any future version (other than Dickens') contain the last twist, the visionary swivel, of the novel's plot, in which Carton dies imaging the very eventuality of a retelling. In this regard the ending does not sketch forth an exhaustive *mise en abyme* but rather a slightly skewed parable of novelistic reception. The freedom upon which the narrative thereby strives to close, vested in the hero as a visionary dispensation, is the freedom to let another discourse do with the inherited story what it will. Carton's withdrawal from writing, his surrender to another kind of record as preservation, is in every understanding of the term—not just emo-

tional and political but etymological—a deeply conservative move on Dickens'
part: a final removal paradoxically sacrificed to continuity, a novelist's eloquence wrung from his hero's silence. But itself wrung silently. Like those stories repeated by (and later about) Nell, you don't read of the tale in its retelling,
for that would only be a kind of rereading. You are to project from your own
immediate literary experience just how moved Carton's eventual namesake is
bound to be by the tale. You thus read *in*—into the blank space of recapitulation—the one pertinent narrative you already have behind you at this point. By
the reverse face of the same token, you thereby extrapolate from a future domestic site (and citing) of the tale to some culminating vantage—personal only
because it remains unsaid—on your own all but elapsed response to Dickens'
version of this tale.

I say "future" citing of the *Tale* as tale. But how far from enactment does it
remain, from simultaneous rather than latter-day fulfillment? In its closural effort to extricate story from textuality, what is the novel's final faith in the orally
told rather than the written narrative but an homage to one important mode
of its own popular dissemination? The historical novel whose heroic climax
seems to sacrifice everything to the perdurance of a family, however displaced
from the hero, and to those familial legends destined to incorporate him into
it, is also consecrated at the formal level to its own oral presentation. For within
the middle-class family setting of Dickens' day, the chief means of transmission for the serial parts of his novels was of course their regular reading aloud,
often by parents to children, at the family hearth. This is as far as possible in
mood from the earlier scene of reading aloud inside the novel: that predatory
listening afforded by the mob, the mass audience gone wrong, to Dr. Manette's
once written and then orally presented narrative. Since Carton's is a story to
be conveyed in an oral version whose chosen words are not specifically anticipated, the hero exits the novel, and textuality per se, by delivering himself to
another and another's telling, time out of mind, a history forever made novel.
This we are asked to believe. It is a way of asking us, at the last, to remember
that *A Tale of Two Cities* is first—and last—a historical novel. What is generated
from the setting of its tragedy is not just a son born to Lucie, and another in
turn to him, but the birth of a new historical order in which Dickens and his
audience together participate. When access to this *Tale* by future generations
is imagined from within its own closing scene, this is less a fantasy than a self-
fulfilling prophecy. Like one Darnay by another, the Victorian public, and we
after it—whether we read the novel or have it read aloud to us—are transported
to France for a myth implicated in our collective sense of the present, heirs to

the revolution as we are, children of history listening to one of the legends of our tribe.

It is for this reason, too, that nothing is uttered out loud or inscribed by Carton in the end about "the thoughts that were inspiring him." But besides the social historiography implied by this narrative ellipsis, there remains as well the private psychology. If the mystery of death as inaccessible difference (like secrecy) permeates the texture of an atomized social life, then the death *scene* loses its leverage on revelation. Always dead to others at the core, the inward self will unload no genuine interiority in the literal moment of death. Such inwardness gives itself over instead to the possibility of pure "popular" narrativizing, pure heroic agency in a never better than superficial recapitulation. It holds back, even as history runs away with it. This view of *A Tale of Two Cities* takes us, tunneling out of the text as it does, directly to the relation of psychology to narrative reception in the whole cultural agenda of popular novel reading which Dickens comes closest of any Victorian to formulating. For one thing, it should now be clear that the *Tale*'s early parenthetical passage about the mystery of self and its links to the awful unknowability of death was introduced seemingly to derail a narrative whose tracks it was actually marking out—a novel that ends up following the roll of the tumbrils to the guillotine. Carton's death, including its interior prolepsis of a better time coming, bears out, by way of completed exemplum, a major proposition of that earlier passage. Something of the "awfulness of death," we remember, "is referable to" that secret which, in life, each of us remains to the other. In the death of others, their absolute remove from us arrives as a parody of their status while alive. Death is, as it were, otherness *de*personified. As such, it is also the empty signifier that "refers" to an unknown signified, to the unnameable, to absence itself.

Carton's death *preserves* his secret in both senses, not just by passing it down through the generations but by keeping it safe all the way. For what is he imagining disclosed when he envisions a child being told "my story"? Certainly nothing more than what we already know about the man, and presumably in far less suggestive detail; nothing he has managed up to this point to keep from himself or others; nothing that Dickensian narrative technique has succeeded in leaving aside without our sense of being denied the aura of psychological complexity. Despite Carton's embittered soul-searching as the novel proceeds, that is, his is a structurally undermotivated as well as emotionally listless existence that only a scene as dramatic as a last-minute sacrifice, for instance, could render narratable. The preceding and still residual mystery of selfhood thereby goes with him to the grave it resembles. Like Lady Dedlock, like other great tormented psychological dignitaries in Dickens, Carton is never revealed, even when narrated to us.[8] So that, as "my story" is told and retold, Carton's phrasing may be found to bear the force of the subjective as well as the objective genitive: *his* version of himself, made transmissible only through conversion and sacrificial death. Carton, for so long impermeable to sympathetic understanding, tries to *turn* his life into a story, a Victorian melodrama, one drawn so broadly that even a child could understand. Despite his life's backlog of opacity, he finds the one public act, even in its final reticence, which will render himself rereadable.

In the process, Carton becomes negotiable as the currency—the very current or conduit—of novelistic ideology. His (and he) becomes one of the stories by which you intuit from symbolic action the buried motives you can never know, even if the action had been your own. Realizing that one day for the Darnay family Sydney Carton will be, will *have* been and may be again, what he is now to the novel's own audience—a spur to rapt and unequivocal attention—that same audience has been definitively *written in*, on the far side of narrative itself, to the "empty space" that Dickens had, two decades before in *Master Humphrey's Clock*, labored impracticably to represent rather than merely to occasion. It is as if Carton dies hoping to be part of the interchange of vocal storytelling, and subsequent "ghostly converse," centering around Master Humphrey's Clock. Then, too, the synecdochic relation of *The Old Curiosity Shop* to the *Clock* from which it was dispensed on schedule is here renewed. There is a cognate relation between *A Tale of Two Cities* and the regularized perennial office of tale-telling suggested by the title of the new journal for which the novel provides the send-off, *All the Year Round*, the last of three serials "Conducted by Charles Dickens" (as the masthead announces). The terms of this relation are sketched forth just at the point when *A Tale of Two Cities* has come to the end of its run in the journal (with Wilkie Collins' *Woman in White* waiting in the wings). At this pass, Dickens, in his role of "conductor," intervenes with an editorial notice on 26 November 1859. He expresses there his "hope and aim, while we work hard at every other department of our journal, to produce, in this one, some sustained works of imagination that may become a part of English Literature." It is up to Collins next, with his new novel; Collins, whose reprinted—and, more important, reframed—stories in *The Queen of Hearts* have already demonstrated, just this same year, that at least one other Victorian popular narrator knows what is socially and culturally at stake in such narration. It is up to Collins now, because Carton's story has certainly done its part. It has laid claim to its place in the historical continuum of literary narrative by thematizing its hero's desire for nothing less. This has been the novel's ultimate reflex action upon its Victorian readership.

So where are we? Where has Dickens brought the Victorian novel? Two chapters in part on the occasional saliencies of interpolated and extrapolated reading in the most popular novelist of the period lead us to summarize as follows: Where *The Old Curiosity Shop* (housed within *Master Humphrey's Clock*) gives us a model of reading as a kind of social formation, *A Tale of Two Cities* (housed within *All the Year Round*) gives us a certain social (hence familial, and finally literary-historical) formation, a lineage of domestic dissemination, as a model of reading. In each case, reading's access to the interpersonal is mounted upon—in order at the same time to preserve—the inalienable singleness of the isolated subject. In each case, therefore, reading is forwarded as exactly the event that keeps otherness and personal subjectivity in touch. As we have seen at length, the parameters of this transaction are staked out by Dickens as early as the 1840s, where its limits are tested and all too quickly reached. By the end of this same decade (as we will find in the next chapter), the Brontës have their own way with a similar impulse to figure reading, even while instigating it, as a mode of desire—and thus to eventuate as well as to portray the fraught dynamic of the reading scene.

"That Very Word, Reading, in Its Critical Use"

In the late and freestanding monthly publication of *Our Mutual Friend* (1864–65), Dickens has no journal apparatus by which to set in place his by now expected parable of reception. Instead, he arranges for plot itself to frame (in two senses) its own reading—capped by a revelation scene that gets structured as a parabolic reminder of exactly your own tactically misled reading up to this point. Following half a decade after *A Tale of Two Cities*, this scene in *Our Mutual Friend* stages yet another narrative exchange at a family hearth. Beyond marking the persistence of this trope for Dickensian fictional response, the episode in question replays in order to defuse the moralizing liberties that Dickens is willing to take with the patience of his readers. For the novel is organized in considerable part around a "plot" (in the conspiratorial sense) by which, along with Bella, the reader has been completely taken in, one about which she and the reader are simultaneously disabused in the climactic scene of explanatory narrative: namely, the extended masquerade of Boffin's hardening greed.

Long before this plot is unraveled by oral disclosure, it has become so entwined, so interchangeable, with the story the Victorian public has been improvingly misinterpreting all along that the climactic parable of reading finds itself glossed by the one and only disquisition on the very word *reading* which I know of in Victorian fiction. As commentator on the high-toned vulgarization of the term *reading*, Eugene Wrayburn is permitted the most defensive of parenthetical digressions just after having congratulated his friend Mortimer on "your reading of my weaknesses" (3,10:605). Let's change the subject, he seems to say; yet the topic into which he sidesteps is more trenchantly relevant than he realizes to the novel's analysis of aimless and imitative subjectivity. On first reaction, though, what follows in his banter sounds like little more than a satiric set piece leveled against a journalist cliché, with Dickens the editorial arbiter of linguistic taste speaking through his languid and mordant mouthpiece: "(By-the-by, that very word, Reading, in its critical use, always charms me. An actress's Reading of a chambermaid, a dancer's Reading of a hornpipe, a singer's Reading of a song, a marine painter's Reading of the sea, the kettle-drum's Reading of an instrumental passage, are phrases ever youthful and delightful.)" (3,10:605). Yet this arch recourse to the term "Reading" (for something like "interpretation" or "impersonation") is "critical" in a different sense than Eugene intends.

To begin with, if Mortimer has in any such sense been responsible for "reading [Eugene's] weaknesses," it is not least by incarnating them, since Mortimer, we long ago learned, "had founded himself upon Eugene when they were yet boys at school" (2,6:337). His whole role in the novel so far is indeed to "do" Eugene in a different voice, just as Sloppy's famous ability at impersonating the police in newspaper reports is in a double sense a "Reading of the police." The phenomenon occurs, too, at a much larger scale. The plot's most extended deception of the reader—not Harmon's mask as Rokesmith, but Boffin's as a greedy reprobate—is of course a ruse designed to penalize and reform Bella's own avarice. When that plan comes to depend on Boffin's being read to by Wegg from numerous accounts of misers, it is indirectly Boffin's own perfect "Reading of the miser" upon which the disciplinary complot turns. The phenomenological exchange that *subjects* a reader to a text is exaggerated here to the monomania of wholesale surrender. And when this text-implicated scheme is turned to further narrative account in a subsequent revelation scene, a scene enacted by parable as yet another locus of domestic literary consumption, this additional device, too, is equally forced—and forcing.

This scene is *put over on us*, displaced upon our own reading, as follows. When the heroine has been renovated beyond fear of backsliding, and the true identity of her husband finally made known, Mrs. Boffin is eager that Bella be set straight as to the balance of the deception, that she "be told all the story. Now I'm a going to tell the story. Once, twice, three times, and the horses is off" (4,14:842). Narrative has an internal momentum, yes, but it also has what we might call, and what is next figured as, a social structure. John takes his wife's hand—as if in ceremonial remarriage under the now unveiled name of Harmon—and the eager narrator, Mrs. Boffin, asks her formerly suspected husband to "come and lay yours a top of his, and we won't break the pile till the story's done" (4,14:842). When the bodies party to the narrative transaction are thus placed literally in contact, Mrs. Boffin—crying "That's capital"—is off and running with the story. In the form of rectification by echo and metaphor, the "pile" of hands thus produced corrects both the repugnant dust mounds and the figurative "mountains" under which Harmon's identity had earlier been "buried" (2,14:443). At the same time, Mrs. Boffin's idiomatic mention of "capital" upends and cleanses the acquisitive obsessions of earlier mercantile amassments in the text, even as Bella's selfish grasping is repaired by the communal clasping of hands.

A dozen and a half paragraphs later, when the "pile of hands dispersed" (4,14:845), you have by that point been told, along with Bella, how Boffin's supposed textually precipitated fall into miserliness was all a fake, a self-conscious fiction (within plot) devised to appall Bella—but no more than you yourself—with the poisonous effects of unearned fortune. Bella's ability not to feel patronized, duped, and abused by all this, but rather edified, is thus a cue to your own gratified response—especially since Dickens has come perilously close here to reminding the reader that a loathsome Boffin is hardly more fictional than a genial Boffin within a novel that has fabricated his very characterization in the first place. If indeed there is any lingering annoyance on the reader's part for being made to abide the extended charade as object lesson, the attempt by Wegg (the reader for hire) to extort workmen's compensation for his own parallel ordeal can only redound against your petulance. Quoting Wegg: "It's not easy to say how far the tone of my mind may have been lowered by unwholesome reading on the subject of Misers, when you was leading me and others on to think you one yourself" (4,15:851). By contrast, and like Bella, you are to have been uplifted rather than "lowered" in your own reading by the fit repulsion you found yourself moved to feel. In the perverse economy of this narrative device, it has been Dickens' "capital" outlay and overextension of plot which have hoarded a surprise for the conscripted audience, leading readers to invest under false pretenses in an ethical stance eminently justified even though locally misplaced.

In a deliberately overworked word, then, the novel depends for effect on your own educed "reading" of Bella, the tutored subject. You assume her role by formal reduplication, especially when positioned to join her in being able to take the reins of narrative disclosure into your own hands: "I want neither you nor any one else to tell me the rest of the story. I can tell it to *you*, now, if you would like to hear it" (4,15:845). Yet because this is the story already elapsed and here merely recapitulated from a clarifying vantage, Bella's elevation to narrator, as yours to second-guesser, is one more mark of your being written with, conscripted, by the novel as correctional institution. Across the transfers of this reflexive scene, Dickensian character psychology appears not only reciprocal (as elsewhere) but identical with reader response. And when Bella's induction into domestic virtue catches up with plot, she can at last assume command of storytelling as a sign of her readiness for a hearthside role as materfamilias and Victorian mouthpiece. Collins again comes to mind. The gradual domestication of the Queen of Hearts by her very patience for narrative has been further moralized by Dickens into a feminine aptitude for dispensing a certain kind of story as admonitory object lesson.

In the last novel whose unfolding plot Dickens lived to complete, therefore, he has given his readers, with the Boffin complot, the most strenuous test of their tolerance and dedication, satirized (in Wegg) the sense of affront to which it might lead, and yet managed to round off the whole as an occasion for the most palpably embodied social congregation of narrative consumption—the redemptive mound of hands—in his fiction, even including the devoted but undemonstrative narratees of Master Humphrey's Clock. By extrapolation from the culminating parable of narrative enlightenment in *Our Mutual Friend*, reading in Dickens is that event of discursive intimacy which makes the members of its audience mutual, interdependent, emotionally symbiotic, which speaks through as well as to them, which circulates and recenters at once. Here is that sociology of reading which has been more or less implicit, often more, from the beginning of his career. A decade or so into the Dickensian ascendancy, however, and only a few years after *Master Humphrey's Clock*, the scaffolding of readerly transmission in the Brontës has already begun raising harder questions about reading's exchanged gratifications, questions having more aggressively to do with voyeurism, psychic dependency, vicarious displacement, and reciprocal self-constitution.

Chapter Nine

"Oh, Romantic Reader"
Relays of Desire in *Wuthering Heights, Jane Eyre,* and *Villette*

Pierre-Auguste Renoir, *Two Girls Reading* (n.d.).
Charles Lachman Collection. The Bettmann Archive

In turning from Dickens, we begin to retrace the century's own multiple turns from a fictional discourse he had brought to such complacent polish. Dickens made it seem luminously easy to read. His is the facilitated audience par excellence. This facility awaits chastening, minimal but various, in Thackeray, the Brontës, Eliot, Meredith, and others. By his favored suppression of address, and the apparent disentrammelment of response, Dickens leaves you alone—with him, his vision and version of things. At least from the authorial crisis of *Master Humphrey's Clock* on, his is the elicited but generally uninvoked reader, seduced even before any advance has been made. With an obvious exception like the peroration that concludes *Hard Times*, Dickens regularly neutralizes the reader as textual object in order to activate the boundless subjectivity of any and all reading. In reference to his audience (or, rather, in its typical avoidance), Dickens' strategy is fairly vigilant and altogether evident: Keep readers on alert but not on call, not called out; let the text both have and make its way with them, while neither obtruding its devices nor leaning on apostrophe; and lest such readers think they are being ignored, dramatize their vested privilege through scenes of narrative reception as imaginative or empathetic access. In narrative discourse rarely fronted by direct address, what results, whenever the reader is let in through this backdoor of plot, is a thematized reading that remains for Dickens a mode of content—and so of containment. With the flag of the vocative seldom flown over the discursive field, the seeding of extrapolated response prepares the ground of conscription while avoiding most spell-breaking nods to the audience.

Where readerly access is meant by Dickens to be magnanimously unimpeded, Thackeray's readers in *Vanity Fair* repeatedly stumble over themselves, over their own denomination, in reading on. And shortly after *Vanity Fair* began its serial run, Charlotte Brontë published *Jane Eyre*, dedicated to Thackeray both on the title page and, implicitly, in its no less than thirty apostrophes to the reader: rhetorical twists—or snags—tagging access as initiation, checking false leads, inflecting melodrama, keeping the course, directing the discourse.[1] Then, too, *Wuthering Heights* appeared in the same year, with its dramatically—and I use the term advisedly—different approach to narrative transmission in an intricate frame tale, every avenue of disclosure enacted by personified response. Which of the Brontë novels seems least Dickensian is the right way to wonder about these departures from his orientation toward the more comfortably accommodated reader, if only because there is no way to choose. Their distance from transparent reading is itself differential. Emily Brontë backs out the process of extrapolation so far toward the outer borders of her narrative that the dramaturgy of response may seem more a structural device than a reading event, a mere, as it were, formality. At the same time, Charlotte Brontë in *Jane Eyre* disperses the complementary interpolative impulse to an equally attenuating extent, so that direct address seems (at least at first glance) more like random punctuation than an active element in the syntax of narration. Charlotte Brontë strips Thackerayan address of its disorienting satire, levels its tone, but only in order to worry its implications for the construction of subjectivity itself around the enunciating center of narration. In *Jane Eyre* the reader is personified without being dramatized, whereas in *Wuthering Heights* reading itself is restaged without being (in the other sense) "characterized," impersonated by Lockwood's place in the enunciative structure rather than specified by epithetical address.

What may at first blush appear dated in *Jane Eyre* (even by contrast with Dickens, let alone Thackeray) and what looks faintly modernist in *Wuthering Heights*—the cozily hailed versus the epistemologically dubious point of reception—are thus obverse but equally combative encounters with that *immanence* coded by Dickensian fiction: a narrative system neutralized as textual event in order to be naturalized as manifest world. It would therefore seem (hence the plan of this chapter) that a comparable distance from Dickens in both Emily and Charlotte Brontë ought to help delineate whatever common problematic their formal options have been driven to solve. In essence: How can the emotive force of a narrative transmission, for sender and receiver alike, be acknowledged and diagnosed, the mutual implicature of reading and writing be revealed, integrally and without digression—and, furthermore, without loss (as in *Master Humphrey's Clock*) of just that force—in the course and conduct of a novel? We turn first to Emily's renowned answer—working round in the end, on the way toward the next chapter on *Villette*, to Charlotte Brontë's earlier implications in *Jane Eyre* about such emotive force as a model of psychic need itself: of desire, lack, and the textual exchanges with which such desire may be said to content itself.

"Too Weak to Read": Narrative Ingestion in *Wuthering Heights*

Emily Brontë's novel sets her narrator (our surrogate, our scapegoat) the task of being the reader of all he surveys, puts him through his paces, and then in the end calls him to task for all he has missed. It has seldom gone unnoted that Lockwood begins *Wuthering Heights* as a reader, a reader in no position to interpret what he reads. On his inaugural visit to Heathcliff's residence, on the second page of the diary that constitutes the narrative he is already idly at work trying to interpret, he lingers on the threshold to decipher an inscription lodged amid ornate carving over the door: "I detected the date '1500,' and the name 'Hareton Earnshaw'" (1:4). To say that he begins a novel *by reading its eponymous site* is to bring out a point that the novel quickly moves to draw out at length: his role as stand-in for the reader, a reader even of what he is there to transcribe. And the next time we see this reader of the Heights reading within *Wuthering Heights* is his first night spent within both, when he is inhospitably shuffled off to a cramped bed closet in Catherine's old room. In a state of "vapid listlessness" (3:15) with which we will become familiar as we get to know him better, an emptiness he is often eager to fill up with stories, he rifles through the well-thumbed and inscribed volumes of Catherine's "select" library on his way—it must have worked for him many times before—to sleep.

In his subsequent and much discussed dream, it is Catherine herself who is materialized from her marginal scribblings in the holy text. Deep within his nightmare, in order to fend off the specter of Cathy in her effort to enter through the window, Lockwood "piled the books up in a pyramid against it, and stopped [his] ears" (3:20). Books as sheer textual bulk cannot, of course, protect against the materialization of what they contain. Nor in the materiality of their inscription can they still the energies they unleash. It is only in dream that they can do so. In waking experience, Lockwood's version of this delusion (that reading—or an experience like it—can defend against reality) is apparent in his sense that the long story told to him by Nelly Dean, first as he is falling ill and later on his sickbed—and then resumed to conclusion nine months later—should be kept at the distance of the diverting and medicinal. In this way he thinks it might provide a catharsis without engagement in only the crudest therapeutic, rather than emotional, sense: "I'll extract wholesome medicines from Mrs. Dean's bitter herbs" (14:120). But the traumatic tale that follows is so much like a scenario of hallucination spun from the original nightmare that, when Lockwood returns to the neighborhood to enjoy the coda of the story, his terms of surprise over Heathcliff's fate cannot help harking back to his first preternatural access to the narrative of the Heights. "I never dreamt of his dying" (32:234), he remarks, with the tacit stress on "him, of all people" and the overt implication that other dream material (like Cathy's death) *has* come to pass. For Lockwood, of course, it is all a bookish dream. In this respect he is prototypical. In "Creative Writers and Day-Dreaming," Freud mentions certain "eccentric" novels in which the protagonist, radically off center, takes "a very small active part; he sees the actions and sufferings of other people pass before him like a spectator."[2] Translate spectator to reader and the eccentricity (or concentricity) of Brontë's frame narrative is lent definition as a kind of *textual* voyeurism, with Lockwood its ironic scribe.

Right from the start, the place—coextensively, the role—of Lockwood the diarist, the amanuensis of narrative, has also suggested his function as a surrogate reader. The lengthy stretch of Nelly Dean's account which composes the first phase of the tale (chaps. 4–7), before Lockwood negotiates for its resumption on his sickbed, begins when he asks Nelly to sit with him while he has his "supper" (4:26). Her ensuing story thus provides a secondary adjunct to his consumption. Lockwood is certainly ready to make whatever use he can of her tale, as he was of his earlier reading in Catherine's old bedroom at the Heights; for if Nelly doesn't "rouse me to animation," at least she will "lull me to sleep by her talk" (4:26). This time, however, his interest is held by, and held to, the realm of apparently conscious response, the realm of leisured narrative in which even Nelly Dean, we may be surprised to find, is well versed. Proudly attributing her storytelling powers to her wide if desultory reading, Mrs. Dean may indeed catch the reader off guard when pinning down the scene of telling with an unexpected demonstrative adjective localizing the ordinary scene of reading: "You could not open a book in *this* library that I have not looked into, and got something out of also" (7:49; emphasis added). Most readers would by now have forgotten just where the dinnertime transmission has been taking place. Once we are reminded of the site of Lockwood's absorption, however, our slight surprise gives weight to one of Frank Kermode's most suggestive insights about Brontë's text: that the cultural otherness of the novel's main locale at the Heights is measured in part by the fact that *Wuthering Heights* is precisely the kind of fiction which would be read only in the cultivated world of the Grange (with its ample library of narrative models for Nelly's telling).[3]

Further, we might add that the rhythms of the tale's consumption at the Grange serve to replicate the patterns of ordinary domestic reading, the story being dispensed only when its oral medium "could spare time from more important occupations" (15:120). So literary, indeed, are both the conditions of reception and the mode of delivery that, as Nelly continues to tell with relish of Heathcliff's depredations, she all but admits that her own language of description—schooled by the library at the Grange and scrupulously preserved by Lockwood—may well be colored by certain literary archetypes that leap to her mind: "'Is he a ghoul or a vampire?' I mused. I had read of such hideous, incarnate demons" (34:250). This one among many Victorian novels of the recent past thus blocks out its own literary-historical (not just intertextual) parameters, with Nelly filling the role of turn-of-the-century midwife to the birth of domestic romance out of gothic melodrama: the story of Hareton and the second Cathy out of the very different tale of Catherine and Heathcliff.

Tacit generic issues are thus braided together with more obvious ironies of the reading scene, and not least in association with the very library now taken over by Lockwood both for listening and for transcription. Contaminated by Heathcliff's return, Catherine quickly became intolerable to Edgar in her ravings, and he fled to the safe confines of this same library. There, as we learn in a curious involution of phrasing, he "shut himself up among books he never opened" (12:93). Though invoking the antithetical relation of "open" and "shut," instead the two levels of designation don't consort, for only the second is literal. The former, idiomatic phrase operates rather like the figurative return of the repressed from Lockwood's own unconscious in his early dream of Catherine: repeating the use of books, closed or otherwise, as a psychic barricade. This is not to say that books themselves, rather than libraries, are not, once opened, readily available for hiding *in* as well as behind. Such is Isabella's strategy after the death of Catherine: "I sat in my nook reading some old books," she tells Nelly, to keep her mind from "continually reverting to the kirkyard and the new made grave" (16:134). In such a counteractive reading, "I dared hardly lift my eyes from the page before me, that melancholy scene so instantly usurped its place" (17:134).

Lockwood the listener, of course, has no such problem, since he is largely indifferent to anything in his immediate environs except as it comes filtered and disinfected through narrative. As a result, he is in fact quite willing to suspend that narration in order to prolong anticipation. His statement to this effect, however, places him doubly at the helm. When he informs his diary that he "felt disposed to defer the sequel of her narrative myself" (9:70), his dead metaphor drawn from the publishing industry ("sequel") is part of an otherwise straightforward sense: that he is as tired as Nelly herself is. But what the delayed reflexive pronoun of his utterance also implies is that, in his own right as transcribing agent, he has the power to "defer . . . himself" the dispensing of her tale to us—if by no less an interregnum than a chapter break to mark yet another hiatus in the turned leaves of his diary. The enfeebled auditor slipping into fever stands confessed as the dilatory strategist of melodramatic narrative's own internal dynamic.[4]

And there is another, more devious strategy at work here. From the beginning, the storyteller has had something more than restorative distraction in mind for her narratee. For Nelly Dean has been telling the tale to Lockwood as its ideal auditor—a resident bachelor with his curiosity up—to generate a fascination with the second Cathy sufficient to save the day. Nelly's is a narrative doled out, that is, to the present tenant at the Grange so as to precipitate its heroine's return on Lockwood's arm as the lady of the manor, with Nelly again in attendance. Lockwood foils her plans; to this leisured and affectless gentleman, the history of the Heights and the Grange remains, for all the fleshed reality of its surviving principals, merely a good story. Desire does not escape the tale, does not leak into the precincts of response. That the irony attaching to this should be so obvious is one measure of the libidinal investments ordinarily incident to narrative contact. In Lockwood's view, the whole tale is instead a diversion for whose sexual intensity a diffuse worldliness is the only antidote, as Lockwood's own very dead sexual metaphor implies: "Stop, my good friend!" cries Lockwood when Nelly's amorous blandishments on Cathy's behalf become too direct; "I'm of the busy world, and *to its arms* I must return" (25:295; emphasis added). Even as he shrinks from the *plot* of Nelly's retold plot, though, Lockwood does ludicrously preen himself about the "romantic" story in which he has forgone a leading role, forgone it in order to remain a listless listener to another version of the tale: "What a realization of something more romantic than a fairy tale it would have been for Mrs. Linton Heathcliff, had she and I struck up an attachment, as her good nurse desired, and migrated together into the stirring atmosphere of the town!" (31:231). This is projected as Nelly's fantasy, not his. For him, instead, a pathological passivity suits his purposes as a reader manqué, an invalid's imagination seeking diversion without engagement: "I am too weak to read," he says as if summing up his hermeneutic default in the novel as a whole, "yet I feel as if I could enjoy something interesting" (10:70). Out from behind his torpor slips the inference that reading itself, not just the ingestion of a tale begun with supper, is a labor that distinguishes, on any number of fronts, our approach to the novel that includes him from his attitude to the storytelling that forms its center.

Certainly sexual activation is the last thing that Lockwood is looking for from the story, whatever Nelly may hope. Yet this is not to minimize the displaced and ironized erotics of his auditory drive. On the last page of the novel, Lockwood offends Mrs. Dean by treating her in effect like a bookseller rather than a reminiscing friend. In the act of "pressing a remembrance into the hand of Nelly Dean, and disregarding her expostulation at my rudeness, I vanished through the kitchen" (34:266). In recompense for a well-turned set of memories, he offers a remembrance. The exchange is complete, the economy of catharsis—degraded to convalescence—kept in place. But it is just this exchange that is in danger of being mistaken by the Bible-spouting Joseph, interpreted instead as the payoff for, of all things, a sexual favor dispensed by Nelly. Instead of letting Joseph feel "confirmed" in "his opinion of his fellow-servant's gay indiscretions," however, Lockwood quickly deploys more money so that the pharisaical pest "recognised me for a respectable character by the sweet ring of a sovereign at his feet" (34:266). In another denotation of the term, however, it is of course Nelly's prolonged "indiscretion"—the candor of her narrativized gossip—for which Lockwood has indeed been just as willing to pay as if he had been an owner (rather than mere tenant) of the Grange, stocking its library with the latest and most tantalizing diversions.

A novel about the relativity of narrative recounting, its *partiality* in both senses, and even more about the subjectivity of response, thus comes across— in oddly direct ratio to its emphasis on orality and audition—as a novel about reading: your reading. Hence the emphasis in this discussion—which I here briefly recapitulate—on the way the citified interloper, Lockwood, arrives as a reader at the threshold of the Heights and has only begun his prolongation of this role by the time he repairs to Cathy's upstairs bed. Rendered ill in the process, he slowly recovers through the auspices of an oral continuation of the same tortured story upon which he has accidentally embarked. This is the fuller narrative unraveled for him first in a library, where he treats it like a novel in parts and "defers" its "sequel." With the strength of mind necessary for any alternative reading having abandoned him entirely, it is this same ongoing tale to which he then passively submits as if to recuperative doses of a tonic—finally to pay good money for the story when all is told, as if he had been engaged the whole time upon a commercial transaction like book buying. And the fact that he writes down this story, or rather that he has already written it down by the time you come to hear of it, is exactly the prod to extrapolation by which his inveterate listening, in lieu of reading, serves as negative model for your own literary rather than aural contact with the story. In the absence of signaled reception, that is, the insinuated rhetorical emphasis of Brontë's frame structure goes to suggest that even a *mere reader*—let alone a sometimes auditor, sometimes bystander at the very scene—would demonstrate more amplitude of response, to say nothing of erotic investment, than does Lockwood in the face of Nelly's harrowing account.

Such, then, was Emily Brontë's solution to the problem that classic realism set itself in its less transparent manifestations: how to integrate the telling without disintegrating the fiction, how to implicate a novel's readers without either placating or admonishing them by address. In the person of Lockwood, she constructs the placeholder of the reader, debilitates him to the point where narrative reception could be dissevered from the activity of narrative reading, and then explores that sheerly receptive capacity in all of its limitations. For what is wrong with Lockwood as auditor is that he is too much the mere sequestered reader, and by no means hermeneutically astute, even of events unfolding to him as real. Yet such debilitated response is only the obverse of his typicality as figured reader. To his defense mechanisms against the ghostly return of the dead through story, in their relation to the usual positioning of the audience by the Victorian frame tale, this chapter must ultimately double back.[5]

"Converting You into a Listener": Jane Eyre's Life Story

By contrast with *Wuthering Heights*, indeed by a deep figurative inversion of narrative logic itself, *Jane Eyre* turns the risk of disappointment over the prominence of textual rather than dramatic encounter directly on its head. Charlotte Brontë can thus ultimately convert reading (narrative reception) to a metaphor for, rather than medium of, those romantic intensifications that it would otherwise subserve by representing. Anticipating such a freighted installation of the reader in *Jane Eyre*, the paradigmatic moment comes as early as Charlotte's juvenilia. In the Angrian story "A Leaf from an Unopened Volume, or The Manuscript of an Unfortunate Author," there is this, a decade and a half before *Jane Eyre*: "Let the reader keep silence whilst I lead him through those splendid halls whose very atmosphere, sweetly laden with perfumes, enervated the soul of him who breathed it & rendered him for the moment more a slave than a free man."[6] This is Brontë's post-Dantean mode of inducted attention: involving so many sensuous entanglements of evocation that the "him" of the reader (commanded to silence—what else?) and the "him" of the enslaved visitor to the described scene appear designed to merge, grammatically and psychologically, in the intoxication called reading. It is only a less unctuous but no less emphatic summons to our attention which interrupts the plot of *Jane Eyre* during the scene where Rochester studies Jane's drawings: "While he is so occupied I will tell you, reader, what they are" (13:110). He gets to see; you must satisfy yourself with word pictures alone. Yet this does not deter you from reading them as you will, interpreting them not as a digression from but as a clue to plot.

With *Jane Eyre*'s dedication to the author of *Vanity Fair* signaling a debt but also a point of departure, all the specified and mutually annulling epithets of the hailed reader from Fielding to Thackeray are scoured of overt satire and then rubbed to essence by the wear of Brontë's repetitions. The uncharacterized reader is constituted not by attribution but by immanent participation. You are just who you think you are in making your way through the rich, overwrought texture of Brontë's narrative prose: the nineteenth-century "reader" per se, processing literary language, projecting identification, not letting the one get in the way of the comparable sensory pleasures native to the other; the reader of romance, the *roman* reader, more broadly at one point (if also ironically) the "romantic reader."

So it goes across the numerous apostrophic asides to your reading in the course of *Jane Eyre*. They provide an interlaced network of checked emotional involvement in the name of fuller textual investment. When this same program is mobilized for *Villette* in the form of a rather extreme experiment, it sheds light in retrospect on the devices of *Jane Eyre*. What you come to recognize is that Brontë's vocative recognitions of your progress through the text are as often peremptory as they are ingratiating. Gestures of acknowledgment which seem anachronistic even in comparison with Dickens (let alone with the frame tales of her sisters, not only *Wuthering Heights* but Anne Brontë's *The Tenant of Wildfell Hall*) are by no means simply a latter-day revamping of eighteenth-century formulas stripped of the often saving because deflationary wit. Rather, they pace off a tacit redrafting of the narrative charter itself as an intermittent negotiation between utterance and presumed—hence presumed upon—response.

The difference between the roughly contemporaneous third-person omniscience of a *Dombey and Son* (1847–48), for instance, and the first-person fictional autobiography of Brontë's first novel allows Jane Eyre, in the name of *Jane Eyre*, not simply to activate but to remotivate the "dear reader" trope of the preceding best-sellers. Apostrophe does less to disrupt than to propel narration if the force of that narration has largely to do with the isolated subject humanizing otherness in the form of an audience for her own otherwise untold desire. To figure this textual reception, this displacement of desire, *Jane Eyre* devises a two-staged parable in which oral rather than written narrative is the vehicle of sublimated transmission. This is where we begin—and for the good reason that the metatextual logic of interpolated address in the entire novel takes its bearings from these sites of extrapolation. We start, that is, by calling up for contrast—as the very fullness of the contrast leads one to suspect they might be rigged to invite—two scenes, early and late, which sketch a single scenario of biographical continuity as oral narration, of self-consciousness as sustained audition. One passage locally interpolates, even as they both prompt you to extrapolate, your condition as responsive anchor of the text. Together, they highlight novelization itself as a metaphor for life lived under the sign of narrative romance. Further, too, and the point can scarcely be overestimated, they outline a view of narrative reception as not only a metaphor for but a mode of self-awareness.

I turn first to the latter, less immediately troublesome, of the two related scenes in *Jane Eyre*. It is a minor episode that might easily (and usually does) pass unnoticed in regard to the systemic pressure exerted upon it from that other, earlier, and more concerted manifestation of portrayed narrative audition. The latter scene in question, usually remembered, if at all, in criticism as a plot device, has St. John Rivers delivering the news to Jane that she is an heiress.[7] What Brontë has him say in order to do so is more to our point. The preparation is meticulous. Rivers has invaded Jane's solitude, interrupting her reading of Walter Scott's *Marmion* "because I got tired," he explains, "of my mute books" (33:332). This is all he is willing to tell her at first. Yet he is every bit as much on the scent of a story—namely, the continuation of Jane's tale— as is Jane herself in her preoccupation with Scott's narrative verse. Rivers has come to appease his "impatience to hear the sequel of a tale" (33:334). Lockwood's itch, too. But with Rivers barely able to distract Jane from the pages of Scott—pleading, "Leave your book a moment, and come a little nearer the fire" (33:334)—he inverts his intended role as listener in order to compete with a literary narrator for Jane's attention. He does so by transforming Jane herself into the virtual reader—the eager auditor, hence narrative recipient—of her own story. Most of it would be properly hers to tell, except for the recent news of the inheritance, but Rivers instead seizes the reins of narrative power. His justification is that "on reflection, I find the matter will be better managed by my assuming the narrator's part, and converting you into a listener" (33:334): a captive audience to her own tale.

In one sense, Jane is used to this. For all the characteristic power play of Rivers' conversionary tactic, the posture of passive reception is scarcely new to the heroine's sense of her own life, especially where anything like an empowering turn of fortune is concerned. Romantic eventualities have always, if at all, come to her as an auditor, usually as a kind of eavesdropper upon her own fantastic scripts for a more expansive contact with the world. This has been the burden of that earlier and notorious passage to which the later conversation with Rivers is indirectly linked. Though involving an incident of explicit address ("oh, romantic reader"), this earlier scene (it is worth some time to notice) is one whose interpolation of the reader merely exerts a further pressure to extrapolate. But there are highly visible objections to this passage which too easily get in the way of such notice. As a matter of fact, the text's unexpected— yet fundamental—stress on Jane as the listener to her own fabulation has been virtually swamped by the critical diatribe against the larger rhetorical episode. Brontë's offending gesture has to do with the way Jane Eyre's rather stunning confession of autonarration as the site of desire is followed, almost before it can be digested—as if Brontë didn't know better—by a strident and narratively digressive stretch of soapbox feminism. This is the long paragraph ending with the insistence that it is "thoughtless to condemn [women], or laugh at them, if they seek to do more or learn more than custom has pronounced necessary for their sex" (12:96). Most famously, Virginia Woolf threw down the gauntlet in her contempt for the supposed aesthetic default of this polemical interruption.[8] Even feminist critics have not fully answered the aesthetic complaint, often taking the break in narrative continuity as symptomatic, even heroic, but, in the working out of its frustrations, not worked *in*. The rent in story has been justified on thematic (that is, mostly psychological) grounds but scarcely on narrative (that is, tacitly psychoanalytic) ones.

What particularly is underplayed, from Woolf forward, in the consensus on this rhetorical sore spot, is the precise location of its narrative (not to say aesthetic) breach. The interlude of private yearning and muted fulmination during Jane's stolen moments on the upper floors or rooftop of Thornfield is abruptly curtailed by that oldest trick in the book: a changing of the topic, if not quite of the subject: "When thus alone I not unfrequently heard Grace Poole's laugh." The goading laugh of her mad counterpart, Bertha, mistaken at this point for that of the servant Grace, intrudes upon Jane's solitude at exactly these moments of defiant aspiration—as if it were the embodiment of that previously noted public dismissal of ambitious women, that tendency to "laugh at them" with blind contempt. At the same time, for the self-governance of Brontë's governess heroine, this cackle of ambiguous origin manifests the other side of agitation and craving, its dark echo in debasing rage: a laugh more structurally parodic than intentionally derisive. In this sense, too, what received opinion often dismisses as a formally egregious paragraph of tendentious meditation on the plight of women is not wrenched from the course of narrative so much as synchronized covertly with it, a manifestation of the Bertha principle—uncontrolled expressive energy—just before the fact.

Moreover, there is Jane's ironic treatment of the reader's putative disappointment right after the mention of that laugh. For when Grace, despite her mysterious aura as assumed source of the deranged chuckling, returns to her lair from her forays below, she is "generally (oh, romantic reader, forgive me for telling the plain truth:) bearing a pot of porter" (12:96). Appearing here only three sentences farther on from that intruded paragraph of vehement feminist plain-speaking, this satiric apology spreads back in application to more than the passing homely detail about the porter.[9] For the "romantic reader" is a category, figuratively understood, into which the autobiographical subject herself—as romantic listener—has recently been slotted. In the mood Jane describes during her elevated solitude at Thornfield, "my sole relief was to walk along the corridor of the third story . . . and, best of all, to open my inward ear to a tale that was never ended—a tale my imagination created, and narrated continuously" (12:96), one "quickened" en route by all that was excluded from her waking duty and drudgery. Commanding a perch on one kind of "stor(e)y," the building's third, she yields to another, to a deep prompting that takes narrative shape in coming to the "inward" audition of desire. So central is this conceit to the mechanisms of subjectivity in Brontë's fiction that it is borrowed two years later for a marked rite of passage in *Shirley*: "Caroline Helstone was just eighteen years old; and at eighteen the true narrative of life is yet to be commenced. Before that time, we sit listening to a tale, a marvelous fiction" (7:121).[10]

Thus has a trivial interpolation ("oh, romantic reader, forgive me") not so much distracted from as recast the reader's prompted extrapolation from the passage as a whole. Twenty-one chapters later, St. John Rivers will try to take charge of, and hold sway over, that "tale" of Jane's and its audition. Five chapters farther on, with Rivers gone, with Rochester reclaimed and embraced again, "My tale draws to its close" (12:396). In between, we have the deferred romantic climax of a novel by the name of a heroine whose secret life is the endless audition of just such a tale. With Jane operating as audience to her own romantic script, a familiar gap yawns in subjectivity, a splitting that proliferates across the texture of enunciation as a recurrent discrepancy. This is the gap that tends to separate social agent from the scenarios of its desire by the distance of auditor from teller, reader from text. The self is at once encoder and decoder in this version of the unconscious structured like a language. And into the space between has stepped Brontë's reader, conscripted as an intermediary relay (a device perfected to the edge of perversity in *Villette*) between Jane and her desire, reading the latter in the form of a romantic novel by her name. Taking up again Erich Schön's claims in the third chapter about the evolution of bourgeois reading, while factoring in the transitional terms of romanticism, we find in Jane's internalized "tale" an epitomizing cultural moment. There above it all, in close proximity at least to an outdoor ventilation of her fantasy redoubled by her inward narrative, the natural supernaturalism of reading finds its quintessential site. And at just this site, too, in a way not predicted within the scope of Schön's historical trajectory, the lost heft of words on the tongue finds a recaptured place, under cover of textual silence and its "empathetic competence," in the sympathetic vibrations of the Victorian mind's ear: reading's reclaimed erogenous zone.

Characterizing the modality of recognition at issue here, the notion of an "inward ear" implies that Brontë's readers cannot fully accede to their place as the stand-ins for Jane's own consciousness until they begin to *listen* while they read. Fleshing out (morphologically embodying) the nature of the subjective narrative whose audition is in turn audited by the reader, Jane further characterizes her inward tale as "quickened with all of incident, life, fire, feeling, that I desired and had not in my actual existence" (12:96). In that quartet of so far substanceless substantives for Jane's unmaterialized desire, the one metaphor, "fire," seems at first tautologically flanked by the twin tenors to its vehicle—in a circular definition of life as sentient spark. But then, true to its nature, "fire" doesn't stay put. Given that the typical interplay of assonance and alliteration in Brontë's prose—all too easy for critics to resist as an overblown lyric drag on narrative momentum—can better be read as a "cryptonymy" of repressed desire, then we have all the more reason to believe our ears here, too, as we subvocalize the immediate lexical pressure points of this writing.[11] The phonemic reading invited by this passage is, I hope to show, no more than the annotated "normal" experience of reading Brontë's prose—as an event of that inner aurality by which Jane's subjectivity is both generated and sustained.

Certainly, in the phrasing at hand, words are far from as "mute" as those in St. John's books. The sensed appositional interchangeability of "life, fire, feeling" disrupts sequence with secret equivalence, so that we come to hear in this phrasing the veritable insistence and slippage of the letter in the unconscious. Words end up signifying only the phantom doubles of themselves as signifiers, with self-identity thus surrendered, structurally sundered, from the lexical level up. Bertha's cackling laughter, the eruptive undoing of all discourse, is not therefore the only appearance made by the Voice of the Other at this point in the novel. For within the phonemic buckling of Jane's own self-utterance, there is the chiastic switch at "life, fire" by which a large part of "life" is, as it were, swallowed up by "fire"—long before Bertha has put the torch to Thornfield. The linguistic engulfment is marked further by an elision releasing from within the juxtaposition of "life, fire" an otherwise bracketed and contained lexeme that obtrudes now as a further appositive. Out of the friction of letters, that is, the ignition of a further signifier: out of "life, fire,"—either "Eyre" if pronounced as in "eyrie (with the optional long *i* rather than long *a* sound) or, more obviously prompted by context here, its homonym (and vocabular succubus) *ire*. At which point we hear named in advance, if by moments only—and only on the sly, or slide, of the signifying chain itself—the vocalized sarcastic rage of Jane's alter ego in Bertha.[12] That this "ire," not the "fire" from which it has been smelted out in the heat of reading, yields up not only a closer alliterative link with "I" but a closer morphemic common denominator with "desire" itself (quoting again: "that *I* desi*re*d and had not") is a coincidence only in the mode of all those other accidents that manifest desire in language—accidents that *Villette* will submit to further psychoanalytic pressure.

In the meantime, there is no reason why my main emphasis concerning this passage in *Jane Eyre*, any more than Brontë's, should get lost in the text's shifting scale of effects. Let me give it again in its broadest outline. At this turning point of the novel, the mock-dialogic gesture of apostrophe is a false lead. We refuse the trivial interpolation as the "romantic reader" if for no other reason than that we have just extrapolated from the preceding passage about inward audition the full *romance of reading* itself, its errancy and its metamorphoses. So that here, in fact, scale is after all just the issue: the minutiae of attention—and its differential slippages. No passage could show forth more succinctly one of the main assumptions informing each of my chapters since its introduction in the third. For this passage in *Jane Eyre* is not best understood to be self-referential as text but rather manifestly reflexive as reading event, inducing upon attention the very reconfigurations (metaphoric, syntactic, phonemic) it sets in motion. To the extent that the passage takes its own narrative status as topic, it is about itself not as written but only and explicitly as listened to: a parable of its own "inward" response, a response internal to language as subjectivity rather than to self as personality. And if the referential ambiguities sprung from such an approach through the subsonic "ear" confirm its model of desire and transference as a rippling corrugation of the unconscious across the integuments of structured subjectivity, then for the reader to stumble over and be momentarily discomposed by these ambiguities, these bivocalizations, is only the narrowest gauge of the passage's reflex action. Brontë's lexical practice, flattened somewhat by the omniscient discourse of *Shirley*, will be fully mobilized again only in *Villette*'s return to so-called first person, where the meshes and rents of subjectivity await once more, and more desperately than before, the transferential displacements of all things "inward" within the reflex equivocations of desire as narrative.

Reading therefore takes on in *Villette* a new form of a not unfamiliar urgency. For Dickens, reading is the prosthetic adjunct of an individuation so immutable that the subject's reach toward otherness through text could never alleviate, but only refigure, the distances upon which all such reading, like all social contract, depends. To see reading in Brontë as an event of desire rather than an event of distance is hardly to change the picture much. Lack becomes another name for separation. When, later in the century, the impossible closing of the gap between subject and otherness is entertained not for its impossibility alone but for the magic of its fantasized overcoming, reading gets repeatedly figured in the *fin de siècle* as preternatural rather than melancholic, weirdly assertive in its willed passivity and depletion, voracious in its vacuity, haunting in the ghostly invasiveness and displacements on which it thrives. To take a text like *Villette* on its own terms keeps us from imagining that any of this will dawn on the later Victorian novel quite by surprise.

Villette's Equivocated Reading

Brontë's last novel drives to one kind of limit that aspect of the Victorian fictional contract by which narrator and reader become cosignatories to the terms of narrative transmission. *Villette*, like *Jane Eyre*, tells its story through as well as to you. Where in the earlier novel the secret life of fantasy is a tale inwardly audited, in *Villette* life's betrayal of wish fulfillment is a story outwardly narrated by its heroine, Lucy Snowe. The related place of the reader in each figurative system does not undo but rather investigates this difference. Whether evoked like a second self listening in on desire, as in *Jane Eyre*, or like a deciphering agent, as in *Villette*, able to exercise a certain editorial control over the course of plot, the reader is made to intervene in each case precisely along the schism that separates self from desire. Figured as eavesdropping alter ego in *Jane Eyre*, as narratorial censor in *Villette*, the reader is subjected in both cases to the otherness that keeps the enunciating subject—as narrating drive—from coinciding with itself.

Anticipating the discursive eruption of linguistic shifters which will bedevil the conclusion of *Villette*, we may recall a briefly sketched literary history of "elocution" in the novel based on a structuralist understanding of the interplay between discourse and narration. This is Gerard Genette's demarcation of fictional evolution into three major periods distinguished by their relative tolerance for the invasion of narrative by discursive markers. For Genette the permeability of eighteenth-century fiction to authorial intrusion is contrasted in modern novels to the stringent exclusion of all storytelling gestures. "The only moment when the balance between narrative and discourse seems to have been assumed with a perfectly good conscience, without either scruple or ostentation, is obviously in the nineteenth century, the classical age of objective narration, from Balzac to Tolstoy."[13] That Genette's paradigm holds true for the British as well as the Continental tradition is shown not least by the obvious perversity of *Villette*'s deviance, where it is ultimately the ordinary "good conscience" of narration which is called into question by the shifters—and shiftiness—of the narrator's discursive evasions.

Villette tacitly raises—which is to say can barely keep down—just such issues of representational good faith across the strain of its own rhetoric in moving toward a conclusion (the death of the hero) that it refuses to narrate in anything like explicit language. Set up early on in *Villette*, as you the reader are, to assume Lucy's position as auditor of a tragic female narrative (Miss Marchmont's tale of lost love) and then to extrapolate from it to the affective nature of your own continuing stance toward the rest of Lucy's story, you ultimately find yourself in Lucy's former position as importunate addressee of a woman's sad looking back. By the end of the novel, even nostalgia foresworn exacts its toll. It is there that the pressure of address upon story, of dialogic byplay against plot's forward drive, is so unyielding that it may be taken—may, more precisely, be read—to bend the very texture of discourse, warping both lexicon and syntax together. After a certain point of evasive double talk, even word borders cannot take the strain of enunciation. In the process, narrative bares itself not just as a carrier but as a structure of sublimated desire. And scenes that tutor (or program) your reading by positive or negative example, like apostrophes that coach or goad you, may still let you think you are learning this for yourself.

Dwelling on such coordination in *Villette* between addressed and encoded reading does not go simply to illustrate once more the way in which interpolative device and extrapolative episode are complementary halves of the same rhetorical, hence figurative, dynamic. This I hope has already been sufficiently brought out. Concerning the textual linkage between narrative's interrelated modes of deployed (rather than merely awaited) attention—an attention externally delegated (by apostrophe) or internally recirculated (by parable)—I would put it this way: Conscripted reading, once recognized as such, makes the fundamental operations of reading visible—and visible as an operation not confined to the written page. Representational construct is not leveled to material inscription. Instead, the reader's role in negotiating between the poles of credited mimetic world and sheerly textual space is simply written into the text. The narratee becomes the phantom protagonist of a continuous phenomenological confrontation that is no less a model of narrative consumption for being at the same time a textual model of desire in production.

This relation of desire to narrative language, glimpsed for the most part at the micrological level of morphology, grammar, and rhetorical address, is also thematized at the manifest erotic climax of the novel. For narrative is indeed what brings Lucy and M. Paul Emanuel together. Just before he makes his proposal, it is as if, by retelling the troubling events of her immediate past, Lucy is reenergizing the impetus of the novel as a whole, an impetus that the narratee's desire must meet half way.[14] Six clauses reiterate the same narrative drive in a flushed tautology of amorous, lubricated release: "I spoke. All leapt from my lips. I lacked not words now; fast I narrated; fluent I told my tale; it streamed on my tongue" (41:591)—not *from* my tongue like speech but *on* it like a slaked need. Since her narrative is a version of the novel's own up to this point, here intimately deputized to Lucy as its chief actor and now discursive agent, the reader need not hear it rehearsed. You willingly cede your status as narratee to Paul Emanuel as the long-preferred object of Lucy's confessed desire. Yet your own need for narrative returns as soon as plot starts up again on the way to closing down.

In fact, *Villette* moves to conclusion by backing the often hailed narratee into an unprecedented corner at precisely the elided moment of the hero's drowning in a shipwreck, a catastrophe that befalls Paul Emanuel while returning to his fiancée, Lucy, after a three-year separation. His is a death not only left entirely to your own reactions in the absence of elegiac gestures on the part of the narrator; his fate is actually left up to you as narrative event it-self in the first place, a death yours to activate, to believe in, if you so choose. Brontë's readers in *Villette* may well be even more egregiously tweaked than in Thackeray, by turns nudged and needled, cheated, rebuked, second-guessed, everywhere manipulated and coerced. Then all of a sudden, right at the close, the narrator would appear to abdicate all storytelling to exactly these readers. It just doesn't sell. The audience is obviously more cornered than capitulated to, since for all the lures of rhetoric there is no real choice.

Yet it is hard to overstate the generic effrontery of Brontë's deflected cli-max. Having had the good grace in *Jane Eyre* to rescue Rochester from Bertha's flames, thus ending on a note of emotional restoration and marital union, Charlotte Brontë is urged by her father, no less, to be equally sparing with the heroine's fiancé at the end of *Villette*, urged to bring him back alive from his sea journey in order to consummate the marriage with Lucy Snowe.[15] Readers will demand it, she is assured. Having planned her story otherwise, however, and confident in its inevitability, Brontë undertakes no narrative, only discursive, revisions, as we will be examining in detail. She thus complies with the plea not to make the hero drown simply by not saying so in so many words. The ef-fect is to leave not only Paul Emanuel but the reader, too, quite at sea. One of the trademarks, indeed mainstays, of Victorian fiction—the ritualized death scene—is thus turned inside out, so that plot is made a function of reader re-sponse rather than the other way around. Brontë has also, as we will be ex-ploring, stage-managed the hero's death in the wings so that its inference be-comes a reenactment, in extremis, of the narrative act itself: a structuring of response even in the absence of event.

"I Will Permit the Reader to Picture Me . . ."

From the jarring intersection of death, address, and premature closure in *Villette*, any reader is likely to be thrown back into the text with a jolt of recog-nition. For at least once before, you have been given enough rope to entangle yourself in a similar fashion. Quitting her godmother's comfortable home at Bretton, Lucy Snowe, we recall, was returned to "the bosom of my kindred" at the opening of the fourth chapter, to remain there, through unspecified tragedy (as the reader shortly, if barely, finds out), for eight years. "It will be conjectured that I was of course glad to return. . . . Well! the amiable conjec-ture does no harm, and may therefore be safely left uncontradicted" (4:94). The litotes (or double negative) of "uncontradicted" is the least of it. The narrator actually goes on to elaborate the reader's options: "Far from saying nay, indeed,

I will permit the reader to picture me, for the next eight years, as a bark slumbering through halcyon weather, in a harbour still as glass" (4:94). Thus begins an extended conceit ascribed to the reader's own supererogatory well-wishing, a conceit attenuated to the point of cultural cliché: "A great many women and girls are supposed to pass their lives something in that fashion; why not I with the rest?" (4:94).

Within the baroque terms of this figuration, this forced image of lulling harborage, Lucy goes overboard in more ways than one. Speaking not only of the original crisis but of the intervening years of anxiety still at work in her unconscious, she writes: "To this hour, when I have the nightmare, it repeats the rush and saltiness of briny waves in my throat, and their icy pressure on my lungs" (4:94). If her nightmares always take this same form, of emotional turmoil and death figured as drowning, then we have all the more reason to understand the bizarre subjective status of Paul Emanuel's closural death. It is a scene, in this light, which "repeats" the originary trauma of violent breach as a watery expulsion from womblike stasis that is both birth and orphaning together, the plunge into mortality. "For many days and nights . . . a heavy tempest lay on us," she nears the climactic moment of this early figurative crisis by recalling. "*In fine*, the ship was lost, the crew perished" (4:94; emphasis added). When another ship is later lost at sea, finally and in "Finis" (the concluding chapter by that name), the hope of a husband and family sunk with it, so has the nightmare come again in "this hour" of autobiographical retrospect.

In just this sense, the proleptic point of the earlier figurative episode may be distilled in its poignantly literal coda: "I complained to no one about these troubles. Indeed, to whom could I complain?" (4:94). This lack of community, this absence of a potentially recuperative audition and response, is one for which only the novelized retrospect itself, as a structure of address, can hope to compensate. Readers, simply by reading, offer the narrator the succor of a hearing. It is a hearing confessional, purgative—even, by the dawning logic of sublimation and displacement, conceivably therapeutic.[16] Such, then, is the more than contractual exchange that can only be played out at the conclusion of the novel, by which point the reader has been many times invoked and jostled, hailed, dodged, enlisted, and rebuffed, at one moment told even to "cancel the whole" of a passage and rewrite it in "alternate text-hand copy" (6:117–18). Amid the novel's webwork of vocative feints, evasions, and prevarications, such a conscription of the reader as inscriber is only the spelling out of an assumption elsewhere at work. Readers can only be taken in, written in, by seeming to have the text given over to the pleasure (even preferential revision) of their own attention.

The Subject of Address

"My reader, I know, is one who would not thank me for an elaborate re-production of poetic first impressions" (5:105–6). As close to the vocative as third-person possessive grammar ("My reader") can come, this (half-accusatory) allusion to your preference for plot over description immediately yields to a miniature—and wholly internalized—plot. It is a plot whose personified abstractions stand at an equal distance from the narrating subject as do the various figurations of the reader elsewhere in the communicative discourse of that subject. *Ex nihilo*, a female character appears who, having "asked the waiter for a room," then "timorously called for the chambermaid" (5:106). Her presence has been sprung a few sentences before as a sheer (and so far ungendered) abstraction: "Into the hands of Common-sense I confided the matter." From there, the reification of a psychic attribute takes over in a circumscribed allegory: "Common-sense, however, was as chilled and bewildered as all my other faculties, and it was only under the spur of an inexorable necessity that she spasmodically executed her trust" (5:106). Indeed, exactly this tendency toward parceled-out self-consciousness in *Villette* is imaged at one point as the very pressure behind writing (a letter of amorous frustration within a novel thereof) as an act of materialized desire: "Feeling and I turned Reason out of doors, drew against her bar and bolt, then we sat down, spread our paper, dipped in the ink an eager pen"—and wrote (23:335). This is a composition that posits a signified (but undefined) self hovering somewhere between the signifying "I" and the momentarily embodied pull of impulse against rationality.

The twofold logic of personification which links, at the site of textual production, the sheerly figural reader with the sheerly figurative facets of an inscribing mentality becomes clearest when the mechanisms of direct address are engaged to catch or channel not the audience's attention but rather that of the narrator herself within the cocoon of self-consciousness: "Courage, Lucy Snowe!" (31:450). If such an apostrophe tropes the self as its own reader—subjectivity taking command from (rather than of) desire—it may also imply that there is no self there at all, in or as retrospect, except as *read into* (both senses) action. When such a state of mind is apostrophized like a second person, like a reader, you may realize how often your own reading is figured in simply so that Lucy—according to the therapeutic motive of the entire autobiographical retrospect—may more easily enter into dialogue with her own conflicting urges. Like apostrophe in romantic verse according to Jonathan Culler, the fictional vocative is once again narrowed to a valence of subjectivity in process.

This is never more obvious, or more urgent, than when *Villette* must call on you in helping to call itself to a halt.

"Those years of absence! How I had sickened over their anticipation," you find in the first paragraph of "Finis," followed by a simile that is soon itself to be literalized: "The woe they must bring seemed certain as death" (42:593). Nevertheless the three years of still hopeful separation turn out to have been far worse in anticipation than in the actual event. Indeed, in the assurance of his love from afar, Lucy can remember them in a direct echo of Jane Eyre's triumphant "Reader, I married him." The intertextual detonation rocks the novel to its foundational logic of address, for marriage has been replaced by sheerly textual congress. "Reader, they were the three happiest years of my life" (42:593). (Transliterate this to "Happiness, these years were your allotted portion," and you have my previous point about the functional interchangeability of reader apostrophe and the reified subdivisions of consciousness.) Such happiness can be affirmed in good part, as the reader readily guesses, because the feared onslaught of Absence has taken another form: the aura of the man in his letters. "By every vessel he wrote" (42:594), Lucy records, in a grammar that elides cause and effect, source and conveyance, so as to convert the verb "wrote" into a designation that spans inscription and delivery, edging the latter toward a mystified presence in reception. That the reader is taken into Lucy's confidence yet again at just this moment of confessed happiness in distance carries a further charge. It is a way of advertising to Brontë's audience the pleasures not only of passionate expressivity (the communicative circuit of Paul Emanuel's correspondence) but also of its receipt as text: in short, the twofold power of eroticized writing to sublimate and rematerialize desire.

Such writing leads on in this novel to no issue "happier" or less strictly textual. Paul Emanuel's appointed vessel never comes, despite the narrator's temporary retreat from fatality into the historical present tense: "And now the three years are past: M. Emanuel's return is fixed" (42:595). There is no comfort for long in this phase of the remembered past, though, since Lucy's recurrent "nightmare" of storm and drowning now begins to "repeat" itself in waking tempest. Six paragraphs from the end of the novel, she is thus precipitated into the immediate scene, the unmediated sense, of anxiety, for "wander as I may through the house this night, I cannot lull the blast" (595-96). As merely an actor in the drama, it is absurd to imagine that Lucy *could* quiet the storm—except of course by a "lull" in narrative. It is only, therefore, as an omniscient discursive agent, elementing the tempest in the present tense of discourse rather than event, that the narrating "I" could conceivably exercise veto power over the fatal course of such a storm. "Peace, be still!" (42:596) begins the third paragraph from the end, as if the imperative grammar marks Lucy's admonition to herself as the momentum of retrospect is carrying her implacably toward the tragic disclosure. Yet by the next sentence it seems otherwise, as if the imperative has been an injunction from above, proleptically quoted and unfulfilled— a case of narrative omniscience kicked up, as it were, to a hoped-for fiat of peace at the providential plane. "Oh! a thousand weepers, praying in agony on waiting shores, listened for *that voice*, but it was not uttered" (emphasis added).

When stillness comes, it is too late to have spared Lucy's lover. All it can do is euphemize his death as such a peace—for him and, as yet provisionally, for her. His name is never mentioned again, even though sentimental readers are apparently licensed to think him returned: "Let it be theirs to conceive the delight of joy born again . . ." Even the narrator's figurative phrasing in this passage ("born again") suggests, without saying so, that there has been a death. To this imperative clause, those parallel clauses that build toward it, and the phrasing that then tapers away—to all this impacted syntactic deflection of the plot we will soon be returning. For now, the only narrative suggestion left in Brontë's "Finis" chapter is that Lucy has lived on past the deaths of the plot's other main participants: "Madame Beck prospered all the days of her life; so did Père Silas; Madame Walravens fulfilled her ninetieth year before she died" (42:596). The plot has one more sentence: "Farewell." Goodbye and good riddance, as addressed to the departed or departing cast? Or is this a sentimental flourish answering at last, years later, to the notably unreciprocal close of the engagement chapter: "We parted: he gave me *his* pledge, and then *his* farewell. We parted: the next day—he sailed" (41:592; emphasis added)? Or a third possibility: Is Lucy's closing "Farewell" (in a non sequitur that nonetheless seems most likely) addressed to her audience instead, the addressed reader invoked one last time in valediction, spoken to across a chasm as absolute as that of the grave?

"What Do You Think, Lucy, of These Things?"

Rounding itself off in this way, however, the text rounds back on its own plot: to a scene of autobiographical storytelling which serves, as microcosm, to reconfigure en route the encompassing motives of narration and inscribed audition in the novel as a whole. This is Miss Marchmont's story, of and by her, an early episode of which we have had no reminder until the "Finis" chapter. Mentioned there, just before the end, is a modest legacy that finally reaches Lucy from one "Mr. Marchmont" (42:593), cousin of her first employer. This "return" of Miss Marchmont in the form of a posthumous remembrance may well direct our attention to an endowment more deeply bestowed at the original scene of her death almost four dozen chapters before: narrative impetus itself, with death in the offing as the structuring antithesis of life writing, of autobiography, of fictional retrospect. Exactly from what vantage Lucy is conducting her own autobiographical narrative is in fact made plain only in the immediate aftermath of Miss Marchmont's death, where Lucy, writing years later, admits to fashioning her retrospect from a distance on lost love comparable to that of her late benefactress, for "my hair which till a late period withstood the frosts of time, lies now, at last white, under a white cap, like snow beneath snow" (5:105). Any romantic narrator seems truest to her name in looking back.

And what Lucy has just recorded in the preceding chapter is not merely the dying retrospect of her predecessor but the story of her own role as audience to that narrative. Remembering the accidental death of her lover on the eve of their intended marriage, Miss Marchmont has called up a fully narrativized form of this tragic past, "its incidents, scenes, and personages" manifested "with singular vividness" (4:98). Quickened into language, the entire ruminated past is sublimated, in its absence, into an embodied object of desire—in a way that anticipates the erotic displacements of Lucy's own later life writing: "I love Memory tonight" (4:98), admits Miss Marchmont uneasily, commandeering Lucy as a confessor figure willing to audit a litany of superannuated yearning. The invested narrator thus attempts to render her listener a mere functionary in the economy of narrative as purgation. "What do you think, Lucy, of these things? Be my chaplain and tell me" (4:101). Even as you are extrapolating this embedded scene of narration to the parameters of the novel as a whole, here you are interpolated by proxy through the inset story's own rhetoric. The ligatures of conscription could scarcely be more strategically coordinated. And Lucy plays her part to perfection. As in the case of a reader rather than auditor of narrative, a reader whose invoked responses can never genuinely be circulated back through the textual system even when courted rhetorically—and even when sometimes ascribed, textually inscribed—Lucy remains mute: "This question I could not answer: I had no words" (4:101). Neither do Lucy's readers, Brontë's readers, have words—except as they are imagined for you. So, too, with Lucy as solicited audience: "It seemed as if she thought I *had* answered it," with Miss Marchmont's "Very right, my child" doing all it needs to do in sustaining the narrative momentum as an interlocutory contract.

Sympathetic audience for Lucy's own later confession, into which this scene is regressively folded as a combined experiment in narrational and enunciative "closure," we are more like therapists than confessors or "chaplains," silently taking in without the need for absolution. But all the while Memory, externalized as plot, is the reader's own object of desire too. So that any yearning for a novelistic ending happier than Miss Marchmont's—with its protracted gap between the death of love and the death of desire, between passion and its still open wounds—may seem to participate in an ultimately closed circle: one whereby the fictions of the teller, once shunted off onto the auditor as narrative expectations, are then projected back upon the narrator herself as the revealed wish fulfillment, the sublimated and substitutive desire, out of which all narrative issues.

Arresting Address: "Here Pause: Pause at Once"

Your place as reader in all this, in and of all this, can only be investigated by experiencing it. At which point the oscillating microtext comes to refigure the larger arcs of displaced closural *resignation* on the narrator's part (both senses: acquiescence and abdication) as a reenacted *acceptance* by the reader (both senses: receipt and understanding). Another way to think of this is to realize that the last two pages of the novel are in the conventional sense impossible to overread, at least impossible not to read over. What is being pulled off? What is being pulled over on you? Positioned to remember Miss Marchmont's earlier story and its structuring of response, you had left Lucy's present ordeal on the brink of denial, carried there by her suspended, present-tense evocation of the storm. It is now time to attend more closely to the verbal skidding that results from her sudden application of the brakes.

"Here pause: pause at once." There are few more sharply drawn instances of the spatiality latent in the very term *figure* of speech than in the arch of this chiasm, where "here" and "at once" flank the imperative as equivalent markers of textual sequencing. But is it, this time, the novel's own reader, as before suspected, who is addressed, asked to relax your engagement with the textual melodrama, to back off and calm down? Or is it, as you have also been led to suspect, the narrator telling herself to halt the forward drive of plot? For at least the next stretch of imperative grammar, the latter possibility looms largest, as if the narrative agency is summoning its own arrest in a further adverbial arc from "here" to "there" as interchangeable deictics: "There is enough said. Trouble no quiet, kind heart; leave sunny imaginations hope." In what amounts to a radical subjectivizing of alleviated inclemency, the cause of hope, the subsided tempest, leaves its dead-metaphoric trace in the induced effect of a brightening optimism ("sunny").

And something else is creeping into the enunciation as it enjoins its own arrest, some resistance to plotted outcome which runs so completely against the grain of written enunciation as to induce a semantic friction. This is a friction, a potential fissuring, which only a psycholinguistics of narrative production can begin to chart. To begin with, the spatial disorientation between locus of remembered event and locus of inscription—in the pitching of *"Here* pause" against the no longer neutral filler of *"There* is enough said" (There where? Here now?)—begins a dizzying slide of mutual displacements between subject and object across those next three apostrophic but perplexingly directed clauses. The entire plot of the novel thus comes bearing down on the internal engineering of direct address. In terms that early work by Julia Kristeva has drawn out from Bakhtin, the compositional "loop" (the message-addressee circuit) is found here to defer the "loop" of retailed event (the plot circuit)—and to do so by intruding upon and derailing it.[17] The novel has become all talk, no action. In the process it has generated one of the most brazen and disjoint stretches of narrative, or antinarrative, in all Victorian fiction, where the reader not only glimpses but gets snarled up within the creaking works of textual production itself.

You linger now (as in any and every reading of the novel) at the rhetorical turning point of those three apostrophes, unsure whether they are turned toward you in their address. In the double grammar of "Trouble no quiet, kind heart," one sense of the clause, perhaps the most likely, allots two nonrestrictive adjectives to the noun "heart," suggesting an audience of readers each left at peace in the kindly disposed expectations of marital closure. The alternative understanding of the clause, by which the imperative is completed by a delayed vocative, with "quiet" become a noun in object position ("Trouble no quiet, I say"), is a reading to which you may well be drawn (on second thought) by analogy with a possible suppressed matrix in the earlier outburst "Peace, be still!"—if understood to be colored in retrospect (as how could it help being?) by Lucy's certain knowledge. To have responded there to a phrasal residue of "Be still my heart!" is to encourage the subsequent sense of "kind heart" as a periphrasis for the feeling subject in dialogue with her own ameliorative instincts. If so, "heart" would take its place as the last of those many reified figurations of her own internal states (Common Sense, Reason, Feeling, and so forth). This is a pattern epitomized, as we saw, in Lucy's attempt virtually to collect herself by apostrophe, to consolidate her fractured attributes through the self-constitutive interjection "Courage, Lucy Snowe!" This is what it once took to go forward. "Lenience, kind heart!" may be what it now takes, at least for the present stalled moment, to go it alone in retrospect.

Supplanting syntactical with lexical byplay is the work of the next imperative clause: "leave sunny imaginations hope." No sooner has the narrator hypostatized a more softening sentiment as the signifying other ("kind heart") to her own narrative enunciation, and given her story over to it, than a surreptitious countermove may now seem to set the subsequent clause in semantic recoil from itself. Just your slight hesitation over something being left to pluralized "imaginations," where you would expect the more idiomatic "left to the imagination," is enough to ripple the syntax into duplicity: unleashing the inference that plot is here leaving behind (in the genitive sense) "sunny imagination(')s hope." This is not what the novel says, not what the narrator writes, but rather what the text may end up uttering in the reflex contingencies of a reader's production.

Any such homophonic shadow play in "imaginations" (when taken as possessive rather than plural) would certainly lead on to the superficially concessive gist of the next paragraph, where once more the lexical sequence may be found even more fundamentally destabilized, not just in the wavering inflection of case versus number but in the matter of syllabic boundary itself. Lucy is referring again to those readers who choose to wish the death away, but to whom is she addressing this reference? "Let it be theirs to conceive the delight of joy born again fresh out of great terror, the rapture of rescue from peril," and so forth, where the imperative seems generalized now, by a formulaic rhetorical expectation, not only to include, as implied vocative recipient, the narrator's own temporizing impulse—Lucy still thinking out loud to herself—but also to enlist the acquiescence of the knowing reader, you yourself, in such a white lie as sop to the popular audience at large. Under the strain of this divisive rhetorical format, however, a further deformation takes place. As with the grammatical ligatures of the plural sibilant loosened in one possible aural response to the phrase "sunny imagination(')s hope"—and testifying again not only to the ambivalence of subvocalizations but to the prevalent mode of hearthside Victorian reception by way of familial reading aloud—a more drastic phonemic splaying may also be activated, against the graphic grain, for the homophonic clue in the spurious dream of rescue "after great (t)error." In this way would a vocalized elision—undermining the narrator's stagy elision of the death scene itself—tell the truer tale of vast *error* in false hope. At micro- as well as macrolevel, phrasing would tell this tale by saying so not in so many words but in their uncanny reshuffling. As in dream slips, lexical spans may snap under stress of the unsaid, so that death as "nonrepresentable" (Kristeva's sense, following Freud) may nevertheless be read not just between the lines but between the words.[18]

In the ambivalent intentionality of the whole passage as plotted discourse, that is, this lexical displacement would be tantamount to the irruptive unconscious of enunciation itself. Here, then, well before the modernist "revolution in poetic language" (Kristeva's term), the thetic force of discourse seems lined with its own antithesis: the symbolic regime submitted to those bucklings of juncture which transiently recover the repressed ripplings of the semiotic as a radical negativity or split in the very sequence of enunciation.[19] Lucy's phrasing even here, of course, is as far from the prelingual throbbing of Kristeva's primal semiotic as it is from the radical symbolic malfunction more recently investigated by her as melancholy's denial of the signifier. Still, these split-second, split-lexical detours from signification may be said to pass through a shudder of this semiotic undoing of the word on their way toward a not much less momentary regrouping as grammar's phantom double in the symbolic. Allowing this aural latitude is one way to bring an earlier Kristevan (Bakhtian) reading not so much up to date as up to the speed, as it were, of reading's own oscillating rhythms.[20]

"Let It Be Theirs to Conceive . . ."

In the draft version of the next-to-last paragraph, beginning "Here pause," there is a final sentence deleted in proof which also, like so much in the passage, straddles the options of closure. Yet Brontë may have seemed to be leaning too much in one direction. Following "Let it be theirs to conceive the delight . . . ," and a further metaphor of suspiciously extratextual activity in "Let them picture union and a happy succeeding life" (direct echo of "I will permit the reader to picture me" in the false lead of the shipwreck conceit of chapter 4), Brontë originally put "So be it."[21] In revision, the performative force of this locution, realizing its own representation, doing what it says, is cleared away to keep the alternative ending, though worded, always unrealized. As the printed version has it, the happy ending is only "theirs to conceive" if they insist on indulging themselves. Between the *saying* that is suspended by the published text ("enough said") and the illicit picturing that is permissively dismissed ("Let them picture") falls the double dead metaphor in "Let it be theirs to conceive . . . joy born again." Though such phrasing operates well this side of an open parodistic barb like one of Thackeray's buttonholings of "madam" or his "fair young readers," we may still sense Brontë's satiric gendering of Victorian domestic sentimentality. For self-delusion is couched in a female "conception" of clutched, unexamined joy that must itself be "born" (or hatched) rather than found narratively bestowed.

Despite all we have noted, there is a more undermining dynamism yet to this final textual constraint ("Let it be theirs . . . ") and its psycholinguistic tensions. What might appear to be *Villette's* radically dialogized and differential (either/or) ending may be taken, as suggested above, to reverse the ordinary mechanisms of romantic fiction—where a protagonist plays out the fantasy life of the reader. Instead, *Villette's* discourse projects onto its reception the return of repressed desire, a desire thus purged by displacement from the site of writing or enunciation. If this sounds—in bare outline as much as in my loaded rendering of it—like that transferential function of story upon which a critic like Peter Brooks has shed such light, then it is a function pushed here to an unprecedented level of countertransference: the enunciating heroine left to fend off, even while feeding off, the lingering fantasies of her own readers.[22] Yet there is more here, or less. After all, this is a Victorian, hence classic, text, and its closural impulses are all but ineluctable. The discursive loop can retard and obfuscate the narrative loop for only so long, until the life/death bracket does after all converge with the speaker/addressee circuit. The grammatical moment of this convergence, in all its resonance, is what we have left to recognize.

Arrived at Brontë's defiant—under the guise of pliant—closure, we may well have sensed how this ending could serve a feminist understanding of the novel by implying that the closure of the female Bildungsroman cannot properly depend on a man, that a woman's story can exist either way, with or without. Or it might ratify those critiques of the closural paradigm itself which expose the deathlike stasis in marital end-stopping. In this sense the ending poses a buried rhetorical question: Even if reunion and subsequent marital unification were to be clung to by some imagined readers as the outcome of the story, what would *not mentioning it* mean but that, formally speaking, there is nothing more to say? Nevertheless, these passing ramifications are, as suggested, subsumed at last to a closure whose ambiguity is itself a ruse. For at just the moment when closure is thrown open to the seeming contingency of reading, you the narratee are in fact entirely constrained by the very form of the novel's address as a directed discourse. To be sure, the narrative does not, will not, say whether or not Paul Emanuel has died, yet the very process of its telling *enunciates* by negative inference the exclusion of the only alternative to such a death. Once the shifters of discursive emplacement, that is, have been foregrounded in the imperative formula "Let it be theirs to conceive," the enunciative position is itself tacitly split. It divides into the narrator of "third persons" (not linguistic "persons" at all, according to Benveniste) and the addressor of that second person ("[You] let it be . . .") who alone can produce every instance of the book as text.[23] By constitutive linguistic fact—rather than just emotional "constitution"—they who could convince themselves to think otherwise about the hero's fate (let us say, contemporaneously, those other and always more sentimental Victorians) are not here, then, at all—not here *now*—in the I/you circuit, the circuit of reading; they are not addressed by this text in its function as message. It is, therefore, not *this* text that they are reading, that their reading produces, even if they hold in their hand the last volume of a three-decker novel by this name. The return of "community" as unified addressee—a culturally consolidating ideal never more than partially banished, according to Bakhtin and Kristeva, by the transformation of epic into novel—is here privatized in the pitting of you against them, and not even them as readers, just an abstract plurality of dupes likely to be fooled by a story to whose text they in fact, as grammar has it, can claim no present access. Thus Brontë's audience finds vexed into recognition that compound vanishing point of both story and address, of heroic narrator and discriminating narratee, neither of whom can finally posit romantic delusion as the condition of closure.

A Valediction for Bidding Mourning

But into what emotional tonality does the narrative thus abruptly fade? If this is an aesthetic question, it may also be a structural—and a poststructuralist—one, a question that ultimately works to league psychology with linguistics. For in the eclipse of that sunny imagination's hope looms the threat of melancholy's Black Sun. In calling up Kristeva's recent title, I am taking Brontë's novel to be neither an act of mourning nor its obsessional reverse face, an act of melancholy, but something in between: something meant to suppress the latter even at the aesthetic expense of the former. In so saying, I must return to the question of transferential relays to ask if their function is in fact exhausted when the reader's lingering hopes seem to keep Lucy's dream alive; whether, at the same time, it is not the case that your inevitable suspicions of the worst also operate, just as importantly, to let the heroine off the hook. On the one hand, in the intrapsychic equilibrium of this closure, it cannot be that Lucy herself is so benighted as to hope still for her hero's survival. That's only a problem for certain kinds of readers ("they"). On the other hand, it is therefore not Lucy's fault if he is presumed dead. And it might have been: This is the ultimate double take in this double voicing of the passage, this ceding to the reader of salvific, but then again lethal, voice.

Such a suspicion takes us, in short, to the logic of *avoided* melancholy in Lucy's move toward closure. It also permits us to reflect on—and textually specify—the pervasive suggestion of Slavoj Žižek's *The Sublime Object of Ideology* that the interpellation of the subject into culture finds its psychoanalytic parallel in the transference, where the ideological truth claims of the Law, of the symbolic system itself, are deferred away to the "one supposed to know."[24] Within the specific literary modalities of a given period, this supposed knowledge resides primarily in its readily assumed generic expectations. *Villette* would appear in this sense to offer the closest point of intersection we have seen between classic fiction's interpolated or apostrophized reader and the interpellated social subject succumbing voluntarily to the law of culture and its literary subcodes. But Brontë's novel operates in this way precisely by negotiating a second, and more specifically textual, intersection with the therapeutic circuit of repetition and working through enacted by the vagaries of the narrative voice. For *Villette* paces Lucy through her concluding ordeal even as Lucy is toying all the while with the predispositions of her readers, their knowledge of literary law: the rule of genre and its closural imperatives. The presumptions of such readers, which could only take effect in the text by virtually rewriting it, would be just that: nothing but presumptive. Yet the artifice of such a viable desire on the reader's part remains in fragile place. In the keep of a knowing narrator who openly withholds her knowledge in deference to *your* desire, or that of some reader not wholly unlike you, the ideology of an entire literary mode is at stake. So it is that *Villette*'s exorbitant transfers of need and loss impose a tax on generic protocol which there is no way for either narrator or reader to collect, only jointly—and defensively—to reinvest.

In this light, the heroine-narrator's extravagant suppression of mourning earlier—her undetailed family tragedy in chapter 4 as an eight-year hiatus in the plot immediately stitched over by the figurative elaboration of her discourse—has come back to haunt the novel in closing. What Freud saw as the luxuriating "self-torments" of the melancholiac, whose grief is exacerbated by the pain of an ambivalence verging on guilt for simultaneously drawing pleasure from the loss (in Lucy's case, ultimately, the preservation of her independence from this rather too overbearing male)—such is exactly the festering pathological aftermath that Lucy's throttled mourning seems meant to forestall. Playing between "sunny imagination" as a mode of desire and a mode of delusion, Lucy's psyche as textual function thus appears to instance an axiom of Kristeva's *Black Sun*: the sense that "if there is no writing other than the amorous, there is no imagination that is not, overtly or secretly, melancholy" (6). Lucy in suspended mourning, that is, rewrites her loss as a continuing eros of the will. Yet the resulting static from these crossed channels of blocked plot and diversionary enunciation cannot be entirely filtered out. As Kristeva puts it in interrogating the symptomatic language of melancholia's divided desire, "Does not such a splitting cut across all discourse?" (26). If it is something like the indulgent romanticism of this morbidity which Lucy Snowe is attempting at once to evoke and forbid, then it is the *effort* of this repression, rather than its seamless success, which the unconscious of her writing has to divulge—has in it to, and must, divulge. In Kristeva's words about melancholic diagnosis (eerily familiar, and not at all accidentally, from her theories of modernist poetry), such splitting comes to the surface in and across the "blanks of discourse, vocalizations, rhythms, syllables of words that have been devitalized . . . in short, the level of imagination, the level of writing—which bears witness to the hiatus, blank, or spacing that constitutes death for the unconscious" (26).

My suggestion is therefore that Lucy's last paragraphs, for all the sometimes stiff rationality of her ordinary discourse, mark the cutting—the rending—edge of an enunciative breakdown discernible even as (and only because) resisted. Accordingly, the semiotic as well as psychic *work* of this bivocal dynamic, this alternating current, between narrator and narratee can be summed up by a recapitulation of Kristeva's answer to her earliest leading question in *Black Sun*: "Is mood a language?" (21). Perhaps so (it certainly seemed to be the case in the audited "inward" narrative of *Jane Eyre*)—but only as some (other) moods can only be traced in their attempted escape from any and all language. Signification for Kristeva, as the replacement by re-presentation of lost objects, lost in the very naming, begins thereby in a negation and a loss that the mood of melancholy seeks to deny: a negation which, precisely to avoid such melancholy, Lucy moves to embrace and redouble. In Paul Emanuel's absence, she has, after all, nothing else to embrace, and so in writing she labors to stave off death's contamination, both its grief and its guilt, both mourning and melancholia at once. The death she would disavow—not by avoiding all signifying negativity but rather by strategically tapping it—is thus a death that remains manifest even in its equivocated denial. And once unleashed, such linguistic instability cannot be readily isolated. At the lexical level, as we have seen, the level where psychosemiotic tolls are taken, it leaks, bleeds over, floods cracks, widens rifts, springs ruptures.[25] What can only be called the return of the depressed is what you, as reader, find flickering in the valleys and crevices, the virtual depressions, of Lucy's enunciation. That you alone can be looked to in order to find them testifies yet again to novelistic conscription as a writing *with*.

In this light, for all the power play of Lucy Snowe's evasive tactics in the recruiting of response, we may come to suspect that the negativity she seeks to exploit is also the presupposition of her textual existence. This sense is perhaps most deviously revealed in a latent trace of the novel's readily conceivable but definitively avoided title. *The Professor, Jane Eyre, Shirley*—these are all we have of the eponymous professor, Jane Eyre, and Shirley. Brontë's last title is more unflinching yet. No Lucy Snowe here. Located on no map of any country, Ville/ette—in its etymology as a grammatically diminutive public space—designates that pseudonymous, feminized, minimal, topography-free, utopic nowhere, always foreign and somewhat estranged—a book by any other name—within whose borders, or at least whose limits, after years of promulgating English language and literature in a schoolroom working space mortgaged to the local "bookseller" (41:589), a formerly "placeless person" (5:103), as Lucy has called herself, has undertaken a text. Where Jane Eyre can be said to create a bounded representation of herself in *Jane Eyre*, her "life," by contrast the titular, fictive space of Villette is all that Lucy produces. Villette, then, as well as the book by its name, can denominate nothing more nor less than the site of a writing, where, for all the shows of vested autonomy, its relentlessly conscripted readers, even when all is over, are left residually to the text's rather than their own devices. But then to be moved is, after all, a passive construction, even when this is what you actively produce a text as causing in you.

If *Villette* is taken finally to manifest the countertransferential charge—and discharge—of invested reading, a reversible displacement at the base of Victorian fiction's rhetorical power, we are thus in a position to register an even more fundamental basis for textual oscillations of all sorts in the execution of Brontë's prose. In such semiotic warpings of the symbolic as the junctural crux at "sunny imagination(')s hope" or "after great t/error"—with their teasing relation to the condensations and displacements of the dreamwork—we can see, or hear, the rifts of subjectivity taking themselves out on enunciation, even as they are locally "dialogized" in the induced double takes of the reading act. It is by just such a counterlogic of ingrained "negativity" that the Voice of the Other has come to invade the compositional, under pressure from the narrational, loop. Moreover, in the fact that Brontë's enunciating heroine has chosen to withhold her name from the title of her published retrospect, one may, I am saying, sense the furthest reverberation of Brontë's phonotext—and this in memory of the multiple phonemic matrix of Jane Eyre's own punning name (or of the "ire" that can't help but flicker in her dreams of "life, fire, feeling"). Rebuking expectation in *Villette*, defying the fates by the silence of her obituary report, yet taking back what she seems to give to the unwary optimist even as she sheathes herself from the charge of secret relief—riding out, in other words, a contradiction and a denial, an elision and an effacement—the narrator, Lucy Snowe, insinuates by this wavering negativity the unwritten entitlement of the text as a whole within the otherwise narrowing strictures of Victorian paradigms: its sustained if unstable materialization of Lucy's No.

Styling Itself Told: Narrative's Invisible Frame

The novel-long push toward Lucy's negative affirmation is in good part the work of reader address in *Villette*, as was the equivocation of "romantic" self-narration in *Jane Eyre*. The mid-Victorian forked paths in a literary history of narrative address thus derive in considerable measure from the linguistically materialized urgency of such writing and its divergence from other modes of novelistic rhetoric. Reader apostrophe comes to seem a crystallizing feature of what used to be discussed as narrative style. But the place of the Brontës in the full spectrum of Victorian stylistic texture—and rhetorical posture—is even more complicated than we began this chapter by noting in their deliberate differentiation from Dickensian omniscience, with its corollary in omnivorous receptivity.

"Reader, I married him" in *Jane Eyre*. In effect: "Reader, I buried him" in *Villette*, all the more *narrative* an act in the marked absence of response. It is up to you, that reader, to perform both ceremonies in your mind. Why else are you called to attention? Yet when is it otherwise in nineteenth-century fiction, even without the apostrophe? Charlotte Brontë's prose takes this both for granted and, incrementally, to a distinct textual limit in the conduct of realist fiction. It is at this limit that rhetoric and narrative structure, individual style and generic format, redefine each other as functions of that institutionalized aesthetic discourse known as the novel but only knowable, finally, as a cultural (not just mercantile) economy with its own psychic exchange value. Devolved through the channels of linguistic subjectivity from the epistolary origins of the novel, Jane's or Lucy's narrative messages seem directed as much at their own self-consciousness as at a potential public. Certain consequences for narrative rhetoric soon grow apparent. When a pinpointed address reverts to sender, and does so as a figure for a definitive rift in the very constitution of the originating consciousness, the reader's apostrophized difference from the enunciating subject is conscripted as a difference within. Between enunciation and response, narrative style is the mediation and the only medium. It induces, in effect, one long reflex of recognition.

Despite their romantic extravagance, then, Brontë's experiments in directed narrative from *Jane Eyre* to *Villette* fall between the extreme polarization of Thackeray and Dickens, on the one side, and the emergent (and in its own way stylistically demanding) psychological realism of George Eliot on the other. Brontë's novels exclude both the battery of satiric apostrophes sported by *Vanity Fair* and the anomalously explicit sociology of the "Dear Reader" in *Hard Times*. They anticipate, instead, what becomes in Eliot's fiction the structuring of empathy through the commanded "imagines" of reader address. In Brontë's case, it is an address bringing in tow an often lush opacity of phrasing which still manages not to compromise the vivid transparency of dramatic evocation. With prose like Brontë's, the emphasis on the fact of your reading—on the textual encounter per se—has a candor that need not come at the price of lapsed intensity. Unbuffered impact (of the Dickensian sort) is still available to the melodrama of her effects, linguistic as well as scenic. Hence her transitional place on the way into the second half of the nineteenth century's fictional testing ground.

Nearing the midpoint of the century with *Vanity Fair*, Thackeray factored his audience into constituencies, special interest groups, regularly by synecdoche ("Jones, who reads this book at his Club"), always by exposure and quarantine. The metatextual irony has both purity and rigor, for the Fieldingesque epithets attached to unsuspecting readers are converted in Thackeray to proper names as if to stress the equally figurative footing of reader and character within the textual field. Yet the satiric mode is by no means to hold sway in the period. Never again after Thackeray will the eighteenth-century habits of subdivided address get such headway in a Victorian text. Emily Brontë transmutes the satiric animus into a frame tale, while Charlotte Brontë transforms it into a device for psychic connection. Mr. Jones becomes Mr. Lockwood in the one sister's work, with the rest of you left to find your footing across the thresholds of the embedded frames. In Charlotte's debut novel of the same year, you are instead kept on a comfortable leash by Jane's occasional tugging at an undetermined second- or third-person "reader." Ensuing fictional address will proceed in this way, giving your reading the slack it needs, the loopholes it seeks (contorted at times in *Villette* to slipknots), without yanking tight the satiric noose.

The issue is larger than at first appears. What sneaks up on us here is a revisionary account of the frame tale not so much as a generic subset but a schematic epitome of the Victorian novel as a whole. Less a specialized epistemological apparatus imported from the discursive brackets of eighteenth-century fiction and willed first to Mary Shelley and Walter Scott, then to Emily Brontë, and on through the late Victorian gothic revival to Conrad's early modernism, the frame tale appears instead as the bared device of the whole Victorian fictional compact. In this sense the structural complementarity of *Wuthering Heights* and *Jane Eyre* is foundational. The frame tale merely narrativizes what the "dear reader" implants, as well as what the whole realist program relies on: the conscription of the audience as a species of intimates, however inhospitably treated at times. With or without framing situations populated by invested interlocutors, Victorian novels tend to figure the scene of their telling as the mobile common border between public and private. It is just this tangency that makes the public communal and the private bearable in its isolation—for narrators as well as readers. "Reader, I married him" is again a quintessential gesture. In the domestic closure of nineteenth-century fiction, there is never more than a narrative ritual in place of a marital one. Put it another way. With or without apostrophe, novels of the period enact the cultural site, even when not setting the dramatic scene, of their own telling. All Victorian novels thus approach to the condition of frame narratives.

With *Master Humphrey's Clock* behind him, Dickens moved on to figure attention by steadily more internal (parabolic) means. There was, however, always the tacit frame, where Boz could be imagined narrating to his eager readers, happily unnamed, in tones unmistakable. Across the subsequent history of Victorian fiction, colored by whatever degree of rhetorical address, style becomes its own discursive framework, the signature effect of transmission. It amounts in this way either to a substitute for or to the considered eclipse of the hearthside inflections and eccentricities of narrative's routine oral delivery. Thackeray's method in *Vanity Fair*—style as cool distanciation—gives way to more amiable stances and tonalities. In Gaskell, style approximates—without exactly simulating—conversational presentation.[26] In Trollope, style is all *rep-resentation*, genial, if at times archly self-conscious, about its fictive invention. In Dickens and Collins, style is hyperbolic manifestation. In Eliot, strenuous imaginative enlargement. In Meredith, an intertextual screen of ironic allusion and reflection. In Hardy, an implacable analytic probe. In all, style is the man—or woman: the narrative voice, source and conduit at once, the telling behind the told. This is the logocentric myth of enunciation as origin which cohabits with another, more particularly Victorian myth: the sense of ritual communion which provides the ideological superstructure for all fictional commerce in its material basis as industrial production. Marketed distribution is merely the facilitation of communal and intrapsychic exchange. Printing houses are thus rightly named: They serve to streamline, by mechanizing, an important cultural aspect of the familial home as a locus of storytelling. With style recognized as its own virtual bracket—or frame—around narrative, its own substitute for a personalized site of telling, our accompanying recognition about the cultural paradigm provided by concentric structure is further secured. The point bears repeating. The special is actually the exemplary case, the offshoot in fact the model. With its enlisted listeners to a read or orally recalled story, the parabolic nature of the frame tale simply delegates to the precincts of explicit narrative that social psychology of motivated telling by which any mainstream Victorian novel is ordinarily rimmed and delimited.

Narrative style might thus be defined as the ensemble of markers which can substitute for a framing metatext in the individuation and direction of a storytelling act. For Brontë, this would only make a start in accounting for the rhetorical force of her writing. According to this definition, Brontë's style would not just include the rhetorical signposts of reader apostrophe but would be found coming clean by such inclusion—such admission of readers rather than listeners—regarding a narrative license that far exceeds the idiomatic resources, not to mention easy flow, of oral discourse. In Brontë, as we have seen by reading, style—lettered textuality—forms the very medium of desire, tortuous and seductive at once. Beyond fulfilling the work of representation, the reader's textual processing has an eroticism and a melodrama all its own. This is as true of *Jane Eyre*, Brontë's first novel, as of *Villette*, her last. But the last goes further yet in overstraining the framework of sociable attention. The potentiated reader—passing without reference in many another Victorian writer, undermined by overexplicitness in Brontë—becomes, after all, not simply the complement of a framing narrative transmission but a worrisome supplement of enunciation itself, forcing confessional narration and libidinal response to mix with and perplex each other.

Still within a retained dynamics of address, even the withdrawal to third-person omniscience in the subsequent novels of George Eliot will not entirely abate the raw nerve of transmission exposed by Brontë's apostrophes—or the questions they breed about realism's psychic identifications. Nor will proliferating metatextual figures for the world as readable text in other canonical writers, familiar figures passed along from earlier best-sellers, successfully deflect the anxieties attendant on the very fact of novelistic attention, on fictional reading within a semiotic cosmos. From Thackeray on through the rest of the century, the alleged book of the world impels a vigilance to which, nonetheless, the affect—and excess—of fiction cannot always be immediately assimilated. At the apogee of psychological realism and its complex emotive demands, it is against the broadspread cultural backdrop of such a hermeneutic postulate—the world as englobing tome—that Eliot's most rigorous figurations of interpretive energy are eventually to be mounted.

Ghost Reading

But before leaving the Brontës to take their collective place in the literary history of Victorian fiction, as we move on to take up their successors, there is a related tendency of classic fiction, in league with the exaggerated or merely tacit framing of its narrative occasions, which the extravagance of the Brontës' storytelling carries to clarification. This is the other side of the phenomenological issue: the psychic function of fictional otherness rather than its routes of delivery. I spoke just now about reading as a libidinal supplement to narrative style. This is also the case, as the next chapter will reveal, with the social subject as always and already appended to the world's book. But the nature of that supplementation needs further consideration.

We start by bearing in mind a not so simple fact: that framing is, among other things, a way of containing. Even before it gets figured as ghoulish in its own right, reading is the simultaneous raising and erasing of specters, their evocation and curtailment. This, too, is what the novels of Emily and Charlotte Brontë, taken together in all their differences, press to recognition. It is indeed another aspect of the merely implicit expressive frame around Victorian narrative, as well as of its structural counterpart in the nested narrative: namely, the sense of elegiac distancing to be regularly inferred from both. In *Frankenstein, Wuthering Heights, Dr. Jekyll and Mr. Hyde, Dracula, Heart of Darkness*—to name but a few narratives structurally preoccupied with the evidentiary transmission of their stories—it is precisely the human extremity of death that is circumscribed and packaged, made manageably phantasmal, kept both at work and at bay. There are so many officially unframed narratives that also provide this service, this taming of death, that one begins to look for an account of Victorian death worship which would grasp how the cult of the dead is not merely instanced discursively in a given novel but ritually performed by its very structure. Death, framed by fiction, becomes haunting. Characters, lost to life, get preserved by text as ghosts: the mode of their manifestation and of their endurance both, as well as the curb on their presence. And in this textual apparatus, this technique of apparition, one may glimpse a latent tropology of literary succession itself, the canon's inherent impetus toward immortalization. Nell's chances of being remembered, that is, are Dickens' own. But the impetus carries its own burden, as the next three chapters will variously come to find, for to figure authorial preservation as an afterlife is to confront a crowded pantheon of predeceased specters.

Within plot, the Brontë novels are quite relentless in their paradoxical laying of the very ghosts they conjure. In them, it would seem that the nineteenth-century novel's founding overlap of epistemology and value (Michael Mc-Keon's closing argument) has come down to the sublimated and fetishized unknowability of death's otherness. Not only drowned but submerged in denial, Lucy's Paul Emanuel, unreturned in body but obsessively present to speculation, is by definition a kind of ghostly agent. As does his equivocated fate, reading in its own right has always kept him in mind without bringing him to view, has satisfied itself with him as a disembodied presence. Indeed, the spooky side of textual engagement is more deeply acknowledged and strenuously policed in the novels of this chapter than in those of the last two. Dickens tries putting to rest the ghost of Mary Hogarth under cover of narrative; in public, that is, he tells instead the story of Nell's preservation in memory. The ghosts fended off in Carton's psyche are permanently interred in the ghost Carton becomes: the legend, the preserved legacy as a communal preservative. Writing pitched against death, a privilege refused by Carton, embraced by Dickens, has its own relation to the unsayable, of course. But for both Carton and Dickens, narrative is the maintained form of what *can* be said. This is to suggest that reading in Dickens (and its allegory in clockside or hearthside audition) transforms the uncanny visitations of the unconscious into the merely *passed on*. In the Brontës, though, the framing elegiac charge of Victorian narrative has an alternative valence. Dickensian sentiment traffics in ghosts, whereas the Brontës troublingly summon in order to defend against such specters. The difference in emphasis is that between the mythologies of legacy and exorcism. Carton is martyred to the former myth. Lockwood travesties the latter with his pile of books at the broken window. Listening later to Nelly's story is a way of getting rid as much as of getting well, so that the ghosts will never come so near again.

On the way to the mortuary irresolution of *Villette*, how can even *Jane Eyre* be construed as a ghost story, and in what relation thereby to the psychology of its reading? To think of Rochester at the end as a virtual revenant is to see at once the hidden prototype of a supernatural thriller. Frustration and lack, the haunted sense of lost opportunity, and finally the willed sacrifice of achieved desire—these are the propulsive drives of Jane's lifelong internal romance. In the continuous but only partial repression of that self-narrated story—a repression effected through none other than the retrospective account she does finally write down about the syncopation of actual event with the pressure of fantasized desire—you participate simply by reading on. You supplement as much as preserve the narrator's yearnings in exactly the way Lockwood cannot allow himself the luxury of doing. Though in his relation to the ghostly hold of narrative, as to other forms of unfulfilled desire, Lockwood is dead wrong, he has not entirely misconceived the process. Some defenses are necessary. Otherwise all fascination becomes, like the dead Cathy's for Heathcliff, a form of possession.

Jane Eyre, whether novel or inscribed subject, tries valiantly to proceed on other grounds. Jane flees the lures of desire, attempts to exorcise them, but finds that they come back like a voice from beyond the grave. For what is Rochester, calling on the wind, but the ghost both of Jane's refused past and of his own robust power? His telepathically received cry of need replaces Bertha's trapped cackle, in the immediate aftermath of her death, by answering to now, rather than mocking, Jane's own des/ire. To permit his communicating with Jane's surviving need, Rochester himself must be dimmed, his overweening energy purged, burnt away. With plot arranging for the muting of his previous self, Jane in turn arranges that the former "romantic reader" should now be made privy to the chastened wish fulfillment of "Reader, I married him." She weds, in short, the shade of his former self to dispossess her imagination of that self's exorbitant erotic mastery. Lucy Snowe, of course, has it harder yet— and thus foists an inordinate share of the burden onto the reader. By your whim, but also in the image of your own projected fantasy, does the masterly Paul Emanuel live or die. Either way, reading is a manner of warding off his ghost—whether by suppressing its recognition or by forestalling the actual advent of its death. In this respect, though, *Villette* only carries the Brontëan agenda to its logical limit in reader complicity.

All told, the Brontës write to quell (without quite dispelling) the otherness of death or loss, Dickens to transmit it into legacy. Style becomes sorcery on the one hand, attempted transfiguration on the other. For literary history, the difference begins to sketch forth separate generic trajectories. All of them equally "romancers," indeed necromancers, Emily and Charlotte Brontë part company with Dickens when the psychic investment of reading is diagnosed (rather than celebrated) in its full mortuary associations. Thus do the Brontës indirectly prepare the way not only for certain textures of psychological realism but for the textual metapsychology of George Eliot in a novel like *Daniel Deronda*, where the emphasis on legacy cannot extricate itself from the spectral—nor from the particular ghostly onus of the literary past. Elsewhere in Victorian narrative prose, the venerable trope of the world's book tends to confirm the two models for reading's relation to the enframed deathwork of elegiac narrative—exorcism and legacy—even as it activates the subtext of belated originality by which the mantle of fiction may become a shroud. This subtext aside, the trope of the read world transcends in its usual instances the death on which it draws: another containment measure concerning the ghosts of the foregone. Like inserting oneself as reading subject into the channels of literary history, reading the world is a way not only of participating in human continuity but of preventing the specters of the past from devouring all succession. The pages of life's big book must be kept turning, its tome the serial entombment of time passing, its ghosts contained but available, its reading a way of living in history. But such reading is a compromise with death which any one novel, as novels like *Wuthering Heights* and *Villette* go to show, may seek to expose by enacting.

Chapter Ten

The Book of the World
Thackeray to Meredith to Hardy

Théo van Rysselberghe, *The Reading* (1903).
Belgium, Ghent, Museum of Fine Arts. Used by permission.

*O*ur continuing investigation has to do with the transactive nature of novel reading; and more, with the self-enactive nature of such transaction; with, in other words, the relations into which reading tends to write the subject. But this conscription can only transpire with full conviction if the text is made in itself to seem (rather than discovered by later criticism to be) embedded in the same social network as the reading agent. Discourse analysis, in other words, is not simply what we practice on the Victorians but what they performed for themselves. To say so is to begin lining up a chapter on the reading of the world's "big book" with the larger emphasis of this study, an emphasis in part corrective.

Accompanying the still proliferating scholarship on the novel as an arma- ture rather than a mirror of cultural indoctrination is, too often, a conde- scending sense of imputed (discovered) rather than implanted (decoded) mo- tive. Commentary frequently proceeds as if classic fiction mistook its own ideological operations or carried them out for the most part unconsciously. The actual evidence resists this position. Within whatever ideologies of liter- acy and privacy Dickens may have worked, he was also working to develop his own myth of reading and individuality, to put his own stamp on the Victorian discourse of social subjectivity. So, too, with Collins and the Brontës. *Villette*, for instance, participates in—by straining to the limit—various contemporary discourses, including nationalist (England versus the Continent), religious (Protestant versus Catholic), medical (female hysteria, hallucinatory drugs), phantasmagoric and supernaturalist (ghostly visitations), as well as phrenological, sexological, economic, and so on. Written out of such prevailing discourses, even when written against them, a novel may, to be sure, fail to write itself out of them in the other sense, may never get wholly free of their prescriptive assumptions. Yet among those discourses, of which it would be absurd to suggest that Brontë's novel was only a sample and not itself a reading, is also the *discourse of literary reading*. In Brontë, for instance, it is the understood therapeutic function of reading, the myth of a communicative circuit made complete, which locates an overriding ideological energy not only of *Villette* but of *Jane Eyre* before it, reminding us that how a story *comes out* has as much to do with receptive destination as with plot and closure.

I repeat the interlocked points most worth insisting on at this stage: The novel always reads rather than merely transmits the prevailing discourses of its day in the very process of advancing one of its own as a mainstay of print culture; moreover, it often enacts itself doing both. Hence the two facets of this chapter, and hence their bearing on the rhetorical function of extrapolation in the Victorian scene of reading. First, the trope of the world as book should help to orient our sense of Victorian fiction as a particular and calculated readout—rather than a just selected printout—of the Victorian social text and its several meshed idiolects (become ideolects). Second, the figured universal conscription of any character into the world's always open book generates what we might call a reduplicative deepening of the trope in more literal, because letteral, scenes of reading: characters narrated in engagement with specific (and always subsidiary) written texts. There is nothing deferential in these generic procedures, nothing subservient to other approximations of the real. For if the world is a kind of book, books like novels are all the more likely to have a self-advertised privilege in relation to that world. Capitalizing on the Western tradition of bibliocentrism, the Victorian novel thus completes the secularization of nature as God's Book whose fortunes Ernst Robert Curtius charts so exhaustively down through Dante and Shakespeare.[1] The weight of this vestigial trope for the Victorian institution of the novel can scarcely be overestimated. Narrative reading garners a unique cultural prestige, both as paradigm and as training ground, when it is figured as largely indistinguishable from being keenly alert to the world.

There is, however, a divided legacy associated with the trope of the universe as text, descended as it is from theological discourse either (1) through the naturalized supernaturalism of romantic poetry into the philosophical subtext of later novelistic prose or (2) through eighteenth-century satire into the nineteenth-century novel's arsenal of irony. Wallace Stevens is a modernist successor to the former lineage, Henry Fielding an immediate forebear of the latter in its Victorian forms. Stevens' little-discussed poem "The Reader" shifts across a simile in the first stanza from an all-night vigil over the pages of a book to the vigilant reading of the night itself.[2] The opening "All night I sat reading a book" becomes the second line's "Sat reading as if in a book," a text whose "sombre pages," reiterated in the last stanza, "bore no print" but merely the "trace" of "burning stars" in the icy night's sky. When, by contrast, the preface to *Joseph Andrews* speaks explicitly of the "book of nature," the import has to do not with inanimate but with human nature. Cited here is the archive of folly and vanity from which all individual satiric portraits have been "copied" (12). Oscillating between the metaphysical poetics of a signifying universe and the mordant typology of human behavior, the trope of the book makes its unsteady way across Victorian fiction.

For major characters of William Makepeace Thackeray and George Meredith, to be sure, life is often no more led than read. To remark as much is a way of noting one of the consequences for English fiction of a phenomenon isolated by Roland Barthes in *S/Z*. His notion of the cultural code—what Meredith's Sir Austin Feverel will incarnate (in Barthes's alternate designation) as the Voice of Science (in Meredith, of Scientific Humanism)—is so completely imprinted on consciousness that all subsequent encodings, all derivative texts, are, for Barthes, mere résumés of the whole. "Reference to what has been written, i.e., to the Book (of culture, of life, of life as culture, [the cultural code] makes the text into a prospectus of this Book."[3] Barthes is of course writing about the structuring unsaid of Balzac's classic fiction. Certain Victorian novels, by contrast, say it in writing, breaking the conspiracy of silence by figuring their own contribution to such an oxymoronic misnomer: the prospectus of the already read.

Thackeray's *Vanity Fair* and Meredith's *The Ordeal of Richard Feverel* are two midcentury texts that tacitly elaborate on the compartmentalized trope of the world's book already noted in Scott and certain later best-sellers (chapter 6). Taking for granted the essentially semiotic fit between the novel and the social world, Thackeray and Meredith refigure the book of that world in ways designed to highlight the intertextual logic that guides the novel reader's extrapolation from the present excerpted instance of such a book. Where for Meredith's tragicomedy the prevailing intertext is the specific literary genre of the Bildungsroman, for Thackeray's social satire it is an unholy mix of theatrical masquerade and journalistic ephemera.

"Numbers of Adventures": Fiction as Serial Fair-going

What does it mean to interrupt the routines of the world ("your books and your business" from our discussion of Thackeray in chapter 3) in order to read in a book about the book of the world? Thackeray approaches this structural conundrum by turning it inside out. "O Vanity Fair—Vanity Fair!" (9:83) exclaims his novel to and about the space it inscribes, as well as to and about the readerly collective (the society) it conscripts. In *Vanity Fair*, the narrative addressing itself as the scene of its own setting—namely, a playground of distractions within the satirized world at large—thus complements the novel's rampant apostrophes to the novel reader per se. Each enlisted "you" becomes a synecdoche for the elsewhere apostrophized Fair as a whole, just as the Fair is a synecdoche—or vice versa—for the *Fair*, that book of the world which portrays it. Coming at us from every direction, Thackeray's addresses pinpoint a momentary response only to veer away to some other tagged interlocutor, as in the irrepressible shuffling, on the same page, from "my dear Madam" to "the carping reader" to "my dear Sir" (12:109).

Things only get more uncomfortable when the reader is pandered to rather than just apostrophized. Thackeray lets his text play openly between providence and plotting, for instance, when the chance of wealthy patronage for Becky and Rawdon "was denied to the young couple, doubtless in order that this story might be written, in which numbers of their wonderful adventures are narrated—adventures which could never have occurred to them if they had been housed and sheltered under the comfortable uninteresting forgiveness of Miss Crawley" (16:153). Thackeray's characters must endure vicissitude—the narratological imperative—so that you should be eager to read on; must, in the exposed sadistic economy of narrative, suffer for your pleasure. Such pleasure is indeed teased out across that reflexive pun on serialization: "*numbers* of their wonderful adventures." It is entirely for your periodical benefit, in other words, rather than for their reward, that Becky and Rawdon must be kept on the move, living from hand to mouth, not only from day to day but, more to the point, from month to month. Even in matters of life and death, the novel's eager serial consumption is linked—by second-person grammar and a pivotal simile—to newspaper accounts of the war: "The lists of casualties are carried on from day to day: *you* stop in the midst *as in a story* which is to be continued in our

next" (35:340; emphasis added). As the locus of extrapolated as well as interpolated reading, the death lists reinscribe the novel into that mode it is never
far from admitting: the memento mori of a serial *vanitas*, a catalogue of futil-
ities in the form of written narrative. Then, too, such a narrative, coterminous
with the "puppet theater" that is Thackeray's novel, finds another mastertrope
related to the book of the world: namely, the *theatrum mundi*, of which Becky's
performance in the Gaunt House charades, as read about later by Rawdon in
a journalistic account, offers a complex microcosm.[4]

When the flight to reading is explicitly (and more traditionally) thematized
at the close of *Vanity Fair*, we know therefore the limits of its attempted abdication from a Fair that has been figured as a pervasive scene of reading all
along. "The Colonel quitted home with reluctance (for he was deeply im-
mersed in his 'History of the Punjaub,' which occupies him *still*)" (68:662; emphasis added). Something is off here, off on an unexpected trajectory within
this novel of the recent past. We would expect "which occupied him still," a
phrasing safely within the historical past tense. But the text says instead that
what Dobbin was doing then, these many years ago, is not merely what he had
so often done before, but what he continues to do, on into the present, even
yet. Portrayed in his reading of India is an escapist territorializing of another
space and time, an imperialism of the imagination, a compensation for domestic failure through the usurpation of cultural otherness. Dobbin thus
moves forward from the novel's explicit time frame to become one of those
mid-Victorian readers still caught up in the expropriated Indian story as a collective imperialist projection of desire, a story that still "occupies" him with
the exoticism of colonial occupation. He becomes, in short, one of those contemporary readers to whom the satire of *Vanity Fair*, should he spare the time
from his preferred reading, is itself addressed.

Turning an Old Leaf

The world of the Fair is the multifarious world of our reading. It diverts attention and turns heads, here inflames and there allays desire. But just as the
world contains reading, is replete with reading, so too—and such is the mastertrope of Meredith as well as Thackeray—does reading contain the world,
the world as reading's decipherable text. This is, again, the bibliocentrism of
Western tradition stripped of the accompanying theological aura that surfaces
even in Dickens' apocalyptic figure in *Dombey and Son* of the "wide firmament
. . . rolled up like a scroll" (16:297).[5] This is an image more or less secularized—
as well as localized—in the dramatic context of the novel by Captain Cuttle's

pride in his range of apt quotation, which, however garbled, is always accompanied by the obligation of its recipient to search the world's files, with an exegetical determination, for chapter and verse. In the Captain's view, all is written, stored somewhere for our fresh application as opportunity presents itself. Having quoted a snippet from the entirely profane story of Dick Whittington in honor of Walter's supposed rise in fortune, the Captain adds in a seaman's metaphor: "Overhaul the book, my lad" (4:99). And later, to a baffled Florence, he boasts in paraphrase about Walter's bravery as being "a out'ard and visible sign of an in'ard and spirited grasp, and when found make note of" (23:406). All of this borrowed evidence of the world's wisdom derives from a distantly religious sense of inscribed law, for on the first appearance of the Captain's citational tic, directing Walter to "Love! Honour! And Obey!" his uncle, the attached injunction takes a paradigmatic form: "Overhaul your catechism till you find that passage, and when found turn the leaf down" (4:97).

So central is this conception, in its broader secular inference, to the self-styled figuration of Dickens' own novel—as breathing hearty new life into the well-thumbed and dog-eared pages of the world's book—that all such imagined searches in the tomes of truth, under energetic command from the Captain, seem pictorially conjured for us on the title page of the 1848 first edition, this time with Rob the Grinder poring over an actual volume, the Captain's hooked arm raised in encouragement. The illustration is brought forward to front the volume from its context much later in the plot, where Rob is indiscriminately "required to read out of some book to the Captain, for one hour, every evening," since the latter "implicitly believed that all books were true" (38:629). The force of this redoubled illustration is prototypical precisely in its abstracting from numerous separate scenes in the novel a vague generalization, however comic, about the improving character of attentive reading: an illustration of the novel itself as humanist illustration, where even the unlikeliest of things may ring true, if only because—in the Master's rather than the Captain's sense—their sponsoring intertexts have been so completely "overhauled," not only thoroughly searched but imaginatively renovated.

The status of narrative event as inevitably referable to the boundless book that precedes it is not, as a rule, so inspiriting a trope in mid-Victorian fiction. Certainly, as we have seen, the internal self-imaging of such fiction by no means consistently refers itself away to revered Scripture as a quotational source for its dramatic exemplifications. In Meredith as in Thackeray, the book of the world, the Fair that is the *Fair*, instead testifies yet again to Victorian culture's absconded godhead, the dying away of the Author from the world as God's Book. But this absconding has, beyond its larger cultural history, a particular generic one as well. The eighteenth-century novel, in its realist ambitions, took into its ambit as a represented part of social life, for instance, that most common reading of the day: personal letters. Yet the evolution of the novel as genre would to some extent inevitably displace, even while initially incorporating, the epistolary habit. Novel readers may find themselves too preoccupied to pen, or even eagerly await, letters. In any event, mass literacy in the nineteenth century, answered by mass fictional publication, alters, at least in one undeniable aspect, the recognizable face of literary representation. The new scope of novelistic realism, in other words, naturally includes the everydayness of fictional consumption. One way of seizing the point is to think of the consolidated genre of the novel as the first inevitably self-referential literary mode. Epics need contain no bards, dramas no subsidiary stagings, lyrics no poets other than their personae. But the representational purview of the realist novel makes novel reading within it, at the very least, a statistical probability.

In this respect, the lessons of life in fiction may run afoul of portrayed fictional expectations. By midcentury, the pattern of chastened novel reading, and of the meretricious desires it may foster, has grown so familiar that it can be rapidly instanced and dispatched within a given plot. What Austen lets her heroine take a whole novel to work out of her system is an addiction to popular fiction which Becky Sharp has overcome by the time of her first letter to Amelia, where she details the mismatch between Lord Crawley and "what we silly girls, when we used to read Cecilia at Chiswick, imagined a baronet must have been" (8:74). As if to counter the ascendancy of print consumption, Becky's return to the epistolary mode castigates the very fiction for which she no longer has the time of day. In another sense, however, the extrication of life from received text is not so easy to arrange from there on in Thackeray's novel, especially when all life is refigured as the already chronicled permutations of the Fair. Here we have Meredith's Book of Egoism by any other name, against which his first novel, like Thackeray's, is internally posed as a kind of antidote. Like *Vanity Fair* before it, *The Ordeal of Richard Feverel* (1859) betrays the paradoxical case of the container contained: a book about exactly that lived world (a *Fair* about the Fair, say) whose universal Book enrolls in large part the social effects of all such subsidiary texts. The conceit waxes metaphysical. If all the world's urges are merely variations on a theme that preexists any one of its human avatars, all thought becomes a (re)reading of this received scheme of things, all writing a new and rearranged transcription of the Book of Egoism, or call it the text of subjectivity. We are—in a way George Eliot would later raise to attempted triumph rather than constraint—each of us interpreters rather than free agents. For Meredith, however, the greatest egoism is not to know your subservience before the Book, before the great text of the world. Such egoism creates a countertext, prescriptive rather than transcriptive, building a System at odds with the manifest lessons of the Book. But what, then, is the status of that cultural misnomer, the "novel," in relation to the universal and all too familiar book of human vanity?

For Meredith, all it can hope to be is Comedy as compendium, a mandate made explicit by the time of *The Egoist* (1879). In the "Prelude" to that novel, we are told that "the world is possessed of a certain big book, the biggest book of earth," as if the phrasing suggested "possessed by" as well. It is a book "that might indeed be called the Book of Earth; whose title is the Book of Egoism, and it is a book full of the world's wisdom" (3). The text is a pitiless surfeit and needs summation. "So full of it," Meredith continues superbly, "and of such dimensions is this book in which the generations have written ever since they took to writing, that to be profitable to us the Book needs a powerful compression" (3). Yet every new précis is of course, if printed, only a further leaf in the volume, as the narrator goes on to acknowledge. So that every reader, in reading a comic novel, for instance, is reading only—such is the inference—a supplement to the world's encyclopedic self-indictment. If all living is rereading, not to mention all writing, then in what relation of productive redundancy—or instructive rehearsal—can a literal reader stand to a published book? Is reading merely a replica of living—hence a kind of tautology? The deliberate trouble, then, with Meredith's mastertrope of the world's book is that it offers no commensurate understanding, no explicit understanding at least, of the books we normally call books. The same could be said of the equation in Thackeray between *Fair* and Fair, since the former, and other novels like it, is for sale in the latter. Long before *The Egoist*, Meredith's debut novel of 1859, *The Ordeal of Richard Feverel*, has sought to mediate this structural incompatibility between the book of the world and the world of books through the carefully demarcated third term of embedded reading scenes. In them, either a distinction or an equivalence can be secured, then investigated, between a world inscribed (in every sense impressed) with its own worldliness and the particular inscriptions that surface in print against the backdrop of this universal open book.

The procedure differs markedly from Thackeray's, affecting the rhetoric of apostrophe as well. In Thackeray's satiric mode, the narrator of *Vanity Fair* never gets very far beyond his admitted role as huckster or "quack" at a Fair booth, his interpolations of the audience being the textual equivalent of the carnival barker's "you there, sir." In Meredith's less irruptive comic mode, interpolated invocations of the reader in a novel like *The Ordeal of Richard Feverel* are excluded because they could only be, by turns, redundant and counter-productive. On the one hand, Meredith's text is attempting to represent (without entirely reproducing) the Book of Egoism, the ultimate book of the world, in its engulfing and solicitation-free legibility for all readers, who assume they come to it unbidden, their perceptions entirely naturalized by spontaneous experience. On the other hand, *Richard Feverel* is working overtime to distinguish itself from that importunate textual vanity that produces such prescriptive micronarratives as those published, under the guise of distilled aphoristic wisdom, by the elder Feverel: recipes for maturation in the imperative mood (do this, don't do that). Eschewing at two related levels the open and coercive interpolation of a readership, then, *Richard Feverel* tends to depend for orientation, instead, on those reframed scenes of narrative attention from which it can thereby induce an extrapolated response: fables of affect, parables of reception.

I have in mind two contrasted pairs of such scenes (or, in the first case, of a narrated scene and its ironic setting in the metaplot as a whole) which divide up the issue at different strata of fit and discomfiture with the novel-making process to which they contribute in regress. The initial contrast is distributed along the diametric axis of desire versus law, the second, more surprisingly, along that of life versus death. The first pair of scenes (one of them pervading the entire narrative as Sir Austin's relentless correctional scenario of human frailty) rests on the pitched contrast between a patriarchal system of overt moral conscription and the attempted escape to popular fiction from within the system's prying vigilance. As such, the rush to fiction offers a defiance in the name of desire meant to redound to the glory of the prose fiction that embeds it. The second pair of episodes (each of them localized this time as isolated dramatic scenes) inscribes preternatural modes of textual encounter, thus operating less directly (more parabolically) in relation to the novel in which we read of such reading. This second set of narrative moments seems arranged to distinguish a successful from a doomed effort to escape altogether from the patriarchal conduit of narrative; one route is back into prenatal dormancy, the second over into mortal absence.

Tome and Epitome

We turn first to the more obvious polarity between a truant flight to fiction and the supposedly benign despotism of Sir Austin's prewritten textbook for living. There is only one extended, however farcical, enactment of Victorian popular reading in *Richard Feverel*. It involves young Ripton Thompson, the lawyer's son who has been handpicked as an appropriate companion for the growing hero. He is supposed to be reading his law books when Sir Austin visits the solicitor's office, but one volume looks out of place. Pretending that it is a book of heraldry, in which the arms of the Feverel family are prominently featured, Ripton is loath to turn over the text itself. When forced to do so, he is discovered to have been reading a cheap romance, "the entrancing adventures of Miss Random, a strange young lady" (16:138). Under cover of the law, so to speak, the formative erotic imagination has found vent in a narrative text. In acid reprisal, Ripton is denied access to the Son, Richard, and thus excommunicated even from his role as satellite of the Feverel System, with its preemptive Law of the Father.

The scandalous scene of reading is thus not only punished by the exile of its perpetrator but neutralized in its own right by being folded into Sir Austin's blanket reading of human nature. Adolescent depravity like Ripton's confirms all of Sir Austin's worst suspicions about the ungovernable nature of youth when not under the surveillance of Scientific Humanism. Indeed, Ripton's reading strikes Sir Austin as part of that larger *story* of human frailty and failed resolve which his own aphorisms are meant to distill and satirize. "I came to visit my lawyer," Sir Austin says to himself, but feels that instead "I have been dealing with The World in epitome" (17:144)—the secular sphere in compressed summary. In its etymological relation to *tome*, however, this phrasing scores a deeper point. Behavior gets summarized, but books get epitomized. Ripton's trespasses, then, only conform to the abridged book of the world, betraying an eroticized irresponsibility in battle against which Sir Austin has published his own corrective book. Certainly, in the mundane sphere whose digest has here been registered, the worldly narratives in which Ripton traffics are only symptomatic. Between the epitomized book of the world's folly, given once again to Sir Austin in précis even before he can find his own wry phrasing for it, and the multifarious books that litter such a world with temptation—those secular stories that supposedly distract and corrode the will—ought to intervene the prophetic program for a better life: namely, the System, the disciplinary *Scrip*(t), into which Richard is born as if mostly for the sake of example.

His father's pre/script is of course already a reading: a reading of such reading as Ripton's, the spirit's self-indulgent waywardness in epi/tome. This trope of the world's folly as book will return, reversed and rectified, in a later vision of reading which offers the very definition of the Comic Spirit—in Meredith's "Essay on Comedy" as well as in the "Prelude" to *The Egoist*. Great comic characters, writes Meredith in the former, "are clear interpretations of certain chapters of the Book lying open before us all."[6] Comic writing, of the kind he aspires to, is thus more an exegetical than a constructive enterprise, an interpretive rereading of the Book of Life. This is what the desiccated wit of Sir

Austin's *Scrip* and Notebook has travestied in advance, squeezing experience dry to wrest into view its monitory quintessence. Having observed the foregoing contrast between an erotics of popular reading and its philosophical interdict in a countervailing script, we are next to examine how such a system of internal contrast organizes a second pair of equally disparate textual experiences, distributed as they are along an axis whereby domestic reading eventually looms homologous with certain preternatural forms of textual access: both reading in utero and reading the posthumous text of the recently dead.

"An Audience Will Come"

Each extremity of transmission bespeaks, indirectly and in different ways, Meredith's sense of his own place in a progressive cultural history of reading. At the height of the most extended commentary in *Richard Feverel* on the spectacle of science warring with human nature, the narrator interrupts himself with an allusion to the current vogue for the muscular school of sensationalist fiction (Collins coming to mind, with his early stories, some of them faintly anticipating this mode, collected the same year as *Richard Feverel* in *The Queen of Hearts*): "At present, I am aware, an audience impatient for blood and glory"— as if this were a euphemistic version of the idiomatic doublet "blood and gore"—is an audience that "scorns the stress I am putting on incidents so minute, a picture so little imposing" (25:226). Like Eliot, however, Meredith imagines that his novel will help to evolve the audience it cannot currently claim. "An audience will come to whom it will be given to see the elementary machinery at work. . . . They will see the links of things as they pass, and wonder not, as foolish people now do, that this great matter came out of that small one" (25:226). This "true epic of modern life"—the prolonged internecine battle of "science at war with Fortune and the Fates"—will be recognized only retrospectively, only after the education of the very society whose story it is.

Yet as Judith Wilt glosses this passage, the reader already "civilized" into responsiveness renders this discursive aside a self-fulfilling prophecy: "But as we read this passage and mentally separate ourselves from that audience of readers impatient for blood and glory we realize it [the better audience] has come. We are it."[7] An only apparently historicized version of the Coleridgean notion that poetic invention must create the taste by which it is to be enjoyed, Meredith's conscripted audience is of course predicted and achieved on the spot. Laminating his self-justification upon the novel of the recent past, Meredith has devised the narrative rhetoric of the future present, as does Dickens the same year with his backdated prophecy of contemporaneous audition at the close of *A Tale of Two Cities*. What we also have here is the central conceit of Mary Shelley's *The Last Man* in reverse. Rather than a narrative for whom all readership has already come and gone, *Richard Feverel* stands in wait for its own present reception, as history will facilitate it. It remains for *Daniel Deronda* two decades later to imagine the fulfillment of this aborning mid-Victorian audience through the closural logic of a novel both set in the present and restaging that present as a hermeneutic perpetuity.

The double perspective involved in such conceits is very much in the spirit of the "Essay on Comedy," which implies—in a teleological paradox—that true Comedy can only exist in the kind of highly evolved society that only true Comedy can help bring to maturity. In *The Ordeal of Richard Feverel*, similarly, the ontogeny of a single reading experience thus recapitulates—in advance— the phylogeny of cultural development, with each new and separate reading aiding in the transformation it singly fulfills. This story about a primal dichotomy in the infancy of the age thus nurtures in embryo the historical transcendence of such tension. And this evolutionary conception is worked out by Meredith in further detail, not merely by the kind of rhetorical excursus we have just examined, but in that second promised set of reading scenes that become parables of fictional reception itself. On the one hand, we encounter an episode of proleptic—indeed prenatal—response: an enacted scene of Victorian hearthside reading which parodies the family romance while ratifying both its domestic and its historical ideology. On the other, we encounter a scene of narration virtually from beyond the grave. These oddly symmetrical passages, in their obverse fantasies, work not to occlude but more strategically to encode the present space of live reading and lived reaction.

If you, outside the text, provide the text's tacit figuration of the finer audience still to come, then you stand allied with the unborn audience yet to emerge from within the plot. It may not be surprising that Richard's young wife, Lucy, victim of the patriarchal monopoly, should take an interest in the decline and fall of historical orders. Such is the reading matter that suits her mood during pregnancy, and her motives are all but as complex as Meredith's in arranging the scene in which historical narratives will be read to her by the same Lord Montfalcon who plots to seduce her. "By heaven! I'd read to her by her bedside, and talk that infernal history to her, if it pleased her, all day and all night" (39:450). Two pages later the narrator follows up with a circumlocution in indirect discourse, diffident on Lucy's part, disingenuous on the narrator's: "Now it was an object of Lucy's to have him reading; for his sake, for her sake, and for somebody else's sake; which somebody else was considered first in the matter" (39:453). We may at this point assume that Richard is the unsaid referent. But there is more quite literally *at issue* in the passage: a bizarre fantasy of cultural gestation in the biological womb of time. As Lucy tries haltingly to explain to the servant, Bessy, a few pages later: "I only read sensible books, and talk of serious things, because I'm sure . . . because I have heard say . . ." (39:461). The point she stammers to make is one that Bessy finally intuits, phrasing it for her: "And that rake of a lord who've been comin' here playin' at wolf, you been and made him—unbeknown to himself—sort o' tutor to the unborn blessed!" (39:462). More than "midwife" (39:450), as he has been mocked for being by his servant, the degenerate patriarch has helped Lucy orchestrate, in advance, a scene of reading as familial tutelage which cannot help but remind us—almost by travesty—of Richard's own inculcation by his father's System *as if from the womb*. It is now left to the novel's other female victim to undermine this paternalistic System, in its benighted reading of the world's book, not so much by parody as by fatal exemplum. For in the death of his cousin Clare, transcribed for him as shadow narrative of his own story, Richard is induced, finally, to read his own doom.

"Breathless Pages": Narrative as Epitaph

Reaching out to the hero from beyond the grave is a voice activated by Richard's only lengthy scene of textual intake in the novel, one of the most prolonged and powerful scenes of reading in Victorian fiction. All the other textual damage has been done by an internalization of the Father's printed Word antecedent to plot itself. The scene of Richard's bereaved reading of Clare's diary is structured now around a close imbrication of text and reception which paces the novel's reader across the hero's own almost line-by-line response. What Richard must here take it upon himself to read rather than to live through, to reread in retrospect, is nothing more nor less than the story of his life—and scarcely less disinterested than if he had penned it himself. "With his name it began and ended" (40:483).

We may recall at this point the inscribed text from which the novel's own doomed Bildungsroman began, just at the time when Clare, we later discover, was first taking up her diarist's burden. We hear in the novel's first paragraph about the publication of *The Pilgrim's Scrip*, that book of aphorisms on which Sir Austin's science of child rearing will later be based. As we are reminded at intervals, the *Scrip*'s subsequent variations, emendations, and amplifications are then jotted in his infamous Notebook: interpretive sequel to the earlier interpretive supplement to the precedent book of the world. The father's finest dream for the son was once that he would have seen an even greater Father's decipherable work in his life—"and could read God's *handwriting* on the earth!" (12:97; emphasis added). But such is the deepest lie of the Book of Egoism, the Book of Earth, that it tends to model the Supreme Plan upon its own desires. By scarcely disguised analogy, Sir Austin's own "handwriting" (and that part of it which has seen print) erects his own image as the Author God of his son's destiny. Other plot contrivances pile up around this irony. Just after Richard's elopement with Lucy, the first news delivered by his cousin Adrian from home is that "the Pilgrim has lost his Note-book" (34:349). It is only found again (44:521) in the chapter of Lucy's death, "The Last Scene," when the worst work of the System has been accomplished. These linked details suggest that in between—across several of the later years articulated in reprise by Clare's diary—has stretched the space of an unscripted but nonetheless doomed wager at autonomy on the hero's part: an attempted suspension of the Script which comes too late. Like the return of the repressed, a metaphor of englobing textuality in fact surfaces right near the end. For in anticipation of Lucy's death, "this last *chapter* of calamity suddenly opened where happiness had promised" (43:517; emphasis added).

The book of books, it seems, cannot be kept closed wholly or for long. To this fact another calamitous "chapter" just before—involving the reading of Clare's diary—desperately attests. For Clare too, like Richard in the figurative sense, has lived and died by the Feverel book, sacrificed to a script that had other plans for its protagonist than a union with herself. We read now through Richard's eyes—later inner ears—as he sits riveted in shock before the open pages of a story that cannot be extricated from, but could never be wedded to, his own: "The first name his eye encountered was his own," the narrator has it, and then quotation from the diary begins: "Richard's fourteenth birthday" (40:479). This is just the age that appears in the first chapter title of the novel. Three texts (finally four) are thus aligned in a complex receding perspective: Sir Austin's, where the fourteenth birthday is already "marked out" (2:12)—as if inscribed—for importance; Meredith's ironic overview of this prescripted "life" in its formative stages (the biographical confused with the biological sense); Clare's later retelling of the tale from the point of view of the desires it denies; and behind them all, the world's remorseless book.

Though Clare closes with the direct quasi-epistolary address of "Good-bye, Richard!" (40:483), for most of her text we have read of him reading of himself in the third person, tracking his growing distance from Clare down to the disruptive adolescent turning point: "Once we laughed all day together tumbling in the hay. Then he had a friend, and began to write poetry, and be proud" (40:483). In this way does Richard review the text of his life in digest form, seeing himself under the sign of the written. "Step by step he saw her growing mind in his history" (40:479)—and vice versa. Though he does not register explicitly the connection with his father's *Scrip*(t) for his life, he feels the grappling hold of death in this narrative act. Yet again he finds his life presided over by denial, her unrequited erotic fixation a kind of mirror image of his own programmatic and joyless self-involvement.

Reading to the unborn; reading the dead. The symmetry is brutally realized. In between prescience and nescience, the reader: conduit, medium, liminal figure, parasite. But given the emphasis on Clare's "voice clear and cold from the grave" (40:481), a voice that "filled his ears" (40:483) as he read, a question nags. To what extent does the power of Clare's undeconstructed and posthumous voice from the dead accrue to the novelist's own sense of his textual agency and agenda? The answer comes as soon as we have let the text lead us to the question. The novelist who dreams of a day when readers not yet in attendance will take to heart his epic of the age; the novelist who so deploys this dream as to induce its local fulfillment, and who then refigures this communicative achievement as an act of narrating history itself to an unborn child—this is the novelist who hopes his words will speak to readers yet unborn, will speak ultimately, that is, from the limit of his death across the receding horizon of the generations. Under the crushing weight of irony, pathos, and marginality, Clare nevertheless emerges as the haunting sacrifice to this ideal, the martyr to narrative force in authorial absentia. Hers is the perverse embodiment of a textuality whose dreamt impact is realized only in its afterlife of reception.

Whereas Brontë in *Villette* carries the closural logic of her plot to the point at which death becomes the ultimate accomplice of narrative—death being what reading is called in to overcome—Meredith goes even farther in a certain direction. He locates the reader at the scene not only of the text's continuance but of its efficacy as critique, its cultural as well as emotional eventuality. This is the direction Eliot follows on from in *Daniel Deronda*, where it is only what comes after that completes. Before that, and before *The Ordeal of Richard Feverel* as well, *Villette* closes in the present tense upon a remembrance it would seem crying out for reading to rewrite. In a not unrelated fashion, though more like *A Tale of Two Cities*, *Richard Feverel*, set also in the recent past and seeking a near future of response, pivots around a temporal gap, a discursive lag that reading seeks to bridge. Similarly, despite its being poised in the contemporaneous moment for a gesture beyond, *Daniel Deronda* is always catching up with its own future in the generative energy of a present response. Achieved thereby (as at least anticipated by Meredith) is an interpretative valence made immanent in the reception of the work: immanent as the cultural work of receptiveness itself. In terms toward which the last chapter led us, however, the question remains—as with Richard under the pall of Clare's prose—whether such an interpretive legacy can be accepted or need be exorcised.

Thus has the preternatural pair of reading scenes we have considered in *Richard Feverel*—reading out loud to the unborn versus the silent reading of the speaking dead—figured forth their parabolic rather than mimetic relation to the novel that contains them. Specifically, a voiced text comes to the fetus in utero, "internalized" twice over as it were, not through normal cognitive channels as a lesson but rather felt along the very pulse, rhythmic and pervasive, lived rather than understood, inhabited as an ambient vocal field rather than processed from inscribed marks. Yet isn't all of this, in exactly its difference from novel reading as we *know* it, merely a hyperbolic version of the novel's englobing affect in reception? So, too, with Clare's diary. As different as is the encounter with this text from reading a published narrative, what does it ultimately amount to if not, yet again, a mystified phenomenology of the novel as literary mode? Line by line, Richard hears himself in Clare's version of his Bildungsroman—just as fiction readers recognize themselves in the identificatory function, if not the vanity mirror, of texts like Meredith's and Thackeray's alike, texts that are always about you under whatever narrative alias, always transcriptions of your place in the big world's book.

Such are the ways of reflexive parable. It is worth stressing, though, that what is downright macabre about both Meredith's episodes of preternatural reading—Clare come back to life in her diary, Richard's child brought to culture while within the womb—is what we are to take as mostly metaphoric in them, at least at this point in Victorian literary history. But not for long. Such metaphors become so insistent later in the century—as reading per se becomes an increasingly questionable enterprise, a queasy gothic in its own right—that mere figuration hardens to diagnosis. Following through on the logic of this offers a last chapter (mine too) in the Victorian book of the world. In the meantime, George Eliot tries closing her final novel so that the Victorian world beyond it becomes the book's own coda—*beyond it* in two senses, offering its social context and its cultural aftermath. The effect, we will see, is certainly no less gothic than Clare's breathing pages in the hands of a reader who cannot believe their impact is that of mere reading. The difference is that Richard reads as he has been written, by both Clare and his father, reads as the ensnared and asphyxiated object of external comment, whereas the reader of Eliot, from *Middlemarch* forward, reads (along with that reader's internal and parabolic surrogates) for a sense of otherness, of contingent possibility, which would keep free some blank and waiting pages in the world's endless text. That this option is in fact the conscripted figuration of a certain mystique of open-ended form does not erase its difference from the contrary figuration of the world as a predigested tome. Where in Thackeray the self (and/as reader) is perpetual understudy to the scripted and then staged vanities of the Fair, and in Meredith the self, as well as its reader, offers a mere footnote to the Book of Egoism, in Eliot the self as cultural subject grows into its role as the collaborative ghostwriter of the world's hermeneutic appendixes.

"Written Out in the Big World's Book"

Before working through to George Eliot's structural suggestion in *Daniel Deronda* of an interpretive energy launched beyond closure, however, this chapter moves forward to its own close by noting five additional, and revealingly divergent, variations on the trope of textualized—hence read and interpreted—reality (from Dickens, Olive Schreiner, H. Rider Haggard, George Moore, and Thomas Hardy). As a Dickensian confidence in textual encounter wanes along with the heyday of realism, we pass to a more suspicious view of the reading motive in the New Woman novel and in late-century exotic romance. Still, though, the lingering trope of the world's book often helps carve out a legitimated space for probative reading from amid the figured perversity of an increasingly gothicized reading habit, addictive and debilitating.

Well before textual engagement itself has fallen under the diagnostic shadow of late Victorian gothic, Dickens' last completed novel finds a typifying figure for the plotted comeuppance of its satiric butts, the Veneerings, in a twist of poetic justice sprung from the worldliest of all possible books-within-the-book. The last chapter of *Our Mutual Friend* (1864–65) is directed toward a final description of the Veneering circle cast up into the perpetual present tense of routinized nouveau riche protocols that began with the second chapter's "This evening the Veneerings give a banquet" (1,2:49). By the end, omniscient narrative interrupts this pattern to take upon itself the privilege of a clairvoyance figured not just in but as text. Despite the implications of grammatical tense, the cycle of the Veneerings' lavish outlay will not go on forever, since "it is written in the Books of the Insolvent Fates that Veneering shall make a resounding smash next week" (4,17:886). In a financial wordplay familiar from *Vanity Fair* (see chapter 3), what we might call this weekly supplement to the Book of Egoism is designated to suggest, with the pluralized "Books," just those accounting ledgers whose close reading would trace Veneering's downfall. It might be said, in sum, that Dickens' pervasive *semiotics* of experience, for which every avid reader like Master Humphrey is only a representative, is suspended between a sacred and a secular bibliocentrism, between the firmament's eternal "scroll" in *Dombey and Son* (or its comic derivation in Captain Cuttle's much overhauled "catechism") and the fiscal rosters of *Our Mutual Friend*. In between, where it goes mostly unmentioned, is the book of the novel as genre.

Tapping directly the theological origins of the trope, the book of the world also makes a late and deflating appearance in Olive Schreiner's 1883 novel *The Story of an African Farm*, whose heroine, Lyndall, having gone into the larger world to seek an education, returns midway in the novel to the colonial farm on which she was raised in order to detail a series of crippling social and spiritual disappointments. Among them is the discovery that one's own life is a kind of recapitulatory footnote to the larger text of society and history. It is indeed "very odd to find all the little follies and virtues, and developments and retrogressions, written out in the big world's book that you find in your little internal self" (2,4:198). In this case, the relation of psychological microcosm to cultural macrocosm is that of reader to read. Eight years later, Hardy's heroine in *Tess of the D'Urbervilles* will literalize the notion of textual prototypes, along with the wilting nature of belatedness, as a reason for the avoidance of actual books: "Because what's the use of learning that . . . there is set down in some old book somebody just like me, and to know that I shall only act her part" (19:107). Schreiner's figurative sense, however, more like Fielding's "book of nature," is the more common Victorian manifestation of this archetype and this potential anxiety.

If the self-accorded semiotic privilege of high Victorian comedic fiction (Dickens, Thackeray, Meredith)—since the world is essentially legible, behold here its digest!—flares to a mocking poetic justice in *Our Mutual Friend* and tapers to desperation in *The Story of an African Farm*, the reigning mastertrope of the scrutinized Book of Life is turned inside out in George Moore's *Esther Waters* (1894). In this naturalistic chronicle of its beleaguered working-class heroine, the thematization of reading has been in one sense drained from the focal center of plot by the abiding fact of her illiteracy. Esther enters the novel carrying the "dead" weight of her mother's books (1:1), the only dowry bestowed upon her in her banishment from the stepfather's home, but having no way to penetrate the "mysteries that this print held *from* her" (2:22; emphasis added on the reversed cliché of the wonders otherwise held *for* the reader by print). Forty chapters later at the novel's final crisis—precipitated by her consumptive gambler husband's latest betting scheme—Esther's illiteracy still haunts her, for she can't read the racing forms to learn the result (42:362).

After a gathering network of self-referential textual turns on "book"-making (32:280) and "reading the omens" (30:257; 33:285), including the clinching mention of "making a book" on a horse named—of all things—"Syntax" (37:312), the final irony of print being closed to a printed heroine is made to pay in a fuller context yet. With reading denied her, even the reading of her private destiny in the racing forms, Esther has nevertheless taken frequent charge of her own story, dispensing it tactically, always second-guessing her audience. Seeking employment in the household of Miss Rice, the retiring novelist, Esther insists, for instance, that "my story is not one that can be told to a lady such as you" (22:184). Yet once hearing some tantalizing sample of it after all, Miss Rice is eager at any point to set aside either a book she may be reading or the one she is penning to attend eagerly to the latest oral installment of Esther's unfolding tale, a narrative that makes her own work seem "pale and conventional" (29:245) by contrast. Ultimately, however, the tale Esther has in her to tell is to be censored in its generational legacy—out of an affectionate deference to her husband, William. It is a censorship for which only omniscient narrative can compensate. By means of a single glance exchanged with William on his deathbed, that is, the full "sad story" we have long been reading places its own pivotal incident under suppression. For "in that look the wife promised the husband that the son should never know the story of her desertion" (43:372), her original jilting by William for a "better" marriage. The closest prototype is Florence Dombey's story of her father's cruelty—in other (Dickens') words, our novel—kept from the ears of the next generation. In *Esther Waters*, the final narrative (in Moore's keep and copyright) is also delegated to the reader as sole repository. It is this reader function that maximizes your potential extrapolation from Miss Rice's attitude in comparing the anemic surface of conventional sentimental fiction to the full-blooded crises of Esther's worldly trials, the latter seeming like nothing so much as "this rough page torn out of life" (29:245).

If naturalism thereby stringently narrows the trope of textualized experience to the "rough" leaves of wearying secular struggle, an antithetical late-century genre, exotic romance (including the gothic revival), widens the conceit to encompass the endless text of unrestrained fantastic wonders. This is a text in which each supposedly bounded life might find itself renewed and cross-indexed from chapter to chapter. In this regard, the metaphoric weft of Haggard's *She* (1887) is baldly revealing. In confronting her would-be lover, Leo Vincey, with the slain body of his millennial double, Kallikrates, the goddess She insists that "I do but turn one page in thy Book of Being, and show thee what is writ thereon" (21:236). Once he has accepted his reincarnation, Leo is promised that he will be able to read not only the narcissistic text of his own enduring beauty but, now vested with the goddess's telepathic powers, the whole book of humanity: "thou shalt read the hearts of men as an open writing, and hither and thither shalt thou lead them as thy pleasure listeth" (25:284). With omniscience entering plot as global voyeurism and further perverted to diabolic control, the very dream of romantic empathy—that mainstay of "openness" in the nineteenth-century novel from Austen forward—has turned to paranoid nightmare.

Textual Immolation and the "Book of Humanity"

Such a variant of the world's book—the figure of universal legibility as obscene prerogative—is of course a dead end for fictional self-advertisement. Closer to the traditional operation of the figure is the sense developed in the fatalist realism of Hardy's *Jude the Obscure* (1895) that the lessons of humanity inscribed in the late Victorian social text may offer Jude an ultimate escape from the tedium and defeat of his claustrophobic book learning. Yet while Jude switches textual allegiances across the course of narrative, what about the book we are all along reading? *Jude the Obscure* is a novel that may be said for much of its length to efface its own namesake even while making his obscurity famous. The realm of intellectual renown into which Jude hopes to insert himself closes against him, and the power of *disinterested* literary reading seldom dawns on him. This is where your attention comes in, shoring up an alternative from within. Interspersed with high-literary quotation from such contemporary Victorian poets as Browning and Swinburne, the novel as a reading event is thus precisely the sort of cultured secular (or "profane") text which mostly eludes Jude in his empty quest to master first classical, then ecclesiastical scholarship.[8] In this prolonged and debilitating process, the figurative book of the world makes a chastening appearance at the turning point in a simultaneously developing pattern of law enforcement as ubiquitous surveillance. This is an exclusionary watchfulness that casts a cold eye on the hero's bookish ambitions.

In noting the novel's frequency of policemen in an overbearing conjunction with the event of reading, we may well recall D. A. Miller's sense, in *The Novel and the Police*, that the escape to reading on the part of characters in Dickens is a scenario which, despite its humanist design, subsumes the would-be privacy of the bourgeois subject within the already carceral (because socially programmed) ideology of imaginative retreat. The abrupt yoking of "the novel" and "the police" in Miller's title is dictated by a violence that is meant to expose culture's own. At least for a while, things *seem* to be falling out otherwise in

Jude. The novel begins by enacting a more stable dichotomy of beleaguered yearning—where bookish exhilaration is just the sort of private emotion which the police, though impeding, cannot reach. Yet to just the extent that one can lose oneself in a book, the neighboring pedestrians of Marygreen are understandably upset that, in the hero's daily rounds on a bread cart, he has devised a method to "ingeniously fix open, by means of a strap attached to the tilt, the volume he was reading" (1,5:28). Here is a late seriocomic derivative of outdoors reading as the emblematic locus of a book's opened cognitive vistas (Erich Schön again). But public protest cannot be ignored: "The policeman thereby lay in wait for Jude, and one day *accosted* him and *cautioned* him" (1,5:29; emphasis added), the cacophonous internal echo being internal as well to the legal system of hailing and curtailing. In the future, Jude has no choice but to keep an eye peeled for this avatar of the law—so that what he has been taught to think of as his continuing transgression will evade further sighting. But by the time the subsequent returns of this figure of enforcement have been relentlessly attached to scenes of reading, we begin to apprehend this consistent association—between bookishness and policing—as more than a pestering ironic disjunction. It comes to suggest, rather, a massive and ineluctable symbolic affinity.

The second intrusion of a constable into Jude's life begins to make this clear. Speaking out loud, and out of his depth, to the ghosts of culture at Christminster from the public space outside the college walls, Jude in his personifying direct address—"like an actor in a melodrama who apostrophizes the audience on the other side of the footlights" (2,1:66)—represents exactly the theatrics of empathy which Hardy's own nonapostrophizing textual mode eschews. But even as audience interpolation is typically ruled out by Hardy (no "dear reader" here), the way is being prepared for an encompassing extrapolation. Jude's fantasy of answering sentiments from this temple and tomb of patrilinear culture—as if the ennobled texts of the past could actually be given voice and speak back—is exploded by a "real and local voice" that reaches him "from a policeman who had been observing Jude without the latter observing him" (2,1:66): the nonreciprocal panoptic of culture's guarded gate. The effect of this disciplinary interruption is to send the hero again into textual retreat in his private quarters, "reading up a little about" his beloved dons "and their several messages to the world" (2,1:66).

Twice so far the police have obtruded their dubious gaze; twice Jude has thought to fortify himself against such authoritarian bureaucracy by taking to textual culture as if it were an alternative to the constraining hierarchy represented by constables on the beat. When Jude is later heard reading aloud from the Greek New Testament in his room, making enough of an audible spectacle of himself that his privacy again goes public, "the policeman and belated citizens passing along under his window might have heard, if they had stood still, strange syllables muttered with fervor within" (2,3:79). Finally, when Jude's ambitions for university learning are entirely dashed and his exile from "the great library" at Christminster (2,7:95) nearly complete, he realizes that he is merely one of the "manual toilers" without whose labor "the hard readers could not read" (2,7:95). With the law of exclusion so clearly in view, it is time for another kind of reading—and another constable.

A page later, Jude lurches from a pub where he has hoped to forget his defeat and ends up standing at a symbolic "Crossway," guilelessly striking up a conversation—voluntarily this time, or so he thinks—with a policeman who dismisses him as drunk. There is, for a change, no attempt to dodge the law at one level in order to embrace the Law of the fathers at another. Appreciating the fact that the Crossway "had more history than the oldest college in the city" (2,6:96), Jude "began to see that the town life was a *book of humanity* infinitely more palpitating, various, and compendious than the gown life" (2,6:96; emphasis added). In this late Victorian instance, the conventional, half-deadened metaphor of the world's "book" is further punned on by its "compendious" manifestation in composite and digest form. When in *Tess of the D'Urbervilles*, the clerically minded Angel Clare finds that, rather than immersing himself in his books, he "soon preferred to read human nature" (28:100) once he has met the captivating Tess, the faint metaphor is faintly comical. For Jude, with the metaphor made explicit in the textualized "*book* of humanity," it is pivotal. Until now, Jude has been a "tragic Don Quixote" (4,1:163) rather than a comic one— addicted to the "Library of the Fathers" (3,3:115) rather than to distracting romances. With Jude seen either evading or stumbling on the police, the Law has all along had him just where it wants him, awed and cowed. Until this moment, at least: when a greater library would seem to throw open its pages momentarily to the hero, one in which he could read freely without the grammar and dictionary that emburden his forays into the dead languages. It is the next logical stage in Jude's disillusionment that, suddenly indifferent to the culturally debarring force of individual policemen—about to face instead, in the second half of the novel, the hounding proscriptions of the marriage law—he should be discovered to have taken fully unto himself the long-policed interdict on his scholarly ambitions. His subsequent behavior confirms this acquiescence to the law when he travesties his own previously laborious textual consumption. He does so in a symbolic auto-da-fé of his once heretical desire for admission to the scholarly establishment: a book burning in which, in Hardy's darkest pun, Jude's volumes were in a new and final sense "more or less consumed" (4,2:173).

Booking the Audience in Advance

Jude later takes to his deathbed in a deserted Christminster, with "neither living nor dead hereabouts," notices Arabella, "except a damn policeman!" (6,9:311). But no contact occurs this time between the constable outdoors and the dying man inside, if for no other reason than that both the constraining and the punitive functions of the law have been wholly internalized by this point as curtailed desire. Jude in his obscurity now escapes all localized notice in order to die alone, watched over on his deathbed by none other than the panoptic ironist of narrative omniscience—in company with, for the first and last time in the novel, the summoned reader. The effect is definitive: "The last pages to which the chronicler of these lives would ask *the reader's* attention are concerned with the scene in and out of Jude's bedroom when leafy summer came round again" (6,2:319; emphasis added). The "book of humanity," having already oriented your attention to Hardy's book at the narrative turning point in Christminster by prodding an extrapolation from Jude's recognitions to your own, now rivets you with a complementary act of interpolation masked as authorial request. Who has ever *not* been eager to read on for one more harrowing chapter? But why should "the reader" appear here for the first time as narrative function—only when the narrative is, as it were, "more or less consumed"? The answer may rest with the most obvious rhetorical force of interpolation itself: that it names in process what might elsewhere be achieved merely in retrospect—a sense of unfolding story become, once read, an encountered book. Interpolation marks, in this way, the moment when narrative is experienced under the aspect of textual process. Though readers "dear," "gentle," or otherwise have no solicited place in the bleak immediacy of Hardy's plot until this point, once the titular obscuration of its hero is about to be rendered lethally complete in the last chapter, a single instance of reader invocation highlights the whole "chronicle" of *Jude* as a digested chapter of the "book of humanity" now available for response and diffusion.

But this may not be all. Maybe we are glimpsing here the deepest utility of the dimly editorial "*the* reader" rather than the more intimate (or more openly consumerist?) "*my* reader" in the rhetorical practice of an age. Maybe what Hardy's strategic insinuation of *the* reader in fact suggests—and only after the turning point signaled by the novel's metanarrative synecdoche, "book of humanity"—is a practiced but always newly enchanced process of only nominally (or partially) *textual* response. As a member of the Victorian publishing industry rendering central his enterprise, Hardy may here have participated in staging, in other words, the very *naturalization* of reading itself: novel reading, yes, but only by extension from an inevitable and involuntary reading by the social subject in the perpetually legible book of the world (rather than exclusively in the written productions of culture). If so, this would be a reading figured not only as a prerequisite but also as an edifying metaphor for any particular refresher course provided by the elected encounter with secondary representations, novels included.

There is another kind of naturalization at stake, as well, in the postmetaphysical conceit of the world as tome and epitome. Such a "book of humanity" as Jude finally prefers to his scholastic volumes may well seem crisscrossed by various discursive systems: class, gender, family, profession, you name it. But when you name it, you may run the risk of normalizing it as inscribed perforce in the text of an essentialist "humanity," invariant, impervious to change. To the extent that Victorian subjects approach the social text as readers not of ideological false leads but of an indisputable book, the very imprint of existence, to just this extent they accede to an overarching discourse about legible givens: a posttheological derivative of God's Book as the very way of the world. This much we have seen, and there is an underlying ideological inference—as well as a literary-historical consequence—that should not be evaded.

A theoretical discrimination that the second chapter took as preliminary may now be pressed into further service. In designating three overlapping orders of mimesis, Paul Ricoeur marks out what amounts to the "prefiguration" (the given constitution) of *the* world on its way to becoming the fictional "configuration" of *a* world. The latter is a narrative structure which, in its strictly textual form, is manifest only in the moment when, in turn, it produces the "refiguration" of y/our world in reception. But what we have been isolating as the reflexive moment in fiction sends shock waves through the whole mimetic system. In the context of this chapter on the world's encompassing book, the reflexive jolt is often twofold. The localized scene of reading reverberates as the marked site, the parabolic (con)figuration, of the novel's own self-meditated reception, but only as that reception depends on appreciating the novel as itself a citation from, a figurative spin on, the always and already (the prefiguratively) written. When this preexistent but now fictionally reconstituted world text is then reoriented toward the very world of reception which it serves to *re*figure, we realize how any such discourse of fictional production (with every text the interpretive variant of its own global intertext) admits to the derivative only to reprivilege its terms as universal. On the one side, the book of the world can be taken to deconstruct the natural and the given, exposing it as an inscribed cultural code. On the other, this same metatextual conceit tends to universalize a specific network of cultural assumptions as fixed, axiomatic, pre-scribed. Suspended on the tension between these tendencies, with the novel no sooner demoted as invention than elevated to mimetic authority, the promulgating of prose fiction as cultural work continues unabated.

This does not mean that it is as easy to produce as to consume. I spoke of a residual literary-historical consequence associated with the mastertrope we have been examining. It has to do with the very fact of the residual, with writing as an aftereffect of the big book. Call it, with Harold Bloom, the anxiety of a belatedness both literary as well as historical. To just the extent that, by the mid-Victorian period, "the novel" has grown wholly untrue to its generic name and gains force only from its accurate quotation of chapter and verse from the given universe of both literary and extratextual experience, the novelist has a correspondingly more difficult task in assuming her title. She (we have Eliot ahead of us) has, of course, read many of those previous books of the world's book and can only don the mantle of her craft by rereading, or in her case more rigorously reinterpreting, them. When her last so-called novel, *Daniel Deronda*, closes with four lines not of her own devising but of Milton's, drawn in turn from his own rereading of the classic tradition (*Samson Agonistes*), she thus puts down the pen where she had no choice but to take it up: in debt and derivation. The rest is up to the reader: site of a restlessness which, at whatever cost to the writer's curbed freedom of originality, keeps the world readable and the world reading.

Early in the downward-spiraling plot of *Jude the Obscure*, Hardy's hero, in the first of many fated accidents, drops on the ground a "little book of tales" (1,3:21). He is never seen reading fiction again. You know better—and are reminded that you do by Hardy's pervasive contrapuntal thematics of (in oscillating senses) *sanctioned* reading.[9] If the world is for reading, books, at least the right ones, are for living. This nineteenth-century mythopoetics of textual production is a far cry from the alternately phobic and utopian modernist trope (from Joyce to Nabokov) of a life lived inside someone else's text. Nonetheless, the Victorian century wore on by wearing away at any novelistic complacency attached to the book of the world as figure. Even well short of the leveling pessimism of Schreiner, Moore, or Hardy, the reciprocity of text and world within both the Victorian society of the sign and the Victorian culture of reading leaves, if we may put it this way, *something to be desired*. Brontë performs this residuum of desire within the raw psychodynamics of transferential response. More philosophically and sociologically at once, George Eliot performs it within—or as—the realm of hermeneutics: a life not merely devoted but promoted to interpretive transmission. How far from a modernist metatrope, how close to a Victorian social program, this novelistic fantasy thrives on remaining, indeed how close to the reflex action of Dickensian fiction it comes to seem, only interpretation can tell.

After a chapter on the spiritual introjection of reading as living in George Eliot (culture as a text for life), and after a transitional look at the degenerated subculture of writing for a living in Gissing, with the associated abjection of reading, we will be tracking the fortunes of the Victorian book of the world into the *fin de siècle* spread of supernatural romance within a new ethos of gothicized reading. This dubious cultural milieu scarcely cuts such texts off from the discursive contexts of the period, but instead embroils their reading itself, more starkly than ever, in the lines of knowledge, power, and desire which articulate such discourse circuits. This is to say that the extraliterary vocabularies crisscrossing the realist text frequently double over themselves in gothic narrative to entangle the reading act, which in its own operations becomes by turns medicalized (pathological), imperialist (territorializing), erotic (voyeuristic), parascientific (hypnotic), and so forth, including what we might call psychoeconomized (libidinally invested). Mid-Victorian bibliocentrism and its constitutive reading agents—delineating an integrated field of semiotic exchange—thus cede to the decentered subject of perverse and vicarious identification. No longer quoting the book of the world, as do realist texts, the fictions of the gothic revival excerpt their fantasies from the lore of the otherworldly. Yet this is itself a complex discursive weave whose very lure is only another name (a second-order allegory, or in our terms a reflexive parable) for the preternatural enticement and menace, the *charm*, of reading per se. With its phenomenology of access by dispossession, just such a dimension of textual submission—of subjected reading—is never more powerfully anticipated in the Victorian narratives of so-called social or psychological realism than by George Eliot's last, most unsettling venture in the form.

Chapter Eleven

Mordecai's Consumption
Afterlives of Interpretation in
Daniel Deronda

Norman Garstin, *A Woman Reading a Newspaper*
(1891). Courtesy, the Tate Gallery, London.

*W*hat makes perhaps the most profound nineteenth-century novelist's last
and perhaps most profound novel such a provoking anomaly in the Victorian
high canon, such a dubious triumph, such (to put it bluntly) a hard read?
How—and why—does George Eliot's *Daniel Deronda* (1876) mount the assault
it does on the readerly? And among recent professional readers, why should
just this resistance to *comprehension* in its twofold aspect, the twin problematic
of rhetorical availability and structural coherence, seem to highlight the crucial relation of this long-marginalized text to George Eliot's undeniable role in
the literary establishment (both active and static senses) of Victorian high culture? These would be questions worth pausing over in any such study as this
on the management of Victorian fictional reception—even if one did not further suspect that the answers are to be found in precisely the conjoint formal-
izations of response known here as interpolation and extrapolation: specifi-

cally, in *Deronda*'s case, reader imperatives and a microcosmic structure of hermeneutic parable.

If in Thackeray and Meredith, in Dickens, Schreiner, Moore, Haggard, and Hardy, as in many Victorian book writers before them, the world is already a book, life in that world is configured more directly in Eliot's last book as already and forever interpretation. Yet the formal modeling of this hermeneutic stance, at any such level of generalization, is so diffusive (or should we say suffused?) that one returns to *Persuasion*'s self-parable of experiential duration for the nearest prototype. The book-inclusive reflex of *Persuasion* consists in the temporal extent or span of its own plotted disclosures set in resonance with the emotional contours of their very reading. More than this, the encompassing reflex of *Daniel Deronda*, guided by extrapolative episodes of interpretive reaction as well as by their interpolative preparation, includes the extension beyond plot not only of the narrative's specifically hermeneutic rather than just affective reverberation but of its residual action in the larger life of the mind.

In Eliot's novel, therefore, we encounter a more troubled and tentative form of Dickens' readerly "field of action" in *Hard Times*, where a socially mobilized audience is conscripted from within narrative as a telos of the story's own omniscient plotting. *Deronda* being also an omniscient narrative, some version of the vexed transferential relays of yearning and deferral which both motivate and forestall a definitive closure at the end of *Villette* can dynamize Eliot's conclusion only at the level of the novelistic discourse itself, not its personification in a first-person narrator. For the impersonal narrator and the no longer apostrophized reader of *Daniel Deronda* to enter, at the end, upon a similarly negotiated exchange concerning the (now cultural more than psychological) valences of generic expectation requires every structural and rhetorical contortion—every involute of extrapolation—which this chapter makes space to examine. Moreover, the difference between Austen's early model of plot as managed temporality and Eliot's as spurred perpetuity comes down to the difference between the aesthetic of domestic realism (in its founding moment as cultural consolidation) and the refined psychological realism of the Victorian high canon (in its later crisis of faith as social agency). To note this is only to begin appreciating how the would-be cultural integration of Eliot's novel makes a visionary last stand (before the multiple disintegrations of the *fin de siècle*) in a continuing literary history of conscripted reading.

Daniel Deronda ends where it famously begins: *in medias res*. This symmetry is perhaps easy to overlook because the "things" (*res*) it leaves hanging are mostly the reader's to comprehend and bring forth. The ethic of reading to which Eliot's novel subscribes is one that must gladly leave every given book behind when attention, nudged by closure, turns to the extratextual matters that need attending to. With book no longer in hand, this is where the insights of literature are meant to come in handiest. Such is the novel's concluding myth of its own efficacy in reception, a reception that thus extends well beyond the duration of response bounded by its covers. Dickens' *A Tale of Two Cities* attempts to build in such a self-fulfilling prophecy as a structural trick: the novel's future becoming, in historical terms, our present. Nothing at the close of *Daniel Deronda* comes near to being this explicit. That is exactly how the novel has already begun to prosecute its muted impact. Though leaning at least as much on the reader, Brontë's strategy at the close of *Villette* could hardly be farther from the opening out of Eliot's novel. Brontë's is the mere contrivance of contingency in the teeth of finality, whereas Eliot's narrator, we are asked to believe, gives way to the undecidable as the genuinely *possible*. In moving toward the novel's closing moment of heavily entailed release, Eliot has offered unusually prominent, indeed almost starkly demarcated, versions of both interpolated address and extrapolative episode: both an intermittent summons to reading as imaginative projection and an inlaid scenario of hermeneutic uncertainty. Dispersed across the text, the former pattern of solicitation lays the ground for the latter episode in its dependence, even as interpretive occasion, on the nuances of imaginative empathy and intuition.

"Imagine . . . All of Us Can"

Eliot is never above recourse to the intimate and companionable address familiar from the best-sellers. It serves more purposes in her fiction, however, than the heightened scene setting we have noted, for instance, in Charles Kingsley. Take an instance of reader positioning (rather than direct apostrophe) which works by allusion to Jane Austen's most famous sentence, the first of *Pride and Prejudice*. The attention-getting power of bachelorhood in provincial neighborhoods, which is a truth "universally acknowledged" in Austen without the need for reader reference or address, is converted to an exclusionary irony in *Daniel Deronda*, skewering a subclass of her "history"-reading public: "Some readers of this history will doubtless regard it as incredible that people should construct matrimonial prospects on the mere report that a bachelor of good fortune and possibilities was coming within reach" (9:123). Austen's "universe" has become Eliot's literate public as reading audience—yet on its own terms totalized, since the demurring reader imagined here in third rather than second person is a false lead. No one really doubts this fact about matrimonial fantasies, and Eliot's audience is harmonized on the spot by the phantom alterity of such social naiveté. You are therefore indoctrinated by what you already know, as elsewhere by what, as fiction readers, you are ready to imagine.

Eliot more often addresses her public without actually naming it as a readership, delivering the imperative of enjoined response without the vocative of denominated status. By the time of *Daniel Deronda* the habit is practiced and tactical, but we find it as early as *Adam Bede* (1859) in the form of the single-word imperatives "look," "imagine," and the like. "See them in the bright sunlight . . . ascending the slope from the Broxton side" (5:114). These tendencies are never wholly foresworn in Eliot, but in *Daniel Deronda* they collect toward a more powerful emphasis on the reader's embroilment. "Look at his [Daniel's] hands" (17:226), the narrator will direct you, as you are stationed before an extended verbal portrait. "Excuse him [Daniel]" (19:247), you are urged, for the Jewish stereotypes that clutter his mind.[1] Later, though, not quite devalued by recurrent use, the device reaches for something like a genuine enlargement of sympathy in the description of Mordecai's wasting illness. Conscripted by second-person grammar at the most rudimentary level, you are slotted for a response well within your grasp: "Imagine—we all of us can—the pathetic stamp of consumption with its brilliance of glance . . . ; and imagine it on a Jewish face naturally accentuated for the expression of an eager mind" (40:533). Such overt prosopopoeia—the textual giving face to an absent person—is thus stressed as reciprocal with another figure: namely, apostrophe. The latter is the (elsewhere tacit) personification of the equally absent reader necessary to realize any scene in reception. Idiom has a way of getting at this conjoint phenomenon, for every textual description presupposes, as it were, *some description of reader* who will be prone to accept the depicted scene in the proper way. Certain demands on "fancy" and "imagination" are precisely what is required for the most routine procedures of narrative. But when the pressure of context is calculated to spring their full implications, these mental processes, these *imperatives* of fiction grammatically laid bare as such, begin to exemplify the more complex phenomenological transfer to which Eliot's cultural project is devoted. Cast wide by rhetoric, the net is later drawn tight by plot. Indeed, by the time the novel has achieved closure, its largest structural imperative has come clear: You are to imagine Mordecai's "consumption" in both senses, the medical but also the aesthetic, and thus to replay any such using up as the novel's own—as recognized in reflex by your very reading.

Having once been told to do what it is said you are well able to do—"Imagine—we all of us can"—the reading audience is soon summoned by a more strenuous demand on the sympathetic imagination. The first word of Eliot's book of "Revelations" (volume 5) is an imperative that launches the last and most prominent of these apostrophes of projected identification: "Imagine the conflict in a mind like Deronda's . . . on the evening after that interview with Mordecai" (41:567). Rehearsed and internalized here is the turning point of the entire novel, when the Jewish visionary, Mordecai, tells the hero, "My hope abides with you" (40:564). Your effort to imagine how this might strike the hero is not as easy as the previous facial evocations of Mordecai. At the very least, it calls on you to call up the psychological texture of the entire work so far. If you heed this grammatical call, you have not simply entered the judicious and probing mind of the hero, and thereby fulfilled the novel's tutelary agenda in the process of carrying it toward completion; you have also inhabited Daniel's stance not just as self-searching consciousness but *as reader*. And this is the case not only within the largest parabolic frame of the plot, as we will find, but in the remainder of the immediate passage. As the paragraph continues, it is less the information of past literature or history than the experience of reading itself—its hold on credulity—which models Daniel's present inclination: "If he had read of this incident as having happened centuries ago," an encounter with a man like Mordecai befalling "some man young as himself, dissatisfied with his neutral life, and wanting . . . some more special duty to give him *ardour* for the possible consequences of his work," he would have had no trouble believing that "the incident should have created a deep impression on that far-off man" (41:567; emphasis added). Daniel's previous *"ardour . . .* given to the imaginary world of his books" (16:206; emphasis added), of which we have heard twenty-five chapters before, is now the term for a similar eros drawing a literary hero like him away to a world of committed action. The event of reading thus promotes as well as enacts its role as a preparation for living. For Daniel is a man whose "sensibilities" have been "enlarged by his early habit of thinking himself imaginatively into the experience of others" (41:570). It is a habit first trained, we are to presume, in the experience of books. It is this experience, in turn, which is now yours for the asking, yours for the taking in. As the reading audience imagines how such sensibilities would be stretched at a time like this, its own are meant to be lent new expanse.

Beyond the "Fashionable Novels"

It is no accident that Daniel first meets Mordecai in a secondhand bookstore, nor that the range of offerings for sale there is laid out in the following polarity: with the "literature of the ages" being "represented in judicious mixture, from the immortal verse of Homer to the mortal prose of the railway novel" (33:435).[2] In an age of the portable romance, Eliot herself strains for the epic dispensation, complete with its extratextual, bardic aura. Yet the exclusion of romance is not in itself the answer, as we know from *Adam Bede*, whose tragic heroine, Hetty Sorrel, "had never read a novel" (13:181). After her seduction, the point is enlarged: "She knew no romance, and had only a feeble share in the feelings which are the source of romance, so that well-read ladies may find it difficult to understand her state of mind" (36:418). Yet composed of such "well-read ladies" as Gwendolen Harleth in *Daniel Deronda*, this narrowly sophisticated female audience is not, of course, Eliot's ideal readership—and therefore, once again, not apostrophied in second person, merely mentioned in passing. The closer model in *Adam Bede* for the intended intimacy of your own participation is set in place during the crisis of Hetty's trial for infanticide, when the narrated experience of the courtroom is projected forward into an anticipated circuit of social storytelling. In a passage that condenses the tactic of extrapolation to a single clause, the benighted creature who knew no literary romance becomes the future protagonist of a homespun local realism, for "the neighbours from Hayslope who were present, and *who told Hetty Sorrel's story by their firesides in their old age*, never forgot to say how it moved them when Adam Bede, poor fellow, . . . came into court, and took his place by her side" (43:476; emphasis added). The free indirect discourse marked by that appositive, "poor fellow," serves to reproduce the very vocabulary and cadence of their narrative. What is more, it does so from a time in the discursive present (looking back on the recent past) which is roughly contemporaneous with the later years of these eventual storytellers. Like Little Nell and Sydney Carton before her, the unlettered Hetty Sorrel nears the end of her history by becoming subsumed to her own story as orally remembered and renewed—renewed, more explicitly even than in Dickens, at the "fireside" of Victorian textual dissemination.

The partnership between direct address to the reader and the thematic of reading in *Adam Bede* returns, with nothing less than a vengeance, in *Daniel Deronda*, where the punitive force of the heroine's literary deficit is once more measured against the reader's own valorized engagement. Hetty Sorrel has read no novels, Gwendolen Harleth too many—and of the wrong sort. Gwendolen has formed her worldly expectations precisely "through novels, plays, and poems" (4:70), but even the low pleasures of railway-style serials cannot be counted on; her usual affinities are reversed to a farcical narcissism when potential blame for a foul mood one morning is laid (by indirect discourse) on "the quality of the shilling serial mistakenly written for her amusement" (7:112). Though at other times Gwendolen "rejoiced to feel herself exceptional," nonetheless "her horizon was that of the genteel romance where the heroine's soul poured out in her journal is full of vague power, originality, and general rebellion, while her life moves strictly in the sphere of fashion" (6:83). When financial trouble comes, the lessons of such literature are found wanting.[3] "Gwendolen's uncontrolled reading, though consisting chiefly in what are called pictures of life, had somehow not prepared her for this encounter with reality" (14:193). By contrast with Gwendolen's taste in fiction, the other sphere of ardent reading in the novel, besides the shared intellectual community of Daniel and Mordecai, is located in the Meyrick household, where the daughters learn by reading their difference from the coarsened "manners of ladies in the fashionable world," as "represented . . . in what are called literary photographs" (18:237)—again, Gwendolen's novelistic "pictures of life." When we first enter their household, "Mrs. Meyrick was reading aloud from a French book" (18:238), Chartrian's *Histoire d'un conscrit*, which, says Mab, "makes me want to do something good, something grand. It makes me so sorry for everybody" (18:239). It thus instills the values of action, or at least the animating will toward action, which is Eliot's broad purpose in her own novel.

This link to the novel's encompassing agenda is furthered by an emphasis on the mother's own taste in reading. Mrs. Meyrick has not the least interest in sensational or romantic fictions; she is instead "a great reader of news, from the widest-reaching politics to the list of marriages; the latter, she said, giving her the pleasant sense of finishing the fashionable novels without having read them, and seeing the heroes and heroines happy without knowing what poor creatures they were" (61:793). Yet her last news of the cruelly "poor" union of Gwendolen and Grandcourt comes to her, not in her favored marriage lists this time, but rather in an obituary notice. For just a paragraph after we have heard of her preferred reading, her son rushes in with the daily paper mentioning Grandcourt's drowning off the Italian coast, the dissolution of the marriage by watery death. Gwendolen's story, though, is only half of what by this time Eliot's audience has long been reading in her double-plotted novel.[4] Like Mrs. Meyrick with her newspapers, you too have given equivalent attention, as in few other novels of the period, to "the widest-reaching politics," a world-historical rather than simply domestic canvas. Here the ambivalent finish of the proto-Zionist narrative comes into a telling relation with the marriage-to-death trajectory of Gwendolen's story, positing indeed its direct symmetrical reversal. In the one storyline: Grandcourt sinking in the sea just when Gwendolen most wishes his death. In the other: Daniel's decision to sanctify his discovered racial origin by marrying the Jewish girl, Mirah, whom he had earlier *saved* from drowning, vowing also his spiritual marriage to her brother Mordecai, self-styled prophet of Hebrew nationalism, who dies floated free on a metaphoric "ocean of peace beneath him" (70:882)—just as Daniel and Mirah begin their overseas pilgrimage to the Jewish East. A moribund marriage ending in death in the one narrative path finds itself matched in the other by a posthumous commitment figured as marriage and doubled, almost interchangeably, by the conjugal event. Such mystical figuration in the Mordecai plot needs pursuing if for no other reason than that, once channeled through further metaphoric conversions, it ends up evoking that unimpedimented marriage of true minds which is the reading act itself.

Confronted in Eliot's novel with the closural overlap of eros and thanatos, of marriage and cultural martyrdom, we may recall Peter Brooks' sense of fraternal-sororal incest as one of the chief tropes in the nineteenth-century novel for the foundering of the metonymic principle of plot—its differential dynamism—upon the stalling metaphors, the undue equivalences, of oversameness.[5] What, then, in the endogamous context of a culture like orthodox Judaism, about the case of fraternal-fraternal incest, which removes gender difference altogether in favor of male priority? Despite her satire of the English patrilineage in the other half of the novel, the Jewish counterplot of Eliot's narrative is structured toward just such a quasi-familial retrenchment, toward its tribal value as a sign of patriarchal bonding. Daniel and Mordecai, soon entwined with "as intense a consciousness as if they had been two undeclared lovers" (40:552), testify in the end to a "willing marriage which melts soul into soul . . . as the clear waters are made fuller" (63:820). Yet Daniel as spiritual bridegroom is also a man Mordecai thinks of "as my brother that fed at the breast of my mother" (63:820). His soul's marriage is thus quite unabashedly imaged by him as a sibling merger, but one very different from the incestuous *Liebestod*—and drowning—of Maggie Tulliver with her brother Tom at the close of *The Mill on the Floss*. In *Daniel Deronda* a community is sustained rather than renounced by the mutual introversion of desire. It is the two men's disclosed genetic sameness, their racial likeness—their function as metaphors for each other, or type and antitype in the exegetical sense—which arrives to rectify the metonymic thinning out of the Jewish "dispersion" (42:591).

The potential incestuous cast of homoerotic bonding, deflected here by Mirah as symbolic midwife (as much as mother) to its presumed communal fruition, is thus an emblem of a beleaguered and earned consolidation, a fending off of otherness, a historically endorsed refusal of difference—all of which fusions find in the internalizing of reading, rather than in the impersonal medium of text, their closest trope. This is what the dying Mordecai goes, as it were, to show. From a consideration of his last scene we will return to an earlier episode—not of reading so much as of hermeneutic rumination on a received text—which has already gone out of its way to anticipate terms for the reading of Mordecai's closural death.

Dying to Transmit

The whole etiology of Mordecai's consumption—its inevitable end postponed until the very last lines of the book and then transpiring in effect *between
them*—makes clear the sense in which his succumbing to tuberculosis is to be
taken not only as a medical fatality but as a sacrificial rite. For it is in the nature, or rather the design, of his martyrdom that he dies so that we might survive to read on, read over. Such are the novel's designs *upon us*. In this sense the
threefold structure of the Victorian death scene which I have elsewhere explored with other texts in mind—in which the "transposition" of imagery from
mundane to mortal register, contrived for the "epitome" of the dying subject,
is then "displaced" onto the consciousness of the survivor—is a structure that
culminates in *Daniel Deronda* as a double displacement.[6] At one level, in this
novel of a drowning English culture, Mordecai's oceanic repose is transferred
in renewal onto the hero's setting sail for the East. At another, the reader is directly entailed in this fatality and this subsequent fate. As in *A Tale of Two Cities*
preeminently, closural death scenes may mark not only the void of narrativity
onto which they open but the space of subsequent response they move to encode and co-opt.

Daniel Deronda anatomizes this structure in the process of dramatizing it.
In his last "deliverance," as his speeches are repeatedly and punningly called,
Mordecai announces a paragraph before his end, "Death is coming to me as
the divine kiss which is both parting and reunion," a severance and perpetuation that "takes me from your bodily eyes and gives me full presence in your
soul" (70:882). Gasped out to Daniel in particular, his soul's bride (or partner
in the husbandry of his racial dream), Mordecai's last quoted words are "Have
I not breathed my soul into you? We shall live together" (70:882). With Daniel
the supposed body to Mordecai's indwelling spirit, the supernatural pact sealed
here has its inescapably ghoulish side: the possession by a tribal incubus from
beyond the grave. After saying his farewell to Daniel, Mordecai then "raised
himself and uttered in Hebrew the confession of the divine Unity, which for
long generations has been on the lips of the dying Israelite" (70:882–83)—always there, waiting, renewed. As indicated, that is, by the generic article of
number—"*the* Israelite" of time immemorial—it is individuality itself that
passes away in this displacement of the single doomed agent by the rituals of
a race. In this last rite of passage, Mordecai has in every sense *become* his people, the delegate of their nationalist adventure, the one subsumed to the many.

"He sank back gently into the chair, and did not speak again." In this his virtual death is confirmed, the end of that rhetorical efficacy by which his life has been defined. "But it was some hours before he had ceased to breath with Mirah's and Deronda's arms around him." Oddly enough, in one of the elusive temporal dislocations of this passage, it is as if some bystander were to have said at the scene: "It will be some hours before he will . . . already have been dead." Within the grammar of a single sentence, that is, in the slide from "*was some hours*" to "*had ceased*" (instead of "ceased"), there passes under suppression the unsaid death moment. In the prevailing rhetoric of the Victorian death scene, the assonant commonplace "had *ceased* to *breath*" is regularly a phonetically dilated circumlocution, or euphemism, for the lingering last of life. Here, instead, it records the clinical aftermath of a final consumptive "deliverance" both of and through breath. In the shunting from past tense into past perfect, Mordecai has in textual terms slipped outside time altogether. He dies in the interstices of syntax rather than in direct mimesis. By never having mentioned death by name, the discourse thus avoids denominating his removal— as if, at the very moment of closure, Mordecai's spiritual presence may have been secreted elsewhere and preserved.

What the unsaid death of Paul Emanuel at the close of *Villette* works in its own way to equivocate is suggested as well by the euphemized death (breathing over; inspiration passed on) of Mordecai: the displacement of the elegiac onto the recuperative at the decisive remove of reader investment. This is a functional shift psychological in Brontë, sociocultural in Eliot. In *Deronda's* four closing lines, unidentified, from *Samson Agonistes*, we encounter the familiar format of one of Eliot's epigraphs (as if to the next chapter that never comes) brought forward now to the position of epitaph. If my last chapter got hold of the problem correctly, this combination of literary deference and effaced attribution grants even to Milton (as to the Old Testament before him) no more than a definitive reading, rather than writing, of the world's tragic book, so that even her great English predecessor, no less than Eliot herself in quoting him unnamed, must become only a footnote to the nonauthorial transmission of that book. Furthermore, wrenched from its Miltonic context, the deictic (or "pointing") form "here" in "Nothing is here for tears," accompanied by the present-tense verb of being, begs every question of textual manifestation and emplacement with which this discussion is concerned. The cathartic gesture of these lines—as Eliot's present text disappears into its own literary prehistory, its own epic tradition—leaves open the question of presence itself ("here" *where?*), especially as that question is directly linked to Mordecai's abdication from textual embodiment, his express and unexpected desire to die without any written trace of his writing available to "bodily eyes." The muted temporal rupture of this death scene has thus opened a loophole in its own finality—its finality as text.

One thing at least is clear: Mordecai's wish to be remembered without scriptive localization, as the remainder of this chapter will consider more closely, is pitched against an opposite compact of writing and reading, of epistolary transmission, in the other plot. There, writing begins to make possible for Gwendolen what it would impede for Mordecai from beyond the grave: the most direct possible contact with Daniel. In an obvious parallel to his parting with Mordecai, Daniel will in all probability never lay "bodily eyes" upon Gwendolen again either, though he does promise her, in effect, "full presence" (Mordecai's term) in the spirit. "I will write to you always," he vows, and "shall be more with you than I used to be" (69:878). It is in fact the first installment of such a verbal communication, Gwendolen's letter to Daniel, which arrives on his wedding day and which is followed, without further comment, by the last half dozen paragraphs detailing the death—without written legacy—of the man who wants no words of his own to come between his vision and Daniel's instrumentation of it. In a heated plea immediately after his virtual marriage vows to Daniel, we discover how completely Mordecai desires a transcendence of the body, of materiality, indeed of the material body of his own writing practice as Jewish historian, philosopher, and poet. Over Daniel's unusually strenuous objections, Mordecai declares, declaims, that "I have judged what I have written, and I desire the body that I gave my thought to pass away as this fleshly body will pass, but let the thought be born again from our fuller soul which shall be called yours" (63:820).

What might at first glance resemble Mordecai's resistance to publication—the diatribe in *Romola* (1863) by the blind fifteenth-century scholar Bardo de' Bardi against the "mechanical printers who threaten to make learning a base and vulgar thing" (5:96)—derives in fact from an opposite motive, a covetous urge for manuscript immortality. As Bardo insists to his daughter, Romola, there will be "nothing but my library" to "preserve my memory and carry down my name as a member of the great republic of letters" (5:100). This is an obsession that has set Bardo up as the enemy of all dissemination in print, a "system of licensed robbery" by which "some other scholar would stand on the title-page of the edition" (5:102). With this manuscript collector being no more than the caretaker of others' words to begin with, his proprietorial obsession blocks transmission and festers in possessiveness. His is a cultural resource narrowed to the perverse familial circuit of the heroine's enforced reading aloud to her blind parent—caught in the original illustration by Frederick Leighton (fig. 9)—as the sole circulation of his holdings.

Figure 9. Frederick Leighton. George Eliot, *Romola* (1863),
from *Cornhill Magazine*

More like Dorothea Brooke dutifully reading to Casaubon in *Middlemarch* than like Gwendolen Harleth avoiding all strenuous text, the martyred feminine role in *Romola* does nothing to redeem the intention behind her servitude.

Mordecai abjures print culture, long after its establishment, for reasons putatively as selfless as Bardo's are vainglorious. Daniel's inspiration from Mordecai must come through unacknowledged, devolving upon him as a legacy engaged only by being wholly internalized, a kind of spiritual plagiarism. Yet, of course, hundreds of this novel's paragraphs have offered permanent form to nothing else but Mordecai's pronouncements, laboriously "transcribed" by Eliot's text. What are we to make of this ironic disjunction? A double bind? A double cross? Has the text necessarily ignored the dying wish of its most relentlessly eloquent hero by emblazoning in print just what he had asked to let pass unrecorded? By some curious extratextual poetic justice, then, do those numerous readers and critics who regret his prominence in the novel as wordy, labored, and tedious, and who react by skimming and dismissal, only grant him his dying wish after all? But, then again, what could be expected even from Eliot's *ideal* reader? Flooded with Mordecai's words, could any reader do much more than carry away from them the spirit rather than the letter of their sentiments? If such a question occurs to you in reading, then the text has braced you for a generalized cultural responsiveness—rather than immediate textual response—within its own antiprovincial agenda. It is in this sense that Mordecai's "yearning for transmission" (38:528) seeks in its highest moments of political lucidity no fixed and so potentially dismissible form, no text. He does everything he can to make the mission of his acolyte, Daniel, as epic, originating, and original as possible.

But the purism of this impulse has not always been easy for Mordecai to sustain. Earlier, his own metaphors reveal more of a desire for authorial permanence than he otherwise admits. Though, nearing death, he looks back on his written words "as the ill-shapen work of the youthful carver who has seen a heavenly pattern, and trembles in imitating the vision" (63:817), this same metaphor of impress and incision has been brought to bear on his earlier wish to carve or inscribe the lines of his own Hebrew poetry on the memory of young Jacob Cohen: "'The boy will get them engraved within him,' thought Mordecai; 'it is a way of printing'" (38:533). In a spurt of logocentric metaphysics, Mordecai further assumes an *inside* to language, to eloquence, an essence that can be accessed even without textual mediation: the place of the spiritual voice, indeed the very "breath of divine thought" (38:557) descended from the Logos itself. This inspiriting influx can enter into secondary transmission (so Mordecai dreams) without the spoiling interposition of script, can pass directly from soul to the body of a spiritual double—a process to be fully achieved only, by definition, at the moment of death. In Mordecai's mystic bonding and *demise* (in the linked etymological senses of demitting and departure, passing on as well as passing away), we come to recognize his yearning beyond the confines of textuality, his fantasy, as the novel's own.

"A Part Possesses the Whole": The Parable of Parables

We are led to this recognition in part by that most resonant of microcosmic episodes—that hermeneutic node to which, as promised earlier, the question of Mordecai's death and extratextual remembrance would lead us round. It is an episode that pointedly exemplifies the workings of its own inclusion—

and, by synecdochic extension, the workings of that enclosing text in whose reading it schools us. In so doing, it outdistances such an earlier *mise en abyme* as Mrs. Meyrick's reading about marriage and politics—and does so by compounding reception with moral and psychological analysis, turning document to interpretive occasion. While illustrating Henry James' unexemplified claim about *Daniel Deronda*—"The mass is for each detail and each detail is for the mass"[7]—this late episode actually goes so far as to stage a scene of "reading" without writing, of interpretation in the absence of the specific text that prompts it, of reading, we might say, the world through text. It thus attempts to let the novel stand back from itself at what could be called an internal remove, emplotting its own organizing logic of response in reduced form.

In putting forward the shape of this episode, as I am about to do, with the delayed disclosure of something like a riddle—"what is this story I'm telling you?"—I am purposefully defying you to try keeping from your mind the subsequent relation of Mordecai's death to the marriage of Daniel and Mirah. On the way toward this climax, the protagonist of the miniature death-closed narrative in question dies as if presiding over a marriage, which thus seems authorized by the finality of that death. Thereafter, the inevitable story of this story, the narrative to be told over or at least never forgotten about such a sacralized dying, is all that will remain—as metanarrative remainder. Does this inherited story of the protagonist's death, however, offer a blessing to marital continuance or a memory meant to eclipse that union, to intrude its own willful self-sacrifice as an ideal more strongly felt than the marriage ties? The death of the protagonist, which is necessary to give meaning to the life leading up to it, has in one sense transpired not as the sheer annihilation of self but in the name of the other, as more a martyrdom than a fortuity or even a virtual suicide. As in Eliot's novel as a whole, heroism is so constructed in this story as to secure a posthumous foothold for identity, a self-effacement that is also a canonization. Is this closural structure a contradiction or a subterfuge, a paradox or an irony, an abnegation or a will to power?

These are questions that do not go away. They return at the end of *Daniel Deronda* to complicate the conclusion of that extended macroplot that this episode so closely resembles in skeletal form: the story of the tubercular, the consumptive, the self-consuming Mordecai ennobling the marriage of Daniel and Mirah, the investiture of his sanctifying power *in absentia*. This is not, though, as I warned above, the story I have just been describing, despite the fact that in moral and psychological outline it corresponds with it at roughly every point. The story whose raised questions I was sketching out is instead the one Mordecai himself recounts, in the economy of a single long sentence, as he nears his death: the parable of the Jewish heroine who goes to her death in the place of the non-Jewish woman who loves the gentile king with whom she too is hopelessly in love. "Somewhere in the later *Midrash*, I think," is this story's source, Mordecai recalls, written once but retrievable now without origin or precise attribution, inherited as part of the wisdom he lives by and the ongoing interpretive energy that keeps such wisdom living. Here is the story in his streamlined version of its plot: "She entered into prison and changed clothes with the woman who was beloved by the king, that she might deliver that woman from death by dying in her stead, and leave the king to be happy in his love which was not for her" (61:802). Though the exemplum is only one sentence long, it follows a rather full disquisition on the confession of "divine Unity" which will be on Mordecai's lips at his deathbed, a wholeness explained in a way that all but explicitly invites the application of the following Midrash narrative *pars pro toto* to the entire novel: "Now, in complete unity a part possesses the whole as the whole possesses every part" (61:802). Advanced as a metaphysical critique of narrowing self-centeredness (the heroic alternative to which is supposedly exemplified by the Midrash text), this doctrinal subsumption of part to whole is sustained as an article of interpretive faith as well. Offered up from within the text itself is, again, the Jamesian notion of the atom for the aggregate, the fraction for the mass. In becoming a microcosm not merely of the larger plot but of the plot as interpreted, the Midrash parable is a story we are not therefore left on our own to interpret. Mordecai "reads" it for us, translating it into his own words and his own import, even while he is challenged in his reading by Mirah, one of the characters who will be most directly concerned in the closure of his own life, the bride he gives away so that he can claim her marriage as his own. One major plotline of *Daniel Deronda* is thus not only miniaturized en route but submitted to a detailed hermeneutic procedure by the very characters involved: a novel worrying in advance the psychological structure of its own closure.

Mordecai, who introduces the Midrash tale by appealing to the gender stereotype that "women are specially framed for the love which feels possession in renouncing," believes that the point of the anecdote is to enshrine a "surpassing love, that loses self in the object of that love" (61:803). Mirah (still afraid that Daniel is smitten with Gwendolen) refuses this reading altogether, insisting instead that the Jewish heroine of the tale "wanted the king when she was dead to know what she had done, and feel that she was better than the other. It was her strong self, wanting to conquer, that made her die" (61:803). Mordecai, the passionate exegete, has thus returned to a cultural parable whose moral he extracts by interpretation, only to have his reading called into question by a character who is no more blatantly projecting onto the heroine her own jealousy than Mordecai is projecting his coveted aspirations to selfless sacrifice, to a death with meaning. His own frail person "framed" like a woman's for "possession in renouncing," Mordecai is structurally identified in his response to this story with the position of a female marginal. Further excluded even from sexuality, however, he seeks vicarious fulfillment in a way that would somehow transform his fatal disease into a nuptial gift, a genetic and spiritual legacy. Rescuing doom from sheer contingency, even if casting himself in the woman's part of the disappointed suitor to the hand of the kingly Daniel, he must die not just *of* but *for* something: call it, again, consumption. It is in this way that the Midrash story, ending in death and opening onto ambiguity, takes shape as a synecdoche of the novel's inclusive narrational mechanism. The story's divergent interpretations are indeed divided between the novel's larger lines of action, not just attached to the Mordecai plot. Mirah's reading of the legend aligns it with that sphere of desire and frustration centering on Gwendolen, associated first with Mirah's jealousy of her, later with hers of Mirah—and finally with the pangs of remorse which Gwendolen causes Daniel himself when he must desert her. As bearing on the counterplot, Mordecai's scarcely disinterested interpretation anticipates, as we have seen, his own desire for enshrinement in a myth of selfless sacrifice as narrative destination, even as it exposes the bid for power which this entails. Once these opposite readings are factored into its structural logic, this synecdochic parable of reprocessed narrative, the sacred text of Eliot's text so to speak, becomes an abbreviated form of, and a brief for, the interpretive activity. This is, in short, its extrapolative charge—or discharge.

Mordecai's unlikely vagueness over the origin of this story ("Somewhere in the later *Midrash*, I think"), whether reflecting Eliot's uncertainty or for some reason dramatizing his own, does more than occlude the story's textual status and highlight its function in oral culture. For Eliot to locate this tale even tentatively in midrashic lore (especially if she has in fact made up the story, as one may suspect) is to go out of her way to evoke the hermeneutic culture of Judaism at its most concentrated.[8] For the Midrash is a compendium of exegetical interventions, a palimpsest of narrative parables and their deciphered application: an extended textual project for which the closest secular equivalent in British culture might well be literature and its criticism (professional or otherwise), literature at its most *productive*, its least fixed and supposedly least commodified. Either to import into (from ballad or folklore) or to concoct for the preeminent hermeneutic site of Jewish tradition a story so clearly resonant with certain landmarks of just this British literary tradition is part of the cultural dovetailing attempted by Eliot's novel as a whole.

For not only does the Jewish heroine smitten with the gentile king recall the self-sacrificing Rebecca of Scott's *Ivanhoe*, but the story of disguise and martyrdom has a yet more proximate intertext. Eliot may here be taken to have rewritten in reduced and corrective form, and glossed with a debunking commentary by Mirah, none other than Sydney Carton's self-aggrandizing effacement at the close of *A Tale of Two Cities*. She thus calls into question the selflessness of Mordecai in his own later elision of self, even as, by contrast with Carton's fantasy of self-maintenance through domestic storytelling, she imagines a broader manner of diffusing the self into history—and by analogy the text into culture. In this light, too, there is a further way to understand the nature of Eliot's embedded story as a formal interruption as well as a thematic recapitulation. By suspending the main narrative line for the duration of the inset text and the debate it occasions, the so-called Midrash episode does what all such synecdochic episodes in Victorian fiction tend to do, especially when they redouble not only the plot but the potential interplay or tension of response. Remember Miss Marchmont's tale to Lucy Snowe. Interrupting narrative to reframe its terms, such reflexive moments mark the very conversion of plot into lesson, of narrative into wisdom.

In this fashion does Eliot's novel finally conspire to end where it began, off the page and in the mind. Mordecai's death into another's mission would redeem his life in the very terms of his own fictional status in the first place: primarily an idea, an inspiration, a prompting in someone else's mind, first his author's, finally his reader's. Or so Eliot hopes, a hope dramatized by the very structure of the novel under the mandate of interpretation. It is also, as with so many issues in this text, a hope—a fictional program—confirmed by the book's contrapuntal thematics. The ramifications of Mordecai's "sacrifice" are in this sense finally sketched forth by negation in the penultimate chapter of the novel, the last of the Gwendolen plot and the last of many allusions to reading as a touchstone of spiritual capacity. There we are given specific terms for Gwendolen's failure in life, her ignorance (steeped as she has been in ephemeral romance) of all those "great movements of the world" and "larger destinies of mankind" which have "lain aloof in newspapers and other neglected reading" (69:875). This is not only the realm of Mrs. Meyrick's interest in political news along with wedding columns, but the domain—and dominion—of that wider understanding brought to bear on private life by such neglected fictions as, say, Eliot's own novels. The power of such reading for Gwendolen, it is clearly implied, would not have been in its momentary diversion, sensation, aesthetic pleasure, or intellectual challenge. It would have resided rather in its very power to *reside*, to linger in and redirect her mind, to *take*—and so to give back its residual influence long after it is no longer before her "bodily eyes."

Epigraphic Displacements

So too with the unprinted "work" Mordecai leaves behind. He comes to his end—coterminous with the text's own—so that others should not simply be moved by, but moved *to*, motivated more generally than any mere reading could contain. His visionary schemes anticipate, in a strange, short-circuited way, what we might call a phenomenology of reading without the text. In the act of reading, according to Georges Poulet, "I am the subject of thoughts other than my own," impressions that I nevertheless think of—and so think— as my own.[9] There is, as it happens, an explicit Victorian prototype not only for this view but for this particular formulation. It comes to us through the dawning recognition of the transcendental farmhand, Waldo, in Schreiner's *Story of an African Farm*, a view of reading's transfiguring influx couched in a novel that elsewhere invokes lived experience as already a reading of the world's englobing book. When he first discovers the demands and rewards of such higher reading as John Stuart Mill, Waldo's is the "startled joy" (1,11:109) of internalization: "—the thoughts were his, they belonged to him. He had never thought them before, but they were his" (1,11:109). So might Daniel say of Mordecai's beliefs. What Poulet calls the "dispossession" by a phenomeno-logical "second self" (57) that takes over in a reading based on "total commit-ment," a reading with no "mental reservation" (57), is just what Mordecai would seem to want from Daniel, while contriving to make the deputized in-spiration appear to his alter ego as if motivated from within. Along with any reader, but without a text before him, Daniel might therefore find himself fol-lowing Poulet in characterizing the nature of his co-optation by another's word: "I am on loan to another, and this other thinks, feels, suffers and acts within me" (57). Mordecai's "possessive" immortality might thus be rethought as the scene of reading displaced from the site of textuality to that of the sur-viving psyche at large in its life. It is, in fact, Mordecai's decisive veto of his own textual legacy which forces us, by the novel's end, not only to revise but directly to reverse Cynthia Chase's suggestion that "Mordecai and Deronda . . . are en-gaged in a kind of reading, a hermeneutic practice, in which the interpreter and the text (or Mordecai and Deronda) stand in a certain mutual relation."[10] Rather, Daniel is the interpreter of a text (the Mordecai effect) so wholly in-ternalized that it can only be read the way one is said to read one's own mo-tives.

Poulet closes his essay by invoking a "subjectivity without objectivity" (68) which he defines as an "anonymous and abstract consciousness presiding, in its aloofness, over the operations of all more concrete consciousness" (68). By relinquishing any hold on authorship, Mordecai would lay claim to just such a freer mode of presiding over his own aftermath, a genius residual rather than simply constructive: the spirit of an epoch as a potent ghost. The "egotism" of such a program, especially as Eliot's own motives attach to it, has been indirectly deconstructed by Michel Foucault in that influential essay (published in the same year as Poulet's) that we have already discussed in connection with the layered and sliding "author-function" of *The Old Curiosity Shop*. I return now to the underdefined "third ego" in Foucault's "What Is An Author?" to entertain its relevance for a sense of the *ongoingness* of Eliot's delegated agenda. As against the two "I's" that respectively anchor and unfold an authorial discourse, the signator and the conductor, this third "I" seems to situate that discourse beyond itself. Whether we call her Evans or Eliot, the authorial "first ego," the starting point (itself a point of no return) for all representation, having been delegated to the "second" or narrative "ego," appears matched at closure by the "third ego" of projected continuance—which is to say the agency of a continuing project. Apart from the clear case of a persisting scientific (or, we might add, political or religious) enterprise articulating its own "goals," however, it is not at all clear whether, or where, Foucault, who mentions no literary writing in this context, would find such a "third ego" in fiction. But one is licensed to suspect, at least, that something very much like this executive dispensation of writing as discursive field—or its diffused nontextual equivalent— can be glimpsed in process at the culmination of *Daniel Deronda*. It manifests itself there across the channeled energies of what I would want to call again the emergent "reader function"—with all its attendant figurations of dependency and delegation.

To follow Foucault's emphasis on the deictic force of linguistic "shifters," the "third ego" would seem materialized on the book's very last page across that now *three*-way "scission" or rift among the discursive localizations incident to the capping quotation from Milton, "Nothing is *here* for tears," with its locative adverb hovering in ambiguity, never quite ready to alight. When, in other words, the middle (mediating) ego of the narrative voice is annihilated at the moment of closure—vanishing into the gap opened by the very transaction with literary history involved in the canonical quotation—it is then that the energies of narrative intentionality on the one hand and a broader literary, hence cultural, project on the other resolve themselves like vectors into the reader function as force field of motivated reception. "Here" is no longer right there; nor is it back in the past, whether it be the narrated past of Milton's biblical drama or the time of Milton's text itself. By "pointing," in part, beyond plot to the immanence of response—"here" in the textual affect as the reader sees it through—this adversion, loosening its grip on antecedence, opens the way forward.[11] At the same time, if we have in fact properly assessed the structural logic of the earlier midrashic parable—as a parable of interpretation itself, an episode of exegetical extrapolation—then there is a further aptness to the closing quotation as an elitist benchmark of literary transmission. For the standard midrashic commentary involves first the parable, then its exegesis and application, and finally its cited textual model, the sacred verses to which it unfolds as narrative exemplum.[12] In this sense, Milton (even as Old Testament poet of *Samson Agonistes* rather than the Christian bard of *Paradise Lost*) cannot be thought to offer a closing gloss on Eliot's novel. It is the other way around. *Daniel Deronda* becomes one long footnote to Milton, preserving what it subserves by the originality of a new narrative illustration. Understood as a field of action rather than of passive acceptance, the readerly site of this intertextual resonance is, after all, rather far from the idealized and abstracted notion in Poulet of sheer consciousness. In *Daniel Deronda*, subjectivity is always in search of a fit object. Rather than offering a reified image of the literary mind, Eliot's text *puts you in mind*: of all that is left to be done by the work of lettered thought in action.

Just as the four lines from Milton read like an epigraph left hanging to a chapter yet to be written in the book of the world, so too does the tactical placement (and self-displacement) of an earlier chapter epigraph also shed indirect light on Mordecai's closural motives as they illuminate in turn Daniel's realization of them (in both senses). Leading off a chapter detailing Daniel's first visit to Mordecai's "Philosophers" club, the Hebrew scholar Zunz is quoted in German as comparing the power of literary genre to Jewish history, "a National Tragedy lasting for fifteen hundred years, in which the poets and the actors were also the heroes" (42:573). Such heroes are among the "great Transmitters" (42:580), part of a collective memory sustained only by that "fresh-fed interpretation" (42:591) championed by Mordecai. And something of this freshness, this immediacy of dissemination, is captured by the actual mechanics of the epigraphic transition that has led us into this chapter. The very form of this transition is the chapter's content in little. For the epigraph is instantaneously translated from one language into another, from an authorial idiom to the linguistic currency of reception. Moreover, coterminous with this translation, the whole passage is displaced from epigraphic into diegetic status, translated *into* the story from the frame of discourse.

It happens like this. There is one quoted paragraph in German with citation given. It is followed, as the typeface enlarges to indicate the real opening of the chapter, by the same paragraph, in English this time. After this, the narrative voice takes over for the first paragraph of actual plot, which begins by taking up the epigraph as antecedent: "Deronda had lately been reading that passage of Zunz" (42:575). Thus is the realm of reading actualized in the plot— and no more here, just more overtly, than in all the other chapters touched by discursive precursors, informed by epigraphic pre-texts, even when of Eliot's own invention. Yet this effortless permeability of plot to epigraph raises questions that retard rather than facilitate our assimilation of the passage in its transition between tongues. Are we to take the translation from German to English as the Victorian narrative equivalent of a cinematic subtitle? Or was Daniel himself reading Zunz in translation? (Unlikely, since I cannot find record of such a translation in the period.) For whom and by whom, then, is the passage translated? By Eliot for us through the poetic leeway of authorial intervention? Or by Daniel for himself, as he makes the Hebraic scholarship his own by *thinking* it in English? Or both? If both, this epigraphic passage about the literary shape of the Jewish national tragedy replays right before your eyes a certain passage—in the sense of a certain passing—from literary or philosophical writing to internalized response. Such is the greatness of the "great Transmitters" like Zunz that their impact on the memory outlasts the immediate reading of their own texts. And every such remembering, every internalization, is a kind of translation. Finessing the radical linguistic indetermination exposed by all acts of translation, Eliot's sense of deracinated language is redeemed here by the spirit rather than the letter of the text in dissemination.

Interpretation's "Fuller Volume"

To elide his own poor texts altogether in reaching out to, and through, Daniel represents Mordecai's eventual alternative to the "fable of the Roman, that swimming to save his life he held the roll of his writings between his teeth and saved them from the waters" (42:590). This is the same fable we have seen him go on to tell in the chapter begun with the epigraph from Zunz. Though Mordecai, of course, is sustained at death upon an "ocean of peace beneath him," needing no texts to guarantee the continuance of his vision, the novel's motif of drowning persists as the hovering structural binary of this trope. A comparison here with Charlotte Brontë is by no means all contrast. Whereas the hero drowns unconfirmed at the close of *Villette* in order to conscript our participation in the narrator's disavowal of his death, the spiritual mate in *Daniel Deronda* is levitated above the waters of annihilation for a similar hermeneutic purpose, though by way of affirmation in this case rather than denial. The language of his death lends figurative impetus to a voyaging out on the hero's part, an uncharted mission, which is primarily a figure in turn for the reader's own internal transmission of the novel's force as a renovating cultural energy. It is this last that the text suggests when it has Mordecai speak loadedly of a desired "fuller volume" (62:802) of cultural engagement, a notion punning on—while outstripping—the textual limitations of just that multivolume genre of Victorian writing which has paved the way for his posthumous effect.

To apprehend more fully what we might call the metatextual psychology of this gesture, we turn to Maurice Blanchot's essay "Death as Possibility" from *The Space of Literature*, naming, as that larger title does, exactly the spatial field that Eliot is engaged in enlarging. Before its application to literary writing is sketched out, Blanchot develops his own sense of the "epitomizing" death one finds so often in Victorian plotting: "To die well means to die with propriety, in conformity with oneself and with respect for the living. To die well is to die in one's own life, turned toward one's life and away from death."[13] From one perspective, one side of the so-called great divide, this is the death died by Mordecai the friend and brother in the arms of those he loved. But those whom Mordecai loves are the foundation of that other death he would colonize, the beyond he would enter through the doors of annihilation and dispersal. In the novel's climactic orientation of narrative plot to cultural discourse, the textual system insinuates a kind of ratio and proportion which swivels upon without actually specifying the reader's position: Deronda (the character) is to Mordecai what *Deronda* (the novel) is to Eliot, the middle term between origin and posterity, between creative ego and audience, between vision and its publicity, between conception and its dissemination. Deronda is, in a word, Mordecai's *translation*. And if Deronda seems to embody such a posthumous reading of Mordecai in the absence of Mordecai's text, so is *Deronda* a translation of Eliot's thoughts. Finally Daniel, like the novel bearing his name, and no less than Mordecai, exists to pass from intention into effect. At which point the ratio Eliot seems to have developed yields certain unruly ramifications. To the extent that the novel is not conceived as an end in itself, but rather a conduit for Eliot's cultural program, to the extent that *Deronda* is a functional structure, so too is Deronda merely being used.

It is just here that Blanchot's sustained speculation on death in relation to the creative urge serves to elucidate the deadlock of scriptive immortality which Mordecai intuitively hopes to avoid. For Blanchot, "art," or call it textual longevity, "is no longer anything but a memorable way of becoming one with history. Great historical figures, heroes, great men of war no less than artists shelter themselves from death in this way: they enter the memory of peoples; they are examples, active presences" (94). Yet the comfort grows cold: "This form of individualism soon ceases to be satisfying" (94). Sensing as much, Mordecai would generate a wisely passive rather than falsely active presence sent forth into history. Blanchot again: "It soon becomes clear that if what is important is primarily the process which is history—action in the world, the common striving toward truth—it is vain to want to remain oneself above and beyond one's disappearance, vain to desire immutable stability in a work which would dominate time" (94). So would Mordecai insist, desiring instead what one might term the reverse face of textual vicariousness: "to act anonymously and not to be a pure, idle name" (94).

Such is also the consolation, beyond renown, offered up—though somewhat paradoxically—at the close of Eliot's earlier narrative, *Middlemarch* (1872), another of those Victorian novels of the recent past which seek their apotheosis not only in present conditions but also (as more explicitly in *A Tale of Two Cities*) in the present conditioning of response. Famously, neither "a new Theresa" nor "a new Antigone" is deemed possible by Eliot's narrator, since "the medium in which their ancient deeds took shape is for ever gone" ("Finale," 577)—"medium" as the very ether of history, yes, but also as the transmissive genres of Christian hagiography and classic drama respectively. From the general run of selfless sufferers and workaday idealists on the contemporary scene, performing "unhistoric acts" in a "hidden life" that leads to an "unvisited" grave (578), Eliot's subsequent designation of her own heroine, amid these "many Dorotheas," as "the Dorothea whose story we know" (578) tilts the restrictive adjectival phrase toward the emphasis of a tacit comma that would not only single her out but set her off. That she is the one whose story we do know is exactly what elevates her—by way of compensation (the unsung finally enshrined) rather than mere synecdochic exemplum (the one for the many)—and this solely by virtue of prose fiction as our new modern genre, our new "medium," for publicized and exemplary self-sacrifice. How else can one read this trumpeted glorying in the power of anonymity? Similarly, the assertion that "things are not so ill with you and me as they might have been" (578), had others like Dorothea not actually lived, operates so that the pronoun "you" (indicating those whose possibilities have been enhanced over time) works to interpolate the novel's readership in its role not only as citizenry but as lettered subjects. Your gradual betterment can thus at least be analogized by, without being narrowed to, your improving encounter with *Middlemarch* itself, both fictional place and fictive book.

Thus in Eliot's most famous novel does a minor and passing interpolation (the apostrophized "you" of the enlisted reading audience standing in for the general public) anchor a parable of the whole plotted text as cultural vector and humanist increment in its own literary right. With its even more strategic interpolations ("Imagine the conflict in a mind like Deronda's"), as well as its tightly circumscribed scene of extrapolated hermeneutic resonance in the midrashic episode, *Daniel Deronda* later reaches for something yet more definitive in this same vein. Developing, as in *Middlemarch*, a view of incremental melioration as part of the narrational as well as the social contract, *Daniel Deronda* takes the latent suggestion of textual power, makes it explicit, renders it parabolic in Mordecai's visionary labors, and then, even as textual transmission is growing firmly entrenched as one figuration for the "medium" of cultural history, rejects it in favor of the more unbound energy of sheer inspiration, orally mediated and dispensed. Mordecai chooses in this way the "incalculably diffusive" (*Middlemarch*, 578) effects of spiritual sympathy instead of textual impress, eschewing in the face of Daniel's offer those "means of publication" which "are within reach" (40:557). Daniel's clinching idiom, after all, has missed the point: "If you rely on me, I can assure you of all that is necessary to that end" (40:557). Mordecai, instead, seeks that reliance on Daniel which will assure that his unpublished thoughts need not be an "end" in themselves.

"Call nothing mine that I have written, Daniel," Mordecai ultimately urges, even "though our Masters delivered rightly that everything should be quoted in the name of him that said it" (63:820). The parodic counterpoint to this idea has found its way much earlier into the mouth of Daniel's rather vapid foster parent, Sir Hugo, insisting as he does that "much quotation of any sort, even in English, is bad. It tends to choke ordinary remark" (16:217). Worse than that, quotation inscribes the subject's own belatedness: "One couldn't carry on life comfortably," adds Sir Hugo, "without a little blindness to the fact that everything has been said better than we can put it ourselves" (16:217). Comfort is not later the issue for Deronda, but "carrying on" certainly is. Mordecai wants to be incorporated rather than quoted, taken up rather than taken down, absorbed rather than deferred to. In this sense his willing, even willful, death escapes all the empty self-assertion, on Blanchot's account, by which artistic vanity, seeking a falsely embodied immortality, "takes a book for the work" (106). Giving up the dream of the book, then, Mordecai would vanish into Daniel's labor of spiritual translation, his "work": a social productivity (the reader's supplemental "field of action" from *Hard Times*) to be accomplished only when Zion is in turn transliterated back into the textual circuit of Eliot's English audience as a figure for the utopic space of responsive reaction, its real-world geography abstracted into the mere horizons of cultural expectation. This is the hermeneutic zone of reception defined (again) by that "fresh-fed interpretation" (42:591) through which all cultural work may be found to outlast the literary instance that has prompted and sponsored it, and where alone its purposes can be carried on if never out.

There is no denying, though, that the abrupt, splayed closure of *Daniel Deronda* can easily be taken for a symptom (of internal and irreconcilable contradictions) rather than an asymptote (of extrinsic destination never wholly fulfilled). The most unflinching rejection of Eliot's novel has come from the Marxist perspective of Franco Moretti, who reads the "terrible" failure of the book as the last gasp of that already depleted genre, the European Bildungsroman.[14] The tension in Eliot's work, for Moretti, between private and public identity, between self-culture and vocation, has become by the time of *Daniel Deronda* an irreparable schism. Daniel need not grow into his role, Moretti argues, nor even go looking for it; it descends on him ex machina, the whole romantic dramaturgy of youth leveled in the process.[15] Against Moretti's charge of generic obsolescence, however, it is one last implication of the present chapter that Eliot, still with the psychological trajectories of this format of maturation in mind, is attempting to resolve novel and romance together into a third narrative genre: a prophetic epic. But this is not first and foremost an epic of Jewish tribal consolidation. The text is instead seen prospectively mounting, by setting its stage, primarily the epic of its own readership, the founding of a newly empowered tribe of moral activists and cultural interpreters.

There remains, too, a way other than Moretti's to historicize the crisis of the Bildungsroman as cultural form in its relation to Eliot's plot—and to the role of reading which subtends it in parable. The motives of textual encasement distinguished at the end of chapter 9, legacy versus exorcism, apply here in revised shape. Mordecai casting his lot entirely with the former, insisting that his vision should be kept viable without the framing containment of subsidiary texts by or about him, is advanced as an act of conferred legacy instead of (deliberately in lieu of) quarantine ghostliness: a bearing (in mind) of the dead. As such, however, and in terms adopted from Esther Schor's study of Britain's emergent politics of sentimentality, Mordecai's intent unsettles the Victorian culture of mourning.[16] Derived from the Enlightenment, this is the humanist tradition by which the polis is seen built upon the necropolis of its own remembered forebears—as a virtual definition of modern national culture, including its ongoing vocations. Mordecai's plan disturbs this logic by shifting the accepted burden of the past away from the whole Anglo-Saxon cultural tradition. What Schor finds in Wordsworth as anticipating the structure of Victorian fictional psychology thus comes to curious fruition in Mordecai's mortuary dictates. In a fraught dialectic of competing models, Wordsworthian retrospection plays between a genuine historical imagination leagued with the sympathetic preservation of the dead, which Schor terms the "elegiac genealogy of morals" (149), and a more internalized history of a single maturing consciousness vitally in touch with its own losses in an "organic genealogy of morals" (149). If the latter closely resembles the psychic evolution of the subject in the Victorian Bildungsroman, then Daniel's attempt to reanimate this novelistic paradigm, but to do so under the hovering influence of Mordecai's inherited political vision, returns the generically prescribed organicism of the hero's development to an elegiac genealogy after all. If not reading, then its spiritual approximation (or afterglow) in imbibed wisdom is the means by which subjectivity in *Daniel Deronda* is ghostwritten by the past and its persisting affiliations.

And not only the hero's subjectivity but your own. Between Gwendolen's disaster and Daniel's triumph, between her unequipped life and his missionary fervor, between her falling short and his forging on, lies (open) all that reading that she has not—but he has, and you in part will have—accomplished when you move on from this book to yet another Victorian text. The model of evolving mentality in the "novel of development" has become less an effectual literary form than a form of literary affect. Austenian social norms, synchronized in her novels to narrative operation, have devolved in Eliot to the recuperative work of fiction alone. Openness, promise, potentiality—these now characterize not a hero's turf so much as the space of reading, where Zion is mostly a sign, as we have seen, for the mission that would instill in Eliot's native English audience an indwelling spirit of enlightened critique.[17] Out of the very dead end of a genre, Eliot's text ends up essaying (as Judith Wilt has claimed on a different count for Meredith) the Bildungsroman of its own ideal reader, imagined en masse: the reader as social subject.[18] By such a concerted mystification of its own status, this novel thereby moves to exceed inscription, to be remembered less for citations than as incitation.

In *A Tale of Two Cities*, the flight from writing, as a conservative defense against an epidemic of fatal revolutionary inscription, yields to bourgeois domestic orality as a supposed antidote. Mordecai's flight from writing as an escape from an equally fatal entombment ("I desire the body that I gave my thought to pass away as this fleshly body will pass") yields to the textual aftermath of freshening interpretation even in the wake of any sponsoring single text still under scrutiny. Both these withdrawals from writing are thematized within novelistic inscriptions that displace onto omniscience, in order to correct, the feared narrowness of private inscription in favor of a broader cultural or familial transmission. This is another way of emphasizing that *Daniel*

Deronda is meant to be a novel never over until we are through with it, until we have finished thinking it through. At loose ends itself at closure, the text has its readers just where it needs them. The Victorian novel becomes here the acknowledged *pars pro toto* of itself as social institution. It goes public in you. What other major fictions of the period ask of you but call giving, what other stories offer up to the process of reception, this story moves to process while your response is still only in the offing. Reading becomes (more obviously than ever) con/scriptive. Pushing to the limit a tendency of certain Victorian novels, straining to override its very textuality in the foreshadowing of its effects, the final reflex action of *Daniel Deronda* thus attempts nothing less than the writing of its own reading. It becomes in the process a compendium of Victorian narrative poetics. From the imperatives of interpolation to the parables of extrapolation, the novel requisitions all its genre's rhetorical resources in order to throw us back on our own. It does so in part to allay its own generic impatience over any contemporary author's inevitably belated relation both with the book of the world and with its long heritage of novelistic retranscriptions. With writing collapsed increasingly into mere cultural rereading, Eliot seeks instead a fictional form that will actually *do* something. She labors, in short, to produce a *work*.

There is, too, an important generic and literary-historical measure of the communitarian dream in Eliot's attempted outdistancing of Victorian social divisions and their psychic rifts. This measure may best be taken by a comparison of Eliot to Dickens which goes beyond the Midrash debate's allusive parody of closural motive in *A Tale of Two Cities*. The severe and irreversible, the severing isolation that the psyche constitutes in Dickens, that the social contract camouflages by ideology (the myth of the *private* citizen), and that reading appeases—this becomes in George Eliot an intolerable, often merely provincial, separateness that a visionary sense of community cannot abide, that an eroticized empathy is therefore devised to overcome, and that reading—textual mediation itself—is elided so as better to bridge. In the last analysis Eliot's final novel, at its most eerily original (hardly its most mastered), Eliot's novel in its closural movement, is not so much the transmission of an ideology (British hero stretching his imperial imagination) but rather a glimpse into the mechanics of ideological transmission itself, where each (always late-coming) inheritor of a culture (here Judaism) signs on to the received discourse of the other as naturally one's own; where, in other words, every initiate like Daniel defers—in ideological transference (Žižek)—to those Mordecai figures always "supposed to know." Recognizing this underlying cultural dynamic may serve to inflect, if not lay to rest, certain recent critiques of (1) Eliot's colonialist blind spot in celebrating her hero's closural reach eastward, (2) the unrepentant nationalism behind her cosmopolitan sympathies, and (3) the stereotypes inherent even in her anti-Orientalism.[19]

What Eliot was up against in yielding up her truncated *story* to the closural balancing act of her *text* in reception can be gauged by a comment of George Gissing's two decades later. At that point Gissing was in a position to look back over a century of aesthetic intransigence and interpretive passivity among those lowbrow readers against whom he had leveled some of his most cynical denunciations. Writes Gissing (with an elliptical passive grammar) in *Charles Dickens: A Critical Study* (1898): "Nothing so abhorred by the multitude as a lack of finality in stories, a vagueness of conclusion which gives them the trouble of forming surmises."[20] Gissing's ironic response to this abhorrence in *New Grub Street* awaits us in the next chapter: his wholly unambiguous closing in upon the double deaths of two novel makers. But it must be remembered that Eliot's parable of consumption and residual "surmise" in *Daniel Deronda* is scarcely less funerary. We are meant to overstep closure the way Daniel is meant to enter upon Mordecai's death as his own renewal. Even when over, a novel like *Daniel Deronda* prides itself on not leaving you alone. Exorcism is the last thing called for. For texts and heroes alike, "haunting" is Eliot's idea of the highest praise.

Where—just where—Sydney Carton sees his life turned at death into a Dickensian family melodrama (as if to preserve his opacity, his carefully guarded superficiality, as character), with the present reader serving as once and future placeholder for the hearthside family audience, and where—just where, in the inescapable but never quite occupied place of reading—Lucy Snowe vests her audience with the double logic of desire and denial which constitutes her own subjectivity, there, too, Mordecai's relation to the reader, through the latter's surrogate in Daniel, is equally a structuring as well as a structure of desire. Turning himself inside out at death—the opposite of Carton's dream—Mordecai gives over his own (albeit impersonal) mentality to delegation. In all three cases—in perhaps the three most histrionically "unfinished" endings in Victorian fiction—closure involves a play for power which outplays narrated life itself (or in Lucy's autobiographical case, life's narrative momentum). In Eliot's last novel, the extremity of the gesture looks forward (as well as back) across a literary history in which the symbiosis typified by the relation of Daniel to Mordecai, of reader to text—a relation all the more *dramatic* when no portrayed text appears, but instead a parable of its own effect—configures an intersubjectivity that will hardly grow to seem any less ghoulish, any less gothic, as the century proceeds.

Chapter Twelve

Grubbing for Readers at the *Fin de Siècle*

Gertrude Hammond, *The Yellow Book,* in
The Yellow Book, volume 6, July 1895

𝓘n promulgating the gospel of hack writing as an income strategy, Gissing's loathsome antihero in *New Grub Street,* Jasper Milvain, blandly grants that "if you can be a George Eliot, begin at the earliest opportunity. I merely suggested what seemed practicable" (1:43). This is the late-century literary businessman speaking, and he knows his market. The high-literary mission of Eliot's realism has by this point fallen on hard times, its particular skid row called Grub Street. And facile reading is at fault, too much of the passive and ephemeral: everything, at a different level, which Mordecai, fearing it so openly, had hoped to avoid by not becoming *merely readable*. It might be said that Eliot in *Daniel Deronda* attempted to plot a way out of this potential literary impasse of degenerated consumption by a socioaesthetic vision whose feasibility she did not quite live to see vanish. But vanish it did: evaporating as the dream of a collectivist high culture submitted to the various "dissipations" of the late Victorian mass appetite, characterized by a growing public for pulp. George Meredith's agenda, explicit early and tacitly reiterated throughout his career, was no bellwether either. If the audience "was to come" which would appreciate the scrupulous discriminations of literary nuance in his diagnosis of the age, it was not to be found among those regularly awaiting the easily devoured fatuity of the grubbers and hacks, who were claiming a larger and more ingrained share of the literary marketplace as Meredith wrote on into the nineties.

"Writing against Writing"

Gissing, too, needed an audience, winning a large one with *New Grub Street* (1891) through a complex narrative gamble that relies in part on a by now familiar (but here uniquely unstable) interplay of direct address with inserted scenes of (or allusions to) literary encounter. Pointed up by these means, the gamble of *New Grub Street*—its emotive balancing act—derives from the book's pervasive irony: the manifest readability both of dedicated literary lives sacrificed to the unreadable and also of the despicably slick careers of popularizers on the make.

Gissing's literary ambience is closely reminiscent of the London periodical circuit represented by Henry Knight in Hardy's *A Pair of Blue Eyes* (1873), one of the earliest novels to diagnose the epidemic of essayistic professionalism. Indeed, Hardy's syntactical irony in having a character explain about Knight that "he writes for *The Present*" (7:113) seems taken up directly by Gissing in such a self-conscious question as Jasper Milvain's "Have you seen the current *Current?*" (6:104). Lampooning a feverish topicality that is symptomatic of what the old-fashioned editor, Yule, sees as the mere "multiplication of ephemerides," a "demand for essays, descriptive articles, fragments of criticism, out of all proportion to the supply of even tolerable work" (3:67–68), such joking verbal formulations as Hardy's and Gissing's score against exactly the expendable writing for hire on which Milvain prides himself: "My writing is for to-day, most distinctly hodiernal" (28:422). In its own topical satire, *New Grub Street* is a novel by no means blind to its lurking ethical contradiction: the sellouts of the literary marketplace critiqued for profit. Indeed, the novel isolates and trivializes this very position in the light banter of Milvain, minion of the new mass audience, who announces the "capital idea" (financial pun no doubt intended) that he "might make a good thing of writing against writing. It should be my literary specialty to rail against literature" (2:55). The lucrative result would be that the "reading public should pay me for telling them that they oughtn't to read" (2:55). It cannot evade notice that Gissing himself gets away with something not a little like this in his remorseless diagnosis of the literary profession's mercantile debasement. Yet through all the sociological acuity and autobiographical rancor, what Gissing's novel is "telling" the "reading public" is of course to read on in at least this one novel, in sympathy with its brutally disappointed novelist hero.

To foster, and at times to force, such sympathy, Gissing resorts to a mode of direct address far from the normative models of the high Victorian period. Closer, for instance, to Thackeray's eccentric metaleptic shifts from plot to extranarrative context are the reader asides that implicate Gissing's audience in the trivial rumor mills of the literary subculture. Of the decline of the Yule newspaper venture: "Well, you probably read all about it" (7:126). Or "Turn to his name in the Museum Catalogue; the lists of works appended to it will amuse you" (7:126–27). Sometimes direct address of this sort is reduced beneath even mock intimacy to the formulaic "see" of a parenthetical imperative citation, as in the description of Milvain's obituary notice on the hero's fiction: "an excellent piece of writing (see *The Wayside*, June 1884)." There is a moment, though, in which the quasi-editorial grammar of command, usually marginalized and impersonal, is turned to a more aggressive address—indeed to an ascription of unfeeling response in second person reminiscent of Mr. Jones at his club in *Vanity Fair*. What Gissing's passage does is to revive the dead metaphor in the expressed desire, on the part of another subliterary denizen, for a tabloid journalism that would *"address itself* to the quarter-educated" (33:496; emphasis added). Though conceived from the opposite end of the social and intellectual spectrum, Gissing's ironic set piece effects its own "address" in precisely the explicit way that cheapjack journalism, in its tawdry transparencies of report, would rigorously avoid. For Gissing shows no hesitation in shattering the invisible pane of omniscience to put epithets into your mouth: "The chances are that you have neither understanding nor sympathy for men such as Edwin Reardon and Harold Biffen," Gissing's fellow suffering heroes. "They merely provoke you. They seem to you inert, flabby, weakly envious, foolishly obstinate, impiously mutinous, and many other things. You are made angrily contemptuous by their failure to get on . . . "(31:462).

Given such a provocation to response from the author who once remarked that "[i]t is better to make no kind of reference to the Reader, I think," the passage is all the more obviously satiric.[1] This accusatory aside in *New Grub Street* is couched statistically ("The chances are . . . ") to stress the fact that an indeterminate majority of the reading public, who may have happened to get this far in Gissing's novel, could still share essentially the same mental disposition as those potential readers who would have shunned the productions of Reardon's or Biffen's own pen, just as they can now be predicted to feel nothing but indifference, if not repugnance, over the fatal plight of these characters. Yet it is just as likely—even without the goading reverse psychology of Gissing's rhetorical ploy—that these present readers are eager to read his story through. For there is a perverse fascination attached to the travail and decline of his heroes in their "shrinking from" that "conscious insincerity of workmanship" (3:83) that panders to "vulgar readers" (3:85). It is exactly your own attitude as reader, then, implicitly interrogated in such a passing adjective, which is later overtly skewered by that extended second-person address as a failure of sympathy—unless, that is, you have escaped the probabilities of the mob in order to read on in an attention bred of empathy. In Gissing, therefore, reading as a mode of social energy is beyond debate but scarcely above suspicion. Hence the novel's embedded briefs against the kind of writing it works to quarantine, if by no other means than by refusing to quote it. Journalism is mulled over in virtually every third scene of *New Grub Street*, yet until the "killing" reviews of Biffen's book (35:522), we hear not a word of it. This follows a kind of extrapolative logic in its own right: In its very topicality, such writing goes, as it were, without saying, each reader of the time knowing the gist of it with tedious familiarity. Yet the social effects of such journalism come in for considerable expository (indeed, virtually journalistic) analysis.

According to Fredric Jameson, the dependence of Gissing's novels on a "naturalist paradigm" of compartmentalized topoi—"a kind of specialized division of official 'subjects,' such as feminism or free-lance journalism"—is "ultimately merely a ruse," since "the two great subjects of marriage and literary production" are in Gissing "profoundly interconnected."[2] More than this (though Jameson himself brings no textual evidence to bear from *New Grub Street*), the "woman question" and the literary marketplace are linked in Gissing's greatest novel by a bond so inextricable as to be causal. For these governing subjects mark off two phases in the same circuit of production and consumption, as follows. In a complementary pattern to the literary-historical complot traced by Gilbert and Gubar (the concerted closing of male-modernist ranks against female scribbling at the turn of the century), Gissing explicitly suggests that literary culture is being diluted by the entrance of women into the marketplace of readers rather than writers.[3] It is not just that published writing has disseminated the stereotype of the New Woman but rather that it has helped produce the type in the first place: through, but not just in, discourse. According to Gissing's editorializing commentary, too much "specialized" reading has sprung the New Woman from the great mass of half-educated domestic functionaries; as we are told in an excursus on the subject of Reardon's estranged wife, Amy: "She read a good deal of that kind of literature which may be defined as specialism popularized," the sort of thing that attracted her to "the solid periodicals" (26:397). By a circular irony, hers is one reaction to that same increasing subdivision among spheres of interest from which the naturalist narrative program itself derives. In sum: "She was becoming a typical woman of the new time, the woman who has developed concurrently with journalistic enterprise" (26:397–98). In the self-adjusted focus of the phrasing within a prevailing past-tense grammar, the shift from the past progressive to the present perfect tense (instead of the more grammatically continuous pluperfect, "had developed") confirms this "new time" as the unfolding present. In a closed circle of precipitated social construction, the woman in question is not just scripted within journalism as topic(al) but conscripted by such publication into her own mold-breaking social mold.

Transfer the terms of this critique from journalistic to novelistic addiction and you have a cartoonish spoof of the New Woman blindly parading through a life of indulgent privilege with her nose buried in the latest improving novel of the genre, her very reading supported from below (in class terms) by the lucrative fruits of patriarchal hegemony and empire. Just such a cartoon appeared in the *London Sketch* of 1896, under the double-edged title "The Pursuit of Knowledge" (fig. 10), where a top-hatted black servant, marching behind the satirized bourgeois lady, holds for her a stack of New Woman novels, featuring in fact two of the prominent "Hill Top" series.

To return to Gissing is scarcely to depart very far from the thrust, if not the lightly dismissive tone, of this visual satire. At the very center of the hero's marital crisis in *New Grub Street* is a literary as well as temperamental difference which, in almost allegorical terms, leads to the recriminatory *estrangement*— the always threatened divorce—of genuine art from the new popular culture. "Anything that savoured of newness and boldness in philosophic thought had a charm for her palate" (26:397), we read of Amy in that same passage—with a double emphasis ("savoured," "palate") on a gustation and consumption which recalls the frequent ironies of dyspepsia, biliousness, and indigestion associated with literary work in *New Grub Street*. The emphasis runs from Biffen's reductio ad absurdum of this motif in his promise "to eat my duplicate of the proofs" (27:407) if and when his novel, *Mr. Bailey, Grocer*, is ever sold (a novel

Figure 10. "The Pursuit of Knowledge," from the *London Sketch* (1896).
The Bettmann Archive

whose very subject is the trade in comestibles), on to the allegorical playing out of the figurative pattern in Reardon's role as the literary aspirant starving for fame. In his wasting, consumptive decline at the end, Reardon appears "written . . . out" (16:240), "cadaverous" (32:490), bled dry by the triple-decker format figured earlier, in a self-consciously gothic metaphor, as a "monster . . . sucking the blood of the English novelist" (15:235).

Yet some readers somewhere, at least you, must be permitted to keep a cleansing distance from all the insatiability associated with literary consumption. A responsible reading of *New Grub Street* cannot proceed on any such foot-

ing, either as a greedy feeding off the labors of the other or as the passive constitution through such labor (as in Amy's case) of a conscribed social role. The
brainwashing power of literary production, as well as its pandering to various
low appetites and unschooled tastes, must be transcended by some sort of aesthetic effect. Both delectation and social engineering must be elevated to interpretive discrimination. Precisely to insist on this, while apparently acting otherwise, Gissing's textual rhetoric indulges in those brazen assays of knowing
address we have considered above, by which "you," even as pandered to, are
forced to disavow the ethical and class affiliations imputed to you by the text.
Whoever the comprehending reader of *New Grub Street* may be, it cannot be
this blatantly interpolated obtuse snob: this rank travesty of a middle-class subject enshrined by an ideological interpellation gone overt. In concluding his
chapter on Gissing, Jameson finds the novelist's mature fiction "generating an
omnipresent class consciousness in which it is intolerable for the bourgeois
reader to dwell for any length of time" (205). The scandal of that socially scan-
dalized "you" in the apostrophic passage quoted earlier may be taken not only
as the badge of intolerance, then, but as the wound of this intolerable dwelling,
leaving its mark as rhetorical scar. In so saying, however, one faces another fact
about Gissing's novel in its blistering social critique, a fact that recalls the displacement of cultural crisis in *Daniel Deronda* onto literary-hermeneutic mission: the fact that (in ways highlighted toward the close by the elegiac ascendancy of the British literary canon itself) the entire numbing socioeconomic
caste system detailed by Gissing's plot, and denied the energy even of class consciousness, is ultimately translated, in rhetorical effect, onto a pitched battle between, as the unsaid but latent cliché would have it, different *classes of readers*.

Through all this, the novel's abiding irony remains: Reardon's own defeated
story of battered idealism and unmarketable talent, if only he could put *that*
on paper, would—and will (in Gissing's hands)—sell quite nicely. And so this
self-referential structure, this portrait of the artist as a doomed young man, in-
curs an immediate reflexivity (more on this distinction in the "terminological
reprise" at the close of this chapter). Your immanent reading act, in other
words, serves to complete the fate of Gissing's autobiographical surrogate and
aesthetic scapegoat. The public taste—so goes Gissing's self-serving inference—
is every reader's obligation. In general, Victorian reading habits only contribute
to that assembly line of salable pages about which Milvain—the personified
vain engine of literary productivity, that paper mill of a character—so shame-
lessly boasts. This will continue to happen unless such public demand can meet
a novelist like Gissing halfway, bringing imaginative sympathy to bear on a psychological study of workaday frustrations and defeats to which the author has

gone out of his way to lend the histrionic cast of fateful incident, jolting reversal, and piercing dramatic irony.

The place of the reader, your conscribed emplacement, is fully realized, however, only in relation to the polarized alternatives of literary production offered by the book's two main novelist figures. Harold Biffen, by contrast to Reardon as "psychological realist" (10:174), has a more stringent mission as a writer: to splice and thereby discipline the competing literary heritages of Dickens and Zola into an "absolute realism in the sphere of the ignobly decent" (10:173). His is a narrative practice purged of "dramatic scene" in order to free it from "conventionalism." In his view, "[f]iction hasn't yet outgrown the influence of the stage on which it originated. Whatever a man writes *for effect* is wrong or bad" (10:175). Warned by Reardon that nothing of this new sort will sell, for it ignores the reader's interests too exclusively, still Biffen persists, surviving Reardon's death only, upon reading the first and mostly indifferent reviews of his "grovelling realism" (35:522), to take his own life. These unmistakably linked deaths are bound up in ways that recall and qualify not only Biffen's attempted transcendence of the realist novel's origin in drama but the specific issue of catharsis, its reading *effect*.

Beaten down and used up, Reardon on his deathbed looks toward Biffen with a last smile: "How often you and I have quoted it!—'we are such stuff as dreams are made on, and our—'" (32:490). The "remaining words were indistinguishable," and Reardon collapses "as if the effort of utterance had exhausted him": an epitome of his lifelong devotion to literary enunciation. He dies shortly after and, as it were, offstage. Even unfinished, however, Reardon's last literary "utterance" is one that most all readers would join Biffen in recognizing, silently completing it for the dying man. This is the case at least with that stratum of readers to which a novel like *New Grub Street* makes its appeal, a readership all but involuntarily recruited to inscribe here the missing material of a literary ellipsis. When Biffen later seeks a secluded country spot in which to take his own life with poison, the "memory of his friend Reardon was strongly present with him" (35:529): the presence of an absence into which he too vanishes. The last you hear of Biffen, as the chapter cuts away from his suicide, comes in an apt grammatical solecism of referent: "Recalling Reardon's voice, it brought to him those last words whispered by his dying companion" (35:529). The dangling participle syntactically anticipates a living subject ("he") that instead gets merged ambiguously with the "it" of the friend's vanished voice; even grammatically, the suffering subject is already receding from the verbal contours of the scene. The chapter then closes by yielding up the full quotation from *The Tempest*, with that "little life" kept from mention in Reardon's arrested last gasp now rounding the corner of the enjambment at "our little life / Is rounded with a sleep" (35:529).

You as reader are thereby triangulated between these two deaths in your counted-upon recognition of the allusive lines and their fabled author—indeed, of their source in that monument of self-referentiality, the preeminent English writer's openly staged valediction to his craft. Earlier suspected of indifference, you the reader have thus been conscripted by the sheer force of intertextuality into an indirect participation in the paired death scenes. Rather than asserting "writing against writing" after all, it would seem, the novel's literary credentials—and their appeal to a common cultural heritage—are meant to sanctify the parallel demise of the two writer figures: those two textual *figures* for the death of serious writing. It is their calling, then, rather than their lives, which you are to assume redeemed by your own part, properly played, in Gissing's metadrama of cathartic effect through reading. The novel thus comes to climax in an attempted rescue of literary aura—of the tradition Reardon (it is time to decrypt his name) was reared on but never nurtured by—from this character's actual death and its supplemental doubling. As in *Daniel Deronda*, the private psychology of the Victorian literary death scene, in its distilled replay of elapsed life, is thus displaced, here twice over, onto the rehearsal of a literary heritage to which two lives are together offered up. By contrast with *Deronda*, however, the nostalgic retrogression of Gissing's closure exposes devotion to the dead past as a repudiation of the future. It thus secures its deference to the canon against any potentially radical class consciousness operating in and behind the doomed efforts at various "realisms" being valorized by their very defeat. The animus of the novel is not, therefore, an impetus for change. Reardon and Biffen simply return to the womb of their acculturation, their individuating ambitions stillborn.

There is not a shadow of the gothic or fantastic falling over the driven realism of Gissing's plot, not even a hint of telepathy—just gloomy fellow feeling—in the nonetheless eerie doubling of the death scene. Yet how can one deny the vaguely preternatural, almost ghoulish quality associated with the intercession of Shakespeare in these paired deaths? For the Bard's most famous literary epigram on the subject of human mortality, ousting any present invention on the part of either modern writer in Gissing's plot, swallows up those writers' own powers of formulation—the immediacy of their deaths with it—into a lineage to which they come too late. Unlike the epic reanimation of Milton by Eliot, the Shakespearean epigram put in play between the dying protagonists of *New Grub Street* produces a bracketed reading act that relates the very activity of reading to the posthumous authority of the fetishized literary masterwork—but with no hint of Eliot's renewed epic energy. We recall again the conflationary terms from Slavoj Žižek by which psychoanalytic transference can be linked conceptually to the interpellative force of an ideological apparatus. The instanciation of the aphoristic Shakespeare as the one-supposed-to-know marks a hailing of the reading subject into the now sepulchral culture of the canon—even (in Gissing) from amidst the socioeconomic critique of its degeneration.[4]

In such a literary-historical light, we may bring this transitional discussion to rest by anticipating the next chapter's investigation of a comparable episode of readerly conscription from the same year as *New Grub Street*. Where Gissing contrives to imply his fiction's need for a reader different from the satirized mob of subliterary taste, Wilde's *Picture of Dorian Gray* (1891) reflexively exposes, even while insuring, the rhetorical vulnerability—bred of literary receptiveness itself—of his own cultivated audience. In Gissing, canonical literary history is, after all, the cultural bond retrieved from attrition (in readers as in characters) just in time to figure for us—and emotionally to measure—the sacrificial surrender of Gissing's failed literati. In Wilde, the more transgressive literary tradition of the decadent avant-garde is revised to incorporate, rather than merely invite, the reader's engrossed response—but wholly in view of the liabilities of such response. To sustain and continually reframe this view is the work of abyssal structure in Wilde's verbal portrait of the manifest power of verbal art. For Wilde's is a *Picture*, we will find, not only of Dorian, slowly growing gray on canvas, but of that manner of verbal sensitivity which, loosely coincident with your own reading, is found to precipitate the entire plot of the transmogrified portrait. The literate empathy valorized in Gissing becomes the high liability of sensitivity itself in Wilde. The difference, ultimately, is between valences of extrapolation. We might put the difference, before pursuing it in the concluding chapter, this way: Gissing's realism meliorates his irony by the conscripting of a compensatory literary response; Wilde's aesthetic fabulation assimilates all response to the scope of his irony.

This is how the funereal morbidity of *New Grub Street* keeps literary-historical company with the demonic metaphysics of textual response typified in Wilde's gothic parable: a natural supernaturalism of literary reception itself. In several major novels roughly contemporary with *New Grub Street*, where an overarching canonical nostalgia vanishes into the underlying deviance of textual encounter itself, reading emerges—emerges as if from within the text—as the uncanny territorializing of other places, times, and minds, voyeuristic, titillating, potentially subject disintegrating, even cannibalistic, but at least not merely palatably routine and instantly digestible. In this last regard, such fictions might have announced—along with Percy Shelley's preface to *Franken-stein* in an earlier gothic revival—that their narratives, like extreme versions of the intervening "sensation" novel, were at least avoiding the "enervating effects" of the current literary scene, including now the increasing late-century flood of hack literary journalism. What makes this avoidance structurally definitive in these *fin de siècle* texts is what the next chapter is scheduled to assess: the parables of unnerved rather than enervated response executed in process by what amounts to a new gothic metagenre.

Terminological Reprise

Gissing's *New Grub Street* strains to almost irreconcilable extremes the reigning methodological checkpoints of the present study: interpolation and extrapolation, apostrophe and reflexive scene. Breaking with his usual rule of reticence ("It is better to make no kind of reference to the Reader, I think"), Gissing obtrudes certain deflationary allusions to second-person attention—apostrophes so compromising that they all but shut down the narrative system. Interpolation, ordinarily removed from anything like naturalist technique by the sterilizing stringency of a pervasive rhetorical tact, erupts here ("you have neither understanding nor sympathy") as a class-exacerbated lesion that threatens to infect the carefully programmed reflex action of the narrative as a whole, its corrective extrapolation from the text's negative exempla of impercipient receipt. Overcoming its own accusatory tone, this is an extrapolation that leads the reader from branded callousness to the tutored and sympathetic reading of the novel in progress.

With such a managed rhetorical crisis in mind, we can now leave this interchapter with a reckoning look back. From at least the end of the third chapter on, where the issue became explicit, this book has been concerned with sustaining a distinction in order to draw (out) a comparison. The comparison is between reader interpolation and reader extrapolation as—each equally—textual, ultimately figural, devices. The distinction is between both these outward orientations and the inward turn of certain more strictly self-referential textual events. Comparison has been maintained, to pick up a new example, between a scene like Jane Eyre reading Bewick's *History of British Birds* (all but inaugurating our own reading of the novel)—together with a later scene like Rochester "reading" Jane's physiognomy, each of them hermeneutic parables—and the climactic address of "Reader, I married him," which even more explicitly inscribes the reader. Our continuing distinction (both hewed to and honed further by these chapters) has been between the former reading scenes rather than reader apostrophes—sites of extrapolation rather than interpolation, as loci for the reflexive action of rehearsed reception—and, by contrast, the tendency elsewhere and in other texts (mostly unpursued here as such) toward self-referential declaration apart from marked response.

As must by now be obvious, however, the grounds for neither the ongoing comparison nor the attached distinction remain entirely stable. Scenes either of Jane's reading or of her being read serve to rewrite by narrative analogue the activity of the novel's own reader, elsewhere named; and, whenever so named, whether addressed or mentioned, such an openly enlisted reader has in turn been made a narrative (rather than just rhetorical) function if not a narrative agent. Similarly, the distinction between textual moments of and about writing and narrative incidents of encoded novel reading operates mostly to delimit the inextricable. For how can the difference between a text recognizing its own textuality, on the one hand, and, on the other, a text recognizing its stance (precisely as text) toward an audience be anything but the difference between sides of a coin?

Indeed, we are now prepared to say that, over against the episode extrapolated from story to the scene of novelistic reception—over against, that is, the quintessential reflexive event—stands something we might fairly designate (but still within the same conscriptive system) as the zero degree of self-reference. Such reference would consist in none other than the explicit acknowledgment of textual transmission and linguistic processing (rather than oral delivery or mind reading, for example) made manifest by the interpolative gesture of "dear reader" or its multitude of stand-ins. And this sense of reader invocation (whether in the vocative case or not) as a text's minimal self-reference only prepares us further to realize that the mentioned as well as the apostrophized reader, in third or second person respectively, is in fact also, and after all, the point of intersection between linguistic self-referentiality and its structural complement, textual reflexivity. For this convergence or switch point signals the momentary jolt to readers which comes from finding a pointedly acknowledged scriptive medium—a legible text rather than any other form of narrative conveyance—using its rhetorical resources to conscribe an attention waiting always outside that text.

As a last test of methodological distinctions, therefore, as well as (more importantly) a last installment in the literary history for which they have been developed, what we have now to confront in the narrative production of the *fin de siècle* is the extrapolative maximum, rather than interpolative minimum, of verbal self-reference and reflexion together. Here is where entire novels, being about the inscription that realizes them as representation—with all the verbal mystery and duplicity involved, the figural conjurations and evasions—also attempt to perform from within the very psychodynamic of reading in which these same novels eventuate. If it is rare enough at any time to find writing's auto-allegory wholly isolated from reading's parable, by the end of the Victorian period, with its fraught sense both of relentlessly self-perpetuating literary output and of a mass audience feverish for novelty, any clear-cut separation between texts about texts and stories about narrative appetite would seem particularly unlikely. Novels that recognize in execution the phantasmal manifestations of language as the signifying filaments of representation are all the more disposed to admit, and this only in order to investigate, the intensities of identification which such language may appear to elicit by virtual hallucination, coerce as if by black magic.

So this is one place among many where ideology comes in—or comes *through*, its assumptions transmitted via text to reader along the rhetorical grooves of conscripted response. The point needs pressing because it underlies every other methodological discrimination of this book: an axiomatic sense that the place of narrative analysis within cultural study is precisely the place of novels within (rather than against the backdrop of) their environing cultural context—namely, a place determined by signaled reception rather than by mere reflection. From one perspective, it may seem a point so obvious that it could well pass without emphasis. This would be the case were it not for the stunning variety of ways in which this understanding of narrative's function is lately (if tacitly) denied in the name of sophisticated historical emplacements derived from a discourse analysis shorn of its crucial rhetorical register. Let us put it this way about the discursive work of nineteenth-century fiction: In the structuring of affect begins ideology; moreover, in the proliferating thrillers of the *fin de siècle* there emerges more clearly than ever before in Victorian fiction, though hardly for the first time, a specific ideology (and structurally contained counterideology) of affect itself. From Dickens forward, the already downgraded function of epic consolidation in a posttribal Victorian ethos results in a psychosocial isolation overcome in good part through the communal exchange of stories. The late-century gothic revival offers time and again a narratively installed scrutiny of just this communal mythology, yet mostly as regards its questionable psychic means rather than social ends.

With these neogothic parables, that is, as well as with the same period's related exotic adventure tales in all their overwrought narrative stimulation, the reflex of reading has become a cognitive recoil from the figure of the subject reader's own surrendered mental integrity. On the verge of modernist textual involution, and as something like an anticipatory last stand against an incremental disengagement from literature's openly rhetorical, hence public, face, the "political unconscious" of the more or less covertly autotelic text of the *fin de siècle* does not merely implicate, but rather incriminates, the telos of its own reception. A lengthy last chapter will be necessary to do justice to the accusations against narrative fascination which are both leveled and extenuated in process by the novels themselves. It is toward this end that our look at late Victorian gothic romance will attempt its double readings of the gothic's own self-conscious doubleness: its impress of reflexive parable upon the allegory of writing, or in other words its imposition of visceral identification upon the linguistic materialization that conscripts such awareness by mere inscription. Yet again, too, the exact texture of such inscription, its syntactic skein, its lexical and phonemic weave, its figurative tension—all such writing effects will be found to mark the spot of readerly arrest. With the entire linguistic substratum seeming at times in these novels a kind of premature cemetery of figuration awaiting artificial resuscitation, such virtual gothicism of language constitutes the most immediate net—or snare—by which the reader is to be caught (off guard) and held (on edge). We proceed, then, to a psychostylistics of textual deviance as a late-century measure of extrapolated response, or in other words of subject reading in narrative reflex.

Chapter Thirteen

The Gothic of Reading
Wilde, du Maurier, Stevenson, Stoker

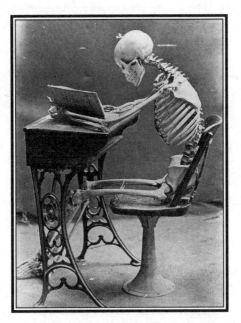

Posture: Skeleton Reading. Photograph, 1870.
The Bettmann Archive

$\mathcal{A}$s never so glaringly before, reading in *fin de siècle* gothic fiction tends to be caught red-handed. This occurs for the most part, as we would by now expect, in narrative parables of which reading is itself the subject—and to which the reading agency is in turn held subject by the necessities and excesses of textual fascination. It occurs, one should add, by unexpected contrast with the generic norms of such fantastic literature. In the reading of gothic fictions, we ordinarily warm to our own chilling excitation, unless something is allowed to block the essential safety valve of such narrative experience: the structured and comforting assurance that *all of that is happening to someone else*. But what about the more immediate *all of this*, the emotive turmoil of reaction? The interest of this chapter centers on those less ingratiating but more directly "engaging" horror stories of the *fin de siècle* in which it gradually dawns on you that *all this is your doing* as well as the author's—and not only your doing, but a figurative rendition of it: of an immanent and activating interest heated, derivative, vicarious, now schizoid, now parasitic, even a little vampiric. These are the horror stories in which plotted monstrosity becomes an image of generic perversity.

It might seem unlikely that a genre would choose to contaminate the attention it demands. Genres, after all, are built upon zones of expectation, not minefields of response. In delimiting the inclinations that they also help to program, they seldom corner and incriminate the very fascination they invite. Detective fiction, for instance, seeks to enlist interest on the side of hermeneutics; historical romance on the side of nostalgia; psychological realism on the side of the autonomous subject; pornography on the side of objectified desire. It is because any and all such generic proclivities are so fully ingrained that the literature of horror, for instance, never fully turns on itself to produce a horror of literature, even while it names as terrible the affective upheavals within plot which its reading is meant to approximate in the audience. Yet I will be arguing that the late Victorian gothic novel does regularly (and regulatively) generate, not a terror of the text, but a carefully controlled gothic of reading: a reflexive disturbance in the circuit of reception which bothers without quite spoiling narrative pleasure, exposing it as participatory, collusive, and two-faced, enticing because in part predatory, feeding off the psychic shock—the depicted horror of characters inside the plot—with which it rushes to identify.

To sense the coordinated nature of late Victorian fiction's reflex action, the sustained recoil of plot upon the dynamics of response, we may contrast the various parables of reading at the *fin de siècle* with the more intermittent conscription of the reader in its midcentury forerunner, the "sensation novel." Named in part for its own affect, this subgenre evokes not just the novel of sensationalism but the sensation(s) of such novels. As D. A. Miller has shown for a text like Wilkie Collins' *Woman in White* (1860), the nervous excitation of various characters is foregrounded like an obtruded mirror of the reader's own disposition in the throes of the genre: a debilitation of internal agency, a "female contagion," whose equivalent in overwrought susceptibility is the very facilitation of fictional impact in the novel's "performative dimension."[1] Hystericized like the narrative agents by plot's whiplash surprises and escalating suspense, the unnerved reader fulfills in his own person the narrative aesthetic: "Like the characters who figure him, the reader becomes . . . paranoid" (160). But this is only half the story, for the violation of "privacy" constituted by reading (a running theme in Miller's book) exposes reading as transmitting not only the feminized receptivity (we might call it masochism) of anxious participation but also a quasi-erotic "sadism" (Miller's term, 164) of penetrating access.[2]

Within reading's passive-aggressive aggravation of the subject, then, the same sadomasochistic pendulum swings of empathy and assault which can tend to derange response in the sensation novel are analyzed more stringently in later neogothic texts as a problematic of identification itself in its weirdly mutating aspects: the drama of the reader's own grotesque metamorphoses.

This chapter thus takes as its subject a last phase in the literary-historical transition toward which the entire study has inevitably been pointed: the transformation of a Victorian culture of literary consumption into a modernist culture of the autonomous text. As the schism between such an elite narrative as Eliot's *Daniel Deronda* on the one side—reflective, exacting, resistant—and the popular best-seller on the other continues to widen along the split path toward modernism, the question of affective participation becomes ever more acute. As fiction closes itself off rhetorically from the relaxed solicitation of an audience on the way to a modernist hermeticism of the aesthetic object, the drama of access can grow downright histrionic. By what strange and estranging means does one enter upon a narrative? According to what desertions of subjectivity? In George Eliot's cognitive paradigm, we think of ourselves as reading any text, sacred or literary, in the same way that Daniel internalizes the unwritten legacy of the dead, offering himself as host to its otherworldly inhabitation. Even this macabre figuration of reading has been anticipated by Eliot's most immediate forebears in nineteenth-century fiction. Where reading for Dickens becomes the very mausoleum of desire, in Meredith textual engagement takes place as a related transgression of the mortal border, both back before birth and over into death. Literary succession is only following suit when the subsequent figures of reading in Hardy, Gissing, Stevenson, Wilde, du Maurier, Stoker, and Haggard tend to gravitate even more obviously toward the perverse or the preternatural, toward the site of reading as corpse, tomb, or ghoulish return.

In scanning the phenomenon of audience endearment in the best-selling Victorian authors, we have already considered the sadistic eroticizing of the textual encounter in Haggard's *Mr. Meeson's Will.* We are now to see that Haggard was by no means alone toward the end of the century in openly figuring the reading act by way of the grotesque, the abject, or the uncanny. In addition to Haggard's game of fetishistic disclosure for the branded feminized text, reading stands variously to writing in numerous later Victorian authors as epitaphic recoil, voyeuristic indulgence, narcotic transfiguration, schizoid self-distancing, mesmeric passivity, parasitic or vampiric devouring—the list goes on—all of it betokening a kind of cannibalizing avidity only barely neutralized by convention. This overstates the case, if at all, only a little. In these fictions, the phenomenology of reading is itself renarrativized as gothic melodrama: in the full luridness of its allure. In the rampant *fin de siècle* multiplication of textual outlets (organs, orifices), and in the frequently mourned decline of literary value, Grub Street has become a teeming necrophiliac ghetto. Hardy saw it coming. Gissing dissected the corpses. From the grave of the aesthetic, Wilde's *Picture of Dorian Gray* veers away, as we will find, into a new level of aestheticized experience, entailing a hedonist and ultimately fatal self-division—even as Stevenson in *The Strange Case of Dr. Jekyll and Mr. Hyde* has already presided over a similar suicide of the subject to which a divorce of desire from social identity can lead. And where du Maurier's *Trilby* exposes in closing the deathless grip of reading (and the eerie coercions that figure it), Bram Stoker's *Dracula* pursues the relation of textual contact to hypnotic co-optation across the entire structure of its gothic plot.

Sinning by the Book: Wilde's *Picture* of Response

Plot must operate in Wilde's *Picture of Dorian Gray* (1891) without the aid of direct address or even any mention of the reader. Either device would seem too comfortably familiar for the novel's arch tonalities. In the Baudelairean tradition, the implied reader of Wilde's novel may well be the Victorian "hypocrite lecteur," yet the direct invocation of that reader's attention would involve too much noblesse oblige on the narrator's part.[3] In another sense, too, any marked intent to gain the reader's ear would inculpate Wilde's discourse—too soon and too symmetrically, that is—with the novelistic cast of Sir Henry's undue and defiling influence upon Dorian Gray.

I begin with Wilde's novel, out of chronological order, because of its paradigmatic relation to late Victorian fantastic narrative. In the rigorous absence (or sometimes pointedly exceptional presence) of direct reader interpolation in other *fin de siècle* texts by du Maurier, Stevenson, and Stoker, the undenominated reader, as in Wilde's novel, tends not to be drawn directly into the systemic alternative of an extrapolative episode or orientation. Another pattern often supervenes, a network of textual self-reference. It is a pattern to which this chapter will be attending from here out—precisely for its ultimate conjunction with the signaling of response. The first stage of this approach involves reading each gothic narrative once through for its displacement of the fantastic onto the textual. It is there that the gothic content finds its macabre counterpart, its analogy and its ground, in the very thanatopraxis (deathwork) of textual operation, with its worried and ultimately spectral relation to reference and subjectivity, to otherness and identity. But since this is not all that *Dorian Gray, Trilby, Dr. Jekyll,* and *Dracula* have in common even in their manifest self-consciousness as texts, a second pass of reading will then move us across the same narrative sequence—alerted, this time through, not just to the self-referential stratum of the story's inscription but to the staged reflex of affect itself. On just this score, suspended disbelief is often in its own way a cover for less flattering susceptibilities. What we will find on this second pass through the novels as self-regarding texts is an exorbitant psychic investment plotted by the narrative even as it is covertly extrapolated to the level of readerly response.

Otherness, mentioned already in connection with the textual level, is an aspect—because a structuring absence—of both writing and reading. This needs stress to prevent any blurring, rather than multivalence, of the term as it recurs in this chapter. Otherness in fiction is the very fiction that grounds (emptily) not only the signifiers that refer elsewhere but also the identifications that make you imagine otherwise. What you think (about) in the activation of the macabre, what you confront in your own collaborative fantasy, is often, of course, violence and death, but not as such mortal turbulence is muted and "framed" by the elegiac factor, for instance, of the Brontë novels. When poltergeists may be real, an aesthetic of ghostly containment cannot seem reliably prophylactic. When the living dead are tangibly imagined by the reader's narrative participation, haunting is no easy way out, no longer a comfortable mode of dramatic distancing. As we move from the pervasive but tamed necromancy of mid-Victorian closure (*The Old Curiosity Shop, Wuthering Heights, Villette, A Tale of Two Cities*, even *Daniel Deronda*), the elegiac weight placed on *loss* redeemed by narrative has been inverted to the dynamics of *appropriation*. Bringing the dead to life becomes not so much a figuration of fiction as a symptom of the vicarious desire that activates such fiction—including, most obviously in *Trilby* and *Dracula*, the hypnotic or telepathic incursions such desire resembles. Language, in short, points to the other across a gap unbridgeable except by the suspect projections of reading. Hence—especially in the verbal texture of these fantastic late-century narratives—the inevitable convergence of textual self-referentiality and readerly self-reflexion.

What follows, then, as an experiment in double reading (untested, so far, in regard to its forced separation of the two trajectories) is also designed as a recapitulation. For if this study has made anything clear, or clearer, it is this: When classic novels own to their very execution as writing, they also foreground their prosecution as read. Novels about the production of textuality tend to entail a metanarrative of reading concerned with reading's own nervous perversity, its surrogate pleasure and pain, its psychosomatic risks rather than institutional stability, less its humanist reach or stretch than its parasitic grasp. Then, too, reading these late Victorian narratives twice over—the second reading superimposed upon the first—carries a point in and of itself. That

such a highly artificial parsing of narrative sequence into contrapuntal trajectories so little violates the felt charge of the tales as gothic thrillers is perhaps the
best measure of the rhetorical differentiations and redoublings on which they
actually depend for their immediate, as well as seek for their ultimate, effect.

At the level of inscriptive self-reflection in Wilde's novel, the punning reciprocity between picture and text sets in early. Once the features of the portrait
are complete, all that remains of the picture, as Basil explains, is "to work up
this background" (2:21)—as happens in another sense when Dorian's family history is disclosed in the next chapter: "Yes; it was an interesting background. It
posed the lad, and made him more perfect as it were" (3:33). The flip side of
such a figure of speech—picture as narrative—recurs at intervals. When the
portrait turns out to have an uncanny temporal dimension in its own creeping
decay, Dorian recoils from it as a thing that "told his story" (7:73). The final
irony of Basil Hallward's share in the "story" comes with Dorian's invitation
to the attic room in which he has locked away the festering portrait: "I keep a
diary of my life from day to day, and it never leaves the room in which it is written" (12:120). If we are in any doubt about this figurative "diary" referring solely
to the painter's once exquisite portrait, whose mut(il)ation over time is a kind
of autobiographical journal of self-abuse, the point is borne home with Dorian's last ominous utterance to Hallward before the murder: "You will not have
to read long" (12:120). The painting as diary thus ironically fulfills the scriptive
dead metaphor used by Basil earlier in the scene, as a way of dismissing the im-
putation of evil to Dorian: "Sin is a thing that writes itself across a man's face"
(12:117).

Writing is an analogy that goes deeper yet, falling through the false bottom
of reference itself. When the painter is later stabbed to death, with all traces of
his body then eradicated by acid, the sequence performs one-half of an inexorable aesthetic purification. It is completed in turn by Dorian's fate—when,
attempting to deface the accusatory text of his own depravity, he ends up stab-
bing himself rather than the painting and is absented forever from its restored
youthful image. As befits the tradition of Victorian fictional melodrama, the
precise death sentence bends its syntax to epitomize the self it expunges. Across
an elliptical chiasmus: "There was a cry heard—and a crash." For a moment,
we can only assume that Dorian hears the lifelike painting utter a shriek of pain
before it crashes to the floor, until—the "trick ending" now clarified—we realize that it is instead the cry of his own falling body, heard from below by ser-
vants and passersby alike. Whether the following phrase, "and a crash," attaches to the grammatical passive of "heard [by]" or is merely a fragmentary
predication hung from "There was," in either case the tactical evacuation of
agency in the preceding phrase cannot be missed. Figured there is the very eli-

sion of consciousness between a final utterance and a protagonist's vanishing self-recognition: a wording that pitches to epitome the novel's abiding rift between (psychological) subject and (pictorial) object.

It is thus that grammar not only carries to completion but articulates in miniature the allegory at issue. With nothing of the painter left, either in the world or on the canvas, and suddenly nothing of the man he once memorialized, what is captured in oil is only the now recovered (no longer decayed) image of a moment. It is a moment whose import we are led to recover in turn through interpretive procedures invited by the textual fable as it has so far unfolded. The deaths of author (Basil) and of referent (Dorian) together complete the thematic of inscriptive self-reference by returning us, in other words, to the problematic of response. And so we begin again, as ordained by the present experiment in double reading. Having run through one trajectory of the plot in its encoding of textuality as the obliteration (by *effect*) of artist and model alike, of origin and referent, we are now ready to rescan the same trajectory for the way it refigures (as *affect*) this very space between viewer and viewed, subject and object. Plot redraws this space as an interpretive zone marking out not the conditions of production so much as the conditioning of response: the objectified subjectivity of reception itself. In so saying, I am directing my argument toward the retrospective vantage achieved by Wilde's subsequently drafted preface to the novel: "It is the spectator, and not life, that art really mirrors" (3). To have removed the life of the subject and the life of the artist from either end of the collapsed representational history of the painting is one sure way to clear space for such a self-recognition on the audience's part.

And that recognition—of the novel's power over you—is implacably caught up in the narrative's own thematic (and critique) of "influence," generated in part under an etymological aegis. For the channeled "in-flow" of affective force, the impress of self (or of culture more broadly), comes into play as a homoerotic penetration (via "subtle fluid" [3:33]) of Dorian by Lord Henry. You as reader of Wilde's text are not left to worry for yourself the analogous consequences of your own fascination, however. The text does it for you in advance, from its first scene forward. It fashions, in short, the extrapolation it would otherwise merely have prompted—fashions and quite literally frames it—in a painted response to the channeled influx of literary suggestiveness ladled out by Lord Henry. Thus does Wilde's narrative inscribe, finally, less the avidities of flesh than those of text: the lust for reading itself, always at performance's remove from life.

Wilde's novel incites desire only to the extent that it cites it, quotes it—it, not its objects. And *The Picture* does so, what is more, anything but evasively. It paints this fact about itself in the boldest eponymous stroke available to it. It is in this way that the ekphrastic principle—the verbal rendering of a visual object—turns inside out to become the imagined image of verbal impact.[4] The *Picture*, in other words, justifies its reflexive title not cheaply but strenuously, precisely because its Picture renders desire as a *function of words* to begin with—words received and savored, words registered in the full materiality of their sensuous persuasion, words lingered over as if read rather than listened to. That the painting of a dashing young man, with no printed text in sight, should inaugurate and ground a novel as the virtual picture of reading is a device whose full apprehension necessitates our rerun of the narrative from that precipitating scene forward.

The young Dorian is a uniquely captive audience in that scene, under injunction to remain motionless as Basil works away on the finishing touches to his portrait. All the while, Lord Henry works Dorian over, virtually makes him over, with one of his lubricious literary pastiches. Announces the painter about the igniting impact upon Dorian of Lord Henry's verbiage: "I have caught the effect I wanted,—the half-parted lips, and the bright look in the eyes"—as it happens, the classic pose of the young male reader from formal portraiture.[5] An extended discourse follows on the power of literary discourse. Added by Wilde to the typescript before letting it go to the printer, it is a passage of verbal expatiation on verbal power itself, with Dorian smitten by the thrill of "Words! Mere words! How terrible they were!" (2:21).[6] In this same added section, Lord Henry remembers an unnamed book which, when read as a youth, "had revealed to him much that he had not known before," and "wondered whether Dorian Gray was passing through a similar experience" (2:21). Analogous to the encounter with a literary text, and explicitly recording the transfixing effect of words, this scene of verbal infusion thus doubles for the very act of reading, whose externally registered (and visually rendered) signs of sensuous introversion complete the expressive content of the canvas. What Basil's portrait thereby captures is aestheticism itself in literary transmission.

The famously unspecified text that Henry much later sends to Dorian—perhaps the same book that had once awakened and redirected his own thought—anticipates Basil's desperate guess about self-corrosive pigmentation on the canvas (his assumption that the "paints I used had some wretched mineral poison in them" [13:122]) by its description as "a poisonous book" (10:98)—poisonous, addictive, hallucinatory in its circuits of identification. The novel's most fateful word occurs again in connection with this book, revised from the word "memory" at the typescript stage: "For years, Dorian could not free himself from the *influence* of this book" (11:98; emphasis added). In its inescapable rehearsal of the novel before us, it is a text concerned with the mental disposition of reading—and not just of reading, but of reading oneself in(to) everything.

In tracing out Wilde's meshes of influence and identification, we need to shuffle for a few moments through the fantastic pages of this untitled volume. As if in a narcissistic travesty of Wilde's axiom about art mirroring its audience, Dorian often feels, in the clutches of this book, that "the whole of history was merely the record of his own life" (11:113). So, too, with the character of whom he reads: "The hero of the wonderful novel that had so *influenced* his life"— that word again—"had himself known this curious fancy. In the seventh chapter he tells how . . ." (11:113; emphasis added). There follows a hyperbolic litany of sensual extravagance through hallucinatory projection, in which the hero, followed in turn by Dorian via the phenomenological identification of reading, lives through various transgressive indulgences "as Caligula . . . as Domitian . . . as Elagabalus." These include such a dramatic irony as the search in marble mirrors for "the reflection of the dagger that was to end his days" (11:113). More deviously ironic yet is the point at which the roster of degeneracy begins. Before mention of Caligula, Domitian, or Elagabalus, the passage has already laid a grammatical snare in the introduction of its first classic prototype. The prepositional framework of analogy, with its controlling grammar of "as," is sprung upon Wilde's reader in momentary ambiguity—wavering between simile and preternatural inhabitation, between "as" for "in the manner of" and "as" for "in the person of." The heady chapter of the book at hand "tells how, crowned with laurel, lest lightning might strike him, he had sat, *as* Tiberius in a garden at Capri, reading the shameful books of Elephantis" (11:113; emphasis added). Until the following subordinate clause, which seems to root the scene not in analogy but in immanent participation—"while dwarfs and peacocks strutted round him [the unnamed reader in the place of Tiberius] and the flute-player mocked the swinger of the censer"—we are for a moment, in our own reading, unsure who is reading what in the role of whom.

In the passage's wholesale inversion of a high Victorian anxiety, the escape from cultural belatedness is to make all history's decadent satiety one's own. Yet access to history remains only textual. Answering to the unnamed book by which the young Lord Henry had himself been intoxicated, and whose diluted influence upon Dorian was first transmitted by Henry's own extemporaneous verbalizing, this later passage offers a direct encounter of the hero with what Lucien Dallenbach would call the "Doppelroman."[7] We are thus caught up, like Dorian *before us* (both senses), in the thrall of fictional writing. This is why Dorian is painted *as us* in the first place, in the very moment of inebriation by the effluence, even before influence, of suggestive language. Here is what distinguishes *The Picture of Dorian Gray* from other abyssal texts: not that it incarnates a "reader figure" but that it textualizes him (transmits him to marked canvas) at the moment of dawning response. What is on view in this irony is pointed up by perhaps the unlikeliest detail of that extended opening scene: the implication that somehow, for the painter Hallward, the contaminating rhetoric brandished by Lord Henry in the presence of the former's "sitting" subject is either out of earshot (improbable) or beyond the focused range of the artist's attention. Supposedly lost in concentration in bringing his painting to a finish, Basil remarks immediately afterward: "I don't know what Harry has been saying to you, but he has certainly made you have the most wonderful expression." Dorian might as well have been reading silently to himself—a process that Jesper Svenbro, in his anthropological study of reading in classic Greek culture (a culture doted on of course by both Henry and Basil), understands as having been modeled in its earliest visual and verbal representations on the ethos of pederastic dominance as a cultural rite of passage: the solicited and submissive silent reader as the passive, internalizing, and mastered recipient of the text's penetrating initiation.[8] Wilde's word for this, again: influence. In sum, then, *The Picture of Dorian Gray* is the late Victorian narrative text figuring in pigment the instigations of its own language—and doing so by eventually eliding authorial intent and referential presence (the deaths of Basil and Dorian) from its arresting manifestation. By synecdochic entitlement, that is, our heady response to Wilde's *Picture* is on preview in that glossed disposition of response to worded sensualities which the title canvas already depicts. It is a depiction that therefore in every sense *draws us in*.

Moreover, if we take a few steps back from Wilde's *Picture*, we can catch it in a different but related media-historical light. In overreaching the limits of traditional pictorial representation, Wilde's conceit of the magic portrait has seized upon, even in yanking it awry, a certain logic of the nineteenth century's newest representational medium. One critic has even suggested that Wilde's novel is a fable of such things: "The live model . . . becomes the photographic 'work' fixed in time while the representational image hanging on the wall becomes the living being," a "lifelike" resemblance.[9] This may not seem to comport well with Wilde's definition of art's mirroring function, however, which is to hold the mirror up to the spectator rather than to the represented subject. In this case, what changes the picture, as it were, is that Dorian constitutes for much of the time his portrait's sole audience: the revenge of voluptuary self-regard turned gradually sadomasochistic.

"As on a Lectern": The Svengali Effect

In moving back from *Dorian Gray* to du Maurier's *Trilby* (1888), both arguably operating within the preternatural overtones of the Victorian discourse on photography, we move from encoded literary effect to encoded literary cause. Still within the literary *topos* of ekphrasis, we turn from a magic portrait as an image of subjected reading to a magnetic photograph as an image of the hypnotic "influence" flowing from a text.[10] Not only does du Maurier's explicit thematics of mesmerism make an extrapolation to the transferential magic of reading even harder to avoid in his novel, it does so across a flash point of minimal second-person interpolation which sutures your attention into line with the heroine's own.

In turning to du Maurier, this chapter is continuing to keep in mind that distinction toward which the examination of Proust led us early on: between the self-referential and the reflexive. It is a difference, of course, which we have just traced out across a double reading of *The Picture of Dorian Gray*. This distinction between textual self-reference and reflexively marked response comes into clearer focus yet in du Maurier's deliberate conflation of the two models. In *The Picture of Dorian Gray*, what is always on view in the painting as "diary," even once it no longer captures the innocent awe of literary influx, is the reflex, the "mirror" in Wilde's sense, of response itself: a response that divides subject from object across the gothic gap (and horrified gaping) between self and its specular image. What the climactic scene of du Maurier's *Trilby* accomplishes, by inserting into an intricate field of textual cross-references an actual photograph, is simultaneously a self-referential inscription of print textuality and a reflexive moment from which the galvanic charge of responsive engagement is once again to be extrapolated, read *out*.

After *Trilby*, the remainder of this chapter is given over to textual developments in which the double tracking of linguistic self-reference and cognitive reflex is no longer attached to a single lynchpin of ekphrastic representation (verbally rendered portraits or photographs) but instead strung out more diffusely across the weave of plot. Yet this will not be entirely new territory, either. After all, this is what Dorian Gray's portrait itself portrays by the fantastic but simple enough fact that, like the rapture of literary intake it begins by replicating, it *changes over time*. This is what makes Wilde's ekphrasis such a close match for his narrativity. With the portrait's bloom long gone, and moral revulsion having taken its slow disfiguring toll, the Picture retains in just this way its mirroring relation to *The Picture* in reception. So, too, with the localized ekphrastic moment of Svengali's photographic portrait, whose effect on Trilby is stationed not just to pinpoint but to replay the novel's previous and continuing effect on the subject reader.

At this final turning point of probably the best-selling English novel of the nineteenth century, du Maurier's heroine, a former mesmeric satellite in the orbit of the maestro Svengali's hypnotic power—a woman whose tone-deaf singing has been transformed under his sway so that she had become the toast of the Continent—is slowly wasting away on her deathbed. Her mind is distracted now only by literary reading until a package of mysterious origin, just arrived on the carefully prepared scene, is "found to contain a large photograph, framed and glazed, of Svengali."[11] All that follows in the episode may seem to devolve from the flickering evocation in "glazed" (for glassed) of the whole cause-and-effect circuit of mesmerism: the glassy-eyed, rapt stare at once of its operative agent and its subjected object. In any case, the reader knows by now that the disclosed photographic icon and catalyst has invaded the space not just of dying but of the whole panoply of death's specifically aesthetic anodynes and preparations in Victorian culture. For Trilby has been taking solace during her declining days by listening to the reading aloud of various improving Christian tracts and sentimental novels, including *The Pilgrim's Progress*, as well as Dickens' masterpiece of sentimental forbearance, *David Copperfield* (8:418).

Into the dramatized place—the prescribed domestic space—of the familiar reading habits of Victorian culture, then, the posthumous photograph of Svengali is unexpectedly inserted, for "Trilby laid it against her legs *as on a lectern*, and lay gazing at it with close attention for a long time" (8:432; emphasis added). She has every reason to be caught, as of old, by his stare, for he is (as if in a present activation of his gaze) "looking straight out of the picture, straight *at you*" (8:432; emphasis added). How idiomatic is this discursive lurch? "Straight *at* you"? Or is it "straight at *you*"? Either way, this confrontation with a photograph of the dead hypnotist while still alive is accompanied by an illustration from the author's own pen (fig. 11)—but one which, compared with the emphasized potency of the photograph, holds no particular spell. The inadequacy of the plate, in fact, throws us back on the narrative itself as a closer approximation to the photographic image's posthumous charge. Just before Trilby is hynotically precipitated into a last song, all we know is that Trilby's body, verbally imaged as "lectern," is ready to receive the image of Svengali's. And reading is what these legible bodies, his to her and both to us, are convened to figure in their mesmeric bond—not least because there is even a verbal underside to Svengali's telekinetic powers in the initial description of the photograph as a "speaking likeness" (8:420).

Such metatextual figuration extends to the narrowest crannies of grammar in the rhetorical torque of that phrase "looking straight at you," surfacing as it does within omniscient narrative. This passing twist on the familiar direct address of Victorian fiction, though muted, plays disruptively, nonetheless, on the shifting differential between grammatical and specular object, since the phrase invokes a second "person" nowhere present in the scene but only present to the page of its representation—namely, the reader. Reduplicating the photo-

postmarks on the case, seemed to have travelled all over Europe to London, out of some remote province in eastern Russia—out of the mysterious East! The poisonous East—birthplace and home of an ill wind that blows nobody good.

Trilby laid it against her legs as on a lectern, and lay gazing at it with close attention for a long time, making a casual remark now and then, as, "He was very handsome, I think"; or, "That uniform becomes him very well. Why has he got it on, I wonder?"

The others went on talking, and Mrs. Bagot made coffee.

"OUT OF THE MYSTERIOUS EAST"

Presently Mrs. Bagot took a cup of coffee to Trilby, and found her still staring intently at the portrait, but with her eyes dilated, and quite a strange light in them.

Figure 11. Svengali illustration, by George du Maurier, for *Trilby*

graph's effect on Trilby, whose body offers its lectern and its target at once, this imaged look even as *verbally* imaged is meant to take in "you," the novel's own reader, at the very moment when you, in taking *it* in, get taken up and over by it. Along with the hinted additional sense of the "glazed" gaze, such is the grammatical (as well as psychophysiological) mystification of du Maurier's storytelling. Especially when doubled by the actual drawing, that passing microsecond of interpolated address ("straight at you") is enough, therefore, to focus the novel's broad-gauged extrapolation—in its full reflex as a parable of textual power.

This is also what the illustrative plate serves to illustrate not only by its place in the text but by its exact placement on the hybrid page. For the pictorial image of Svengali is embedded within the ongoing printed narrative as a half-disruptive, half-continuous segment of the textual surface. As the immediately adjacent type is compressed into a column, its indented justification delineates a marked parallel with the vertical pole of the music stand just visible at the far right of the etching, angled away from Svengali toward an unseen performer at just the point of the image's truncation by the encroaching space of print. Typeset narration thus displaces any sheet music on this podium as the only visible text for the maestro's captivating raised baton—summoning the reader in this sense, along with Trilby, to performative readiness.

Despite the specificities of *Trilby*'s page, a common denominator here dawns within the apparent contrast between du Maurier's novel and Haggard's *Mr. Meeson's Will* (chapter 6) in their figurative deployment of the impressed female body (and its association with photography) in relation to the affective charge of reading. Such is the fluidity of the feminine as trope in the nineteenth-century metapoetics of male writers, or let us say its suspect availability, that it can be recruited to convey both allure *and* impressionability by turns, the tantalizing accessibility of a text or the reader's vulnerability (permeability) to *it*. Ever since Coleridge's gender-based diatribes against the novel, what often goes unsaid is that there is something at least a little feminine about stories themselves, as well as something at least a little feminine about reading stories.[12] If, in *Mr. Meeson's Will*, textual unfolding is feminized to figure (via photographic mediation) the reader's subjective, quasi-erotic fascination with narrative's always titillating procedures, in *Trilby* the textual recipient is feminized into aggravated passivity to figure (via photography again) narrative's indomitable power over what we are led to think of as the subjected reader. This is the reader who, in avid textual encounter, is always occupied not only *with* but *by* the psychic apparatus of the other.

Locking Trilby into position just where it wants her, the photograph thus emerges as a reflection of and upon nothing less than narrative art's complex hallucinatory aura. The Victorian novel's whole modality of addressed discourse (always in one sense directed "straight at you") is replayed in a representation that draws you into that discourse, galvanizes you, and organizes your own transfixed reaction. Here again is where a novelistic ekphrasis divulges the ruling interplay between textual (linguistically self-referential) and reactive (reflexive) models not just within its own circumscribed image but along the temporal axis of narrative. In the case of *Trilby*, such a multilayered textual portrayal of a photographic portrait can be taken in this way as a *mise en abyme* of the novel as a continuous reading act because, at the narrative climax of the tale, it *resumes* the power of narrative in two senses, renews and reviews it, propels it while offering its précis, its quintessential reinscription. It is thus, in a mirroring duplication hinged about a pivotal narrative moment, that we come upon the representation of hypnosis as the hypnosis of narrative representation.

Here again, too, is where the rank inadequacy of the drawing to evoke the electrifying "look" of the mesmerist serves the novel's larger purpose. On the eve of literary modernism, with its heightened insistence on the graphic and phonic materiality of language rather than its strictly mimetic powers, it is only the narrative, not the stare of the drawing, which gets (through) to you. Within a linguistic and rhetorical conception of the novelistic text, the figural is eclipsed by the figurative. That fictional images derive their often bizarre power from the merely legible language inducing you to conjure them is a fact owned up to, so as not to be thought suppressed, by such a compound textual moment. Novelistic illustrations aside, always at least to one side, what you see is what you beget. Never more than with the eroticized and subservient body of the victimized gothic heroine, this is the true guiltiness of reading's pleasure—and the deepest reflex action of its textuality: the gothic of reading, by any other name.

Svengali joins a long line of characters divided from their own self-image: the subject doubled, hence radically exceeded, by an extruded *textual* emblem. Dorian by his portrait, Svengali by his photograph, Jekyll by Hyde, the ancient corpse of Dracula by the regenerative lineage of the Undead as well as by the multiplied typescripts that track his wanderings: Such is the psychic energy overstepping or outliving itself which comes to figure—either directly or by the way its excess (or outreach) is taken up in response—both the overweening projective impulses and the libidinal vulnerabilities that circulate through the reading moment in an age of sensationalist literary production. In all this, it might have gone without saying that the contract between reader and text grew strained. Instead, Robert Louis Stevenson said it explicitly in a poem called "The Reader" (first collected posthumously in 1896), a text that might be read both as a send-up of the easy securities of the apostrophic habit and as a retrospective glance at Stevenson's own detractors a decade earlier in response to *Dr. Jekyll and Mr. Hyde*. The poem's philistine reader is an indignant puritanical bully, a "hypocrite" reader who tosses a book on the floor for its impiety (fig. 12). The violent respondent is urged by the personified and speaking volume to blame instead the author of such narrative material rather than the material pages of the bound book. After further attempts to appease this irate audience of one, the animated book quite literally *tells* a fable, metonymic for the volume of "Fables" in which it is contained, only to be tossed on the fire in contempt.[13] What is enacted in this miniature dramatic dialogue with the most ferocious of readers is precisely what is overruled within the circuit of address in Stevenson's often sanguine and conversational version of Victorian fiction's inscribed audience (as in his

Figure 12. E.R. Herman, illustration for "The Reader,"
from Robert Louis Stevenson, *Fables,* 1914 edition, Charles Scribner's Sons.

prefatory poem to *Treasure Island* [see chapter 6 above]): the fatal recalcitrance
of absolute emotional disengagement—hence textual obliteration. What "The
Reader" thus offers at century's end is the reductio ad absurdum of the book-
reader dialogue of the whole Victorian era, with the text here pleading for its
very life. The "fable" is just that, its coded generalization as follows: When any
reader turns against any book, the latter is destroyed—as functional text
whether or not as bound volume.

Stevenson's Text/duality

Stevenson's most famous novella is able to fabulate the text's contract with its audience even more explicitly as a kind of aesthetically contained devil's pact. With Svengali in mind, one remembers that it is a signal fact about *The Strange Case of Dr. Jekyll and Mr. Hyde* (1886) that the said Hyde has "never been photographed" (50). For much of the novella, indeed, he is only said: whispered about, reported, unseen. To bring him to life is the act of story and its reading. In moving on from Wilde and du Maurier, we may take the absence of Hyde's photograph as itself emblematic. Our examples so far have turned on ekphrastic moments of human portraiture, a photograph and its pictorial counterpart in a magic canvas. But Hyde's initial magic is that he seems to exist only as narrative impetus—or animus—not as a depictable human figure. In Stoker, too, as well as in Stevenson, ekphrastic icons, as punctuating nodes in the development of narrative parable, are exchanged for more thoroughly dispersed analogues of reading's diabolic fixations, analogues that nonetheless unfold once more across the linked strata of verbal self-reference and reflexive recognition. Conscripted and placed under analysis, your narrative desires are held hostage to their own imaginative projections in the distorting mirror of preternatural plotting. This is the way you see yourself in the late Victorian gothic: not as an ontological perversion (deformed double, devolving portrait, mesmeric alter ego, sepulchral bat-man), but as fascinated by all such aberrations to the point of self-disfiguring (self-decentering) perversity. The transferential interchange of reading has grown more than ever self-diagnostic, though still well within an institutional regime of programmed rehabilitation. Reading, as we are to see, takes its own potentially sickly temperature without finally taking the heat.

Since it is advisable at times to recast the general question to which these several chapters have been gathering in answer, let us recognize that one version of what we have been asking is how Victorian fiction, even though scuttling the full-scale pedagogy of response inherited from the eighteenth-century novel, still manages not only to induce its desired mode of reading but to inculcate reading itself as a mode of desire. To inculcate it—and often to inculpate (but only up to a point) its underlying psychology. No Victorian narrative reviewed so far has freed your reading entirely from the carefully cultivated taint of suspect pleasure or morbid libidinal investment, and none less than Stevenson's story of Dr. Jekyll and his nocturnal delegate. The metatextual operation proceeds, of course, with impunity. It cannot even be dignified with the name of irony, let alone paradox. Nothing keeps you reading more surely than the prolonged hint that reading is a kind of guilty pleasure—or, more to the point here, a *form* of such pleasure, a structuring of desire as the plundering of otherness. As interpolation drops away in the late Victorian gothic, the gothic of reading emerges by extrapolation in the mode of what we might today call reverse psychology.

As with *The Picture of Dorian Gray*, we begin by moving once through the story of *Dr. Jekyll and Mr. Hyde* as if it were (which it is) a self-referential thriller, a text about perverse textual materialization. We can then move through it once more along the reactive track of response. It hardly needs reiteration that the strands of such double reading, temporarily separated here, are in fact part of an entwined and simultaneous encounter with the story as "normally" read. What *Trilby* brings together in that single climactic scene is (1) a self-referential emblem of mimetic inscription in a photograph whose (2) reflexive effect is to evoke the whole ensemble of readerly response. This double encoding is, in the (strange) case of *Dr. Jekyll and Mr. Hyde*—as also in *Dorian Gray*, from its first moment of deceptively stabilized ekphrasis forward—assigned instead to narrative *succession* across the overall patterning of plot. Concerning the self-referential thread of Stevenson's story, the metaplot (of inscription as a mode of self-division) leads on to a monstrous co-optive doubling. It reaches its destination with the death of the author in the last sentence, where grammar falls away from first to third person: "Here, then, as I lay down the pen, and proceed to seal up my confession,"—as if it were a tomb—"I bring the life of that unhappy Henry Jekyll to an end" (54), with "that" a fatal deictic pointing only backward on a life. In our now familiar effort at double reading, we will be following earlier versions of such textually fraught leads (culminating in the overlapped biological and biographical senses of "life") for as long as the story lets us—before it throws us back on our own, as it were, recognizance as readers.

Where Dorian differed from his degenerative portrait as both referent and reader from text, so, too, Jekyll differs from Hyde as the presumed unitary subject from his (its) disintegration in language, in text. Put the other way around: Like all textual conjuration, Hyde must be read into being—in his case, like an embodied double entendre. Indeed the "profound duplicity" (42) of the title character(s) seems to manifest itself in verbal byplay at the very first materialization of the actual Doppelgänger. Following the throes of his alchemical transformation, Jekyll's degeneration into the dwarfish, stooped Hyde is a loss in "stature" (44)—spiritual as well as the intended physical—against which the ethical force of "my more *upright* twin" (43; emphasis added) becomes a play on the stalwart versus the groveling. Well before the transformation scene (in fact, as its first medical clue), the repeated entry of "the single word: double" (38) in Jekyll's log book (in reference to the dosage of his magic antidote) evokes both the corrective po(r)tion and the specter of doubleness it is meant to quell.

Beyond localized duplicities of this sort, echoes across the text institute their own doublings. A negligible idiom of split identity at one early point—the dead metaphor of dissociated personality in Enfield's being "surprised out of himself" (34) in a first discussion of Hyde—can, returning in a variant form, seem burdened with the weight of the entire tale, as when Jekyll "came to myself once more with the character, the stature, and the face of Henry Jekyll" (85).

As lexical doubleness further distills itself to the special case of homophony, the metatext is all the more exacerbated. Even the name "Hyde" enters into duplication beyond its almost farcically obvious pun (not to mention the syllabic play of "Jekyll is ill" [57]). For "Hyde" is activated in its garish hint of sequestration by Jekyll's own contrary and contemptuous description of Lanyon as a "hide-bound pedant" (43)—as opposed, one presumes, to something like a Hyde-released profligate.[14] The self-referential text thus turns at its narrowest compass on the breached self-identity of referential language per se, especially when the grammar of identity is itself on the line. Where the lawyer Utterson would hope to "set eyes on [Hyde]" (37), Jekyll cannot set his "I" free from him in what we might call the phonemic stream of split consciousness. By Jekyll's own admission, Hyde "was knit to him closer than a wife" (53)—closer even (the comparison could scarcely be more explicit) than a bed partner to the implementation of his desires. To this Jekyll adds, just as oddly, and with an assonant echo of the long vowel in "wife": "closer than an eye." By this he would seem to mean, beyond the timeworn homophonic pun on an "I" hereby undergoing drastic redefinition, that Hyde is actually *inside* rather than adjacent to or embraced by him—as he later puts it, "caged in his flesh" (53).

Even the homoerotics of doubling is made manifest as a bent of diction itself. And putting the *I* back in "wife" is not the only echoic thickening of this sort in which Jekyll is caught up. Twice before he has stumbled over an interjection as if it were the redundant designation of his own faltering—stuttering—identity. To Utterson, in explaining why he can't say more, Jekyll multiplies the monosyllables of selfhood even as he is trying to keep his own multiplicity under wraps: "I would trust you before any man alive, *ay*, before myself, if *I* could" (44; emphasis added). When explanation can no longer be postponed, Jekyll's reflexive grammar, turning back on itself, again snaps open more selves than it has intended, for "by the sleeplessness to which I now condemned myself, *ay*, even beyond what *I* thought possible to man, *I* became, in my own person, a creature eaten up" (95; emphasis added)—the "ay" stammered out only as the affirmation of negativity and self-division.[15] A page before, in fact, grammar has all but abrogated its own role in self-definition. "He, I say—I cannot say, I" (94), Jekyll writes of Hyde. Without quotation marks around the cited pronouns, the second clause would seem to trumpet the impossibility of any first-person self-enunciation whatsoever for a writing subject soon to close his document with reference to himself as "that unhappy Henry Jekyll."

From homophony to syntactical metonymy, all such "profound duplicity" at the linguistic level keeps not just writing—with its internal differentials—but finally the slack between writing and reading constantly before us. In making that last distinction I am of course anticipating a transition between the self-referential and the reflexive dimensions of this text: a shift of emphasis (I stress again) within the inseparable. Let me put the second half of the matter as baldly as possible: An alternative or double meaning (whether homophonic or merely semantic) stands to a primary signifier—a read suggestion to a written sign—as Hyde stands to Jekyll. This does not exhaust the macabre physiology of the double, to be sure, but it goes far toward naturalizing it within the only range of experience which usually (and here) counts for its realization: the experience of the readerly (rather than the civil) subject in the grips of the self-alienating morphology of literary language. Where else but in language can the one be made two (or more)? In dream and nightmare, of course, as well as in their waking pharmacological equivalent—where His Majesty the Ego (Freud's personification) shivers into multiplicity like a rogue signifier. But, for most of us, only in literary language: that is, in language *recognized* for its layered and multivalent associations. Textual polysemy, in and of itself, thereby engages a uniquely self-conscious intensity of reading, before any local deployment turns a particular ambiguity thematic. We have seen this at work in *The Picture of Dorian Gray*, where the play on "background" serves early on, as does the whole conceit of the mutating portrait later, to narrativize the pictorial text. Even more centrally in *Dr. Jekyll and Mr. Hyde*, the pun, as a paradoxically duplex singular, generates a kind of metalinguistic matrix (multiple signification per se) for this narrative of the dual personality.

To think of such textual double folds as signaled effects of writing, of textual work and its by-products—as if the monster were sprung from the ungovernable nature of language itself (as it inheres, insists, and slips away in the unconscious)—to think in this way becomes scarcely less tempting at the moment when the story itself, the story as written narrative, arrives at that underlying pun for which the others may be taken to prepare and extend the context. Without a mirror available on the spot, the first visible sign for Jekyll of his eventually uncontrollable transformations into Hyde is the appearance of the latter's hand at the end of the doctor's sleeve. And yet it is with this appendage, alone at times, that Jekyll is able to produce (in the other sense) his own identifying hand: "I remembered that of my original character, one part remained to me: I could write my own hand" (51), where even "part" sustains the pun by suggesting the bodily part-object rather than merely an implied portion or fraction of individual agency. This is to say that the one site of convergence between the warring principles, become principals, of the doctor's psyche is the organ of text production itself: the limb, to redouble the pun, by which desire is limned in words. As switch point between identities, this mutating appendage is, of course, also the origin of the orthographic "hand" of Hyde himself, a writing whose similarity to Jekyll's script has been noted early on by a keen-eyed clerk as a "rather singular resemblance" (21)—another passing phrase playing double with the reader by playing between idiom and oxymoron.[16] An even more telltale idiom makes a two-faced appearance when Enfield explains the impossibility of characterizing Hyde's looks as if it were a default of inscription: "No, sir: I can make *no hand of it*; I can't describe him" (34; emphasis added).

Biographical information actually intersects this path of speculation about Hyde's ultimately textual relation to Jekyll. To say, for instance, that the anatomical hand in question is regularly the first "sign of Hyde" in transformation is to recall that Stevenson, hemorrhaging in bed during the long illness that led to the drafting of *Dr. Jekyll*, not only scribbled in pain when he could but at other times used his hand as a signifying organ in the development of a private sign language between him and his wife.[17] Then, too, if "hand" is a pivotal ambiguity for the rift between Hyde as body versus Hyde as legible trace, Hyde as stalking monster versus Hyde as demonstrable only in writing and its reading, it is a pun confirmed by yet another at an even more specific level of textual connotation. This is the "transforming draught" (49) that—as exuded textual production (either "draft" or "draught") rather than ingested potion—actually produces the mutation it appears to record. Bringing to mind the *pharmakon* in the twin Derridean sense, as at once poisonous alien additive and textual supplement, such is the "draught" necessary to effect Jekyll's shift from one subject position to another. Since Stevenson's wife famously convinced him to burn the first draft of the story (the outline of which had come to him, like Hyde to Jekyll, out of his sleep), biography again comes to the extrinsic aid of homonymy.[18] The biographical circle is immediately complete when we recall from other sources that Stevenson, as reader, thought of pulp fiction—reversing Coleridge's antipathetic metaphor—as a kind of homeopathic medicine for the troubled mind, preferring popular to highbrow novels when mentally distressed: "I take them like opium . . . a drug."[19]

How, we might ask, can the drug taking that both produces and presumably later (in other forms—and at his own hands) degrades Hyde be operably transferred to a figure of speech for the psycholinguistics of text production, whether in manuscript or reception? Or cast the question in reverse: Drawing on the etymological unconscious of *manus* for hand, how does Hyde in his bio-chemical deviance become the phantasmal *man you script*? We make a way forward toward an answer only by appreciating fully the devious byways of figuration itself, and other forked paths of enunciation, in the generative mixed signals of the unfolding text. To entertain Stevenson's story as approaching the de Manian paradox of an allegory of its own reading in a fully historicized context of late-century literary production, I return to my suggestion in chapter 3 that inscription offers itself most directly to the reflexivity of response at the moment of textual slippage, syntactic or lexical. This is the site of either momentary friction or outright fracture and its necessitated *double take*. To read on in Stevenson's story of split personality while keeping in mind the textually material and mutating term "draught" is thus to pursue the braiding of inscriptive self-reference—some of whose threads we have just sketched out under the rubric of pun's "singular resemblance"—with that drama of re-agency which makes for both plot (the scandal of the vicarious) and its reading (the aesthetic institution of deputized desire).

We benefit, though, from prolonging our concentration on the self-referential stratum of the textual parable for a moment more. As it happens, the notion that Stevenson's story is about literary writing—not to say subliterary hackwork—and its reception, about literary production and consumption, is not a new thought about *Dr. Jekyll and Mr. Hyde*, not at least until certain further specifications are set out. The ratio has elsewhere been suggested, for instance, that Hyde stands to Jekyll as the writer in Stevenson, in all the transgressiveness of inventive license, stands to the man as socialized Victorian citizen.[20] My emphasis so far, of course, is instead on deviance as a figure for writing itself (and its recognitions), rather than for the writer, so that Hyde would in this sense embody in order to externalize the sort of thing writers *write out* so they don't have to live through them. It has more recently been suggested that the split between Jekyll and Hyde represents the division not between Stevenson as creative and as social being but instead, within the writer himself, between higher and lower callings.[21] Whether this makes the hunched, brutish Hyde the figure of the misshapen popular text, the "crawlers," "shilling shockers," and "penny dreadfuls," or a figure of the low reader himself, whose voracious tastes ("drug"-like, as Stevenson well knew) must be placated, remains undecided in this last line of argument. It is likely to be the former possibility that Stevenson stresses in speaking of the story itself, rather than its savage protagonist, as a "Gothic gnome"—like the "hideous progeny" of Mary Shelley's deformed literary production.

In any case, the various symbolic determinations of Hyde in the leading criticism of the story might well appear to exhaust the semiotic field. The potent malformation offers a figure for writer or writing, reading or reader; the symmetrical possibilities seem complete. But not quite. One of the terms claims priority in being required by the rest. For if Hyde stands to Jekyll at the distance, on the one hand, either of writer from citizen or of writing from writer, or, on the other, either of popular reader from artist or of subliterary potboiler from its more aesthetically ambitious authorial source, nevertheless any such distance is manifested only as the recoil incident to recognition: only, in short, by decipherment through reading. And it is here that we move (or flip) from the self-referential linguistic network to the reflexive snares of the textual encounter. As we have come to understand it, the reflexive parable is thus once again transactive in content as well as in form, an affective negotiation played out by plot even as it is played to in response. This is what makes reflexive episodes parabolic rather than merely rhetorical: a narrative *of* as well as *for* acknowledgment, an acknowledgment including identification, distancing, purgation, and release. In such episodes, story carries the burden of its own discursive effect. In the case of Stevenson's narrative, just as a pun requires a kind of multiple consciousness, so does that narrated punning of autonomy into aberrant multiplicity for which wordplay paves the reader's way.

Furthermore, Jekyll's relation to his alter ego is motivated by the kind of one-way identification we associate with literary experience, where characters take no notice of (even while sometimes illustrating) the very psychic impulses that are necessary to manifest them in the reading act. By this controlling design, Hyde is materialized over against the civilized but never again *self-contained* subject, Jekyll, who reads his own desire in the deviant's every move. Rendering this configuration most like the novel reading that makes us aware of it, Jekyll's is a fraught attention unreciprocated in its raw self-consciousness. By the asymmetrical structure of this particular narrative, that is, Hyde remains mostly oblivious to the subject he must eclipse in order to exist, just as Jekyll contemplates Hyde with the vicarious abandon necessary to keep that side of himself alive. And so we are returned by the internal logic of this structure to the role of vicariousness in the frame, where Utterson prefigures Jekyll as proxy for the displaced energies of the reading event.

"Vicarious Depravity": Reading Jekyll-eyed

Vladimir Nabokov, in his lecture on Stevenson's story, detects a "curious problem" in this regard, one which, in my view, he stops just short of solving.[22] Noting that both Utterson and Enfield are too "stolid" in their ordinary walks of life to wax eloquent, as they do, over the stories that have come to them about Hyde, he surmises that Hyde must bring out "the hidden artist" (193) in them. "Otherwise . . . the colorful imaginings of Utterson's dreams after he has heard the story," for instance, "can only be explained by the abrupt intrusion of the author with his own set of artistic values and his own diction and intonation. A curious problem indeed" (193). To be sure. It might even be a problem (thinking of Wilde again, and of Dickens before him) of curiosity itself and its deflected channelings. But let me rephrase it this way—to make an alternative explanation as obvious as possible: Why isn't a character's reaction to a narrative, whether the narrative is told to him or conveyed in writing, a closer guide to his role *as reader* than as artist?[23]

Before he becomes a focal point for the stories, oral and written, which circulate around the eminent Dr. Jekyll, Utterson is described early on in his customary position "close by the fire, a volume of some dry divinity on his reading desk" (35), spelling away the hours in ascetic dedication to denial itself—as he will later, and unsuccessfully, attempt to "mortify curiosity" (59) in regard to the unfolding plot. By the novel's very first paragraph, we have heard that Utterson is a man whose hospitality to "downgoing men" (29), especially to their stories, leaves him "wondering, almost with envy, at the high pressure of spirits involved in such misdeeds" (29). To recall the aspect of triangular desire in René Girard's work by which "external mediation" is provided not through a flesh-and-blood rival but through a literary prototype, we might cast up Utterson's vicarious psychology as follows: His is an impulse mediated not by an erotic rival but by the envied degenerate, whose dangerous indulgence is just what Utterson (to use the kind of idiom which Stevenson's text ends up punning upon while deconstructing) *denies himself*. Utterson's homosocial envy is the functional obverse, in short, of our narrative urge. But between intake and uptake in such a response, between recognition and identification, falls the unnerving logic of "projection" (Dr. Jekyll's own term, as we will see)—and its parables. The result is that the conservative, stabilizing allegory of bipolar good and evil in the main schema of the plot is in fact sabotaged rather than bolstered by its vicarious reframings.

It is said of Utterson that "few men could read the rolls of their life with less apprehension" (42). Since this is precisely the "apprehension" one wants from a good story, yet since he has sworn off any reading but "dry divinity," other stimuli will have to suffice—as, for instance, when Utterson "seemed to read a menace" (42) in the convivial firelit decor of Dr. Jekyll's front room. Jekyll himself is so self-conscious about the narratability—hence readability— of his woes that he uses it as a metaphor for them, soliciting help from Lanyon so that "my troubles will roll away like a story that is told" (75). The literal rather than figurative "story" arrives, finally, in two private documents that come into Utterson's possession, one from Lanyon, one from Jekyll. In the last we read of Utterson, he "trudged back to his office to read the two narratives in which this mystery was now to be explained" (73). He has promised Jekyll's servant, Poole, that he will peruse them as quickly as possible, returning by midnight to help "send for the police" (73). He never does return within the plot, and any policing function, whether of deposition or verdict, is deputized to the speechless reader, whose reactions are cut adrift from any explicit post-mortem after Jekyll's own exit line at the end of his document.

What division of consciousness Utterson's reading of these pages is by now presumed to involve can only be brought out by its correlation with the preter-natural (yet at another level quite recognizable) nature of the monstrosity he reads about. Whenever Hyde is dormant, Jekyll must indulge the forbidden pleasures he craves in the old-fashioned way: "It was in my own person that I was once more tempted to trifle with my conscience" (92). This mundane sin-ning *in propria persona* is thus dramatically contrasted with its alternative: a "vi-carious depravity" (86) that supposedly sets him apart from all precedent. "Men have before hired bravos to transact their crimes, while their own person and reputation sat under shelter. I was the first that ever did so for his pleasures" (86). Book buyers might have cause to object to this boast, for they too pay di-rectly (in purchase price) for the surrogate experience Hyde generates as de-monic *vicar*, being taxed for such guilty pleasures without (unlike Jekyll) the ultimate forfeit of their identity.

There is no need to inflate the point in order to make it. One needs only to quote. Jekyll "projected and shared in"—both generated and inhabited—"the pleasures and adventures of Hyde" (48). He does so in just the way a reader would in the case of a fictional character, where you participate in the very ef-fects you begin by producing in your own textually spurred imagination. At a more explicitly linguistic level, unguarded reading has already been found to risk identification—and this in the case of your own longstanding stand-in. When Utterson comes upon Jekyll's will, he is startled to find himself inscribed there as the usurper of Hyde, the previously designated inheritor, "for in the place of the name of Edward Hyde, the lawyer, with indescribable amazement, read the name of Gabriel John Utterson" (35). Across the normative linkages of grammar, the false flicker of equivalence through apposition ("Hyde, the lawyer") gets ahead of itself in making the point about the exchangeability of Utterson and Hyde. Not only legatee of the will, Utterson will also end up the recipient (if not exactly the beneficiary) of the later document, the final "nar-rative," which goes out as well over Jekyll's signature. This is a story that remains inert, for him as for any reader (reading over his shoulder as it were), unless you can each find yourself, amazed, in Hyde's place as well as Jekyll's. It is, therefore, part and parcel of Jekyll's Faustian overreaching to exaggerate his uniqueness in being the first to delegate his pleasure as well as his dirty work, to project and imaginatively embody it elsewhere. For not only do writing and masturbatory fantasy, say, those two effects of the secretive hand, come to mind as counterexamples, but more precisely reading—where the projections of another, of the narrator, return upon you in the all but involuntary promptings of response. Such a response, Utterson would be the first to think, is by nature predatory, divisive, in every sense un*wholesome*.

To this dynamic of projection there is a further and purely discursive clue, one that happens to tap the very tradition of literary address—of interpolated and so ensnared reading—which elsewhere in the story is left to the inference of plot rather than the deference of rhetoric. In a passage detailing Utterson's obsessive curiosity to behold the features of Mr. Hyde, indirect discourse swells to a fever pitch of speculation—until an unexpected reader address punctures the cocoon of Utterson's own musings, suddenly diverting the exact nature of the Jekyll/Hyde relationship into an inoculated parenthesis that leaves all suspicions in the reader's keep. I refer to the mention of Jekyll's "preference or bondage *(call it which you please)*" (8; emphasis added). Pivoted around the idea of desire versus entrapment, the unexpectedly evoked immanence of reception in this seemingly inconsequential rhetorical gesture nonetheless justifies its own aside—at this charged moment—as a telling acknowledgment of the necessary (and hence conscripted) pseudovoluntarism of the reading agency, where a certain version of interpretation (guesswork) is exactly the audience's *pleasure*. The most negligible of interpolations—the parenthetical "which you please" (like *Trilby*'s "straight at you")—thus finds itself lodged strategically within one of the most exhaustive structures of extrapolation since the one-sided frame of *Frankenstein*.

Like Shelley's novel, *Dr. Jekyll and Mr. Hyde* simply closes by opening upon such an underdetermined space of reception, as if Utterson were in the position of Mrs. Saville rather than Walton, with just a bit more characterization for us to go on when taking his tacit intensity of investment for our own. Then, too, it is scarcely to be doubted that in all of this implied metapsychology of reception, Dr. Jekyll himself should know whereof he speaks. Suggesting to Lanyon that he not press for further details of the mystery, Jekyll taunts him rhetorically: "Or has the greed of curiosity got too much command of you?" (79). Jekyll thus anticipates what he will later describe as the "greedy gusto" (89) with which he himself indulged his wildest fantasies through the mediation of Hyde. If the loss of self-control, in some drastically literal sense, is exactly what constitutes the long-shrouded aberration named Hyde, then even the narratee of secrets is hereby tainted with the contagion into which he inquires too closely. The same insinuation surfaces a good deal more explicitly across the verbal echo between Jekyll's "till I fell in slavery" (85)—as a description of his thrall to debauchery—and Utterson's response to Enfield's mere "story" as a kind of fall into fascination with the faceless "figure" of evil: "Hitherto it had touched him on the intellectual side alone; but now his imagination also was engaged, *or rather enslaved*" (37; emphasis added). Indeed, it is Utterson's early "wondering, almost with envy" (29) about the sins of the other which is answered by Jekyll's state of mind when "plunged into a kind of wonder at my vicarious depravity" (86), a wonderment that cannot be separated from further insatiable speculation and enactment. Surprise, curiosity, engagement, dependency; eager gusto, greedy gustation, addictive voracity, enslavement—the tainted metonymic shuttle of associations generates *in reading* the metaphoric link between a reader's internal projections and the supernal nightmare of their actual embodiment.

What Utterson's vicarious travail diagnoses is the very principle of romance attraction analyzed four years earlier, and without anxiety, by Stevenson in "A Gossip on Romance" (1882). This was an unabashed defense of a genre whose neogothic variant would in his own hands turn that defense back on itself as (anticipating his later poem) a sustained cautionary "fable" of "the reader." In "A Gossip," Stevenson insists that it is "incident" (romance) and not characterization (psychological realism) in fiction (as, for instance, in *Dr. Jekyll's* three flatly named chapters, "Incident of the Letter," "Remarkable Incident of Dr. Lanyon," and "Incident at the Window") which "woos us out of reserve"—or, in other words, eroticizes our indentification.[24] In a language of embodied self-extension closely anticipating that of his later novella ("plunged into a kind of wonder" above), he writes that at such moments "we plunge into the tale in our own person and bathe in fresh experience" (233). His emphasis in the essay falls on heroic rather than depraved incident, of course, but only within a rejection of anything like deceptive "illusion," since "the reader consciously plays at being the hero" (232): an effort of willed removal from self-identity. We violate nothing in the logic of his defense of romance to recognize in it the condition of possibility for the reader's identifying as well with the villain, especially if the latent villainy in question is unchecked vicariousness itself.

The more one reads in that essay on romance, the more does it seem a gloss on the later gothic novella as a parabolic deviation from the norm. "The pleasure we take in life is of two sorts—the active and the passive" (217) might be

Jekyll confessing, rather than Stevenson expositing. Or here is a version of Utterson's insomniac unrest after first hearing of Hyde, without the tacit critique of such unacknowledged sublimations of desire: a state where we are "rapt clean out of ourselves, . . . our mind filled with the busiest, kaleidoscopic dance of images, incapable of sleep or of continuous thought" (214). I quote from a sentence, the first of the essay, which begins: "In anything fit to be called by the name of reading, the process itself should be absorbing and voluptuous" (214). Change the paired terms of this beckoning otherness of romance to self-expunging and libidinal and you have a narrative rather than an essay. So complete is the reader's surrender that "there are lights in which we are willing to contemplate even the idea of our own death" (233), an assertion less surprising than it might have been when, by this point in the essay, it is clear that the very structure of reading as self-surrender already produces a tentative figure for that death, one that *Dr. Jekyll and Mr. Hyde* will narrate into an entire plot. Whereas Stevenson in the essay wants to distinguish these romance effects from the deliberative attention one gives to high realist fiction in a psychological vein, such is the power of the novella that it exposes the phenomenological displacements incident to any and all invested narrative reading, where "natural appetites" (221) and the "narrative longings of the reader" (222) must find vent and venue and where the reader who "dwells upon" (234) a story has already participated in its indwelling force. That an author so eloquently devoted to the strange psychic displacements of reading could produce an apparently monitory fable on this theme suggests exactly the retrenchment at the back of all such critique, the celebration beneath diagnosed morbidity, which this chapter will finish by considering in the parables of reading with which it is concerned.

Conscripted Interest, Drafted Manifestations

Nothing makes clearer the primacy of textual encounter and its elusive materializations in *Dr. Jekyll* than the first extended description of Utterson's obsessive interest in finding a credible face for the rumored Hyde: "If he could but once set eyes on him, he thought the mystery would lighten" (37). Mr. Hyde and myster/y: They each need a face, or they remain merely distorted mirror images of each other in the ripplings of discourse. In this way does the figure of prosopopoeia—the figure that serves famously for Paul de Man and J. Hillis Miller as the trope of tropology itself—begin to coagulate in the passage around a tacit dead metaphor, as if it were the clichéd matrix (Riffaterre) of the entire story: *the very face of evil*.[25] Here again is a rather free indirect discourse inhabiting Utterson's feverish ruminations across the threefold iteration of their absent cause: "And still the figure had no *face* by which he might know it . . . a *face* worth seeing: the *face* of a man who was without bowels of mercy" (37)— in short, the almost disembodied or eviscerated mask of depravity. But Hyde remains for a long while virtually featureless and therefore virtual, retaining in this way his usefulness as the perfect backdrop for "projecting."

To rerun in brief the overall procedures of this chapter in their bearing on Stevenson's tale: If the punning turn can seem to deconstruct "itself" through its mordant homophonic parody of discrete self-presence, in other words through a split moment of linguistic autoreferentiality, it can do so only by way of the reflex of reading. To the naked eye, there is no more than one "I," for instance, on hand in Jekyll's utterances; only in reading do you start sensing, if not seeing, double(s)—and by a specific sort of projection: the subvocal throwing of your own voice. Along these (not entirely written) lines, we come now upon a crux of textual processing in which the overdetermined reflex of *graphonic* response—the tendency, so to speak, to *hear things* when reading, to audit linguistic materiality itself—serves to structure in microcosm the extrapolative logic of the entire plot as a cognitive projection, a reading in.

Utterson's role is again central: the reluctant reader whose indirect discourse is left by us to decode as if it were the texture of his own (and the story's) unconscious. A couple of sentences before that triple iteration (quoted above) of "face" as a password for embodied rather than nebulous deformity, we find this twofold stress: "And still the figure had no *face* by which he [Utterson] might know it; even in his dreams, it had no *face*" (37; emphasis added). In the sentence just before this, as if precipitating the fivefold litany of "face" to come, the text offers a summary of the hyperactive "figure" of Hyde, now running down a girl in the street, now appearing at Jekyll's bedside to will the latter into doing his bidding: "The figure in these two faces haunted the lawyer all night." So Stevenson had originally written, striking "faces" at the last minute (as if effacing it) and writing "phases" above the line.[26] The trace of this excision may be taken as the crux of the whole novella *as narrative*. Trying to get a fix on Hyde, Utterson's effort is to arrest the reports about him long enough to figure him, to give him face. He does so in a way that resembles the ekphrastic localization of textual analogues in painting and photography discussed earlier, where we find dramatized the principle of "ekphrastic fear" postulated by W. J. T. Mitchell.[27] But since this effort is only meant to figure in turn Utterson's desire to *read* Hyde, the underlying pressure toward narrativity shows through—and wins out—in the redrafting, even if defensively normalized in the process. In other words, the logical constraint of a linear *distinction* (phases or stages) is exerted

upon the intolerable *composite* (double-facedness)—all in the unconscious service of a credible reading rather than sighting, yet with the revised word achieving only the limited success of a partial suppression.

There is a suggestive point of comparison between this knot of self-refer-
encing textual alterity and the homophonic undulation of Jane Eyre's discourse
when describing that persistent, if continually interrupted, "romance" never
more than audited by her inward ear (chapter 9). As banked "fire" turns to "ire"
in Dr. Jekyll's case as well, the inward clefts, defiles, and drifts of subjectivity
are delivered from latency (here through the projection of Utterson's indirect
utterance) in the syncopated phasing in and out of desire as well as in the reified—and so rent—facets of the subject's contradictory impulses. That this verbal turmoil is figured, within the narrative, as itself a kind of a reading event,
a manner of (vicarious) recognition, is a fact condensed here, by this reflex of
Stevenson's text, into what we might want to term a monosyllabic parable—
like the homophonic cloning of "I" and "ay" earlier. With one word taking the
place of another, "phases" gets read in echo and exchange with "faces." At such
a moment the reader of the published novel rather than the manuscript draft
is quite literally enacting Utterson's own wish fulfillment by projecting a "face"
on the "phase" in question.

What I don't mean to be saying about this linguistic crease in *Dr. Jekyll and
Mr. Hyde* is either of the things that might seem most obvious about the authorial revision involved, beyond the fact that five appearances of the word
"face" in such close quarters may have seemed more effective than six: either
that Stevenson didn't want the fantasized manifestations of Hyde in his different roles to be confusingly two-faced in their own right (reserving this distinction for the Janus-like Jekyll); or that Stevenson's manuscript alteration has
fended off a virtual dead metaphor ("faces" for something like "aspects") in
order to postpone any foreshadowings for Utterson of the Doppelgänger's actual countenance at this premature point in the arc of building anticipation. I
wouldn't put it this way precisely because the erasure is actually retained in the
shadow of a pun. I want, therefore, to suggest instead that homophobic shock
(Utterson's shudder at the thought of Hyde at Jekyll's bedside) is taken up
rather than kept down by the (merely?) textual scandal of homophonic recoil.
In the imposed sequential logic, that is, of "phases" (temporal rather than corporeal), we nevertheless—by a metamorphosis, or anamorphosis, internal to
language—catch the alternative face of a phrasing which, like its referent, refuses self-identity. We catch it, moreover, as if glimpsing it in superimposition:
the prosopopoeia of the pun itself as a kind of lexical mirage, a specter, a deformed aural double—the result of Stevenson's own "transforming draught."

This phantom manifestation operates, on the model of a dreamlike parapraxis, as a working (out) of fleeting, amorphous apprehensions (both senses) in and through language—the reader's apprehensions as well as those of the character's subjectivity within which discourse labors to situate you.

Quite apart from the manuscript's apparent corroboration of (however unconscious) wordplay, then, the published text as we have it has its divided way with you. Even while in a state of quickened, edgy alertness—a kind of textual paranoia—you may think it is you who are writing over, by reading in, the given by its equivocation, the stable substantive by the pun ("phases" by the "faces" that demarcate them). Instead, you are all the while being written with—conscripted at the (lowest) level of phonemic demarcation itself. Such a split-second thought has, I repeat, an extrapolative force as novelistic reading event precisely because the linguistic palimpsest—read in and thus read off as a psychic projection (yours in Utterson's place)—is in its own right the narrativization of the strictly verbal image: the displacement onto plot's phased events of a radically figural ekphrasis (the verbal evocation of the unenvisaged face).

Like the secret face of fear he materializes, it remains the very nature of Hyde to be always hidden in his very naming. Never fixed by an accurate designation, he lingers instead as that always renewable projection in and through whom you take your gothic pleasure, haunting, insistent, residual. You do so not by reading Hyde per se but by *going out of yourself* (like Jekyll) in order to make Hyde not so much visible as narratively viable. To say so is to retrieve from within the deconstructive rhetoric of tropes (Hyde the figure of writing)—as has been the work of this book as a whole—something of the original suasive force of rhetoric itself (Jekyll/Hyde as a dynamized figure of textual response). In summing up the way this discussion differs from recent approaches to the story, therefore, I would stress that Jekyll's projection into Hyde represents, centrally, neither aesthetic inspiration nor creative product (neither writerly sensibility nor writing itself). Nor does this cloning represent primarily either the groveling and sensual audience or the sensationalist reading matter of just such an audience. Hyde's manifestation would appear to demarcate instead the very sensation of narrative reading: a both insatiable and sapping fascination, with the reader drafted into complicity by the least turn of phrase.

Thus does *The Strange Case of Dr. Jekyll and Mr. Hyde* not only trope reading but diagnose it. The tale, that is, dissects precisely reading's initially split motive in encounter with any such tale. This is the urge to divide subjectivity into passive and projective agencies in a multifarious will toward otherness, toward fictive extensions of the self, which quickly outstrips the mere doubleness on which it is built. The whole process, in its late-century inflammation, may thus lay itself open to the "genealogical perspective" applied to its immediate aftermath, the commercial advent of film in the next decade, by Fredric Jameson. Understanding the tension in film spectatorship between active and passive impulse "as the material reinforcement of an ongoing tendency in social life as a whole," Jameson finds the experiential condition institutionalized by the cinematic apparatus to mark a symptomatically reified division of human labor induced by the alienating effects of capitalism—cognitive labor as well as physical.[28] Stevenson's terms for this take his own text to court for exactly the fragmentations of labor it exploits as well as portrays. Both introvert and extrovert at once, reading stands inscribed by *Dr. Jekyll* as a will toward psychic dispersion which remains, from the midst of its caution and complacency, nonetheless "greedy" and engorging—a tendency "vicarious" and voyeuristic, "enslaved" and ultimately self-consuming.

Jekyll is the riven because *divisible* subject, the subject become object, while you the reader (despite, if also because of, the passive versus projective aspects of your stance) are ultimately the *dissipated* subject: diffused and spent. There is nothing in the divided intentionality of Jekyll, the battle of higher against lower in his own person and of the two together against the reification of the latter in Hyde—nothing in that dutiful Victorian polarization which assaults at any depth the ideology of the unitary subject which persists across, as if to heal, the rifts of self-alienation. For units can be halved within the stable system of calibration which identifies them. Jekyll's "transcendental medicine" (80) is indeed in service to what we would now dub a transcendental subject, a subject whose bastion in the corporeal body it only appears to blast open. Jekyll must be one self or the other, the mixed compound of aspiration or the precipitated monster, at which point the only thing not appalling about the latter is perhaps that Hyde is at least always *so much himself.* You as reader, on the other hand, can be, as it were, *anyone you think.* And this is a more genuinely transgressive indeterminacy. As such, and though fostered under the aegis of the aesthetic, this tendency must also be chided, or at least bridled, by a parable that links the reader not so much to Hyde as to the Hyde effect: a defection from fixed subjectivity. Such transference of affect in identification is a vicariousness which, grown avid and wasting, must be quenched by a constraining ethics of curiosity familiar to the nineteenth-century novel at least from Dickens forward—and about which I will have more to say, in respect to its late-century cultural work, at the end of this chapter.

For now, it is time to call in the more immediate dramaturgical yield of a distinction borrowed in my opening chapter from Barthes's *S/Z*: that between "character" and symbolic "figure." If it helped there to suggest a figuration of "the reader" sliding between and across both rhetorical loci as well as various characters who may or may not be caught reading, it might now be adapted to clarify the narrative structure of Stevenson's Doppelgänger plot. For one of Barthes's major analytic purposes is a defamiliarization of character as self-identity. Intermittently surfacing across a text, figures are fluid, skittish, indeterminate, multiple, whereas characters are fixed in a social role. Dr. Jekyll, however, explodes the myth of character by embodying, in a body itself fatally unstable, the intersection (I would want to say) of the figures of alert reading as well as moral passivity (figures manifested also in Utterson) with the radically incompatible and so divisive figure of unchecked craving. This symbolic crossing of vicariousness with realized desire, once released into and discharged by plot, issues both in monstrosity and in parable: gothic mayhem and the reflexive tumult of reading.

As with many a neogothic plot, textual consumption in Stevenson's story is both internal to and beyond the text, extrapolated to response from within, contextualizing the parable from without. In an age where published stories are so relentlessly engorged by the addicted body politic, consumption (rather than reflective contemplation) is indeed a kind of structural mastertrope, the apotheosis of which we saw Eliot struggling for in *Daniel Deronda*. Parable is one name for the way this works. Dorian Gray is finally used up by his *Picture* in its closing paragraph, as will Dracula be consumed at the very last in and by *Dracula*. In this same way Dr. Jekyll and his psychopharmacological double, in the former's final "Statement of the Case," are consumed both by that text and by *The Strange Case* it brings to a close. In all of these gothic metatexts, a certain vein of literary history is tapped and exploited by structural irony as well. Having worked the artificial climacteric of the gothic out of her textual system with her first novel, Jane Austen achieved by the time of her last a mode of plotting which served as a veritable paradigm for patient and capacious temporality. The gothic revival of the late Victorian period borrows the overarching logic of narrative fullness and postponed closure with a mortal vengeance. It recruits the deferrals of plot as the macabre superannuation of the self-destructive or already defunct protagonist (painted icon, hypnotizing photographic image, split and haunted agent of desire, nosferatu). And it goes further—by breaking out of its plot into the queasy zone of reception, holding the mirror up to your own devouring captivation. Taking the ambiguities of story, or its local wording, any way you "please," you are still led to extrapolate from them to the psychology of your own prolonged and complicit projections, reminded *in the event* that reading is always a rather weird circus of goblinish telepathic doubles operating by an occult logic of dispossession and inhabitation which remains preternaturally invasive, parasitic, a bit creepy, a shade vampiric. This is just what the reading of gothics tends to remind you about the courted grotesquerie of reading in general: that you are always in one sense, if not in the other, at least a little spooked by narrative, visited in it by the shades of otherness.

We may let Stevenson's story distill what we have been seeing. It is as if the whole plot of his novella hinges tacitly on a twofold rhetorical question: By analogy with what in "normal" experience can the reader be expected to understand (a) the splintering of identity in the very manifestation of its desires and (b) the experience of taking one's pleasure and enduring one's pain (if "one" is even the word for such a subject) through the agency of another? The answers: (a) in writing and (b) in reading. Moreover, these two allied and finally reciprocal decenterings converge in the pursuit of a third implicit question: On what sort of everyday experience do we draw in order to recognize the plotted phenomenon of an ineradicable alterity dogging the individuated form, shadowing it with self-estrangement? The answer: on writing registered intensively, in all its self-alienating overtones and ambivalent voicings; that is, on literary reading. Bram Stoker's *Dracula*, while itself contextualized both by developments in media technology and by contemporaneous literary debate, also finds in linguistic metamorphoses the shifting material base—and most familiar analogue—for its own very different (but no less reflexive) thematic of "vicarious" depravity.

There is a way to think of this in generic terms as well. Franco Moretti borrows Todorov's notion that the "supernatural" is always the literalization of a metaphor.[29] My more specific point is that this fact is insinuated by certain texts in their local metaphoric and lexical structure. This difference of emphasis from Moretti has direct consequences for conscripted reading. Let us grant that a gothic or "supernatural" story is born by making palpable a notion (and dead metaphor) like "something terrible is afoot in the land," a notion never materialized in so many words but embodied instead in, let us say, a man-made organism, werewolf, or vampire. Beyond this global conversion from figuration to personification, however, there are texts like *Dracula* in which such dead metaphors will in fact be multiplied and dispersed across the textual surface, albeit reactivated only by a certain oversensitive—again, paranoid—attentiveness. This is the gothic of reading at ground zero, where recognition is itself a kind of deviance.

Animating the Undead: Dracula's Composite Manifestations

As part of the evolution of nineteenth-century realism from Austen forward, the Victorian novel will mostly inter without quite embalming, where *Northanger Abbey* embeds and disinfects, the gothic thriller. The lid is to be kept on this generic tomb for most of a century. In the late 1890s, though, Bram Stoker may be seen to turn the recent gothic revival into a fable of revivalism itself. In the process, as if in a bookend for the Victorian century answering to Austen's early prognosis, Stoker drafts a tacit palinode for the aesthetics of realist fiction. With an emphasis on reception which recalls Austen's critique of gothic overindulgence, narrative in *Dracula* is found holding an uncertain ground between documentary and fantastic models, between transparent and hypnotic modes of access. Our question: As the reader recognizes the way in which hoary folkloristic materials are being rejuvenated in this novel of contemporary terror, how does the sensationalist pleasure in that revival bear comparison with—or bear up under—the self-regenerative nature of vampiric monstrosity itself?

I put it this way to draw out again the dubious role of reading in yet another *fin de siècle* tale of the otherworldly. Reading borrows once more from the content of fantastic narratives the form of its own interrogation. If the realist novel, with its aesthetic of suspended disbelief, arose from the dialectical transformation of empiricist versus romance models, a century later we find the renewed pull of romance, of a broadly supernatural variety, throwing the equation out of balance once more. It might even be argued that another dialectic is taking hold. On the slope of decadence, the long rule of realism as a seamless aesthetic seems pitched now against its antithesis in the preternatural narrative of vicarious aestheticism in Wilde—as well as of neogothic fantasy both in Wilde and in other writers of the period. What might subsume these alternatives in a new dialectical synthesis is a question to which *Dracula* will eventually lead.

Like *Frankenstein*, *Dracula* is in part the story of its own literary prehistory. Broaching the comparison has a way of recalling, in fact, that our earlier investigation of Shelley's novel involved something of the same approach through double reading attempted more systematically in this chapter, considering the novel first as a self-referential text about writing, revising, editing, and transmitting, then as a multiply framed parable of reception. To come to life, the Creatures of both Shelley and Stoker must resuscitate past material as present force. They must convert formative influence into continuing vitality. The deviant antihero of each plot, like the novel itself as an amalgam of legends, is a textual pastiche, spatial in one case (a congeries of body parts), temporal in the other (a palimpsest of historical incarnations): the former sutured together and artificially galvanized, the latter renewed from the hideously literalized *pulse* of otherness and then, in the reverse process of detection by his enemies, stitched into legibility as a quiltwork of separately incriminating textual evidence adding up to "a whole connected narrative" (17:269). The nosferatu is thus ultimately destroyed by information, by journalism manqué, by a data feedback system that borrows the documentary mosaic of a Wilkie Collins sensation novel, with one partial text after another piecing together the puzzle.[30]

And this is not all. In *Dracula*, finally, the metatextual logic of plot turns inside out. Just as Count Dracula is tracked and cornered by the transcription of raw data on the part of his adversaries, so in the long run does this same material become aligned with the mysteriously transfused energies of the Count himself: the telepathic correlative of what one can only call his powers of penetration. In this way, the two strands of gothic fabulation with which we have been concerned do converge after all upon the Count's showcased monstrosity. At the level of textual self-reference: Dracula hovers as the elusive signified of a rampant signifying energy whose new discursive technology of the keyboard actually repeats the sharp impress of his own assault.[31] At the level of the reader's extrapolated orientation toward the narrative: As Dracula lives off otherness within the plot, and constitutes as character an otherness living off you, so do you in turn draw off his energy in keeping alive your interest. Stoker thus rethinks (as did Stevenson before him) the very workings of realist identification as yet another gothic of reading.[32] I have dwelled on the self-referential dimension of *Dracula*'s manuscript composite in a separate essay, one concerned in part with the attempted textual containment of the vampire (himself introduced to us as a voracious reader about English culture) and his subversive return in the doubleness of dead metaphor.[33] To save space here, I will give only enough evidence to begin suggesting, first, the relation of this self-referential system to received critical opinion on the novel and, then, the interrelation of all such evidence with the simultaneous aspect of reflexive reading.

First, then, the critical coordinates. Above and beyond the insistent textuality of his reported manifestations, Count Dracula, as deracinated aristocrat and nosferatu both, is ferociously overdetermined in his role by a number of historical ironies concerning the British culture into which he inserts his spectral presence. As Franco Moretti has argued by comparison with *Frankenstein*, Dracula represents not only the aristocratic will in anemic attenuation but also its conversion to capital, to portably deployable investment.[34] He is defeated, in turn, by the collective entrepreneurial energies of the professional bourgeois cabal—or cartel—marshaled against him. In addition to Moretti's sense of his economic determinations, Dracula is also a kind of negative or reverse image of British imperialism, sailing to England as parasite on *its* vitality, yet doing so with a subaltern's fear of insufficient linguistic assimilation.[35] As elsewhere proposed, he is the transmitter of a kind of "venereal" infection that figures an epidemic of sexual "decadence" and biological degeneration.[36] Furthermore, in his sapping the will of his already passive female victims, his very modus vivendi represents a fantasized escape from, while in the end a heightened vulnerability to, the independent energies of the New Woman (in the conservative form of working wife). And in his powers of telepathy, he is the necromantic counterpart of the new telegraphic (25:398) and phonographic (24:374 and passim) technologies of electrically displaced origin which labor together to outmode and obliterate him. For critical readers attempting to recover the phobic context of the novel's original publication, this mélange of menace seems most revealing, finally, in its very divergences. With the anxiety disinterred by *Dracula* seeming all things to all people—the embodiment of all socioeconomic and psychosexual nightmares at once in elusive mutation—the act of reading spawns a general distress under the aegis of its aesthetic counterpart in nervous pleasure.

It is in this context of free-floating signification that the enunciative eruptions of neutral idiom into revived dead metaphor, unmentioned in the criticism, serve to figure something like a dynamic of continuous revamping at the level of the readerly unconscious. This is apparent as early as the Count's first double-edged sign of aristocratic hauteur in mentioning "we of the Dracula blood" (3:42). One further example among many—this in connection with Mina Harker, typist and dossier keeper on the Count—will have to suffice. Confessing her personal internalization of the disciplinary regime that her schoolteaching job has served to enforce, Mina admits the way she cannot help but respond when her fiancé takes her arm in public: "I felt it very improper, for you can't go on for some years teaching etiquette and decorum to other girls without the pedantry of it biting into yourself a bit" (13:207). The play of "biting" against "bit" only goes to underscore a trope of punctured skin which could scarcely find a novel in which it would be likelier to set off an alarm. The socially repressive, patriarchally sanctioned tradition of sexual law and order has already left its mark, sunk its teeth, into Mina well before its supposed antithesis in vampiric abandon arrives to literalize the dead metaphor in another version of coercive violence.

Noting the subterranean connection between *Dr. Jekyll* and *Dracula* on the score of such polysemic markers, we need also to recognize that such gothicism of language—this tapping of the uncanny through semantic instability, this polymorphousness of form as well as content—is by no means deployed exclusively as a discursive counterpart to story. Both Stevenson's and Stoker's narratives do operate with this self-figurative dimension as one armature of their narrative development, with textuality becoming an immanent metaphor for the site of doubling and vampiric renewal alike. Just as importantly, though, the signals emitted by pun and by dead metaphor redivivus, in thematizing linguistic perversity within the respective plots of doubling and resurrection, become the signs of the reader's own dubiety and second thoughts: the metalinguistic programming of reception itself as a participatory decoding of occulted energy.

Self-referential layering once again induces the reflex of reading. Yet the latent figuring of response does not stop there. Across the plot of *Dracula*, even as the documents that track the Count's whereabouts are read aloud by Mina to her cohorts in detection as a normative exercise in parafamilial transmission, another mode of reception is being progressively thematized—one that bypasses altogether the materiality of the written text. In trying to convince Dr. Seward of the vampire's existence, Van Helsing attempts early on to insinuate the possibility by leading rhetorical questions: "I suppose now you do not believe in . . . the reading of thought. No? Nor in hypnotism—" (14:229–30).[37] In Stoker's novel, not only do telepathy and hypnotism open the door to the off chance of vampirism, but they offer complementary figurations of its insidious—its both mentally and bodily invasive—threat. Since Seward is a bit of a psychoanalytic mesmerist himself, with a curious habit, as Lucy Westenra mentions, "of looking one straight in the face, as if trying to *read one's thoughts*" (5:72; emphasis added), he of all people is vulnerable to Van Helsing's argument.[38] Yet it is Mina Harker's peculiar vulnerability to the Count's own uncanny powers which brings this whole motif of telepathic transgression to a head. It is a case of preternatural double cross: the stalking, indomitable reader become herself thought-read.

Trancescription: Toward a Phenomenology of the Vampiric

To be sure, Wilde, du Maurier, and Stevenson each had a way of figuring textuality in scientific terms, chemical (poisonous) and photochemical alike, even while they explored a psychosomatics of reading. Stoker drives their diagnoses one step further in imagining a psychotechnology of reading itself: a wireless circuitry of unconscious dictation which, once textualized, must be reread by its doubly subjected agent—the read character turned reading medium. This clinching episode of the readerly metaplot develops as follows.

Mina has been involuntarily hypnotized by the Count so that she might transmit to him long-distance the secret machinations of his enemies. But it is Van Helsing's triumphant stroke to realize that telepathy—what he has earlier called "thought-reading"—can go both ways once the circuits have been opened. The result is that Mina is rehypnotized by the professor to invade Dracula's own mind by using the Count's psychic wiring, even when he is interred in his shipboard coffin, as an antenna to broadcast his whereabouts. While Mina is thus unconsciously engaged, it falls to Dr. Seward, as Van Helsing puts it in one of his telling solecisms, to "be scribe and write him all down" (25:408)—as if the nosferatu could be translated wholesale and per se to a textual form, Dracula become *Dracula*.

No one could be more interested in eventually studying this text than its unconscious conduit and oracle. Here is Mina, eagerly reinternalizing the narrative at the very moment of its first encounter by the novel's audience: "I read in the typescript that in my trance I heard cows low and water swirling level with my ears and the creaking of wood. The Count in his box, *then*, was on a river in an open boat" (26:419; emphasis added). In this preternatural access to a temporal simultaneity across great spatial distance, "then" marks the space of present inference rather than the space of the past: "therefore" instead of (or as well as) "at that time." Mina's "reading of thought," once reread, has thus sucked the enemy dry by identification, located his "where" here and now in the psychic field of countersurveillance. The apogee of dramatic irony—the vampire vampirized in his own encoffined passivity—is accompanied by a no less obvious metadramatic irony: the transcriber transcribed in order to read of herself at one remove, read of herself as if she were the other, here and now. At such a nodal moment in the media network within the plot, such a telepathic chiasm and hypnotic switch point of the text itself, the reading of gothic and the gothic of reading collapse upon each other.[39] The "figure" of vampirism as, finally, a baroque but manageable emblem for textual negotiation and its parasitic transfers of psychic energy is thus foregrounded by this regulatory reversal, where invasiveness (of mind by text, of text by mind) becomes reciprocal and liberating. Plot's telepathology seeks its homeopathic cure in the hermeneutics of reading.

So proceeds the least adventitious scene of reading in the late Victorian gothic. Quite apart from its implications for fictional consumption in a literary-historical overview, this scene is the covert thematic climax of Stoker's entire novel. It may in fact not only suggest why Mina is excluded from the last stages of the *man*hunt for Dracula but also go further than Moretti in explaining why Stoker's figure for the vampire is, despite the precedents of elite literature, cast instead by Stoker into masculine gender, thereby avoiding in part a too manifest conversion of mother to succubus.[40] With the vampire made male, a role is also left over in Stoker's plot for the energy of the feminine as the worried site of merely glimpsed or *disclosed* rather than incarnate and assailable perversity. In finally tracking the Count to his castle, that is, or in other words hounding the revived trope of vampirism back to its source, the confederacy of male sleuths is in fact *reading the unconscious of the woman*, reading as if in neural code what she herself would never consciously recognize as being shared with or derived from the brainwaves of the vampire: namely, the sleeping secret and nightmarish obverse of the novel's own courtship of domestic idealism in its parafamilial collective. Such is the plot's bizarre epistemological access, through hypnosis, to the horrific reverse nurture of an erotically devouring and solely self-regenerative desire. No parable of reading, I repeat, could be less peripheral to the narrative crisis of its text. Anxieties geopolitical (colonialist), psychosexual (phallic), familial (conjugal, maternal), medical (venereal), socioeconomic (monopolist)—all of them and more, swept up under the rank grave clothes of the Transylvanian invader, converge upon the body of the woman, not inscribed but internalized there: as something that must be deciphered—decrypted—from her mutterings, even and especially by the subject herself, through at once a technology and a necromancy of transmission.

All that remains of Stoker's novel after the summary execution of the Count—where, stabbed to the heart, he crumbles, dust to dust, at prolonged last—is a final textual reflection on his namesake, *Dracula*, after its own consumption.[41] In his closing "Note," Jonathan Harker speaks for the discursive collective when he laments that, with the whole ordeal now behind them, they had little to show for it but the questionable evidence of nonholographic prose, "nothing but a mass of typewriting" (27:449). They might as well be packing it off to a publisher. Yet the story, we are told, as, for example, with the story of Nell, stays private—becoming in effect a domestic version of one of those male-bonding narratives to which a member of the cadre alludes early on as part of the narrative's own prehistory: "We've told yarns by the camp-fire in the prairies, and . . . [t]here are more yarns to be told" (5:79). When finally unraveled, that is, the Dracula yarn, with Mina its unsung heroine, is putatively to become only a family legend in the Harker household, like the Darnays' story of Sydney Carton's sacrifice. Yet you know better, or else you wouldn't know anything about the story at all. Despite disclaimers of publishing intent—as in the punning "we want no proofs" (27:449)—any member of Stoker's audience well realizes that, once buried in the lead-lined grave of set type, Dracula can be revived and consumed ad infinitum. This is not an isolated trope of the supernatural genre but, rather, the gothic novel's figurative view of fiction at large in its constitutive rereadability. As we saw at the close of *Villette*, literary characters provide the Victorian novel's running equivalent of the perpetual Undead. But this is only because you vampirize them as much as they you—as they fuse with you. This, then, is the recognition that Stoker's antihero suffers for you. As he lives, invasively, so he dies. Penetration replies to penetration. In *Dracula*, it is the double vulnerability of reading, the penetrability of its objects and its subjects alike, which is ultimately and perilously *at stake*.

In this and other novels drawing the Victorian period toward its close, the picture of reading sketched forth is not particularly flattering. We have seen how the inaugural crisis of *The Picture of Dorian Gray* figured (painted) the hero at the moment when he was invaded and occupied, as smitten initiate, under the novel-like literary impress of Lord Henry's penetrating verbal dominance. In the heterosexual register, Trilby, too, lives in a relation of overt erotic subjection to her mesmeric master, Svengali. Stevenson refracts the terms in a somewhat different manner. What Hyde seems to represent is neither the incursive text nor the buggered or colonized reader. He stands, rather, for the imaginative violence done in reading which allows the figuration of such a splintered agency as Hyde to begin with. Wavering indeterminately as he does between an image of the textually ravenous masses and their degraded choice of books, between readers and read, Hyde, through it all, represents those overextensions of identity to which the abandoned self (whether through debauch or rapt attention) is prone. When we come to *Dracula*, there can be no doubt that writing and reading—as equally aggressive modes of self-extension—each violate thresholds and rend surfaces, puncture, invade, and engorge in the name of both initiation and satiation.

In this light, one final emblem of reading as bloodletting lies coiled within the convoluted turns of Stoker's text: the contextually overdetermined means by which Mina decides to bind shut her husband's troubled diary. This is of course the increasingly frantic document that has provided a first impetus to the unfolding textual pastiche we have all along been reading. In a burst of exquisitely quaint sentiment, Mina chooses to seal the evidence "with a little bit of pale blue ribbon which was wound round my neck" (9:129). If a silenced text would now need its decorative neck ribbon ripped away before it could grant access, then reading is every bit as much like vampirism as it is often figured to seem, here and elsewhere, in late Victorian narrative.

The Gothic Diagnostic: Modernism in the Offing

It is time to make plain what I have not been arguing—before pulling together the conclusions pointed toward by the evidence of this chapter. First, let me dispel the specter of any necessary intentionalism once and for all. As far as we know, Stoker had nothing more against reading than George Eliot did, or Dickens before them. Yet in telling their separate stories, they each came upon the story of reading itself. In its power, it is not always pretty. If we may want to say that Stevenson, like Gissing in his way, thought as much at some level of explicit consciousness, still what we have of this thought in *Dr. Jekyll* is mostly by indirection.[42] Stoker's later novel needs to be no more overt than Stevenson's in order to drive home the point along two correlative trajectories. Read through once, *Dracula* is about the writing-to-death of the vampiric. Read through once again, even if simultaneously, it is about the reading-to-death of the vampiric, in a calculated reversal of the nosferatu's own territorializing techniques. Once through (in the sense of over), with its title character consumed, the narrative also turns out to have been about the vampirism and hypnotic interchange of reading any such literary narrative through to its finish. This scarcely singles it out in its day, as we have seen, for even in commandeering an entire gothic archetype for its neogothic parable of story, it has only done with the nosferatu what Stevenson did with split personality. Stoker's legendary vampirism is to Stevenson's demonic doubling what each is to reading: virtual paraphrases of each other in the *fin de siècle* climate of print culture.

Which brings me to the second point I am not, or not simply, making. With its enshrinement of the reality principle in bourgeois culture, high Victorian realism can readily be seen as giving way to a denaturalizing counterswing in the late Victorian revival of romance—a transitional mutation of genre on the path toward a postrealist modernism.[43] But there is a more particular verdict to be reached from the evidence of this chapter. I have been investigating such exotic romances (by Wilde, du Maurier, Stevenson, and Stoker) as constituting not so much a welcome alternative to as, instead, an analysis and critique of realist representation in its *channels of reception*. And realism not only as it is inevitably mystified in consumption but also as it had always been recognized in its greatest texts to elude or exceed the reality principle. With the neogothic plots of the *fin de siècle*, this is where the romance of reading comes in: interceding in, rather than reversing, a tradition. We have noted in previous chapters how saturated by rhetoric and figure, and thus in one sense how persistently denaturalized, the Victorian novel has always been, and been known to be—how stylized its mimesis. Time wore away further at the edifice of autonomous world building, the reader's constructionist investment increasingly showing through. It is in this sense that what I have called the gothic of reading emerges from the reading of supernatural romance as, in its own right, a rereading of the whole realist aesthetic. Conscription enters the dramatic script itself, psychic coercions inflecting the plot. The commodified objectivity of the real transforms itself before your reading eyes into the paid or stolen pleasures of subjection.

At just this point in an attempt to think through the transition from realism to its melodramatic critique in late Victorian gothic fiction, one may take counsel from a tacit debate about literary modes within one of the central (central because most self-conciously transitional) texts of the period. I refer to a passing glance at genre theory couched in the defeated discriminations of Harold Biffen in *New Grub Street*. Whereas his friend Reardon, in Biffen's view, aspires to be a "psychological realist in the sphere of culture" (10:174)—read: George Eliot—Biffen's asperity of technique, as we have seen, struggles for "absolute realism in the sphere of the ignobly decent" (10:173). For "absolute," put "vulgar," as in the contemptuous imagination of Wilde's Lord Henry: "I hate vulgar realism in literature. The man who could call a spade a spade should be compelled to use one" (17:149). But what is the inevitable—or should we say logical—affiliation between the "real" and the "ignoble" (or "vulgar")? And what other categorical distinctions are consequent upon it?

Cognitive mapping can begin here, starting us toward not just an answer but that answer's wider field of inference. Following Fredric Jameson's use of the semiotic square adopted for narrative analysis by A. J. Greimas, we find that an ideological field of interdependent dichotomies derives from a cross-mapping of governing binaries at the level not only of narrative but of genre itself and, ultimately, of reception.[44] One possible quadratic logic would fall out as follows at the generic level, determining narrative construction and its underlying assumptions. Against the ignoble is counterposed the ennobled, which thus stands in preliminary contrast to the real (see fig. 13). But what, then, is neither real nor artificially ennobled, and what, if conceivable, is both? Again (as repeatedly in Jameson) the problem of the complex and contradictory fourth term (in this case, the neither quite real nor the wholly unreal) is raised and schematically resolved—here in the oxymoronic mold of idealist real*ism*: the transformation of the mundane into both its aestheticized ideality and its reigning bourgeois ideology. This can occur, however, only after something like the logical (rather than merely tonal) divergence between Biffen's literary practice and that of Reardon has served to distribute—to the sectors of a doubly bipolar model—the whole panoply (become grid) of late Victorian generic options.

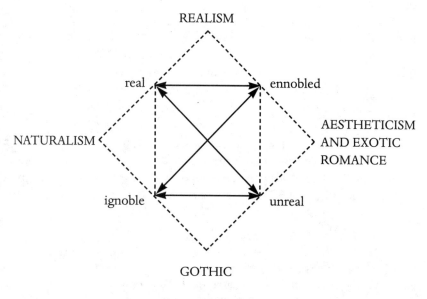

Figure 13. Genre Grid

In charting the ideologemes of narrative (Jameson's theory), not at the scale of conflicting values and the agencies they generate (Jameson's usual practice) but rather at the generic level, the squared ideological horizon ends up inscribing the subject positions of reading itself, as figure 14 will momentarily bring out. For now, one notes a curious return to the launching dichotomies of the novel form per se, recalling terms set out for early English fiction by Michael McKeon. Truth and value seem polarized as never before. Opposite the naturalist stance, and sharing with the gothics the indifference to factual reality, lie the self-gratifying ennoblements of both aestheticism (Wilde) and exotic romance (Haggard), with their very different transcendence of brute fact—one into the sensual otherworldliness of art-for-art's-sake, one into the heroic apotheosis of derring-do. In categorical terms, so far so good—even though this broader schematic view makes strange bedfellows of just such antithetical writers as Wilde and Haggard. This, after all, is the revelatory force of such semiotic analysis. The nagging binary that remains, however, is the one whose founding opposition makes dialectical resolution most strenuous and tentative. Setting itself up against its contrary in the gothic thriller (in the diagram's bottom quadrant) is this logical impasse transformed to cultural blind spot. Sharing the aspect of transcendence (ennoblement) but with one foot in the real, that is, stands (in the upper quadrant) the straddling giant of what Biffen would reject as "psychological realism" (his term for idealized, hence no longer "absolute," realism): a literary practice supposedly cleansed of the preternatural—until it returns by the back door of the reader's own quasi-spectral participation. A novelist like George Eliot would, preeminently, represent the distilled form of the realist enterprise. Hardy's skepticism and sociological diagnosis would lean heavily toward the naturalist pole on one end (joined there by certain New Woman novelists, with only the humanist vestiges of his tragic vision holding him back). By contrast, Dickensian melodrama and sentimentalism would edge toward the zone of romance on the other (though not in the particular *fin de siècle* mode of muscular male fantasy).

If this chapter is traveling in the right direction—if generic determinants are indeed caught up with self-enacted orientations of reading even more dramatically in *fin de siècle* texts than elsewhere in Victorian fiction—then we should be able to commute between such a generic taxonomy as sketched in figure 13 and a correlative model of response, one in which the tenor of the human events represented gives its coloration, not always protective, to the posture of reception. Taking our lead once again from Gissing's opposition between "psychological realism" (Reardon) and "absolute realism" (Biffen), we may assume the absence—or negation—of attempted depth psychology (or call it of subjectivity) in the latter's radically objective treatment. With such absolutism rejecting, in Biffen's terms, all evaluative "point of view save that of honest reporting" (10:174), the dispassionate scientism of this naturalist method often seems leagued with the flat acceptance of the socioeconomic given by the wearied characters within plot, an internalized empirical distance on their own lives. As with this permeating affective neutrality, the other categories so generated also slip between diegetic agency and formal attitude, exposing the way characters are made at once to endure and to induce the emotional tonalities of both representation and reception. Hence naturalism's zero point of affective intervention as the point of departure for the following corollary schema, with its implications for the reading (as well as fictional) subject (fig. 14). The clinical remove of radical objectivity (as in naturalism) finds its negating counterpart in the solipsistic self-involvement of rampant subjectivity—whether in decadent aestheticism or in the narcissistic mold of pulp adventure, with the world reduced to febrile projections of hypertrophic sensibility on the one hand, of heroic prowess on the other. A structural irony cannot be avoided: If you identify with the protagonists of either subjectivist mode, you do so with characters who do not themselves generically subscribe to the fictional ideology of empathetic self-divestment. The remaining counterparts in this grid may seem more elusively—we may wish to say subversively—interrelated. I am suggesting that, in the bottom quadrant, the objective and the subjective are together canceled (or

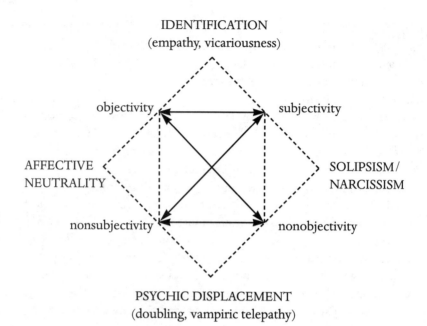

IDENTIFICATION
(empathy, vicariousness)

objectivity   subjectivity

AFFECTIVE   SOLIPSISM/
NEUTRALITY   NARCISSISM

nonsubjectivity   nonobjectivity

PSYCHIC DISPLACEMENT
(doubling, vampiric telepathy)

Figure 14. Metapsychological Grid

at least suspended) by the rules of generic fantasy as they operate in the gothic thriller. This is a narrative and hermeneutic terrain best understood in the terms of Todorov's influential account: fantasy defined, in other words, as a field of undecidable explanatory options.[45] On whether the monstrous is to be explained away by the marvelous or supernatural, with its own "objective" laws, or by the uncanny, with its exclusive recourse to psychic phenomena—on this postponed determination rests the very genre of the fantastic: defined as a space (text)—that is, a duration (reading experience)—of structured uncertainty hovering (in our terms) between explanations objective (however unverifiable) and subjective. A case in point for the double negation at issue here: The moment Mr. Hyde gets objectified as a second self, he can only be read as subjectivity itself personified.

Opposed to this, indeed formally dependent on its suppression, is the imagined transparent access to objectified (textualized) subjectivity which is continually paraded in the idealized "selves" of psychological realism. At this horizon (and ideological vanishing point) of expectation in the realist (organicist) novel, the communitarian—and equally organicist—values that hold (together) the autonomous subject in a represented network of sympathetic social affinities *may at any moment be extended to, and confirmed by, the participatory interest of the reader.* We may formulate the analogy as follows: The autonomous social subject enters into communal filiation through empathetic participation—but only within certain stringent limits—in just the way that the reader enters into identification. In this sense, as we saw in Dickens most clearly, reading tutors the subject in the intractable basis of all bourgeois confederation: an ineradicable otherness whose transcendence even reading can only begin to effect. Here, then, the always problematical resolution of antithesis in the initial Greimassian binary is achieved only when the text is oriented beyond itself toward reception, only in an interpenetration of objective and subjective registers made possible through the reciprocally invaded inwardness of the reading subject in encounters with fictional character. But there is a catch. The diffuse calculus of response ends up depending on a rudimentary arithmetic of mystified humanist assumptions: Autonomy (of character as of reader) plus empathy equals vicariousness, where the doubling of subjectivity in identification begins to resemble the psychotic breaks of an antithetical gothic mode.

We may now rewrite the field of affect plotted by figure 14 in the following terms: If realism under the sign of empathy is one definition of the mainstream Victorian reading act, then (at the lower level of the diagram) gothic fantasy under the sign of libidinal investment—with its perverse reifications and splittings of psychic energy—also seems a good deal like reading. This latter investment is, in fact, not only the topic of this chapter but the often unsaid subject of much that has gone before (here, and in the novel's own literary history): namely, the gothicizing of desire in textual response. If the diagrammatic approach shows nothing else, it manifests the semiotic fact that, though opposites repulse, they are also encroached upon at certain pressure points by the mirror reversals of their common (even when negated) terms. The degenerative trajectory of *Dorian Gray* offers, for example, a particularly illuminating series of generic swing cases, with the determinations of plot growing variously contaminating in response. We can track Dorian's moral decline as a virtual slippage around the zones of our two (now superimposed) grids. The narcissistic solipsism of his hermetic luxuriation closes him off in an empire of the senses contemptuously far removed from anything like the empirics of social observation. A tendency fertilized early on by the vicarious displacements of sensuous reading, then externalized in its deforming effects as a monstrous Doppelgänger in poison pigment, this indolent self-pleasuring rotates on the downside toward a gothic spectrality that extrudes, after all, a perverse objectification of his foul spirit on view in the vulgar empiricism of this portrait's implacable report—the mocking antithesis of everything imagined as art-for-art's-sake. The quadratically mapped course of generic erosion and overlap becomes a punitive vicious circle. And a no less incriminating hermeneutic spiral: For you in the audience end up where Dorian began, swept away by the vicarious pleasures, overriding all moral strictures, of the scandalous text.

Wilde's elusive allegorizing aside, our second grid serves to sketch again one of the abiding distinctions of this book: the difference between self-referential texts (where narratives theorize, among other things, their own genres—as well as their linguistic foundations) and reflexive ones (where narratives theatricalize their own reception). What shifting from generic to metapsychological terms (from fig. 13 to fig. 14) has allowed is, in short, a schematic view of the way reading is inextricably entailed by the dynamics of plot. More particularly, what the symmetries of semiosis lay bare in this case is the manner in which the doublings of fantasy are in fact the uncomfortable dark doubles of realist credence in operation. Biffen's dispassionate naturalism may remain the opposite of solipsistic aestheticism, but when the telos of empathy, even curiosity, gravitates toward radical inhabitation, the psychological and the uncanny have grown all too weakly differentiated. In the annexed mentalities it feeds on and the transfusions of affect it demands, reading begins to feel as much vampiric as evocative. Hence the bothered gothic of reading, to whose literary-historical implications we return.

The fantastic narratives of the *fin de siècle* seem repeatedly to thrive on this perversity of response, to batten upon the drama of their own consumption. They take a good (and strange) part of their thematic bearing from the specified psychic eventuality of just such response. What we find, from the tacit backward vantage of these late-century texts, is that along the downslope of generic erosion, certain preternatural parables work to expose the underlying risk of the whole realist establishment: not identification *of* but identification *with* the rendered world, a matter not of empirical match but of emotional fit, less evidentiary certification than vicarious surrender. In this sense, the romantic and Victorian agendas of suspended disavowal have degenerated in these stories to the suspended will of libidinal fixation or hypnotic thralldom. Literary history has thus closed in recoil upon its own staying power, its own hold on the imagination.

The move toward a more hermetic modernism, toward a textual surface at once seductive, resistant, and opaque, may be one attempted way out of the perceived impasse of this weird permeability of text to consciousness in classic narrative. The textual surface simply (or, rather, not so simply) thickens in retreat. This is what Fredric Jameson finds inaugurated in Flaubert as "the depersonalization of the text, the laundering of authorial intervention, but also"—and more to our point—"the disappearance from the horizon of its readership, which will become the *public introuvable* of modernism" (221). In our terms, the text no longer fronts its audience by attempting to conscribe it directly. In this fashion does the modernist novel—withdrawing from fiction's suspect appeals to participatory reading, the novel now as object rather than as world—contrive something of a dialectical synthesis of a polarized literary aesthetic within the pervasive tensions of *fin de siècle* culture. As crystallized in eighteenth-century British fiction, the prerealist poles of epistemology versus ethics, truth versus value, empiricism versus romance, the dichotomies that bracketed the formative epoch of the novel (McKeon), seem recast more than a century later under pressure from the antirealist animus of such adventure novelists as Stevenson, Haggard, and Kipling, as well as such affiliated gothic writers as Wilde and Stoker. The novel's founding oppositional paradigms thus come forward in reworked form as the counterpull of the exotic (valued for its falsity) against the domestic (routine in its truth to life), the fantastic versus the psychological "real." As such, this polarity swivels on an antithesis that is pro-grammatically subsumed in turn by the next century's concerted *exoticism* of literary language itself, the romance of textuality in its own right, with the modernist novel distanced and fetishized in technique now more often than in topic. On the *fin de siècle* brink of this transition, the vexed distinction in late Victorian gothic narrative (implicit in or actually plotted by it) between low and high culture, marketing and art, often seethes as a distinction between pan-dering to and parodying the insatiable appetite of mass consumption. Such is a lust for narrative which *Dracula*, three years before the end of the century, renders unmistakable. We might say that Gissing's mere figure of speech in *New Grub Street* (1891) for the triple-decker novel as a "monster . . . sucking the blood of [the] English novelist" (Gissing 15:235) meets in *Dracula* an answering mastertrope for the complementary relation of audience to the drained body of the lurid popular text.

Yet it must be apparent that the gothic of reading, whatever its prognostic value for modernism's beaten retreat from the mass audience, meant finally to pose no real and lasting threat to the institution of reading. All intentionality aside, when the phobic texts we have been discussing bulldoze whatever social oppressions they might otherwise be taken to conjure as monstrous, deform-ing, parasitic—or at least radically unnatural (that is, cultural)—when these novels level such fears to the status of reading's own uneasy self-recognition, when they turn social allegory into reflexive parable, they neutralize under the sign of the aesthetic the social traumas they might have addressed more force-fully, even if not more directly. Lest reading be seen as a culturally encouraged flight from the social violence of culture, it is found instead to mobilize its own aggressive and territorializing drives, deflecting to just that extent the unrest literature might instead have incited rather than merely, in its own consumption, indulged, scrutinized, and temporarily exhausted. In their parabolic alternative to simply working through our fears of the unknown—or the frightfulness of the too well known—the texts in question, that is, enact rather than merely tap our more perverse, but all the while generically contained, embrace of such fear in fiction.[46] This is their ideology—and finally their dialectic—of the aesthetic.

The truant detour from the real which such narratives provide is thus routed, via its own partial critique, toward a return to the status quo. Allowing that the terrors of any "supernatural tale" (Victor Frankenstein's phrase—having never, we are to regret on his behalf, trembled at one) are not simply chills but also thrills, and hence questionable as either, such fictions unload the burden of psychological disturbance from content onto form. You are made to fear the lurking morbidity of your reading. Just a little. Just enough. It is exactly the metatextual gothic of reading, in short, which keeps the reading of gothic from the rank escapism it so obviously courts on the open market. Such parables disinfect the same emotive sore spots they have stung into recognition. The intermission from the real is subsumed to a recuperative aesthetic mission: to reconcile the reading subject to textual experience more than the social subject to the world. All under the blanket of a cultural continuance strengthened by such controlled testing, it is thus the text, in its full reflexivity, which saves the book from itself, from its own worst indictment as *unexamined* pathological gratification—and does so in order to keep neither the narrative (plotted thriller) nor the text (linguistic and phenomenological construct) but precisely the book, the literary commodity per se, in the healthiest possible circulation. Though under internal siege, reading never had it so good.

Afterword
Caveat Lector

The reader is privileged to remain, and try what he can make of the discourse.

—Anne Brontë

One writes only half the book: the other half is with the reader.

—Joseph Conrad

Eternal curse on the reader of these pages

—Manuel Puig

René Magritte, *La lectrice soumise* (1928) © 1996
C. Herscovici, Brussels / Artists Rights Society
(ARS), New York. Used by permission

$\mathcal{F}$rom Brontë to Puig, allotted privilege to anathematizing sacrilege, discursive effect to ineffectual curse, may be one dead-ended route in the evolution of fictional rhetoric from mid-Victorian to postmodern fiction. If so, the indulged position of the reader during the nineteenth-century leg of this journey was meant to seem as comfortably provided for from novel to novel as one would suspect in hindsight. As an effort of such hindsight, this has been a book about the manipulated fact, rather than the presumptive substance, of audience reaction, but only as the two are inseparable; a book, that is, about rhetorical means rather than delivered meaning, but only as the one repeatedly—and reversibly—folds over upon in order to trope the other. In this proviso, this crucially suspended distinction, lies the intended difference between these pages and numerous other efforts at a theory of a reader's generative relation to prose fiction. The reader functionally "implied" in order to facilitate narrative continuity is, yes, the reader whose own inferences keep a narrative going across its inevitable gaps in presentation—this along the lateral axis. But these chapters approach the matter from a different angle. Perpendicular to such horizontal progression, the rhetorical axis is where, incident by incident in reception, a narrative happens as text. The definitive gaps encountered and transacted there are those between fiction and the subjectivity that animates it from the outside in—by being turned inside out in the process. In classic fiction, this is how the accomplice reader is accomplished by the text's own operation. This is the conscriptive event.

Fiction's concerted structural effort to extend the marked interpenetration of form and substance beyond even the narrative confines of a given novel into the space between text and reception may be—this book is now ready to propose—the definitive ideological index of nineteenth-century narrative: the moment when storytelling is doubly naturalized, not only as a sequence of transparently available human events but as the conscribed eventuation of a humanizing response. Such a moment signals the discursive pressure point where the formative imposition of narrative device so completely pervades, and seems so effortlessly to exceed, mere story that it, in every sense, takes you in. On the evidence before us, the various ideological constraints of nineteenth-century prose fiction are most obviously exposed, in short, at exactly the moment when form, overstepping plot, makes claims on the very content of attention.

What remains of this book is a final consideration of the effort by which the "privileged" reader of narrative—Anne Brontë's epithet, as well as Conrad's in *Lord Jim* for that "privileged man" (36:205) who alone reads rather than hears the conclusion of Marlow's narrative—is reoriented toward the world beyond written "discourse" (Brontë again). This is a world whose own broader idiom of interaction includes certain received and variously formulaic terms for the social establishment of the literary reader as lettered subject. What is lately called discourse analysis (where novels become polyphonic switchboards for the intersecting sociolects and institutional vocabularies of an epoch)—if such analysis is to help in achieving any comprehensive view of the novel as a cultural form—needs, therefore, to factor in the specific discourse attached to literary reading, the vernacular of the novel's own publicity machine and its self-advertising internal figures. It must pay heed to the way a text subjects its readers, as understudies, to a rehearsal of their literate roles in society: middle-class agents buying this or that kind of fiction on the advice, or not, of this or that journalistic assessment, programmed readers treasuring the spiritual currency of a novel's sentiment and its complexity at once, conscribed by both its therapeutic and its hermeneutic ideologies. This is the reader as literary (even subliterary) textual initiate as well as methodically accustomed customer. And if reading closely was a form of cultural study for the Victorians (because a form of acculturation), why not for us in critical retrospect? The institution of the novel as mass cultural product, in other words, demands investigation as the structuring of an intermittent leisured subject whose vacation from social commerce is made legible by rhetorical designation or plotted delegation, by interpolation or extrapolation, within the very texts that not only obligingly invite this imaginative diversion from the world but which figure it as part of the subject's cultural obligation to just that world—an obligation at once emotive and interpretive.

Idiom seldom fails to hit the ideological mark. What you *make of* a classic novel is the way you are led to believe yourself privileged to construe it, without quite wanting the responsibility for having spun it out entirely in your own mind. This middle ground is nicely held by a related idiom: the *construction* you *put upon* a text, collaborating with what already exists. Here Conrad takes up where Brontë's "privileged . . . discourse" leaves off, spelling out the culturally mandated division of labor in the most equable fashion. But what exactly is Conrad's emphasis? "One *writes* only half the book," the rest being merely pondered? Or "One writes only *half* the book," the rest being virtually written by— or "with"—its readers? Either way, it sounds democratic and ecumenical enough: the myth of hermeneutic freedom as textual facilitation. Either way, though, what goes unsaid is that these collaborative readers—either scripting their half of the book or honoring their share of the interpretive bargain—are themselves made, written, constructed by the text in its own likeness, in other words *figured in*: both imaged and so accounted for.

The rhetorical issue remains in productive flux. Conrad's transitional modernism offers a revelatory balancing act between Victorian assumptions and revisionist protocols. Looking back on the reader orientation of his major novels, Conrad sums up the deliberately mystified osmosis of his narrative transmission: "My manner of telling, perfectly devoid of familiarity as between author and reader, aimed essentially at the intimacy of a personal communication, without any thoughts for other effects."[1] Putting a definitive distance between his own textual stance and the authorially invoked "dear reader" of a Trollope or (by satiric inversion) a Thackeray, still the seeming conundrum of Conrad's double talk (a privately communicative discourse intimate and personal without being familiar) appears, when so described, at least as Dickensian as it does Joycean—and not least because its contradictions are best resolved in imagining intermediate narrators like Marlow or Master Humphrey: framers, scribes, exorcists. Conrad's manipulation seems especially complete. Even as they conscript you, his novels pride themselves on leaving you be.

Puig's "eternal curse" on the reader is, by contrast, a decidedly postmodernist gauntlet thrown down to travesty a vanished illusion of textual power, the once magic potency of the page. In between lies something like the modernist irony of Magritte's *La lectrice soumise* at the head of this chapter. While parodying the quiescent absorption of a whole subtradition of female readers in Western portraiture, Magritte's image of the astounded reader drags to heights of laughable exaggeration (in part through his past-participial adjective) the "submissive" position of being overly taken with a text, thus providing a pictorial bookend to the frontispiece of ravished reading by Antoine Wiertz. Who has ever, Magritte's canvas asks, been *that* shocked or shaken by mere reading? Nonetheless, in curious tune with the late-century potboilers (and their twentieth-century pulp legacy) to which it alludes, this image, by displacing modernism's shock of the new onto a popular medium of ready consumption, produces, every bit as much as does Wiertz's painting in a different key, a *soumise en abyme* of Magritte's own modernism after all—as an effect less of passive viewing than of genuine interpretation, which is to say a reading effect. So, too, in many a Victorian novel is the reader submitted to fiction as topic and subject together.

The main question we have been turning over in these chapters is not what readers think of novels, but how they are thought by such novels. Yet this is something only reading can produce, not simply disclose. And in so doing, reading becomes what the shape of all thought in fiction must be: formal. Reading is mapped, paced, codified, contractual, overdetermined, and often, in our specialized sense, whether mentioned or emblemized, conscripted. But reading is not thereby fixed and unitary. Let the reader be aware, beware. But be where? Depending, as literary reading always does, on social subjects at least fractionally estranged from themselves by their gravitation to fictional life stories, the high station of literature is inseparable from its internal destabilization. Fictional reading leeches identity in the name of identification. And whether through the auspices of address or parable, this estranging fact about reading is not likely to go for long in a Victorian narrative without letting itself get (t)roped in or actually narrated. As this reflexive tendency recurs across the Victorian evolution of the novel, the narrative indices of reading steadily proliferate, migrate, subdivide, and turn on themselves in an increasingly suspicious (but never disabling) scrutiny.

So it is in nineteenth-century narrative practice (calling back again certain theoretical checkpoints from introductory and later chapters) that the conative (formerly appellative) function of any addressed utterance (Jakobson) may be recast within a fictional text, within the "poetic message" per se, as a psychodynamic index of motoring narrative desire (Brooks). So it is that such potentially symbolic "figures" (Barthes) as projection, psychic truancy, libidinal infringement, surrogacy, hypnotic dependency, vampiric co-optation, and so on may outplay the weave of narrative coding and pass from fictional "characters" to the figured reading function in its own right. So, therefore, may the overlapping stages of mimesis (Ricoeur) be configured to emplot audience orientation itself. In this way is Victorian prose fiction able to subordinate reader interpolation to reader extrapolation, dispersing the mirror effect of reading more broadly across the text of the plot, the plot of the text. And so it is, as with the deconstruction of fictional character in the service of a consolidated model of the Victorian bourgeois self (J. Hillis Miller), that the decentering of the manifestly textual "dear reader" serves to reorient rather than efface the deciphering social subject in its own supposedly autonomous sphere, a subject policed into liberal submission (D. A. Miller) by the very comforts of its supposed difference from fictional characters so transparently available to it.

If, during the inception of the novel as genre, the rhetoric of Fielding and Sterne, for instance, worked to mentor the reader, submitting the anonymous *lector* to a running lecture on the codes of the new narrative form, then Victorian fictional procedures labor more completely to process the cognitive act on which these codes depend. One way to understand the development of the nineteenth-century novel, including mass-market best-sellers as well as the prestige product of the high canon, is thus to read it as a history of the steady narrativizing of its own reading—and this within the period's whole cultural shift toward a psychology (not just an epistemology) of verbal interchange, fraught with desires that would, without containment, repeatedly overstep their prescribed bounds. By the time of the gothic revival in the eighties and nineties, what certain parabolic narratives of necromantic representation, mesmeric corpses, deformed doubles, otherworldly reanimations, you name it— name it so as not quite, at first, to recognize it in yourself as you read—what these parables achieve is to *de*sublimate the latent violence of reading as mental trespass. Once again we encounter the culturally freighted dialectic of plot and its provocations to response: the content of invasive penetration, passed through the self-conscious form of narrative fascination, emerging in reflex as the story of reception itself as an ideology of the vicarious.

A fairly simple contrast can summarize the largest literary-historical development to which this book has been witness. Whereas the eighteenth-century novel tends to read you your rights as member of an interpretive audience, the novel of the next century conspires, by narrating with and through you, to write you more directly, though often less explicitly, into plot. Nor would it serve the nineteenth-century novel's ultimate sociological function to hide or deny this artifice for a second. A tacit caveat against complacent credulity is part of the fun. What the best-sellers and the high-canonical texts alike have shown is how little room there is for a rank naiveté of reaction to the stagy machinations of either interpolation or extrapolation. As endeared or enacted reader, you are left with delusions neither about the supposed purity of your motives, their freedom from perverse desire, nor about your laying claim to anything but a strictly textual "field of action" while reading. Yet this latter is a circumscription never quite thought to coincide with you yourself.

Glancing all the way back to the first chapter's opening example from Forster's *The Longest Journey*, we see now the full two-sided irony of "the reader who has no book" and who is thus obligated to audit the narrative scene. Placing you at ontological cross-purposes with yourself in appointing you both textual reader and internal eavesdropper, the passage only attests once more to the general role of the conscribed reader as both the fixture of novel reading and its figment, a symbiotic shadow, a gothic adjunct, truly the ghost in the machine. That is one side of Forster's trick coin. To this extent, his text is still working very much within, if on the outer edge of, the classical paradigm of nineteenth-century prose fiction. So, too, with its dimly imprinted obverse suggestion. For sometimes the devoted habitué of fictional space, though known still as a "reader," in fact "has no book." At such times, in the intermission between narrative, you are simply the literate subject: the subject between—and behind—textual engagements. Such is the cultural safety net of all textual false bottoms in classic fiction, which Forster's taunting paradox depends upon even while upending. The will to read is turned so completely inside out by his metatextual trope of textlessness that we see exposed the whole inner lining along which, in traditional practice, the rhetoric of reading is invisibly stitched into a larger fabric of bourgeois self-image. Just as we are citizens and social subjects—and, more to the point, in order to be—we are all of us readers, of the world's book and others, even when no particular volume is in our hands. This is why audience apostrophe or reference slips so easily into—and out of—the prose of actual Victorian books. For nineteenth-century culture, reader is the most common of nouns.

The lures of fictional reading in classic narrative solicit a subject that remains liminal, shifting, figurative, and centerless, a receptive subjectivity articulated ad hoc and finally unlocalized. But once you are released from your particular fictional book, and even if you always remain something of a decoding and interpretive agent in society at large, what you inevitably think to rejoin is that world system in which you yourself, at least, are supposedly otherwise constituted than by mere signs. Micromanaged within the pivoting differentials of content and form (sheer story and its plotted shape, narrative textuality and the attempted substance of your structured reaction to it), you are always, by whatever designation, there where the expenditure of reading is scheduled to pay off. Apart from its own profit margins in a commodity market, classic fiction as an institution of cultural literacy thus operates as the surplus that insures the center, a hypertrophy of signifiers which leaves certain signifieds inviolable. The novel conjures a mimetic world reveling so self-contentedly, so containedly, in its own writtenness that it can even write you in as textual function without compromising your autonomy as social agent outside the story. Your hovering absentation in the isolated event of reading is what makes the ambient event of communal living seem so much more solidly based in self-presence. Fictional discourse becomes in effect the cultural bonus, supplemental and founding at once, in a psychosocial economy of the subject.

There might, then, have been one more epigraph preceding this coda, coming after Anne Brontë at the very midpoint of the century. Yet the passage from *Moby Dick* (1851) seemed not to line up so much as to sum up. The chapter called "Fast-Fish and Loose-Fish" ends on this distillation of a century's narrative rhetoric: "And what are you, reader, but a Loose-Fish and a Fast-Fish, too?" (89:510). Ishmael's rhetorical question is of course Melville's as well, and the disingenuous freedom of the interrogative gets right to its point. Between an internal reader secured by rhetoric and an audience of voluntary subjects charting their own courses, as between the harpooned capitulation of a rhetorical question and the open seas of interpretive response, falls the limited captor text—from which every reading must and should escape. Call me reader, keep me hooked for as long as possible, but cast me off again.

So goes the ritual of textual consumption as an ideological rite. It is rite, at once, of estranging passage and of cultural repatriation. Even if the world is a book, you want to think, then there is still at any moment a reader outside it somewhere. And that reader is, as if by definition, you yourself. Not so much fast and loose in the everyday sense, you are regularized in the rhythm of your uptake, now fastened by rhetoric, now loosed to interpretation—and to social *return*: the yielding of text to the world and, in the bargain, the giving over of your reading's cultural yield. This is to say, finally, that when conscripting your attention, the nineteenth-century novel as cultural form, as book of the world, has much good will to gain—indeed the very concept of your own will to secure—from figuring the image of your held attention in tacit contrast to the countless ways in which you presume yourself, when not reading, to go about unwritten, unsubjected. By "dear reader" and its derivatives, the pages of Victorian fiction thus punctually countersign your traveling papers back to a world you had no hand in constructing and within which, therefore, you can count on resuming your communal (hence present) rather than focal (because absent) place. Such texts come to closure just where you once came in. Exit the conscripted audience. Ready or not, reader.

Notes

John Frederick Peto, *Nine Books* (n.d.). The David and Alfred Smart
Museum of Art, the University of Chicago. The Mary and
Earle Ludgin Collection

Portions of chapter 6, 8, 9, 11, and 13 have appeared, respectively, in

"Reading Figures: The Legible Image of Victorian Textuality," in *Victorian Literature and the Victorian Visual Imagination,* ed. Carol Christ and John O. Jordan (Berkeley: University of California Press, 1995): 345–67.

"Leaving History: Dickens, Gance, Blanchot," *Yale Journal of Criticism* 2, no. 2 (1989): 145–82.

"A Valediction for Bidding Mourning: Death and the Narratee in Brontë's *Villette,*" in *Death and Representation,* ed. Sarah Webster Goodwin and Elisabeth Bronfen (Baltimore: Johns Hopkins University Press, 1993): 51–79.

"'Beckoning Death': *Daniel Deronda* and the Plotting of a Reading," in *Sex and Death in Victorian Literature,* ed. Regina Barreca (London: Macmillan, 1989): 69–109.

"'Count Me In': *Dracula,* Hypnotic Participation, and the Late-Victorian Gothic of Reading," *Literature Interpretation Theory (LIT)* 5 (1994): 1–18.

Chapter One   Readers in the Making

Epigraph: Maurice Blanchot, "Reading," in *The Space of Literature,* trans. Ann Smock (Lincoln: University of Nebraska Press, 1982), 193.

1. Parenthetical citations by volume (where applicable), chapter, and page are from Penguin editions unless otherwise mentioned, except for the Riverside editions of *Joseph Andrews* and *Vanity Fair;* the Norton Critical editions of *Jane Eyre, Wuther-*

ing *Heights, Middlemarch, The Picture of Dorian Gray, Jude the Obscure,* and *Lord Jim;* the Signet Classic edition of *Frankenstein;* the World's Classics (Oxford) edition of *Esther Waters* and *The Ordeal of Richard Feverel;* and the Vintage editions of *The Longest Journey* and *Howards End.*

2. Henry James, "George Eliot," in Henry James, *American Writers, English Writers* (New York: Library of America, 1984), 922.

3. Dickens to John Forster, 21 September 1840, *The Letters of Charles Dickens,* Pilgrim Edition, ed. Madeline House and Graham Storey (Oxford: Clarendon Press, 1965, 1969), 2:129. Dickens wrote to Forster in connection with a potentially misleading passage in *The Old Curiosity Shop* revised at Forster's suggestion: "Of course I had no intention to delude the many-headed into a false belief concerning opera nights." Quoted in Easson (see chap. 7 below, n. 7), 116.

4. In *Modes of Production of Victorian Novels* (Chicago: University of Chicago Press, 1986), N. N. Feltes pursues a rigorously materialist account of the forces that shaped the commercial circuit of fiction's production and consumption. It is an account to which occasional forays into narrative strategy, linguistic address, even scenes of reading are subordinated, with these textual manifestations understood as traces of commercial imperatives external to the book as literary structure. The way in which Feltes *places* the phenomenon of Dickens' first best-seller, *Pickwick Papers,* sets the agenda—and the tone: "For the future, the new literary mode of production determined by the developing structures of Victorian capitalism lay . . . in the ever more self-conscious, ever more assured exploitation of the surplus value of commodity-texts, within the dominant ideology of the commodity-book and the dominant economic structure in which it was embedded" (17). What is striking here is how the book/text distinction has lost much of its poststructuralist valence, employed now in strictly mercantile terms to distinguish the expensive bound artifact, token of privilege, from the infinitely reprintable mass-market item. Generalizing more broadly from an economic base, Terry Lovell's *Consuming Fictions* (London: Verso, 1987) builds a feminist argument about the ideology of production as well as consumption on the earlier groundbreaking scholarship of Kathleen Tillotson's *Novels of the Eighteen Forties* (Oxford: Clarendon Press, 1954), Richard Altick's *The English Common Reader: A Social History of the Mass Reading Public, 1800–1900* (Chicago: University of Chicago Press, 1957), and such recent work by John Sutherland as *Victorian Novelists and Publishers* (London: Athlone, 1976) and *Fiction and the Fiction Industry* (London: Athlone, 1978).

5. Samuel Taylor Coleridge, *The Statesman's Manual,* in *Lay Sermons,* ed. R. J. White (Routledge & Kegan Paul, 1972), 36; quoted by Jon Klancher, *The Making of English Reading Audiences, 1790–1832* (Madison: University of Wisconsin Press, 1987), 4, 47. For Coleridge, this is "as strange a phrase, methinks, as ever forced a splenetic smile on the staid countenance of Meditation; and yet no fiction!" (36–37). In ways unremarked by Klancher, however, this is nonetheless a "public," at least in its more cultivated subclass, which Coleridge is by no means above borrowing the techniques

of "fiction" to address, apostrophize, and otherwise conversationally position by his own group rhetoric, here and throughout the *Manual*. See, for instance, his pluralized mention of "you, my friends, to whom the following pages are more particularly addressed, as to men moving in the higher class of society" (7).

6. Frances Burney, *Evelina*, ed. Edward A. Bloom (London: Oxford University Press, 1968), 7.

7. Klancher's *The Making of English Reading Audiences, 1790–1832* (see n. 5 above) is the most instructive study to date in the historicizing of nineteenth-century audiences. Klancher wields a nuanced stylistic vocabulary to analyze the prose of literary and political periodicals as they fashioned the new mass audience to which they simultaneously catered. Arguing against "an enclosed empirical sociology of literature" (3) in favor of a subtler and broader-ranging analysis of the rhetoric of cultural formation, Klancher examines the means by which "carving out readerships" meant "evolving readers' interpretive frameworks and shaping their ideological awareness" (4). Informed by the voluminous attention already given to that "protean 'reader' that empowers so much contemporary criticism and cultural theory," he sees such a view of the reader as "an important outcome of the struggle for audiences in the Romantic period" (5), part of a continuing move beyond coterie circulation to the "public sphere" of mass audience. For a coherent view of this transformation at the stylistic level, Klancher borrows theoretical support from Bakhtin, holding that the audience fashioned by literature is "mutually produced as an otherness within one's own discourse" (12). Balancing, via Bakhtin, a social against an individual "dialogism," Klancher stresses the "moment of transition—when . . . one's orientation as individual 'reader' shifts to an intimation of the larger 'audience' in which one may be inscribed" (12), an aggregate related to its larger cultural context as "social text" (see chap. 2 and following).

8. Pierre Macheray, *A Theory of Literary Production*, trans. Geoffrey Wall (London: Routledge & Kegan Paul, 1978), 70.

9. This is a part of my argument in *Reading Voices: Literature and the Phonotext* (Berkeley: University of California Press, 1990), a book to which the present investigations offer a kind of sequel: here an account of emplaced and enacted reading pursued to complement the microlinguistics of sublexical text production. Together, I have it in mind with these studies to map out the overlapping regions as well as regimes of reading, on the one hand the vocalizing body, on the other hand the psychological and socialized (rather than merely social) space marked out and paced off by reading.

10. I won't take space here to round up the usual suspects. It is indeed a function of the relative unanimity of such reader-response approaches that each new volume tends to recapitulate in a fairly noncombative way the work of its predecessors. Two of the more recent and less well known books in this line, as expected, provide extensive bibliographies. Elizabeth Freund's *The Return of the Reader: Reader Response Criticism* (London: Methuen, 1987) is a useful overview of the field, with emphasis

on Culler, Fish, Riffaterre, Holland, and Iser. Inge Crosman Wimmer's *Poetics of Reading: Approaches to the Novel* (Princeton: Princeton University Press, 1988), after distilling familiar theoretical approaches, turns to practical applications in French fiction. Besides these latest in a string of studies, two prominent anthologies always bear mention: Susan R. Suleiman and Inge Crosman, *The Reader in the Text: Essays on Audience and Interpretation* (Princeton: Princeton University Press, 1980), and Jane P. Tomkins, ed., *Reader-Response Criticism: From Formalism to Post-Structuralism* (Baltimore: Johns Hopkins University Press, 1980).

11. Exceptions exist. One recent study, Susan Noakes' *Timely Reading: Between Exegesis and Interpretation* (Ithaca, N.Y.: Cornell University Press, 1988), works to avoid this reductiveness by stressing the difference between hermeneutic reflection and mere exegetical reading. Concerned specifically with the nineteenth century, an approach closer in emphasis to my own is Tillotama Rajan's *The Supplement of Reading: Figures of Understanding in Romantic Theory and Practice* (Ithaca, N.Y.: Cornell University Press, 1990). Examining the hermeneutic incitations of high romantic poetry, where meaning is not "activated" in the text but left to be generated in the slippage between signifier and signified, Rajan takes unfinished poems like *Christabel* or *The Fall of Hyperion* as paradigmatic of the age, where meaning does not come to closure in the manifest text but awaits instead the heuristic and dialectical engagement of a reader. My own understanding, below, of such postromantic novels as *Villette* and *Daniel Deronda*, to name but two, finds them operating in just this vein: reconceiving with their suspensive conclusions the deconstructive "supplement of writing," its indeterminacy and decentered voicing, as the locus of a readerly interaction and/or continuance. See especially Rajan's opening chapter, "The Supplement of Reading," 15–35.

12. Tony Bennett, "Text, Readers, Reading Formations," *Literature and History* 9, no. 2 (Autumn 1983): 221.

13. Jacques Derrida, *Writing and Difference*, trans. Alan Bass (Chicago: University of Chicago Press, 1978), 103.

14. Walter J. Ong, "The Writer's Audience Is Always a Fiction," *PMLA* 90 (January 1975): 9–21.

15. Wayne C. Booth, *The Rhetoric of Fiction* (Chicago: University of Chicago Press, 1961), 206.

16. Judith Wilt has commandingly elaborated upon this notion in her study of the reader's identification with certain interpreter characters in Meredith's fiction. See *The Readable People of George Meredith* (Princeton: Princeton University Press, 1974).

17. Roland Barthes, "The Five Codes," in *S/Z: An Essay*, trans. Richard Miller (New York: Hill and Wang, 1974), 18–20.

18. See Wolfgang Iser, *The Implied Reader: Patterns of Communication in Prose Fiction from Bunyan to Beckett* (Baltimore: Johns Hopkins University Press, 1974).

19. Except by analogy, that is. The moments I am attempting to specify emerge

by contrast with D. A. Miller's commentary on that "turn" to reading in Dickens which is most explicitly rendered in *David Copperfield*. It is there that David finds in books "the free, liberalizing space" he seeks precisely because, in reading, "he is not there," his will to vicariousness fulfilled (*The Novel and the Police* [Berkeley: University of California Press, 1988], 215). For Miller this thematic level appears directly translatable to the field of response: "What goes for the subject of *David Copperfield* goes in *a different dimension* for the subject who reads it," who also "defines his subjectivity in absentia" (215; emphasis mine). Miller means to evoke here, I take it, the whole phenomenological assumption of the reading act: the sense that when we are in its grips, a text absconds with our interiority in order to substitute another. But moving between this fact and its narrativization by text is not a simple matter. What my concept of extrapolation is meant to capture is the way in which the reflexive parables of certain Victorian texts actively negotiate rather than simply elide the two reading "dimensions" noted by Miller.

20. Catherine Belsey puts the term *interpellation* into circulation in *Critical Practice* (London: Methuen, 1980) as the name for a strategy to be exposed in "classic realist fiction, the dominant literary form of the nineteenth century and arguably of the twentieth," a literary mode that "'interpellates' the reader, addresses itself to him or her directly, offering the reader as the position from which the text is most 'obviously' intelligible, the position of the *subject in (and of) ideology*" (56–57). With the phrase "addresses itself" being merely metaphoric for something like "is directed at" (anticipating no specific account of audience apostrophe), Belsey's further derivations from this Althusserian concept proceed at the same level of generalization: "The reader is invited to perceive and judge the 'truth' of the text, the coherent, non-contradictory interpretation of the world as it is perceived by an author whose autonomy is the source and evidence of the truth of the interpretation" (68–69).

21. Without reference to Belsey's application of the term (see n. 20 above), N. N. Feltes, in *Modes of Production of Victorian Novels* (see n. 4 above), introduces the notion of interpellation (with detailed reference to Althusser) as a close correlate of the "commodity-text," whose devices "interpellate by constituting the bourgeois subject" (9).

22. In her *Epistemology of the Closet* (Berkeley: University of California Press, 1990), taking the provenance of the term *interpellation* and its textual application for granted while putting them through their most sophisticated paces, Eve Kosofsky Sedgwick detects its operations in *Billy Budd*'s moments of "rhetorical impaction" (97), moments where "the reader . . . is invented as a subject in relation to the 'world' of the novel by an act of interpellation that is efficacious to the degree that it is contradictory, appealing to the reader on the basis of an assumed sharing of cognitive authority whose ground is hollowed out in the very act of the appeal" (99). See also the "demeaning interpellatory terms" (111) of a later passage, or, by a subsequent periphrasis for interpellation, the "double message by which the reader *is constituted here*" (121; emphasis added).

Chapter Two   On Terms with the Reader

Epigraph: Maurice Blanchot, "Reading," 193.

1. See Michael Wheeler, *Death and the Future Life in Victorian Literature and Theology* (Cambridge: Cambridge University Press, 1991), 43.

2. Roman Jakobson, "Linguistics and Poetics," in *Essays in Stylistic Analysis*, ed. Howard Babb (New York: Harcourt Brace Jovanovich, 1972), 296–332.

3. Gerald Prince, "Introduction to the Study of the Narratee," *Poetique* 14 (1973): 177–96; rpt. in Jane P. Tompkins, ed., *Reader-Response Criticism* (see chap. 1 above, n. 10), 7–25.

4. See, for instance, Mary Louise Pratt, *Toward a Speech Act Theory of Literary Discourse* (Bloomington: Indiana University Press, 1977), for a sense of "directive" in the roster of illocutionary acts (81). In surveying discursive strategies in *Jane Eyre* (54–58), Pratt quotes the "Reader, I married him" sentence (58) without considering it specifically in light of the illocutionary surplus of direct address.

5. Jonathan Culler, "Stanley Fish and the Righting of the Reader" and "Apostrophe," in *The Pursuit of Signs: Semiotics, Literature, Deconstruction* (Ithaca, N.Y.: Cornell University Press, 1981), 119–31, 135–54.

6. Culler, "Apostrophe" (see n. 5 above), 149.

7. One recent book has, however, taken up this matter as a literary-historical issue. Without the psychological emphasis I mean to place on readerly urges, the presumption of a narrator beyond and behind narration is what Karl Kroeber emphasizes in *Retelling/Rereading: The Fate of Storytelling in Modern Times* (New Brunswick, N.J.: Rutgers University Press, 1990) by asserting that "the central feature of fictional modernism is its replacement of the traditional *teller* with an *author*" (98). His own contrastive examples come from *Vanity Fair* and *Ulysses* (89–98), and in their light we can see that Joyce's blunt-edged satire on overt Dickensian apostrophe, to be discussed shortly, bespeaks just this modernist animus against embodied omniscience, against the myth of *telling* as in fact an irresponsible illusion of textual signification.

8. For a useful discussion of this postmodern tendency, and of Thomas Pynchon's place within it, see Brian McHale, "'You Used to Know What These Words Mean': Misreading *Gravity's Rainbow*," *Language and Style* 18, no. 1 (Winter 1985): 93–117.

9. Italo Calvino, *If on a winter's night a traveler*, trans. William Weaver (1979; New York: Harcourt Brace Jovanovich, 1982), 260.

10. See Erich Auerbach, "Dante's Addresses to the Reader," *Romance Philology* 7, no. 4 (May 1954): 268–78. Leo Spitzer replies in "The Addresses to the Reader in 'The Commedia,'" *Italica* 32, no. 3 (September 1955): 143–65. This critique is then taken up in turn, by way of a passing rejoinder, for Auerbach's later discussion of Dante in *Literary Language and Its Public in Late Latin Antiquity and the Middle Ages* (New York: Pantheon, 1965), 297–317. Lowry Nelson Jr.'s "The Fictive Reader and Literary Self-Reflexiveness," in *The Disciplines of Criticism: Essays in Literary Theory, Interpretation,*

and History, ed. Peter Demetz, Thomas Greene, and Lowry Nelson Jr. (New Haven: Yale University Press, 1968), though with no examples from British fiction, distinguishes between "the confessional or conversational mode, on the one hand, and, on the other, the direct, seemingly impersonal or formal, presentation in fiction"— the latter in such writers of "the realistic novel" as "Balzac, Flaubert, or Tolstoy," where "the reader is in some degree kept at a distance." (184). Nelson stresses throughout that the reader's active involvement as "accomplice, communicant, collaborator" (190) stands in direct rather than inverse proportion to the text's reflection on (rather than denial of) its own textual status. What he seems properly to assume at the back of all this is the following: If there is a fictive reader, even though treated in the manner of an interlocutor, then the fiction is self-admittedly a thing to be *read*, a text. Nelson also discusses in some detail the role of reading in the epistolary tradition, where the fictive reader becomes a "reconstructive historian" (182) laboring in close collaboration with the author, piecing together a plot from its discrete documents. My own different point, below, about the epistolary paradigm is that the addressed reader of even nonepistolary fiction is figured into a text in something like the privileged, if vestigial, status of a letter's personal addressee.

11. See John Freccero, "Infernal Irony: The Gates of Hell," *MLN* 99, no. 4 (1984): "For the modern reader, familiar with the funerary inscriptions of romantic poetry, the beginning of Canto III is not unlike an epitaph, written in the first person and marking with a presence in stone an absence of the spirit" (776). The inscription in question is incised upon the portals of hell as the first manifestation in words of that solely text-materialized access to the otherworld which not only evokes the epitaphic model but invites its subsidiary manifestations in the ushering function of address throughout.

12. A hint of this appears in Spitzer's critique of Auerbach (see n. 10 above): "Dante pauses to announce to the reader the necessity of proceeding on a higher stylistic level which is only meet for the sublimity of the scene he must describe— a thought which he could also have rendered in the form of an invocation to the Muses" (147).

13. Wolfgang Iser does begin *The Implied Reader* (chap. 1 above, n. 18) with an essay on Bunyan's "Shaping of the Novel," drawing on Lukács's account (5, 27) of the gestation of the novelistic mode from the decline of the epic. For Iser, *Pilgrim's Progress* "is meant to appeal to each individual reader, whatever his disposition, and its aim is to lead the believer to recognize himself" (7), yet he does not take up the addresses and apostrophes by which such induction is guided in the "Apology."

14. John Bunyan, *The Pilgrim's Progress* (Oxford: Clarendon Press, 1960), 5.

15. Jonathan Swift, *A Tale of a Tub*, in *Gulliver's Travels and Other Writings*, ed. Miriam Kosh Starkman (New York: Bantam, 1962), 1:317; 7:360; 9:377; 11:391. J. Paul Hunter, in *Before Novels: The Cultural Contexts of Eighteenth-Century English Fiction* (New York: W. W. Norton, 1990), serves to contextualize such quasi-editorial citations when he mentions those prenovelistic fictional prologues that provide a "buffer be-

tween reader and text" (159), especially the sort of prefatory addresses headed "To the Reader" or even "An Epistle to the Reader." Hunter claims that they institute a "personal-impersonal passport to the private closet" (159), to that newly demarcated domestic space that offers, as he has been arguing at greater length, the "primary locus for secret contemplation and private reading" (157), in other words the "enabling architecture for fiction" (157). Though part of the incipient "closet culture" of the late seventeenth century, with the private cabinet as a new individualistic site in the middle-class home, these intimate addresses also reflect a "nostalgia for community" (159) in a postepic culture, with the result that there were "'gentle readers' and 'learned readers' and 'candid readers' in books long before the novel" (159). I will be placing more emphasis on the peculiar valences of the self-consciously editorial (rather than merely prefatory and authorial) intertext for such address in the subsequent era of the novel, not to mention a variety of other influences. But Hunter offers a valuable sense of the convergence between a social history of an increasingly privatized domestic space and the prenovelistic textual markers of a reconstituted communality, all within a technological history of the rise of print culture.

16. Of Fielding's novels in general, John Preston notes simply that, though mentioning the reader often, Fielding "projects him in surprisingly impersonal terms, usually as 'the reader,' not so often 'my' or 'our' reader, still less often 'thee,'" the whole panoply of reference being "all rather formal and remote." See Preston, *The Created Self: The Reader's Role in Eighteenth-Century Fiction* (New York: Barnes and Noble, 1970), 197. In comparing Fielding's novels with Sterne's *Tristram Shandy*, Preston sets in place a pertinent distinction, resulting as it does from the two authors' differing practice of direct address. Stressing the way in which narrator and reader more closely "collaborate" in the "making" of Sterne's kind of novel, Preston summarizes: "Fielding imagines situations for the reader: Sterne imagines the *only* situation for the reader. And the text of the novel is that situation" (199). As against the kind of figuration we get in Fielding, of the reader as coach-traveler, Preston offers in illustration of his point one of Sterne's notorious direct addresses: "—How could you, Madam, be so inattentive in reading the last chapter?" (199). The surprise of this textual directive in second person is mitigated only if one weighs the influence of editorial practice on the novelistic guiding of the reader.

17. For a literary-historical discussion of this motif, see Geoffrey H. Hartman, "Wordsworth, Inscriptions, and Romantic Nature Poetry," in *Beyond Formalism: Literary Essays, 1958–1970* (New Haven: Yale University Press, 1970), 211 ff., and a dissertation by Lorna Clymer, "Lessons of the Dead: Genres, Modes, and Attitudes in Eighteenth- and Early Nineteenth-Century Poetry about Death," University of California, 1994.

18. See Alexander Welsh, *Strong Representations: Narrative and Circumstantial Evidence in England* (Baltimore: Johns Hopkins University Press, 1992), 41, quoted from Henry Fielding, *Tom Jones*, ed. Martin C. Battestin and Fredson Bowers (Middletown, Conn.: Wesleyan University Press, 1975), 916.

19. Culler's essay "Apostrophe" (see n. 5 above) begins: "Quintilian, speaking of oratory, defines apostrophe as "'a diversion of our words to address some person other than the judge'" (135).

20. Vladimir Nabokov, *The Annotated Lolita*, ed. Alfred Appel Jr. (New York: Vintage, 1991), 9, 123, 132.

21. The confusion of subject positions between narrative voice and its personified reception continues in *Pale Fire* (New York: Vintage, 1989), in which the unhinged editor, Kinbote, describes the second canto of Shade's poem as "your favorite" (13) and later confounds the mere parenthetical conventions of editorial shorthand with a schizoid self-instruction that needs correction to a reader imperative: "(see again— I mean the reader should see again—the note to line 49)" (257).

22. See John Schad, *The Reader in the Dickensian Mirrors* (London: Macmillan, 1992), who opens his first chapter with this address (17) and proceeds through a catalogue of free-form associations between the so-called sovereignty of Dickensian readers and allied notions of power, enthronement, majesty, and kingly prerogative (14–16). Elsewhere in his study, there is an erratic alternation between "reader-characters" and a mode of textual attention very close to Stanley Fish's "affective stylistics" (unmentioned), in which the reader is put through the text's own thematic paces by oblique recognitions sprung from alleged verbal ambivalences of all sorts. In view of my own chapters on Dickens, it is worth noting that though Schad turns intermittently to *The Old Curiosity Shop*, there is no mention, let alone examination, of the novel's structurally embedded place within the reading circle of its frame tale, the serial *Master Humphrey's Clock*.

23. James Joyce, *Ulysses: The Corrected Text* (New York: Random House, 1986), 343.

24. See Emile Benveniste, *Problems in General Linguistics*, trans. Mary Elizabeth Meek (Coral Gables, Fla.: University of Miami Press, 1971), chap. 5.

25. William Makepeace Thackeray, *Vanity Fair*, ed. Geoffrey and Kathleen Tillotson (Boston: Houghton Mifflin, 1963), 1:15.

26. In *The Politics of Reflexivity: Narrative and the Constitutive Poetics of Culture* (Baltimore: Johns Hopkins University Press, 1986), Robert Siegle places *Vanity Fair* in a self-referential tradition running down through *The French Lieutenant's Woman*, but he does so with a proper emphasis on the quintessential Victorian character of Thackeray's overloaded text, which is continually "predicating different roles for the reader in his own act of interpretation" (31). About this predicated reader Siegle has more to say under the suggestive subheading "The Reader as a Narrative Stance" (62–65), where he concentrates on the rhetorical questions (rather than direct vocatives) by which the reader is made "cocreative" (48) with the narrator in the puzzling out of ethical quandaries.

27. J. Hillis Miller, "The Function of Rhetorical Study at the Present Time," in *Theory Now and Then* (Durham, N.C.: Duke University Press, 1991), 213.

Chapter Three   Reflex Action

Epigraph: Maurice Blanchot, "Communication," in *The Space of Literature,* 200–201.

   1. See Michael Fried, *Absorption and Theatricality: Painting and Beholder in the Age of Diderot* (Chicago: University of Chicago Press, 1980), 9, 12, 16, 17, 18, 26, 32, 46, 47, 49, 50, 54, 57, for discussion or reproductions of absorptive compositions associated with reading by such painters as Chardin, Greuze, and Van Loo, including on 137 the Fragonard that illustrates the present chapter. See also Roger Chartier, *The Cultural Uses of Print in Early Modern France,* trans. by Lydia G. Cochrane (Princeton: Princeton University Press, 1987), 219–21, where discussion of the new architectural accommodations for sequestered reading in the eighteenth century, the private "reading closets," adduces in evidence the prevalent pictorial representation of women reading alone, often personal letters, in the throes of unespied emotion.

   2. André Kertesz, *On Reading* (New York: Penguin, 1971).

   3. And then there are the trick shots, the visual double entendres, the compositional ironies: the skylights and angled planes of New York roofs redoubling and enlarging the barely visible shapes of held books; a beetle crawling across the surface of Voltaire's title page, following the print without reading it; books piled in the absence of any human form to gaze upon them but gargoyle or portrait. There are also shots in which no books at all, let alone readers, appear except in pictorial simulation: images where the only reader is glimpsed in a street vendor's painting behind the legs of New York pedestrians or in relief on the frieze that has closed off a defunct fireplace and has thus supplanted, in effect, one former site of household reading.

   4. While drafting these introductory pages, I chanced upon an article by Fredric Jameson on the generic determinants of science fiction, "Science Fiction as a Spatial Genre," *Science-Fiction Studies* 14 (March 1987): 44–59. That essay speculates in the direction of my own project, and just as tentatively as I had once begun to do. For Jameson was following little more than an informed hunch about the collateral (and broadly rhetorical) devices of address and emblematic scene: "I suspect that most kinds of texts—and in particular those of mass culture—include within themselves not merely directions about the reading process and the way in which its operations are to be performed, but also symbolic references to that process itself" (56). His example of the "symbolic"—or one might say emblematic—reference is the fictional detective relaxing with a book of fiction. As far along as I was in my own research into the evolution of mass cultural fiction as a reading grid when coming upon this remark, I was certainly in a position to hope Jameson wrong in thinking it "too ambitious to try to document this hypothesis in detail" (56). But I nevertheless took encouragement from his intuitive stress both on the distinction that guides these pages, that between directive and symbol in his words—or address and reflexive emblem (reading's self-parable) in mine—and on their interlinked service to generic maintenance.

5. On this recurrent Victorian *topos* there is much scattered and topical as well as consolidated discussion. In *The Sense of an Audience: Dickens, Thackeray, and George Eliot at Mid-Century* (Athens: University of Georgia Press, 1981), Janice Carlisle's chapter "The Bonds of Reading" considers scenes in Dickens' *Dombey and Son*, Thackeray's *Henry Esmond*, and George Eliot's "Janet's Repentance" from *Scenes of Clerical Life* in which "the novelist depicts the storyteller in action," with attending characters who "serve as 'readers'" (16). That third narrative, in which Janet's waywardness is cured through a cautionary autobiographical narrative by the Reverend Mr. Tryan, is particularly revealing, since Carlisle can explain the excessive conventionality of the story as a "recognizable fiction-within-a-fiction" (20), one whose effect on the hearer thus doubles all the more closely for the power of popular fiction in dissemination. A more extended discussion of such moments in Dickens can be found in John Kucich's chapter "Storytelling" (17–42) from *Excess and Restraint in the Novels of Charles Dickens* (Athens: University of Georgia Press, 1981). Before this, there was Barbara Hardy's *Tellers and Listeners: The Narrative Imagination* (London: Athlone Press, 1975), with chapters on Dickens, Hardy, and Joyce as writers who gravitate toward restagings of the narrative situation within their stories. Ranging over French and British fiction, Carla L. Peterson takes up the more purely thematic rather than dynamic issue of characters fixated upon reading in *The Determined Reader: Gender and Culture in the Novel from Napoleon to Victoria* (New Brunswick, N.J.: Rutgers University Press, 1986). Similarly, in the closing chapter of *Desire and Domestic Fiction: A Political History of the Novel* (New York: Oxford University Press, 1987), entitled "Seduction and the Scene of Reading," Nancy Armstrong uses as her extended Victorian example the reading of *Coriolanus* in Brontë's *Shirley:* as evidence for the evolving feminization of literary transmission within the cult of domesticity.

6. Paul Ricoeur, *Time and Narrative*, 3 vols., trans. Kathleen McLaughlin and David Pellauer (Chicago: University of Chicago Press, 1984–88), 1:71.

7. See Macheray, *A Theory of Literary Production* (chap. 1 above, n. 8), "Pact and Contract," 69–73. A complementary notion appears in Elizabeth Deeds Ermarth's *Realism and Consensus in the English Novel* (Princeton: Princeton University Press, 1983), where the effective merger of separate points of view in realist fiction is imagined as a perspectival consensus among them which also implicates the consent of a reader.

8. See Gilles Deleuze and Félix Guattari, *A Thousand Plateaus: Capitalism and Schizophrenia*, trans. Brian Massumi (Minneapolis: University of Minnesota Press, 1987). Such at least would seem to be one implication of the always "territorialized" (9) structure of the rhizomelike text machine, a material body without organs whose presence deconstructs the book/world dualism (317).

9. Henry Fielding, *Joseph Andrews*, ed. Martin C. Battestin (Boston: Houghton Mifflin, 1961), 4,9:270.

10. Mikhail Bakhtin, *The Dialogic Imagination*, ed. Michael Holquist, trans. by Caryl Emerson and Michael Holquist (Austin: University of Texas Press, 1981), 166.

See the brief gloss on this passing concept by Gary Saul Morson and Caryl Emerson in *Mikhail Bakhtin: Creations of a Prosaics* (Stanford: Stanford University Press, 1990), where the authors assume that the embedded theatricality at issue centers around the Fair as puppet spectacle, as highlighted by the novel's synecdochic title: "Bakhtin's prime example is *Vanity Fair*, the title of the work referring to the intervalic chronotope that interrupts and casts light upon the chronotope of the main narrative" (404).

11. Paul de Man, *Allegories of Reading: Figural Language in Rousseau, Nietzsche, Rilke, and Proust* (New Haven: Yale University Press, 1979).

12. See *Allegories* (n. 11 above), 57. Though de Man insists that "the sections in the novel that literally represent reading are not to be privileged," still he does grant that this "should not prevent us . . . from questioning the passage on actual reading, if only to find out whether or not it does make paradigmatic claims for itself" (58).

13. Georges Poulet, *Proustian Space*, trans. Elliott Coleman (Baltimore: Johns Hopkins University Press, 1977), 21.

14. This is the translation given by Poulet (see n. 13 above), 21–22. His claim for the rarity of such address in *Jean Santeuil* can be contrasted with the several citations from the *Recherche* offered in connection with metalepsis by Gerard Genette in *Narrative Discourse: An Essay in Method*, trans. Jane E. Lewin (Ithaca, N.Y.: Cornell University Press, 1980), 239.

15. I quote here from the English translation by Gerard Hopkins of *Jean Santeuil* (London: Weidenfeld and Nicolson, 1955), 110, 111.

16. Marcel Proust, *Jean Santeuil* (Paris: Gallimard, 1952), 3 vols. The passage Poulet discusses is found on 1:194–95.

17. Erich Schön, *Der Verlust der Sinnlichkeit oder die Verwandlungen des Lesers: Mentalitätswandel um 1800* (Stuttgart: Klett-Cotta, 1987), 328. Coming to my attention well after completing *Reading Voices* (chap. 1 above, n. 9), Schön's is a project that encourages a further dialectical history of the mutings and returns of phonemic texturing I discuss there. I want to thank Martin Zerlang for directing me to Schön's work. The translations here are by Nataša Ďurovičová

18. G. Hermans, ed., *Musée Wiertz: Album Illustré* (Bruxelles: Musées royaux des Beaux-Arts de Belgique, n.d.).

19. This opening, canceled by the time of the first edition, is reprinted as an appendix in Roger Ebbatson, ed., *A Pair of Blue Eyes* (Harmondsworth: Penguin, 1980), 466–69. The rhetoric of the chapter happens also to mark Hardy's ironic distance from the "dear reader" trope, for the text's gesture of conscription is held in play between the ascribed "kindly curiosity" of Hardy's own audience in surveying the listed cast of characters and a contrived climax of the unnamed internal "romance" mockingly celebrated as "the saddest *contretemps* that ever lingered in *a gentle and responsive reader's mind* since fiction has taken a turn—for better or for worse—for analysing rather than depicting character and emotion" (467; emphasis added). Hardy's rhetoric will later have largely exiled to the prefatory margins the "too genteel reader" dismissed in his "explanatory note" to the first edition of *Tess of the*

D'Urbervilles (1891). Explicitly interpolating the "curious" reader, however, into the first serial chapter of 1873's *A Pair of Blue Eyes* (in a publishing format where no table of contents makes possible a cheating discovery of the heroine's fate), at the same time that the chapter extrapolates from her all too impatient curiosity a corrective stance for his reading audience, Hardy would seem to suggest in context that he aligns the epithetical specification of a "responsive" readership with the latter-day "analysis" of character—where, by contrast, the dramatic incidents of story alone might suffice.

20. The "picture of life had changed" so drastically for Angel Clare after Tess's honeymoon disclosure, that "humanity stood before him . . . in the staring and ghastly attitudes of a Wiertz Museum, and with the leer of a study by Van Beers" (29:217). To be specific in a way that Hardy is not, Angel's repudiation of tainted female sexuality would certainly have made its contemplation as leering as that of the purient viewer of "The Romance Reader."

21. Only in person can a viewer make out the title of one of the books, the one being slipped onto her bed: *Antony* by Alexandre Dumas fils.

22. According to the museum's curator, André Moerman, the screens have not been in place for at least three decades now. The paintings are currently displayed in a small back gallery together with other canvases.

Chapter Four   "Whomsoever It May Concern"

1. Iser, *The Implied Reader* (see chap. 1 above, n. 18), xii.

2. Lewis's *The Monk* (1796) is more self-conscious yet about its initiatory apparatus yet also quickly enough peels away its layers of mediation to permit unreflective access to the events of its plot. In an ennobling "Imitation of Horace," the verse preface addresses by turns both the text itself and its reader in alternating—and equidistant—second person, with a grammar at play between "your page" and "Kind Reader."

3. In the cluster of gothic novels alluded to at one point in *Northanger Abbey* (6:61), all published during the decade in which Austen began her novel (and reprinted collectively under the title *The Northanger Set of Jane Austen Horrid Novels* [London: Folio Press, 1968]), one of the seven, *The Necromancer* (1793), partly epistolary in format, ends with an addressed and signed letter; another, *Horrid Mysteries* (1796), couched in first person, begins its last chapter with the dying voice of the narrator—"I now shall bid an eternal adieu to my friends"—in a way that places those friends in the position of readers and vice versa; and only one, *Clermont* (1798), concludes with an indirect appeal to lenience in the reception of the tale: "an humble hope, that however unworthy of public favour it may be deemed, its not aspiring to fame will guard it from severity" (373). The rest precede from first to last at a pitch of vividness undeterred by allusions to that intense participation which, having conspired to generate, they choose not to call attention to as mere reading.

4. A further example, this time from *The Mysterious Warning* (1796): "From the

characters of Rhodophil and Fatima, we may trace the progression of vice, and its fatal termination!" (381), where the reader is subsumed to an editorial plural.

5. Gerald Prince, "Introduction to the Study of the Narratee," in Jane P. Tompkins, ed., *Reader-Response Criticism* (see chap. 2 above, n. 3), 14.

6. The *OED*'s last instance of such usage is taken from Smollett in 1757–58 ("literary correspondence"), while the next entry gives Todd (1818) as an authority for the fact that *"literary* is not properly used of missive letters."

7. The memoir of Jane Austen by her nephew, J. E. Austen-Leigh (reprinted in the Penguin edition of *Persuasion*), contains an "extract from one of her letters" in which Edgeworth is given pride of place on her preferential list of fiction: "I have made up my mind to like no novels really, but Miss Edgeworth's, E's [her sister's], and my own" (332; see also 398 n. 20).

8. Maria Edgeworth, *Belinda* (London: Pandora, 1986), 3:28.

9. See Genette, *Narrative Discourse* (chap. 3 above, n. 14), 101 n, 234–37.

10. See Michael McKeon, *The Origins of the English Novel, 1600–1740* (Baltimore: Johns Hopkins University Press, 1987), 398–408.

11. The strategy of resolution in *Joseph Andrews* becomes one of those points of conversion, rather than simple convergence, where "Fielding's subsumption of questions of virtue by questions of truth transfers the major challenge of utopian projection from the substantive to the formal realm" (McKeon, 408; see n. 10 above), so that "the end of *Joseph Andrews* . . . is less a social than an epistemological event" (408).

12. On Barthes's view of narrativity in relation to carnal disclosure, see Peter Brooks, *Body Work: Objects of Desire in Narrative* (Cambridge: Harvard University Press, 1994), 19–21.

13. Willoughby seems at first a "young man of good abilities, quick imagination, lively spirits, and"—last but not least—"open, affectionate manners" (*Sense and Sensibility*, 10:80). Of another character, Colonel Brandon, it is said that "his heart seemed more than usually open to every feeling of attachment to the objects around him" (14:100). Edward Ferrars, however, though surprised to find himself criticized as "reserved" (17:120), is soon again described as suffering from "want of spirits, of openness" (19:126). Measuring the formalities of public behavior against a similar touchstone, the Dashwoods do everything they can to "promote" the "unreserve" of newcomers to their neighborhood (21:147). Later, whatever information is available to "open [Willoughby's] character further" (31:214) is seen as desirable, this loaded term operating now within an epistemological circuit linked all the while to the moral value of the unreserved self. The talismanic term crops up even in light banter as the sign of an interpersonal necessity, when Marianne teases Edward that "those who will accept of my love and esteem must submit to my open commendation" (35:248). Further, it is incumbent upon Willoughby to allay misunderstanding in the novel's penultimate revelation scene by deciding to "open my whole heart

to you [Elinor]" (44:313). With Edward's disclosures next resolving the details of his former entanglement, the narrator's climactic phrasing, "His heart was now open to Elinor" (49:314), is able at last to evoke the two-way transit upon which marital—and narrative—closure depends. Revelation become invitation, for as he opens up to her in a confessional mode, he is simultaneously opened out toward her in a receptive—and reciprocated—emotional mood.

14. My view of *Persuasion*'s effort to plot its way *back* to felicity is informed throughout by the paradigm established for a certain mode of post-Shakespearean romantic comedy in Cavell's *The Pursuits of Happiness: The Hollywood Comedy of Remarriage* (Cambridge: Harvard University Press, 1981), where something like a Freudian Eden, attended by the all but inevitable fall into too much knowingness, takes nostalgic shape as an idyll of virtually familial closeness, a time when a couple's invigorating differences carry no threat of divorce—and at the same time no promise, if only because no need as yet, of strengthening reaffirmation.

15. Michael McKeon (see n. 10 above) claims that the novel as genre is sprung from an early-modern rupture in confidence concerning historical valuation when reduced (as by Sir Walter) to aristocratic lineage: "From Hesiod to Chrétien, lineage existed to resolve questions of virtue and truth with a tacit simultaneity, making both a causal claim of genealogical descent attesting to an eminence of birth, hence worth, and a logical claim of testimonial precedent validating all present claims as true. The origins of the novel's mediatory project mark the discovery not of the relation between these realms but of an increasing division between them that is too great to ignore" (420). In this sense, the opening of *Persuasion*, well after the divisive recognition McKeon has been at pains to chart, is Austen's version of ontogeny recapitulating phylogeny: a novel inaugurated by an encapsulation of its own conflictual prehistory as genre.

16. Between these two relatedly ironic instances are two other plays in this vein on Anne's name which have in fact to do with potential suitors. When Mr. Elliot eyes her with interest for the first time, Wentworth's triangulated glance "seemed to say" that "even I, at this moment, see something like Anne Elliot again" (12:125)—something like the family good looks ("an Elliot") as well as the spirited young lady he once admired. And there is Mary's consternation, in the case of Captain Benwick's rumored attraction to Anne, over his being a man not "entitled by birth and situation to be in love with an Elliot" (14:125).

17. This is a pun that Mark Schorer passes over without mention in his otherwise astute three pages on the economic subtext of *Persuasion* in "Fiction and the 'Analogical Matrix,'" in Babb, *Essays in Stylistic Analysis* (see chap. 2 above, n. 2), 340–42.

18. Here Cavell's notions (see n. 14 above) of a fraternal-sororal closeness in the marriages of a certain subgenre of romantic comedy, marriages that need to be redifferentiated in order to be revitalized, converge in their psychological emphasis with the psychopoetics of Peter Brooks' *Reading for the Plot: Design and Intention in*

Narrative (New York: Alfred A. Knopf, 1984), 308–9, where incest is a figure of metaphoric excess (oversameness) stalling the drive of metonymy (or plot sequence).

19. My stress on the "open" *rendering* as well as characterizing of Austen's narrative agents touches upon the concerns of D. A. Miller in *Narrative and Its Discontents: Problems of Closure in the Traditional Novel* (Princeton: Princeton University Press, 1981). Miller explores the momentum of plot as a continuous repression of the unnarratable (the unspeakable) en route toward the closural horizon of the nonnarratable (the invariant, the unchangeable). His point is well taken as an account of the instabilities that make for narrative succession but tends to downplay the interchange between plot and discourse generated by the withholding of narrative information. In this sense (to adopt Miller's schema to my own examples from Austen) the unnarratable (in the form of secrecy) and the nonnarratable (in the form of inveteracy), once thematized as character psychology (Mr. William and Sir Walter Elliot respectively), bear in turn upon the discursive tactics of subjectivity, its construction and disclosures. My emphasis thus falls less on narratability than on *readability*, broadly conceived—and broadly executed—as a textual strategy.

20. See John Bender, *Imagining the Penitentiary: Fiction and the Architecture of Mind in Eighteenth-Century England* (Chicago: University of Chicago Press, 1987), esp. 177–78, 211–13.

21. I say "virtual" to describe their restoration of and to the past because no passage in English fiction so clearly anticipates the idea of "the same but different" which Cavell borrows from *The Awful Truth* for the title of his last chapter (see n. 14 above). The past recaptured by hero and heroine in *Persuasion* is one in which, as in film's comedies of remarriage, the couple is "more exquisitely happy, perhaps, in their re-union, than when it had first been projected: more tender, more tried, more fixed in a knowledge of each other's character, truth, and attachment" (23:243), where the epistemology of "fixed" knowledge closes the circle of wavering indeterminacies, the circle of plot, by doubling for the virtuous fixity of marital *attachment*.

22. Anne is herself the champion, for instance, of a less introvert and claustrophobic reading than that to which the character Benwick is addicted, with his exclusive fondness for lyric poetry. In response, Anne "ventured to recommend a larger allowance of prose in his daily study; and on being requested to particularize" (12:123) seemed inclined to advertise, within a presumed emphasis on nonfiction, many of the salient strengths of the novel in which she finds herself. Anne, that is, "mentioned such works of our best moralists, such collections of the finest letters, such memoirs of characters of worth and suffering"—again that privileged term "worth"—"as occurred to her at the moment," all offering "the strongest examples of moral and religious endurances" (12:123). Endurance is what Benwick must achieve after the death of his fiancée, just as endurance is what Anne herself has learned, presumably from some of the same reading she now recommends. Benwick's indulgences aside, certainly any reading is better than none, as *Northanger Abbey* has long ago suggested in its genial tolerance for the gothic and the senti-

mental. Reading is that to which neither of Anne Elliot's sisters is able to turn for comfort, however, for Mary has "no resources for solitude" (5:64) and the vapid Elizabeth returns a book unfinished to Lady Russell in high dudgeon over its dreary demands on her time (22:211). With no inner life to harbor or release in solitude, a character like Mary or Elizabeth is seen from the outside. So too their father, who is the only character, as patriarchal figurehead, about whom he never tires of reading.

23. In line with his overall argument (see n. 17 above), Mark Schorer does note, without mentioning the "worth" of Wentworth, the largely dead metaphor ("pay the tax") in the novel's last sentence (342).

24. My emphasis thus falls less on the thematic transmutations of gothic ingredients in Victorian through modern fiction, so well detailed in Judith Wilt's *Ghosts of the Gothic: Austen, Eliot, and Lawrence* (Princeton: Princeton University Press, 1980), than on the ghosting of the reader within the text, the preternatural inhabitation of narrative space by the ambiguous powers of identification.

Chapter Five   In the Absence of Audience

1. Here one might follow out a recent suggestion by Peter Brooks about narrative interaction. Having pursued Roland Barthes's notion of "contract narrative" with illuminating results in *Reading for the Plot* (see chap. 4 above, n. 18), Brooks expands further on the psychodynamic of such narrative exchanges in a chapter on *Frankenstein* in *Body Work* (see chap. 4 above, n. 12), where the relation between Walton and Mrs. Saville is conceived on the "transferential" model: "As a 'subject supposed to know,' the listener is called upon to 'supplement' the story . . . , to articulate and even enact the meaning of the desire it expresses in ways that may be foreclosed to the speaker" (200). Though Brooks doesn't mention this, Mrs. Saville's structured silence as narrative recipient may contribute to the sense that she fills the role of therapeutic sounding board in this fable of vicarious interchange. Moreover, it is Walton's own anticipation of one day taking up the role of reader rather than narrator of the story which may imply his urge for an imaginative access otherwise "foreclosed" by his role as storyteller. Only by reading, perhaps, can he "articulate and even enact the meaning of the desire" he has begun by half confessing on his own part, half reporting on Victor's.

2. Charles E. Robinson, ed., *Mary Shelley: Collected Tales and Stories* (Baltimore: Johns Hopkins University Press, 1976), 121.

3. The protagonist of the *History of the Inconstant Lover*, "when he thought to clasp the bride to whom he had pledged his vows, found himself in the arms of the pale ghost of her whom he had deserted" (viii–ix). Anticipating Victor's dream of his mother's corpse replacing his fiancée, Elizabeth, in his arms (5:57), this fictional prototype also captures the ambivalence of erotic desire and marital drive in Victor's whole story. Then there was "the tale of the sinful founder of his race"—the very periphrasis for paternity offering a proleptic hint—"whose miserable doom it was to bestow the kiss of death on all the younger sons of his fated house" (ix). Prefigured

here is the negating effect of Frankenstein on all his "progeny," both the natural children he fails to have and that monstrous issue he seeks to eradicate.

4. Mary Shelley, *The Last Man* (Lincoln: University of Nebraska Press, 1965), 3.

5. Two of Shelley's other narratives instance in closure the renormalized poles of this clash between forecast and epitaphic commemoration. The year after *The Last Man*, the novel *Falkner* (New York: Saunders and Otley, 1837) concludes in speculative ambivalence over its audience's subsequent response—namely, the reader's judgment about the rightness of the characters' final domestic arrangements: "Whether the reader of this eventful tale will coincide with every other person, fully in the confidence of all, in the opinion that such was the necessary termination of a position full of difficulty, is hard to say" (316). The book's future, as it were, is the eventuation of our assessment. Against this open-endedness, albeit rhetorically coercive, stands the flatly memorial emphasis of an epitaphic final judgment in Shelley's historical novel *Valperga: Or, The Life and Adventures of Castruccio, Prince of Lucca* (London: G. and W. B. Whittaker, 1923). Preceding by three years the higher epitaphic stakes of *The Last Man*, this novel closes with the reproduction in untranslated Latin of the "antient [*sic*] tombstone" of the hero, since "its inscription may serve for the moral and conclusion of this tale" (269).

6. Georges Poulet quoted in Paul de Man, *Blindness and Insight: Essays in the Rhetoric of Contemporary Criticism*, 2d ed., rev. (Minneapolis: University of Minnesota Press, 1983), 95.

7. My point here is informed by, just where it departs from, an emphasis of Jay Clayton's in *Romantic Vision and the Victorian Novel* (Cambridge: Cambridge University Press, 1987). In his section "Phenomenology of Lyric and Narrative" (104–8), Clayton stresses subjective "internalization" (106) as the readerly effect more of lyric utterance than of fictional narrative. In closer connection to the romantic poets, however, what it seems to me that Mary Shelley's narrative texts engineer into view, especially through the conduits of their dramatized first-person writers, is indeed the phenomenological abdication of self in all reading: a constitutive deputizing of subjectivity which leads to an internalization of the other in the form of story. "My dear sister" (Walton to Mrs. Saville) might in this sense be taken to mark the transit site for a proxying out of consciousness through internalizable utterance which is equivalent for its genre to the lyric delegation of visionary experience in contemporaneous verse (Wordsworth to his sister, let us say, in a one-way conversation poem like "Tintern Abbey").

Chapter Six   In "Dearing" the Reader

1. Both the phrase's montagelike blurring of phonetic matter and its literary-historical precedents are captured in the title of Laurie Anderson's 1974 film *Dearreader*, with its descriptive gloss: "How to turn a book into a movie. Dedicated to Lawrence [*sic*] Sterne." In *Stories from the Nerve Bible: A Retrospective, 1972–1992* (New York: Harper Perennial, 1994), 16–20.

2. Both for the culling of best-selling sales figures and for a detailed sense of the publishing context, this chapter is indebted to the pioneering archival work of Q. D. Leavis, *Fiction and the Reading Public* (London: Chatto and Windus, 1932), and Altick, *English Common Reader* (see chap. 1 above, n. 4), as well as to John Sutherland's invaluable guide to the major and minor fiction of the period, *The Stanford Companion to Victorian Fiction* (Stanford: Stanford University Press, 1989).

3. W. Harrison Ainsworth, *Rookwood: A Romance* (London: J. M. Dent and Sons, 1952), 3,5:202.

4. W. Harrison Ainsworth, *The Tower of London: A Historical Romance* (Bath: Chivers, 1974), 2,4:172.

5. Edward George Bulwer-Lytton, *Pelham, or The Adventures of a Gentleman*, ed. Jerome J. McGann (Lincoln: University of Nebraska Press, 1972), 22:444–45. Subsequent quotations are from this edition, in which the "Preface to the Second Edition" is placed before the text (xxxiii–xxxv) and the appendixes contain the "Preface to the Edition of 1840" (449–53) and "Advertisement to Edition of 1849" (454–57).

6. Charles Reade, *The Cloister and the Hearth* (London: Collins, 1962), 101:667.

7. Thomas Carlyle, *Sartor Resartus*, ed. Kerry McSweeney and Peter Sabor (Oxford: Oxford University Press, 1987), 1,11:62.

8. Charles Kingsley, *Westward Ho!*, Everyman's Library (London: J. M. Dent and Sons, 1960), 16:325.

9. George Gissing, *Workers in the Dawn* (New York: P. F. Collier and Son, 1880), 1:1. Note the clash (a further signaling of irony) between this apostrophe and Gissing's subsequent advice against such address, as discussed below (chap. 12, n. 1).

10. Nathaniel Hawthorne, *The Scarlet Letter*, Norton Critical Edition, ed. Sculley Bradley, Richmond Croom Beatty, E. Hudson Long, and Seymour Gross, 2d ed. (New York: W. W. Norton, 1978), 1:8, 1:40, 20:153.

11. Mark Seltzer, in "Reading Foucault: Cells, Corridors, Novels," *Diacritics* 14, no. 1 (Spring 1984), quotes this sentence, along with more of the passage as well, in support of his claim that "the novel is thus both for commuters and a commuter itself, representing and enacting an exchange between domesticity and the market-place of the world" (88).

12. Although Trollope's texts are riddled with references to the reading act, usually in third rather than second person, it is of course not these moments of acknowledged reception in themselves which so famously annoyed Henry James, for he might have found them in his beloved Hawthorne as well. Rather, it was the admission not of textuality but of fictionality, of sheer manipulable invention, which for James broke the novelistic contract with the reader, the reader who should be led to believe in the coherence of the world described. See Henry James, "Anthony Trollope," from *Century Magazine* (1883), rpt. in James, *American Writers, English Writers* (see chap. 1 above, n. 2), 1330–54, where James rebukes Trollope for taking a "suicidal satisfaction in reminding the reader that the story he was telling was only, after all, a make-believe" (1343). A striking instance of the alleged transgression (not cited by James) occurs in the disquisition on the "poor fictionist" and his burdens of

verisimilitude in *Phineas Finn* (1869), in Anthony Trollope, *The Palliser Novels* (London: Oxford University Press, 1973), 29:267–68.

13. Mrs. S. C. Hall, *Can Wrong Be Right?*, in *St. James Magazine* 1–2 (April 1861): 438.

14. Marie Corelli, *The Sorrows of Satan, or The Strange Experience of One Geoffrey Tempest* (London: Methuen, 1895), 1:9. Corelli's first novel was rejected by the then best-selling novelist Hall Caine, a "reader" for the firm of George Bentley, which in the final event overrode his advice. See John Sutherland (n. 1 above), 148.

15. Marie Corelli, *A Romance of Two Worlds* (London: Richard Bentley, 1886), 17:308.

16. George Moore, *Confessions of a Young Man*, ed. Susan Dick (Montreal: McGill-Queens University Press, 1972), 12:190.

17. See Elaine Showalter's back-to-back chapters "Queen George" and "King Romance" in *Sexual Anarchy: Gender and Culture at the Fin de Siècle* (New York: Viking, 1990), 59–104.

18. Rudyard Kipling, *Kim*, ed. Alan Sandison (Oxford: Oxford University Press, 1987), 15:286.

19. H. Rider Haggard, *King Solomon's Mines*, ed. Dennis Butt (Oxford: Oxford University Press, 1989), 1:7–8.

20. Norman Etherington, ed., *The Annotated She* (Bloomington: Indiana University Press, 1991), 5–6.

21. H. Rider Haggard, *Beatrice* (New York: P. F. Collier, 1894), Envoi: 319.

22. For Peter Keating in *The Haunted Study: A Social History of the English Novel, 1875–1914* (London: Secker and Warburg, 1989), the literary experimentation of the 1880s and 1890s "marked the decline of one of the most treasured of Victorian conventions—the direct authorial address" (397). In its emphasis on strict rhetorical exhortation, his rather monolithic view of address corresponds to that of Robyn Warhol (below, n. 24) as a quasi-oratorical procedure. George Moore, for example, is cited as a writer who hastened the decline of address "in his early naturalistic novels" (397). Moore's later recourse to direct address as a self-conscious anachronism (as I discuss below) does not undermine the general tendency Keating is out to chart. Where I part company with Keating's account, however, is with his handling of the negative evidence, the absence of apostrophe. He sees its very suppression deployed, too symmetrically, as the opposite of rhetorical persuasion, generalizing that writers of the nineteenth century tended to use authorial address in direct proportion "to the degree of importance they attached to the social message of their work" (397), with the "cajoling, hectoring, bullying" tone of H. G. Wells given in partial evidence. Yet the practice of certain New Woman novelists, we will see, would go to show that there may well be a tacit "social message" precisely in withdrawing from either the deferential pleading or the avuncularity, as it were, of address.

23. Sarah Grand (Frances Elizabeth Bellenden McFall), *The Heavenly Twins* (New York: Cassell, 1893). "'The Vicar of Wakefield' makes me think a good deal" (3:16), Evadne Frayling writes in an early entry in her commonplace book. "What strikes me first and foremost . . . is that the men were educated and the women were ig-

norant" (3:16). So dawns an inchoate feminism in the young girl's consciousness, a resentment against those men who have withheld the advantages of education "by main force" (3:17). Dutifully pursuing, and patiently uninterested in, both *Roderick Random* and *Tom Jones*, with their prototypical male heroes (3:19), she returns at intervals to *The Vicar* until she is able to articulate her social critique, as if matured in part by recurrent literary encounter, "with greatly improved power of expression" (3:16).

24. Given her account of the feminine valence of direct address (one sided especially in view of the eighteenth-century literary rather than oratorical predecessors of the technique), it is not a little surprising that Robyn Warhol's evidence in *Gendered Interventions: Narrative Discourse in the Victorian Novel* (New Brunswick, N.J.: Rutgers University Press, 1989), concerned throughout with both "engaging" and "distancing" narrators in Victorian women's writing, involves no attention to Charlotte Brontë, the period's most relentless and varied manipulator of reader apostrophe.

25. Here is where literary history itself charts some of the same resistances in which, according to Robyn Warhol's virtual conspiracy theory, only critics have colluded. In the last chapter of *Gendered Interventions* (above, n. 24), called "Direct Address and the Critics: What's the Matter with 'You'?" (192–206), Warhol adds to Jonathan Culler's list of reasons why critics shy away from apostrophe in romantic poetry a further sense that, in Victorian fiction, direct address is—at least for "androcentric" or "more extremely misogynist critics"—a "sign of feminine presence" and a "gesture of connection between the worlds inside and outside the text" (205). This alleged allergic reaction "can account, too, for objections to signs of the feminine that surface in moments of direct address in men's texts: the oratorical sentimentality of Dickens and Thackeray, the 'instrusive' chattiness of Kingsley and Trollope" (205). In the face of such claims, one at least needs the reminder that there is oratorical rhetoric that is not necessarily sentimental, and women writers capable of it (like Eliot) whose model other women writers may still choose to refuse.

26. Schreiner to Havelock Ellis, 5 April 1889, in Olive Schreiner, *Letters*, vol. 1, 1871–1899, ed. Richard Rive (Oxford: Oxford University Press, 1988), 154.

27. H. Rider Haggard, *Mr. Meeson's Will* (New York: Arno Press, 1976), 10:135.

28. See chap. 4 above, n. 12, xi, 25, 77. Brooks' most striking example concerns the case of an eponymous heroine from another nineteenth-century novella, Balzac's *La Duchesse de Langeais*, a woman threatened with a male branding that is never performed and who, when dead, passes into memory as if she were merely "a book read during childhood" (77).

29. George Moore, *A Story-Teller's Holiday* (New York: Cumann Sean-eolais n h-Éirann, 1918), 1:4.

30. In *Modes of Production of Victorian Novels* (see chap. 1 above, n. 4), N. N. Feltes concentrates his otherwise economic argument upon linguistic indices for a closing discussion of *Howards End*, including the archironies of this passage of direct address as an example of interpellation.

31. Nathaniel Hawthorne, "Preface" to *The Marble Faun* (New York: Library of America, 1983), 853.

32. Hugh Kenner, the F. W. Bateson Memorial Lecture, "Modernism and What Happened To It," *Essays in Criticism* 37, no. 2 (April 1987): 97–109. "Reading Matter, consisting almost wholly of Easy Books, was the principal mass-produced artifact of the late 19th century" (106), as opposed to "a certain textual obduracy, never quite subduable" that characterizes the modernist textual surface.

Chapter Seven   Telling Time

1. I discuss the relation of these inset tales to the main narrative of *Pickwick Papers* in *Dickens and the Trials of Imagination* (Cambridge: Harvard University Press, 1974), chaps. 1–3. In this respect, the frontispiece to the novel, showing the sublimely unbookish Sam Weller reading to Pickwick—as if from the book of life—seems designed as a corrective for Pickwick's resistance to reading's impact in the course of the novel.

2. See Gerald Prince, "Introduction to the Study of the Narratee," in Jane P. Tompkins, ed., *Reader-Response Criticism* (chap. 2 above, n. 3), 7–27, where one of his examples of this zero-degree marking is the corrective negative interjection "no" (14).

3. In her commentary on omniscient technique and ideology in Dickens, for instance, it is the latter Foucault (of *Discipline and Punish*) that gives direction to Audrey Jaffe's *Vanishing Points: Dickens, Narrative, and the Subject of Omniscience* (Berkeley: University of California Press, 1991). See her discussion of the panopticon (11–12) as preparation for her investigation of *The Old Curiosity Shop* (45–70).

4. Michel Foucault, "What Is an Author?" in Donald F. Bouchard, ed., *Language, Counter-Memory, Practice*, trans. Donald F. Bouchard and Sherry Simon (Ithaca, N.Y.: Cornell University Press, 1977), 144.

5. Sigmund Freud, "Creative Writers and Day-Dreaming," in *The Standard Edition of the Complete Psychological Works of Sigmund Freud*, trans. James Strachey (London: Hogarth Press, 1959), 9:143–53, where Freud speaks of "His Majesty the Ego, the hero alike of every day-dream and of every story" (150).

6. See chap. 1 above, n. 15.

7. See Angus Easson, "*The Old Curiosity Shop*: From Manuscript to Print," in *Dickens Studies Annual*, ed. Robert B. Partlow (Carbondale: Southern Illinois University Press, 1970), 93–128.

8. There are the giants who, when their legs get too rickety to perform, are pensioned off to the circus caravan, lest their presence afoot in the land create a deficit of interest in other, agile giants (see 19:204). More centrally, there is the case of Little Nell's star value. Mrs. Jarley, entrepreneur of the waxworks where she puts Nell to work, can only have learned her sense of economized attractions from Dickens himself, with his calculated oscillation between Nell's story and the alternative Lon-

don scene. For "lest Nell should become too cheap" by overexposure, Mrs. Jarley regularly removed her from view as public inducement and "kept her in the exhibition rooms" (29:286), where "she described the figures every half-hour." Even when displaced from center stage, Nell is thus secured (in shrewd Dickensian fashion) as a narrative focal point of other salable "curiosities."

9. For background on the social disquiet of this period, see Paul Schlicke, "The True Pathos of *The Old Curiosity Shop*," *Dickens Quarterly* 7, no. 1 (March 1990): 191.

10. Beyond the Chartist unrest, Paul Schlicke, in *Dickens and Popular Entertainment* (London: Allen and Unwin, 1985), has provided (without pursuing) another context for understanding the disruptive street theater fomented, as it were, by the single gentleman. Schlicke takes note (though without reference to the heavily revised comic passage on the conversion of Bevis Marks to urban fairground) of the curious coincidence of the closing of the fabled Bartholomew Fair at Smithfield—with its implications for the curtailment of proletarian leisure—during the very publication of *The Old Curiosity Shop* (94–95).

11. Horace's "the many-headed multitude," alluded to, for instance, in Shakespeare's *Coriolanus* (II.iii.18) and adopted by Pope as "the many-headed monster" (*OED*), is transformed by Dickens into an abstract plural (first *OED* citation as an "absolute").

12. See chap. 1 above, n. 3.

13. Until now, the invasive threat to Nell, looked at from one angle, has all along been a kind of quasi-capitalist greed figured as ravage. This is the case because Quilp incarnates in compressed and stunting form the fever of mercantile aggression, rapacious, devouring, a self-fulfilling and self-punishing extroversion of the work ethic. Rejecting the notion of Quilp as a satanic figure, Theodor Adorno saw him as a "goblin or gnome," closer to a "cannibal" than a demon, indeed the "very epitome of the bourgeois profit-seeker." See Theodor Adorno, "An Address on Charles Dickens's *The Old Curiosity Shop*," trans. Michael Hollington, *Dickens Quarterly* 6 (1989): 96–102, quotation 98; orig. publ. in *Frankfurter Zeitung* 75, no. 285 (18 April 1931): 1–2. Adorno gives no textual evidence, but it is abundant. "Mr. Quilp could scarcely be said to be of any particular trade or calling, though his pursuits were diversified and his occupations numerous. He collected the rents of whole colonies of filthy streets and alleys by the waterside, advanced money to the seamen and petty officers of merchant vessels, had a share in the ventures of divers mates of East Indiamen, smoked his smuggled cigars under the very nose of the Custom House, and made appointments on Change with men in glazed hats and round jackets pretty well every day" (4:72–73). Quilp is at once master and slave to that "law of supply and demand" we saw alluded to in the canceled passage about the single gentleman's interest in Punch troupes. Agent of colonialist venture, moneylender, and frequenter of the stock exchange, Quilp represents capitalist energy run amok, self-employed but inextricably intertwined with the funds of others, a conduit of business transactions and investments that are all energy without labor, all surplus. Dickens' fabled

industry is here mocked by an uncreative expenditure whose diametrical opposite is figured in Birmingham as enforced and listless nonproductivity.

14. For Adorno (see n. 13 above), Nell is a "sacrificial victim of the mythical system of life in which she must live, atoning for the injustice that prevails there" (100).

15. Easson (see n. 7 above), 117.

16. Lucien Dallenbach, *The Mirror in the Text* (Chicago: University of Chicago Press, 1989), 100.

17. There is a minor but telling inverse of this process built into the plot itself, when the autobiographical agent (the single gentleman as Master Humphrey) seems debarred from the characterological space of narrative. The inferred link between Dickens (a.k.a. Master Humphrey) and the single gentleman (a.k.a. Master Humphrey) inflects in this way the pathos attending the gentleman's failed attempt to make his presence known to old Trent. The latter goes to his grave without acknowledging the reunion, as if the secret fraternal narrator and his protagonist were separated all along by the distance of art from life. As narrative functionary within and around the tale, there seems no way for the single gentleman to break through the screen of discourse into the story in order to claim the attention of his closest living kin. It is a kind of aborted metalepsis whereby narrator is blocked from intruding upon narrative *in propria persona*. From this moment of stymied contact through to the close of the novel, grandfather Trent "never understood, or seemed to care to understand, about his brother" (71:660). It is, in sum, as if the single gentleman has abdicated his status as character within the fiction—and can no longer be realized as such.

18. *The Letters of Charles Dickens* (see chap. 1 above, n. 3), 2:190–91, 22 January 1841, quoted in Easson (see n. 7 above), 109.

19. Georges Poulet, "Phenomenology of Reading," *New Literary History* 1 (October 1969): 56.

20. This scene of closural telling figures importantly in Audrey Jaffe's arguments about the novel (see above, n. 3): "Kit's mode of storytelling might serve as a model for the reader, or for Dickens's own 'working through.' Treating Nell as his children must—as legend—he incorporates her story into and subordinates it to his own, so that their tears are replaced (rather than displaced) by laughter" (70). See also John Kucich's mention of Kit's narrative, in connection with other Dickensian happy endings converted to 'stories within the novel,' in his chapter "Storytelling" in *Excess and Restraint in the Novels of Charles Dickens* (see chap. 3 above, n. 5), 33.

21. It is also, and eerily, a fantasy come true for Dickens. Its deserted quarters establish the functional—the textually revivifying—equivalent of the cenotaphic memorial he once would have made of Mary's death chamber itself. "I shall never be so happy again," Dickens wrote in a diary he kept only briefly in the years following her death, "as in those Chambers three Stories high—never if I roll in wealth and fame. I would hire them to keep empty, if I could afford it." See diary entry for Saturday, 6 January 1838, from the diary covering the months January 1838 through September 1839, in *The Letters of Charles Dickens* (see chap. 1 above, n. 3), 1:630. Within

a decade, Dickens has in fact become both famous and financially comfortable through just such activity as letting a similar space to the multitude of Victorian readers, who take to Nell as to the very enshrinement of loss. Appended to the capitalized "Stories" by the editors of the Dickens letters (one of them, Graham Storey, no doubt particularly alert to the orthographic issue at stake) is a terse—and presumably noninterpretive—footnote, the equivalent of "*sic*": "Thus in MS." Let stand indeed. It remains unclear whether this alternate spelling of the common British "storeys" counts as a true Freudian parapraxis, by which Dickens takes fleeting dictation from his unphrasable desire—from his need eventually, and even in different forms repeatedly, to write out, and himself out of, Nell's sad "story." Certainly it might be said, in his career-long preoccupation with the deathbeds of innocence, that Dickens left to Mary Hogarth a monument at least three or more stories high.

22. This and the next quotation are from a later passage not reprinted in the appendix to the Penguin Edition. See *Master Humphrey's Clock and A Child's History of England* (London: Oxford University Press, 1958), 37.

23. Dickens, "An Address Announcing the Termination of 'Master Humphrey's Clock,'" *Sketches by Boz and Early Minor Works* (Bloomsbury: Nonesuch Press, 1938), 693–94 (dated September 1841).

24. "Preface to the First Volume," in Nonesuch ed. (see n. 23 above), 689.

25. A literary-historical comparison may clarify the attenuation of narrative content which results from Dickens' formal reflex of narrative attention. It has not escaped critical notice that Dickens owes much to the high-journalistic periodicals of the eighteenth century as regards the serialized dissemination of Master Humphrey's narratives and the interludes of commentary between them. What has not been remarked is that Addison's *Spectator* offers a very particular model for that congregational microcosm of the reading public which Dickens has adapted to his own different purposes in the *Clock*. "The Club of which I am a Member," explains the Spectator, "is very luckily compos'd of such Persons as are engag'd in different Ways of Life, and deputed as it were out of the most conspicuous Classes of Mankind." See Joseph Addison, *The Spectator*, ed. Donald F. Bond (Oxford: Clarendon Press, 1965), 1:142. One result of this is that "[m]y Readers too have the Satisfaction to find, that there is no Rank or Degree among them who have not their Representative in this Club, . . . who will take Care of their respective Interests" (142). In Dickens, however, the deputized members *represent* Dickensian readers in a different and far more diffuse sense, without class or vocational specification: represent by *picturing* them, and this solely in their role as fascinated auditors. Put succinctly: Where in the *Spectator* the delegated club members look out for the reader's plural "interests," in *Master Humphrey's Clock* they instead stand in collectively for the reader's *interest*, his wholesale curiosity, first encapsulated in the opening attitudes of Humphrey himself. Contrasting Addison's "new paper" to its predecessor, the *Tattler*, Donald Bond explains that it is designed to "record the more sober reflections of a silent and even diffident man, withdrawn from the strife of the market-place, an observer of life—in short, a Spectator" (xviii). This exact description would apply equally well to Mas-

ter Humphrey, whose unlikely (yet still disinterested) trespass into the peripheral marketplace of the Curiosity Shop precipitates the novel by that name.

26. Illustrations reprinted in *Master Humphrey's Clock and A Child's History of England* (see n. 22 above), facing 8 and 118 respectively.

Chapter Eight   On *Abymes*

1. Collins happens to be the only Victorian novelist to have received a book-length treatment centering on his strategies of reaching and retaining—of *assuring*—a readership. Sue Lonoff's *Wilkie Collins and His Victorian Readers: A Study in the Rhetoric of Authorship* (New York: AMS Press, 1982), however, does not conceive of such "rhetoric" in specifically linguistic or textual terms; nor, more to the point here, does her commentary direct itself to overdetermined scenes of narrative response within Collins' plots, so it is no surprise that she passes over *The Queen of Hearts* without discussion.

2. Wilkie Collins, *The Queen of Hearts* (New York: Harper, 1859; rpt., New York: Arno Press, 1976), 15.

3. Most of the stories are collected in Edgar Wright, ed., *Lady Ludlow and Other Stories* (New York: Oxford University Press, 1989), with an appendix (433–44) that gives the original framing prologue and the "links" between separate tales in the "chain" format of *Round the Sofa*. Whereas Collins builds into his prologue an explanation for the written, hence implicitly publishable, form of the stories as transcribed reminiscences, Gaskell's explanation, following the first of the tales, comes after the fact of spontaneous oral delivery: "Miss Duncan thought it would be a good exercise for me, both in memory and composition, to write out on Tuesday mornings all that I had heard the night before; and thus it came to pass that I have the manuscript of 'My Lady Ludlow' now lying by me" (440–41).

4. Thomas Hardy, *A Group of Noble Dames* (London: J. R. Osgood, McIlvaine, 1891), 56.

5. The appearance of "ye" instead of "you" in the manuscript (259) was perhaps thought by Dickens to have overdone the rhetorical satire and hence blunted its thrust. Even when, elsewhere in the novel, it is instead to a general and more disinterested reader that address is directed, the cue is likely to remain specified (and thus a little distanced) in some way, as in "none of us in our sober senses and acquainted with figures" (1,5:19) or "Never fear, good people of an anxious turn of mind" (1,11:53).

6. This is a different point from the Foucauldian one driven home by D. A. Miller in *The Novel and the Police* (Berkeley: University of California Press, 1988), where domestic "privacy" (both the space dedicated to reading and the value system to which the novel is in turn devoted) is invaded as well as fortified by the bureau of fiction as an armature of social discipline and ideological surveillance.

7. I have developed at fuller length the contrast of Carton's last hours and mo-

ments, in their complicated avoidance of writing, with the revolutionary dependence on accusatory inscription (as against a similar problematic in Abel Gance's film *Napoleon*) in "Leaving History: Dickens, Gance, Blanchot," *Yale Journal of Criticism* 2, no. 2 (1989): 145–82.

8. It is here again (see n. 6 above) that I would resist the generalizations to which D. A. Miller is led by his striking analysis of the Dickensian minor grotesques in *David Copperfield*, such figures as Ham Peggotty, Mr. Mell, Betsey Trotwood, and Uriah Heep. These are characters who harbor their "open secrets" (from Miller's chapter title) in a presumed inwardness that leads the reader to wonder "what value can be put upon the hidden innerness that like the miser's hoard can never see the light of day . . . upon an innerness that is never realized in intersubjectivity" (204). Though the rhetorical question can't be decided from Miller's evidence directly, the answer is there in Dickens—and Miller takes an important step toward it. His insights into the phenomenological interspace of reading, that is, get us to a certain depth in the operation of Dickensian fiction which that fiction's own readerly contract would like us to think is exceeded by the further recesses of personal essence. For Miller, the "novel-reading subject can never resemble Dickens's characters, conspicuously encased but so transparent that they are always inside-out, because the novel-reading subject as such has no outside" (208). All seeing, that subject is never seen, "invisible both to himself (he is reading a novel) and to others (he is reading it in private)" (208). Yet the withheld and mystified innerness of a Humphrey or a Carton or a Carker or a Lady Dedlock or an Arthur Clennam or a Eugene Wrayburn, even a David Copperfield, is not, as Miller claims in connection with the comic caricatures, "refuted or transcended in any reader's experience" (208) but rather redoubled and confirmed by the positioned subjectivity of just such a reading act, which meets otherness seldom more than part of the way toward self-surrender. (When the tendency toward such surrender is unchecked, we move beyond the Dickensian model of the Victorian novel's parasocial "field of action" into the psychic no-man's-land of reading's own gothic metadrama [cf. chapter 13].)

Chapter Nine   "Oh, Romantic Reader"

1. See Sylvère Monod, "Charlotte Brontë and the Thirty 'Readers' of *Jane Eyre*," in Charlotte Brontë, *Jane Eyre*, Norton Critical Edition (1971), ed. Richard J. Dunn, 496–507. Only the parodic clotting of "readers" in *Shirley*—as if an ironic clearinghouse for all the apostrophic baggage of the best-sellers—exceeds the overload of address and mention in *Jane Eyre*, as typified by the later novel's warning, "If you think, from this prelude, that anything like a romance is preparing for you, you never were more mistaken" (1:40), and concluding with "I think I now see the judicious reader putting on his spectacles to look for the moral" (37:599).

2. Sigmund Freud (see chap. 7 above, n. 5), 151.

3. Frank Kermode, *The Classic* (Cambridge: Harvard University Press, 1983), 124.

4. In this sense, Lockwood offers a negative parallel to the evolution of Hareton Earnshaw as reader, which also takes shape in terms of textual suspension and suspense. When all of Cathy's "ingenuity was at work" in attempting to generate a desire for reading on Hareton's part, she would strategically interrupt her reading aloud to Nelly; with Hareton in view, "she generally paused at an interesting part, and left the book lying about" (32:236), hoping to inflame his curiosity. It might be said that Lockwood conspires with Nelly to produce the same effect in himself.

5. These matters have been previously linked in John T. Matthews, "Framing in *Wuthering Heights*," *Texas Studies in Literature and Language* 27 (1985): 25–61, where ghostly incursion is seen resisted by the framing device: "Writing, for Lockwood, is a way of dispossession" (46).

6. Charles Lemon, ed., *A Leaf from an Unopened Volume, or The Manuscript of an Unfortunate Author: An Angrian Story by Charlotte Brontë* (Haworth: Brontë Society, 1986), 14. The use of third person singular in the masculine gender seems entirely formulaic here, as later in *Jane Eyre*. The point becomes important if one wants to take some distance from Sylvère Monod's sense of similar address in Brontë's novels (see n. 1 above). For him, the reader (in *Jane Eyre* and elsewhere) is "constantly referred to in the masculine" so as to evoke the "conventional, silly, cowardly, ignorant, and vain" attributes that "the Brontë girls" associated with "the average male," as "embodied especially in the narrator of *Wuthering Heights*, the unspeakable Lockwood" (504). My own point is rather that a major rhetorical difference between Emily Brontë's frame tale and Charlotte's first-person retrospect is marked by the way in which Lockwood's flaccid response is overruled by the conscripted attention enforced by Jane's emphatic, wry, but by no means consistently satiric (or Thackerayan) asides.

7. One exception to the critical indifference concerning this scene is the essay by Mark M. Hennelly Jr., "*Jane Eyre*'s Reading Lesson," *ELH* 51 (Winter 1984): 693–717, though he notices only the first half of what we might call Rivers' advance (709), not the subsequent "conversion" of Jane into a "listener," a virtual reader, of her own life. Still, Hennelly's general remarks about the way Brontë's fiction links "hermeneutics and love" are apposite to this scene: "Both relationships demand flexible perspectives, intimacy and distance alike" (708). Hennelly has come to this conclusion by considering many aspects of the novel related to the present inquiry, from "Brontë's direct, explicit invocations of 'the Reader'" (700) to "some of the major reading experiences in the novel" (694)—in particular, Jane's reading of the world for the blind Rochester at the close. In the famous passage given elliptically by Hennelly, Jane in fact says more than that "he saw books through me." The full sentence is as follows: "He saw nature—he saw books through me; and never did I weary of gazing for his behalf, and of putting into words the effect of field, tree, town, river, cloud, sunbeam—of the landscape before us, of the weather round us" (38:397), and so forth. He thus stands in our place, his entire access to the world of the novel mediated through her words about it.

8. Virginia Woolf, *A Room of One's Own* (New York: Harcourt Brace Jovanovich, 1957), 68–70.

9. Again I take exception to Sylvère Monod's view (n. 1 above) of this epithet (along with "gentle," one of only two attached to any of the novel's thirty mentions of the reader). Contributing to his notion of the reader's belligerent male perspective, here forced to confront the uneuphemized thirsts of a female servant, the readerly attribute denotes "our attitude as conventionally romantic persons" (502). Instead, I would stress the thirsts of the other servant on the scene, the heroine herself, and the internalized romantic tale just dredged from the well of repressed desire to allay them. Following Linda Kauffman's lead in *Discourses of Desire: Gender, Genre, and Epistolary Fictions* (Ithaca, N.Y.: Cornell University Press, 1986), I would thus associate such an apostrophe to the "romantic reader," however ironic, with those moments of self-address discussed by Kauffman ("'*You*,' I said, 'a favorite with Mr. Rochester? *You* gifted with the power of pleasing him?'" [178]): interlocutions with the self's own desire which Kauffman sees operating in conjunction with the "Reader, I married him" format as an assimilation of the epistolary modality to the genre of first-person fiction.

10. So has Caroline sat listening just paragraphs before—and there, too, with her "mind's ear" (6:115) as well as her corporeal audition—to a reading aloud by Robert Moore of Shakespeare's *Coriolanus*, in a scene treated at length by Nancy Armstrong in *Desire and Domestic Fiction* (see chap. 3 above, n. 5), 213–24 ("Seduction and the Scene of Reading"). For Armstrong, this episode functions "to give the reader procedures for reading not only such an openly political text as Shakespeare's but the fictional narrative to follow as well" (214). On her account, Shakespeare himself is domesticated and dehistoricized, appropriated "for middle-class culture" (214) by means of "procedures of reading that were developed in the curricula for women during the eighteenth century" (215). Armstrong's discussion of *Shirley* is part of her larger claim about the politics of the Brontës' fiction: less that history is filtered through their works than that their fictional structures enter into history as discursive paradigms of middle-class subjectivity and have ever since been too acquiescently read in terms of their own "psychologizing tropes," their own preferred "figures of desire" (187). On this showing, the scene of reading in *Shirley* would compress and reprise the logic of the entire Brontë canon. In it, a representative literary woman instructs her public, via the hero as book-reading proxy, in how to *read our way* into history as acculturated subjects. Yet Armstrong's view of self-referential thematization in this particular scene from *Shirley* tends to stop short at what the hero is to learn from Shakespeare, as we from Brontë. Despite the link in the heading of Armstrong's subsection between "seduction" and the "scene of reading," it is as if the lures of reading were largely ideological, offering primarily an appliance of domestic virtue and its public extensions (more humility and fellow feeling with the laborers in Moore's employ) rather than a psychodynamic *act*, a form (if not a "figure") of desire in its own right.

11. For a testing out with *Jane Eyre* of the work by Nicholas Abraham and Maria Torok on "cryptonomy," see Herman Rapaport's *"Jane Eyre* and the *Mot Tabou,"* *MLN* 94, no. 5 (1979): 1093–1104, which attempts a tentative and site-specific rapprochement between their version of psychoanalytic reading and that of Lacan. Rapaport's claims about a "poetic of hauntedness" (1093) center on the mourninglike effects of those encrypted signifiers in Brontë which circle the unsaid bilingual *mère* both of Jane's patriarchal "nightmare" (1101) and of the orphaned Jane's own paternal name: the Law of the Father thus manifest and evaded at once in the "psychotic voices" (1103) of a signifying maternal other. In the context of such echoing phonic chains as "'ere, air, aware, beware, nightmare, glare, terror, but also eye, ire, Ireland, I, Vampyre, wild" (1098), Rapaport finds a subterranean "verbarium" strung together in Brontë's novel out of what Abraham and Torok call lexical "allosemes." These are ghostly, self-haunted echoes of each other slipping into signification along "paths of avoidance" (1101) which one might call repression were it not for their perpetual return, a return both within and upon themselves. As for the passage currently under discussion from *Jane Eyre*, my own sense of "ire" and "I" in relation to the "Eyre" of both "Ireland" and "Eyrie" finds such lexical dissemination taking a different "path of avoidance"—via the frictional erosion of what might instead be called overlapping "allophonic" variants. For the theoretical implications attaching to such a syntagmatic activation of the *simultaneous* echo, see my *Reading Voices* (chap. 1 above, n. 9).

12. Concerning the phonemic (or "allosemic") network of "Eyr(i)e"—rather than "ire"—see Rapaport (above, n. 11) on the association of Jane's name, via imagery of the "condor," with a "mad wife's nest" (1102).

13. Gerard Genette, *Figures of Literary Discourse*, trans. Alan Sheridan (New York: Columbia University Press, 1982), 142.

14. In *Charlotte Brontë and the Storyteller's Audience* (Iowa City: University of Iowa Press, 1992), Carol Bock aptly notes that the last quoted words of Lucy's in the novel are (to Paul Emanuel) "I want to tell you something, . . . I want to tell you all" (129; 41:590). Borrowing Naomi Schor's category "fiction of interpretation" to characterize *Villette*, however, Bock puts her main emphasis on Lucy as an "interpretant" rather than a narrator.

15. See Elizabeth Gaskell, *The Life of Charlotte Brontë* (London: Smith, Elder, 1877), in which Gaskell includes a letter from Brontë pleading with her not to make the heroine of her own novel, *Ruth*, die at the end—"And yet you must follow the impulse of your own inspiration. If *that* commands the slaying of the victim, no bystander has a right to put out his hand to stay the sacrificial knife" (24:391). The notion of fictional death as ritual sacrifice reverberates in the next chapter's mention of Mr. Brontë being "anxious that [Charlotte's] new tale should end well. . . . But the idea of M. Paul Emanuel's death at sea was stamped on her imagination, till it assumed the distinct force of reality. . . . All she could do in compliance with her father's wish was so to veil the fate in oracular words, as to leave it to the character and discernment of her reader to interpret her meaning" (25:399–400).

16. My sense of the emotional tonality of Brontë's conclusion coincides up to a point with the feminist reading by Brenda R. Silver, "Reflecting Reader in *Villette*," in *The Voyage In: Fictions of Female Development*, ed. Elizabeth Abel, Marianne Hirsch, and Elizabeth Langland (Hanover, N.H.: University Press of New England, 1983). I would agree both that Lucy is finally appealing on the last page, in her direct address to the reader, to "the community she herself has created to grant credence to the highly unconventional conclusion of her tale" (110); and that we are to believe she prospers without Paul Emanuel (in his absence—though in and through the memory of his love, I might add) during the intervening years between his death and her narration. Indeed, it is for just these reasons that my own analysis can be taken to begin with the question: Why, even though her *life* goes on, is her *narrative* so precipitously over with this distant and unnarrated death?

17. I discuss Kristeva's early essays on Bakhtin, in connection with their tacit debt to the semiotic narratology of A. J. Greimas, in "A Valediction for Bidding Mourning: Death and the Narratee in Brontë's *Villette*," in *Death and Representation*, ed. Sarah Webster Goodwin and Elisabeth Bronfen (Baltimore: Johns Hopkins University Press, 1993), 51–79.

18. See "Is Death Nonrepresentable?" in Julia Kristeva, *Black Sun: Depression and Melancholia*, trans. Leon S. Roudiez (New York: Columbia University Press, 1989), 25–29, where her answer is that death is manifest, not mimetically but textually, in the very lacunae of representation.

19. See Julia Kristeva, *Revolution in Poetic Language*, trans. Margaret Waller (New York: Columbia University Press, 1984).

20. It is this activation of phonemic overtones by the reading act, an act understood as the coproduction of textual discourse and its deciphering agency, which I pursue in *Reading Voices* (see chap. 1 above, n. 9). Included among numerous other contingent (but nonetheless thematically charged) instances of the Victorian proclivity for such homophonic shadow play are examples in particular (not repeated here) from *Jane Eyre* (194–95) and *Villette* (195–96). The bearing of Kristeva's "semiotic" on such textual apprehension is discussed on 270–71.

21. Herbert Rosengarten and Margaret Smith, eds., *Villette* (Oxford: Clarendon Press, 1984), 715; see description of the Sterling ms. and proof sheets of the first edition, "Introduction," xxxvii ff.

22. See Peter Brooks, *Reading for the Plot* (chap. 4 above, n. 18), especially the chapter "Narrative Transaction and Transference" (216–37), as well as remarks scattered throughout his commentary.

23. See Emile Benveniste, "Relationships of Person in the Verb," in *Problems in General Linguistics* (see chap. 2 above, n. 24), 196–204.

24. Slavoj Žižek, *The Sublime Object of Ideology* (New York: Verso, 1989); after frequent references to "interpellation," Žižek makes clear his case for its psychoanalytic equivalent (38).

25. I take it as corroborating the malleability of syntactic constraints in certain prose that an early proofreader of my chapter admits to finding herself so much in

the Kristevan groove by this point that she was momentarily disposed to read my own serial predicate here as even more verb-heavy than its punctuation was meant to suggest—that is, "it leaks, bleeds over, floods, cracks, widens, rifts, springs, ruptures."

26. As a local measure of Gaskell's Dickensian resistance to the flagging of textuality through apostrophe, there is this closural passage of immediate scenic manifestation in the anonymous narrative voice of *Mary Barton* (1848), a device of "presencing" familiar from the earlier best-sellers: "I see a long low wooden house, with room enough, and to spare" (38:465).

Chapter Ten   The Book of the World

1. See chap. 16, "The Book as Symbol," in Ernst Robert Curtius, *European Literature and the Latin Middle Ages*, trans. Willard Trask (Princeton: Princeton University Press, 1953), 302–47. Curtius's wide-ranging evidence comes to a head midway through the chapter: "Summing up, we find that the concept of the world or nature as a 'book' originated in pulpit eloquence, was then adopted by medieval mystico-philosophical speculation, and finally passed into common usage. In the course of this development the 'book of the world' was frequently secularized, i.e., was alienated from its theological origin, but this was by no means always the case" (321). Some of this same medieval ground is gone over again, with an emphasis on Dante and without reference to Curtius, by Gabriel Josipovici, *The World and the Book: A Study of Modern Fiction* (London: Macmillan, 1971), in his chapter called "The World as a Book," 25–51.

2. Wallace Stevens, *Collected Poems* (New York: Alfred A. Knopf, 1954), 146–47.

3. Roland Barthes, *S/Z* (see chap. 1 above, n. 17), 2–21.

4. For an account of the way the semiotic decoding of images into words in the charade episode complicates our reaction to the interplay between Thackeray's prose and his illustrative plates in the novel as a whole, see my essay "Reading Figures: The Legible Image of Victorian Textuality," in *Victorian Literature and the Victorian Visual Imagination*, ed. Carol Christ and John O. Jordan (Berkeley: University of California Press, 1995), 345–67.

5. Curtius (see n. 1 above) mentions the "eschatological" force of this figure from Isa. 34:4 (310).

6. George Meredith, "An Essay on Comedy," published with Henri Bergson, "Laughter," in *Comedy*, ed. Wylie Sypher (Garden City, N.Y.: Doubleday, 1956), 51.

7. Judith Wilt, *The Readable People of George Meredith* (see chap. 1 above, n. 16), 114. This response to the passage is very much in line with her overall claim, derived in part from Wayne Booth, that this parodic education novel, like many nineteenth-century texts, also effects, as its incremental "subplot," the *"Bildungsroman"* of the "civilized reader" (19). The residual conscription, even beyond closure, of the reader as world citizen in Eliot's *Daniel Deronda* will also seem aptly characterized by this formulation.

8. The term "profane" is Sue Bridehead's, in her boast that "I can only quote profane writers" (5,4:222). Though Jude has already admitted that "I know hardly any poetry" (4,5:195), her subsequent quotation from Shelley strikes a chord. "What a terrible line of poetry!" Jude reacts, adding, "though I have felt it myself about my fellow-creatures, at morbid times" (5,4:227). It is exactly to the point of the novel, in its encoded rehearsal of the evolution of classical and theological writing into the mordancy (as well as morbidity) of modern literature, that Jude's openness to nineteenth-century poetry would follow from—and only after—the pattern of policed classical ambition which can be traced out in the first half of the book. Only when the worst tragedy strikes, the death of their three children, does Jude draw personally on his secular reading by bringing to mind a line from the *Agamemnon* about the "destined issue" (6,2:268) of things, with its unwitting pun on *fated offspring*.

9. Yet again (see chap. 8 above, n. 6), one can appreciate the position to which D. A. Miller's approach might well lead as regards the attempted rescue of Hardy's novel from a textual "consumption" whose inert or debilitating effects it satirizes: namely, that the text in reception instills a cultural policing in the key of high literature. One may do so, however, without having to ignore or deny the way in which the novel's theory of selfhood posits a space of identity more fully withdrawn from panoptic scrutiny than the always and already invaded "privacy" of a would-be scholar's—and/or reader's—room. What Dickens calls "innermost personality," Hardy calls the "secret center of [the] brain" (1,9:48). It is from this supposedly harbored core of being that any of Jude's reading in the "book of humanity" must proceed, including his later interpretation of Sue's behavior, which he scrutinizes "as if to *read* more carefully the creature he had given shelter to" (3,4:119; emphasis added). At the same time, none of this rules out the sense, especially given Hardy's ironies of selfhood, that a later iteration of inward depth in connection with Sue—"that mystery, her heart" (4,5:191)—may seem nothing more than a reified social construction of contradictory impulses figured as interiority.

Chapter Eleven   Mordecai's Consumption

1. At other times this imperative habit is reduced to the sheer scene setting of the best-seller: "Fancy an assemblage where the men had all that ordinary stamp of the well-bred Englishman" (10:136), or "Imagine a rambling, patchy house" (30:384).

2. On the evolution of the railway novel of the forties, including the publication of Bulwer-Lytton and Dickens in this format, into the late Victorian "shilling shocker" and the "rack-marketing" of popular genres, see John Sutherland, *The Stanford Companion to Victorian Fiction* (chap. 6 above, n. 2), 519.

3. Cf. "Readers and Readings in *Daniel Deronda*," in Tony E. Jackson, *The Subject of Modernism: Narrative Alterations in the Fiction of Eliot, Conrad, Woolf, and Joyce* (Ann Arbor: University of Michigan Press, 1994), 47–65, where he discusses the "hierarchy of readers" (59) in the novel, including Gwendolen's role as a romance reader "conventionally condemned by realism in its desire to authorize itself" (48).

4. See Peter K. Garrett, *The Victorian Multiplot Novel: Studies in Dialogical Form* (New Haven: Yale University Press, 1980). Following a tendency descended from the earliest reviewers of *Daniel Deronda*, Garrett sees the novel divided between "novelistic" and "romance" treatments of the Gwendolen and Deronda plots respectively (168), each functioning dialogically as (according to his chapter title) "equivalent centers."

5. See Peter Brooks, *Reading for the Plot* (chap. 4 above, n. 18), 109.

6. See Stewart, *Death Sentences: Styles of Dying in British Fiction* (Cambridge: Harvard University Press, 1984), 11–20, for an initial summary of this threefold constitution of the death scene.

7. Quoted in *George Eliot: The Critical Heritage*, ed. David Carroll (London: Routledge & Kegan Paul, 1971), 431.

8. I can find no reference to this tale in midrashic commentary or the commentary thereon. What does emerge from the secondary scholarship, however, is a sense—see David Stern, *Parables in Midrash: Narrative and Exegesis in Rabbinic Literature* (Cambridge: Harvard University Press, 1991)—that the episode of the Jewish woman and the king would function like a "king-mashal" (a royal parable) normally to be followed by the "nimshal" (its narrative application) as an exegetical gloss (8). For elucidations of the role of interpretation both built into these "mashal" narratives and accrued over time in rabbinic disquisition, see 44–45, 86–93. Further, Stern's description of the midrashic commentary as mediator between Torah and everyday existence, a transmissive as much as exegetical function, offers a sacred parallel to the subordination in Eliot's novel, both as plot and as cultural program, of rigorous hermeneutics to the perfusion of spiritual influence: "Rather than primarily determining the Torah's meaning, or its multiple meanings, midrashic interpretation seems often to be more concerned with maintaining the Torah's presence in the existence of the Jew, with bridging the gap between its words and their reader, with overcoming the alienation, the distance of Torah, and with restoring it to the Jew as an intimate, familiar presence" (44).

9. Georges Poulet, "Phenomenology of Reading" (see chap. 7 above, n. 19), 56.

10. Cynthia Chase, "The Decomposition of the Elephants: Double-Reading *Daniel Deronda*," *PMLA* 93 (March 1978): 393.

11. I thus take the final emphasis on Milton as seriously as does Janice Carlisle in *The Sense of an Audience* (see chap. 3 above, n. 5), even as I come to a rather different conclusion. In a chapter called "Severing Relations," Carlisle sees the deferral to Milton as an index to Eliot's self-conscious divorce from the previous popular readership of her storytelling, a deliberate surrender of narrative voice and its consequent authority: "Storytelling as a source of relation and mediation is no longer the powerful force it has been" (218). There seems little doubt that *Daniel Deronda* is addressed directly to Eliot's crisis of faith in the venues of popular fiction, as part of the crisis of British culture she diagnoses. Rather than marking an abdication from narrative, however, I take the excerpt from Milton (like the epigraphs it resembles) to be rais-

ing the stakes of the Victorian novelistic vocation, channeling narrative momentum into a literary continuity that might be able to sustain its values at a more strenuous, even elitist, level of reception.

12. See Stern, *Parables in Midrash* (n. 8 above) on the hermeneutic aftermath of the initial "mashal" or parable: "In addition, the nimshal usually concludes by citing a verse, the mashal's prooftext" (8). When Eliot's entire Mordecai plot, having been condensed and rethought by the episode of the sacrificial Jewish heroine, comes to its own rather than her finish, the delayed citation is dropped into place: "Nothing is here for tears."

13. Maurice Blanchot, "Death as Possibility," in *The Space of Literature*, trans. Ann Smock (Lincoln: University of Nebraska Press, 1982), 100.

14. Franco Moretti, *The Way of the World: The "Bildungsroman" in European Culture* (London: Verso, 1987), 226.

15. One way around Moretti's objections might be implicit in an argument that does not actually confront his position. In *Figures of Conversion: "The Jewish Question" and English National Identity* (Durham, N.C.: Duke University Press, 1995), Michael Ragussis shifts the generic terms of discussion from the Bildungsroman to the novel of conversion and sees the spiritual reformation of Gwendolen in one half of the plot, the Jewish initiation of Daniel in the other, as twin corrective reversals of a Victorian subgenre: the novel of Jewish conversion to Christianity (260–98). This argument might also go some way toward explaining why the usual Jewish cultural weight placed on textual transmission via citation and elaboration can be thrown over so completely by Mordecai, who wants Daniel—more like a Christian convert (Eliot's reversal may indeed be this thoroughgoing)—simply to *believe*, to internalize the faith more as spiritual disposition than as *doxa* or text.

16. Esther Schor, *Bearing the Dead: The British Culture of Mourning from the Enlightenment to Victoria* (Princeton: Princeton University Press, 1994). Part of what Schor's work accomplishes is to entwine a social history of sentimentalism with the origins of the Victorian cult of death in ways that reveal in the widespread elegiac rhetoric over the death of Princess Charlotte in 1817, for instance, a veritable politics of tropology. With the image of familial bonds annealed by grief passing back and forth between characterizations of the royal family and descriptions of the private domestic household, the latter serves to delimit a social space that becomes, in national mourning, a synecdoche for the reconsolidation of the state. Such a picture of an intimate though thoroughly public "discourse of the dead" (4, following de Certeau) might also broaden our perspective on the sense of communal mutuality fostered by grief's literary manifestations in the Dickensian fellowship of sorrow, including especially the parafamilial reach of the framing material surrounding Little Nell's death or the preface alluding to Paul Dombey's (see chapter 7).

17. I thus see Eliot working deliberately to circumvent the impasse noted by Deirdre David in *Fictions of Resolution in Three Victorian Novels: North and South, Our Mutual Friend, Daniel Deronda* (New York: Columbia University Press, 1981). David

claims, like Moretti after her, that no Victorian domestic or even native English consolidation—or even consolation—serves to resolve the cultural crisis exposed by Eliot and that in this regard her novel "displaces her critical imagination right out of English society" (204). English society as monolithically conceived is left behind, perhaps, but not—quite elaborately not—a persisting attachment to its intellectual readership. Building on Cynthia Chase's deconstruction of the novel's visionary mode (above, n. 10), Jay Clayton's *Romantic Vision and the Novel* (see chap. 5 above, n. 7) sees Eliot's attempted prophetic text moving beyond a Wordsworthian model of personal "transcendence," as in *Adam Bede* and *Middlemarch*, toward an open-ended "apocalyptic" tenor: "Rather than privileging a particular structure of experience, *Daniel Deronda* forces the reader to look beyond anything the text can claim as 'a genuine fact or a genuine act' (Chase 223) for the source of the narrative's meaning and power" (161). I would further specify that readerly "beyond" as precisely a reconstitution of the readerly imagination itself.

18. See Wilt, *The Readable People of George Meredith* (chap. 1 above, n. 16), where the reader is taken as hero of the novel's "subplot" (a term Wilt borrows from Wayne Booth [6]).

19. Patrick Brantlinger surveys these critical positions in "Nations and Novels: Disraeli, George Eliot, and Orientalism," *Victorian Studies* 35 (Spring 1992): 255–75, where he stresses the ascendancy of "romantic nationalism" (a kind of internationalist nationalism) over "provincial nationalism" in *Daniel Deronda* (268).

20. George Gissing, *Charles Dickens: A Critical Study* (London: Blackie and Son, 1898), 82.

Chapter Twelve   Grubbing for Readers at the *Fin de Siècle*

1. In a letter to his brother Algernon in 1883, reprinted in *George Gissing on Fiction*, ed. Jacob and Cynthia Korg (London: Enitharmon Press, 1978), 26. Gissing's words to the wise against reader interpolation are quoted by Peter Keating (chap. 6 above, n. 22) with the (unexemplified) addendum that "Gissing never followed his own advice" (397). The present evidence does bear out Gissing's principle at least to some extent, however, since the tongue-in-cheek "you" addressed here is closer to the ironies of E. M. Forster (see chap. 6 above, n. 30)—as well as to Thackeray before them—than to the explicit, highly codified, calculatedly endearing, and rhetorically unironic "references" to the reader in earlier Victorian fiction.

2. Fredric Jameson, *The Political Unconscious: Narrative as a Socially Symbolic Act* (Ithaca, N.Y.: Cornell University Press, 1981), 196.

3. Sandra M. Gilbert and Susan Gubar, *No Man's Land: The Place of the Woman Writer in the Twentieth Century*, vol. 1: *The War of the Words* (New Haven: Yale University Press, 1987). See especially chap. 3, "Tradition and the Female Talent: Modernism and Masculinism," 125–64.

4. See Žižek, *The Sublime Object of Ideology* (chap. 9 above, n. 24).

Chapter Thirteen   The Gothic of Reading

1. See Miller, *The Novel and the Police* (chap. 8 above, n. 6), 152, 149.

2. The distinction is powerfully sketched by Miller (n. 1 above), but not as the two modes might be seen to inhere within the same figurative (or psychosomatic) system. Whereas the nervous reader is a sustained presumption of the text, projected by example upon the characters, in other words thematized, the violative reader—reciprocal aspect of what we might call the sadomasochistic system—is separately disclosed, in Miller's treatment, by the superimposed subjectivities of an explicit scene of reading. This occurs at the narratively (and textually) shocking moment when we realize—just as Marian Holcombe does by reading a note from the villainous Count Fosco appended to her diary—that he has all along been devouring her words, with mounting sexual fascination, as if over the reader's own shoulder. Fosco's "rape" (Miller, 164) of her privacy—which also, on Miller's account, takes *us* from behind as well—thus prods the recognition of our own intrusive and emotionally dubious access. Passively excited on the one hand, complicit in an aggressively invaded intimacy on the other, straddling the divide of gendered figuration itself, part effete and twitchy victim, part violator, now paranoid, now predatory, the reader focuses a range of associations whose inherent contradiction is never explored, let alone resolved, either by Miller or by Collins' text. In the mid-Victorian sensation novel, such deviance (and figurative self-deviation) in the positioning of the reading subject remains an implicit test of realism at its outer limits. Openly violating those limits, the supernatural parables at the end of the century add to such a reflexivity of narrative response a litany of magical empowerments and transgressions whose figuration of reading, by being more flagrantly oblique than mere nervous suspense or visual eavesdropping (even when called paranoia and rape), can also be more pervasive and detailed (more steadily parabolic): exposing the contradictions of reading through the psychodrama of such preternatural aberrations as phantom doubling, rampant and chemically induced vicariousness, diabolic projection, and vampiric telepathy.

3. Given Eve Kosofsky Sedgwick's remarks in *Epistemology of the Closet* (chap. 1 above, n. 22), 174, on the implication of the reader inherent in Wilde's recurrent epithet "curious," one may well recall the double valence of the adjective in Dickens—playing there, too, between cause and effect as part of the novel's paranoid epistemology of attributed desire. In the case of Wilde's text, there is a particularly tantalizing break with the novel's rhetorical decorum, outlawing as Wilde does all direct reference to the reading customer, when the Norton editor interpolates his own scholarly audience by setting "the curious reader" (xi) on the trail of manuscript variants.

4. I therefore resist Françoise Meltzer's dismissal of Wilde's novel (as an instance of ekphrastic displacement of one art form by another) in *Salome and the Dance of Writing: Portraits of Mimesis in Literature* (Chicago: University of Chicago Press, 1987),

where she writes that *"Dorian Gray* is, it seems to me, too contrived to be convincingly unsettling" in this regard (111).

5. Consider, for example, Frans Hals' *Youth Reading* (1580) alongside Rembrandt's later apparent allusion to this intertext in his portrait of his own son reading (c. 1600). In each painting we see the slightly ajar mouth either of rapt (literally breathtaking) interest or of a more homely and serviceable lip-reading—or both. In the Hals portrait, part of the held volume being scanned by the youth is open before us, too, on the boy's desk, its facing pages and the hatchwork used to indicate written lines being partly visible to us at an oblique angle before they are truncated by the right frame. Rembrandt's trumping—and further troping—of the motif rests with the way his subject has averted the open book (its back passing out of frame at the right) from any possibility of our gaze. With no pretense of our conceivably being able to read along with the enthralled youth, as we might have thought to do with Hals' subject, the effect does more than highlight the invaded but nonetheless unapproachable intimacy of the reading moment. Rembrandt's absorptive portrait, once absorbing us into it, produces the metatrope of reading itself as an activity one performs upon the entire image rather than upon the subsidiary rendering of an almost legible text within it. Whereas Hals depicts reading, then, Rembrandt thematizes its relation to painting. The latter's scene of reading might thus be said to be the more obviously extrapolative of the two.

6. Cf. Norton Critical Edition of *The Picture of Dorian Gray*, ed. Donald L. Lawler (New York: W. W. Norton, 1988), 186 n. 4.

7. See Lucien Dallenbach, *The Mirror in the Text* (chap. 7 above, n. 16), 37. Later commentary bears also (without mention) on Wilde's novel as what we have been calling a parable of reading. "The implicit reader," writes Dallenbach, "like the implicit author, has a minimal existence in the text." In order to overcome this "radical anonymity," the imaging of a reader "requires the introduction of an auxiliary reflexion," serving both as "narrative guarantee" of reception itself and as the "material underpinning" for the mode of reading being advanced (78). The *figure* of Dorian constitutes both strata of this secondary "reflexion": both the auxiliary receptive consciousness and, as Picture, the material homology for our own two-dimensional text as processed over time.

8. See Jesper Svenbro, *Phrasikleia: An Anthropology of Reading in Ancient Greece* (Ithaca, N.Y.: Cornell University Press, 1993).

9. Jane M. Gaines, *Contested Culture: The Image, the Voice, and the Law* (Chapel Hill: University of North Carolina Press, 1991), 43. This is an allegorical reading Gaines offers in passing, as an appendage to her larger account of Wilde's copyright battles over the American publication of his image in a famous photograph. In aid of the purported connection between canvas and photograph there is the further fact (unmentioned by Gaines) that Lord Henry, in lieu of the portrait, has collected at least seventeen photographic studies of Dorian (4:40).

10. I have discussed the emergence of photography and photographic analogy

within Victorian fiction at greater length in "Reading Figures" (see chap. 10 above, n. 4).

11. George du Maurier, *Trilby* (New York: Harper and Brothers, 1894), pt. 8, 430. Subsequent text references are to part and page numbers.

12. It was Coleridge who may be taken to have set the tone for a nineteenth-century animus against the gendered submission to novelistic narrative. In his view, "popularness" itself leads to the sagging of literary virility, the decline of "manly vigor of intellect" and "masculine fortitude of virtue." See *The Friend*, in *The Collected Works of Samuel Taylor Coleridge*, vol. 4, ed. Barbara E. Rooke (Princeton: Princeton University Press, 1969), 24.

13. Robert Louis Stevenson, "The Reader," in *Fables* (New York: Charles Scribner's Sons, 1896), 2:40–41; the illustration by E. R. Herman appears in the 1914 Scribner's edition.

14. See William Veeder, "Children of the Night: Stevenson and Patriarchy," in *Dr. Jekyll and Mr. Hyde after One Hundred Years*, ed. William Veeder and Gordon Hirsch (Chicago: University of Chicago Press, 1988), where this particular double entendre, "hide-bound," is noted in passing as a "wonderful pun" that "bonds Lanyon with Hyde" (117). A recent undergraduate student of mine, caught up in the network of verbal duplicity in the text, suggested that "Hyde" as lower-class emanation of Jekyll, perhaps a kind of Cockney double, might have pronounced his own name more like "I'd."

15. Verbal polysemy of this sort should not surprise us from the master stylist of the exotic mode. Even a lesser gothic writer like Haggard can have his self-perpetuating millennial heroine in *She* seem to achieve her present manifestation, her immanent subject position, by an anagrammatic wrench of syllabic and lexical raw material: "I, yes I, Ayesha—for that is my name" (13:149). Gothic apparition often begins in the most tortured of merely lexical congestions.

16. In *Sexual Anarchy* (see chap. 6 above, n. 17), Elaine Showalter connects the handwriting Jekyll shares with Hyde and the phallic associations of the latter's "'lean, corded, knuckly,' and hairy hand" (115). As such a penislike appendage is conflated with the organ of signification, one might add, the symbolic phallus emerges in and as writing.

17. See J. C. Furnas, *Voyage to Windward: The Life of Robert Louis Stevenson* (New York: William Sloan Associates, 1956), 215–16.

18. See Furnas (above, n. 17), 244–45.

19. Stevenson to John Meiklejohn, 1 February 1880, *The Letters of Robert Louis Stevenson*, ed. Sidney Colvin, 2 vols. (New York: Charles Scribner's Sons, 1923), 2:104. In *The Friend* (see n. 12 above), Coleridge's metaphors for the epidemic of novel reading, in particular for the mass addiction to the first epoch of gothic thrillers, prefigure late-century anxieties, during the gothic revival, about dependent readers who "dwarf their own faculties" (21)—as if he already had in view a stooped and shrunken double like Mr. Hyde. As Coleridge puts it elsewhere, such degeneration

comes about through the drug of textual intake, including "the grossest and most outrageous stimulants" (*Biographia Literaria, or Biographical Sketches of My Literary Life and Opinions*, ed. James Engell and W. Jackson Bate, 2 vols. [Princeton: Princeton University Press, 1983], 2:229). For more on these matters, see my own illuminating source in Dino Felluga's "The Novel Poet: Ideology and the Instability of Genre, 1798–1885" (Ph.D. diss., University of California at Santa Barbara, 1995), where the denigration by feminine gender of literary forms in the popular press of the day is also surveyed.

20. Jerome Charyn, afterword to *The Strange Case of Dr. Jekyll and Mr. Hyde* (New York: Bantam, 1981): "Hyde is Stevenson's portrait of the artist as a bad little boy. His 'littleness' helps identify his rage. . . . He's that saddest of monsters, the artist who can find no shape to please him" (107).

21. Patrick Brantlinger and Richard Boyle, "The Education of Edward Hyde: Stevenson's 'Gothic Gnome' and the Mass Readership of Late-Victorian England," in *Dr. Jekyll and Mr. Hyde after One Hundred Years*, ed. William Veeder and Gordon Hirsch (see n. 14 above), 265–82. The story as "shilling shocker" (265) was designed for what its author (joining, as we have seen, Fanny Burney, Coleridge, Dickens) thought self-consciously to designate "the public"—for Stevenson, indeed, "that fatuous rabble of burgesses called 'the public'" (273). In the process, according to Brantlinger and Boyle, Hyde comes to represent this "atavistic" (273) populace, whereas elsewhere they take Hyde as the personification of the grotesque story itself as literary structure. Their pervasive equivocation—which may be true enough to the tale but would be more revealing if acknowledged and pursued—crystallizes in a formulation like this: "Stevenson as popular author shares in the criminal 'popularity' or populace-like nature of Hyde" (274). The monstrosity is thus at once the promiscuousness of textual appeal and certain comparable deformations at the receiving end. My own sense is closer to the former pole: Hyde as read rather than Hyde as reader, but read not as a definable creature but only insofar as such reading alone materializes him as a psychic—or psychosomatic—event.

22. Vladimir Nabokov, "The Strange Case of Dr. Jekyll and Mr. Hyde," in *Lectures on Literature*, ed. Fredson Bowers (New York: Harcourt Brace Jovanovich, 1980), 179–204.

23. My line of thought converges with that of Jerrold E. Hogle's densely suggestive reading of the novella, via Lacan and Kristeva, precisely when his own terms diverge from—to generalize at a higher level—those of Brantlinger and Boyle in the same volume. In "The Struggle for a Dichotomy: Abjection in Jekyll and His Interpreters" (see Veeder and Hirsch, n. 14 above), Hogle's recurrent notion of the Father/Reader (170, 195, 196), under whose gaze and auspices the subject enters into the symbolic, is related to the various abjections of the Jekyll/Hyde pairing by which the narrativized "readers" (Lanyon, Enfield, Utterson) try to make sense of such self-division while avoiding a recognition of the figurality that underwrites all supposed self-identity. Hogle's pursuit of these issues comes to its own kind of alle-

gorical head (reminiscent of Brantlinger and Boyle's, indeed as an implicit rejoinder to their topical and historical, rather than tropological, argument) when Stevenson the writer is thought to have staged this effort in order to submit the mystery of such "body languages" (186) to a hegemonic (i.e., rigidly dualistic) "grid of intelligibility" (200), staged it as a mirror of his own relationship to the literary marketplace, where meaning must be packaged and commodified: "If that is the inescapable situation of the multiple self and the writer all at once, why not construct a narrative that makes such a world order explicit?" (200). Where for Brantlinger and Boyle Hyde represents ambiguously (or simultaneously) the mob and its favored reading, for Hogle the fiercely dichotomized structure of the Jekyll/Hyde dynamic represents the binary constraints of symbolization itself—the law of the Father—awaiting the popularly sanctioned gaze of the other in reading. My own related (and, I suppose, more specific) claim is that Hyde represents in his own material apparition that which is readable about Jekyll's monstrosity, by Jekyll himself as well as by others—detectable only by being externalized into legibility and then introjected again by psychic identification.

24. Robert Louis Stevenson, "A Gossip on Romance" (1882), in *Memories and Portraits* (Boston: Small, Maynard, and Co., 1907), 233. See Barry Weller's spirited defense of reading along lines sketched out by Stevenson, in "Pleasure and Self-Loss in Reading," *ADE Bulletin* 99 (Fall 1991): 8–12. With evidence drawn in part from Dickens, where the chief reader figure of *Our Mutual Friend*, Lizzie Hexam, is seen tagged as such by the play in her name on *liseuse* (11), Weller explores what used to be called "the romance of reading" in ways that parallel what I find Stevenson rendering parabolic in *Dr. Jekyll and Mr. Hyde* as the more complex and disturbing gothic of reading.

25. Though not taking up the matter of prosopopoeia explicitly, much less its particular de Manian resonance, Hogle's line of attack seems very much in this spirit, with Hyde emerging as "the figural being in which the doctor can conceal the figural nature of *all* being" (see above, n. 23, 188). Jekyll/Hyde is in this sense the deconstructed version of a self otherwise presumed unitary, a phenomenon thus zealously quarantined from the presumed normal state it serves to travesty.

26. See William Veeder, "Collated Fractions of the Manuscript Drafts of *Strange Case of Dr. Jekyll and Mr. Hyde*," in Veeder and Hirsch (n. 14 above), 20.

27. In "Ekphrasis and the Other," *South Atlantic Quarterly* 91, no. 3 (Summer 1992): 695–719, Mitchell notes "the moment of resistance or counterdesire that occurs when we sense that the difference between the verbal and visual representation might collapse, and the figurative, imaginary desire of ekphrasis might be realized literally and actually" (697). Where Mitchell finds this fear persisting in, among other current strongholds, the "deconstructionist efforts to overcome 'formalism' and 'closure'" (698), I would locate it more specifically in the deconstructive critique of prosopopoeia as literary mastertrope. In this respect, Mitchell's speculation that "our ambivalence about ekphrasis is simply that it transfers into the realm of literary art

sublimated versions of our ambivalence about . . . merging with the Other" (702) is redoubled by those texts examined here which verbally summon a noxious and personified otherness whose tendency to merge with and usurp us—as crystallized within plot by the transgressive power, for instance, of magic portraits or photographs—is refigured by the encompassing narrative as the occasion of reading's own phobic reflex.

28. Fredric Jameson, *Signatures of the Visible* (New York: Routledge, 1990), referring to "Lukács' concept of 'reification' in its broadest sense of a gradual fragmentation and division of labor within the psyche, as the latter is retrained and reprogrammed by the reorganization of the traditional labor processes and human activities by emergent capital. The sharp structural differentiation of active and passive *within* a single mental function . . . would then be seen as a historic intensification of the reification process" (125–26).

29. Franco Moretti, "The Dialectics of Fear," in *Signs Taken for Wonders: Essays on the Sociology of Literary Forms*, rev. ed., trans. Susan Fischer, David Forgacs, and David Miller (London: Verso, 1988), 106.

30. On this aspect of the novel, see Friedrich Kittler, *Discourse Networks, 1800/1900*, trans. by Michael Metter, with Chris Cullens (Stanford: Stanford University Press, 1990), 353–56. In a discussion independent of Kittler's, Regenia Gagnier's "Evolution and Information, or Eroticism and Everyday Life, in *Dracula* and Late Victorian Aestheticism," in *Sex and Death in Victorian Literature*, ed. Regina Barreca (London: Macmillan, 1990), touches in passing on some of the same issues. For Gagnier, the Count's links to an antiquated oral culture are to be contrasted with the "graphomania" of "intelligence techniques" (150), the "modern systematic data processing of the English" (151). A similar stress is laid on the secretarial dimension of the novel by Geoffrey Wall in "'Different from Writing': *Dracula* in 1897," *Literature and History* 10, no. 1 (Spring 1984): 15–23, as part of his Marxist argument about the "crisis of the bourgeois family" of the period (15). "The narrative movement of *Dracula* is toward a social synthesis of these private writings, toward a knowledge which can only be constituted as the relation between diverging phantasies" (16). The rest of the essay explores the role of "Mina, the woman who writes" (18) as she "represents a certain historical transition" (16) in the English institution of the family.

31. Kittler (see n. 30 above), 356: "Whereas Mina types, her friend ends up on the nocturnal side of machine writing. Two tiny bite wounds on the throat materialize Beyerlen's law that eyeteeth or a piece of type, through a single, brief application of pressure, place the entire engram in the proper position on skin or paper."

32. My sense of a "gothically" implicated reading in the aberrant as well as the bureaucratic dimension of the plot, its hypnotic thrall as well as its textual palimpsest, is meant to complement the sort of structural inevitability noted by David Seed in "The Narrative Method of *Dracula*," *Nineteenth-Century Literature* 40, no. 1 (1985): 73: "Whereas *The Woman in White* moves toward an end point where all the pieces will fall into place, *Dracula* narrates its own textual assembly. The reader participates in

this formation of continuity. He becomes a reader among other readers," an agent of "collaboration."

33. See Garrett Stewart, "'Count Me In': *Dracula*, Hypnotic Participation, and the Late-Victorian Gothic of Reading," *Literature Interpretation Theory (LIT)* 5 (1994): 1–18.

34. Franco Moretti, "The Dialectics of Fear" (see n. 29 above), 83–108.

35. Judith Wilt attaches Dracula to imperialism more directly than by the linguistic route I am tracing out. In "The Imperial Mouth: Imperialism, the Gothic and Science Fiction," *Journal of Popular Culture* 14, no. 4 (Spring 1981), she reminds us that the Count "sees himself as part of that race of great nationalist heroes, variously Hungarian, Romanian, Czech, Wallachian, who were obliged to defend the fatherland century after century from the hordes of imperialists—Mongols, Bulgars, Turks. . . " (621).

36. See Carol A. Senf, "*Dracula*: Stoker's Response to the New Woman," *Victorian Studies* 26, no. 1 (Autumn 1982): 43–44, for the prominence of venereal disease as a topic in the New Woman writers. At a far pole from the somatic manifestation of the body's erotic functions and their social or moral "decadence," and beyond the subordination of language to information systems at the turn into technological modernity (Kittler and Gagnier above, n. 30), there is another level at which the relation of linguistic mutability to the novel's vampiric transmutations may be contextualized within a potentially phobic cross-current of Victorian thought. The novel's play with a polymorphous perversity of wording itself, like that of the other late-century gothics we have been considering, may indirectly reflect, by putting into popular practice, the last stages of a gradual evolution in linguistic theory that has moved away from a transcendental or Adamic view of the signifier and drifted—in the resultant "decay" of stable referential grounding—toward both the differential linguistics and the literary relativity of a materialist verbal modernism. For an expert detailing of these nineteenth-century transformations in language theory, see Linda Dowling, *Language and Decadence in the Victorian Fin de Siècle* (Princeton: Princeton University Press, 1986).

37. Jacques Derrida, in "Telepathy," trans. Nicholas Royle, *Oxford Literary Review* 10 (1988): 3–41, is at admitted pains to separate such an effect as "the reading of thoughts" from his concept of telepathy: "I'm desperately trying to distinguish between telepathy and 'thought transference,' to explain why I have always had greater difficulty in accepting the first than the second" (29). Stoker takes no such pains, his parable of reading depending in part on a merger between preternatural communication or suasion and the one-way "exchange of ideas," we might say, which takes place in routine textual experience.

38. In *Telepathy and Literature: Essays on the Reading Mind* (Oxford: Basil Blackwell, 1992), Nicholas Royle's consideration of George Eliot, beyond a treatment of preternatural empathies in *Daniel Deronda*, includes remarks on Eliot's story of explicit telepathy, "The Lifted Veil." More to the point of our present discussion, however, is Royle's chapter on "cryptaesthia" in *Wuthering Heights*. Developing the theories

of Abraham and Torok on the "cryptanalysis" of interred verbal associations or "al-
losemes" (for an exaggeratedly mortuary instance, the *urn* in "Earnshaw" [39]),
Royle comes closest to the effects noted before with the "faces"/"phases" of Mr.
Hyde and here with the punning dead metaphors associated with Stoker's vampire.

39. The power of telepathy (not so called in Stoker) is linked, a little more than
a decade after its first *OED* appearance, with other related phenomena mentioned
in *Dracula*. Cited is an 1888 passage from the *Athenaeum* listing it alongside "thought-
reading, and hypnosis" as "after-dinner experiments . . . trifled with for amusement."
The literary use to which Mina's parapsychic powers are put in Stoker's novel is not
mentioned by Nicholas Royle in *Telepathy and Literature* (see n. 38 above), despite
the prominence in that text of those epistolary and detective elements that Royle is
led to connect with his sense, via Derrida and the cryptonomy of Abraham and
Torok, of literature as a telepathic discursive system. In *Over Her Dead Body: Death,
Femininity, and the Aesthetic* (New York: Routledge, 1992), Elisabeth Bronfen is drawn
to Mina's ordeal by hypnotic or telepathic transcription, even to its relation with
previous scenes of reading in the novel, while discounting the larger issue of reading in and of the text which it might be found to allegorize. Quoting Van Helsing
on the way Mina's hypnotized voice sounds like "she is interpreting something," as
when "reading her notes," yet minimizing the hermeneutic emphasis in favor of the
supernatural, Bronfen stresses Mina's trance as a communication with the specific
"Otherness" of death in the person of Dracula (319). In the process, she dismisses the
more general otherness of transgressed psychic boundaries: "the banal sense that
[Stoker's] entire text works by exciting the reader's imagination, drawing her or him
into the dangerous realm of uncanniness, duplicity and longing for Otherness" (321).
This objection misses the mark, since the "excitation" of Stoker's reader is produced
not only by the specific otherness of the uncanny but by the uncanny otherness inherent in reading itself—uncanny precisely because it is so completely internalized.
Engrossed by the final transcripts of her suspended animation, Mina reading her
way to the conclusion of the Dracula plot *as if she were reading her own mind*, spooked
by all that she has taken in, is the text's ultimate reflexive turn.

40. "At the root of vampirism . . . lies an ambivalent impulse of the child towards
its mother," but the vampire "is transformed into a man by mass culture" in order
"to protect the conscious mind, or more precisely to keep it in a state of greater un-
awareness" (Moretti, n. 29 above, 104).

41. Like Dracula disintegrating when his blood-sucking intent has been bled dry
by the transcripts of relentless textual detection, Haggard's female version of the
Undead in *She* (the heroine's own name italicized throughout as if to coincide with
the title) arrives at her annihilating apotheosis, following one too many zaps from
the flaming pillar of life, only after she has been virtually read to death, like the novel
before us, by the gaze of the males who invade her realm. In ways impossible, says
the narrator, to "define or explain on paper" (292), the millennially superannuated

She shrivels in a matter of seconds to a condition "yellow, like an old piece of withered parchment" (293), which exactly echoes one of the ancient documents, the "roll of parchment . . . yellow and crinkled with the passage of years" (25), upon which we first read her story in translation.

42. Brantlinger and Boyle (n. 21 above) call *The Strange Case of Dr. Jekyll and Mr. Hyde* "a kind of gothic version of George Gissing's *New Grub Street*" (266).

43. See, for instance, the chapter-long sophistication of such a premise—for Conrad, via James and Flaubert—in Fredric Jameson, "Romance and Reification," in *The Political Unconscious* (see chap. 12 above, n. 2), 206–80.

44. Pressing this analytic template to the level of genre—let alone to the parameters of reception, as I will next attempt—takes it beyond the semiotic prototype borrowed and redeployed by Jameson. See his foreword to Algirdas Julien Greimas's *On Meaning: Selected Writing in Semiotic Theory*, trans. Paul J. Perron and Frank H. Collins (Minneapolis: University of Minnesota Press, 1987), as well as the analysis of character positions in Balzac and Conrad in *The Political Unconscious* (see chap. 12 above, n. 2), 154–84, 253–57, and 275–80. Recently, Jameson has in fact followed his dialectician's instincts to the point of mapping "high modernism" and "stylistic postmodernism" as opposed aesthetic modes—according to the irreconcilable contradiction in the former between the mystiques of totality and innovation, with fragmentation and replication their respective opposites. See *The Seeds of Time* (New York: Columbia University Press, 1994), 133.

45. See Tzvetan Todorov, *The Fantastic: A Structural Approach to a Literary Genre*, trans. Richard Howard (Ithaca, N.Y.: Cornell University Press, 1975).

46. This is where my argument is bound to differ from Franco Moretti's, not so much on the role of fiction in maintaining bourgeois cultural cohesion as on the precise nature of those reversals and dialectical returns that implement this maintenance in the reading event. Moretti includes *The Strange Case of Dr. Jekyll and Mr. Hyde* as another instance, along with *Frankenstein* and *Dracula*, of that nineteenth-century "literature of terror" (n. 29 above, 107) which, "while professing to save a reason threatened by hidden forces, . . . merely enslaves it more securely" (107), binding it over to a conservative and repressive rationalism—tool of corporate society—which narrates the grotesquerie and doom of all genuine individualism. Yet Moretti distinguishes absolutely, as I would not, between Shelley and Stevenson on the one side, Stoker on the other, in regard to "the *effect* they mean to produce on the reader" (106). Retrospective to a considerable extent, the former novels analyze terror on the part of the protagonists, whereas *Dracula* alone, according to Moretti, actually generates such fear in the very reading. "Such, finally, is the bond between the reader and the literature of terror. The more a work frightens, the more it edifies. . . . It is a fear one *needs*: the price one pays for coming contentedly to terms with a social body based on irrationality and menace" (108). But since—I would add—this voluntarily contracted terror (felt to whatever degree) is part of the marketable plea-

sure of such novels, we are left with the economy of vicariousness rather than the social therapeutics of fear as the real common denominator of Shelley, Stevenson, and Stoker.

Afterword

Epigraphs: Anne Brontë, *The Tenant of Wildfell Hall* (1848); Joseph Conrad, letter to R. B. Cunninghame Graham, 5 August 1897, in Gerard Jean-Aubry, *Joseph Conrad: Life and Letters,* 2 vols. (Garden City, N.Y.: Doubleday, Page, & Co., 1927), 1:208; Manuel Puig, *Eternal Curse on the Reader of These Pages* (New York: Random House, 1982), 102.

   1. 14 July 1923 to Richard Curle, in Jean-Aubry, *Joseph Conrad* (see epigraph source above), 2:317.

Index